SELECTED WRITINGS
— OF —
ROBERT L. MILLET

GOSPEL SCHOLARS SERIES

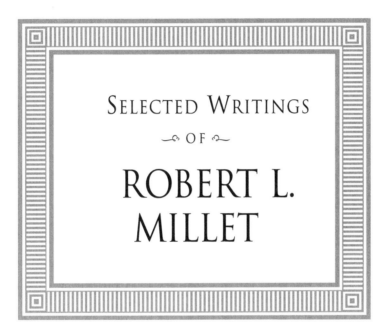

SELECTED WRITINGS

_✿ OF ✿_

ROBERT L.
MILLET

DESERET BOOK COMPANY

Library of Congress Cataloging-in-Publication Data

Millet, Robert L.
  [Selections 2000]
  Selected writings of Robert L. Millet/Robert L. Millet.
    p. cm.—(Gospel scholars series)
  Includes bibliographical references.
  ISBN 1-57345-550-4
  1. Church of Jesus Christ of Latter-Day Saints—Doctrines. I. Title. II. Series.
BX8637.M552   2000
230'.9322–dc21   99-086125

Printed in the United States of America   72082-6475

10   9   8   7   6   5   4   3   2   1

CONTENTS

PUBLISHER'S PREFACE

In recent decades, a number of exceptional Latter-day Saint scholars have expanded our understanding of many gospel subjects. In many cases, however, much of what they have written (or given as speeches) has been published for relatively small audiences, or it was published so long ago as to be unavailable or inaccessible to most readers; in some cases an article or paper has never been published at all. Now Deseret Book is pleased to bring together some of "the best of the best" in the Gospel Scholars Series.

KEY TO SHORTENED REFERENCES

Conference Report
Conference Reports of The Church of Jesus Christ of Latter-day Saints. Salt Lake City: The Church of Jesus Christ of Latter-day Saints, 1898 to present.

Doctrinal New Testament Commentary
Bruce R. McConkie. *Doctrinal New Testament Commentary.* 3 vols. Salt Lake City: Bookcraft, 1965–73.

Doctrines of Salvation
Joseph Fielding Smith. *Doctrines of Salvation.* Compiled by Bruce R. McConkie. 3 vols. Salt Lake City: Bookcraft, 1954–56.

Gospel Doctrine
Joseph F. Smith. *Gospel Doctrine: Selections from the Sermons and Writings of Joseph F. Smith.* Salt Lake City: Deseret Book Co., 1971.

History of the Church
Joseph Smith. *History of The Church of Jesus Christ of Latter-day Saints.* Edited by B. H. Roberts. 2d ed. 7 vols. Salt Lake City: The Church of Jesus Christ of Latter-day Saints, 1932–51.

Hymns
Hymns of The Church of Jesus Christ of Latter-day Saints. Salt Lake City: The Church of Jesus Christ of Latter-day Saints, 1985.

Journal of Discourses
Journal of Discourses. 26 vols. London: Latter-day Saints' Book Depot, 1854–86.

Lectures on Faith
Joseph Smith. *Lectures on Faith.* Salt Lake City: Deseret Book, 1985. References are to lecture number, followed by a colon, followed by the page number (i.e., *Lectures on Faith,* 7:4).

Messages of the First Presidency
> *Messages of the First Presidency.* Compiled by James R. Clark. 6 vols. Salt Lake City: Bookcraft, 1965–75.

Millennial Messiah
> Bruce R. McConkie. *The Millennial Messiah.* Salt Lake City: Deseret Book Co., 1982.

Mortal Messiah
> Bruce R. McConkie. *The Mortal Messiah.* 4 vols. Salt Lake City: Deseret Book Co., 1979–81.

Promised Messiah
> Bruce R. McConkie. *The Promised Messiah.* Salt Lake City: Deseret Book Co., 1978.

Teachings of the Prophet Joseph Smith
> Joseph Smith. *Teachings of the Prophet Joseph Smith.* Selected by Joseph Fielding Smith. Salt Lake City: Deseret Book Co., 1976.

Times and Seasons
> *Times and Seasons.* 6 vols. Nauvoo, Illinois: The Church of Jesus Christ of Latter-day Saints, 1839–46.

Words of Joseph Smith
> Edited by Andrew F. Ehat and Lyndon W. Cook. *The Words of Joseph Smith: The Contemporary Accounts of the Nauvoo Discourses of the Prophet Joseph.* Provo: Religious Studies Center, Brigham Young University, 1980.

SCRIPTURE

HOW THE BIBLE
CAME TO BE

Just prior to his last winter in Rome, while he lay in prison awaiting the death sentence, the Apostle Paul petitioned Timothy, his beloved associate and traveling companion: "The cloke that I left at Troas with Carpus, when thou comest, bring with thee, *and the books, but especially the parchments*" (2 Timothy 4:13; emphasis added). Some students of the New Testament have suggested that the cloak mentioned may well have been a piece of cloth used to cover books as well as to protect one from the cold. As to the content of the books (literally, rolls of papyrus) and parchments, we can only surmise; but does it require too great a stretch of the imagination to reason that they contained portions of the holy scripture?[1] Surely after a lifetime of immersion in the scriptures, Paul would want to spend his last days and weeks in pondering once again upon those inspired messages that had so forcefully shaped his life.

What was this book of books, this work heralded by the humanists as a classic literary and historical document but revered by the Saints in all ages as a work containing the words of eternal life? How did it come to be?

WHAT IS THE BIBLE?

In reminding us that prophecies of the past came not by the will of man, Peter declared that "holy men of God spake as they were moved by the Holy Ghost" (2 Peter 1:21). Latter-day Saints affirm that holy men have from the beginning not only spoken but written as they were so prompted. President Joseph Fielding Smith has stated: "We are informed that Adam and the Lord carried on conversations. How was this done unless Adam had been taught to speak? Therefore, all who have faith in the word of the Lord must know that Adam had a language; that his language was pure and perfect for it came from the Lord. All Latter-day Saints know this to be the case, for the Lord revealed to Moses, and later to Joseph Smith in the writings of Moses, that not only did Adam have the power of speech but *he was taught also to read and to write, and records were kept by him and by his posterity.*"[2]

The people of God from the days of Adam recognized the wisdom and necessity of collecting the revelations of the Lord to man, and thus from the early "book of remembrance" spoken of in the Pearl of Great Price (Moses 6:5, 46) came those compilations known later as the holy scriptures.

How were the sacred words recorded? It appears that anciently two main substances were used in writing. Papyrus was made from the inner bark of a reed plant that grew beside rivers and marshes. To make the papyrus the "reeds were stripped and cut lengthwise into thin narrow slices before being beaten and pressed together into two layers set at right angles to each other. When dried the whitish surface was polished smooth with a stone or other implement."[3] Separate pieces could be joined together end to end to form a long strip that could then be rolled into a scroll of manageable size, called in the Greek a *biblios* or *biblion*. "This name was derived from one of the names of the plant itself, *byblos,* which is related in turn to the name of a town in Phoenicia which the Greeks knew as Byblos."[4] It is from the word *biblion* that our word *Bible* is derived. The plural of *biblion* is *biblia,* literally, "the books."

The second material on which writing was done was parchment. Parchment was formed through shaving and scraping clean the skins of sheep, goats, antelope, and other animals in order to produce a material for writing which was more durable than papyrus. "In New Testament times parchment, being more durable and more costly than papyrus, was used chiefly for documents of greater value, or for such as were constantly in use and were, therefore, exposed to greater wear and tear."[5] Other types of materials on which the written word could be recorded included unglazed pottery, stone, and clay and wax tablets. Though tablets of this sort were more durable, their weight and bulk made them extremely inconvenient. On the other hand, papyrus, which was very convenient, was not very durable—in humid climates the papyri soon rotted away. Pen and ink were used to write on papyrus or parchment. The pen was a reed "fashioned from rushes about 6–16 in. long, the end being cut to a flat chisel-shape to enable thick and thin strokes to be made with the broad or narrow sides."[6] The ink was made of charcoal, gum, and water.[7] Note the scriptural reference to "paper and ink" in 2 John 1:12 (see also 3 John 1:13). Writing instruments for the more durable substances were usually a chisel or a metal stylus.

Rollers were provided around which the papyrus could be wound. As the roll of papyrus was read, it would be unwound with one hand and wound up with the other. F. F. Bruce has given an interesting insight into the importance of the size of the rolls: "The longest books of the New Testament (which, in descending order of length, are Luke, Acts, Matthew, John) represent the amount of written matter which a roll of normal size contained. A roll could not exceed a certain length without becoming inconvenient for use. One of the reasons why Christian communities so quickly adopted the codex form [i.e., a "book" with pages] in preference to the roll form . . . was probably that the new form allowed them to have several documents together in one book."[8]

Another biblical scholar has written: "We must remember that an ancient book was in form a roll—as the Jews made them, scrolls of skin, finished smooth on one side to be written on. These might be of most inconvenient length; Jesus in the synagogue was handed 'the roll of the Prophet Isaiah,' and he 'found the place where it was written'—a difficult thing to do in the long series of columns of that book, which amounts in print to 125 large pages and must have made at least that many columns of Hebrew, with no chapter-numbers, capitals, or column numbers (there were no pages) to aid the reader in his search.

"The Hebrew Bible—the Old Testament—as Jesus knew it, consisted of from twelve to twenty such scrolls of different sizes. They were never united into what we would call one 'book' until the invention of printing made that possible, in the fifteenth century."[9]

Perhaps one final thought will help us appreciate our modern age: until the invention of printing, all copying had to be done by hand, one copy at a time.

FORMATION OF THE CANON

The word *canon* goes back through Latin to the Greek *kanon*. The root meaning of the word is "reed" and seems to have been understood to refer to a type of ruler or measuring device or (later, in a metaphorical sense) a standard. Origen, the great Alexandrian scholar (A.D. 184–254) used the word *kanon* to refer to what he called the "rule of faith," the standard by which we are to measure and evaluate everything that may be offered to us as an article of belief. In this sense the word is "closely linked with the authority of Scripture."[10] In another sense, *canon* came to be associated with a list or index or collection of documents that served as the rule of faith, though such a use of the word seems not to have been made earlier than Athanasius (A.D. 296–373).

Bruce is quick to maintain a distinction between the canonicity of a book and its authority: "Its canonicity is dependent upon its authority. For when we ascribe canonicity to a book we simply mean that it belongs to the canon or list. But why does it so belong? Because it was recognized as possessing special authority. People frequently speak and write as if the authority with which the books of the Bible are invested in the minds of Christians is the result of their having been included in the sacred list. But the historical fact is the other way about; they were and are included in the list because they were acknowledged as authoritative." He concludes this thought by stating simply, "Both logically and historically, authority precedes canonicity."[11] One group of scholars feels that there were five guiding principles used to determine whether a book belonged within the canon:

"*Is it authoritative?* . . . Does this book come with a divine 'Thus saith the Lord'? . . .

"*Is it prophetic?* . . . Was this book written by a man of God? . . .

"*Is it authentic?* . . . 'Does the book tell the *truth* . . . as it is already known by previous revelation?' [The Fathers had the attitude of 'if in doubt, throw it out.'] . . .

"*Is it dynamic?* . . . Does the book come with the *power* of God? . . .

"*Was it received?* . . . Has this book been *accepted* generally by the *people* of God?"[12]

There were a number of factors that pointed out the need for a canon of Old Testament scripture. For one thing, the Jewish sacrificial system was ended by the destruction of Jerusalem and the temple in A.D. 70. The Jews were scattered and needed to determine which books were the authoritative word of God because of the numerous extrascriptural writings of the time. Exiled Jews returned to ancient scripture to rekindle the hope of deliverance and reestablishment as a nation, all of which had been the burden of so many of the Old Testament prophets. Thus, "for the study and preservation of this the synagogue arose, and Judaism was enabled to survive the destruction of its Temple and the interruption of its national worship."[13]

The debates raged for centuries as to exactly what should be constituted as scripture. For example, there was repeated dispute as to the status of such books as Proverbs, Ecclesiastes, Song of Solomon, and Esther. The book of Esther, for example, did not contain the name of God; Ecclesiastes was difficult to square with contemporary orthodoxy. The Synod at Jamnia, which took place about A.D. 90, proved to be critical in the review and collection of these works and others that came to be the twenty-two books of the Hebrew Bible.[14]

It is interesting to note Christ's reference to the canon of scripture in the meridian of time. In the upper room (after the Resurrection) he spoke to the disciples regarding the scriptures as a witness to his divine Sonship: "These are the words which I spake unto you, while I was yet with you, that all things must be fulfilled, which were written in the law of Moses, and in the prophets, and in the psalms, concerning me" (Luke 24:44). Jesus here made reference to the threefold division of the Hebrew Bible—the Law, the Prophets, and the Writings (although he called the Writings "the psalms" here, probably because the book of Psalms is the first and longest book in the third section). It appears that by the time of Jamnia a sort of unofficial canonization had been accomplished, so that "the Council of Jamnia," as one writer has indicated, "was the confirming of public opinion, not the forming of it."[15]

Though there seems to be no evidence of any dispute between Jesus and the Jews with regard to the canonicity of any Old Testament book,[16] one particular clarification by the Prophet Joseph Smith in his inspired translation attests to the fact that at least some of the "plain and precious truths" of the scripture had been removed or ignored by his day: "Woe unto you, lawyers! For ye have taken away the key of knowledge, the *fullness of the scriptures;* ye entered not in yourselves into the kingdom; and those who were entering in, ye hindered" (JST, Luke 11:53; emphasis added). The doctors of the law had removed the "fullness of the scriptures" from their writings or from their teachings.

Another matter resolved (or confirmed) at Jamnia was the status of the Old Testament Apocrypha. St. Jerome in the fourth century was the first to call certain works "apocryphal," meaning "secret or hidden." One group of writers gave a number of testimonies of antiquity against accepting the Apocrypha:

"1. Josephus (A.D. 30–100), Jewish historian, explicitly excludes the Apocrypha, numbering the books of the Old Testament as 22.

"2. Jesus and the New Testament writers never once quote the Apocrypha.

"3. The Jewish scholars of Jamnia (A.D. 90) did not recognize the Apocrypha.

"4. Many of the great Fathers of the early church spoke out against the Apocrypha, for example, Origen, Cyril of Jerusalem, Athanasius.

"5. Jerome (340–420), the great scholar and translator of the Vulgate, rejected the Apocrypha as part of the canon.

"6. Many Roman Catholic scholars through the Reformation period rejected the Apocrypha.

"7. Not until A.D. 1546, in a polemical action at the Counter Reformation Council of Trent, did the Apocryphal books receive full canonical status by the Roman Catholic Church."[17]

When Martin Luther finished his translation of the Bible in 1534, he placed the apocryphal books in a group by themselves at the end of the Old Testament. This same pattern was followed by Myles Coverdale in 1535 in the first Bible printed in English. Thereafter all the great historic English Bibles followed the same procedure. Only in the Catholic Old Testament of 1610, which was translated from the Latin Vulgate, did the apocryphal books remain scattered throughout the Old Testament, as they are today in the Douai Version of the Bible.[18]

There were at least three reasons for determining a New Testament canon. First of all, there was the problem of heresy. For example, Marcion, a teacher from Asia Minor, came to Rome (A.D. 140) with a novel approach to the teaching of the gospel. Marcion rejected the Old Testament and proposed a new canon to take its place, consisting of two parts—the "Gospel" and the "Apostle." The Gospel would be represented by an expurgated Gospel of Luke, and the Apostle would contain the Pauline letters (excluding Timothy and Titus). "Even the books which he did accept as canonical Scripture were edited in accordance with what he believed to be pure Christian doctrine. No doubt he believed that by this process of editing he was removing interpolations introduced by those who followed the teaching of the Twelve, as distinct from Paul, who in Marcion's eyes was the only faithful apostle. Thus anything, even in Paul's epistles, which seemed to recognize the authority of the God of Israel or to identify Him with the God and Father of our Lord Jesus Christ was cut out; it could not, on Marcion's premises, be genuine. All Old Testament references were likewise excised."[19] Second, many Eastern churches had begun to use in their services books whose authority was questionable. A decision was needed with regard to canon. Finally, there came a time when, for extremely practical reasons, it was crucial that serious thought be given to the canonicity of certain books. The Edict of Diocletian (A.D. 303) decreed the destruction of the sacred books of the Christians. Simply stated, who wanted to die for a nice book that happened to have religious overtones? These people needed to know.

As was the case with the Old Testament, much debate ensued through the years with regard to the status of particular books in the New Testament. Of special note is the fact that Origen had devised his own canon, made up of his "acknowledged" and his "disputed" books. His disputed books consisted of 2 John, 3 John, 2 Peter, Jude, and two apocryphal works—the Letter of Barnabas and the Shepherd of Hermas.[20] Others quarreled over Hebrews, James, and Revelation. Even during the Reformation, we find Martin Luther speaking of a canon within a canon, evidencing his own discomfort, for example, with the Epistle of James. On the whole, however, most scholars agree that the canon of our present New Testament was fixed by the end of the fourth century.

THE SCRIPTURES: FROM HEBREW TO ENGLISH

Let us back up for a moment now, and recount some of the more critical incidents associated with the development of our own King James Version of the Bible. The formation of the Septuagint (from the Latin word *septuaginta,* meaning "seventy"), the Greek version of the Old Testament (often designated in Roman numerals as LXX), is an excellent place to begin this discussion. The story is told that Ptolemy Philadelphus, king of Egypt (285–246 B.C.), became fascinated with the Jewish Law as a piece of literature. Ptolemy was known as a patron of literature and founder of the great library at Alexandria. One account of these happenings describes how the king was encouraged by his aides to send a delegate to the high priest at Jerusalem. The high priest thereafter chose six elders from each of the twelve tribes of Israel to serve as translators of the Hebrew scripture into Greek, and these were sent to Alexandria with an accurate and beautiful parchment of the Torah. After being wined and dined, these men were taken to Pharos, in the harbor of Alexandria, where they took up residence while undertaking the translation. In seventy-two days they completed their task and, upon comparison, found their individual results to be remarkably similar.[21] Other versions of the same incident tell how the seventy-two translators did their work in seventy-two separate cells, and after seventy-two days their versions were found to be identical. Thus was born the LXX, a version of the scriptures vital to the gradual spread of the word of the Lord through his prophets to the peoples of the earth. The LXX is important to us not only because of the myriad of other translations that follow from it but also because of the fact that when the New Testament authors quote from the Old Testament, most of them quote, not from the original Hebrew, but from the LXX or other Greek translations.[22]

It appears that the first translation of the scriptures into Latin took place in northern Africa sometime during the last part of the second century after Christ. The translation into Latin was not from the Hebrew language, but rather from the old Greek text. The name "Old Latin" is used to designate those translations of the

Bible which existed prior to, or at least independent of, the work of Jerome at the end of the fourth century. Bruce M. Metzger has written: "By the close of the fourth century the limitations and imperfections of the Old Latin versions had become evident to the leaders of the Roman church. In the OT renderings rested on the Greek of the LXX instead of the original Hebrew, and in both testaments scribal corruptions had disfigured still further what had never been scholarly translations. It is not surprising, therefore, that ca. 382 Pope Damasus requested the most capable Biblical scholar then living, Eusebius Hieronymus, known today as Jerome, to undertake a revision of the Latin Bible."[23]

Jerome's translation of the Bible, called the Latin Vulgate (written in the vulgar, or common, language of the people) helped to fill the need for one standard text with which to combat heresy and unify the Western church. On 8 April 1546 the Council of Trent declared the Vulgate to be the authoritative version of the Bible to be used by the church, and even today it is accepted as such by the Roman Catholic Church.[24]

It is fascinating to consider that by the middle of the twentieth century much of the Bible had been translated into more than a thousand different languages and dialects. But significant to this discussion is the fact that less than a score of these translations had been made before the year 1000.[25] Also worthy of note is the fact that eighteen editions of the complete German Bible were in print prior to Martin Luther's translation. And yet, the translation by Luther is unique. It "marks an epoch in the history, not only of the German Bible, but of the German language as well."[26] Luther's work (published in 1534) had a profound influence upon the rise of modern German literature. Through the years Luther's personal ambition had been to give to the people a version of the Bible that truly spoke their language. He seems to have succeeded, for so influential was his rendering that for almost a century few other attempts at translations were made.

William Tyndale was a young Englishman, a reformer at heart, who had studied at Oxford and Cambridge. He had concluded that it was "'impossible to establish the lay people in any truth except the scripture were plainly laid before their eyes in their mother tongue'—'which thing only moved me to translate the New Testament.'"[27] Unable to elicit church support for his project, Tyndale went abroad to work and began the printing of the scripture in English in Cologne in 1525. But officers of the Catholic Church learned of his work and interrupted it. Thereafter Tyndale fled to Worms, where he was able to finish the printing by the end of that same year. His translation into English was not from the Latin Vulgate but from the original Greek. This seeming obsession with the need for providing a translation of the Bible with the average man in mind was not original with either Tyndale or Luther. In 1383 John Wyclif had produced the first complete Bible in English. In commenting upon Wyclif's role in this grand drama, one writer has stated: "The work of John Wyclif is different from any translations before him. He planned and executed the translation of the entire Bible with the average man in mind and for the specific purpose of placing the Bible in the hands of laymen. His work of translation was a part of more comprehensive effort to reform the church which caused him to be called the 'morning star of the Reformation.'"[28]

Copies of the Tyndale translation reached Britain by 1526, and although welcomed by the Reformation-minded among the people, these documents were sought out for destruction by church authorities. After a study of Hebrew, Tyndale went on to complete the Pentateuch and published it in 1530. But in 1535 his enemies finally overtook him and imprisoned him near Brussels. In that same year, 1535, while Tyndale was in prison, Myles Coverdale produced the first printed English Bible.[29] The next year, on the sixth of October, William Tyndale was brought forth to the place of execution, strangled, and finally burned at the stake.[30]

That which follows is easily recounted—one translation after another.[31] Only two years elapsed after the Coverdale Bible before another English Bible made its appearance, under the name of Thomas Matthew. This name seems to have been a pen name for John Rogers, who later became the first of the Smithfield martyrs in Queen Mary's persecution in 1555. The John Rogers Bible has the distinction of having become the first licensed English Bible. As such, it could be bought and sold, owned and read without fear of interference by the authorities. In 1539 came the so-called Great Bible, a large pulpit-style book intended to be placed on the lectern at church. Now for the first time Englishmen could listen as the Bible was read in church, not in Latin but in English. And thus we have the first authorized English Bible. In 1560 the Geneva Bible came forth. This particular Bible had two significant features: first, it incorporated the recent innovation of versification that had been established in 1551 by Robert Etienne, the French printer; second, it was printed not in the old black letter, but in the new Roman type, which is in universal use today. It was this Geneva Bible (also known as the Breeches Bible because its wording for Genesis 3:7 reads, "And they sewed fig leaves together, and made themselves breeches") that passed through more than one hundred editions. This was the Bible of Shakespeare, of Cromwell, and of the Pilgrim fathers. In 1568 there appeared the Bishops' Bible, a revision of the authorized Great Bible. The Bishops' Bible became the second authorized English Bible.

English Catholics had no English Bible as yet, but in 1578 Gregory Martin began a translation of the Latin Vulgate into English. He began this work at the Catholic College at Rheims, in France, but by the turn of the century the college had removed to Douai. Thus, in 1610 came the Douai Version of the Bible.

"In 1604 this period of Bible translation and revision reached its climax: On February 10, 1604, the king ordered 'that a translation be made of the whole Bible, as consonant as can be to the original Hebrew and Greek, and this to be set out and printed without any marginal notes and only to be used in all churches of England in time of divine service.' By July, 1604, King James says that he had 'appointed certain learned men to the number of four and fifty for the translating of the Bible.' These men were to be the 'best learned' in Westminster and in 'both the Universities' and their work was to be 'reviewed by the bishops and the chief learned of the church,' and 'to be ratified by Privy Council and by royal authority.' The men appointed were to be able, efficient biblical scholars and were chosen from among Anglican churchmen, Puritans, and laymen. Only forty-seven names have been included on the list of those who actually worked on the edition. Those men divided into six groups, four working on the OT and two on the NT."[32]

Regarding the role of the Divine in the development of this collection, our own King James Version of the Bible, Elder Mark E. Petersen taught: "When I lived in England a few years ago I went to the British Museum in London and studied the history of the King James Version of the Bible. I learned that *its translators fasted and prayed for inspiration in their work. I am convinced that they received it.*"[33] And thus the year 1611 proved to be a year of deep significance in the continuing struggle for the children of God to obtain the word of God.

IN RETROSPECT

To the Latter-day Saints the Bible is a special revelation of the Divine to man. We love the Bible as much, perhaps, as any people on earth. And yet this attitude is most strange to those who are not Latter-day Saints, for we claim a belief in this stick of Judah *"as far as it is translated correctly"* (Articles of Faith 1:8; emphasis added). Though we are aware of the fact that many plain and precious truths have been taken from the Bible through the years; that there are obviously many missing books of the Bible; that "many important points touching the salvation of man, [have] been taken from the Bible, or lost before it was compiled";[34] and, finally, that "ignorant translators, careless transcribers, or designing and corrupt priests have committed many errors" in their work with the Bible;[35] yet, we have a special respect and reverence for this divine collection. Our faith in the hand of the Lord in its compilation is a firm faith in the overall process by which it has come to us, for we recognize that "there will be, there can be, no absolutely reliable translation . . . unless it be effected through the gift of translation, as one of the endowments of the Holy Ghost. The translator must have the spirit of the prophet if he would render in another tongue the prophet's words; and human wisdom alone leads not to that possession."[36]

Errors in the Bible should not tarnish its image, for there is still very much within its covers that is beautiful and wholesome and ennobling. Our duty, President George Q. Cannon reminded us, is to engender faith in the Bible:

"As our duty is to create faith in the word of God in the mind of the young student, we scarcely think that object is best attained by making the mistakes of translators the more prominent part of our teachings. Even children have their doubts, but it is not our business to encourage those doubts. Doubts never convert; negations seldom convince. . . . The clause in the Articles of Faith regarding mistakes in the translation of the Bible was never inserted to encourage us to spend our time in searching out and studying those errors, but to emphasize the idea that it is the truth and the truth only that the Church of Jesus Christ of Latter-day Saints accepts, no matter where it is found."[37]

Notes

From an address delivered at a CES Symposium on the Old Testament, Brigham Young University, Provo, Utah, August 16–18, 1979.

1. See F. F. Bruce, *The Books and the Parchments,* 3d ed. rev. (Westwood, N. J.: Fleming H. Revell Co., 1963), 12.
2. Joseph Fielding Smith, *The Way to Perfection* (Salt Lake City: Deseret Book Co., 1970), 67; emphasis added.
3. P. R. Ackroyd and C. F. Evans, eds., *From the Beginnings to Jerome,* vol. 1 of *Cambridge History of the Bible* (London: Cambridge University Press, 1963), 30; see also Bruce, *Books and Parchments,* 11.
4. Bruce, *Books and Parchments,* 11.
5. Ibid., 12.
6. Ackroyd and Evans, *From the Beginnings to Jerome,* 31.
7. Bruce, *Books and Parchments,* 13.
8. Ibid., 12.
9. Edgar J. Goodspeed, *How Came the Bible?* (New York: Abingdon Press, 1940), 10.
10. Bruce, *Books and Parchments,* 95.
11. Ibid., 95–96.
12. Norman L. Geisler and William E. Nix, *A General Introduction to the Bible* (Chicago: Moody Press, 1968), 138–43.
13. Goodspeed, *How Came the Bible?* 23.
14. George Arthur Buttrick, ed., *The Interpreter's Dictionary of the Bible,* 4 vols. (New York: Abingdon Press, 1962), s.v. "Jabneel"; see also Bruce, *Books and Parchments,* 98; Goodspeed, *How Came the Bible?* 41.
15. J. S. Wright, in *Evangelical Quarterly,* April 1947, 97, as cited in Bruce, *Books and Parchments,* 98.

16. See Edward J. Young, "The Authority of the Old Testament," in *The Infallible Word* (Philadelphia: Presbyterian and Reformed Publishing Co., 1946), 73, as cited in Josh McDowell, comp., *Evidence That Demands a Verdict* (n.p.: Campus Crusade for Christ, 1972), 37.

17. Geisler and Nix, *General Introduction to the Bible*, 173, as cited in McDowell, *Evidence That Demands a Verdict*, 40.

18. Goodspeed, *How Came the Bible?* 49–50.

19. Bruce, *Books and Parchments*, 108. It was soon after the time of Marcion, in the last quarter of the second century, that the term New Testament (from the Greek *diatheke*, literally, "covenant or agreement") began to be used to refer to the collection of Christian scripture, while Old Testament was used to refer to the Jewish scriptures.

20. Goodspeed, *How Came the Bible?* 78–79.

21. See Bruce, *Books and Parchments*, 146–47; see also Buttrick, *Interpreter's Dictionary of the Bible*, s.v. "Versions, ancient."

22. Buttrick, *Interpreter's Dictionary of the Bible*, s.v. "Versions, ancient"; see also Goodspeed, *How Came the Bible?* 13.

23. Buttrick, *Interpreter's Dictionary of the Bible*, s.v. "Versions, ancient."

24. See William Smith, *The New Smith's Bible Dictionary*, ed. Reuel G. Lemmons (Garden City, New York: Doubleday and Co., 1966), s.v. "Vulgate," 411–12.

25. See Buttrick, *Interpreter's Dictionary of the Bible*, s.v. "Versions, medieval."

26. Ibid., s.v. "Versions, medieval."

27. As cited in Goodspeed, *How Came the Bible?* 97.

28. Buttrick, *Interpreter's Dictionary of the Bible*, s.v. "Versions, English."

29. Goodspeed, *How Came the Bible?* 97–99.

30. See Bruce, *Books and Parchments*, 10.

31. See chapter 10 in Goodspeed, *How Came the Bible?*

32. Buttrick, *Interpreter's Dictionary of the Bible*, s.v. "Versions, English."

33. Mark E. Petersen, in Conference Report, October 1977, 18; emphasis added.

34. See Preface to D&C 76; *Teachings of the Prophet Joseph Smith*, 9–10.

35. *Teachings of the Prophet Joseph Smith*, 327.

36. James E. Talmage, *The Articles of Faith*, 14th ed. (Salt Lake City: The Church of Jesus Christ of Latter-day Saints, 1925), 237.

37. Jerreld L. Newquist, comp., *Gospel Truth: Discourses and Writings of President George Q. Cannon*, 2 vols. in one (Salt Lake City: Deseret Book Co., 1987), 472.

HOW THE FOUR
GOSPELS CAME TO BE

W hy seek ye the living among the dead? He is not here, but is risen" (Luke 24:5–6). This divine announcement, uttered by two angelic ministrants to a group of faithful and sensitive women, affirmed the hope and stilled the fears of a troubled lot of early Christian disciples. It was a testimony, a witness of the bodily resurrection of Jesus of Nazareth, and thus the physical assurance of his divine Sonship. The word of their Master was attested: he was literally the Son of God, and had power over life and death. From this singular hour the plain declarations of those with apostolic commission were delivered with greater fervor than before. Not only had the Messiah come among them, established the kingdom of God on earth, and left timely and timeless messages; but most important, he had put into effect the conditions of the plan of the Eternal Father: he had trodden the winepress alone, and through the agonies of the Atonement had "brought life and immortality to light" (2 Timothy 1:10). In short, he had established the *gospel,* the God-news, truly the good news, the theological center and hub from which all other ethical principles and practices receive meaning and context. A modern revelation declared the gospel to be "the glad tidings . . . that he came into the world, even Jesus, to be crucified for the world, and to bear the sins of the world, and to sanctify the world, and to cleanse it from all unrighteousness; that through him all might be saved whom the Father had put into his power and made by him" (D&C 76:40–42).

THE TRANSMISSION OF THE GOSPEL MESSAGE

Prior to his ascension into heaven, the Lord delivered a charge to the Apostles to go into all nations, teach, testify, and make disciples through baptism of those who would give ear to their words. In addition, these earliest messengers were to perfect their converts through proper instruction and discipline, through "teaching them to observe all things whatsoever [Christ had] commanded" (Matthew 28:20). They were to proclaim the Lord and teach what he had taught.

Acceptance of Christ and his gospel was accomplished first through the power of verbal human testimony: faith came by hearing the word of God, as taught by legal administrators whose oral witness was attended by the spirit of prophecy and revelation.[1] Much of the earliest scripture in the meridian dispensation (as perhaps in all dispensations) existed in an oral and unrecorded form.[2] The *kerygma* or proclamation of the gospel, the *logia* (sayings of Christ), and the *agrapha* (unwritten things) circulated as the witness of the Apostles spread from Jerusalem to the ends of the known world (see Acts 1:8). And as we shall observe shortly, these oral testimonies spread at the same time that written documents were being prepared and circulated concerning the majesty of the ministry of the Master. Then, as now, the gospel was preached by word and by power, whether that was by mouth or by pen; either system of delivery, oral or textual, has its underlying purposes, its strengths, and its limitations. In our own day, genuine faith-promoting stories circulate throughout the Church orally at the same time that written accounts of the events are readily available. Does it require a stretch of the imagination to suppose that in the first-century Church, written documents recounting many of the events of the life of Jesus were contemporaneous with the Saints' reminiscences and personal oral testimonies of the same? The manner in which oral traditions were valued is highlighted in the following statement of Papias, bishop of Hierapolis in Asia Minor (ca. A.D. 130–140):

"I will not hesitate to set down for you alongside my interpretations all that I ever learned well from the elders and remembered well, guaranteeing their truth. For I did not, like the majority, rejoice in those who say most, but in those who teach the truth; not in those who regard the commandments of others, but in those who relate commandments given by the Lord to faith, and proceeding from him who is truth. Also, if ever a person came my way who had been a companion of the elders, I would inquire about the sayings of the elders—what was said by Andrew, or by Peter, or by Philip, or by Thomas or James, or by John or Matthew or any other of the Lord's disciples? . . . For I did not suppose that what I could get from books was of such great value to me as the utterances of a living and abiding voice."[3]

THE TASK OF THE GOSPEL WRITER

It would be the grossest understatement to suggest that the task facing the Gospel writer was a formidable one. How does one write the biography of a God, sketch the outlines or prepare the epoch of the Infinite One? It would seem, therefore, that an initial obstacle facing the inspired author/editor was one of being able to discern the words and ideas that could most closely approximate that which is basically ineffable. Indeed, some matters are such that "no tongue can speak [of them], neither can [they] be written by any man, neither can the hearts of men conceive so great and marvelous things" (3 Nephi 17:17; see also 2 Corinthians 12:4). But to certain chosen representatives it *was* given to construct a limited but living and descriptive testimony of the Messiah—a carefully constrained chronicle of the life of the Son of God.

A second potential obstacle facing the Gospel writer was the passage of time, the interval between the actual events and the accounts of those events. We are in no position at this date to state exactly when Matthew, Mark, Luke, and John produced their individual Gospel narratives. Reason would dictate, however, that much of the material in our present canonical Gospels did not take final form until a number of years after the death and resurrection of Christ. The passing of time often leads to a loss of detail. Yet the passing of time also leads to an enhanced perspective and a breadth of clarity and context. Nephi began his small plates approximately thirty years after leaving the land of his father's inheritance (see 2 Nephi 5:28–32), but we as readers and recipients of his offering are much the richer as a result of a period of rare and valuable spiritual gestation. With eyes open to the works and wonders of the Lord during the previous three decades, Nephi the prophet/writer set forth in remarkable fashion his "outline," an intriguing account of how the "tender mercies of the Lord are over all those whom he has chosen" (1 Nephi 1:20). Joseph Smith's account of the First Vision as recorded in the Pearl of Great Price was dictated some eighteen years after the initial opening of the heavens. During that interval Joseph the Prophet grew in spiritual graces and gained a maturity and spiritual frame of reference that sharply defined the significance of the appearance of the Father and the Son. In similar fashion the Gospel writers, moved upon by the Holy Ghost, reflected upon personal or reported experiences with the Master, and finally with mature minds and a grander vision set out to construct an extended written testimony of Jesus the Christ. Time frequently yields a peak in overall perception.

Eusebius, the fourth-century church historian, reported that "of all the disciples, Matthew and John are the only ones that have left us recorded comments [concerning the ministry of Christ], and even they, tradition says, *undertook it from necessity.*"[4] What was the *necessity* for written Gospels? Why was it essential that *the* gospel be formed into *a* Gospel, that the oral become textual? First of all, it is important to note that the power and impact of oral traditions are bounded by the limitations and inabilities of human transmitters. Two early Latter-day Saint writers thus suggested that the written Gospels took shape to ensure continuity and orthodoxy of doctrine. They explained:

"It may be supposed that those Disciples of Christ . . . like Matthew and John, would keep journals while they followed their Master, witnessing His works and listening to His teachings. These journals would, after the Crucifixion and Ascension, naturally be read in private and in public. They would be copied and distributed in the various branches of the Church and from texts for sermons and otherwise discourses, and thus be augmented with such incidents or sayings which were still retained in the memories of those who had been eyewitnesses. In this way several versions of the doings and sayings of our Lord began to circulate, some no doubt contradicting others, until the necessity became universally felt to have some authentic record showing exactly what was reliable of the many circulating reports, and what was not reliable. And the result is the four Gospels according to Matthew, Mark, Luke and John."[5]

Then, as now, there was a need for a standard work, a written testimony whereby the first-century Saints might "speak the same thing," and thus "be perfectly joined together in the same mind and in the same judgment" (1 Corinthians 1:10). The authorized Gospels helped to establish precise doctrinal and historical lines between orthodoxy and heresy, between the accepted and the aberrant. One theologian has described the process as follows: "In the Graeco-Roman world, the Palestinian Gospel came into contact with all sorts of religious and philosophic movements. Men challenged it and could have perverted it by turning it into a metaphysical system or a mystery or Gnostic cult, without connection with that historic figure who gave it birth; that is, they could have cut it from its root. To prevent this, the Gospels came into being; they kept the Church attached to its base."[6]

Secondly, the Gospels were written to secure and maintain the precious witness of those who had originally walked and talked with the Savior. "When these witnesses began to pass away," W. D. Davies has written, "their testimony had to be preserved. This is one of the fundamental reasons for the emergence of the Gospels—in part, at least, they were designed to supply the witness of those witnesses who were no longer alive."[7] In analogous fashion, one might ask where we would be as a church today had it not been for the handy and faithful pens of such persons as Wilford Woodruff and William Clayton and Willard Richards and Thomas Bullock, men who conscientiously recorded and preserved critical elements of the sermons of Joseph Smith for a future day. In prophetic fashion the Gospel writers prepared documents and thus preserved traditions that were both timely and timeless.

THE FOUR GOSPELS: FORMATION AND FUNCTION

In speaking against doctrinal heresies of the second century, Irenaeus (ca. A.D. 180) taught that "it is not possible that the gospels can be either more or fewer in number than they are." He further referred to the four Gospels as like unto the "four zones of the world in which we live," as well as the "four pillars" of the Church. Irenaeus then added that Christ "has given us the Gospel under four aspects, but bound together by one spirit."[8] Irenaeus' statement is obviously intended to discourage and discount any and all apocryphal gospels. At the same time, it is wise for us to recognize the hand of Providence in the formation, inspiration, and preservation of the four canonical Gospels that we have. Surely Matthew, Mark, Luke, and John were foreordained in premortality and raised up in mortality to make their particular contributions. "Every man who has a calling to minister to the inhabitants of the world," Joseph Smith taught, "was ordained to that very purpose in the Grand Council of heaven before this world was."[9] The ministries of our Gospel writers did not end with their own deaths; their compositions continue to turn men's minds toward their Savior twenty centuries later.

Matthew. Matthew (Levi) was one of the original Apostles, a publican or tax gatherer before his call. One noted theologian has written concerning Matthew as the scribe or recorder of the Twelve:

"Matthew was probably a man of somewhat more education, as we would call it, than some of his fellow disciples. He must have been able to read and write, and to use the elements at least of arithmetic, in his work as a tax collector. . . . Matthew is more likely to have known Greek than any of the rest, for he was a tax collector. He is likely to have been readier with the pen than most, perhaps than any, of the group, and he may even have jotted down for his own use not a few of Jesus' striking sayings, especially after the missionary travels of the Twelve about the Jewish towns."[10]

In the preparation of his Gospel, Matthew would have drawn upon his own reminiscences and notes, and possibly upon other extant oral or written sources. After providing the genealogy of Jesus Christ, Matthew records (1:18): "Now the birth of Jesus Christ was on this wise. . . ." The Matthean infancy narrative follows. Joseph Smith's translation of the same verse (JST, Matthew 2:1) reads: "Now, *as it is written,* the birth of Jesus Christ was on this wise." This alteration of the King James text by the Prophet may well point toward a written source available to the Apostle that predates his own Gospel.

Traditionally Matthew is said to have collected the *logia* (sayings) of Jesus in Hebrew (presumably meaning Aramaic) and later translated the same into Greek. From Papias, we have the following fragment: "Matthew put together the oracles [of the Lord] in the Hebrew language, and each one interpreted them the best he could."[11] In commenting on the statement of Papias, one scholar has written: "If Matthew had made notes from time to time of things of especial interest and importance that Jesus had said, he would naturally have done so in Aramaic, the language Jesus spoke and they all used." Further, "In Antioch [the traditional source of Matthew's Gospel], of course, his public was largely Greek, and he naturally translated the sayings into that language as he had occasion to use them, or unwritten things that he simply remembered. This is doubtless the background of Papias' remarks."[12]

Mark. John Mark's Gospel bespeaks an awareness of much detail concerning the comings and goings of Jesus Christ. Mark became a traveling companion of Paul, and certainly would have received and imbibed much information from this Apostle to the Gentiles. Most important, however, the early Church leaders recognized Mark's Gospel as being tied directly to his personal experiences with Simon Peter.

"So greatly . . . did the splendour of piety enlighten the minds of Peter's hearers, that it was not sufficient to hear but once, nor to receive the unwritten doctrine of the gospel of God, but they persevered in every variety of entreaties, to solicit Mark as the companion of Peter [see 1 Peter 5:13], and whose gospel we have, that he should leave them a monument of the doctrine thus orally communicated, in writing. Nor did they cease their solicitations until they had prevailed with the man, and thus become the means of that history which is called the gospel according to Mark. They say also, that the Apostle (Peter), having ascertained what was done by the revelation of the spirit, was delighted with the zealous ardour expressed by these men, and that the history obtained his authority for the purposes of being read in the churches."[13]

Luke. Luke is the author of the two-part work, Luke-Acts, an inspiring narrative which documents the ministry of the Savior and describes the struggles and growth of the first-century Church. Also a missionary companion of Paul, Luke seems to have drawn widely from a number of sources to tell the gospel story. The first four verses of Luke's Gospel provide the background and motivation for his work: "Forasmuch as many have taken in hand to set forth in order a declaration of those things which are most surely believed among us, even as they delivered them unto us, which from the beginning were eyewitnesses, and ministers of the word; it seemed good to me also, having had perfect understanding of all things from the very first, to write unto thee in order . . . that thou mightest know the certainty of those things, wherein thou hast been instructed" (Luke 1:1–4). The Joseph Smith Translation identifies Luke as "a messenger of Jesus Christ" (JST, Luke 1:1). In the words of Elder Bruce R. McConkie, "Luke was a legal administrator. He held the Melchizedek Priesthood, served as an official minister of Christ, *quite likely wrote his gospel by assignment of the church officers,* and spoke as one having authority."[14] In further commenting on Luke's role as a divinely directed author/editor, Elder McConkie has written:

"Many of the early saints recorded their testimonies or gospels, bearing eyewitness accounts of the divinity of our Lord and of his ministry among men, just as many with personal knowledge of Joseph Smith and his work of restoration have written journals, letters, and histories delineating what took place in the ushering in of this dispensation. *Luke had access to many of these ancient gospels.*"[15]

Luke prepared his Gospel "in order to free [the Saints] from the uncertain suppositions of others," and therefore "delivered the certain account of those things, that he himself had fully received from his intimacy and stay with Paul, and also his intercourse with the other apostles."[16] After countless interviews with the Apostles, with various lesser-known disciples, and certainly with people like Mary, the mother of Jesus,[17] the "beloved physician" sought inspiration and gave birth to his masterpiece, the Gospel of Luke.

John. The Apostle John, known as the Beloved Disciple or the Revelator, bequeathed to the world one of the most remarkable treasures in religious history in the form of his Gospel narrative. It is generally held (though difficult to establish beyond all doubt) that the Gospel of John, known early as "the spiritual Gospel," was the last of the canonical Gospels to be committed to writing. One ancient tradition states that after Mark and Luke had published their Gospels, John "admitted them, giving his testimony to their truth." John, however, recognizing the fact that "the other three evangelists only wrote the deeds of our Lord for one year after the imprisonment of John the Baptist," set out to fill in those historical gaps of the synoptic Gospels. "John, it is said, being entreated to undertake it, wrote the account of the time not recorded by the former evangelists, and the deeds done by our Savior, which they have passed by."[18] It is reasonable to suppose that John collected and drew upon available sources beyond his own personal records. If indeed John's Gospel was written last, it may well be—in those few areas where his Gospel follows the course of the synoptics—that he would have been acquainted with, had before him, and thus utilized in a discerning manner details from the other three Gospels.[19] An analogous situation in Latter-day Saint literature would be that of Elders James E. Talmage and Bruce R. McConkie, who, in the preparation of their masterworks on the life of Christ, would have had before them such earlier works as *The Life of Christ* (Farrar) and *The Life and Times of Jesus the Messiah* (Edersheim) and, in the case of Elder McConkie, Elder Talmage's *Jesus the Christ.*

In addition to the possibility that John had access to the synoptics, there is a strong probability that the forepart of his Gospel was based on the earlier writings of John the Baptist. A modern Apostle has written regarding this ancient Apostle's resources: "There is little doubt but that the Beloved Disciple had before him the Baptist's account when he wrote his gospel. The latter John either copied or paraphrased what the earlier prophet of the same name had written. The only other possibility is that the Lord revealed to the gospel author the words that had been recorded by the earlier messenger who prepared the way before him."[20]

There should be no doubt among Latter-day Saints that the canonical Gospels were compiled and composed and organized and written under the spirit of revelation. At the same time, we do not remove any of the importance or spiritual significance from these inspired authors by acknowledging Matthew, Mark, Luke, and John as divinely directed *editors* as well as creative authors. Moses was a choice seer and a man open to the revelations of the Almighty. He was also a gifted compiler and editor of earlier records. From the beginning men had been commanded to keep records in order that the history of man's existence (as well as the dealings of God with man) might be preserved. "How else," President Kimball has asked, "do you think Moses, many hundreds of years later, got the information he compiled in the book of Genesis? These records had been kept, and he referred to them and got the history of the world, which wasn't in any library other than that."[21] Likewise, Mormon was an inspired editor/author whose "and thus we see" passages in the Nephite record help wondrously to achieve the "wise purposes" of the Lord. The

Gospel writers undertook the task of producing authorized and written testimony-narratives, based upon accurate and authentic accounts and directed by the Spirit which their Master had promised to send. Undoubtedly, the Holy Ghost instructed the writers and brought things to their remembrance that were critical to the assignment at hand (see John 14:26).

All four Gospel writers knew of the divine Sonship of Jesus of Nazareth; they all loved and served the same Lord. And yet their testimonies of the Christ were expressed in varying ways and in a manner peculiar to each author.

"It appears that Matthew was directing his gospel to the Jews. He presents Christ as the promised Messiah and Christianity as the fulfillment of Judaism. Mark apparently wrote with the aim of appealing to the Roman or Gentile mind. Luke's gospel presents the Master to the Greeks, to those of culture and refinement. And the gospel of John is the account for the Saints; it is pre-eminently the gospel for the Church, for those who understand the scriptures and their symbolisms and who are concerned with spiritual and eternal things."[22]

Each Gospel writer "had especial and intimate knowledge of certain circumstances not so well known to others," and thus "each felt impressed to emphasize different matters because of the particular people to whom he was addressing his personal gospel testimony."[23]

Another matter worth considering is the fact that our four Gospels may not always have existed in their present state or condition. On the one hand, we need to recognize the appropriateness of a writer—even an inspired writer—adding to or taking away from his work as he matures spiritually or gains new or added perspective. In our Book of Mormon story, Moroni returned to his record after a period of fearful anticipation and (since he was still alive) provided additional doctrinal and historical insights to that which had previously been written. In the preparation of the 1835 edition of the Doctrine and Covenants, Joseph Smith made prophetic editorial changes as he felt impressed to do so. What is now section 7 of the Doctrine and Covenants (concerning the continued ministry of John the Beloved), for example, is a broadened and extended version of what had appeared in the 1833 Book of Commandments. The same is true of Joseph Smith's inspired translation of the King James Bible: whereas the Prophet and his scribe had formally completed the work of translation by July of 1833, Joseph Smith continued to labor with the manuscripts (making changes where he felt the need to do so) until the time of his death. We might, therefore, want to remain open to the possibility that different editions of the Gospels may have existed through the years. In this connection it is worthwhile to consider an excerpt from the somewhat controversial "Secret Gospel of Mark." This document was discovered in 1958 by Morton Smith in the Mar Saba monastery, some twelve miles southeast of Jerusalem.

"[As for] Mark, then, during Peter's stay in Rome he wrote [an account of] the Lord's doings, not, however, declaring all [of them], not yet hinting at the secret [ones], but selecting those he thought most useful for increasing the faith of those who were being instructed. But when Peter died as a martyr, Mark came over to Alexandria, bringing both his own notes and those of Peter, from which he transferred to his former book the things suitable to whatever makes for progress toward knowledge [*gnosis*]. [Thus] he composed a more spiritual gospel for the use of those who were being perfected. Nevertheless, he yet did not divulge the things not to be uttered, nor did he write down the hierophantic teaching of the Lord, but to the stories already written he added yet others and, moreover, brought in certain sayings of which he knew the interpretation would, as a mystagogue, lead the hearers into the innermost sanctuary of that truth hidden by seven [veils]."[24]

It may be that the Gospels as we have them now represent a truncated version of the Gospels as they were first written by the evangelists. Nephi saw in vision the day when the Bible record (the book which would proceed "out of the mouth of a Jew") would suffer a willful interference by the great and abominable church, such that "many plain and precious things [would be] taken away from the book, which is the book of the Lamb of God" (1 Nephi 13:28). We need to be extremely grateful that the Lord has seen fit to preserve those portions of the Gospels that have been secured for us; at the same time, we must be aware that the "fulness of the gospel of the Lamb" is not to be had in our present canonical Gospels, but that the Lord is revealing and restoring many of those precious truths through the "other books" (the Book of Mormon, the Doctrine and Covenants, the Pearl of Great Price, the Joseph Smith Translation, and other materials yet to be revealed) which have and will come forth by the power of the Lamb of God (1 Nephi 13:39).

THE GOSPELS: A UNIQUE CREATION

In forming the message of *the* gospel into what we have come to call *a* Gospel, the writers became the initiators of a unique literary genre, a form which is not seen elsewhere in ancient literature. The Gospels are not wholly biographical, in the modern sense of revealing or developing the thoughts or personalities of the main characters; possibly not more than thirty days of the life of Christ receive treatment through all four Gospel accounts. On the other hand, the Gospels represent laudatory biographies written to elicit faith and emulation.

The presence of sensational and titillating elements often evident in the apocryphal gospels are absent in the canonical Gospels. Absent also are attempts to explain the unexplained or to reconcile the seemingly estranged or disparate. There are no attempts to "lie for God," to appease the questioning mind, to conciliate by appending the authoritative. The canonical Gospels combine simplicity with the power of their message, and present a dignified and appropriate glimpse into the life and words of the Savior.

The Gospels are testimonies of Christ, and as such they "do not claim to be exhaustive accounts of all that Jesus said or did." Rather, "each gospel was selective according to the purpose of the author, and is complete in the sense that it carries out his intent."[25] The Gospels were "standard works," in the sense that they were given to guide the Saints in emulating the Sinless One, and given to transmit the witness that Jesus died, was buried, rose again on the third day, and ascended into heaven (see 1 Corinthians 15:3–4). The Gospels were written to convey the "portion of the word" (to use Alma's words) that is appropriate for Christians who are gaining or strengthening a conviction of Jesus as the Messiah. They were not written to convey the esoteric teachings of the Master, those sacred truths preserved for those persons able to bear the added enlightenment. In a sense, the Gospels are public documents, created for display purposes. Surely there are "many other things which Jesus did, the which, if they should be written every one, I suppose that even the world itself could not contain the books that should be written" (John 21:25).

CONCLUSION

The process by which the four Gospels came into being as written documents is a fascinating field of study, a field worthy of the consideration and attention of Latter-day Saints. Obviously the complete story of the transmission of the Gospels is not available; we are left with fragments and particles of tradition and history, and we thus seek to piece together the overall drama associated with the formation, inspiration, and preservation of four books now accepted with sacred appreciation the world over. Without question, the story of the sources and the sequences of events of the overall formation of the texts is not as important as the message delivered in the Gospels themselves. A serious study of this process, however, may lead one to a deeper awareness of the Lord's ability to make bare his mighty arm and preserve through millennia the essence of the gospel message. Such a process also reveals the infinite love of God for his children.

Notes

From an address given at a symposium sponsored by the BYU Religious Studies Center on Apocryphal Literature and the Latter-day Saints, Brigham Young University, Provo, Utah, Fall 1983.

1. See Romans 10:17; see also *Teachings of the Prophet Joseph Smith,* 148.
2. See *Doctrinal New Testament Commentary,* 1:55.
3. Eusebius, *Ecclesiastical History,* trans. C. F. Cruse, popular edition, 10 vols. (Grand Rapids, Mich.: Baker Book House, 1977), III.39; see also "Fragments of Papias," in Alexander Roberts and James Donaldson, eds., *The Ante-Nicene Fathers* (Grand Rapids, Mich.: Eerdmans Publishing Co., 1981), 1:153.
4. Eusebius, *Ecclesiastical History,* III.24.
5. George Reynolds and Janne M. Sjodahl, *Commentary on the Pearl of Great Price* (Salt Lake City: Deseret Book Co., 1965), 21–22.
6. W. D. Davies, *Invitation to the New Testament* (New York: Doubleday & Co., 1969), 83.
7. Ibid., 81.
8. Irenaeus, *Against Heresies,* III.8, in Roberts and Donaldson, *Ante-Nicene Fathers,* 1:428.
9. *Teachings of the Prophet Joseph Smith,* 365.
10. Edgar J. Goodspeed, *The Twelve: The Story of Christ's Apostles* (New York: Holt, Rinehart, and Winston, 1957), 27, 42–43; see also Edgar J. Goodspeed, *Matthew: Apostle and Evangelist* (Philadelphia: John C. Winston Co., 1959), 13, 16–17.
11. "Fragments of Papias," in Roberts and Donaldson, *Ante-Nicene Fathers,* 1:155; see also Eusebius, *Ecclesiastical History,* V. 8.
12. Goodspeed, *Matthew: Apostle and Evangelist,* 101, 103. Note the following statement from Eusebius regarding the spread of the gospel to all parts of the earth, particularly the ministry of one Pantaenus of Alexandria (ca. A.D. 180): "Pantaenus also was one of them and [is] said to have gone to India, where the story [goes] that he found the gospel according to Matthew, [which] had preceded his arrival, among certain people there who had learned of Christ; that Bartholomew, one of the apostles, had preached to them; and that *he had left the writing of Matthew in Hebrew letters,* which also was preserved to the time indicated" (*Ecclesiastical History,* V. 10). A detailed study of this tradition regarding Matthew's Gospel is Matthew Black, *An Aramaic Approach to the Gospels and Acts,* 3d ed. (London: Oxford University Press, 1967). See also J. Reuben Clark Jr., *Why the King James Version?* (Salt Lake City: Deseret Book Co., 1956), 11; Werner Georg Kummel, *Introduction to the New Testament* (London: SCM, 1975).
13. Eusebius, *Ecclesiastical History,* II.16; see also VI.14.
14. *Doctrinal New Testament Commentary,* 1:69–70; emphasis added.
15. Ibid., 69; emphasis added.
16. Eusebius, *Ecclesiastical History,* III.24.
17. See *Mortal Messiah,* 1:324.
18. Eusebius, *Ecclesiastical History,* III.24.
19. See *Doctrinal New Testament Commentary,* 1:69.
20. Ibid., 71; see also D&C 93:6–18; Matthew 3:16–17.
21. Spencer W. Kimball, *President Kimball Speaks Out* (Salt Lake City: Deseret Book Co., 1981), 55–56.
22. *Doctrinal New Testament Commentary,* 1:65.
23. Ibid., 69.
24. Morton Smith, *The Secret Gospel* (New York: Harper & Row, 1973), 15.
25. Merril C. Tenney, *New Testament Survey* (Grand Rapids, Mich.: Eerdmans Publishing Co., 1961), 133.

PROPHETS AND PRIESTHOOD
IN THE OLD TESTAMENT

The prophetic voice is a voice of authority, divine authority. Those called to speak for the Lord Jehovah are empowered by Jehovah and ordained to his holy order. Thus it seems appropriate to devote some attention to the nature of prophetic authority—the power of the holy priesthood among the prophets in ancient Israel.

Joseph Smith the Prophet wrote in 1842: "We believe in the same organization that existed in the primitive Church, namely, apostles, prophets, pastors, teachers, evangelists, and so forth" (Articles of Faith 1:6). When the time was right, when God the Eternal Father elected in his infinite wisdom to reestablish his kingdom on earth, he began to restore the basic priesthoods, offices, quorums, and councils that had been put in place by Jesus in the meridian of time. The "marvellous work and a wonder" foreseen by Isaiah (Isaiah 29:13–14) would also entail a restoration of the Church of Jesus Christ that had existed in the centuries preceding the mortal ministry of Jesus (see D&C 107:4). That restoration would consist of Old Testament truths, powers, priesthoods, covenants, and ordinances, such that "a whole and complete and perfect union, and welding together of dispensations, and keys, and powers, and glories should take place, and be revealed from the days of Adam even to the present time. And not only this, but those things which never have been revealed from the foundation of the world, but have been kept hid from the wise and prudent, shall be revealed unto babes and sucklings in this, the dispensation of the fulness of times" (D&C 128:18).

The Melchizedek Priesthood, that "Holy Priesthood after the Order of the Son of God" (D&C 107:3), is, like its Author, infinite and eternal (see Alma 13:7–9).

"The Priesthood is an everlasting principle," Joseph Smith explained, "and existed with God from eternity, and will to eternity, without beginning of days or end of years."[1] It is about that Holy Priesthood that we shall speak in this chapter—more specifically, the Melchizedek Priesthood of the Old Testament, the manner in which this divine authority operated from Adam to Malachi. Sadly, the Old Testament is almost silent in regard to the High Priesthood. Thus we must rely heavily in our study upon the doctrinal teachings of Joseph Smith as set forth in his sermons, revelations, and translations. Further, we will turn to clarifications and expansions provided by those who knew Brother Joseph firsthand, as well as those apostolic and prophetic successors to whom is given the divine mandate to build on the doctrinal foundation he laid.

ADAM AND THE PRIESTHOOD

Once the church of God is organized on earth with legal administrators, there is the kingdom of God. "The kingdom of God was set up on the earth from the days of Adam to the present time," the Prophet Joseph Smith explained, "whenever there has been a righteous man on earth unto whom God revealed His word and gave power and authority to administer in His name. And where there is a priest of God—a minister who has power and authority from God to administer in the ordinances of the gospel and officiate in the priesthood of God—there is the kingdom of God."[2]

From the days of Adam to the time of Moses, men and women lived under the patriarchal order of the Melchizedek Priesthood. That is, they lived in a family order presided over by a patriarch. It includes the new and everlasting covenant of marriage.[3] "Adam held the priesthood," Elder Russell M. Nelson observed, "and Eve served in matriarchal partnership with the patriarchal priesthood."[4] President Ezra Taft Benson explained that "Adam and his descendants entered into the priesthood order of God. Today we would say they went to the House of the Lord and received their blessings. The order of priesthood spoken of in the scriptures is sometimes referred to as *the patriarchal order* because it came down from father to son. But this order is otherwise described in modern revelation as *an order of family government where a man and woman enter into a covenant with God—just as did Adam and Eve—to be sealed for eternity, to have posterity, and to do the will and work of God throughout their mortality.*"[5]

Though we are uncertain as to the precise organization of the Church during the so-called pre-Christian times, the priesthood leaders among the ancients sought to follow the will of God in all matters. Such persons as Adam, Seth, Enos, Cainan, Mahalaleel, Jared, Enoch, Methuselah, Lamech, and Noah were all high priests; they governed the church and kingdom in righteousness and by virtue of their civil (kingly) and ecclesiastical (priestly) positions. Other worthy men held the higher priesthood, but these patriarchs were the presiding officers and held the keys or right of presidency.[6] "Adam, our father, the first man, is the presiding high priest over the earth for all ages," Elder Bruce R. McConkie observed. "The government the Lord gave him was patriarchal, and . . . the righteous portion of mankind were blessed and governed by a patriarchal theocracy.

"This theocratic system, patterned after the order and system that prevailed in heaven, was the government of God. He himself, though dwelling in heaven, was the Lawgiver, Judge, and King. He gave direction in all things both civil and ecclesiastical; there was no separation of church and state as we now know it. All governmental affairs were directed, controlled, and regulated from on high. The Lord's legal administrators on earth served by virtue of their callings and ordinations in the Holy Priesthood and as they were guided by the power of the Holy Ghost."[7]

Adam was Earth's first Christian. He was baptized, confirmed, born of the Spirit, quickened in the inner man, ordained, and received into the holy order of God (see Moses 6:64–68). "The Priesthood was first given to Adam; he obtained the First Presidency, and held the keys of it from generation to generation."[8] In the book of Moses, the Prophet Joseph Smith's inspired translation of the early chapters of Genesis, he recorded the revelation of the gospel to Adam. We read there of Adam's baptism and spiritual rebirth. "And he heard a voice out of heaven, saying: Thou art baptized with fire, and with the Holy Ghost. This is the record of the Father, and the Son, from henceforth and forever." And now note the language of the scripture: "And thou art after the order of him who was without beginning of days or end of years, from all eternity to all eternity. Behold, thou art one in me, a son of God; and thus may all become my sons. Amen" (Moses 6:66–68).

Adam was born again and became through adoption a son of Christ. President Joseph Fielding Smith wrote, "To Adam, after he was driven from the Garden of Eden, the plan of salvation was revealed, and upon him the *fulness* of the priesthood was conferred."[9] Truly, as President John Taylor wrote, "Adam was the *natural* father of his posterity, who were his family and over whom he presided as patriarch, prophet, priest, and king."[10]

THE SONS OF ADAM

The account of Cain and Abel's offerings in Genesis 4 is brought to life and given a doctrinal context by the Prophet's inspired translation. We learn that God had commanded Adam, Eve, and their posterity to "offer the firstlings of their flocks" as an offering, "in similitude of the sacrifice of the Only Begotten of the Father" (Moses 5:5–7). Cain, one who "loved Satan more than God," turned away from his parents' teachings and entered into league with the father of lies. At Satan's urging, and in what seems to be a defiance of the command to offer a blood sacrifice,[11] Cain "brought of the fruit of the ground an offering unto the Lord." On the other hand, Abel "hearkened unto the voice of the Lord" and "brought of the firstlings of his flock." The Lord "had respect unto Abel, and to his offering; but unto Cain, and to his offering, he had not respect." Cain then entered into an unholy alliance with Satan, plotted and carried out the death of his brother Abel, and instigated secret combinations in the land (Moses 5:18–51).

The Prophet Joseph explained that by faith in the atonement of Christ and the plan of redemption, "Abel offered to God a sacrifice that was accepted, which was the firstlings of the flock. Cain offered of the fruit of the ground, and was not accepted, because he could not do it in faith, he could have no faith, or could not exercise faith contrary to the plan of heaven. It must be shedding the blood of the Only Begotten to atone for man; for this was the plan of redemption; and without the shedding of blood was no remission [see Hebrews 9:22]; and as the sacrifice was instituted for a type, by which man was to discern the great Sacrifice which God had prepared; to offer a sacrifice contrary to that, no faith could be exercised, because redemption was not purchased in that way, nor the power of atonement instituted after that order; consequently Cain could have no faith; and whatsoever is not of faith, is sin." The Prophet went on to say that however varied may be the opinions of the learned "respecting the conduct of Abel, and the knowledge which he had on the subject of atonement, it is evident in our minds, that he was instructed more fully in the plan than what the Bible speaks of. . . .

" . . . How could Abel offer a sacrifice and look forward with faith on the Son of God for a remission of his sins, and not understand the Gospel?" Now note what the Prophet asks: "And *if Abel was taught of the coming of the Son of God, was he not taught also of His ordinances?* We all admit that the Gospel has ordinances, and if so, had it not always ordinances, and were not its ordinances always the same?"[12]

Further, Brother Joseph stated that God had "set the ordinances to be the same forever and ever, and set Adam to watch over them, to reveal them from heaven to man, or to send angels to reveal them." That Adam "received revelations, commandments and ordinances at the beginning is beyond the power of controversy; else how did they begin to offer sacrifices to God in an acceptable manner? And *if they offered sacrifices they must be authorized by ordination.*" The Prophet then quoted from the Apostle Paul: "'By faith Abel offered unto God a more excellent sacrifice than Cain, by which he obtained witness that he was righteous, God testifying of his gifts; and by it he being dead, yet speaketh' (Hebrews 11:4). How doth he yet speak?" Joseph asked. "Why *he magnified the Priesthood which was conferred upon him,* and died a righteous man, and therefore has become an angel of God by receiving his body from the dead, *holding still the keys of his dispensation;* and was sent down from heaven unto Paul to minister consoling words, and to commit unto him a knowledge of the mysteries of godliness."

And then, as a type of summary on these matters, the Prophet spoke concerning Cain and Abel: "The power, glory and blessings of the Priesthood could not continue with those who received ordination only as their righteousness continued; for *Cain also being authorized to offer sacrifice, but not offering it in righteousness, was cursed.* It signifies, then, that the ordinances must be kept in the very way God has appointed; otherwise their Priesthood will prove a cursing instead of a blessing."[13]

We know little concerning the keys of Abel's dispensation, spoken of above, except for the fact that a modern revelation indicates that one line of the priesthood descended "from Noah till Enoch, through the lineage of their fathers; and *from Enoch to Abel,* who was slain by the conspiracy of his brother, *who received the priesthood by the commandments of God, by the hand of his father Adam,* who was the first man" (D&C 84:15–16; emphasis added). With the murder of Abel and the defection of Cain to perdition, God provided another son for Adam and Eve through which the blessings of the evangelical priesthood or patriarchal order would continue. Seth was "ordained by Adam at the age of sixty-nine years, and was blessed by him three years previous to his (Adam's) death, and received the promise of God by his father, that his posterity should be the chosen of the Lord, and that they should be preserved unto the end of the earth; because he (Seth) was a perfect man, and his likeness was the express likeness of his father, insomuch that he seemed to be like unto his father in all things, and could be distinguished from him only by his age" (D&C 107:39–43; see also Moses 6:10–11).

ENOCH AND HIS CITY

Enoch, the son of Jared, was the seventh from Adam. Jared "taught Enoch in all the ways of God" (Moses 6:21). "Enoch was twenty-five years old when he was ordained under the hand of Adam; and he was sixty-five and Adam blessed him" (D&C 107:48). He was called by God as a prophet and seer to declare repentance to a wicked generation. Because Enoch was obedient and submissive, Jehovah transformed a shy and hesitant young man into a mighty preacher of righteousness. The Lord put his Spirit upon Enoch, justified all his words, and walked with him (see Moses 6:26–34). "And so great was the faith of Enoch that he led the people of God, and their enemies came to battle against them; and he spake the word of the Lord, and the earth trembled, and the mountains fled, even according to his command; and the rivers of water were turned out of their course; and the roar of the lions was heard out of the wilderness; and all nations feared greatly, so powerful was the word of Enoch, and so great was the power of the language which God had given him" (Moses 7:13). That is to say, Enoch was faithful to the covenant of the Melchizedek Priesthood, which allowed God to swear an oath unto him, an oath that granted unto Enoch godlike powers (JST, Genesis 14:27–31; see also Helaman 10:4–10; D&C 84:33–44).[14]

Because of his own righteousness and the power of his witness, Enoch established a society of the pure in heart. He established Zion, a people who "were of one heart and one mind, and dwelt in righteousness; and there was no poor among them" (Moses 7:18; see also D&C 97:21). Zion represents the pinnacle of human interaction, the ideal community, or, as President Spencer W. Kimball taught, "the highest order of priesthood society."[15] Through preaching righteousness and incorporating the doctrines of the gospel into all they did, including applying the pure love of Christ into their social relations and thereby consecrating themselves completely, Enoch and his people founded a holy commonwealth and were eventually translated or taken into heaven without tasting death. The people of Enoch "walked with God, and he dwelt in the midst of Zion; and it came to pass that Zion was not, for God received it up into his own bosom; and from thence went forth the saying, Zion is fled" (Moses 7:69). "And men having this faith, coming up unto this [priesthood] order of God, were translated and taken up into heaven" (JST, Genesis 14:32). "And [Enoch] saw the Lord, and he walked with him, and was before his face continually; and he walked with God three hundred and sixty-five years, making him four hundred and thirty years old when he was translated" (D&C 107:49).

Enoch's society became the pattern, the prototype for all faithful men and women who lived thereafter. The Apostle Paul could therefore write of Abraham as one of many who "looked for a city which hath foundations, whose builder and maker is God" (Hebrews 11:10).

The Prophet Joseph Smith explained that translation is a power that belongs to the Melchizedek Priesthood, a dimension of the holy order of God.[16] John Taylor added that "the translated residents of Enoch's city are under the direction of Jesus, who is the Creator of worlds; and that he, holding the keys of the government of other worlds, could, in his administrations to them, select the translated people of Enoch's Zion, if he thought proper, to perform a mission to these various planets, and as death had not passed upon them, they could be prepared by him and made use of through the medium of the holy priesthood to act as ambassadors, teachers, or messengers to those worlds over which Jesus holds the authority."[17]

NOAH AND THE PRIESTHOOD

Noah, the tenth from Adam, was ordained a patriarch at the age of ten years (see D&C 107:52). "God made arrangements beforehand," Elder John Taylor explained, "and told Methuselah that when the people should be destroyed, that a remnant of his seed should occupy the earth and stand foremost upon it. And Methuselah was so anxious to have it done that he ordained Noah to the priesthood when he was ten years of age. Noah then stood in his day as the representative of God."[18]

Noah was thus more, far more, than a weather prophet; he was a legal administrator, one empowered by God to call a wicked generation to repentance. "And *the Lord ordained Noah after his own order,* and commanded him that he should go forth and declare his Gospel unto the children of men, even as it was given unto Enoch. And it came to pass that Noah called upon the children of men that they should repent; but they hearkened not unto his words" (Moses 8:19–20; emphasis added). Further, his call to repentance was not just a warning of impending disaster; it was a call to come unto Christ and be saved. "Believe and repent of your sins," Noah said, "and be baptized in the name of Jesus Christ, the Son of God, even as our fathers, and ye shall receive the Holy Ghost, that ye may have all things made manifest" (v. 24). In speaking of the patriarchal order of the Melchizedek Priesthood in the days of Noah, John Taylor stated that "every man managed his own family affairs. And prominent men among them were kings and priests unto God."[19]

The Prophet Joseph explained the position of Noah (the angel Gabriel) in the priesthood hierarchy. Noah "stands next in authority to Adam in the Priesthood; he was called of God to this office, and was the father of all living in this day, and to him was given the dominion."[20] The Prophet also observed that "the keys of this Priesthood consisted in obtaining the voice of Jehovah that He talked with him [Noah] in a familiar and friendly manner, that He continued to him the keys, the covenants, the power and the glory, with which He blessed Adam at the beginning."[21]

MELCHIZEDEK AND ABRAHAM

Abraham, known to us as the "father of the faithful," sought for the "blessings of the fathers" and the right to administer the same (Abraham 1:1–3). He "was not only a prince on the earth but a prince in the heavens, and by right came to the earth in his time to accomplish the things given him to do. And he found by tracing his genealogy that he had a right to the priesthood, and when he ascertained that, he prayed to the Lord, and demanded an ordination."[22] His father Terah was an idolater and so Abraham's blessings could not come to him in father-to-son fashion. And so it was that he looked to Melchizedek, the great high priest of that day, for counsel, direction, and authority. In his discussion of the ancients who entered the rest of the Lord, Alma chose Melchizedek to illustrate his doctrine. "And now, my brethren," he said, "I would that ye should humble yourselves before God, and bring forth fruit meet for repentance, that ye may also enter into that rest. Yea, humble yourselves even as the people in the days of Melchizedek, who was also a high priest after this same order [the holy order of God] which I have spoken, who also took upon him the high priesthood forever" (Alma 13:13–14). God swore the same oath to Melchizedek that he had sworn to Enoch and granted him the same godlike powers. Melchizedek obtained peace in Salem, "and his people wrought righteousness, and obtained heaven, and sought for the city of Enoch which God had before taken" (JST, Genesis 14:25–36).

The Saints of God who lived at this time, "the church in ancient days," called the Holy Priesthood after Melchizedek (D&C 107:2–4). A modern revelation informs us that "Esaias . . . lived in the days of Abraham, and was blessed of him— which Abraham received the priesthood from Melchizedek, who received it through the lineage of his fathers, even till Noah" (D&C 84:13–14). Further, it appears that Abraham received additional rights and privileges from Melchizedek. The Father of the Faithful sought for the power to administer endless lives, the fulness of the powers of the priesthood. According to Joseph Smith, the power of Melchizedek was "not the power of a prophet, nor apostle, nor patriarch only, but of a king and priest to God, to open the windows of heaven and pour out the peace and law of endless life to man. And no man can attain to the joint heirship with Jesus Christ without being administered to by one having the same power and authority of Melchizedek."[23]

James Burgess recorded a sermon by Joseph Smith, a kind of doctrinal commentary on Hebrews 7, in which he spoke of three orders of the priesthood: the Aaronic, the patriarchal (the new and everlasting covenant of marriage, that which Abraham held), and the fulness of the priesthood (the realization of the blessings promised in the eternal marriage covenant). The Prophet is reported to have said: "Paul is here treating of three different priesthoods, namely, the priesthood of Aaron, Abraham, and Melchizedek. Abraham's priesthood was of greater power than Levi's [Aaron's], and Melchizedek's was of greater power than that of Abraham. . . . I ask, Was there any sealing power attending this [Levitical] Priesthood that would admit a man into the presence of God? Oh no, but Abraham's was a more exalted power or priesthood; he could talk and walk with God. And yet consider how great this man [Melchizedek] was when even this patriarch *Abraham gave a tenth part of all his spoils and then received a blessing under the hands of Melchizedek, even the last law or a fulness of the law or priesthood, which constituted him a king and priest after the order of Melchizedek or an endless life.*"[24] In summary, Joseph the Prophet explained, "Abraham says to Melchizedek, I believe all that thou hast taught me concerning the priesthood and the coming of the Son of Man; so Melchizedek ordained Abraham and sent him away. Abraham rejoiced, saying, Now I have a priesthood."[25] The keys of the priesthood then continued through Isaac, Jacob, Joseph, Ephraim, and so on through the centuries, down to the time of Moses. To what degree the Melchizedek Priesthood and its powers were utilized among the people of Israel during their Egyptian bondage is unclear.

FROM MOSES TO CHRIST

We learn from modern revelation that Moses was ordained to the high priesthood by his father-in-law, Jethro the Midianite. That priesthood line then traces back from Jethro through such unknown ancient legal administrators as Caleb, Elihu, Jeremy, Gad, and Esaias. The revelation then speaks of the divine authority coming through Abraham, Melchizedek, Noah, Enoch, Abel, and Adam (see D&C 84:6–16). That the priesthood had been given to Jethro through Midian implies—

once again, as was the case with the priesthood descending through Abel, in addition to Seth (see D&C 84:6–16; 107:40–52)—that there was more than one line of authority. It may be that the priesthood was transmitted through several lines but that the keys or right of presidency remained with and were passed on by the ordained patriarchs.

In speaking of the children of Israel, the Prophet stated: "Their government was a theocracy; they had God to make their laws, and men chosen by Him to administer them; He was their God, and they were His people. Moses received the word of the Lord from God Himself; he was the mouth of God to Aaron, and Aaron taught the people, in both civil and ecclesiastical affairs; they were both one, there was no distinction."[26] Moses sought diligently to bring the children of Israel to a point of spiritual maturity wherein they could enjoy the highest blessings of the priesthood—the privilege of entering into the rest of the Lord, into the divine presence. Jehovah's desire was that the Israelites become "a kingdom of priests, and an holy nation" (Exodus 19:6). "But they hardened their hearts and could not endure his presence; therefore, the Lord in his wrath, for his anger was kindled against them, swore that they should not enter into his rest while in the wilderness, which rest is the fulness of his glory. Therefore, he took Moses out of their midst, and the Holy Priesthood also; and the lesser priesthood continued" (D&C 84:19, 24–26; see also 107:18–19). That is, Israel's unwillingness to enter the Lord's presence (see Exodus 20:19) signaled their lack of preparation as a nation to see God and thus the need to bear the holy priesthood and enjoy its consummate privileges. For one thing, as Abinadi pointed out, many of the children of Israel did not comprehend the place of the Law of Moses as a means to a greater end. "And now," he asked, "did they understand the law? I say unto you, Nay, they did not all understand the law; and this because of the hardness of their hearts; for they understood not that there could not any man be saved except it were through the redemption of God" (Mosiah 13:32).

"And the Lord said unto Moses, Hew thee two other tables of stone, like unto the first, and I will write upon them also, the words of the law, according as they were written at the first on the tables which thou brakest; but it shall not be according to the first, for *I will take away the priesthood out of their midst; therefore my holy order, and the ordinances thereof, shall not go before them; for my presence shall not go up in their midst,* lest I destroy them. But I will give unto them the law as at the first, but it shall be after the law of a carnal commandment; for I have sworn in my wrath, that they shall not enter into my presence, into my rest, in the days of their pilgrimage" (JST, Exodus 34:1–2; emphasis added; see also JST, Deuteronomy 10:1–2).

When Moses was translated, the keys of the Melchizedek Priesthood were taken from among the Israelites as a body and the patriarchal order of priesthood ceased. True, there were still men like Aaron, his sons, and the seventy elders of Israel who bore the Melchizedek Priesthood. But no longer did the Melchizedek Priesthood pass from father to son. Thereafter, the priesthood of administration among the people generally was the Aaronic Priesthood. The ordination of men to the Melchizedek Priesthood and the bestowal of its keys came by special dispensation.[27] President Joseph Fielding Smith therefore pointed out: "In Israel, the common people, the people generally, did not exercise the functions of priesthood in its fulness, but were confined in their labors and ministrations very largely to the Aaronic Priesthood. *The withdrawal of the higher priesthood was from the people as a body, but the Lord still left among them men holding the Melchizedek Priesthood, with power to officiate in all its ordinances, so far as he determined that these ordinances should be granted unto the people. Therefore Samuel, Isaiah, Jeremiah, Daniel, Ezekiel, Elijah, and others of the prophets held the Melchizedek Priesthood,* and their prophesying and their instructions to the people were directed by the Spirit of the Lord and made potent by virtue of that priesthood which was not made manifest generally among the people of Israel during all these years." President Smith adds this detail: "We may presume, with good reason, that never was there a time when there was not at least one man in Israel who held this higher priesthood (receiving it by special dispensation) and who was authorized to officiate in the ordinances."[28] Or, as he wrote on another occasion, "The Lord, of necessity, has kept authorized servants on the earth bearing the priesthood from the days of Adam to the present time; in fact, there has never been a moment from the beginning that there were not men on the earth holding the Holy Priesthood. Even in the days of apostasy . . . our Father in heaven held control and had duly authorized servants on the earth to direct his work and to check, to some extent at least, the ravages and corruption of the evil powers. These servants were not permitted to organize the Church nor to officiate in the ordinances of the gospel, but they did check the advances of evil as far as the Lord deemed it necessary."[29]

Joseph Smith was asked by John Taylor: "Was the Priesthood of Melchizedek taken away when Moses died?" The Prophet stated—and this principle guides our understanding of who held the High Priesthood from the translation of Moses to the days of Christ—that "all Priesthood is Melchizedek, but there are different portions or degrees of it. That portion which brought Moses to speak with God face to face was taken away; but that which brought the ministry of angels remained." Now note this important clarification: "*All the prophets had the Melchizedek Priesthood and were ordained by God himself,*"[30] meaning that God himself performed the ordination or sent a divine messenger to do so. In a meeting of the First Presidency and Quorum of the Twelve on 22 April 1849, John Taylor asked Brigham Young, "If Elijah, David, Solomon and the Prophets had the High Priesthood, how it was," inasmuch as "the Lord took it away with Moses." After much discussion, President Young "said he did not know, but wished he did." Elder Taylor, who had not been with the Prophet Joseph when the answer was first given in 1841 (he was in England), "thought perhaps the Lord conferred it himself upon some at times whom he had considered worthy, but not with permission for them to continue it down upon others."[31]

And so we operate from a perspective that all the Old Testament prophets held the Melchizedek Priesthood. Exactly how Isaiah and Micah, who were contemporaries, related to one another or who supervised whom, we cannot tell. Who was in charge when Jeremiah, Ezekiel, Habakkuk, Obadiah, or Lehi ministered in the prophetic office, we do not know. It is inconceivable to me that they went about their prophetic labors independent of one another. That Lord who called and empowered them is a God of order and not of confusion (see D&C 132:8), and we would suppose that their labors were coordinated and directed by one holding the appropriate keys of the kingdom—the right of presidency, the directing power (see D&C 107:8). These principles are, unfortunately, nowhere to be found in the Old Testament record.

It is from modern revelation that we learn that the ordinances of the house of the Lord have been delivered from the beginning. The book of Abraham speaks of "the grand Key-words of the Holy Priesthood, as revealed to Adam in the Garden of Eden, as also to Seth, Noah, Melchizedek, Abraham, and all to whom the Priesthood was revealed" (explanation to Figure 3 in Facsimile no. 2); that sacred ordinances such as washings and anointings were carried out in ancient temples, which, the Lord said, "my people are always commanded to build unto my holy name" (D&C 124:39); and that Nathan and "others of the prophets" held the keys of the sealing power associated with eternal marriage and the everlasting union of families (see D&C 132:39). Surely if and when God elected to make available the ordinances of the priesthood to certain individuals—including the endowment and sealing blessings—he could do so in the wilderness or on mountain tops. The scriptural passages quoted above also seem to imply that the ancient tabernacle and temples allowed for more than Aaronic Priesthood sacrificial rites. The exact relationship between the prophet (who held the Melchizedek Priesthood) and the literal descendants of Aaron (who held the keys of the Levitical ordinances) is unclear. Elder Bruce R. McConkie has, however, made the following clarification: "Do not let the fact that the performances of the Mosaic law were administered by the Aaronic Priesthood confuse you. . . . Where the Melchizedek Priesthood is, there is the fulness of the gospel; and all of the prophets held the Melchizedek Priesthood." He continues: "The Melchizedek Priesthood always directed the course of the Aaronic Priesthood. All of the prophets held a position in the hierarchy of the day."[32] In short, "in all ages of the world, whenever the Lord has given a dispensation of the priesthood to any man by actual revelation, or any set of men, this power has always been given" (D&C 128:9).

The Lehite colony, a branch of ancient Israel that was brought by God to the Americas, took the priesthood with them to the New World. Lehi was a prophet, and, as we have seen, would have held the Melchizedek Priesthood. The Nephites enjoyed the blessings of the fulness of the everlasting gospel, a gospel that is administered by the higher priesthood. There were no Levites among the Nephites, and so we would assume that they offered sacrifice and carried out the ordinances and ministerial duties as priests and teachers by virtue of the Melchizedek Priesthood.[33] John Taylor explained that the higher priesthood was held by "Moroni, one of the prophets of God on this continent. Nephi, another of the servants of God on this continent, had the gospel with its keys and powers revealed unto him."[34]

ELIJAH AND THE KEYS OF THE PRIESTHOOD

There is a statement from Joseph Smith that seems, to some extent at least, to contradict what has been said heretofore in regard to the keys of the priesthood in ancient Israel. Brother Joseph stated: "Elijah was the last Prophet that held the keys of the Priesthood, and who will, before the last dispensation, restore the authority and deliver the keys of the Priesthood, in order that all the ordinances may be attended to in righteousness."[35] Elijah lived about 850 B.C. If this statement were taken at face value, then no prophet after Elijah, at least in the Old Testament or Book of Mormon, would have held the keys of the Holy Priesthood. That would include such men as Elisha, Joel, Hosea, Jonah, Amos, Isaiah, Micah, Nahum, Jeremiah, Zephaniah, Obadiah, Daniel, Habakkuk, Ezekiel, as well as Lehi and the American branch of Israel. Are we to understand that none of these men held keys? Was there no right of presidency, no directing power in regard to the covenants and ordinances of the gospel?

The troublesome statement is from a discourse on priesthood delivered at a conference of the Church held in Nauvoo in October 1840. The Prophet Joseph began by defining the priesthood and then observed that the Melchizedek Priesthood "is the grand head, and holds the highest authority which pertains to the priesthood, and the keys of the Kingdom of God in all ages of the world to the latest posterity on the earth; and is the channel through which all knowledge, doctrine, the plan of salvation and every important matter is revealed from heaven." He went on to say that "all other Priesthoods are only parts, ramifications, powers and blessings belonging to the same, and are held, controlled, and directed by it. It is the channel through which the Almighty commenced revealing His glory at the beginning of the creation of this earth, and through which He has continued to reveal Himself to the children of men to the present time, and through which He will make known His purposes to the end of time."[36]

The Prophet then discussed the role of Michael or Adam as the one designated to oversee the revelations and ordinances of God to his people, emphasizing, as Joseph did so often, that the ordinances of the gospel are forever the same.[37] He went on to describe the descent of priesthood powers and rites to Abel, Cain, Enoch, Lamech, and Noah. The Prophet provided very important information regarding Enoch and the doctrine of translation. "Now the doctrine of translation," he taught, "is a power which belongs to this Priesthood. There are many things which belong to the powers of the Priesthood and the keys thereof, that have been kept hid from before the foundation of the world; they are hid from the wise and prudent to be revealed in the last times."[38]

Joseph Smith then began to discuss at length the restoration of sacrificial offerings as a part of the restitution of all things, for "all the ordinances and duties that ever have been required by the Priesthood . . . at any former period, shall be had again, bringing to pass the restoration spoken of by the mouth of all the Holy Prophets. . . . The offering of sacrifice has ever been connected and forms a part of the duties of the Priesthood. It began with the Priesthood, and will be continued until after the coming of Christ, from generation to generation. We frequently have mention made of the offering of sacrifice by the servants of the Most High in ancient days, prior to the law of Moses; which ordinances will be continued when the Priesthood is restored with all its authority, power and blessings." He continued: "Elijah was the last Prophet that held the keys of the Priesthood, and who will, before the last dispensation, *restore the authority and deliver the keys of the Priesthood, in order that all the ordinances may be attended to in righteousness.* It is true," the Prophet continued, "that the Savior had authority and power to bestow this blessing; but the sons of Levi were too prejudiced. 'And I will send Elijah the Prophet before the great and terrible day of the Lord,' etc., etc. Why send Elijah? Because he holds the keys of the authority to administer in all the ordinances of the Priesthood." He added once again that "these sacrifices, as well as every ordinance belonging to the Priesthood, will, when the Temple of the Lord shall be built, and the sons of Levi be purified, be fully restored and attended to in all their powers, ramifications, and blessings. This ever did and ever will exist when the powers of the Melchizedek Priesthood are sufficiently manifest; else how can the restitution of all things spoken of by the Holy Prophets be brought to pass?"[39]

Remember, this sermon was delivered in October 1840, over four years *after* Elijah had come to the Kirtland Temple (see D&C 110). But Joseph Smith stated that Elijah "*will*, before the last dispensation"—meaning, presumably, at some *future time* before the dispensation is complete—"restore the authority and deliver the keys of the Priesthood, in order that all the ordinances may be attended to in righteousness." The context of the sermon seems to suggest that a part of Elijah's role as one who would restore the "fulness of the priesthood"[40] is to restore the keys associated with *all the ordinances,* including animal sacrifice, an event prophesied by Malachi (4:5–6; emphasis added), quoted by Jesus to the Nephites (3 Nephi 25:5–6), rendered differently by Moroni (D&C 2), and described in modern revelation (D&C 84:31–32). One wonders whether Elijah will not deliver those particular keys at the Council of Adam-ondi-Ahman, that grand gathering of priesthood leaders—those who have held keys of authority in all ages—just before the coming of the Lord in glory.[41]

I am grateful to my friend and colleague, Robert J. Matthews, for suggesting the following principles, each of which adds somewhat to our understanding of this matter of the keys of the priesthood.

1. It is evident that a person who holds the keys can "give" them to another without losing them himself.

2. There is a difference between holding the keys sufficiently to function, and being the person designated to convey those keys to others. Both Moses and Elijah gave Peter, James, and John the keys on the Mount of Transfiguration,[42] yet it was still Moses and Elijah that brought them to Joseph Smith and Oliver Cowdery in 1836. No doubt Peter had sufficient of "Elijah's keys" to operate the Church during the meridian dispensation, yet the Lord did not choose Peter to convey those sealing keys to Joseph and Oliver.

3. It is clearly stated in the Book of Mormon, more than once, that the Twelve in the Western Hemisphere were subject and would be subject to the Twelve in

Jerusalem (see 1 Nephi 12:9; Mormon 3:18–19). This suggests, again, that a people may have sufficient keys of the priesthood to operate the Church without having the right to pass those keys to future dispensations.

4. Truly, all of the keys and powers of the priesthood have not yet been delivered to us in our day; there is much that lies in futurity, including the keys of creation, translation, and resurrection.[43]

In summary, the keys of the kingdom of God have always been on earth when the higher priesthood was on earth; there must be order in the house of God. Those keys would have been held by the Lord's anointed after the time of Elijah. Elijah was not the last man to hold keys in the Old Testament period, since many did after him, but he was the last one in the Old Testament commissioned to return in the dispensation of the fulness of times to see to it that "all the ordinances may be attended to in righteousness."[44]

CONCLUSION

Ammon explained to King Limhi that "a seer is a revelator and a prophet also; and a gift which is greater can no man have, except he should possess the power of God, which no man can; yet a man may have great power given him from God. But a seer can know of things which are past, and also of things which are to come, and by them shall all things be revealed, or, rather, shall secret things be made manifest, and hidden things shall come to light. . . . Thus God has provided a means that man, through faith, might work mighty miracles; therefore he becometh a great benefit to his fellow beings" (Mosiah 8:16–18).

As Latter-day Saints we love the Old Testament. We cherish the lessons and language of its sacred pages. We know, however, that it has not come down to us in its pristine purity. Many plain and precious truths and many covenants of the Lord have been taken away and kept back by designing persons (see 1 Nephi 13:20–32). The understanding that the fulness of the gospel of Jesus Christ was once among the ancients is missing. The insight that prophets in the Old Testament were Christians who taught Christian doctrine and administered Christian covenants and ordinances is lacking. But thanks be to God that a seer has been raised up, even a "choice seer" (2 Nephi 3:6–7), Joseph Smith, who began the work of restoring many of those plain and precious truths to the Bible. Jehovah instructed Moses to write the things that would be spoken to him. "And in a day when the children of men shall esteem my words as naught and take many of them from the book which thou shalt write, behold, I will raise up another like unto thee; and they shall be had again among the children of men—among as many as shall believe" (Moses 1:40–41).

A study of the Old Testament by the lamp of the restored gospel ties the Latter-day Saints to the former-day saints. Such a study becomes far more than a lesson in history, for as the revelation declares, "Now this same Priesthood, which was in the beginning, shall be in the end of the world also" (Moses 6:7). What was true for the ancients is true for us. What inspired and motivated them can and should entice us to continuing fidelity and devotion to our covenants. The same authority by which they were baptized, confirmed, endowed, washed, anointed, married, and sealed unto eternal life—that same authority has been delivered to Joseph Smith by heavenly messengers. Let us all study the gospel with the goal of believing, accepting, and rejoicing in the treasure house of doctrinal understanding delivered to us through modern revelation.

Notes

From *Voices of Old Testament Prophets, The 26th Annual Sidney B. Sperry Symposium,* ed. Dennis A. Wright et al. (Salt Lake City: Deseret Book Co., 1997), 192–215.

1. *Teachings of the Prophet Joseph Smith,* 157.
2. Ibid., 271.
3. See D&C 131:1–4; Bruce R. McConkie, in Conference Report, October 1977, 50.
4. Russell M. Nelson, *The Power Within Us* (Salt Lake City: Deseret Book Co., 1988), 109.
5. Ezra Taft Benson, "What I Hope You Will Teach Your Children about the Temple," *Ensign,* August 1985, 9; emphasis added.
6. See Joseph Fielding Smith, *The Way to Perfection* (Salt Lake City: Deseret Book Co., 1970), 72–74.
7. Bruce R. McConkie, *A New Witness for the Articles of Faith* (Salt Lake City: Deseret Book Co., 1985), 35.
8. *Teachings of the Prophet Joseph Smith,* 157.
9. *Doctrines of Salvation,* 3:81.
10. John Taylor, *The Gospel Kingdom,* ed. G. Homer Durham (Salt Lake City: Bookcraft, 1987), 148.
11. See John Taylor, in *Journal of Discourses,* 22:301; Charles W. Penrose, in *Journal of Discourses,* 25:47–48, 339.
12. *Teachings of the Prophet Joseph Smith,* 58–59; emphasis added.
13. Ibid., 168–69; emphasis added.
14. See Joseph Fielding Smith, in Conference Report, April 1970, 59; see also Boyd K. Packer, *The Things of the Soul* (Salt Lake City: Bookcraft, 1996), 153.
15. Spencer W. Kimball, in Conference Report, October 1977, 125.
16. See *Teachings of the Prophet Joseph Smith,* 170–71.
17. John Taylor, *The Gospel Kingdom,* ed. G. Homer Durham (Salt Lake City: Bookcraft, 1987), 103; see also *Teachings of the Prophet Joseph Smith,* 170–71.
18. Taylor, *Gospel Kingdom,* 103–4.
19. Ibid., 139.
20. *Teachings of the Prophet Joseph Smith,* 157.
21. Ibid., 171.
22. Taylor, *Gospel Kingdom,* 104.
23. *Words of Joseph Smith,* 245.

24. Ibid., 245–46; emphasis added, spelling and punctuation corrected.
25. *Teachings of the Prophet Joseph Smith*, 322–23.
26. Ibid., 252.
27. See *Mortal Messiah*, 1:60.
28. *Doctrines of Salvation*, 3:85; emphasis added.
29. Joseph Fielding Smith, *Answers to Gospel Questions*, 5 vols. (Salt Lake City: Deseret Book Co., 1957–66), 2:45.
30. *Teachings of the Prophet Joseph Smith*, 180–81; emphasis added.
31. *Words of Joseph Smith*, 82–83.
32. Bruce R. McConkie, "The Bible: A Sealed Book," *Eighth Annual Church Educational System Religious Educators' Symposium* (Salt Lake City: The Church of Jesus Christ of Latter-day Saints, 1984), 6.
33. See *Doctrines of Salvation*, 3:87; *Promised Messiah*, 412, 421, 427.
34. Taylor, *Gospel Kingdom*, 140.
35. *Teachings of the Prophet Joseph Smith*, 172.
36. Ibid., 166–67.
37. Ibid., 59–60, 264, 308.
38. Ibid., 168–71.
39. Ibid., 171–73; emphasis added.
40. Ibid., 337.
41. Ibid., 157; see also Joseph Fielding Smith, *The Progress of Man* (Salt Lake City: Deseret Book Co., 1964), 479–82; McConkie, *Millennial Messiah*, 578–88.
42. *Teachings of the Prophet Joseph Smith*, 158.
43. Spencer W. Kimball, in Conference Report, April 1977, 69–72; see also John Taylor, in *Journal of Discourses*, 23:32.
44. *Teachings of the Prophet Joseph Smith*, 172.

JOSEPH SMITH
AND THE NEW TESTAMENT

Joseph Smith loved the Bible. In his sermons he frequently explained biblical passages and gave deeper insights into matters treated only briefly in that sacred volume. The revelations given to the Prophet during his brief ministry opened his mind to the things of eternity and taught him doctrines and principles that transcended anything known by the religionists of either his day or ours.

In July 1830 the Lord told Joseph Smith to "continue in calling upon God in my name, and writing the things which shall be given thee by the Comforter, and expounding all scriptures unto the church" (D&C 24:5). Joseph Smith came to know the mind of God not only by reading of the divine encounters of earlier prophets, but also by having personal experiences with Deity. The Prophet was given access to an understanding of scriptural matters that both sanctifies and soothes the soul—an understanding that comes from the Holy Ghost. He translated through his knowledge of the language of revelation, the language of the Spirit: "I have the oldest book in my heart," he said in 1844, "even the gift of the Holy Ghost."[1]

Let's take a brief walk through the New Testament with Joseph Smith and sample the many contributions latter-day revelations have made to our understanding of the New Testament.

THE BOOK OF MORMON AND THE NEW TESTAMENT

The Lord explained to the Saints at the time of the organization of the restored Church that the Book of Mormon had been given for the purpose of "proving to the world that the holy scriptures are true" (D&C 20:11). Nephi had learned in vision that the sacred record kept by the Nephites would help restore many of the plain and precious truths lost through the centuries, as well as establish the essential truthfulness of the "record of the Jews"—the Bible (see 1 Nephi 13:20–40; Mormon 7:8–9).

The Book of Mormon successfully fulfills these purposes. It is another testament of Jesus Christ, bearing companion witness with the Bible that our Lord has "abolished death, and hath brought life and immortality to light through the gospel" (2 Timothy 1:10). The Nephite-Jaredite record is remarkably Christ-centered, affirming that "Jesus is the Christ, the Eternal God" (2 Nephi 26:12).

In addition, the Book of Mormon witnesses of the truthfulness of the biblical record by establishing the historical veracity of events discussed in the New Testament. For example, both Nephi and Alma testify of the miraculous virgin birth of our Lord (1 Nephi 11:13–21; Alma 7:10). Nephi also verifies the account of the baptism of Jesus Christ by John the Baptist (2 Nephi 31:4–11). The historicity and authenticity of the Sermon on the Mount are confirmed by the Book of Mormon account of the resurrected Savior delivering essentially the same sermon to the Nephites (3 Nephi 12–14).

An angel taught King Benjamin concerning the condescension of the "Lord Omnipotent who reigneth, who was, and is from all eternity to all eternity" (Mosiah 3:5), and further affirmed the significance of the Savior's experience in Gethsemane (mentioned only briefly in Luke 22:44):

"And lo, he shall suffer temptations, and pain of body, hunger, thirst, and fatigue, even more than man can suffer, except it be unto death; for behold, blood cometh from every pore, so great shall be his anguish for the wickedness and the abominations of his people" (Mosiah 3:7).

Book of Mormon prophets knew and prophesied that the Master would be crucified. Signs of his death—such as the three days of darkness, as well as the tempests and cataclysms of the earth—were known centuries before he died and rose again (1 Nephi 19:10).

Some of the other New Testament doctrines that receive a marvelously clear explanation in the Book of Mormon include the nature and definition of the resurrection (Alma 11:40–45; 40:23), the necessity for and the nature of the new birth (Mosiah 5:1–8; 27:24–27; Alma 5:14), the Savior's cryptic message concerning his "other sheep" (3 Nephi 15:16–16:5), worthiness to partake of the sacrament of the Lord's supper (3 Nephi 18:26–34), and the ministry of John the apostle and other translated beings (3 Nephi 28).

THE DOCTRINE AND COVENANTS
AND THE NEW TESTAMENT

A surprising number of revelations in the Doctrine and Covenants, given through the Prophet Joseph Smith, add to our understanding of the New Testament account. For example, the record and testimony of John is given in extended form in section 93, along with a promise that the complete record of John will come forth in the Lord's due time (see vv. 6–18).

The Savior's parable of the wheat and the tares is given in more detail, and its interpretation is extended to the latter days (see D&C 86:1–7).

The transfiguration of Jesus on the mount is discussed in the Doctrine and Covenants, along with insight into the extensive vision Peter, James, and John received on that occasion—a vision of the earth in its future glorified state (see D&C 63:20–21). In addition, we can read in the Doctrine and Covenants about a modern transfiguration and conferral of keys in the Kirtland Temple (see D&C 110); this experience suggests that priesthood keys were bestowed also during the Transfiguration, which took place some six months before the Lord's death.

The doctrine of eternal marriage as outlined in the Doctrine and Covenants sheds light on Jesus' answer to the Sadducees concerning the final status of a woman who had been married seven times. "In the resurrection whose wife shall she be of the seven?" they had asked. The Lord's answer, as given in Matthew, was: "Ye do err, not knowing the scriptures, nor the power of God. For in the resurrection they neither marry, nor are given in marriage, but are as the angels of God in heaven" (Matthew 22:23–30). In a revelation recorded on 12 July 1843, the Lord explained that unless a marriage is sealed by the power of the holy priesthood, the marriage ends with death. If it is sealed, however, men and women might eventually qualify for eternal lives—the everlasting continuation of the family unit (see D&C 132:1–25).

A description of Christ's suffering during the hours of atonement is given in his own words—a poignant pronouncement concerning the awful agony but supreme submission of the Son of Man to the Man of Holiness (see D&C 19:15–20).

The story of the ministry and destiny of John the Beloved—a matter debated for centuries in the Christian world—is contained in an unusual but fascinating revelation given to Joseph Smith and Oliver Cowdery (see D&C 7). In addition, invaluable aids in understanding the Book of Revelation are provided in Doctrine and Covenants 77.

Section 74 of the Doctrine and Covenants is an explanation of the Lord's direction concerning circumcision, the innocence of little children through the Atonement, and Paul's statement in 1 Corinthians 7:14 concerning the believing Christian and the unbelieving spouse.

Section 76 of the Doctrine and Covenants—the vision of the glories of heaven—came as a result of the Prophet's inspired translation of John 5:29, a passage related to the doctrine of the Resurrection. It is a heaven-sent commentary upon this verse, upon John 14:1–2, and upon 1 Corinthians 15:40–42.

One of the most intellectually challenging sections in the New Testament is the epistle of Paul to the Hebrews; the language and imagery of the Old Testament utilized by Paul are particularly difficult to follow. D&C 84 is a tremendous lens through which the honest seeker after truth may come to grasp many of the profound realities regarding sacrifice, temples, and the ordinances of the priesthood.

Sections 127 and 128 of the Doctrine and Covenants deal with salvation for the dead. In a sense, they are commentaries upon Paul's statement regarding baptism for the dead in 1 Corinthians 15:29.

Finally, among the most frequently discussed subjects in the Doctrine and Covenants is the matter of the signs of the times—the scenes just incident to the Savior's Second Coming—as well as the glorious events of the millennial day and the final celestialization of the earth and its inhabitants (see D&C 29, 45, 88, 130, 133). All these revelations help us understand better Matthew 24 and other New Testament references to the Second Coming and the destiny of the earth.

JOSEPH SMITH'S INSPIRED TRANSLATION OF THE NEW TESTAMENT

Speaking of the Lord's plans for the "doctrinal restoration," Elder Bruce R. McConkie stated: "It was his design and purpose to bring forth the Book of Mormon as a new and added witness of the Lord Jesus Christ. Then he would endow his prophets with keys and power and give them direct revelation as to how and in what manner his earthly kingdom should be established anew among men.

"After this—as a crowning achievement—he would begin the perfection of the Bible, a work destined to be greater and have more significance than any of us have yet realized."

Continuing, Elder McConkie observed: "Thus, the doctrinal restoration is destined to come to pass, first, through the Book of Mormon, second, by direct revelation—a re-revelation—of the doctrines known anciently, and third, by the restoration, by revelation, of [parts of] the Bible, which in spite of its faults has been the most stabilizing force on earth since the day it came into being."[2]

The work of biblical revision was a mission appointed to the Prophet Joseph Smith (see D&C 76:15); it was an integral "branch of [his] calling."[3] The Latter-day Saints came to rejoice in the fact that the Bible was "undergoing the purifying touch by a revelation of Jesus Christ."[4]

On page one of Joseph's New Testament Manuscript No. 1 is the following inscription: "A Translation of the New Testament translated by the power of God."[5] Working under the influence of the spirit of revelation, the Prophet altered some 2,096 verses in the King James text of the New Testament—in addition to his work on the Old Testament. It isn't possible to discuss here all of the changes, but let's look at some important doctrinal contributions from the Joseph Smith's translation of the New Testament.

The early years of Christ. In the infancy narrative, we note a reference in the JST to Jesus as the *Messiah,* as well as the *king.* The Wise Men from the east, seeking to behold and participate in the marvelous event at hand, asked, "Where is the child that is born, the *Messiah* of the Jews?" (JST, Matthew 3:2; emphasis added).

In a passage that does not occur in the King James Version, the JST gives us a remarkable insight into the childhood and early preparation of Christ:

"And it came to pass that Jesus grew up with his brethren, and waxed strong, and waited upon the Lord for the time of his ministry to come.

"And he served under his father, and he spake not as other men, neither could he be taught; for he needed not that any man should teach him.

"And after many years, the hour of his ministry drew nigh.

"And in those days came John the Baptist, preaching in the wilderness of Judea" (JST, Matthew 3:24–26; Matthew 3:1).

These verses supply an excellent transition between Christ's infancy and the beginning of John's ministry. (Note the lack of transition in the KJV from Matthew 2:23 to 3:1.) They also explain that the Lord received instructions from the heavens. This suggests one of the reasons Jesus, at age twelve, was spiritually adept and insightful enough to be found in the temple teaching the doctors of the law (see JST, Luke 2:46–47).

The ministry of John the Baptist. Jesus taught that "among those that are born of women there is not a greater prophet than John the Baptist" (Luke 7:28). Joseph Smith explained that John's greatness consisted largely of his critically important mission to prepare the way for the Son of Man and then baptize the Lord by proper authority.[6] John "came into the world for a witness, to bear witness of the light, *to bear record of the gospel through the Son, unto all,* that through him men might believe" (JST, John 1:7; emphasis added).

The JST provides a clearer rendition of John's preaching and baptism than that contained in other translations. Note the following:

KJV, Matthew 3:11–12

"I indeed baptize you with water unto repentance: but he that cometh after me is mightier than I, whose shoes I am not worthy to bear: he shall baptize you with the Holy Ghost, and with fire:

"Whose fan is in his hand."

JST, Matthew 3:38–39

"I indeed baptize you with water, upon your repentance; and when he of whom I bear record cometh, who is mightier than I, whose shoes I am not worthy to bear, *(or whose place I am not able to fill,) as I said, I indeed baptize you before he cometh, that when he cometh he may* baptize you with the Holy Ghost and fire.

"*And it is he of whom I shall bear record,* whose fan shall be in his hand" (emphasis added).

John was a prophet who spoke with power. His message not only touched the hearts of the common people but also stirred both fear and respect in some of the leaders of the Jews. For example, "Herod feared John, knowing that he was a just man, and a holy man, and one who feared God and observed to worship him; and when he heard him he did many things for him, and heard him gladly" (JST, Mark 6:21).

Further, John the Baptist's message included more than announcing the coming Messiah. In the JST, specific doctrines preached by John are given—doctrines that are absent from the King James Bible and that provide a crucial bridge between the events of the Savior's first and second comings.

"And he [John] came into all the country about Jordan, preaching the baptism of repentance for the remission of sins.

"As it is written in the book of the prophet Esaias; and these are the words, saying, The voice of one crying in the wilderness, Prepare ye the way of the Lord, and make his paths straight.

"For behold, and lo, he shall come, as it is written in the book of the prophets, to take away the sins of the world, and to bring salvation unto the heathen nations, to gather together those who are lost, who are of the sheepfold of Israel;

"Yea, even the dispersed and afflicted; and also to prepare the way, and make possible the preaching of the gospel unto the Gentiles;

"And to be a light unto all who sit in darkness, unto the uttermost parts of the earth; to bring to pass the resurrection from the dead, and to ascend up on high, to dwell on the right hand of the Father,

"Until the fulness of time, and the law and the testimony shall be sealed, and the keys of the kingdom shall be delivered up again unto the Father;

"To administer justice unto all; to come down in judgment upon all, and to convince all the ungodly of their ungodly deeds, which they have committed; and all this in the day that he shall come;

"For it is a day of power; yea, every valley shall be filled, and every mountain and hill shall be brought low; the crooked shall be made straight, and the rough ways made smooth;

"And all flesh shall see the salvation of God" (JST, Luke 3:3–11).

Jesus and the Jews. The leaders of the Jews in the first century had perverted the Law of Moses through confusing tokens with covenants, ritual with religion, means with ends. Jesus came as the pure fulfillment of the Law and sought to heal the spiritual blindness that had come from "looking beyond the mark" (Jacob 4:14). The JST is even clearer than the KJV, revealing Jesus' challenge to the Jewish intellectuals of his day in the form of a call to a higher righteousness. He questioned their authority and their right to teach and guide the masses in accordance with their narrow interpretation of the Law. The Jewish leaders were deeply schooled in commentary upon the Torah but lacked the animation that comes with the Spirit of God. Jesus was different; he "taught them *as one having authority from God, and not as having authority from the Scribes*" (JST, Matthew 7:37; emphasis added).

Some of the most important alterations made by the Prophet Joseph Smith are in the Sermon on the Mount. For one thing, the JST witnesses that this sermon was predominantly for the purpose of apostolic preparation. Note that the following section on judging righteously (chapter seven) is followed in the JST by a scathing denunciation: "And Jesus said unto his disciples, Beholdest thou the Scribes, and the Pharisees, and the Priests, and the Levites? They teach in their synagogues, but do not observe the law, nor the commandments; and all have gone out of the way, and are under sin.

"Go thou and say unto them, Why teach ye men the law and the commandments, when ye yourselves are the children of corruption?

"Say unto them, Ye hypocrites, [note here who it is that the Lord calls a hypocrite], first cast out the beam out of thine own eye; and then shalt thou see clearly to cast out the mote out of thy brother's eye" (JST, Matthew 7:6–8).

Many of the Jews of Christ's day had reached a state of sterile self-sufficiency wherein they trusted alone in the Law. "We ourselves are righteous," they were prone to say, "and need not that any man should teach us" (JST, Matthew 7:14). Because some had "taken away the key of knowledge, the fulness of the scriptures" (JST, Luke 11:53), people stumbled in spiritual matters. Many of the leaders of the Jews no longer trusted in the efficacy of personal prayer and the spirit of revelation; others had come to doubt the very existence of God (see JST, Luke 16:19–21). Those in the meridian of time who were earnest in their hearts partook of the living fruit from the living tree of life offered by Christ and his appointed servants; those who rejected the fruit denied themselves access to God's new covenant with Israel and spurned fellowship with the Mediator of that covenant.

Doctrinal teachings of Paul. We will here consider segments of two of the Apostle Paul's epistles—doctrinal areas that have been misunderstood for centuries. Again, through the clarifying lenses provided by the JST, matters that seemed obscure or foreign are made plain and inspiring.

Chapter seven of Romans might well be labeled "Paul: Before and After." It might also be classified as an explanation of how the power of Christ can change men's lives. In the King James Version, Paul sounds very much like a helpless and largely depraved individual who has little power to choose good and live according to the things of God. Paul is "carnal, sold under sin" (Romans 7:14). Further, those things which he knows he should do, he does not do; that which he should not do, he does. "Now then it is no more I that do it," he adds, "but sin that dwelleth in me" (Romans 7:17). It is not difficult to understand how many, from Augustine to Luther to Bible students in our own day, could conclude from Romans 7 that man is basically a depraved creature, incapable of moving in wisdom's paths.

Through the Prophet's inspired translation, we come to discern more clearly the character of Paul the apostle. The JST emphasizes man's inability to effect righteousness *without Christ:*

"For we know that the commandment is spiritual; but *when I was under the law, I was yet carnal,* sold under sin.

"*But now I am spiritual; for that which I am commanded to do, I do; and that which I am commanded not to allow, I allow not.*

"For what I know is not right I would not do; for that which is sin, I hate." Continuing, Paul stated: "Now then, it is no more I that do sin; but *I seek to subdue that sin which dwelleth in me.*

"For I know that in me, that is, in my flesh, dwelleth no good thing; for to will is present with me, but to perform that which is good I find not, *only in Christ*" (JST, Romans 7:14–16, 18–19; emphasis added).

Secondly, some Latter-day Saints have concluded that Paul's discussion of marriage in 1 Corinthians 7 is inconsistent with the other teachings of the restored gospel. In the King James Version of this chapter, we find the following: "Now concerning virgins. . . . I suppose therefore that this [the unmarried state] is good for the present distress, I say, that it is good for a man so to be. . . .

"But this I say, brethren, the time is short: it remaineth, that both they that have wives be as though they had none" (1 Corinthians 7:25–26, 29). Now note the same verses from the JST: "Now concerning virgins. . . . I suppose therefore that this is good for the present distress, *for a man so to remain that he may do greater good. . . .*

"But *I speak unto you who are called unto the ministry.* For this I say, brethren, the time that remaineth is but short, *that ye shall be sent forth unto the ministry.* Even they who have wives, shall be as though they had none; *for ye are called and chosen to do the Lord's work*" (JST, 1 Corinthians 7:25–26, 29; emphasis added).

The JST restores the needful insight that Paul was addressing himself to *members of the Church who had been called as missionaries,* those for whom the postponement of marriage would be most appropriate. Of this contribution from the JST, Robert J. Matthews has written: "Paul's counsel is similar to that given in the Church today, as established in the mission field and as obeyed by the young elders and sisters. Many have had the experience of listening to a mission president counsel the elders and sisters to remain at arm's length while on the mission assignment and then preach marriage to the people of the mission. [As Paul does in 1 Corinthians 11:11; Hebrews 13:4.] If all we knew was the instruction given to the missionaries, we would have an incomplete sampling of the teachings of the church, and consequently an incorrect notion. In like manner, 1 Corinthians 7 is not a true picture of Paul's whole concept of marriage, but is directed to a temporary situation in the lives of those called into the ministry. There is no contradiction, simply a change in situation."[7]

CONCLUSION

Latter-day revelation sheds a brilliant light upon the Bible and allows those who seek to read by that light to become more acquainted with the doings and doctrines of prophets and seers who preceded us by many centuries. In particular, the Book of Mormon, Doctrine and Covenants, and Joseph Smith Translation of the scriptures provide a treasure house of knowledge concerning the Lord Jesus Christ and the former-day Saints. Another entire area of study (beyond the scope of this chapter) is the Prophet Joseph Smith's sermons and addresses, many of which contain the Prophet's explanation and discussion of biblical passages.[8]

Latter-day revelation both confirms and clarifies many of the vital verities contained in the biblical record. We are deeply indebted to the Prophet Joseph Smith and other living oracles of this dispensation for receiving the revelations, collecting the revelations, printing and publishing the revelations, and thus making available to the Saints plain and precious principles once had by earlier peoples. May the Lord grant us the wisdom to walk in the light of those great beacons of understanding which he has revealed in our day.

Notes

From "Joseph Smith and the New Testament," *Ensign,* December 1986, 28–34.

1. *Teachings of the Prophet Joseph Smith,* 349.
2. Bruce R. McConkie, as quoted in Monte S. Nyman and Robert L. Millet, eds., *The Joseph Smith Translation: The Restoration of Plain and Precious Things* (Provo: Religious Studies Center, Brigham Young University, 1985), 10, 12.
3. *History of the Church,* 1:238.
4. *The Latter-day Saints' Messenger and Advocate* (Kirtland, Ohio: The Church of Jesus Christ of Latter-day Saints, 1834–35), vol. 2, no. 3, December 1835, 229.
5. See Robert J. Matthews, *"A Plainer Translation": Joseph Smith's Translation of the Bible, A History and Commentary* (Provo: Brigham Young University Press, 1975), 267.
6. See *Teachings of the Prophet Joseph Smith,* 275–76.
7. Matthews, *"A Plainer Translation,"* 358.
8. See *Teachings of the Prophet Joseph Smith; Words of Joseph Smith.*

THE MOUNT OF TRANSFIGURATION

Approximately one week after Peter's great confession to the Lord that "thou art the Christ, the Son of the living God" and of Jesus' promise that the keys of the kingdom would be given (Matthew 16:13–19), the Master took Peter, James, and John to a high mountain to pray (see Luke 9:28). It is the fall of the year, a time when the Feast of Tabernacles is celebrated among the Jews. It is six months before Passover, six months before the Redeemer will be crucified, buried, and resurrected. It is a time of sober reflection for the Lord and of inquiry for the Apostles. Mark thus writes that Jesus took "Peter, and James, and John, who asked him many questions concerning his sayings" (JST, Mark 9:1).

THE SAVIOR PREPARED

The Spirit of God was poured out abundantly on this occasion. Christ and his meridian First Presidency[1] were transfigured—lifted spiritually to a higher plane for a brief season—in preparation for what they were about to see and receive.[2] "Transfiguration is a special change in appearance and nature which is wrought upon a person or thing by the power of God. This divine transformation is from a lower to a higher state; it results in a more exalted, impressive, and glorious condition."[3]

According to the synoptic Gospels, Moses and Elias appeared. Luke points out that they "appeared in glory, and spake of [Jesus'] death, and also his resurrection, which he should accomplish at Jerusalem" (JST, Luke 9:31). Elder James E.

Talmage observed: "In faithfully treading the path of His life's work, He had reached the verge of the valley of the shadow of death; and the human part of His nature called for refreshing. As angels had been sent to minister unto Him after the trying scenes of the forty days' fast and the direct temptation of Satan, and as, in the agonizing hour of His bloody sweat, He was to be sustained anew by angelic ministry, so at this critical and crucial period, the beginning of the end, visitants from the unseen world came to comfort and support Him."[4]

KEYS CONFERRED

These ancient prophets appeared not only to comfort and prepare our Lord for what lay ahead, but also to join with him in conferring priesthood keys or directing powers; these keys would enable the Twelve to lead the Church of Jesus Christ after the Savior's mortal ministry was completed. Both Moses and Elijah had been translated in their own day, taken from the earth without tasting death. They came to the holy mount with physical bodies in order to confer sacred authority.[5] Moses the Lawgiver, Moses who gathered and led ancient Israel for forty years, appeared. If we may draw upon modern revelation as a commentary upon ancient scripture, we conclude that Moses conferred upon Peter, James, and John the keys of the gathering of Israel. This is precisely what he did during that pentecostal season in Kirtland, Ohio, at the time of the dedication of the temple (D&C 110:11). Gathering consists of coming to Christ, to his gospel, to his true church, and to the congregations and gathering sites of his Saints.[6]

Elias appeared. As we know, the word *Elias* in the New Testament generally refers to the Old Testament prophet Elijah. Again, if we may lean heavily upon modern revelation, we would suppose that Elijah assisted the Savior in conferring upon Peter, James, and John the sealing powers, the right of presidency associated with binding and sealing on earth and in heaven, the very power Jesus had promised earlier and which he would soon deliver to all the Twelve (see Matthew 16:19; 18:18). The Prophet Joseph Smith explained that "the spirit, power, and calling of Elijah is, that ye have power to hold the key of the revelations, ordinances, oracles, powers, and endowments of the fulness of the Melchizedek Priesthood and of the kingdom of God on the earth; and to receive, obtain, and perform all the ordinances belonging to the kingdom of God." He taught further, "Then what you seal on earth, by the keys of Elijah, is sealed in heaven; and this is the power of Elijah, and this is the difference between the spirit and power of Elias and Elijah; for while the spirit of Elias is a forerunner, the power of Elijah is sufficient to make our calling and election sure."[7]

The messenger Elias who appeared in 1836, whose specific identity is not mentioned in the revelation, "committed the dispensation of the gospel of Abraham, saying that in us and our seed all generations after us should be blessed" (D&C 110:12). That is, in modern times Elias restored the Abrahamic covenant, the patriarchal order, the keys associated with that order of the Melchizedek Priesthood we know as the new and everlasting covenant of marriage (see D&C 131:1–4). Elias conferred the power whereby men and women who have been gathered out of the world may then, through temples, be organized into eternal family units. We would suppose, because celestial marriage is at the heart and core of the gospel covenant, that some heavenly messenger restored like powers in the meridian of time.

Indeed, the powers of Elias and the powers of Elijah are inextricably tied. Elder Bruce R. McConkie has written: "Elijah brought back the sealing power so that marriages and other ordinances that are bound on earth shall be eternally sealed in the heavens. Those married by this authority are husband and wife in this life, and they so remain in the life to come, if they are true and faithful in all things. When Elias appeared to Joseph Smith and Oliver Cowdery on the third day of April in 1836 in the Kirtland Temple, he . . . restored the great commission, given of God to Abraham our father, whereby the seed of Abraham has power to gain eternal blessings forever through eternal marriage; that is, Elias restored the marriage discipline that had eternal efficacy, virtue, and force in the days of Abraham, Isaac, and Jacob."[8]

"Jesus himself gave [Peter, James, and John] all else that they needed to preside over his earthly kingdom; to lead all men to eternal salvation in the mansions on high; to send the gospel to the ends of the earth; and to seal men up unto eternal life in the kingdom of his Father."[9] Or as the Prophet Joseph Smith pointed out, "Men will set up stakes and say thus far will we go and no farther. Did Abraham, when called upon to offer his son? Did the Savior? No. View him fulfilling all righteousness again on the banks of Jordan, also on the Mount transfigured before Peter and [James and] John, there receiving the fulness of priesthood or the law of God, setting up no stake but coming right up to the mark in all things."[10]

JOHN THE BAPTIST PRESENT

Mark adds the fascinating detail that John the Baptist was also present on the Mount of Transfiguration (JST, Mark 9:3). Whereas Moses and Elijah, both of whom had been translated and taken to heaven without tasting death, would have come with physical bodies to confer priesthood authority, the Baptist would still be a spirit. He, like myriad others, would wait but six months more before "their sleeping dust was to be restored unto its perfect frame" (D&C 138:17). Peter, James, and John were Apostles. They held the Melchizedek Priesthood. There would therefore be no need for John to confer any authority upon those who led the Twelve. "Perhaps he was there, as the last legal administrator under the Old Covenant, to symbolize that the law was fulfilled and all old things were done away, thus contrasting his position with Peter, James, and John who were then becoming the 'first' legal administrators of the New Kingdom."[11]

Endowed with Power

Modern prophets have suggested that Peter, James, and John may have received the temple endowment on the mount. President Joseph Fielding Smith taught that "when there is no house of the Lord and the work is urgent, the Lord makes it possible that . . . the ordinances that pertain to the house of the Lord may be performed in the wilderness, on a mountain top, or in a lake or a stream of water. I am convinced in my own mind that when the Savior took the three disciples up on the mount, . . . he there gave unto them the ordinances that pertain to the house of the Lord and that they were *endowed*. That was the only place they could go. That place became holy and sacred for the rites of salvation which were performed on that occasion."[12]

In addition, the Apostle Peter, in speaking of this supernal experience many years later, implies that the First Presidency received on the Mount of Transfiguration the more sure word of prophecy, the knowledge that they were sealed up unto eternal life (see D&C 131:5–6).[13] "Moreover I will endeavor," Peter wrote, "that ye may be able after my decease to have these things always in remembrance. For we have not followed cunningly devised fables, when we made known unto you the power and coming of our Lord Jesus Christ, but were eyewitnesses of his majesty. For he received from God the Father honour and glory, when there came such a voice to him from the excellent glory, This is my beloved Son, in whom I am well pleased. And this voice which came from heaven we heard, when we were with him in the holy mount. We have also a more sure word of prophecy; whereunto ye do well that ye take heed, as unto a light that shineth in a dark place, until the day dawn, and the day star arise in your hearts" (2 Peter 1:15–19).

Joseph Smith, in offering prophetic commentary upon this passage, said: "And though they had heard an audible voice from heaven bearing testimony that Jesus was the Son of God, yet [Peter] says we have a more sure word of prophecy. . . . Now, wherein could they have a more sure word of prophecy than to hear the voice of God saying, This is my beloved Son.

"Now for the secret and grand key. Though they might hear the voice of God and know that Jesus was the Son of God, this would be no evidence that their election and calling was made sure, that they had part with Christ, and were joint heirs with Him. They then would want that more sure word of prophecy, that they were sealed in the heavens and had the promise of eternal life in the kingdom of God. Then, having this promise sealed unto them, it was an anchor to the soul, sure and steadfast. Though the thunders might roll and lightnings flash, and earthquakes bellow, and war gather thick around, yet this hope and knowledge would support the soul in every hour of trial, trouble and tribulation."[14]

A bright cloud overshadowed the three chief Apostles, followed by a voice: "This is my beloved Son, in whom I am well pleased; hear ye him. And when the disciples heard it, they fell on their face, and were sore afraid. And Jesus came and touched them, and said, Arise, and be not afraid. And when they had lifted up their eyes, they saw no man, save Jesus only" (Matthew 17:5-8). It was the voice of the Eternal Father bearing record of the Word of his power. The *Shekinah* or dwelling cloud manifested the glory and presence of God, even as it had in ancient Israel (see Exodus 33:9-11; Numbers 9:15-22; 11:25). It "came down from heaven to shield the face and form of God from his earthbound creations," Elder McConkie has written. "Elohim was there in the cloud. That he was seen by the Son we cannot doubt. Whether our Lord's three companions saw within the veil we do not say."[15]

CONCLUSION

A modern revelation speaks of a vision that came to Peter, James, and John on the mount. "He that endureth in faith and doeth my will," the holy word attests, "the same shall overcome, and shall receive an inheritance upon the earth when the day of transfiguration shall come"—that day we know as the Millennium, initiated by the second coming of the Son of Man in glory. "When the earth shall be transfigured, even *according to the pattern which was shown unto mine apostles upon the mount; of which account the fulness ye have not yet received*" (D&C 63:20-21; emphasis added).

And so the three chief Apostles descended the holy mount different men than when they had ascended it. They were lifted spiritually, empowered, endowed, sealed, and prepared. Theirs was a perspective of what was, a view of what was to be, and a confidence in the God of heaven that would enable them to lead the Church of Jesus Christ into a difficult and uncertain future.

Notes

From "Transfiguration Was Lifting to Higher Plane," *Church News,* 1 July 1995, 11–12.

1. See *Doctrines of Salvation,* 3:152.
2. *Teachings of the Prophet Joseph Smith,* 158.
3. Bruce R. McConkie, *Mormon Doctrine,* 2d ed. (Salt Lake City: Bookcraft, 1966), 803.
4. James E. Talmage, *Jesus the Christ* (Salt Lake City: Deseret Book Co., 1973), 373.
5. See *Doctrines of Salvation,* 2:110–11.
6. See Spencer W. Kimball, *Teachings of Spencer W. Kimball,* comp. Edward L. Kimball (Salt Lake City: Bookcraft, 1982), 439.
7. *Teachings of the Prophet Joseph Smith,* 337, 338.
8. Bruce R. McConkie, *A New Witness for the Articles of Faith* (Salt Lake City: Deseret Book Co., 1985), 508.
9. *Mortal Messiah,* 3:57.
10. *Words of Joseph Smith,* 246; spelling and punctuation corrected.
11. *Doctrinal New Testament Commentary,* 1:404.
12. *Doctrines of Salvation,* 2:170; emphasis in original; see also page 165; McConkie, *Doctrinal New Testament Commentary,* 1:44; McConkie, *Mortal Messiah,* 3:57–58.
13. See *Doctrinal New Testament Commentary,* 1:400; *Mortal Messiah,* 3:58.
14. *Teachings of the Prophet Joseph Smith,* 298.
15. *The Mortal Messiah,* 3:60–61.

C h a p t e r   6

LOOKING BEYOND THE MARK

Seven hundred years before Jesus walked the roads of Palestine, Isaiah spoke of the coming Messiah as one who would mature "as a tender plant, and as a root out of a dry ground" (Isaiah 53:2). This root, or "stem of Jesse" (Isaiah 11:1), would grow to godhood in a sterile and barren religious soil, in the midst of great learning but gross darkness.

The social and religious setting of first-century Judaism in Palestine provides a stark contrast with Jesus' ministry of salvation. On the one hand was the Anointed One who was the light that shone; on the other hand was a tradition-bound generation who refused to comprehend the light.

After ages of bondage, the Jews had fixed themselves upon the hope of deliverance. Anticipation was great, and expectations were legion, for "the Jews taught that the kingdom of God should immediately appear" (JST, Luke 19:11). And yet, the results were quite different from what they expected.

It has been written that "the Jews were looking for a redeemer quite different from the Christ. It was a temporal salvation that they desired. It was an earthly kingdom for which they longed. It was not faith, repentance, and baptism for which they sought, but national vindication, the destruction of gentile oppressors, and the establishment of a kingdom of peace and justice."[1] With such limited vision and perspective, it is not difficult to see how a people could "discern the face of the sky" but "not discern the signs of the times" (Matthew 16:3). Jesus the Christ was the fulfillment of numerous prophecies and Mosaic ordinances; nevertheless, a stiff-necked generation refused to focus upon the mark and chose instead to look for a messiah of their own making. In this, they parallel very closely a modern generation who refuses the living prophets and limits their belief to ancient scriptures and dead prophets only.

THE LAW FULFILLED IN CHRIST

Jesus himself was an observant Jew: he loved and honored the Law of Moses and sought to keep the statutes and ordinances associated with it. He taught that he was "not come to destroy, but to fulfil" the law (Matthew 5:17). Joseph Smith said that "Christ Himself fulfilled all righteousness in becoming obedient to the law which he had given to Moses on the mount, and thereby magnified it and made it honorable, instead of destroying it."[2]

Until the time of the Atonement was past, the Master taught that the law was to be observed and kept:

"Heaven and earth must pass away, but one jot or one tittle shall in no wise pass from the law, until all be fulfilled.

"Whosoever, therefore, shall break one of these least commandments, and shall teach men so to do, he shall in no wise be saved in the kingdom of heaven; but whosoever shall do and teach these commandments of the law until it be fulfilled, the same shall be called great, and shall be saved in the kingdom of heaven" (JST, Matthew 5:20–21).

The law was, as Paul observed, a "schoolmaster" (literally, *pedagogue* or *supervisor of children*) for a wayward people in need of structure and direction (Galatians 3:24). Unfortunately, the law wasn't sufficient for the Jewish elders. To it, and often replacing it, was added the oral law of the Pharisees. Often called "the tradition of men" or "the traditions of [the] fathers" (Mark 7:8; Galatians 1:14), these interpretations and commentaries on the law in large measure came to govern Jewish life. Had the Pharisees been more intense in their study of the law itself rather than in the commentaries upon it, they might have recognized Jesus as the promised Messiah. And had they been more eager to apply its teachings rather than to seek for further things they could not understand, they might have been able to accept him. Such, however, was not the case.

Jesus knew that Judaism carried the promise of salvation, telling a Samaritan woman that "salvation is of the Jews" (John 4:22). Yet the failure of individuals to accept living oracles resulted in the Lord's rejection of them. Jesus made this clear when the Pharisees asked why he did not receive them:

"Then said the Pharisees unto him, Why will ye not receive us with our baptism, seeing we keep the whole law?

"But Jesus said unto them, Ye keep not the law. If ye had kept the law, ye would have received me, for I am he who gave the law.

"I receive not you with your baptism, because it profiteth you nothing" (JST, Matthew 9:18–20).

Said one scholar about Jewish baptism: "Now the process by which a man was made a proselyte [convert to Judaism] was threefold: it consisted of circumcision, immersion in water (i.e., baptism), and the presentation of an offering in the Temple. Of these rites baptism assumed a growing importance."[3]

Jesus explained to the Pharisees that mixing the old (the traditions and misunderstood ordinances of the Pharisees, represented by their "old" baptism) with the new (Christ and the ordinances of the new covenant) would not work. It would be like sewing new cloth onto an old garment (see JST, Matthew 9:21–22). Clearly, those who accept and follow divine direction will recognize and accept the divine director. Those who reject Jesus the lawgiver have not known Moses the lawgiver and the other prophets. If the Law of Moses and the law that the Jews had developed were compared to salt, one would be good, and one would have lost its savor:

"Then certain of them came to him, saying, Good Master, we have Moses and the prophets, and whosoever shall live by them, shall he not have life?

"And Jesus answered, saying, Ye know not Moses, neither the prophets; for if ye had known them, ye would have believed on me; for to this intent they were written. For I am sent that ye might have life. Therefore I will liken it unto salt which is good;

"But if the salt has lost its savor, wherewith shall it be seasoned?

"It is neither fit for the land, nor yet for the dunghill; men cast it out" (JST, Luke 14:35–38).

THE LAW CORRUPTED BY TRADITION

Not only had the traditions of the Jewish elders leached spiritual power from the Mosaic law, they had even caused the Jews to transgress God's commandments. When the scribes and Pharisees from Jerusalem accused the disciples of transgressing the traditions of the elders by not washing their hands when they ate bread, Jesus replied that the Jewish leaders transgressed the commandment of God by their tradition. He then cited one example whereby tradition had nullified the commandment to honor one's parents (see Matthew 15:1–6).

The tradition of the elders was manmade, and obeying it rendered worship meaningless, as the Lord explained:

"In vain do they worship me, teaching for doctrines the commandments of men" (Mark 7:7).

In the eyes of the Lord, to present oneself as an expert of the law and then to miss the intent and purpose of the law was the height of hypocrisy:

"Well hath Esaias prophesied of you hypocrites, as it is written, This people honoureth me with their lips, but their heart is far from me" (Mark 7:6; see also Matthew 23:23–28).

In a sense, such people were guilty of profaning and violating the whole law. "Ye blind guides," Jesus said in a scathing denunciation, "who strain at a gnat, and swallow a camel; who make yourselves appear unto men that ye would not commit the least sin, and yet ye yourselves, transgress the whole law" (JST, Matthew 23:21).

Jesus stood as a marked contrast to the rabbis of his day. He taught "as one having authority from God, and not as having authority from the Scribes" (JST, Matthew 7:37). The ability to teach with spiritual authority is a gift granted to those who pay the price of fasting, prayer, and scripture study (see Alma 17:2–3). Both Jesus and the Jewish leaders had done those, but one difference is that the latter had studied what the learned had said *about* the law while Jesus knew what was actually said *in* the law.

When the Sadducees hypothesized a problem dealing with marriage and resurrection, Jesus scolded them: "Do ye not therefore err, because ye know not the scriptures, neither the power of God?" (Mark 12:24.)

The Jews could have enjoyed a power and authority behind the words they spoke if they had carefully studied and taught from the scriptures of the day. They would have enjoyed the ratifying influence of the Holy Ghost in their declarations if they had accepted Jesus as the Christ and entered in at the strait gate.

Bruce R. McConkie has written that "many great doctrinal revelations come to those who preach from the scriptures. When they are in tune with the Infinite, the Lord lets them know, first, the full and complete meaning of the scriptures they are expounding, and then he ofttimes expands their views so that new truths flood in upon them, and they learn added things that those who do not follow such a course can never know."[4]

First-century Judaism produced a generation who, for the most part, did not follow such a course. The teachers of the day lacked the confirming spiritual power that was so evident in the works and words of Jesus Christ.

A DEARTH OF REVELATION

Many of the rabbis themselves had noted the absence of the spirit of prophecy and revelation in ancient Judaism. Some dated the loss of the Holy Spirit from the destruction of the first temple; others dated it after the deaths of the Old Testament prophets.[5]

The Mishnah says that "when the First Prophets died, Urim and Thummim ceased." Herbert Danby, the translator, explains this by noting, "Here [is meant] . . . all the Prophets except Haggai, Zechariah, and Malachi. . . . [The Jews] ceased to have power to indicate God's will."[6]

The Babylonian Talmud, a fifth- or sixth-century body of Jewish civil and canonical law, confirms this: "After the later prophets Haggai, Zechariah, and Malachi had died, the Holy Spirit departed from Israel."[7]

E. R. Goodenough spoke of later Judaism and identified what he called the "horizontal" and "vertical" paths to holiness. The Pharisees had trod a horizontal path, but others had looked to a vertical path:

"Man walked through this life along the road God had put before him, a road which was itself the light and law of God, and God above rewarded him for doing so. Man was concerned with proper observances to show respect to God, and with proper attitudes and acts toward his fellow men. . . . This seems . . . [to be the essence of] rabbinic or talmudic or Pharisaic Judaism. . . .

"Alongside rabbinic Judaism in Palestine in the century or so before the fall of Jerusalem there sprang up a rash of other sects. We have documents, . . . whose interest seems to be in a hero who had trod not a horizontal path but a vertical one up to the throne of God, and had returned to tell men of another world."[8]

Goodenough proposed that Judaism experienced a "tension between the two basic types of religious experience everywhere, the religion of the vertical path by which man climbs to God and even to a share in divine nature, as over against the legal religion where man walks a horizontal path through this world according to God's instructions."[9] In the end, rabbinic or Pharisaic Judaism won out, and the vertical path to God within Judaism was suppressed and forgotten.

The fact that many at the time of Jesus had personally apostatized to the degree that they no longer accepted modern prophets or even personal revelation is evident in the following passage from the Sermon on the Mount:

"Then said his disciples unto him, they will say unto us, We ourselves are righteous, and need not that any man should teach us. God, we know, heard Moses and some of the prophets; but us he will not hear.

"And they will say, We have the law for our salvation, and that is sufficient for us.

"Then Jesus answered, and said unto his disciples, thus shall ye say unto them,

"What man among you, having a son, and he shall be standing out, and shall say, Father, open thy house that I may come in and sup with thee, will not say, Come in, my son; for mine is thine, and thine is mine?" (JST, Matthew 7:14–17.)

Perhaps more than any other place in the Gospels, the above passage demonstrates the static condition in the days of Jesus. Much like the people in our day who say that the Book of Mormon is an unnecessary addition to the "complete" Bible, the Jews of the first century had stumbled into a pathetic state of blindness: "God, we know, heard Moses and some of the prophets; but us he will not hear."

How typical of those who are "past feeling" (1 Nephi 17:45). "Have ye inquired of the Lord?" Nephi asked his rebellious brothers. "We have not," they responded, "for the Lord maketh no such thing known unto us" (1 Nephi 15:8–9).

In Christ's day the spirit of true inquiry among the majority of the Jews was all but gone. Absent was the awareness of the need for the spirit of prophecy and revelation. Orson Pratt described their state:

"The Jews had apostatized before Jesus came among them to that degree, that there were sects and parties among them, just as we find in the Christian world since; and these Jewish sects were destitute of the spirit of prophecy which their ancient fathers had. . . . It was because of this that the Jews were broken off, and the Gentiles were grafted in, and were made partakers of the riches, blessings and glories formerly enjoyed by the ancient Jews."[10]

The odd point of view that rabbinic Judaism developed is exemplified by this statement from a Jewish writer:

"Although the gift of prophecy was taken away from the prophets, it remained with the wise; hence it may be inferred that the wise are greater than the prophets."[11]

A rather humorous yet tragic rabbinic anecdote is given in the Babylonian Talmud. Rabbi Eliezer and some colleagues are debating a point and arguing about proof:

"On that day, R. Eliezer brought forward every imaginable argument, but they did not accept them. Said he to them: 'If the halachah [laws supplementing or explaining Old Testament law] agrees with me, let this carob-tree prove it!' Thereupon the carob-tree was torn a hundred cubits out of its place. . . . 'No proof can be brought from a carob-tree,' they retorted. Again he said to them: 'If the *halachah* agrees with me, let the stream of water prove it!' Whereupon the stream of water flowed backwards. 'No proof can be brought from a stream of water,' they rejoined. . . . Again he said to them: 'If the *halachah* agrees with me, let it be proved from Heaven!' Whereupon a Heavenly Voice cried out: 'Why do ye dispute with R. Eliezer, seeing that in all matters the *halachah* agrees with him!' But R. Joshua arose and exclaimed: *'It is not in heaven.'* What did he mean by this?—Said R. Jeremiah: 'That the Torrah had already been given at Mount Sinai; we pay no attention to a Heavenly Voice, because Thou hast long since written in the Torah at Mount Sinai."[12]

LIVING SCRIPTURE

An absentee and unresponsive God exerts little influence upon the hearts and minds of his children. Those who believe in such a being are only a stone's throw away from an outright denial of God's existence.

"Why teach ye the law," the Lord asked the Jewish leaders, "and deny that which is written; and condemn him whom the Father hath sent to fulfil the law, that ye might all be redeemed?

"O fools! for you have said in your hearts, *There is no God.* And you pervert the right way; and the kingdom of heaven suffereth violence of you; and you persecute the meek; and in your violence you seek to destroy the kingdom" (JST, Luke 16:20–21; emphasis added).

The Jews of the New Testament time denied their salvation when they denied both established and continuing scripture: "Woe unto you, lawyers! For ye have taken away the key of knowledge, the fulness of the scriptures; ye enter not in yourselves into the kingdom; and those who were entering in, ye hindered" (JST, Luke 11:53).

One way of taking away "the fulness of the scriptures" is hindering or denying the spirit of revelation, inasmuch as scripture represents what is uttered through the power of the Holy Ghost (D&C 68:3–4). Elder Bruce R. McConkie wrote concerning Luke 11:53:

"The devil wages war against the scriptures. He hates them, perverts their plain meanings, and destroys them when he can. He entices those who heed his temptings to delete and discard, to change and corrupt, to alter and amend, thus taking away the key which will aid in making men 'wise unto salvation.' (2 Tim. 3:15–17.)

"Accordingly, Jesus is here heaping woe upon those who have contaminated and destroyed scriptures which would have guided and enlightened the Jews."[13]

There stood One among the Jews who, with his associates, offered to the world living scripture—seed cast upon different kinds of soil. Many of the Jews who were earnest in their hearts proved to be good ground, bringing forth fruit many-fold. Yet Judaism as a whole missed the mark, much as modern-day Christianity as a whole is missing the mark of living prophets and living scripture. Too many proved to be soil by the wayside, stony ground, and ground full of thorns, subject to Satan, persecution, and the cares of the world (see Matthew 13:3–23). Those who chose "walking in darkness at noon-day" (D&C 95:6) rejected God's new covenant with Israel and fellowship with the Mediator of that covenant.

Notes

From "Looking Beyond the Mark," *Ensign*, July 1987, 60–64.

1. Joseph Fielding McConkie, "Messianic Expectations Among the Jews," in *CES Symposium on the New Testament* (Salt Lake City: The Church of Jesus Christ of Latter-day Saints, 1980), 128.
2. *History of the Church*, 5:261.
3. W. D. Davies, *Paul and Rabbinic Judaism: Some Rabbinic Elements in Pauline Theology* (London: SPCK, 1955), 121.
4. McConkie, *Promised Messiah*, 515–16.
5. See Louis Ginzberg, *The Legends of the Jews*, 13 vols. (Philadelphia: The Jewish Publication Society of America, 1939), 6:441–42.
6. *The Mishnah*, trans. Herbert Danby (Oxford: Oxford University Press, 1933), 305.
7. *Yoma*, in *The Babylonian Talmud*, ed. I. Epstein (London: The Soncino Press, 1938), 41.
8. E. R. Goodenough, *Jewish Symbols in the Greco-Roman Period*, 13 vols. (New York: Pantheon Books, 1953), 1:18–19.
9. Goodenough, *Jewish Symbols*, 1:19–20.
10. Orson Pratt, in *Journal of Discourses*, 16:345.
11. Cited in Ginzberg, *Legends*, 6:442.
12. Baba Mezi'a, in *The Babylonian Talmud* (1938), 352–53.
13. *Doctrinal New Testament Commentary*, 1:624–25.

DOCTRINAL TEACHINGS OF PAUL

It is given to but few to wield a more powerful influence over Christian history than to Saul of Tarsus, the persecutor who became a prophet, the Pharisee who became the apostle to the Gentiles. The life and teachings of the Apostle Paul stand as bright reminders of the power of Christ to transform the souls of men and women, to remake the human heart, and to refocus one's misdirected zeal into the way of the Master. When the risen Lord appeared in vision to Ananias of Damascus and instructed him to send for the stricken and blinded Saul, Ananias answered: "Lord, I have heard by many of this man, how much evil he hath done to thy saints at Jerusalem: and here he hath authority from the chief priests to bind all that call on thy name." The response that followed bespeaks the Redeemer's insight into the wonders that would be done at Paul's hand: "Go thy way: for *he is a chosen vessel unto me,* to bear my name before the Gentiles, and kings, and the children of Israel" (Acts 9:11–15; emphasis added).

I will leave to others a discussion of the early life, education and training, and conversion of Saul. In this chapter I will consider briefly some of the more significant doctrinal messages from his epistles. Many of these are, in the language of Simon Peter, "things hard to be understood, which they that are unlearned and unstable wrest, as they do also the other scriptures, unto their own destruction" (2 Peter 3:16). I begin with the testimony that the message of Paul was a proclamation of the gospel—Jesus Christ and him crucified—and that he was no more the originator of Christianity (as some foolishly suppose) than Abraham was the originator of the everlasting covenant. Further, as F. F. Bruce observed: "Paul himself is at pains to point out that the gospel which he preached was one and the same gospel as that preached by the other apostles—a striking claim, considering that Paul was neither a companion of Christ in the days of His flesh nor of the other apostles, and that he vigorously asserts his complete independence of these."[1] And yet Paul knew as Peter knew. He knew as Thomas knew. And what he knew— whether from the teachings of Stephen, from the other apostles, from his own study of the Old Testament with new eyes, or by means of personal revelation—he taught. And he taught with a power, a persuasion, and a holy zeal known only to those who, like Alma and the sons of Mosiah, have gone from darkness to light and whose whole soul yearns to lead others to that same light.

"ALL HAVE SINNED . . ."

One cannot fully appreciate the need for medication until he is aware of a malady. One does not pant after the cooling draught until he has nearly died of thirst. In the same way, as President Ezra Taft Benson observed, people do not yearn for salvation in Christ until they know why they need Christ, which thing they cannot know until they understand and acknowledge the Fall and its effects upon all mankind.[2] The atonement of Jesus Christ is inextricably and eternally tied to the Fall of Adam and Eve. To attempt to offer the solution without a knowledge of the problem is to teach the Atonement in the abstract, to lessen its impact, to mitigate its transforming power in the lives of men and women. Thus it is that the Apostle Paul began at the beginning; he laid stress where it needed to be. Quoting the Psalmist, he affirmed: "There is none righteous, no, not one: there is none that understandeth, there is none that seeketh after God. They are all gone out of the way, they are together become unprofitable; there is none that doeth good, no, not one" (Romans 3:10–12; see also Psalm 14:1–3; 53:1–3).

Though we as Latter-day Saints do not subscribe to a belief held by many in the Christian world as to the depravity of humankind, yet the burden of scripture, including the New Testament, is that there was a Fall and that it does take a measured toll on all humanity. Paul taught plainly that men and women must be extricated and redeemed from the Fall. Because our first parents partook of the forbidden fruit, death and sin entered the world. We are, as God taught Adam in the earliest ages, "conceived in sin," such that when children "begin to grow up, sin conceiveth in their hearts, and they taste the bitter, that they may know to prize the good" (Moses 6:55). In the words of Lehi, God revealed to the ancients that all persons "were lost, because of the transgression of their parents" (2 Nephi 2:21). Truly, "because of the fall our natures have become evil continually" (Ether 3:2). We do not believe that there is sin in the sexual act, so long as it is undertaken within the bonds of marriage. Nor do we subscribe to the belief in men and women's inability to even choose good over evil. To say that we are conceived in sin is to say, first of all, that we are conceived into a world of sin. But, more significantly, it is to declare that conception is the vehicle, the means by which a fallen nature, what we know as mortality or what Paul calls "the flesh," is transmitted to all the posterity of Adam and Eve. The revelations declare that little children are innocent, not because they are that way by nature, but rather because Christ's atonement declares them to be so (see Moroni 8:8, 12, 22; D&C 29:46; 74:7). In short, "as in Adam, or by nature, they fall, even so the blood of Christ atoneth for their sins" (Mosiah 3:16). Thus all of us struggle not only for forgiveness for individual sins, but also for relief and redemption from a fallen nature that yields to sin. That is to say, salvation in Christ consists not only in meeting and satisfying the demands of God's justice (which forbids uncleanness), but also in enjoying the renovating and cleansing powers of Christ's blood such that we begin to die as pertaining to unrighteousness and the ways of sin.

"All have sinned, and come short of the glory of God," Paul wrote to the Romans (Romans 3:23). In speaking of life before coming unto Christ, Paul further taught: "For when we were in the flesh, the motions of sin, which were not according to the law, did work in our members to bring forth fruit unto death. . . . For I know that in me, that is, in my flesh, dwelleth no good thing; for to will is present with me"—that is, to do what is right is in my heart—"but to perform that which is good I find not, *only in Christ*" (JST, Romans 7:5, 19; emphasis added). Herein lies the solution: though all of us are subject to sin and to the pull of the flesh, there is hope for liberation through Jesus. The Son of God has "delivered us from the power of darkness" (Colossians 1:13). He truly "hath abolished death, and hath brought life and immortality to light through the gospel" (2 Timothy 1:10).

JUSTIFICATION BY FAITH

The scriptures are consistent in their declaration that "no unclean thing can enter into [God's] kingdom" (3 Nephi 27:19). In theory there are two ways by which men and women may inherit eternal life. The first is simply to live the law of God perfectly, to make no mistakes. To do so is to be justified—pronounced innocent, declared blameless—by works or by law. To say this another way, if we keep the commandments completely (including receiving the ordinances of salvation), never deviating from the strait and narrow path throughout our mortal lives, then we qualify for the blessings of the obedient. And yet we have just attended to the terrible truth that all are unclean as a result of sin. All of us have broken at least one of the laws of God and therefore disqualify ourselves for justification by law. Moral perfection may be a possibility, but it is certainly not a probability. Jesus alone trod that path. "Therefore," Paul observed, "by the deeds of the law"—meaning the Law of Moses, as well as any law of God—"there shall no flesh be justified in his sight" (Romans 3:20; see also 2 Nephi 2:5).

The second way to be justified is by faith; it is for the sinner to be pronounced clean or innocent through trusting in and relying upon the merits of Him who answered the ends of the law (Romans 10:4; see also 2 Nephi 2:6–7). Jesus owed no personal debt to justice, the Holy One who can now "claim of the Father his rights of mercy which he hath upon the children of men" (Moroni 7:27). Because we are guilty of transgression, if there had been no atonement of Christ, no amount of good deeds on our part, no nobility independent of divine intercession, could make up for the loss. Truly, "since man had fallen he could not merit anything of himself" (Alma 22:14). Thus He who loved us first (1 John 4:10, 19) reaches out to the lost and fallen, to the disinherited, and proposes a marriage. The Infinite One joins with the finite, the Finished with the unfinished, the Whole with the partial—in short, the Perfect with the imperfect. Through covenant with Christ and thus union with the Bridegroom, we place ourselves in a condition to become fully formed, whole, finished—to become perfect in Christ (see Moroni 10:32).

The means by which the Savior justifies us is wondrous indeed. It entails what might be called "the great exchange." It is certainly true that Jesus seeks through his atoning sacrifice and through the medium of the Holy Spirit to *change* us, to transform us from fallen and helpless mortals into "new creatures in Christ." But there is more. Jesus offers to *exchange* with us. In his epistle to the Philippians, Paul speaks of his eagerness to forsake the allurements of the world in order to obtain the riches of Christ. "I count all things but loss," he said, "for the excellency of the knowledge of Christ Jesus my Lord: for whom I have suffered the loss of all things, and do count them but dung, that I may win Christ"—and now note this important addition—"and be found in him, *not having mine own righteousness, which is of the law, but that which is through the faith of Christ, the righteousness which is of God by faith*" (Philippians 3:8–9; emphasis added). Paul's point is vital: justification comes by faith, by trusting in *Christ's righteousness,* in his merits, mercy, and grace (see Romans 10:1–4; compare 2 Nephi 2:3; Helaman 14:13; D&C 45:3–5).

Though our efforts to be righteous are necessary, they will forevermore be insufficient. Paul teaches a profound truth—that as we come unto Christ by the covenant of faith, our Lord's righteousness becomes our righteousness. He justifies us in the sense that he *imputes*—meaning, he reckons to our account—his goodness and takes our sin. This is the great exchange. To the Corinthians Paul explained that "God was in Christ, reconciling the world unto himself, not imputing their trespasses unto them. . . . For *he* [God the Father] *hath made him* [Christ the Son] *to be sin for us,* who knew no sin; *that we might be made the righteousness of God in him*" (2 Corinthians 5:19, 21; emphasis added). As Paul explained elsewhere, Christ "hath redeemed us from the curse of the law, being made a curse for us" (Galatians 3:13; see also Hebrews 2:9). Sidney Sperry thus spoke of being justified as not only a matter of "acquittal" from guilt and sin but also of "being regarded as righteous in a future divine judgment."[3] Those who enter the gospel covenant and thereafter seek to do their duty and endure to the end the Lord "holds guiltless" (3 Nephi 27:16; see also D&C 4:2). It is not that they are guiltless in the sense of having never done wrong; rather, the Holy One removes the blame and imputes—accounts or decrees to the repentant sinner, the one who comes unto Christ by covenant—His righteousness. "For as by one man's disobedience"—the fall of Adam—"many were made sinners, so by the obedience of one"—Jesus Christ—"shall many be made righteous" (Romans 5:19).

One Evangelical theologian, John MacArthur, has written: "Justification may be defined as an act of God whereby he imputes to a believing sinner the full and perfect righteousness of Christ, forgiving the sinner of all unrighteousness, declaring him or her perfectly righteous in God's sight, thus delivering the believer from all condemnation. . . . It is a forensic reality that takes place in the court of God. . . ."[4] MacArthur also explained: "Justification is a divine verdict of 'not guilty—fully righteous.' It is the reversal of God's attitude toward the sinner. Whereas He formerly condemned, He now vindicates. Although the sinner once lived under God's wrath, as a believer he or she is now under God's blessing. Justification is more than simple pardon; pardon alone would still leave the sinner without merit before God. So when God justifies He imputes divine righteousness to the sinner. . . . Justification elevates the believer to a realm of full acceptance and divine privilege in Jesus Christ." The harsh reality is that "the law demands perfection. But the only way to obtain perfect righteousness is by imputation—that is, being justified by faith."[5] "Therefore being justified by faith, we have peace with

God through our Lord Jesus Christ: by whom also we have access by faith into this grace wherein we stand, and rejoice in hope of the glory of God" (Romans 5:1–2). Since all have sinned and come short of the glory of God, we are "justified only by his grace through the redemption that is in Christ Jesus," or in other words, "justified by faith alone without the deeds of the law" (JST, Romans 3:24, 28). The comforting message of the gospel is that Jesus the Messiah has, "according to his mercy," offered to save us, "by the washing of regeneration, and renewing of the Holy Ghost; which he shed on us abundantly . . . ; that being justified by his grace, we should be made heirs according to the hope of eternal life" (Titus 3:5–7).

SALVATION BY GRACE

As we are all aware, the theological debate between whether we are saved by grace or by works has continued for centuries. In reality, it is a meaningless argument that generates more heat than light. Perhaps because Latter-day Saints have been so hesitant to acknowledge any virtue in the argument that we are saved by grace alone, some of us have not taken the Apostle Paul seriously enough; sadly, we have too often robbed ourselves of sacred insights, understanding, and comfort to be found not only in the New Testament, but also in the Book of Mormon.

Paul certainly understood that the works of righteousness are necessary to our salvation. He taught that God "will render to every man according to his deeds" (Romans 2:6). Of course we must receive the ordinances of salvation. Of course we must strive to live a life befitting that of our Christian covenant. Of course we must do all in our power to overcome sin, put off the natural man, and deny ourselves of all ungodliness. These things evidence our part of the gospel covenant. They allow us, in fact, to remain in the covenant with Christ, even as we occasionally stumble and fall short of the ideal. The question is not whether good works are necessary—they are. As we have already observed, they are not sufficient. The harder questions are: In whom do I trust? On whom do I rely? Is my reliance on Christ's works, or do I strive to save myself?

Paul asked: "What shall we say then that Abraham our father, as pertaining to the flesh, hath found? For if Abraham were justified by the law of works, he hath to glory in himself; but not of God. For what saith the scripture? Abraham believed God, and it was counted unto him for righteousness. Now to him who is justified by the law of works, is the reward reckoned, not of grace, but of debt. But to him that seeketh not to be justified by the law of works, but believeth on him who justifieth not the ungodly, his faith is counted for righteousness" (JST, Romans 4:1–5).

To summarize, Abraham's faith—his willingness to believe the promises of God, trust in Jehovah's power to accomplish what to him seemed like the impossible, and thus to sacrifice Isaac—was what gained him the approval of the Almighty. It is with us as it was with Abraham; if in fact we are saved by our deeds and our merits alone, then we might have something about which to boast, namely the fact that our own genius, our own resources, our own righteousness were what allowed us to bound into glory.

Paul was not saying that only those who *do not* work are the ones who receive eternal life, but rather that they who receive eternal life are those who labor but, knowing their own fallibility and limitations, never trust in their own works. Paul taught what James taught—that true faith is always manifest in righteous works (see James 2), and that one who relies wholly on the merits of Christ, who has faith in him, will evidence that faith through noble actions and Christian conduct. To argue that we are saved by our works is to argue that Christ's atoning mission was unnecessary. "I do not frustrate the grace of God," Paul wrote; "for if righteousness come by the law, then Christ is dead in vain" (Galatians 2:21). John MacArthur has suggested that the word *grace* makes an acronym for a glorious concept—"God's Riches At Christ's Expense."[6]

"How else could salvation possibly come?" Elder Bruce R. McConkie asked. "Can man save himself? Can he resurrect himself? Can he create a celestial kingdom and decree his own admission thereto? Salvation must and does originate with God, and if man is to receive it, God must bestow it upon him, which bestowal is a manifestation of grace. . . . Salvation does not come by the works and performances of the law of Moses, nor by 'circumcision,' nor by 'the law of commandments contained in ordinances' . . . nor does it come by any good works standing alone. No matter how righteous a man might be, no matter how great and extensive his good works, he could not save himself. Salvation is in Christ and comes through his atonement."[7]

NEW CREATURES IN CHRIST

Paul taught that to come unto Christ was to enter into a new realm of existence, a spiritual realm. It was to forsake death and come unto life, to put away evil and darkness and learn to walk in righteousness and light. "Know ye not," Paul asked the Romans, "that so many of us as were baptized into Jesus Christ were baptized into his death? Therefore we are buried with him by baptism into death: that like as Christ was raised up from the dead by the glory of the Father, even so we also should walk in newness of life. For if we have been planted together in the likeness of his death, we shall be also in the likeness of his resurrection: knowing this, that our old man is crucified with him, that the body of sin might be destroyed, that henceforth we should not serve sin" (Romans 6:3–6). The new life in Christ entails a new energy, a new dynamism, a new source of strength and power. That power is Christ. So often people simply go through the motions, do good and perform their duties, but find little satisfaction in doing so. One Christian writer offered this thought: "There are few things quite so boring as being religious, but there is nothing quite so exciting as being a Christian!

"Most folks have never discovered the difference between the one and the other, so that there are those who sincerely try to live a life they do not have, substituting religion for God, Christianity for Christ, and their own noble endeavors for the energy, joy, and power of the Holy Spirit. In the absence of reality, they can only grasp at ritual, stubbornly defending the latter in the absence of the former, lest they be found with neither!

"They are lamps without oil, cars without gas, and pens without ink, baffled at their own impotence in the absence of all that alone can make man functional; for *man was so engineered by God that the presence of the Creator within the creature is indispensable to His humanity.* Christ gave Himself for us to give Himself to us! His presence puts God back into the man! He came that we might have life—God's life!

"There are those who have a life they never live. *They have come to Christ and thanked Him only for what He did, but do not live in the power of who He is.* Between the Jesus who 'was' and the Jesus who 'will be' they live in a spiritual vacuum trying with no little zeal to live for Christ a life that only He can live through them."[8]

The disciples of Jesus must strive to do what is right. They should do their duty in the Church and in the home, even when they are not eager to do so. They cannot just leave the work of the kingdom to others because they have not been changed and reborn. But that doesn't mean they must always remain that way. Each of us may change; we can change; we should change, and it is the Lord who will change us. Coming unto Christ entails more than being cleansed, as important as that is. It entails being *filled.* We speak often of the importance of being cleansed or sanctified. It is to have the Holy Spirit, who is not only a revelator but a sanctifier, remove filth and dross from our souls as though by fire. We refer to this as a baptism by fire. To be cleansed is essential, but to stop there is to stop short of great blessings. Paul presents the idea of (in a sense) nailing ourselves to the cross of Christ—

nailing our old selves, the old man of sin. He writes: "*I am crucified with Christ: nevertheless I live; yet not I, but Christ liveth in me:* and the life which I now live in the flesh I live by the faith of the Son of God, who loved me, and gave himself for me" (Galatians 2:20; emphasis added).

This is a new life in Christ. To the Ephesian Saints Paul wrote: "For by grace are ye saved through faith; and that not of yourselves: it is the gift of God: not of works, lest any man should boast. For *we are his workmanship, created in Christ Jesus unto good works,* which God hath before ordained that we should walk in them" (Ephesians 2:8–10; emphasis added). To the Hebrews he explained: "*Now the God of peace, that brought again from the dead our Lord Jesus,* that great shepherd of the sheep, through the blood of the everlasting covenant, *make you perfect in every good work to do his will, working in you that which is wellpleasing in his sight, through Jesus Christ*" (Hebrews 13:20–21; emphasis added). When we have been filled, the Spirit is with us, and Christ comes to dwell in us through that Spirit. Then our works begin to be motivated by that Holy Spirit and they are no longer our works; they are his works.

The risen Lord said to the Nephites that there were certain things required before his church would be truly his Church: it must have his name, and it must be built upon his gospel. If these two conditions are met, then the Father would show forth his own works in it (see 3 Nephi 27:5–10). How? Through the body of Christ, through the members of the Church. The Father's Spirit motivates them to greater righteousness. It is not expected that we "go through the motions" all our lives. There can come a time when the Spirit changes our motives, desires, and yearnings, and we begin to do the works the way God would do them, because he has now begun to live in us through that Spirit.

On one occasion Paul wrote: "Wherefore, my beloved, as ye have always obeyed, not as in my presence only, but now much more in my absence, work out your own salvation with fear and trembling." If we stop our reading there, and that's usually where we stop, we wonder about the phrase "work out your own salvation." How? There's not a person living on this earth that can work out their own salvation, at least not without divine assistance. There aren't enough home teaching visits; there aren't enough cakes and pies to be delivered to the neighbors; there aren't enough prayers to be uttered for a person to work out their own salvation. But Paul doesn't stop there: "For *it is God which worketh in you both to will and to do of his good pleasure*" (Philippians 2:12–13; emphasis added). The works are the Lord's works through us, and thus we are doing not our works, but his works.

Through the atonement of Christ we do more than enjoy a change of behavior;

we have our *nature* changed. "Therefore if any man be in Christ, he is a new creature: old things are passed away; behold all things are become new" (2 Corinthians 5:17). Isn't that what the angel taught King Benjamin—that the natural man is an enemy to God and will stay that way unless and until he yields himself to the enticings of the Holy Spirit (Mosiah 3:19)? John Stott explained: "*We may be quite sure that Christ-centeredness and Christ-likeness will never be attained by our own unaided efforts. How can self drive out self?* As well expect Satan to drive out Satan! For *we are not interested in skin-deep holiness,* in a merely external resemblance to Jesus Christ. We are not satisfied by a superficial modification of behavior patterns. . . . No, *what we long for is a deep inward change of character, resulting from a change of nature and leading to a radical change of conduct.* In a word we want to be like Christ, and that thoroughly, profoundly, entirely. Nothing less than this will do."[9]

Elder Glenn Pace put it this way: "We should all be striving for a disposition to do no evil, but to do good continually. This isn't a resolve or a discipline; it is a disposition. We do things because we want to, not just because we know we should. . . . Sometimes we overlook the fact that a spiritual transformation or metamorphosis must take place within us. It comes about through grace and by the Spirit of God, although it does not come about until we have truly repented and proven ourselves worthy. . . . My conclusion is that we will not be saved by works if those works are not born of a disposition to do good, as opposed to an obligation to do good."[10] This, of course, is what President Ezra Taft Benson meant when he taught that although the world deals in externals, the Lord works from the inside out.[11]

Bob George, a Protestant writer, described the spiritual transformation this way: "Being made into a new creation is like a caterpillar becoming a butterfly. Originally an earthbound crawling creature, a caterpillar weaves a cocoon and is totally immersed in it. Then a marvelous process takes place called metamorphosis. Finally a totally new creature—a butterfly—emerges. Once ground-bound, the butterfly can soar above the earth. It now can view life from the sky downward. In the same way, as a new creature in Christ you must begin to see yourself as God sees you.

"If you were to see a butterfly, it would never occur to you to say, 'Hey, everybody! Come look at this good-looking, converted worm!' Why not? After all, it was a worm. And it was 'converted.' No, now it is a new creature, and you don't think of it in terms of what it was. You see it as it is now—a butterfly."[12]

The Fruit of the Spirit

The Apostle Paul declared that one of the marks of true discipleship, one of the significant evidences of our growth into this new life in Christ, is the degree to which we enjoy the fruit of the Spirit. In three different books of scripture the Lord discusses the *gifts* of the Spirit—such things as discernment, tongues, interpretation of tongues, gifts of administration, prophecy, healing, etc. In 1 Corinthians 12, Paul suggests that the gifts of the Spirit are intended to enhance, build up, and make perfect the body of Christ, meaning the Church. They are for the good of the Church and the kingdom. In addition, Paul spoke of the *fruit* of the Spirit. In Galatians 5, Paul begins by contrasting the works of the flesh with the fruit of the spirit: "Now the works of the flesh are manifest, which are these; adultery, fornication, uncleanness, lasciviousness, idolatry, witchcraft, hatred, variance, emulations, wrath, strife, seditions, heresies, envyings, murders, drunkenness, revellings, and such like: of the which I tell you before, as I have also told you in time past, that they which do such things shall not inherit the kingdom of God" (Galatians 5:19–21).

There is a natural birth and there is a spiritual birth. The natural birth comes with mortality, and the natural birth creates the natural man. The spiritual birth comes later. The natural birth has its own set of fruits or works. Paul has just mentioned several of them. The spiritual man or woman brings a different kind of fruit. "But the fruit of the Spirit is love, joy, peace, longsuffering, gentleness, goodness, faith, meekness, temperance: against such there is no law. And they that are Christ's have crucified the flesh with the affections and lusts. If we live in the Spirit, let us also walk in the Spirit" (Galatians 5:22–25).

Some of the gifts we know as the gifts of the Spirit may have begun to develop within us before we came here.[13] Many aptitudes, capacities, talents, etc., may thus come quite naturally for us. For some, the gift of speaking or the gift of teaching come naturally, and these are spiritual gifts. For others, discernment and wisdom are an integral part of their lives. But there are people who are wonderful speakers, who are poor Christians. There are people who do remarkable things in the classroom and do hurtful things outside the classroom. Talk to their family, secretary, staff, or co-workers. The gifts of the Spirit are one thing, the fruit of the Spirit another. Patience, mercy, meekness, gentleness, longsuffering, and, of course, charity or the pure love of Christ—these are the kinds of things that characterize men and women who have begun to live in Christ. Such persons are simply more Christlike. Elder Mark E. Petersen once asked a haunting question that strikes at the core of this matter of being Christlike. He inquired: "If you had to prove in court that you are a Christian, what would you use as evidence?"[14]

The interesting thing about the fruit of the Spirit is that such attitudes and such actions do not seem to be situational. In other words, a person is not just very fruitful in the Spirit while the sun shines, pleasant and kindly only when circumstances are positive. Rather, those who enjoy the fruit of the Spirit feel "love for those who do not love in return, joy in the midst of painful circumstances, peace when something counted upon doesn't come through, patience when things are not going fast enough, kindness towards those who treat others unkindly, goodness towards those who have been intentionally insensitive, faithfulness when friends have proven unfaithful, gentleness towards those who handle us roughly, self-control in the midst of intense temptation."[15]

NOT ALL ISRAEL ARE ISRAEL

Once Christ came into his life, nothing was quite the same for Saul of Tarsus. The Old Testament was a new book to him. He saw the life and ministry of Jesus Christ in and through all things, and he became a witness of the fact that all things bear testimony of the Redeemer (see Moses 6:63). Paul knew, for example, that the gathering of Israel was first and foremost a gathering to Christ and only secondarily a gathering to lands of inheritance. He taught that to be a true son or daughter of the covenant was to be fully Christian, to have accepted completely Jesus Christ, the mediator of God's new covenant with Israel. "They are not all Israel, which are of Israel," he pointed out. "Neither, because they are all children of Abraham, are they the seed" (JST, Romans 9:6–7). Descent from Abraham, Isaac, and Jacob was significant to the degree that one received the God of Abraham, Isaac, and Jacob. In Nephi's words, "as many of the Gentiles as will repent are the covenant people of the Lord; and as many of the Jews as will not repent shall be cast off; for *the Lord covenanteth with none save it be with them that repent and believe in his Son, who is the Holy One of Israel*" (2 Nephi 30:2; emphasis added).

In bearing witness of Christ, Paul drew upon the prophetic promise that through Abraham's seed all humanity would be blessed (see Genesis 12:1–3; 17:1–7; JST, Genesis 17:11–12). "Now to Abraham and his seed were the promises made. He saith not, And to seeds, as of many; but as of one, And to thy seed, which is Christ" (Galatians 3:16). Paul's point might be restated as follows:

It is certainly true that all nations would be blessed through Abraham's seed—meaning his endless posterity, through which the blessings of the gospel, the priesthood, and eternal life would be dispensed to the world (see Abraham 2:8–11). However, the ultimate fulfillment of the Abrahamic promise came through the One who was truly the Chosen Seed, Jesus of Nazareth, son of David and thus son of Abraham (see Matthew 1:1–16).

Paul also taught that many of the performances and ordinances of the ancients (animal sacrifice being the most obvious) had their fulfillment and thus their ultimate meaning in Christ and his redemption. For example, circumcision was given originally as a token of God's covenant with Abraham; male children were to be circumcised at *eight days old,* for example, as a reminder that because of the Atonement little children are not accountable until they are *eight years old* (see JST, Genesis 17:11–12). "For he is not a Jew, which is one outwardly," Paul wrote; "neither is that circumcision, which is outward in the flesh: but he is a Jew, which is one inwardly; and circumcision is that of the heart, in the spirit" (Romans 2:28–29). Stated another way, "in Jesus Christ neither circumcision availeth any thing, nor uncircumcision; but faith which worketh by love" (Galatians 5:6). Truly, in Christ we "are circumcised with the circumcision made without hands, in putting off the body of the sins of the flesh by the circumcision of Christ: buried with him in baptism, wherein also [we] are risen with him through the faith of the operation of God, who hath raised him from the dead" (Colossians 2:11–12).

In short, Paul's message was clear to those who took pride and license in their lineage. He declared boldly that it is a blessed privilege to be a chosen people, to be heirs to the adoption, the glory, the covenants, and the promises (see Romans 9:4). But true heirship is to be secured through adoption into the family of the Lord Jesus Christ. "For there is no difference between the Jew and the Greek: for the same Lord over all is rich unto all that call upon him. For whosoever shall call upon the name of the Lord shall be saved" (Romans 10:12–13). "For ye are all the children of God by faith in Christ Jesus. For as many of you as have been baptized into Christ have put on Christ. *There is neither Jew nor Greek, there is neither bond nor free, there is neither male nor female: for ye are all one in Christ Jesus. And if ye be Christ's, then are ye Abraham's seed, and heirs according to the promise"* (Galatians 3:26–29; emphasis added; see Colossians 3:11).

A NAME ABOVE ALL OTHERS

Paul affirmed that Jesus Christ transcends all things, is superior to the gods of the pagans, has preeminence over the mystical deities of the Gnostics, and is, under the Eternal Father, the One before whom all creatures bow in humble reverence. Paul wrote to the Ephesians that he did not cease to "give thanks for you, making mention of you in my prayers; that the God of our Lord Jesus Christ, the Father of glory, may give unto you the spirit of wisdom and revelation in the knowledge of him." The apostle then added that the Father's power had been "wrought in Christ, when he raised him from the dead, and set him at his own right hand in the heavenly places, far above all principality, and power, and might, and dominion, and every name that is named, not only in this world, but also in that which is to come: and hath put all things under his feet, and gave him to be the head over all things to the church, which is his body, the fulness of him that filleth all in all" (Ephesians 1:16–17, 20–23).

Many of the ancients believed that names held power and that to know the name of a deity was to possess power with or over it. Paul let it be known that Christ was the name above all other names and that salvation, the greatest of all the gifts of God, was to be had only in and through that holy name. "Let this mind be in you," he pleaded with the Philippian Saints, "which was also in Christ Jesus: who, being in the form of God, thought it not robbery to be equal with God: but made himself of no reputation, and took upon him the form of a servant, and was made in the likeness of men: and being found in fashion as a man, he humbled himself, and became obedient unto death, even the death of the cross. Wherefore God also hath highly exalted him, and given him a name which is above every name: that at the name of Jesus every knee should bow, of things in heaven, and things in earth, and things under the earth; and that every tongue should confess that Jesus Christ is Lord, to the glory of God the Father" (Philippians 2:5–11; see Ephesians 3:15).

The united testimony of the apostles and prophets is that God the Eternal Father has delivered us from the power of darkness and "translated us into the kingdom of his dear Son: in whom we have redemption through his blood, even the forgiveness of sins: who is the image of the invisible God, the firstborn of every creature"—meaning, all creation—"for by him were all things created, that are in heaven, and that are in earth, visible and invisible, whether they be thrones, or dominions, or principalities, or powers: all things were created by him, and for him: and he is before all things, and by him all things consist. . . . For it pleased the Father that in him should all fulness dwell" (Colossians 1:13–17, 19; see Hebrews 1:1–3). Thus in the spirit of adoration and worship, Elder Bruce R. McConkie wrote: "The name of Jesus—wondrous name—the name in which the truths of salvation are taught; the name in which the ordinances of salvation are performed; the name in which miracles are wrought, in which the dead are raised and mountains moved;

"The name of Jesus—wondrous name—the name by which worlds came rolling into existence; the name by which redemption comes; the name which brings victory over the grave and raises the faithful to eternal life;

"The name of Jesus—wondrous name—the name by which revelation comes and angels minister; the name of him by whom all things are and into whose hands the Father hath committed all things; the name of him to whom every knee shall bow and every tongue confess in that great day when the God of Heaven makes this planet his celestial home."[16]

CONCLUSION

I love the Apostle Paul. I love his personality—his wit, his charm, his firmness, his unquestioned allegiance to the Christ who called him. I love his breadth, his vision, his flexibility, and his capacity to be "all things to all men" (1 Corinthians 9:22). And, most important, I love his doctrine—particularly as revealed in his epistles, the timely but timeless messages in that regulatory correspondence by which he set in order the branches he helped organize within the Church. Jesus of Nazareth, Savior and King, was the Lord of his life and the burden of his message to the world.

As he closed his last epistle, Paul said: "I am now ready to be offered, and the time of my departure is at hand. I have fought a good fight, I have finished my course, I have kept the faith: henceforth there is laid up for me a crown of righteousness, which the Lord, the righteous judge, shall give me at that day: and not to me only, but unto all them also that love his appearing" (2 Timothy 4:6–8). The "chosen vessel" (Acts 9:15) ran the race of life and did all he had been commanded to do, namely, open the eyes of the people far and wide to the gospel of Jesus Christ and "turn them from darkness to light, and from the power of Satan unto God, that they [might] receive forgiveness of sins, and inheritance among them which are sanctified" (Acts 26:18). And surely his was a glorious reunion with the Master whose name he had declared and whose gospel he had defended. In Christ Paul had found a newness of life, and through Christ Paul inherited the greatest of all the gifts of God—that life which is eternal and everlasting.

Notes

From Paul Y. Hoskisson, ed., *The Apostle Paul: His Life and His Testimony, The 23rd Annual Sidney B. Sperry Symposium* (Salt Lake City: Deseret Book Co., 1994), 132–50.

1. F. F. Bruce, *The New Testament Documents: Are They Reliable?* (Grand Rapids, Mich.: Eerdmans, 1974), 79.
2. See Ezra Taft Benson, *A Witness and a Warning* (Salt Lake City: Deseret Book Co., 1988), 33.
3. Sidney B. Sperry, *Paul's Life and Letters* (Salt Lake City: Bookcraft, 1955), 176.

4. John MacArthur, *The Gospel According to Jesus: What Does Jesus Mean When He Says, "Follow Me"?* rev. ed. (Grand Rapids, Mich.: Zondervan, 1994), 197.

5. John MacArthur, *Faith Works: The Gospel According to the Apostles* (Dallas: Word Publishing, 1993), 89–90, 103.

6. MacArthur, *Faith Works,* 57.

7. *Doctrinal New Testament Commentary,* 2:499–500.

8. W. Ian Thomas, as cited in Bob George, *Classic Christianity* (Eugene, Oregon: Harvest House, c. 1989), foreword; emphasis added.

9. John Stott, *Life in Christ* (Wheaton, Ill.: Tyndale House, 1994), 109; emphasis added.

10. Glenn L. Pace, *Spiritual Plateaus* (Salt Lake City: Deseret Book Co., 1991), 62–63.

11. See Ezra Taft Benson, in Conference Report, October 1985, 5.

12. George, *Classic Christianity* (Salt Lake City: Deseret Book Co., 1991), 79.

13. See Bruce R. McConkie, *A New Witness for the Articles of Faith* (Salt Lake City: Deseret Book Co., 1985), 4, 34, 359.

14. Mark E. Petersen, "Honesty, A Principle of Salvation," *Ensign,* December 1971, 73.

15. Charles Stanley, *The Wonderful, Spirit-Filled Life* (Nashville: Oliver Nelson, c. 1992), 108.

16. *Promised Messiah,* 300.

REVELATION: THE PLAINEST BOOK EVER WRITTEN

Perhaps no book of scripture has led to more speculation, spawned more foolishness, and resulted in more spiritual imbalance than the Apocalypse, the Revelation of John the Beloved. It was an important book in the first century of the Christian era, one that provided hope and perspective for the former-day Saints. And, when properly approached and understood, it provides a like hope for the Latter-day Saints who live in the closing years of the twentieth century and the opening years of a new millennium. Although it is not likely that even the most serious students of scripture will uncover every symbol and thereby come to understand every particular of the Revelation, there are certain doctrinal refrains, recurring lessons, and basic principles that may be grasped by all of us.

BACKGROUND

The author of Revelation is John, the brother of James and son of Zebedee. This is the same John who served as an apostle and as a member of the First Presidency of the meridian church, the one who wrote the Gospel of John and the three epistles. He is known variously as John the Beloved, John the Revelator, and the one Jesus loved (see John 21:20). We know from the Book of Mormon (see 3 Nephi 28:6) and from modern revelation (see D&C 7) that John was translated— changed to a terrestrial state so as to no longer be subject to the effects of the Fall, including physical suffering, bodily decay, and death. Like the three Nephites, he is still ministering among the peoples of the earth and will do so until the Second

Coming of Jesus Christ, at which time he and they will be changed from mortality to immortality (see 3 Nephi 28:8, 27–30).[1] This book of scripture is called "The Revelation of John, a servant of God, which was given unto him of Jesus Christ" (JST, Revelation 1:1; see also 1:4, 9; 22:8).

Though most modern biblical scholars are prone to cast doubt on the authorship of John the Beloved, Johannine authorship has been attested from as early as the second century A.D. by Justin Martyr. The actual time of the writing is unknown, and debates continue among New Testament scholars: some date the Apocalypse during the reign of the Roman emperor Domitian (81–96 A.D.), while others propose a date some time during the reign of Vespasian (69–79 A.D.). What we do know is that John wrote this book from the island of Patmos (1:9), a small volcanic island just southwest of Ephesus. The Revelation contains specific counsel, condemnation, warning, and prophetic promises to the seven churches of Asia—Ephesus, Smyrna, Pergamum, Thyatira, Sardis, Philadelphia, and Laodicea—branches of the Christian Church that had been organized by the Apostle Paul during his missionary journeys.

APOCALYPTIC LITERATURE

As most readers of Revelation can attest, reading this book is unlike any other experience we have with scripture. Whereas most of the Book of Mormon, for example, is given to us "in plainness" (2 Nephi 25:4; 31:3; 33:6), Revelation is not terribly plain to the generality of the Saints. John's messages are not always clear, and coming to understand what is intended often requires extensive cross-referencing, searching out historical details, and much pondering and discernment. It does not help that many plain and precious truths have been taken from the Bible (see 1 Nephi 13:20–40), and specifically from Revelation. Nephi was given a panoramic vision, a view of things from beginning to end (see 1 Nephi 11–14). He was told, however, that he would not be permitted to write the whole of the vision in the Nephite record but that another, the Apostle John, would be asked to do so. "Wherefore, the things which he shall write are just and true; and behold they are written in the book which thou beheld proceeding out of the mouth of the Jew; and at the time they proceeded out of the mouth of the Jew, or, at the time the book proceeded out of the mouth of the Jew, the things which were written were plain and pure, and most precious and easy to the understanding of all men" (1 Nephi 14:18–23).

Like Lehi's dream/vision and Nephi's vision, John's Revelation was "a

God's-eye view" of things from eternity past to eternity future. "John had the curtains of heaven withdrawn," the Prophet Joseph explained, "and by vision looked through the dark vista of future ages, and contemplated events that should transpire throughout every subsequent period of time, until the final winding up scene."[2] John's book is an example of apocalyptic literature. *Apocalypse* is a Greek work meaning revelation or unveiling. Other examples of apocalyptic literature include chapters in Ezekiel and Daniel, Matthew 24 (sometimes called the "little Apocalypse"), Mark 13, and 1 Nephi 13–14. These all contain some apocalyptic elements. Chronology seems irrelevant in apocalyptic writing. The writer seems to jump back and forth through time, darting from distant past to distant future in the blink of an eye. Thus we would read of two prophets who will be killed at the time of the Battle of Armageddon for their testimony (in Revelation 11) and then discover the war in heaven in the next chapter (chapter 12). To God, for whom the past, the present, and the future are "one eternal now,"[3] time apparently is not reckoned in the same way.

The following are additional elements and characteristics of apocalyptic writings (Revelation contains all of these):

1. *Symbols.* This literary genre is filled with symbols—objects or messages that stand for, represent, or typify other things. We find in Revelation such figures as lambs, dragons, candlesticks, stars, white stones, a sea of glass, animals filled with eyes and wings, books with seals, a bottomless pit, a huge cubic city, trumpets, vials with bitter potions, various colored horses, white robes, seals on the forehead or right hand, locusts and scorpions, little books that are eaten, olive trees, a great whore, and a tree with twelve manner of fruit. These all point to greater realities and deeper messages. They are symbols. In some cases we are able to uncover the symbolism through a careful reading of Revelation itself, while frequently we must turn to other revelations (particularly modern revelation) to uncover the meaning. And in some cases we are left without scriptural or prophetic commentary.

2. *Beasts.* There are many types of beasts mentioned in Revelation, and some are easier to understand than others. The Prophet Joseph Smith explained: "It is not very essential for the elders to have knowledge in relation to the meaning of beasts, and heads and horns, and other figures made use of in the revelations. . . . I make this broad declaration, that whenever God gives a vision of an image, or beast, or figure of any kind, He always holds Himself responsible to give a revelation or interpretation of the meaning thereof, otherwise we are not responsible or accountable for our belief in it. Don't be afraid of being damned for not knowing the

meaning of a vision or figure, if God has not given a revelation or interpretation of the subject."[4]

3. *Numbers.* It is common in apocalyptic writings to find numbers everywhere—three, seven, twelve, and forty. The number seven, for example, which represents wholeness or perfection in Greek, occurs 52 times in Revelation; everything in Revelation seems to be done in sevens—seven seals (5:1–8:5), seven trumpets (8:6–11:19), seven significant signs (12:1–14:20), and seven last plagues (15:1–16:21).

4. *Astral phenomena.* Often we read of things taking place in the heavens, as well as on the earth—stars falling, the heavens being shaken, the moon turning to blood, a burning fire from heaven hitting the earth, etc. These signs and symbols seem to represent unrest in the universe, God's anger, or the coming destruction of the wicked.

5. *Cosmic dualism.* In apocalyptic literature the world is a battleground between light and darkness, good and evil, the kingdom of God and the kingdom of the devil. Satan rules and reigns now in a fallen world, but the time is not far distant when the God of heaven will step to the forefront, defeat the powers of darkness, and bring to an end all wickedness on earth. Today may be the day of Lucifer's power, but the future belongs to Jehovah. Thus the plea of Revelation to the true and faithful on earth is essentially "Hold on! The day of the Lord is at hand. Don't give up, don't give in, don't compromise or concede to diabolical forces; the time of deliverance is near."

SOME GUIDES TO INTERPRETATION

There is no substitute for reading Revelation, straight through, looking for key themes and seeking to understand the grand overarching and undergirding messages of the book. It is worth our while to read Revelation several times to simply recognize the doctrinal refrains and recurring precepts that John chose to weave through this remarkable document. The big picture is crucial. As the Prophet Joseph Smith suggested, it probably doesn't matter a great deal whether we know exactly what this beast, that horn, or some poisonous vial represents; it does matter whether we get the point of the book.

Second, to paraphrase Nephi, the book of Revelation, though a sealed book to many, is clear to those who have the spirit of prophecy (see 2 Nephi 25:4). There is absolutely no way for us to grasp what was intended by John unless we are moved upon by the same Spirit that moved upon the Revelator. That is to say, it takes revelation to understand Revelation. The spirit of prophecy, which is the spirit of revelation, the same spirit that plants within our souls the testimony of Jesus (see Revelation 19:10)—even that Spirit will lead us to that level of understanding the Lord intends for each of us.

Third, the greatest commentary on scripture is scripture. Indeed, the best way to understand Revelation is to rely on other books of scripture, particularly the scriptures of the Restoration. President Marion G. Romney emphasized the need to search and study modern revelation. "In each dispensation, . . . the Lord has revealed anew the principles of the gospel. So that while the records of past dispensations, insofar as they are uncorrupted, testify to the truths of the gospel, still each dispensation has had revealed in its day sufficient truth to guide the people of the new dispensation, independent of the records of the past. I do not wish to discredit in any manner the records we have of the truths revealed by the Lord in past dispensations. What I now desire is to impress upon our minds that the gospel, as revealed to the Prophet Joseph Smith, is complete and is the word direct from heaven to this dispensation. It alone is sufficient to teach us the principles of eternal life. It is the truth revealed, the commandments given in this dispensation through modern prophets by which we are to be governed."[5]

For example, there are certain sections of the Doctrine and Covenants (29, 45, 77, 84, 88, 133) that provide invaluable insight into John's work. Section 77 is especially helpful; it explains details concerning people and events in Revelation 4, 5, 7, 8, 9, 10, and 11. First Nephi, chapters 13–14, and Ether 4 and 13 in the Book of Mormon are instructive. Joseph Smith's translation of the Bible is an indispensable aid; some 20 percent of the Book of Revelation was altered by the Prophet under inspiration (including about 95 percent of chapter 12). Finally, a sermon delivered by Joseph Smith on 8 April 1843 in Nauvoo, Illinois, contains several valuable insights regarding Revelation.[6]

One other guiding principle may be useful. The Prophet Joseph explained that "the things which John saw had no allusion to the scenes of the days of Adam, Enoch, Abraham or Jesus, *only so far as is plainly represented by John, and clearly set forth by him. John saw that only which was lying in futurity and which was shortly to come to pass.*"[7] The first three chapters of Revelation are directed to the seven churches of Asia and address current problems in John's day, problems of conversion, immorality, idolatry, and apostasy in general. In addition, other than the brief glimpse into the past in the first eleven verses of chapter six, in which John reviews the history of the world from the beginning down to the meridian dispensation,[8] Revelation deals with "things which must be hereafter" (Revelation 4:1).

To put this in perspective, only eleven verses are used to discuss the events of the first five seals, meaning the period of time from the Creation to 1000 A.D. This is approximately 3 percent of the total number of verses in Revelation. On the other hand, 281 verses, or about 70 percent, deal with the sixth and seventh seals, the time from 1000 A.D. to the end of the Millennium.

MAJOR MESSAGES

Even if we are uncertain as to the meanings of many of the unusual symbols in the Apocalypse, we can grasp and appreciate the overarching messages of this book of holy scripture. Some of these include:

1. Those Saints who overcome the world shall receive from Christ the supernal rewards of the faithful: they will eat of the tree of life, that is, they will gain eternal life (Revelation 2:7; Alma 32:41); they shall not be overcome by the second death (Revelation 2:11); they shall come to know all things, even as God does (2:17; D&C 130:9–11); they shall gain power over many kingdoms and rule with the word of God, even as Christ, who is the bright and morning star (JST, Revelation 2:26–27; 22:16); they shall be adorned in white, the robes of righteousness (3:4; 19:8); they shall have the name of God written upon them; that is, they shall be gods (3:12)[9]; and they shall sit with Christ on his throne, even as Christ also overcame and is set down on the throne of the Father (3:21; compare D&C 93:20).

2. Jesus Christ, who is the Lion of the tribe of Judah, the root of David, has power to loose the seals on the record of men's dealings on this earth (Revelation 5:1–10). In other words, the Master knows the end from the beginning—he knows what was, what is, and what is to be. His is the eternal perspective, and we can trust in and rely upon his omniscient and all-loving wisdom in orchestrating the events of our lives.

3. "Worthy is the Lamb that was slain to receive power, and riches, and wisdom, and strength, and honour, and glory, and blessing" (5:12). Indeed, if any people in all the wide world have reason to rejoice in the Lord, it is the Latter-day Saints. When we contemplate what has been restored to earth—knowledge and power and gifts abounding—we ought to lift our voices to heaven and exult with the Revelator, "Alleluia: for the Lord God omnipotent reigneth" (19:6).

4. The war that began in heaven continues on earth; it will be waged until the Savior returns in glory. Many in our day are afflicted with the same poison that once afflicted Lucifer and his followers—they are accusers of the brethren. But the faithful overcome dissidence and opposition and persecution "by the blood of the

Lamb, and by the word of their testimony," for they love "not their lives unto the death" (12:1–12).

5. Despite rising tides of wickedness, the Lord saw fit to restore the fulness of his gospel. John "saw another angel fly in the midst of heaven, having the everlasting gospel to preach unto them that dwell on the earth, and to every nation, and kindred, and tongue, and people" (14:6). President Gordon B. Hinckley testified: "That angel has come. His name is Moroni. His is a voice speaking from the dust, bringing another witness of the living reality of the Lord Jesus Christ. We have not as yet carried the gospel to every nation, kindred, tongue, and people. But we have made great strides. We have gone wherever we are permitted to go. God is at the helm and doors will be opened by His power according to His divine will. Of that I am confident. Of that I am certain."[10]

6. All people will be judged by their works out of the books that are written on earth and in heaven (20:11–13; see also D&C 128:6–7). "He that overcometh shall inherit all things; and I will be his God, and he shall be my son" (Revelation 21:7). The faithful will become kings and priests, queens and priestesses unto God forever (1:5–6; 5:10; 20:6).

7. Wickedness will widen, malevolence will multiply, and the forces of evil will cover the globe. But the great and abominable church will eventually fall, and Satanic influences will be no more (see chapters 17–19). There will be an eventual triumph of good over evil on this earth. A day of righteousness will be ushered in at the time of our Savior's return in glory. Satan will be bound and the work of God will go forward without distraction for a thousand years. At the end of that glorious era, the devil will be loosed for a little season, but he and his minions will be defeated by the powers of God, and a final cleansing will take place. The earth shall then become the celestial kingdom (see chapters 21–22; D&C 88:17–20).

CONCLUSION

The Prophet Joseph Smith taught: "The book of Revelation is one of the plainest books God ever caused to be written."[11] Some of us who struggle with understanding this rather esoteric book of scripture might be prone to suggest that such a point of view is appropriate for one who, like Joseph Smith the Seer, has essentially seen and experienced what John the Revelator saw and experienced. I sense, however, that the Prophet had reference to the key themes, the unmistakable principles that are found in Revelation, more than to the seemingly infinite number of symbolic details. These central messages we can all understand. We can, like the former-day Saints, watch and be ready. We can be vigilant, ever alert to evil in all its diverse forms. We can take heart that the God of heaven is in charge, that he presides over the affairs of men and women, and that divine justice and pardoning mercy shall yet deliver and reward the Saints. In short, we can yield our hearts to God and look to heaven. In harmony with the soul-cry of the beloved Revelator, we can exclaim: "Even so, come, Lord Jesus" (Revelation 22:20).

Notes

From "Revelation of John Offers Recurring Lessons, Doctrinal Refrains and Hope," *Church News,* 23 December 1995, 7, 10.

1. See *Teachings of the Prophet Joseph Smith,* 191.
2. Ibid., 247.
3. Ibid., 220.
4. Ibid., 287, 291.
5. Marion G. Romney, "A Glorious Promise," *Ensign,* January 1981, 2.
6. See *Teachings of the Prophet Joseph Smith,* 287–94.
7. Ibid., 289; emphasis added.
8. See *Doctrinal New Testament Commentary,* 3:476–85.
9. See Orson Pratt, in *Journal of Discourses,* 14:242–43.
10. Gordon B. Hinckley, "Stay the Course—Keep the Faith," *Ensign,* November 1995, 70–71.
11. *Teachings of the Prophet Joseph Smith,* 290.

THE BOOK OF MORMON, HISTORICITY, AND FAITH

The historicity of the Book of Mormon record is crucial. We cannot exercise faith in that which is untrue, nor can "doctrinal fiction" have normative value in our lives. Too often the undergirding assumption of those who cast doubt on the historicity of the Book of Mormon, in whole or in part, is a denial of the supernatural and a refusal to admit of revelation and predictive prophecy. Great literature, even religious literature, cannot engage the human soul and transform the human personality like scripture. Only scripture—writings and events and descriptions from real people at a real point in time, people who were moved upon and directed by divine powers—can serve as a revelatory channel, enabling us to hear and feel the word of God.

FAITH IN THAT WHICH IS TRUE

My memories of the first class I took in a doctoral program in religion at an eastern university are still very much intact. It was a course entitled "Seminar in Biblical Studies" and dealt with scripture, canon, interpretation, authorship, eschatology, prophecy, and like subjects. We were but weeks into the seminar when the professor was confronted by a question from a fundamentalist Baptist student on the reality of miracles among Moses and the children of Israel. The response was polite but brief: "Well," the professor said, "I'm not going to state my own position on the matter in this class. Let me just say that I feel it doesn't really matter whether the Israelites crossed the Red Sea as a result of Moses parting that body of water in a miraculous way, or whether they actually tiptoed across the waters of the Reed Sea. What matters is that the Israelites then and thereafter saw it as an act of divine intervention, and the event became a foundation for a people's faith for centuries."

About a year later I found myself in a similar setting, this time in a seminar entitled "Critical Studies of the New Testament," the first half of a two-semester encounter with biblical criticism. The composition of the class made for fascinating conversation: a Reformed Jew, two Methodists, two Southern Baptists, a Roman Catholic, a Nazarene, and a Latter-day Saint. By the time we had begun studying the passion narratives in the Gospels, the question of "historical events" vs. "faith events" had been raised. The professor stressed the importance of "myth" and emphasized that such events as the miracles and bodily resurrection of Jesus— because in them the narrative detaches itself from the ordinary limitations of time and space such that the supernatural breaks into human history—should be relegated to the category of faith events or sacred story. And then came the interesting phrase: "Now whether Jesus of Nazareth came back to life—literally rose from the dead—is immaterial. What matters is that Christians thought he did. And the whole Christian movement is founded upon this faith event."

Perhaps one can appreciate how I felt when I read an article written by a non-member a few years ago in which he suggested that we Latter-day Saints tend to concern ourselves with all the wrong things. "Whether or not Joseph Smith actually saw God and Christ in a grove of trees is not really crucial," he essentially said. "What matters is that young Joseph thought he did." There was a haunting familiarity about the words and the sentiments. Other prominent Latter-day Saints have described the First Vision as mythical, a vital and significant movement in Mormonism's past upon which so many things turn, and yet a "faith event" which may or may not represent an actual historical occurrence. More recently, it seems fashionable by some to doubt and debate the historicity of the Book of Mormon; to speak of the contents of the Nephite record as "doctrinal fiction"; to question the reality of Book of Mormon personalities or places; or to identify "anachronisms" in the book, specifically doctrines or principles that they feel reflect more of Joseph Smith and the nineteenth century than antiquity. Others go so far as to deny outright the reality of plates, angels, or authentic witnesses.

SACRED BUT HISTORICAL

Though not a secular history of the Nephites per se, the Book of Mormon is a sacred chronicle, or to use Elder Boyd K. Packer's language, "the saga of a message."[1] The book claims to be historical. Joseph Smith said it was a history. He even went so far as to suggest that one of the major characters of the story, Moroni, appeared to him and delivered golden plates upon which the Nephite narrative was etched. Now in regard to the historicity of the book, it seems to me that only three possibilities exist: Joseph Smith told the truth, he did not know the truth, or he told a lie. The latter two alternatives are obviously not very appealing to believers. If Joseph Smith merely thought there were Nephites and supposed that such persons as Nephi and Jacob and Mormon and Moroni wrote things which they did not, then he was deluded or remarkably imaginative. He is to be pitied, not revered. If, on the other hand, the Prophet was solely responsible for the perpetuation of the Book of Mormon story—if he created the notion of a Moroni, of the golden plates and Urim and Thummim, and of a thousand-year-old story of a people who inhabited ancient America, knowing full well that such things never existed—then he was a deceiver pure and simple. He and the work he set in motion are to be feared, not followed. No matter the intensity of his labor, his own personal magnetism, or the literary value of his embellished epic, the work is a hoax, and the word of the New York farm boy is not be trusted in matters of spiritual certainty any more than Hawthorne or Dostoyevski.

My colleague Stephen D. Ricks addressed himself to those who question the historicity of the Book of Mormon. He spoke of a "view of the Book of Mormon" that "accepts its inspiration but rejects its historicity, viewing it as inspired in some sense or senses, but not the product of antiquity, coming, rather, from the pen of Joseph Smith."[2]

Brother Ricks continues, "But if the Book of Mormon was simply a spiritual manifesto of Joseph, why could he not have chosen some other genre than one that appears to be making specific historical claims? One thinks, for instance, of the Doctrine and Covenants. Further, it is precisely the internal claims of the Book of Mormon as divine history that give it its normative religious value (a value maintained in the Doctrine and Covenants, since the individual sections claim to be revelations from God). If the Book of Mormon is simply an unhistorical yarn, even a deeply religious one, it would have no more normative, sacramental value for me (impelling me, that is, to repent, be baptized, and live an upright life before God) than would the Sermons of Wesley or the Imitation of Christ of Thomas á Kempis, and perhaps less, since these latter make no claims to the intervention of the Divine, while the Book of Mormon does."[3]

One who chooses to assume the posture that the Book of Mormon is doctrinal fiction must come face to face with the issues and implications that automatically flow from such a stance; to pick up one end of this historical/theological stick is to pick up the other.

The "expansionist" position of the Book of Mormon history is what some have assumed to be a middle-of-the-road posture. It propounds the view that the Book of Mormon represents an ancient core source as elaborated on by a modern prophet. I feel this is basically an effort to have it both ways, to contend that certain sections of the Nephite record are ancient, while certain identifiable portions are unmistakably nineteenth-century, reflecting the culture, language, and theological world view of Joseph Smith. Any reference to such matters as the Fall, the Atonement, resurrection, new birth, or the Godhead before the time of Christ are seen to be anachronistic—evidence, that is, of theological perspectives obviously out of place, perspectives which were written into the narrative by the translator but which would not originally have been on the plates themselves. For example, any discussion of resurrection or atonement through Jesus Christ in the writings of Lehi or Jacob would be classified as expansion text, inasmuch as such notions are not to be found among the pre-exilic Jews, at least according to the extant materials we have, such as our present Old Testament or other Near Eastern documents. But, Ricks has observed:

"If we use the Bible or other documents from the ancient Near East as the standard, this seems an implied admission that the Book of Mormon has no independent evidentiary value as an ancient document. It also seems to imply that what can be known about pre-exilic Israelite religion is already to be found in the extant sources, principally the Bible. If this is the case, and nothing not previously known will be accepted, what unique contribution can a new document make? This reminds me of the reply falsely attributed to Umar when asked why he wished to burn the library at Alexandria: 'If it is already in the Qur'an, we have no need of the book; if it is not in the Qur'an, we have no need of the book; if it is not in the Qur'an, then it is suspect of heresy and ought for that reason to be destroyed.' But can we be so certain that we know that what can be known about pre-exilic Israelite religion is available in the extant sources? . . . Are we authorized to believe that Israelite religion before the exile is given its complete account in the Bible and other available documents? I, for one, am not so certain."[4]

Nor am I. Nor can I grasp how one can deal with a major inconsistency in the reasoning of such a position. Why is it, for example, that God can reveal to the Lehites how to construct a ship and cross the ocean, but that same God cannot reveal to them the plan of salvation, together with Christian conceptions of creation, fall, atonement, and redemption through bodily resurrection? Why is it that God can speak to Abinadi, call him to ministerial service, send him to Noah and his priests, and yet not make known to that same prophet the doctrines of the condescension of Jehovah and the ministry of Christ as the Father and the Son? Why is it that God can raise up a mighty prophet-king like Benjamin, can inspire that holy man to gather his people for a large covenant renewal ceremony (an occasion, by the way, which according to expansionists, bears the mark of Israelite antiquity), and yet not reveal doctrine to him—doctrine pertaining to the natural man, the coming of the Lord Omnipotent, and the necessity for the new birth? The selectivity is not even subtle.

THROUGH JOSEPH, NOT FROM HIM

We need not jump to interpretive extremes because the language found in the Book of Mormon (including that from the Isaiah sections or the Savior's Sermon in 3 Nephi) reflects Joseph Smith's language. Of course it does! The Book of Mormon is translation literature: practically every word in the book is from the English language. For Joseph Smith to use the English language with which he and the people of his day were familiar in recording the translation is historically consistent. On the other hand, to create the doctrine (or to place it in the mouths of Lehi or Benjamin or Abinadi) is unacceptable. The latter is tantamount to deceit and misrepresentation; it is, as we have said, to claim that the doctrines and principles are of ancient date (which the record itself declares), when, in fact, they are a fabrication (albeit an "inspired" fabrication) of a nineteenth-century man. I feel we have every reason to believe that the Book of Mormon came through Joseph Smith, not from him. Because certain theological matters were discussed in the nineteenth century does not preclude their revelation or discussion in antiquity.

Unless. Unless we deny one of the most fundamental principles of the Restoration—Christ's eternal gospel: the knowledge that Christian prophets have taught Christian doctrine and administered Christian ordinances since the days of Adam. "Taking it for granted that the scriptures say what they mean, and mean what they say," Joseph Smith explained in 1842, "we have sufficient grounds to go on and prove from the Bible [that is, through utilizing the supplementary scriptural resources available through the Restoration] that the gospel has always been the same; the ordinances to fulfill its requirements, the same, and the officers to officiate, the same."[5] This is evident in the Book of Mormon, is found throughout the Doctrine and Covenants, and is central to the Pearl of Great Price, especially Joseph Smith's inspired translation of Genesis (the book of Moses). I contend that there is little reference to Christian doctrine in our present Old Testament or other Near Eastern texts, simply because that was a time in ancient Israel of spiritual darkness and apostasy. The Book of Mormon is a report and an account of a restoration, a renewal, a re-evaluation of the nature of God and the plan of salvation. Kent P. Jackson has written that in the Book of Mormon, "we follow the history of one family of Israelites which proved itself worthy to be blessed with great light and knowledge concerning Christ. . . . Even a superficial comparison of the content of the Book of Mormon with that of the Bible enables one to see that the level of understanding concerning sacred things was greater among Lehi's descendants than among the people from which they came. With the separation of Lehi and his family from their native society came a revelation—perhaps more accurately a restoration—of gospel principles that were unknown to the mainstream of their countrymen."[6]

Too often the real issue—the subtle but certain undergirding assumption of those who question the historicity of the Book of Mormon, in whole or in part—is a denial of the supernatural, a refusal to admit of divine intervention, of revelation and miracles and predictive prophecy. It is the tendency, unfortunately, to adopt uncritically the secular presuppositions and methodologies of those who have neither faith nor direction. "It should be noted," Stephen E. Robinson observed, "that the rejection of predictive prophecy is characteristic of the secular approach to the scriptures, for the exclusion of any supernatural agency (including God) from human affairs is fundamental to the methodology of most biblical scholarship."[7]

Robinson continued, "The naturalistic approach gives scholars from different religious backgrounds common controls and perspectives relative to the data and eliminates arguments over subjective beliefs not verifiable by the historical-critical method. However, there is a cost to using the naturalistic approach, for one can never mention God, revelation, priesthood, prophecy, etc., as having objective existence or as being part of the evidence or as being possible causes of the observable effects.

" . . . If one starts with the a priori that the claims of Joseph and the Book of Mormon to predictive prophecy are not to be accepted, then that a priori is bound to force a conclusion that where the Book of Mormon contains predictive prophecy it is not authentic and must therefore be an 'expansion.' But clearly, this conclusion flows not from the evidence but from the a priori assumption. If one allows the possibility that God might have revealed future events and doctrines to Nephi, Abinadi or Samuel the Lamanite, then the so-called anachronisms disappear and this part of the argument for 'expansion' collapses.

"Naturalistic explanations are often useful in evaluating empirical data, but when the question asked involves empirical categories, such as 'Is the Book of Mormon what it purports to be?,' it begs the question to adopt a method whose first assumption is that the Book cannot be what it claims to be. This points out a crucial logical difficulty in using this method in either attacking or defending the Church."[8]

CAUTION ABOUT CRITICISM

I candidly admit to caution rather than eagerness when it comes to applying many of the principles of biblical criticism to the Book of Mormon. The quest for the historical Jesus of Nazareth has led thousands to the demythologization and thus the de-deification of Jesus the Christ. "It would be incredibly naive," Robinson noted, "to believe that biblical criticism brings us closer to the Christ of faith. After 200 years of refining its methods, biblical scholarship has despaired of knowing the real Jesus, except for a few crumbs, and has declared the Christ pictured in scripture to be a creation of the early church."[9] I for one am reluctant to assume that certain scholarly movements represent progress. Change, yes. Progress, not necessarily. Our faith as well as our approaches to the study of the Bible or the Book of Mormon must not be held hostage by the latest trends and fads in biblical scholarship; our testimony of historical events must not be at the mercy of what we know and can read in sources external to the Book of Mormon or to the witness of revelation. In the words of Elder Orson F. Whitney:

"We have no right to take the theories of men, however scholarly, however learned, and set them up as a standard, and try to make the Gospel bow down to them; making of them an iron bedstead upon which God's truth, if not long enough, must be stretched out, or if too long, must be chopped off—anything to make it fit into the system of men's thoughts and theories! On the contrary, we should hold up the Gospel as the standard of truth, and measure thereby the theories and opinions of men."[10]

Professor Paul Hedengren of the philosophy department at BYU made a specific request of those studying the historicity of the Book of Mormon: "If someone wishes to consider the Book of Mormon as other than historical, do not make subtle this deviation from its obvious historical structure as some have done to the Bible. Make the deviation bold so that it is clear and unmistakable. Do not take the book Joseph Smith had printed in 1830 and say that its truths are not historical but are of some other type, for the simple logical structure of the sentences in it falsifies this claim. Instead create from the Book of Mormon another book which asserts what the Book of Mormon simply reports to have asserted. If someone claims that actually no one said what the Book of Mormon claims someone to have said, but these actually unspoken utterances are true, let them compose a book of these sentences without the historical reports of these sentences being said. Do not say in this new book, 'Jesus said to some Nephites, "Blessed are the meek."' Simply say in this new book, 'Blessed are the meek.' In doing this the person will not have to overlook or ignore the historical claims taken to be either false or inessential."[11]

In summary, "If we deny the historicity of the Book of Mormon or consider it inessential, let us compose a book in which claims are not inherently historical and attend to whatever truths we may find there. But in no case, let us say of the new book we compose that it is either the book Joseph Smith had printed in 1830 or that it is the Book of Mormon, for it is neither."[12]

THE DISTINCTIVE POWER OF SCRIPTURE

I believe in regard to faith (and thus faithfulness and adherence to a cause) that it matters very much whether there is an actual event, an objective occurrence toward which we look and upon which we build our faith. One cannot exercise saving faith in something untrue (see Alma 32:21) or that did not happen, no matter how sweet the story, how sincere the originator or author, or how committed the followers. Though it is true that great literature, whether historically true or untrue, may lift and strengthen in its own way and even contain great moral lessons, such works cannot result in the spiritual transformation of the soul as only scripture can do. Scripture becomes a divine channel by which personal revelation comes, a significant means by which we may hear the voice of the Lord (see D&C 18:34–36). The power of the word, whether spoken or written, is in its source—even God our Father and his Son, Jesus Christ. We are able to exercise faith in a principle or doctrine taught by real people who were moved upon by the power of the Holy Ghost, actual persons in time and space whose interactions with the Lord and his Spirit were genuine and true and whose spiritual growth we may imitate. Huck Finn may have given the world some sage advice, but his words cannot sanctify. Even the sweet testimonies of Demetrius the slave and Marcellus the Roman centurion from the novel *The Robe* cannot enliven the soul in the same way that the teachings of Alma to Corianton or the letters of Mormon to Moroni do. There is a difference, a big difference. "Doctrinal fiction" may be entertaining. Its characters may demonstrate wisdom and their lives provide noble examples. But doctrinal fiction cannot engage the sons and daughters of God as does "the will of the Lord, . . . the mind of the Lord, . . . the word of the Lord, . . . the voice of the Lord, and the power of God unto salvation" (D&C 68:4).

Our faith in Christ is grounded in the work of redemption that was accomplished in a specific garden and on a designated cross in a particular moment in our earth's history. It is not the exact site that matters so much as it is that there was such a site. If Jesus did not in reality suffer and bleed and die and rise from the tomb, then we are spiritually doomed, no matter how committed we may be to the "faith event" celebrated by the first-century Christians. And so it is in regard to the occasion in Palmyra. It matters very much that the Eternal Father and his Only Begotten Son did appear to a young boy in a grove of trees in New York state. Exactly where the Sacred Grove is, as well as what specific trees or ground were hallowed by the theophany, is much less significant. If Joseph Smith did not see in vision the Father and the Son, if the First Vision was only the "sweet dreams" of a naive boy, then no amount of goodness and civility on the part of the Latter-day Saints will save us. And so it is in regard to the people and events and teachings of the Book of Mormon. That there was a Nephi and an Alma and a Gidgiddoni is vital to the story, and, in my view, to the relevance and truthfulness of the Book of Mormon. That the prophetic oracles from Lehi to Samuel preached and prophesied of Christ and taught and administered his gospel is vital in establishing the dispensational concept restored through Joseph Smith; these items reveal far more about the way things are and have been among the people of God in all ages than they do about the way things were in the nineteenth century. Joseph Smith the Seer, in harmony with the principle taught by Ammon to Limhi (see Mosiah 8:17), may well have restored as much knowledge of things past as of things future.

FUNDAMENTALS OF THE FAITH

There is room in the Church for all types and shapes and sizes of people, and certainly all of us are at differing stages of intellectual development and spiritual maturity. Further, there are myriad doctrinal issues over which discussion and debate may lead to diverse conclusions, particularly in matters that have not been fully clarified in scripture or by prophets. At the same time, there are certain well-defined truths—matters pertaining to the divine Sonship of Christ, the reality of the Atonement, the appearance of the Father and the Son in 1820, and the truthfulness of the Book of Mormon—which, in the uncompromising language of President J. Reuben Clark, "must stand, unchanged, unmodified, without dilution, excuse, apology, or avoidance; they may not be explained away or submerged. Without these two great beliefs"—the reality of the resurrection and atonement and the divine call of Joseph Smith—"the Church would cease to be the Church." Further, "any individual who does not accept the fulness of these doctrines as to Jesus of Nazareth or as to the restoration of the Gospel and Holy Priesthood, is not a Latter-day Saint."[13]

I have often sensed that ours is not the task to shift the Church about with its history, practices, and beliefs—as though the divine institution were on casters—in order to get it into the path of moving persons who desire a religion that conforms with their own private beliefs or attends to their own misgivings or doubts. At a time of intellectual explosion but of spiritual and moral corrosion, I am persuaded that no Latter-day Saint needs to surrender cherished values to live in a modern world; that a member of the Church need not fall prey to the growing "alternate voices" offering alternative explanations for our foundational events and institutions; and that one can have implicit trust in the Church and its leaders without sacrificing or compromising anything. In the end, as we have been counseled repeatedly, the reality of golden plates and Cumorah and angels may be known only by an independent and individual revelation. Such an experience, as well as the reinforcing and renewing ones thereafter, comes to those who demonstrate patience and faith. "The finished mosaic of the history of the Restoration," Elder Neal A. Maxwell taught, "will be larger and more varied as more pieces of tile emerge, adjusting a sequence here or enlarging there a sector of our understanding. There may even be a few pieces of the tile which, for the moment, do not seem to fit. We can wait, as we must." One day, he promised, "the final mosaic of the Restoration will be resplendent, reflecting divine design. . . . At the perfect day, we will see that we have been a part of things too wonderful for us. Part of the marvel and the wonder of God's 'marvelous work and a wonder' will be how perfect Divinity mercifully used us—imperfect humanity. Meanwhile, amid the human dissonance, those with ears to hear will follow the beckoning sounds of a certain trumpet."[14]

Notes

From *Journal of Book of Mormon Studies* 2, no. 2 (Fall 1993): 1–13.

1. Boyd K. Packer, "The Things of My Soul," *Ensign*, April 1986, 59.
2. Stephen D. Ricks, "The Historicity of the Book of Mormon: Perspectives and Problems," remarks at a Sunstone panel discussion on the historicity of the Book of Mormon, Salt Lake City, December 1988.
3. Ibid.
4. Ibid.
5. Joseph Smith, in *Times and Seasons* 3 (1 September 1843): 904; see also *History of the Church*, 2:15–18; 4:208.

6. Kent P. Jackson, "The Beginnings of Christianity in the Book of Mormon," in Paul R. Cheesman, ed., *The Keystone Scripture* (Provo: Religious Studies Center, Brigham Young University, 1988), 92.

7. Stephen E. Robinson, "The Expanded Book of Mormon?" in Monte S. Nyman and Charles D. Tate Jr., eds., *Second Nephi: The Doctrinal Structure* (Provo: Religious Studies Center, Brigham Young University, 1989), 393.

8. Ibid., 393–94.

9. Ibid., 395.

10. Orson F. Whitney, in Conference Report, April 1915, 100.

11. Paul Hedengren, "The Book of Mormon as an Ancient Document," unpublished manuscript, 20 September 1986.

12. Ibid.

13. J. Reuben Clark, "The Charted Course of the Church in Education," in David H. Yarn Jr., ed., *J. Reuben Clark, Selected Papers* (Provo: Brigham Young University Press, 1984), 245.

14. Neal A. Maxwell, "Out of Obscurity," *Ensign*, November 1984, 11.

THE BOOK OF MORMON
AND THE NATURE OF GOD

M any Latter-day Saints have just begun to sense the power of the Book of Mormon. It is indeed a day of discovery. We have had a precious gift in our midst for more than a century and a half and have just begun, in a sense, to remove the wrapping. But the excitement is mounting, and the thrill associated with intense spiritual encounter for an entire people is perhaps just around the corner.

USING THE BOOK OF MORMON

There has been some hesitation in the past to utilize the Book of Mormon as the supreme missionary tool it was intended to be. Some have worried that they would give offense to those of other faiths by suggesting the need for another book of scripture. Some have sought to "prove" the Restoration from the Bible alone, trying to stay with what they perceive to be "common ground" between themselves and the rest of the Judaeo-Christian world. The Lord's plan for effective proselyting is set forth plainly in modern revelation. The following verses from the Doctrine and Covenants are but a few examples of that plan:

"This generation shall have my word through you [Joseph Smith]" (D&C 5:10).

"Lift up your heart and rejoice, for the hour of your mission [Thomas B. Marsh] is come; and your tongue shall be loosed, and you shall declare glad tidings of great joy unto this generation.

"You shall declare the things which have been revealed to my servant, Joseph Smith, Jr." (D&C 31:3–4; emphasis added).

"Again I say, hearken ye elders of my church, whom I have appointed: Ye are not sent forth to be taught, but *to teach the children of men the things which I have put into your hands by the power of my Spirit"* (D&C 43:15; emphasis added).

"Hearken unto my word, my servants Sidney [Rigdon], and Parley [P. Pratt], and Leman [Copley]; for behold, verily I say unto you, that I give unto you a commandment that you shall go and preach my gospel which ye have received, *even as ye have received it,* unto the Shakers.

"Behold, I say unto you, that they desire to know the truth in part, but not all, for they are not right before me and must needs repent.

"Wherefore, I send you, my servants Sidney and Parley, to preach the gospel unto them.

"And my servant Leman shall be ordained unto this work, *that he may reason with them* [the Shakers], *not according to that which he has received of them, but according to that which shall be taught him by you my servants; and by so doing I will bless him, otherwise he shall not prosper"* (D&C 49:1–4; emphasis added).

Joseph Smith was a mature and independent witness of the truths of salvation. Parley P. Pratt related the following incident, which provides an important pattern for all those within the faith who desire to influence those outside the faith:

"While visiting with brother Joseph in Philadelphia, a very large church was opened for him to preach in, and about three thousand people assembled to hear him. Brother [Sidney] Rigdon spoke first, and dwelt on the Gospel, illustrating his doctrine by the Bible. When he was through, brother Joseph arose like a lion about to roar; and being full of the Holy Ghost, spoke in great power, *bearing testimony of the visions he had seen, the ministering of angels which he had enjoyed; and how he had found the plates of the Book of Mormon, and translated it by the gift and power of God.* He commenced by saying: 'If nobody had the courage to testify of so glorious a message from Heaven, and of the finding of so glorious a record, he felt to do it in justice to the people, and leave the event with God.'"[1]

We will not accomplish the task of carrying the message of the Restoration to the ends of the earth through stressing the *similarities* between ourselves and other faiths. Only as we teach and proclaim those things which have been communicated specifically and by revelation to us (see D&C 84:61)—the *differences* between the Latter-day Saints and the rest of the world, the things which we have to offer to the world—will we make the difference we ought to make in the world. No one desires to be disliked or to be ridiculed for his peculiar beliefs. No one wants to be suspect or to be considered cultic or unchristian. At the same time, we have some truths to tell, truths not had as fully elsewhere. With the dawning of a brighter day, the knowledge of God and the authority to act in his behalf have been delivered to man again; a knowledge of Christ and the fulness of salvation available through him are to be had only by an acceptance of the doctrines and powers vested in The Church of Jesus Christ of Latter-day Saints.

The Book of Mormon is a guide to understanding persons and events in antiquity. The Nephite record provides, as it were, an interpretive lens through which we may view much in the Old Testament, for example, and supply missing or obscure parts to the story.[2] Much of what we understand about the Old and New Testaments is clear to us because of the Book of Mormon. There are those, however, who are hesitant to "read into" the biblical record what we know from modern revelation, those who feel that to do so is to compromise the "integrity" or unique contribution of the Bible itself. In response to this posture, let me suggest an analogy. If one were eager to locate a valuable site, should he utilize a map which is deficient in detail or inaccurate in layout, simply on the basis of the fact that the map had been in the family for generations and was highly prized? Should he choose to ignore the precious information to be had on a more reliable and complete map, if such were made available? Of course the whole matter is related to the question of whether the traveler is sincerely desirous of reaching his destination: maps have real value only to the degree that they guide us to a destined location. To change analogies, would a scholar in any discipline choose to maintain a position or defend a point of view when subsequent but available research had shed further (and perhaps clarifying) information on the subject? To do so would represent at best naïveté, and at worst shoddy and irresponsible scholarship. So it is with the Bible and the Book of Mormon: the latter is a supplementary doctrinal witness as well as a helpful historical guide. "Just as the New Testament clarified the long misunderstood message of the Old," Hugh Nibley observed, "so the Book of Mormon is held to reiterate the messages of both Testaments in a way that restores their full meaning."[3] Its strengths and supplementary contributions, however, will be fully appreciated only by those who are eager to be led to the fulness of truth, who seek the glory and approbation of God more than the praises of the secular synagogue.

"The Book of Mormon has not been, nor is it yet, the center of our personal study, family teaching, preaching, and missionary work. Of this we must repent," counseled President Ezra Taft Benson.[4] Our near neglect of the Book of Mormon has been a serious concern for some time. "Your minds in times past," the Lord warned the Saints in 1832, "have been darkened because of unbelief, and because you have treated lightly the things you have received—which vanity and unbelief have brought the whole church under condemnation." The condemnation, a "scourge and judgment" upon all the children of Zion, is to be lifted only as the members of the Church "remember the new covenant, even the Book of Mormon and the former commandments" which the Lord has delivered in this day of restoration (D&C 84:54–61). Our modern Church leaders have likewise warned us that the Church is still under condemnation and have thus encouraged us to "daily sup from its pages and abide by its precepts." In so doing, President Benson has promised, "God will pour out upon each child of Zion and the Church a blessing hitherto unknown."⁵

THE DOCTRINAL SUPERIORITY OF THE BOOK OF MORMON

The Prophet Joseph Smith identified the Book of Mormon as the "most correct of any book on earth."⁶ A modern apostle has declared: "As far as learning the gospel and teaching the gospel are concerned, the Book of Mormon, by all odds, is the most important of the standard works, because in simplicity and in plainness it sets forth in a definitive manner the doctrines of the gospel."⁷ Some things we simply understand better because of the Book of Mormon.

Some years ago at a university in the East I sat in a doctoral seminar on Paul. The course was taught, interestingly enough, by a Jewish professor who obviously did not believe in the divinity of Jesus. In one particular session during the term, we centered our attention on 1 Corinthians 15. As the three-hour session rolled on, it became very clear to me that I was the only person in the group (including, of course, the instructor) who believed that the resurrection was a physical phenomenon, that the resurrected body is a tangible, corporeal entity. I wondered why such a plain and simple matter would have escaped their understandings. Then I read the chapter more carefully. Speaking of the resurrected body, Paul wrote: "It is sown a natural body; it is raised a spiritual body" (1 Corinthians 15:44). Suddenly it was clear why they misunderstood. But why did I understand that a "spiritual" body was a physical body, a glorified immortal body not subject to death? Only a moment's reflection was needed to remind me that I knew what I knew because of the Book of Mormon and modern revelation (see Alma 11:45; D&C 88:27; Moses 3:9). It was a sobering but soul-satisfying occasion.

Frequently the Bible will tell us *what* happened, while the Book of Mormon will tell us *why* it happened. We know from the Bible that there was a fall of Adam, but we learn from the Book of Mormon *why* there was a fall and thus why an atonement was necessary (see 2 Nephi 2). We learn early in the Old Testament that Jehovah gave a "law of carnal commandments" to rebellious Israel; we turn to the Book of Mormon to discover why he gave the Law of Moses and what the law symbolized (see 2 Nephi 11:4; 25:24–27; Jacob 4:5; Mosiah 13:30; Alma 34:14). We know that Paul and the early apostles preached the gospel, but we may come away from the New Testament lacking understanding on some essentials; the Book of Mormon leaves no doubt as to the meaning of the gospel and what its principles are (see 2 Nephi 31–32; 3 Nephi 27). We are exposed to the doctrine of the election of Israel in the Old Testament and also read in Paul's writings about the status of the house of Israel (e.g., Romans 11), but we turn to the Book of Mormon for a more complete scriptural account concerning the destiny of the Lord's covenant people (see, for example, 1 Nephi 19–22; 2 Nephi 6:4–11; 10:3–8; Jacob 5–6; 3 Nephi 20–21).

And so it goes through most of the doctrines we might consider. In the words of Elder Bruce R. McConkie, in undertaking a serious doctrinal comparison between the stick of Judah and the stick of Joseph, "it will not be long before you know that Lehi and Jacob excel Paul in teaching the Atonement; that Alma's sermons on faith and on being born again surpass anything in the Bible; that Nephi makes a better exposition of the scattering and gathering of Israel than do Isaiah, Jeremiah, and Ezekiel combined; that Mormon's words about faith, hope, and charity have a clarity, a breadth, and a power of expression that even Paul did not attain; and so on and so on."[8] Elder McConkie's observation is in no way intended to denigrate the goodness and value of the Bible, but to point out the infinite worth of a supplementary scriptural source.

THE NATURE OF GOD IN THE BOOK OF MORMON

The Lord has chosen to bring about the restitution of all things in process of time; the truths of heaven, as well as the priesthoods and powers associated with establishing the kingdom of God, have been delivered to the Latter-day Saints "line upon line, precept upon precept," evidencing the Lord's sensitivity to our "bearing capacity," where the matters of salvation are concerned. What the Prophet understood as he left the Sacred Grove was no doubt a small amount when compared with what he had come to know by the time of his death in 1844. It is just so with the growth and development of the Latter-day Saints collectively: time and patience and maturity resulted in greater understanding. And yet the wisest among the

Latter-day Saints—in Joseph Smith's day and certainly in our own—have come to recognize in the Book of Mormon not only a timely guide for living but also a timeless sacred record and rich repository of doctrinal insights.

Some historians and writers have sought to contrast Joseph Smith's theology before 1835 with that which came to be taught in and after the Nauvoo experience. Of these treatments, there have been those who have included the Book of Mormon as a part of the doctrinal development, an aspect of the "early" thinking of the Mormon prophet. Some persons have gone so far as to suggest that the Book of Mormon represents a "trinitarian" concept of God, one beyond which Joseph Smith and the Church gradually evolved. What of such propositions?

1. *A Nineteenth-Century Product?* From the days of Alexander Campbell, people have been eager to discount the divine story behind the Book of Mormon by suggesting alternative explanations for its origins. Campbell himself proposed that the Book of Mormon had been produced by Joseph Smith as a means of dealing with such commonplace issues in nineteenth-century America as "free masonry, republican government, and the rights of man."[9] Richard Bushman has successfully pointed out the fallacies of this approach to explaining the Book of Mormon, demonstrating convincingly that the socio-political setting of Nephite America is worlds apart from that of nineteenth-century America.[10] Others have suggested alternative authorship for the book, such as Sidney Rigdon[11] or Solomon Spaulding,[12] all of which are superficial ideas but terribly resistant to extinction. In considering the whole question of alternative explanation—and here specifically the possibility of the Book of Mormon as a nineteenth-century book—Hugh Nibley has observed: "The idea that the Book of Mormon was simply a product of its time may be a necessary fiction to explain it but it is a fiction none the less. If they may be trusted in nothing else, the voluminous writings of the anti-Mormons [and of some misguided or myopic Mormons] stand as a monumental evidence for one fact: that Mormonism and the Book of Mormon were in no way a product of the society in which they arose."[13]

One of the things readily apparent to a careful reader of the Book of Mormon is what some would term "anachronistic" elements in the record. Matters such as faith and repentance and baptism, constant mention of Jesus Christ and his atonement, and repeated reference to the gift of the Holy Ghost are found throughout the Book of Mormon in the sermons of prophets who are supposed to have predated the Savior by many centuries. How do we explain such things? If he indeed wrote the Book of Mormon (as some contend), was Joseph Smith so careless or simpleminded as not to recognize that he was mixing time periods?

The answer to this query is quite simple to the person willing to fully accept Joseph Smith and his works and words: the Book of Mormon—with the Doctrine and Covenants, Pearl of Great Price and Joseph Smith Translation of the Bible—restores many of the "plain and precious truths" lost before the Bible was compiled into its present form. One of the central verities of the Restoration—a matter totally hidden from the religious world until the "times of restitution" began—concerns "Christ's Eternal Gospel," the realization that Christian prophets have declared Christian doctrines and administered Christian ordinances since the days of Adam. In counseling with his errant son, Corianton, in approximately 73 B.C., Alma declared:

"And now, my son, I would say somewhat unto you concerning the coming of Christ. Behold, I say unto you, that it is he that surely shall come to take away the sins of the world; yea, he cometh to declare glad tidings of salvation unto his people.

"And now, my son, this was the ministry unto which ye were called, to declare these glad tidings unto this people, to prepare their minds; or rather that salvation might come unto them, that they may prepare the minds of their children to hear the word at the time of his coming.

"And now I will ease your mind somewhat on this subject. Behold, you marvel why these things should be known so long beforehand. Behold, I say unto you, is not a soul at this time as precious unto God as a soul will be at the time of his coming?

"Is it not as necessary that the plan of redemption should be made known unto this people as well as unto their children?

"Is it not as easy at this time for the Lord to send his angel to declare these glad tidings unto us as unto our children, or as after the time of his coming?" (Alma 39:15–19; see Jacob 4:4). In the same vein, the Lord—after having spoken concerning the purposes for which the Book of Mormon was given to the world—explained in April 1830 what doctrines and principles we now know as a result of the delivery of the Book of Mormon and modern revelation. Concerning the ministry of the Master, the Book of Mormon (with the Bible) testifies that "he was crucified, died, and rose again the third day; and ascended into heaven, to sit down on the right hand of the Father, to reign with almighty power according to the will of the Father; that as many as would believe, and be baptized in his holy name, and endure in faith to the end, should be saved." Now note the following, a recitation of truths which are made known primarily through the Book of Mormon and the revelations given to the Prophet Joseph Smith: "Not only those who believed after he came in the meridian of time, in the flesh, but *all those from the beginning, even as many as were before he came, who believed in the words of the holy prophets, who spake as they were inspired by the gift of the Holy Ghost, who truly testified of him in all things,* should have eternal life, as well as those who should come after, who should believe in the gifts and callings of God by the Holy Ghost, which beareth record of the Father and of the Son" (D&C 20:23–27; emphasis added). In short, the Book of Mormon is gospel centered and Christ centered and stands as a witness that all true believers and their scriptural records from the beginning have also been gospel centered and Christ centered.

Because some matters in the Book of Mormon (social, economic, political, religious, philosophical) seem so relevant to modern man—as those who have suggested alternative explanations have pointed out—must we therefore conclude that the book is a product of modern man? Could we not conclude just as easily—given a slight propensity to accept divine intervention, miracles, and angels—that the record was produced by ancient persons with prophetic insight to meet the needs and address issues of a modern time? Is that not what the Book of Mormon compilers/writers intended? In the words of President Ezra Taft Benson, *"The Book of Mormon was written for us today. God is the author of the book.* It is a record of a fallen people, compiled by inspired men for our blessing today. Those people never had the book—it was meant for us. Mormon, the ancient prophet after whom the book is named, abridged centuries of records. *God, who knows the end from the beginning, told him what to include in his abridgment that we would need for our day."*[14] Moroni, the man who received the records from his father, finished the compilation and writing, and buried the records in Cumorah, said: "Behold, I speak unto you as if ye were present, and yet ye are not. But behold, Jesus Christ hath shown you unto me, and I know your doing" (Mormon 8:35; see 9:30; 1 Nephi 19:21).

2. *Joseph Smith's "Early" Theology?* To place the Book of Mormon within the developmental process is to accentuate the man (Joseph Smith) at the expense of the record (the Book of Mormon). Most believing Latter-day Saints accept without reservation that the process of translation involved a significant labor on the part of the Prophet and his scribes, and that mental exertion was frequently necessary to frame into words that which had been received by revelation. At the same time, to ascribe to Joseph Smith the *theology* of the Book of Mormon is to give him more credit than is due, and likewise to call into question the historicity of the record and its ancient contents. For Joseph Smith to utilize the English language with which he was familiar in recording the translation is one thing; to create the

theology (or to place the theology into the mouths of Benjamin or Alma or Moroni) is quite another. The latter situation is tantamount to deceit and misrepresentation: it is to claim that the doctrines and principles are of ancient date (which the record itself declares), when, in fact, they are a fabrication of a nineteenth-century man.

In November of 1831 William E. McLellin, who later became one of the original twelve Apostles in this dispensation, criticized some of the revelations received by Joseph Smith. He was invited to write a revelation himself, one on a par with even the least of those recorded by the Prophet (see D&C 67:5–8). McLellin tried and failed miserably. In speaking of this episode, Joseph Smith said: "After the foregoing was received [D&C 67], William E. M'Lellin, as the wisest man, in his own estimation, having more learning than sense, endeavored to write a commandment like unto one of the least of the Lord's, but failed; *it was an awful responsibility to write in the name of the Lord.* The Elders and all present that witnessed *this vain attempt of a man to imitate the language of Jesus Christ,* renewed their faith in the fulness of the Gospel, and in the truth of the commandments and revelations which the Lord had given to the Church through my instrumentality."[15] It is difficult for me to imagine that a man who would make such a statement about the seriousness of imitating the language of Jesus Christ could be involved in the creation of a story about pre-Columbian Americans or insert Christian doctrine into their mouths. Why should we assume the theology of the Book of Mormon (and particularly, for our purposes here, the doctrines associated with the Godhead) to be a part of the doctrinal development of the modern seer and his followers? Because the Book of Mormon was published in 1830, must it be viewed as "early theology"? Is it not just as reasonable to suppose that the doctrines regarding the Godhead in the Book of Mormon reflect not the contemporary New England religious mind but rather the understanding had by the ancients?

My position is that the doctrine of the Godhead in the Book of Mormon is actually deeper and more penetrating than that found in any other book of scripture; that the Book of Mormon theology was not a part of a line-upon-line unfolding of doctrine in this dispensation; and that if Joseph Smith had been asked, prior to his death, to provide a reading list of recommended works detailing an in-depth look at God, Christ, and the Holy Ghost, the Book of Mormon would have been high on (if not at the top of) that list.

One of the perspectives a reader gains early in the Book of Mormon is the centrality of Jesus Christ, the majestic role he played as both premortal Jehovah and mortal Messiah. The Book of Mormon prophets declare with consistency the fact that Jesus is not only the Christ but also the Eternal God (see title page; 2 Nephi

26:12). In fact, the power and position of Christ are put forward with much more emphasis than in the Bible, the Doctrine and Covenants, and the Pearl of Great Price. Though, as we shall see shortly, God the Eternal Father (Elohim) is the ultimate object of worship in the Book of Mormon, Jesus Christ is the focus of the testimonies of all the prophets. Consistent with the teachings of latter-day prophets that all revelation since the fall of Adam has been by and through Jehovah-Christ,[16] the Nephites talk of Christ, rejoice in Christ, preach of Christ, and prophesy of Christ (see 2 Nephi 25:26). They emphasize that he is the God of Abraham, Isaac, and Jacob (see 1 Nephi 19:10); that he is the creator and upholder of all things and thus the very Eternal Father of heaven and of earth (see Alma 11:39; 3 Nephi 9:15); and that he is the Holy One of Israel, the Eternal Judge of both quick and dead (see 1 Nephi 19:14–15; 2 Nephi 9:41; Moroni 10:34). The testimony of Elder Bruce R. McConkie echoes the testimonies of the Book of Mormon prophets:

"Christ-Messiah is God!

"Such is the plain and pure pronouncement of all the prophets of all the ages. In our desire to avoid the false and absurd conclusions contained in the creeds of Christendom, we are wont to shy away from this pure and unadorned verity; we go to great lengths to use language that shows there is both a Father and a Son, that they are separate Persons and are not somehow mystically intertwined as an essence or spirit that is everywhere present. Such an approach is perhaps essential in reasoning with the Gentiles of sectarianism; it helps to overthrow the fallacies formulated in their creeds.

"But having so done, if we are to envision our Lord's true status and glory, we must come back to the pronouncement of pronouncements, the doctrine of doctrines, the message of messages, which is that Christ is God. And if it were not so, he could not save us."[17]

Nephi wrote: "My soul delighteth in proving unto my people that save Christ should come all men must perish. For if there be no Christ there be no God; and if there be no God we are not, for there could have been no creation. But *there is a God, and he is Christ,* and he cometh in the fulness of his own time" (2 Nephi 11:6–7; emphasis added).

The depth of the Book of Mormon doctrine of Christ is also to be seen in its treatment of the ministry of Jesus Christ as the Father and the Son.[18] Consistent with prophets whose testimonies are recorded in the other Standard Works, the Book of Mormon prophets revealed Christ as the Father by virtue of his role as *Creator* (see Mosiah 3:8; D&C 14:9; Moses 1:33; 7:30), as well as through spiritual rebirth (see Mosiah 5:5–7; D&C 25:1; Moses 6:58–60). Christ is also called Father by *divine investiture of authority.* In the Doctrine and Covenants and the Pearl of Great Price we find numerous occasions wherein the Lord Jesus speaks in the name of his Father, on behalf of the Father, in the first person as though he were the Father (see D&C 29:1, 5; 49:5, 28; Moses 1:4, 6; 6:51–52).

One of the powerful witnesses of the Nephite-Jaredite record is that Jesus Christ is Father because Elohim has literally *invested* his Son with his own attributes and powers. Our Lord is Father "because he received power from his Father to do that which is infinite and eternal. This is a matter of his Eternal Parent investing him with power from on high so that he became the Father because he exercises the power of that Eternal Being."[19] Abinadi's penetrating testimony of Christ in Mosiah 15:1–5 might be paraphrased as follows:

a. God himself—Jehovah, the God of ancient Israel—will come to earth, take a body of flesh and bones, and accomplish the work of redemption for all mankind.

b. Because Jesus will have a physical body and dwell in the *flesh*—he will be known as the *Son* of God. His growth—like all men's—will be gradual, line upon line, precept upon precept.

c. The will of the Son is to be swallowed up in the will of the Father. That is, the *flesh* will be subject to the *spirit,* the mortal subject to the immortal. In short, Jesus will do what the Father would have him do.

d. Thus Christ will be known as both the Father and the Son. He will be called the Father because he was conceived by the power of God and inherited all of the divine endowments, particularly immortality, from his exalted Sire. He will be called the Son because of his flesh—his mortal inheritance from his mother, Mary. Therefore Christ will be both flesh (will have a physical body) and spirit (will possess the powers of the Spirit, the powers of his Father), both man and God, both Son and Father. "And they"—the Father and the Son, the spirit and the flesh, the God and the man—"are one God, yea, the very Eternal Father of heaven and of earth" (Mosiah 15:4). That is, the elements of mortality and immortality—flesh and spirit, Son and Father, man and God—are blended wondrously in one being, Jesus Christ.

Indeed, the Book of Mormon evidences a highly developed Christology, a doctrine of Christ as God that has no equal in the rest of our scriptural canon. Such views are neither primitive nor out of harmony with what Joseph Smith later taught the Saints, nor with what we teach today.

3. A "Trinitarian" Concept of God? Presumably people who take this posture concerning the Book of Mormon assume that the book reflects the prevailing sentiments of the nineteenth century concerning God. First of all, it is worth stating what is fairly obvious: trinitarian ideas concerning God—that the Father, Son, and Holy Ghost are simply three manifestations of one and the same being—are unscriptural, foreign to the spirit or content of the New Testament, and doctrinally untenable. Trinitarianism is a creation of man, a costly compromise between Greek philosophy and Christian doctrine that was perpetuated when the Christian church had fallen into apostasy after A.D. 100.

Secondly, although the Book of Mormon prophets speak of the "oneness" of the members of the Godhead, this does not imply trinitarianism. There were, in fact, large groups of people in the nineteenth century who believed in the oneness of the Godhead but rejected the mysterious notions associated with trinitarianism. One religious leader, David Millard, a minister who organized an Eastern Christian church, published a pamphlet in 1818 in which he attacked the prevailing view of the Trinity. He undertook a scriptural analysis of the New Testament to prove his point. "The whole tenor of scripture," he asserted, "concurs in the testimony, that Christ is verily the Son of God, as really so as Isaac is the son of Abram." He further stressed the illogical nature of the Nicean concept: "Three Gods are not one God, any more than three times one are one or two and one are one: which not only destroys the rules of multiplication and addition, but is flat inconsistency."[20] Likewise, William Ellery Channing, the Father of Unitarianism, contended in a famous 1819 Baltimore sermon that God can no more be three persons than man can be.[21]

William W. Phelps wrote a letter dated 19 May 1835 concerning his beliefs before conversion. His perception might well reflect the views of other lay persons in nineteenth-century New England: "I was not a professor at the time, nor a believer in sectarian religion, but *a believer in God, and the Son of God, as two distinct characters,* and a believer in sacred scripture."[22] There is no reference in the *Messenger and Advocate* letter that such a belief was contrary in any way to the teachings of the restored Church; in fact, the statement implies that his preconversion beliefs were in harmony with the teachings of the Latter-day Saints.

The presentation of the Godhead in the Book of Mormon is remarkably similar to that in the New Testament concerning separateness yet oneness of the members of the Godhead. At the same time, and as we have observed already, the Book of Mormon is more complete in regard to establishing the centrality of Jesus Christ as God. The Book of Mormon is a mighty witness of the fact that although the Father, Son, and Holy Ghost are separate and distinct individuals, they are infinitely more one than they are separate. They are one God—one Godhead, united in purpose, power, and glory (see 2 Nephi 31:21; Alma 11:44; Mormon 7:7). And yet they are separate Persons. Consider the following areas in which the Book of Mormon establishes their individuality:

a. We pray to the Father in the name of the Son.

"But behold, I say unto you that ye must pray always, and not faint; that ye must not perform any thing unto the Lord save in the first place *ye shall pray unto the Father in the name of Christ,* that he will consecrate thy performance unto thee, that thy performance may be for the welfare of thy soul" (2 Nephi 32:9; emphasis added).

"Therefore ye must always pray unto the Father in my name;

"And whatsoever ye shall ask the Father in my name, which is right, believing that ye shall receive, behold it shall be given unto you" (3 Nephi 18:19–20).

"O then despise not, and wonder not, but hearken unto the words of the Lord, and *ask the Father in the name of Jesus for what things soever ye shall stand in need"* (Mormon 9:27; emphasis added).

"Behold, when ye shall rend that veil of unbelief which doth cause you to remain in your awful state of wickedness, and hardness of heart, and blindness of mind, then shall the great and marvelous things which have been hid from the foundation of the world from you—yea, when *ye shall call upon the Father in my name,* with a broken heart and a contrite spirit, then shall ye know that the Father hath remembered the covenant which he made unto your fathers, O house of Israel" (Ether 4:15; emphasis added).

"*O God, the Eternal Father, we ask thee in the name of thy Son, Jesus Christ,* to bless and sanctify this bread to the souls of all those who partake of it" (Moroni 4:3; emphasis added; see also 5:2; 10:4).

"I am mindful of you always in my prayers, *continually praying unto God the Father in the name of his Holy Child, Jesus,* that he, through his infinite goodness and grace, will keep you through the endurance of faith on his name to the end" (Moroni 8:3; emphasis added).

b. We worship the Father in the name of the Son.

"And when that day shall come that they [the Jews] shall *believe in Christ, and worship the Father in his name,* with pure hearts and clean hands, and look not forward any more for another Messiah, then, at that time, the day will come that it must needs be expedient that they should believe these things" (2 Nephi 25:16; emphasis added).

"For, for this intent have we written these things, that they may know that we knew of Christ, and we had a hope of his glory many hundred years before his coming; and not only we ourselves had a hope of his glory, but also all the holy prophets which were before us.

"Behold, *they believed in Christ and worshiped the Father in his name,* and also *we worship the Father in his name*" (Jacob 4:4–5; emphasis added).

c. Christ received powers from his Father.

"And because he [Christ] dwelleth in flesh he shall be called the Son of God, and having subjected the flesh to the will of the Father, being the Father and the Son—

"*The Father, because he was conceived by the power of God;* and the Son, because of the flesh; thus becoming the Father and the Son" (Mosiah 15:2–3; emphasis added).

"And remember also the words which Amulek spake unto Zeezrom, in the city of Ammonihah; for he said unto him that the Lord surely should come to redeem his people, but that he should not come to redeem them in their sins, but to redeem them from their sins.

"*And he hath power given unto him from the Father to redeem them from their sins* because of repentance" (Helaman 5:10–11; emphasis added).

"Know ye that ye must come to the knowledge of your fathers, and repent of all your sins and iniquities, and believe in Jesus Christ, that he is the Son of God, and that he was slain by the Jews, and *by the power of the Father he hath risen again,* whereby he hath gained the victory over the grave; and also in him is the sting of death swallowed up" (Mormon 7:5; emphasis added).

d. Christ's atonement reconciles us to God.

"For we labor diligently to write, to persuade our children, and also our brethren, *to believe in Christ, and to be reconciled to God;* for we know that it is by grace that we are saved, after all we can do" (2 Nephi 25:23; emphasis added).

"But God did call on men, in the name of his Son, (this being the plan of redemption which was laid) saying: If ye will repent, and harden not your hearts, *then will I have mercy upon you, through mine Only Begotten Son;*

"Therefore, whosoever repenteth, and hardeneth not his heart, *he shall have claim on mercy through mine Only Begotten Son,* unto a remission of his sins; and these shall enter into my rest" (Alma 12:33–34; emphasis added).

"For behold, God knowing all things, being from everlasting to everlasting, behold, he sent angels to minister unto the children of men, to make manifest concerning the coming of Christ; and in Christ there should come every good thing. . . .

"And after that he came men also were saved by faith in his name; and by faith, they become the sons of God. And as surely as Christ liveth he spake these words unto our fathers, saying: Whatsoever thing he shall ask the Father in my name, which is good, in faith believing that ye shall receive, behold, it shall be done unto you.

"Wherefore, my beloved brethren, have miracles ceased because Christ hath ascended into heaven, and *hath sat down on the right hand of God, to claim of the Father his rights of mercy which he hath upon the children of men?*" (Moroni 7:22, 26–27; emphasis added).

e. The voices of the Father and the Son are distinguished.

"And [Christ] said unto the children of men: Follow thou me. Wherefore, my beloved brethren, *can we follow Jesus save we shall be willing to keep the commandments of the Father?*

"And *the Father said:* Repent ye, repent ye, and *be baptized in the name of my Beloved Son.*

"And also, *the voice of the Son came unto me,* saying: *He that is baptized in my name, to him will the Father give the Holy Ghost,* like unto me; wherefore, follow me, and do the things which ye have seen me do.

"Wherefore, my beloved brethren, I know that if ye shall follow the Son, with full purpose of heart, acting no hypocrisy and no deception before God, but with real intent, repenting of your sins, *witnessing unto the Father that ye are willing to take upon you the name of Christ,* by baptism—yea, by following your Lord and your Savior down into the water, according to his word, behold, then shall ye receive the Holy Ghost; . . . and then can ye speak with the tongue of angels, and shout praises unto the Holy One of Israel.

"But, behold, my beloved brethren, *thus came the voice of the Son unto me,* saying: After ye have repented of your sins, and witnessed unto the Father that ye are willing to keep my commandments, by the baptism of water, and have received the baptism of fire and of the Holy Ghost, and can speak with a new tongue, yea, even with the tongue of angels, and after this should deny me, it would have been better for you that ye had not known me. "And *I heard a voice from the Father,* saying: Yea, *the words of my Beloved are true and faithful.* He that endureth to the end, the same shall be saved" (2 Nephi 31:10–15; emphasis added).

The above passages are only a sample of a much larger group of scriptures that demonstrate that the Book of Mormon prophets understood very clearly the separate and distinct natures of the Father and the Son. Only eleven days before his death, Joseph Smith the Prophet said: "I have *always* declared God to be a distinct personage, Jesus Christ a separate and distinct personage from God the Father, and that the Holy Ghost was a distinct personage and a Spirit: and *these three constitute three distinct personages and three Gods."*[23] Any thinking Latter-day Saint should ask the question: Would Joseph Smith expound doctrine—the distinctness of the Father and the Son—that was seemingly at variance with the teachings of a book he claimed to have received from God?[24] "Clearly," Elder Neal A. Maxwell has written, "this book came *through* a 'choice seer'—Joseph Smith—but not *from* that seer.

"Some, desperate for an alternative explanation, almost seem to suppose Joseph was getting help from some theological mail-order supply house.

"To the human mind it is amazing that such rich revelations and translations should come through an untrained individual such as Joseph was. The reason, of course, is that, though Joseph did not spell perfectly, he came to know the grammar of the gospel, because he was God's apt pupil."[25]

IN PERSPECTIVE

It was in Nauvoo in 1841, during the zenith of his ministry, only three years before his death, that Joseph Smith made the statement that the Book of Mormon was "the most correct of any book on earth, and the keystone of our religion."[26] It would seem that by that time in his life and ministry, he could speak not only with authority but also with perspective. After having received literally hundreds of revelations from God, after having seen numerous visions and preached myriad doctrinal sermons, surely the modern Seer knew where truth and light were to be found. And those in this generation who are truly intent on growing in light and truth—those who literally seek for the glory of God (see D&C 93:36)—know where lasting inspiration is to be found. The Book of Mormon is indeed "the book that will save the world and prepare the sons of men for joy and peace here and now and everlasting life in eternity."[27]

Notes

From a presentation to the BYU Religious Education faculty, Provo, Utah, 1986.

1. Parley P. Pratt, *Autobiography of Parley P. Pratt* (Salt Lake City: Deseret Book Co., 1972), 298; emphasis added.
2. See Joseph F. McConkie, "Modern Revelation: A Window to the Past," in Robert L. Millet, ed., *"To Be Learned Is Good If . . ."* (Salt Lake City: Bookcraft, 1987), 115–28.
3. Hugh Nibley, *Nibley on the Timely and the Timeless* (Provo: Religious Studies Center, Brigham Young University, 1978), 150.
4. Ezra Taft Benson, in Conference Report, April 1986, 4.
5. Ibid., 100.
6. *Teachings of the Prophet Joseph Smith,* 194.

7. Bruce R. McConkie, *The Foolishness of Teaching*, address to LDS Church Educational System employees (Salt Lake City: The Church of Jesus Christ of Latter-day Saints, 1981), 6.

8. Bruce R. McConkie, in Conference Report, October 1983, 106.

9. Alexander Campbell, *Delusions: An Analysis of the Book of Mormon* (Boston: B. H. Green, 1832), 13.

10. Richard L. Bushman, "The Book of Mormon and the American Revolution," in Noel B. Reynolds, ed., *Book of Mormon Authorship* (Provo: Religious Studies Center, Brigham Young University, 1982), 189–211.

11. The ludicrous nature of this claim is to be seen in the fact that Sidney Rigdon was converted by the Book of Mormon.

12. For an excellent survey on the use and abuse of this theory, see Rex C. Reeve Jr., "Spaulding Theory and the Origin of the Book of Mormon," First Annual Symposium on the Book of Mormon, Provo, Utah, October 1985.

13. Hugh Nibley, "Mixed Voices," *Improvement Era*, July 1959, 565.

14. Ezra Taft Benson, in Conference Report, April 1975, 94; emphasis added.

15. *History of the Church*, 1:226.

16. See Joseph Fielding Smith, *Man: His Origin and Destiny* (Salt Lake City: Deseret Book Co., 1954), 304, 312; *Doctrines of Salvation*, 1:27; Joseph Fielding Smith, *Answers to Gospel Questions*, 5 vols. (Salt Lake City: Deseret Book Co., 1965–75), 3:58.

17. *Promised Messiah*, 98.

18. For a detailed discussion of this subject, see my article entitled, "The Ministry of the Father and the Son," in *The Book of Mormon: The Keystone Scripture*, Papers from the First Annual Book of Mormon Symposium, Religious Studies Center, Brigham Young University, October 1985. See also "The Father and the Son: A Doctrinal Exposition of the First Presidency and the Twelve," in James E. Talmage, *The Articles of Faith* (Salt Lake City: Deseret Book Co., 1975), 465–73.

19. *Promised Messiah*, 371.

20. David Millard, *The True Messiah Exalted, or Jesus Christ Really the Son of God, Vindicated; in Three Letters to a Presbyterian Minister* (Canandaigua, N.Y.: n.p., 1818), 5–8.

21. William E. Channing, *The Works of William E. Channing* (Boston: American Unitarian Assocation, 1886), 371, as cited in Milton V. Backman Jr., *American Religions and the Rise of Mormonism* (Salt Lake City: Deseret Book Co., 1970), 210.

22. William W. Phelps, in *The Latter-day Saints' Messenger and Advocate* 1, no. 8 (May 1835): 115; emphasis added.

23. *Teachings of the Prophet Joseph Smith*, 370; emphasis added; see also *Words of Joseph Smith*, 63, 378.

24. I am aware of the fact that the early leaders of the Church in this dispensation did not always distinguish as clearly as we do today between the name-titles of Jehovah and Elohim. At the same time, there seems to have been no doubt in their minds as to the separateness of the Father and the Son. The issue is an issue of nomenclature, not theology. See my article, "The Ministry of the Father and the Son" for a more detailed treatment of this matter.

   Some persons have even suggested that the Book of Mormon is "Calvinistic" in scope. Such an idea is even more radical than the proposition that the book is trinitarian. Do the Nephite prophets teach such doctrines as the total depravity of man (including man's inability to choose the right)? unconditional election of individuals to eternal life? a limited atonement (reserved only for the elect, those predestined to salvation)? irresistible grace? perseverance of the Saints (one's inability to fall from grace)? These ideas are as remote and foreign to the theology of the Book of Mormon as they could possibly be.

25. Neal A. Maxwell, *But for a Small Moment* (Salt Lake City: Bookcraft, 1986), 44; emphasis in original.

26. *Teachings of the Prophet Joseph Smith*, 194.

27. Bruce R. McConkie, in Conference Report, October 1983, 107.

LESSONS FROM THE
JOSEPH SMITH TRANSLATION

Joseph Smith was called of God in this final dispensation to be a prophet, seer, revelator, and translator (see D&C 21:1; 107:92; 124:125). Not only was he ordained to make known truths that had never been given to people on earth before (see D&C 121:26; 124:41; 128:18), but he was also empowered to translate ancient records and restore and clarify doctrine and understanding from previous dispensations. To Oliver Cowdery the Lord said: "Assuredly as the Lord liveth, who is your God and your Redeemer, even so surely shall you receive a knowledge of whatsoever things you shall ask in faith, with an honest heart, believing that you shall receive a knowledge concerning the engravings of old records, which are ancient, which contain those parts of my scripture of which has been spoken by the manifestation of my Spirit" (D&C 8:1). Within a short time, the Savior spoke again to Oliver. He was instructed that when the translation of the golden plates was completed, "other records have I, that I will give unto you power that you may assist to translate" (D&C 9:2). These two revelations refer to the Prophet's work as translator—of the Book of Mormon, the Book of Abraham, and the Bible.

MAKING THE NEW TRANSLATION

Some time prior to June of 1830 the Lord commanded Joseph Smith to begin a serious study of the King James Version of the Bible (KJV). On 8 October 1829 Oliver Cowdery purchased a large pulpit-style edition of the Bible from E.B. Grandin in Palmyra, New York. This was the Bible used in what we have come to know as the Joseph Smith Translation of the Bible (JST). The Prophet would read from the Bible and, under inspiration, dictate to a scribe, who would then write what was said on manuscript pages. Though the Prophet was assisted briefly in the translation by Oliver Cowdery, Emma Smith, and John Whitmer, the preeminent scribe was Sidney Rigdon. The work with the Bible was done without the aid of the Urim and Thummim. The first thing revealed, dated June 1830, was what we call Moses 1, an account of an experience had by the prophet Moses on an unnamed mountain. Following this account, the Prophet and his scribe began to move through Genesis, making alterations in the text as they were inspired to do so. What we now have as the book of Moses in our Pearl of Great Price is the Joseph Smith Translation of the opening chapters of Genesis. The translators worked with the text of Genesis until 7 March 1831, when a revelation instructed them to begin the translation of the New Testament (see D&C 45:60–62).

Translation activity continued until February of 1833, until the New Testament was completed. Then the translators returned to the Old Testament. On 2 July 1833 the Prophet wrote to the leaders of the Church in Missouri and indicated that he and his scribe had just completed their translation of the Bible.[1] In fact, Joseph worked with the text for the next eleven years of his life, editing, correcting, refining that which had come to him by revelation. In total, over 3,410 verses from the KJV were altered through corrections, additions, and an occasional deletion. There is no question in my mind but that in many cases these changes represent a restoration of ancient texts that had been corrupted or lost before the compilation of the Bible. This is certainly the case in regard to insight that came to Joseph Smith pertaining to the Creation, Fall, and Atonement and the work of Adam and Eve (Moses 2–6), the life and ministry and translation of Enoch (Moses 6–7), the Christian ministry of Noah (Moses 8), the person and powers of Melchizedek (JST, Genesis 14), and the prophecies of Joseph of old (JST, Genesis 50). In the New Testament, significant doctrinal details concerning the ministry and teachings of John the Baptist (JST, Luke 3), Jesus as the Word (JST, John 1), the baptism of Christ (JST, John 1), the Sermon on the Mount as a kind of missionary training center for the Twelve (JST, Matthew 5–7), and scores of other changes point toward a divinely directed restoration.

It may be that Joseph the Prophet restored conversation and teachings, as well as episodes in the lives of the ancients (in both Old and New Testaments), that actually took place but were never recorded. In addition, we cannot overlook the possibility that in some cases the Prophet's alterations to the KJV represent a type of inspired prophetic commentary on the text, a prophetic prerogative that surely must be received with as much enthusiasm as restorations. And certainly one reason we must take the entire JST seriously is that the Prophet never delineated which changes were restorations, which were harmonizations, which were prophetic commentary, and so forth.

TRUTHS LEARNED THROUGH THE TRANSLATION OF THE BIBLE

Some of the most important truths of our dispensation came as a direct result of the translation of the Bible. Many of these came from the translation itself, while others came in the form of revelations (now recorded in the Doctrine and Covenants) that arose from questions during the translation. In the former category, consider the following matters, from the Old Testament alone, that came directly from the translation:

- The spirit creation and the spiritual creation (Moses 2–3);
- The premortal existence of mankind (Moses 4);
- The revelation of the gospel to Adam by heavenly messengers; the baptism, confirmation, and ordination of Adam (Moses 5–6);
- The call and prophetic ministry of Enoch; the establishment of the ancient city of Zion and its translation (Moses 6–7);
- The gospel teachings of Noah (Moses 8);
- The ministry of Melchizedek and the translation of Salem (JST, Genesis 14);
- The age of accountability of children (JST, Genesis 17);
- A difference between the two sets of tablets Moses brought down from Sinai (JST, Exodus 34; JST, Deuteronomy 10). And on and on.

In addition, the following sections of the Doctrine and Covenants came as a direct result of the translation: Section 74 (dealing with 1 Corinthians 7), section 77 (dealing with the Revelation of John), section 91 (dealing with the Old Testament Apocrypha), and section 132 (dealing with eternal and plural marriage). Perhaps most important, Doctrine and Covenants 76, the Vision of the Glories, one of the greatest and most sublime revelations ever received, came as Joseph Smith and Sidney Rigdon pondered over a change they had made in John 5:29.

The JST proved to be a vital dimension of the spiritual education of Joseph Smith himself. As the Prophet studied the text of the KJV, he came to know by revelation what had been taken, altered, added, etc., what things needed to be changed to open the scriptures more fully to the Latter-day Saints and the world. The Prophet considered this work to be a branch of his calling.[2] He warned the Saints:

"God [has] often sealed up the heavens because of covetousness in the Church. The Lord [will] cut short his work in righteousness and except the Church receive the fulness of the Scriptures that they would yet fail."[3] The Lord himself took this labor very seriously. To Sidney Rigdon, the preeminent scribe in the JST, He said: "And a commandment I give unto thee—that thou shalt write for him [the Prophet]; and *the scriptures shall be given, even as they are in mine own bosom, to the salvation of mine own elect*" (D&C 35:20; emphasis added).

OTHER LESSONS

In addition to the sublime doctrinal messages that came from or through the JST, there are lessons to be learned from this remarkable labor of Joseph Smith. For example:

1. *The Bible has not come down to us in its pristine purity.* Nephi learned from an angel that at one time the Bible contained the "fulness of the gospel of the Lord" that went forth "from the Jews in purity unto the Gentiles." He saw, further, "the formation of [a] great and abominable church, which is most abominable above all other churches; for behold, they have taken away *from the gospel* of the Lamb many parts which are plain and most precious; and also many covenants of the Lord have they taken away." These were not the unintended scribal errors—the errors of eye or ear, the errors created and perpetuated through human limitations. The angel explained: "And all this have they done that they might pervert the right ways of the Lord, that they might blind the eyes and harden the hearts of the children of men." The mother of abominations not only tampers with the gospel and its meaning, but also "there are many plain and precious things taken away *from the book,* which is the book of the Lamb of God." And because of these plain and precious truths "taken away" and "kept back" by malicious mortals, "an exceedingly great many do stumble, yea, insomuch that Satan hath great power over them" (1 Nephi 13:24–32; emphasis added; see also D&C 6:26).

Most biblical scholars acknowledge that scribal errors inevitably took place in the transmission of the Bible, and even that thousands of errors were introduced purposefully by scribes adding to or taking from the manuscripts.[4] But because the Bible is all they have, because it is the only sacred scripture in their possession, they feel the need to make statements like the following: "We must trust that the same Holy Spirit who inspired the original text was able to protect it through the centuries of handwritten copying." This same writer then proceeds to acknowledge that while the secular Greek classics, for example, were generally copied by professional scribes "and checked against accepted copies or originals by professional proofreaders," the New Testament texts were probably copied "mostly by ordinary Christians who were not professional scribes but who wanted a copy of a New Testament book or books for themselves or for other Christians." These did not have "the same opportunity as the secular copyists to compare their manuscripts with other manuscripts." He continues by observing that "as scribes copied these copies, they continued to make changes through the centuries. Most of these changes were insignificant; those that were of importance—the ones with which we are concerned—were introduced during the first two centuries after the New Testament was written. . . . The textual variants that concern us, of course, are those that affect the meaning of the New Testament in some way. There are a few thousand of these," he states, and then hastens to add, "but we should be clear on the fact that they affect only a small portion of the New Testament text."[5]

One New Testament scholar suggested that the theological debates during the first few centuries of the Christian Church had a major impact on the biblical texts. "The New Testament manuscripts were not produced impersonally," he states, "by machines capable of flawless reproduction. They were copied by hand, by living, breathing human beings who were deeply rooted in the conditions and controversies of their day. Did the scribes' polemical contexts influence the way they transcribed their sacred Scriptures?" He contends that "they did, that theological disputes, specifically disputes over Christology, prompted Christian scribes to alter the words of Scripture in order to make them more serviceable for the polemical task. Scribes modified their manuscripts to make them more patently 'orthodox' and less susceptible to 'abuse' by the opponents of orthodoxy."[6]

Even if biblical scholars should never acknowledge that significant doctrinal matters were excised from the Bible, Joseph Smith explained otherwise: "From Sundry revelations which had been received," he said, "it was apparent that many important points touching the salvation of man had been taken from the Bible, or lost before it was compiled."[7] "From what we can draw from the Scriptures relative to the teaching of heaven," he declared some two years later, "we are induced to think that much instruction has been given to man since the beginning which we do not possess now. . . . We have what we have, and the Bible contains what it does contain."[8] In short, "I believe the Bible, as it ought to be, as it came from the pen of the original writers."[9] That the Prophet Joseph Smith should be "appointed" by God (D&C 42:56; 76:15) and called to undertake a "new translation" of the Bible implies of itself that the message of the Bible, though essentially true, needed clarification, correction, and supplementation at the hands of an inspired translator. The early Latter-day Saints thus exulted in the fact that the Bible was "undergoing the purifying touch by a revelation of Jesus Christ."[10]

2. *The greatest commentary on scripture is scripture.* Further, a careful study of scripture brings forth additional light and truth. One of the fascinating discoveries of a careful study of the new translation—and thus one of the reasons the history of the Church cannot be prepared or told without adequate attention to the work with the Bible—is the manner in which matters in the translation, both doctrinal topics and specific phrases, are reflected in the revelations given to the Prophet at about the same time. We have sometimes been too prone to impose artificial distinctions, to study the translations and the revelations as separate endeavors, when in fact they went forward concurrently in the daily activity of the life of Joseph Smith. Generally the knowledge gained through the Prophet's work with the Bible preceded a revelation addressing the same subject. Shortly we will note exceptions to this order—times when the revelations seemed to precede the translations. For now, we will consider some specific illustrations of doctrinal topics first revealed through the JST and later discussed in the Doctrine and Covenants.

3. *Revelation comes line upon line to prophets, just as it does to us.* There is no question but what Joseph Smith knew far more, worlds more, than he ever revealed to the Latter-day Saints. What is also clear, however, is that very often the Lord required his "choice seer" to labor and ponder and reflect and ruminate upon a doctrinal matter before clarity came. It is one thing to receive a revelation, to come to know the mind and will of God; it is another thing to record what one has learned. Certainly most of the revelations in the Doctrine and Covenants were dictated by Joseph Smith as God spoke through him. On other occasions, such as is the case with the JST, Joseph was required to put into words what God had put into his mind. This is reflected in the different manuscripts of the Old and New Testaments, evidencing a process of inspired but laborious refinement of the JST.

Robert J. Matthews has written: "In the face of the evidence it can hardly be maintained that the exact words were given to the Prophet in the process of a revelatory experience. Exact words may have been given to the Prophet on occasion, but the manuscript evidence suggests that generally he was obliged to formulate the words himself to convey the message he desired. Consequently, he might later have observed that sometimes the words were not entirely satisfactory in the initial writings. They may have conveyed too much or too little. Or they may have been too specific or too vague, or even ambiguous. Or the words may have implied meanings not intended. Thus through (1) an error of recording, (2) an increase of knowledge, or (3) an inadequate selection of words, any passage of the New Translation might be subject to later revision."[11]

4. *A passage may be rendered more ways than one.* When Moroni first appeared in September of 1823, he quoted numerous passages of scripture to Joseph Smith. He rendered Malachi 4:5–6 differently (see D&C 2). Moroni's rendition did not necessarily invalidate the KJV, but rather Moroni shed light on a doctrine—the "promises made to the fathers"—that is less clearly set forth in the KJV. Indeed, in this case, both renditions are correct and either could be cited, depending upon what point needed to be made at the time. In an epistle written by Joseph Smith at Nauvoo in 1842, the Prophet quoted the KJV of Malachi 4:5–6 in referring to work for the dead. "I might have rendered a plainer translation to this," he then wrote, "but it is sufficiently plain to suit my purpose as it stands" (D&C 128:18).

Extensive changes in the JST occur on such matters as God repenting, God hardening people's hearts, predestination, man's capacity to see God, Christian covenants and ordinances in antiquity, and the ministries of such otherwise enigmatic characters as Enoch and Melchizedek. In other places, changes in the JST seem to reflect not a correction so much as a clarification or even a different meaning entirely. For example, when the Prophet translated Hebrews 11 (sometime between February 1832 and February 1833), he altered verse 40 from "God having provided some better thing for us, that they without us should not be made perfect" to "God having provided some better things for them through their sufferings, for without sufferings they could not be made perfect." Hebrews 11 is the New Testament's "Who's Who in Faith" chapter, the equivalent to Ether 12 in the Book of Mormon. It is a statement of what was required of the ancients to gain faith unto life and salvation, including enduring suffering and trials. The change in the JST fits perfectly the doctrinal context of the chapter. It seems clear to me that at this point in time the Prophet and the Saints did not yet comprehend the doctrine of work for the dead. It was probably not until the Vision of the Celestial Kingdom (D&C 137), given in January of 1836, that the doctrinal door seemed to open to the idea that men and women could gain the blessings of the gospel after they had departed this life. Later in his ministry, and operating with added light and knowledge concerning this supernal gem in the plan of salvation, Joseph Smith quoted Hebrews 11:40 as scriptural support for the importance of work for the dead (see D&C 128:15).[12]

The same is true with Revelation 1:5–6. The KJV of this passage refers to the work of Christ the Redeemer who has "made us kings and priests unto God and his

Father; to him be glory and dominion for ever and ever." When the Prophet translated this passage (sometime between February 1832 and February 1833) he rendered it as follows: Christ "hath made us kings and priests unto God, his Father." The JST of this passage is true and accurate. It also seems to indicate that the Prophet and the Saints may not have understood the doctrine of the plurality of Gods at this point in time. It was in the Sermon in the Grove, delivered in Nauvoo just eleven days before his martyrdom, that the Prophet quoted Revelation 1:5–6 in the KJV and added: "It is altogether correct in the translation." He then spoke at length of the plurality of Gods. "Where was there ever a son without a father? And where was there ever a father without first being a son? . . . Hence if Jesus had a Father, can we not believe that *He* had a Father also? I despise the idea of being scared to death at such a doctrine, for the Bible is full of it."[13]

5. *Loyalty to a living oracle entails an acceptance of what he brings forth.* We cannot afford to pick and choose what we will accept and what we will not, even if it is not well received by the learned of the day. So far as I can tell, Joseph Smith (or the Lord, for that matter) did not view the Bible translation as of any lesser worth than he did the Book of Mormon, the revelations in the Doctrine and Covenants, or the book of Abraham. They are all products of the Restoration, fruits of a modern oracle, evidences of his prophetic call. The JST was no sideline, no prophetic parlor game; it was serious business. In the words of Elder Dallin H. Oaks, it is "a member of the royal family of scripture" and should be "noticed and honored on any occasion when it is present."[14] As we noted earlier, the Lord explained that through the Bible translation the scriptures would be given, "even as they are in mine own bosom, to the salvation of mine own elect" (D&C 35:20). Salvation itself is at stake here. The issue is whether or not we will in fact receive and utilize the JST—with enthusiasm, not with tolerance.

Why have we been somewhat hesitant to use the JST in the past? Simply stated, for many years we were ignorant of both the process and the product. Over the years we have been a bit prejudiced, have assumed that the Reorganized Church of Jesus Christ of Latter Day Saints made changes in the Prophet's work. Robert Matthews's groundbreaking work with the original manuscripts helped to dispel these myths.

In addition, some have suggested that we should not use the JST because the Prophet never finished the work. They quote the following scripture for support: "It is expedient that thou shouldst hold thy peace concerning [the changes in the translation], and not teach them until ye have received them in full" (D&C 42:57). This simply cannot mean, as some have concluded, that Joseph and the Saints were not to teach that which was found in the JST until all changes that were ever to be made in the Bible were made. Earlier in that same revelation, section 42, the Lord had directed that the elders, priests, and teachers of the Church were to teach the principles of the gospel as found in the Bible and the Book of Mormon. In addition, the Saints were to "observe the covenants and church articles to do them, and these shall be their teachings, as they shall be directed by the Spirit. . . . And all this ye shall observe to do as I have commanded concerning your teaching, *until the fulness of my scriptures is given*" (D&C 42:12–15; emphasis added). "At that time," Elder Bruce R. McConkie noted, "they had only the imperfect King James Version of the Bible and the near-perfect Book of Mormon. These were their only scriptural sources for the principles of the gospel. When the Joseph Smith Translation of the Bible—included in this revelation [D&C 42] under the designation 'fulness of my scriptures'—came forth, then teachers were to use it and the various additional direct revelations. This, then, is a command to teach the changes and additions now found in the so-called Inspired Version."[15]

As indicated, Joseph Smith was not permitted to make every possible change. The fact is, the Prophet did teach from the new translation during his ministry, and many parts of the JST were published during his lifetime—in *The Evening and the Morning Star,* the *Lectures on Faith,* and the *Times and Seasons.* He obviously did not perceive the Lord's command to be other than a warning against sharing the "mysteries of the kingdom" prematurely with those unprepared to receive them. (The Prophet did ask that William W. Phelps not print the New Translation in a serial format in *The Evening and the Morning Star.* He had plans of publishing it all as a unit; see Moses 1:42; 4:32.) Again from Elder McConkie, who had such strong feelings on this matter, "True, the Joseph Smith Translation, though completed to the point that the early Brethren were going to publish it at one time, has not been completed in the full and true sense. But for that matter neither has the Book of Mormon. I am as anxious to read and study what is in the sealed portion of the Book of Mormon as I am to give the same attention to those parts of the Bible yet to be revealed.

"I am clear in my mind that the sealed portion of the Book of Mormon will not come forth until the Millennium. The same thing is undoubtedly true of the fulness of the Bible, though some additions could well be made before that time.

"Of what will the Bible consist when it is perfected?

"Surely it will contain the writings of Adam and Enoch and Noah; of Melchizedek and Isaac and Jacob; and certainly Abraham wrote much more than the Prophet found on the Egyptian papyrus. The Book of Abraham in our Pearl of Great Price is obviously a restored biblical record.

"Does anyone think we have all of the words of Isaiah or Jeremiah or Malachi? And are there not prophets and apostles without number, whose names we do not even know, who have recorded their teachings and testimonies?"[16]

THE JST AND THE CANON OF SCRIPTURE

Why do some feel comfortable accepting the parts of the JST that are in the canon of scripture (the standard works), such as the book of Moses and Joseph Smith—Matthew, but feel less inclined to accept the other JST alterations? There is no question but that we are firmly committed to the canon, the standard works, and that these books of scripture serve as the rule of faith and practice for the Latter-day Saints; they are binding upon us. At the same time, if any people in all the wide world should have reason to be nervous about sealing the canon, it is the Latter-day Saints. For us nothing is more fixed, set, and established than the eternal fact that the canon of scripture is open, flexible, and expanding. What is scripture one day may become part of the canon the next, as was the case in 1976 with the Vision of the Celestial Kingdom (D&C 137) and the Vision of the Redemption of the Dead (D&C 138). These were, according to the definition provided in modern revelation (D&C 68:3–4), *scripture* from the time they were given; they were just as true before they were canonized in 1976. The same is so in regard to the entire JST before it was printed by the Reorganized Church.

Further, in our study or our inquiry after the mind and will of the Lord, we as a people are not bound by a single collection of sacred books. We are called upon to "live by every word . . . of God" (D&C 84:44), to open ourselves to new truths as they may come forth through proper channels. The addresses delivered by the President of the Church at general conference are not in the canon, nor are such official doctrinal declarations of the First Presidency as "The Origin of Man" (1909) or "The Father and the Son" (1916) or the Proclamation on the Family (1995), but they certainly represent the mind and will and voice of the Lord to the Saints; the members of the Church are expected to "give diligent heed to the words of eternal life" (D&C 84:43) as they come from the lips of the Lord's anointed servants. Does anyone really believe that what is said in scripture by Alma or Paul or John the Beloved is any more binding on the Saints in our day than President Ezra Taft Benson's messages on the Book of Mormon or President Howard W. Hunter's pleas for greater Christian charity and more devoted service in the temples?

In writing on the subject of the biblical canon, the respected Evangelical scholar F. F. Bruce observed that "there is a distinction between the canonicity of a book of the Bible and its authority. Its canonicity is dependent upon its authority. For when we ascribe canonicity to a book we simply mean that it belongs to the canon or list. But why does it so belong? Because it was recognized as possessing special authority. People frequently speak and write as if the authority with which the books of the Bible are invested in the minds of Christians is the result of their having been included in the sacred list. But the historical fact is the other way about; they were and are included in the list because they were acknowledged as authoritative." Bruce concludes: " Both logically and historically, authority precedes canonicity."[17]

Within our own history there are examples of doctrinal practices that were in effect long before the actual revelation was a part of the canon. For example, the Latter-day Saints were gathering Israel—bringing people into the kingdom through conversion—even before the Church was officially organized. But the keys of the gathering of Israel were not actually conferred until the coming of Moses to the Kirtland Temple in April of 1836. In fact, those keys formalized and empowered a work that was already well under way. Joseph Smith seems to have learned of eternal and plural marriage as early as 1831, as a result of his inspired translation of Genesis. Plural marriage was introduced to some of the Saints in Nauvoo. It remained for Elder Orson Pratt to deliver the first public discourse on the subject in 1852. Section 132 of the Doctrine and Covenants was first recorded on 12 July 1843 but was not included in the Doctrine and Covenants until 1876. The practice of plural marriage continued until the Manifesto issued by President Wilford Woodruff called for its cessation in 1890.

Elder McConkie noted in 1984 that the JST "contains various additions, deletions, and emendations to the King James Version. But most importantly it contains the book of Moses and the twenty-fourth chapter of Matthew as published in the Pearl of Great Price.

"These portions have been formally canonized by us, which should establish that any changes made by the Prophet are true and should be used. Does anyone think that the pure revelation found in Genesis 14 about Melchizedek or in Genesis 50 about the Nephites and Joseph Smith and the latter days is any less a revelation than Moses 1? Does anyone think the [JST of the] first chapter of John's Gospel is of any less worth than the twenty-fourth chapter of Matthew's?"[18]

We are not bound solely by the written word nor limited by our devotion to texts. It is the spirit of revelation, not specific texts, that leads the Church of Jesus

Christ. It is the living voice, not the standard works alone, that directs the kingdom of God. Elder Dallin Oaks observed that "those who will not rely on revelation and who insist on a manuscript so they can concentrate on the original meaning and intent of the words spoken by the author can be expected to ignore the Joseph Smith Translation. In contrast, those who understand that the importance of the scriptures is what the Lord would have us understand today are anxious for revelatory insight into the current significance of scriptural texts and concepts. They understand that some things we have already received are hard to understand without the Lord's help (see 1 Nephi 15:1, 3, 8, 11), and that we can never receive enough of the word of God. Persons with this attitude are anxious to have every source of revelation to help us know what the Lord would have us understand from the scriptures today. Such persons will welcome the revelatory insights—even additions—by the prophets of this dispensation."[19]

We love the Bible. We cherish the Bible. And we thank God that so many truths in the Bible have been preserved for us. But if it were necessary—and thank God that it is not—we could move forward without the Bible. God has revealed sufficient truth and knowledge through his latter-day prophets for us to be sustained and directed.

CONCLUSION

Joseph Smith was not a linguist, at least by this world's standards. But he possessed the mind of God, enjoyed all of the gifts of the Spirit, and was in tune with the Infinite. On one occasion he said: "I . . . have witnessed the visions of eternity, and beheld the glorious mansions of bliss, and the regions and the misery of the damned. . . . I . . . have heard the voice of God, and communed with angels, and spake as moved by the Holy Ghost for the renewal of the Everlasting Covenant, and for the gathering of Israel in the last days."[20] In speaking of his affection for an old German translation of the Bible, he stated: "I thank God that I have got this old book; but I thank him more for the gift of the Holy Ghost. I have got the oldest book in the world; but I [also] have the oldest book in my heart, even the gift of the Holy Ghost."[21] Thus the Prophet's schooling was of the Spirit. His instructors were heavenly beings. And the light and intelligence by which he operated were pure and undiluted.

In the future we will surely come to understand how the Prophet translated the golden plates, the Egyptian papyri, and the King James Bible. We shall see, one and all, that he was a man of integrity, knew whereof he spoke, and accomplished superhuman tasks by means of divine assistance. In the meantime, an acceptance of Joseph Smith's work as translator transcends what is currently known or available in the world of scholarship and thus enters the realm of faith. If we cannot for the present time understand how he translated Reformed Egyptian from golden plates, we can still taste the sweetness of the fruit. If we cannot reconcile the text of the Book of Abraham with what scholars translate from the facsimiles of the few papyrus fragments in our possession, we can still recognize the spirit of truth in that which he recorded. If we find that the Prophet's Bible translation does not match what may be found on the oldest extant Hebrew or Greek manuscripts, we yet recognize the spirit and genius of a prophet in this sacred labor and treat the JST with the same respect we would treat doctrinal insights from the Book of Mormon or Doctrine and Covenants.

If we are true and faithful to what we believe and know in our hearts, the Lord will yet open our minds and bring forth great discoveries in the land. If, on the other hand, we let what we have discovered by study alone drive our faith and commitment, we close ourselves to a vital realm of reality and block the hand of God. Our study must always be tempered by faith if we desire to be loyal to the work of Joseph Smith. For in Joseph Smith we have a man who walked and talked in the light of divine truth. "His mind was opened by the visions of the Almighty," Elder Wilford Woodruff testified, "and the Lord taught him many things by vision and revelation that were never taught publicly in his day; for the people could not bear the flood of intelligence which God poured into his mind."[22] A major part of that marvelous flood of intelligence came as a result of his inspired translation of the Bible. The Lord and his preeminent prophetic witness in this dispensation referred to this work as "the fulness of the scriptures" (D&C 42:15; 104:58),[23] a designation well worth pondering on. That we will receive and believe and utilize all that has come through the "Choice Seer" is my sincere prayer.

Notes

From a Symposium on Ancient Scriptures and the Restoration, Brigham Young University, Provo, Utah, 7 June 1997.

1. See *History of the Church,* 1:368.
2. Ibid., 1:238.
3. *Teachings of the Prophet Joseph Smith,* 9.
4. See, for example, Bruce M. Metzger, *The New Testament: Its Background, Growth, and Content,* 2d ed. (Nashville: Abingdon, 1983), 280–81.
5. J. Harold Greenlee, *Scribes, Scrolls, and Scripture* (Grand Rapids, Mich.: Eerdmans, 1985), 35–38.
6. Bart D. Ehrman, *The Orthodox Corruption of Scripture* (New York: Oxford, 1993), 3–4.
7. *Teachings of the Prophet Joseph Smith,* 9–10.
8. Ibid., 61.

9. *Words of Joseph Smith,* 256.
10. *Messenger and Advocate* 2 (December 1835): 229.
11. Robert J. Matthews, *"A Plainer Translation": Joseph Smith's Translation of the Bible, A History and Commentary* (Provo: BYU Press, 1975), 86.
12. *Teachings of the Prophet Joseph Smith,* 193, 356.
13. Ibid., 369, 373.
14. Dallin H. Oaks, "Scripture Reading, Revelation, and Joseph Smith's Translation of the Bible," in Robert L. Millet and Robert J. Matthews, eds., *Plain and Precious Truths Restored: The Doctrinal and Historical Significance of the Joseph Smith Translation* (Salt Lake City: Bookcraft, 1995), 13.
15. Bruce R. McConkie, "The Doctrinal Restoration," in Monte S. Nyman and Robert L. Millet, eds., *The Joseph Smith Translation: The Restoration of Plain and Precious Things* (Provo: Religious Studies Center, Brigham Young University, 1985), 3.
16. Ibid., 15.
17. F. F. Bruce, *The Books and the Parchments* (Westwood, N.J.: Fleming H. Revell Co., 1963), 95–96; see also F. F. Bruce, *The New Testament Documents: Are They Reliable?* (Grand Rapids, Mich.: Eerdmans, 1974), 27.
18. McConkie, "The Doctrinal Restoration," 15.
19. Oaks, "Scripture Reading," 13.
20. *History of the Church,* 6:77–78.
21. *Teachings of the Prophet Joseph Smith,* 349.
22. Wilford Woodruff, in *Journal of Discourses,* 5:83–84.
23. *Teachings of the Prophet Joseph Smith,* 9.

DOCTRINE

PRAISE TO THE MAN

In speaking of his beloved prophet-leader, Brigham Young declared: "When you hear a man pour out eternal things, how [good] you feel, to what a nearness you seem to be brought with God. What a delight it was to hear brother Joseph talk upon the great principles of eternity; he would bring them down to the capacity of a child, and he would unite heaven with earth."[1] On another occasion, President Young said, "When I saw Joseph Smith, he took heaven, figuratively speaking, and brought it down to earth; and he took the earth, brought it up, and opened up, in plainness and simplicity, the things of God."[2] And later, he added: "This should have convinced every person that ever heard of him of his divine authority and power, for no other man was able to teach as he could, and no person can reveal the things of God, but by the revelations of Jesus Christ. When we hear a man that can speak of heavenly things, and present them to the people in a way that they can be understood, you may know that to that man the avenue is open, and that he . . . has communication with the highest intelligence that exists."[3]

Brigham Young maintained a loyalty to Joseph Smith that people in the modern age cannot even comprehend, and as a result became a mighty man of God in his own right. I want to discuss loyalty, more specifically loyalty to the work Joseph Smith set in motion, as well as to the work as it goes forward today.

LOYALTY TO HIS REVELATIONS

The Restoration began by a revelation, a re-revealing of doctrine, principles, and precepts. It started, of necessity, with the First Vision, the beginning of the revelation of God to man. It would be followed by the coming forth of the Book of Mormon. Revelation upon revelation came to and through Joseph Smith, including the restoration of plain and precious truths once taken away or kept back from the Bible.

But there was more—more to come by way of truth, more than theology. The Restoration was destined to be a significant revolution. It must have been a mighty vision that filled the mind of Joseph Smith the Seer when he announced: "I calculate to be one of the instruments of setting up the kingdom [of God envisioned by] Daniel by the word of the Lord, and I intend to lay a foundation that will revolutionize the whole world." And how was this to be realized? "It will not be by sword or gun that this kingdom will roll on," the Prophet said. *"The power of truth is such that all nations will be under the necessity of obeying the gospel."*[4] Joseph Smith's vision of the kingdom of God—and of the power and ultimate reach of the Restoration—was cosmic. It consisted of more than preaching, study, and Sabbath services; it entailed the entire renovation of the order of things on earth, the transformation of man and the elevation of society. The Restoration was to be as broad and as deep as the Apostasy. Eventually the people of Zion would be in a position to know and acknowledge the truth, to discern and dispel error, and to teach and live the truth in all they said and did, in all facets of human endeavor—intellectual, moral, and spiritual. "Behold, I, the Lord, have made my church in these last days like unto a judge sitting on a hill, or in a high place, to judge the nations. For it shall come to pass that the inhabitants of Zion shall judge all things pertaining to Zion" (D&C 64:37–38).

Largely because of repetitive emphasis by President Ezra Taft Benson in recent years, we have become very much aware of the condemnation, scourge, and judgment that rests upon the members of The Church of Jesus Christ of Latter-day Saints because of our neglect of the Book of Mormon and modern revelation. The Lord's censure has come because we have "treated lightly the things [we] have received." The solution for ridding ourselves of this curse—extricating ourselves and subsequent generations of Saints—is simple: "They shall remain under this condemnation until they repent and remember the new covenant"—or the new Testament—"even the Book of Mormon and the former commandments which I have given them, not only to say"—that is, to teach or discuss or declare—"but to do"—to incorporate, to inculcate, to live—"according to that which I have written." The Master also explains: "I will forgive you of your sins with this commandment—that you remain steadfast in your minds in solemnity and the spirit of prayer, in bearing testimony to all the world of those things which are communicated unto you" (D&C 84:54–61).

Some six centuries before the coming of Jesus in the flesh, Nephi offered a haunting warning. Speaking of those in the last days, he prophesied: "They wear stiff necks and high heads; yea, and because of pride, and wickedness, and abominations, and whoredoms, they have all gone astray save it be a few, who are the humble followers of Christ; nevertheless, they are led"—i.e., many of the humble followers of Christ—"that *in many instances they do err because they are taught by the precepts of men*" (2 Nephi 28:14; emphasis added). In a modern revelation a similar warning is sounded: "And when the times of the Gentiles is come in"—i.e., our time, the day when the gospel is delivered to the Gentile nations—"a light shall break forth among them that sit in darkness, and it shall be the fulness of my gospel; but *they receive it not; for they perceive not the light, and they turn their hearts from me because of the precepts of men*" (D&C 45:28–29; emphasis added). It should be clear to most of us that this prophecy will not be fulfilled solely through the rejection of Mormonism by non-Mormons. Sadly, it will find its fulfillment also in the lives of those baptized members who choose to live beneath their privileges, who exist in twilight when they could bask in the glorious light of noonday sun (see D&C 95:5–6). The doctrines of the Restoration assist us immeasurably in sifting and sorting through the views and philosophies of men and staying ourselves to that which is true and enduring.

Being loyal to the Restoration entails being ready and willing to bear witness of the truths made known to us, primarily through Joseph Smith, in this latter day. We love the Bible. We cherish its truths, treasure its marvelous stories of faith, and seek to live according to its precepts. But the scriptures of the Restoration carry a spirit all their own, particularly the Book of Mormon. There is a light and an endowment of spiritual power that comes into our lives through searching modern revelation. It can come in no other way. Being loyal to the Restoration entails teaching from and giving preferential treatment to the things that have been delivered to Joseph Smith and his successors.

An acceptance of Joseph Smith's work transcends what is currently known or available in the world of scholarship and thus enters the world of faith. If we cannot for the present time understand how he translated Reformed Egyptian from golden plates, we must still receive his work in all patience and faith. If we cannot reconcile the text of the Book of Abraham with what scholars translate from the facsimiles or the few papyrus fragments in our possession, we must still receive his work in all patience and faith. If we find that the Prophet's Bible translation does not fit with Hebrew or Greek manuscripts, we must still receive his work with all patience and faith. "Search diligently," the Lord implored in a modern revelation, "pray always, and *be believing,* and all things shall work together for your good, if ye walk uprightly and remember the covenant wherewith ye have covenanted one with another" (D&C 90:24; emphasis added). The Lord does not ask that we suspend mental activity, that we compromise our integrity, or that we rely upon cunningly devised fables. What he does ask is that we be willing to exercise faith, to believe in the reality of the unseen, and to trust in things beyond the works of our own hands or the wisdom of our own discoveries. If we are true and faithful to what we believe and know in our hearts, the Lord will yet open our minds and bring forth great discoveries in the land. If, on the other hand, we let what we have discovered by study alone drive our faith and commitment, we close ourselves off from a vital realm of reality and block the hand of God. Our study must always be tempered by faith if we desire to be loyal to the work of Joseph Smith.

Loyalty in How We Tell Our Story

Jesus of Nazareth was rejected by some for eating and drinking with publicans and sinners; surely, many thought, no true Messiah would lower himself to affiliate with the scourges of society. Joseph Smith was condemned for wrestling and joking and playing ball; certainly, some insisted, prophets ought to be made of more austere stuff!

Lorenzo Snow said: "I can fellowship the President of the Church, if he does not know everything I know. . . . I saw the . . . imperfections in [Joseph Smith]. . . . I thanked God that he would put upon a man who had those imperfections the power and authority he placed upon him . . . for I knew that I myself had weakness[es], and I thought there was a chance for me."[5]

Unfortunately, not all Latter-day Saints have been as sensitive or considerate of Joseph Smith and his successors as was Elder Snow. It has become somewhat fashionable, in fact, to emphasize the humanness and weaknesses of those called to lead the Church, to cast aspersions on their motives or character, and to reveal their personal and intricate details, the context and true meanings of which are often lacking.

President Gordon B. Hinckley noted that "we have critics who appear to cull out of a vast panorama of information those items which demean and belittle some men and women of the past who worked so hard in laying the foundation of this great cause. They find readers of their works who seem to delight in picking up these tidbits, in chewing them over and relishing them. . . . My plea is that as we continue our search for truth . . . we look for strength and goodness rather than weakness and foibles in those who did so great a work in their time.

"We recognize that our forebears were human. They doubtless made mistakes. . . . There was only one perfect man who ever walked the earth. The Lord has used imperfect people in the process of building his perfect society. If some of them occasionally stumbled, or if their characters may have been slightly flawed in one way or another, the wonder is the greater that they accomplished so much."[6]

Prophets are called and approved of God—what further and greater recommendation do we need? We ought to be grateful that God can utilize imperfect beings and that these men—molded into vessels of holiness over time—can prove such a benefit to their fellow imperfect humans. Joseph Smith, Brigham Young, Lorenzo Snow, Joseph F. Smith, or others of our leaders cannot be with us now to answer all the charges against them. But be it remembered again that God called them and God has evidenced his approbation of their labors.

We simply do not have the whole story yet. Joseph and Brigham and John and Wilford are not here to fill in the gaps in our knowledge, nor are the rank-and-file members of the Church from bygone days available for oral interviews and clarifications. We must do all that we can in the present to reconstruct the past, to write the story of the Latter-day Saints and prepare that sacred history, that saga of a message, which will yet touch the hearts and build the faith of many. But we must be patient in writing it, avoiding the temptation to attribute improper motivation or to jump prematurely to conclusions, seeking earnestly to give the leaders of the Church the benefit of the doubt. The Lord, in time, will vindicate the words and works of his anointed servants; of this I have no doubt.

In the meantime we must receive their words, as the revelation declares, "in all patience and faith" (D&C 21:5). Elder Neal A. Maxwell stated: "The finished mosaic of the history of the Restoration will be larger and more varied as more pieces of tile emerge, adjusting a sequence here or enlarging there a sector of our understanding. There may even be a few pieces of the tile which, for the moment, do not seem to fit. We can wait, as we must. . . . The final mosaic of the Restoration will be resplendent, reflecting divine design. . . . At the perfect day, we will see that we have been a part of things too wonderful for us. Part of the marvel and the wonder of God's 'marvelous work and a wonder' will be how perfect Divinity mercifully used us—imperfect humanity. Meanwhile, amid the human dissonance, those with ears to hear will follow the beckoning sounds of a certain trumpet."[7]

LOYALTY TO HIS SUCCESSORS

The grief associated with the death of the Prophet and the Patriarch in June 1844 must have been almost unbearable. To know that one of such vision and spiritual magnitude as Joseph Smith had been taken from among them must have been a source of great agony for the stunned Saints. Elder Bruce R. McConkie stated: "We do not have language or capacity or ability to extol the greatness and the glory of the ministry and mission of the Prophet Joseph Smith. And yet when he was taken the Lord had Brigham Young. Brigham Young stepped forth and wore the mantle of leadership. With all respect and admiration and every accolade of praise resting upon the Prophet Joseph, still Brigham Young came forward and did things that then had to be done in a better way than the Prophet Joseph himself could have done them."[8]

I believe Joseph Smith would shout "Amen" to that observation of Elder McConkie. We all know that Joseph Smith was vital to this work because he, as the dispensation head, was the preeminent revealer of God and Christ to the world and the legal administrator through which priesthoods and keys and authorities were restored once again to earth. But each prophet-leader has a role to play, and God puts his hand upon the man who holds the fulness of the keys of the priesthood. For us, what is and what is to be is just as significant as what went before.

Because God had raised up Brigham Young to succeed the Prophet Joseph, the Saints in Nauvoo—at least those who enjoyed the spirit of revelation and were in tune with that divine influence that guides this work—were pleased to be able to sustain another whose personality, administrative abilities, and even approach to teaching the gospel were somewhat different than his predecessor. In temporal matters Joseph was not to have strength (see D&C 24:9), but in temporal matters Brigham had great strength. Brigham was not Joseph, but the spirit of Joseph was with Brigham. And so it was with John Taylor and Wilford Woodruff and Lorenzo Snow and Joseph F. Smith and Heber J. Grant and George Albert Smith. And so it is in our own time with David O. McKay and Joseph Fielding Smith and Harold B. Lee and Spencer W. Kimball and Ezra Taft Benson and Howard W. Hunter. They have worn the mantle of Joseph Smith, the mantle of authority needed to guide the Lord's Church and kingdom in these last days. They worshiped and were led by the same Lord God of Joseph Smith.

As members of the Church at the close of the twentieth century and the beginning of a new millennium, we can be loyal to Joseph Smith only to the degree that we are loyal to the leaders of the Church in our own day. As I have become aware of many movements in our day, I have asked myself, "What would Joseph think?" I believe he would be delighted in:

1. The progress of The Church of Jesus Christ of Latter-day Saints.
2. The fact that the message of salvation is spreading to all lands.
3. The refinements and improvements of the past 150 years.
4. The fact that Latter-day Saints are making a difference in the world in the academic community, in business and industry, and in the arts.

I also sense that he would be troubled, perhaps even incensed, by certain recent trends such as

efforts to downplay or deny outright the historicity of the Book of Mormon or the book of Abraham;

a failure to take seriously his inspired translation of the Bible or the Lectures on Faith;

efforts to utilize his name, teachings, and ministry to legitimize the aberrant and the unauthorized;

the arrogance of some who suppose they know better how to lead the Church than those who now bear the keys of the kingdom which were originally restored to him.

I think he would grieve over the unnecessary worry, heartache, and burden imposed on today's apostles and prophets by those who seek to run before their file leaders; by those who claim allegiance to Brother Joseph and then walk contrary to the law and order of the Church and kingdom; by self-proclaimed experts, Mormon gnostics, who lay claim to some secret and sacred knowledge available only to those initiated into the mysteries.

The spirit of Brother Joseph is with the leaders of this Church. Of this I have no question. President Joseph F. Smith testified:

"I feel quite confident that *the eyes of Joseph the Prophet, and of the martyrs of this dispensation, and of Brigham and John and Wilford, and those faithful men who were associated with them in their ministry upon the earth, are carefully guarding the interests of the Kingdom of God in which they labored and for which they strove during their mortal lives. I believe they are as deeply interested in our welfare today, if not with greater capacity with far more interest, behind the veil, than they were in the flesh.* I believe they know more; I believe their minds have expanded beyond their comprehension in mortal life, and their interests are enlarged in the work of the Lord to which they gave their lives and their best service. . . . I have a feeling in my heart that I stand in the presence not only of the

Father and of the Son, but in the presence of those whom God commissioned, raised up, and inspired, to lay the foundations of the work in which we are engaged."[9]

If the leadership of the Church does not feel the need to stress a given point that seems to be an obsession with some, then we would be wise to ask ourselves why such things are not being spoken of by our leaders. Are they unaware? Are they aware but unwilling to reveal these things to us? Though as a people we have miles to go before we rest and much spiritual development ahead of us, I bear witness that the Church is in excellent hands, is in the line of its duty, and is preparing a people for the second coming of the Son of Man. What is spoken by the General Authorities of the Church is what we need to hear, what the Lord would have his Saints know; those messages should become, as President Harold B. Lee once said, "the guide to [our] walk and talk."[10] If the Lord desires to warn his people, to provide appropriate interpretation of difficult prophetic passages, then that warning will surely come, but it will come through the channels he has established.

In March of 1844 the Prophet Joseph Smith gave an unusual assignment to a group of Church leaders: they were asked to amend the Constitution of the United States, so as to make it "the voice of Jehovah."[11] Later in the week, Elder John Taylor, as a representative of a special committee of three, responded that no progress had been made toward the preparation of a constitution for the kingdom of God. The Prophet acknowledged their failure, indicating that he knew "they could not draft a constitution worthy of guiding the kingdom of God."[12] The Prophet himself had gone before the Lord, seeking that such a constitution be made known by revelation. The answer came: "Ye are my constitution and I am your God and ye are my spokesmen, therefore from henceforth keep my commandments."[13] In a revelation given to President John Taylor on 27 June 1882, the Savior said: "Verily, thus saith the Lord, I have instituted my Kingdom and my laws, with the keys and power thereof, and have appointed you as a spokesman and my Constitution, with President John Taylor at your head, whom I have appointed to my Church and my Kingdom as Prophet, Seer and Revelator." Later in the same revelation the Lord affirmed: "*Ye are my constitution, and I am your God.*"[14] In short, this Church is to be governed by revelation—current, daily, modern revelation—and not by written documents alone. All of God's purposes for his children cannot be codified. Nothing is more fixed, set, and established than the fact that among the people of God the canon of scripture is open, flexible, and expanding.

As a sign of our loyalty to Joseph Smith, we need to look to the presidency of the Church, heed the counsel of those called and appointed to direct its destiny, and follow the Brethren as they point the way to eternal life. Though there will be individual casualties from the faith as we move toward the end, we need not be anxious about the future of the Church and kingdom of God. We need not be anxious about the leadership of the Church; we need only cultivate the little plot of ground assigned to us and leave the government of the kingdom to the King. The Lord does not ask us to magnify other people's callings.

CONCLUSION

So much of what I know to be true I know because of what God revealed through Joseph Smith. I know that there is a God—that he is our Father in Heaven, the Father of our spirits, that he has a body of flesh and bones, that he is an exalted Man of Holiness—because of Joseph Smith. I know that there is purpose in life— a plan, a divine timetable, a carefully constructed program for the edification and exaltation of all—because of Joseph Smith. I know that we are eternal beings—that we lived in a premortal existence for endless ages of time, that this life is the time for men to prepare to meet God, and that we shall live forever and ever after mortal death—because of what has been made known through Joseph Smith. I know that Jesus is the Christ—the Savior and Redeemer, the Lord God Omnipotent, the God of the ancients, and that his atonement is infinite and eternal—because of Joseph Smith. I know that the consummate power of God—including the keys of the kingdom of God, the power to seal men and women unto eternal life—is on the earth because of the ministry of Joseph Smith. I know that my wife and I can truly become eternal companions, that my children have indeed been born in the covenant, and that the sweetest joys in time and eternity can be maintained and multiplied—because of what God has revealed in this final dispensation through the Choice Seer, Joseph Smith.

Is it any wonder, then, that we feel to sing praise to the man who communed with Jehovah? Truly, Jesus anointed that Prophet and Seer. In 1837 Wilford Woodruff, one who knew Joseph the Prophet intimately, said:

"There is not so great a man as Joseph Smith standing in this generation. The gentiles look upon him as he is like a bed of gold concealed from human view. They know not his principles, his spirit, his wisdom, his virtues, his philanthropy, nor his calling. His mind, like Enoch's, expands as eternity, and only God can comprehend his soul."[15]

I pray most sincerely that we will be loyal and true to the memory and ministry of so great a one who has walked among us, and that one day, having demonstrated that loyalty through faithful living, we shall have association with him and the Gods of whom he stands as a preeminent witness.

Notes

From a fireside address in Chicago, Illinois, summer 1993.

1. Brigham Young, in *Journal of Discourses,* 4:54.
2. Ibid., 5:332.
3. Ibid., 8:206.
4. *Teachings of the Prophet Joseph Smith,* 366; emphasis added.
5. Lorenzo Snow, as cited by Neal A. Maxwell in Conference Report, October 1984, 10.
6. Gordon B. Hinckley, "The Continuous Pursuit of Truth," *Ensign,* April 1986, 5.
7. Neal A. Maxwell, in Conference Report, October 1984, 11–12.
8. Bruce R. McConkie, "Succession in the Presidency," *1974 BYU Speeches of the Year* (Provo: Brigham Young University Press, 1974), 24.
9. Joseph F. Smith, "In the Presence of the Divine," in *Messages of the First Presidency,* 5:6; emphasis added.
10. Harold B. Lee, in Conference Report, April 1946, 68.
11. Joseph Smith Diary, 10 March 1844, LDS Church Archives, Salt Lake City, Utah, as quoted in Andrew F. Ehat, "'It Seems Like Heaven Began on Earth': Joseph Smith and the Constitution of the Kingdom of God," in *Brigham Young University Studies* 20, no. 3 (Spring 1980): 259.
12. Minutes of the Council of Fifty, 8 April 1881, as quoted in Ehat, "It Seems Like Heaven Began on Earth," 259.
13. Joseph F. Smith, Minutes of the Council of Fifty, 21 April 1880, as quoted in Ehat, "It Seems Like Heaven Began on Earth," 259.
14. Fred C. Collier, *Unpublished Revelations of the Prophets and Presidents of The Church of Jesus Christ of Latter-day Saints* (Salt Lake City: Collier's Publishing Co., 1979), 132, 134; emphasis added.
15. Journal History, entry for 9 April 1837.

THE ETERNAL GOSPEL

The scriptures of the restoration and latter-day prophets affirm that God our Father has a plan for his children, a program established to maximize our growth and ensure our happiness. And yet that fact alone—that there is some divine plan to life—is not as obvious from the Bible as from latter-day scripture. Knowing what we know, we are able to recognize divine design, but seldom can we turn to a specific Old or New Testament passage that speaks with clarity of a plan. How very different is the Book of Mormon! The Nephite prophets speak with grateful hearts for the merciful plan of the great Creator (2 Nephi 9:6), the plan of our God (2 Nephi 9:13), the great plan of mercy (Alma 42:15, 31), the plan of redemption (Jacob 6:8; Alma 12:25–26, 30, 32; 17:16; 18:39; 22:13–14; 29:2; 34:31; 39:18; 42:11, 13), the eternal plan of deliverance (2 Nephi 11:5), the plan of salvation (Jarom 1:2; Alma 24:14; 42:5), and the great plan of happiness (Alma 42:8, 16). We know that the plan of salvation is "always and everlastingly the same; that obedience to the same laws always brings the same reward; that the gospel laws have not changed . . . ; and that always and everlastingly all things pertaining to salvation center in Christ."[1]

AN ETERNAL ATONEMENT

Jesus is truly the "Lamb slain from the foundation of the world" (Revelation 13:8; Moses 7:47). That is, the atoning sacrifice is not only timely (for those of us who regularly need its cleansing powers) but *timeless.* Though the act of atonement would not take place until Jesus suffered in Gethsemane and on Golgotha in the meridian of time, earth's earliest inhabitants were taught to call upon God in the name of his Beloved Son for deliverance (Moses 5:5–8). Again, this central truth is not to be had in Christendom. Indeed, one of the fascinating attacks on the Book of Mormon is that it is too Christ-centered! That is, critics contend, the Book of Mormon has too much Christ within it, long before there was a Christ.

The Latter-day Saints know that God has revealed himself, his plan, and the Mediator of his sacred covenant to men and women from the beginning. The voice of the Father came to Adam: "If thou wilt turn unto me, and hearken unto my voice, and believe, and repent of all thy transgressions, and be baptized, even in water, in the name of mine Only Begotten Son . . . , which is Jesus Christ, the only name which shall be given under heaven, whereby salvation shall come unto the children of men, ye shall receive the gift of the Holy Ghost" (Moses 6:52). Further, Adam was commanded to teach his children that all men and women, because of the effects of the Fall, "must be born again into the kingdom of heaven, of water, and of the Spirit, and be cleansed by blood, even the blood of mine Only Begotten; that ye might be sanctified from all sin, and enjoy the words of eternal life in this world, and eternal life in the world to come, even immortal glory" (Moses 6:59).

The Prophet Joseph Smith observed that "we cannot believe that the ancients in all ages were so ignorant of the system of heaven as many suppose, since all that were ever saved, were saved through the power of this great plan of redemption, as much before the coming of Christ as since; if not, God has had different plans in operation (if we may so express it), to bring men back to dwell with Himself; and this we cannot believe, since there has been no change in the constitution of man since he fell."[2] And so it is that we learn through the scriptures of the Restoration that, in addition to Adam, such prophetic personalities from the Bible as Enoch (Moses 7), Noah (Moses 8), Abraham (JST, Genesis 15:9–12), and Moses (Moses 1) had revealed unto them the particulars of the Father's plan and knew and taught of the coming redemption in Jesus Christ. Truly, as the Apostle Peter proclaimed, "To [Christ] give all the prophets witness" (Acts 10:43).

It was no different in the Western Hemisphere. With Lehi and his family came the fulness of the gospel, including the holy priesthood, the knowledge of salvation, and the intercessory role of Jesus the Christ. Very early in the Book of Mormon account, Nephi stated that "six hundred years from the time my father left Jerusalem, a prophet would the Lord God raise up among the Jews—even a Messiah, or, in other words, a Savior of the world" (1 Nephi 10:4). Nephi saw in vision that Jesus would be "lifted up upon the cross and slain for the sins of the world" (1 Nephi 11:33). Almost six hundred years before the birth of Jesus in Bethlehem, Lehi taught his son Jacob that "redemption cometh in and through the Holy Messiah; for he is full of grace and truth." Further, he explained, "there is no flesh that can dwell in the presence of God, save it be through the merits, and mercy, and grace of the Holy

Messiah, who layeth down his life according to the flesh, and taketh it again by the power of the Spirit, that he may bring to pass the resurrection of the dead, being the first that should rise" (2 Nephi 2:6, 8). Alma taught an erring son that because the souls of men and women who live before the meridian of time are just as precious in the sight of God as those who live during or after that age, it is necessary that redemption in Christ should be made available to people of all ages (Alma 39:17–19). Indeed, "none of the prophets have written, or prophesied, save they have spoken concerning this Christ" (Jacob 7:11; compare 4:4; Mosiah 13:33).

ETERNAL COVENANTS AND ORDINANCES

Because we know that the great plan of happiness is eternal and that salvation in any age is accomplished only in and through the mediation of the Redeemer, we also know that the covenants and ordinances are likewise eternal and unchanging. "Now taking it for granted that the scriptures say what they mean, and mean what they say," the Prophet Joseph noted, "we have sufficient grounds to go on and prove from the Bible that the gospel has always been the same; the ordinances to fulfill its requirements, the same, and the officers to officiate, the same; and the signs and fruits resulting from the promises, the same." He continues with an illustration of this principle: "Therefore, as Noah was a preacher of righteousness he must have been baptized and ordained to the priesthood by the laying on of the hands."[3] In short, the Lord "set the ordinances to be the same forever and ever."[4] That is, "ordinances instituted in the heavens before the foundation of the world, in the priesthood, for the salvation of men, are not to be altered or changed. All must be saved on the same principles."[5]

It is in this light that we speak of the restored gospel as comprising the new and everlasting covenant. Modern revelations affirm: "Wherefore, I say unto you that I have sent unto you mine everlasting covenant, even that which was from the beginning" (D&C 49:9). "Verily I say unto you, blessed are you for receiving mine everlasting covenant, even the fulness of my gospel, sent forth unto the children of men, that they might have life and be made partakers of the glories which are to be revealed in the last days, as it was written by the prophets and apostles in days of old" (D&C 66:2; see also 1:22; 39:11; 45:9; 49:9; 133:57). In the words of President Joseph Fielding Smith, *"The new and everlasting covenant is the sum total of all gospel covenants and obligations."*[6] The gospel covenant is *new* in the sense that it is revealed anew following a period of apostasy. It is *everlasting* in the sense that it was had from the beginning.

In that spirit, and knowing what we do about the everlasting nature of the gospel, the Church and kingdom, and the principles and ordinances pertaining thereto, we know that many of the ancients had the gospel. Many of them knew the Lord, taught his doctrine, and officiated as legal administrators in his earthly kingdom. Isaac, Israel, Joseph, and all the patriarchs enjoyed personal revelation and communion with their Maker. We would suppose that Eve and Sarah and Rebekah were baptized; that Jacob received the temple endowment; that Micah and Malachi stood in the prophetic office by divine call and not because they assumed that role on their own. Surely Nephi, son of Lehi, was baptized by water and received the gift of the Holy Ghost, as well as the high priesthood, although an account of the same is not stated directly in the Nephite record. That the blessings of the holy temple were available to the ancient Saints is made clear in the Prophet's translation of the Egyptian papyri. We are told that one particular figure represents "the grand Key-words of the Holy Priesthood, as revealed to Adam, in the Garden of Eden, as also to Seth, Noah, Melchizedek, Abraham, and all to whom the Priesthood was revealed" (explanation of Figure 3 in Facsimile no. 2). Because of what has been made known through Joseph Smith—principles of doctrine and priesthood government—we know what it takes to operate the kingdom of God and what things the people of God must do to comply.

OUR FATHER LOVES ALL HIS CHILDREN

Several years ago on a Sabbath day I sat with an associate in his beautiful cathedral and listened as the priest spoke of the body and blood of Jesus. Out of the corner of my eye I noticed tears making their way down the cheeks of my friend. My mind ambled back over the years of our association, and memory impressed upon me the reality of my friend's commitment to his faith, his goodness as a human being, and his genuine, heartfelt desire to be true to what he understood. There came over me the quiet but compelling realization that the Almighty loved this man as much as he loved me; that he was a child of heavenly parents just as I was; and that the Lord would do all that was possible to maximize this man's opportunities and ensure his ultimate happiness.

That was an important moment in my life. I grew up with a testimony. It has not been difficult for me to believe. Though I was reared in a part of the country where there were few members of the Church around me, I somehow sensed deep in my bones that what we are about in The Church of Jesus Christ of Latter-day Saints is true, is right, and is meant for the blessing of the entire world. On that particular occasion, however, as we sat reverently in a place that was somewhat foreign to my spiritual upbringing, there sprouted within me an inner awareness that God loves all men and women of all ages and is no respecter of persons. Oh, I knew then as I know now that this is the only true and living church and that the Latter-day Saints are the custodians of the fulness of the gospel and the holy priesthood. There was and is no question whatsoever about that. But I seemed to perceive then—and as I grow older I perceive even more clearly—the goodness and mercy and infinite patience of our Heavenly Father toward all his sons and daughters. As Enoch observed: "Thou art there, and thy bosom is there; and also thou art just; thou art merciful and kind forever" (Moses 7:30).

I had a somewhat similar experience not long after that visit to my friend's church. I picked up a copy of *Reader's Digest,* only to discover an insert on how to communicate more effectively with family members. It was prepared by The Church of Jesus Christ of Latter-day Saints. I was aware that the Church had begun placing these brief advertisements in the *Digest* but had never taken the time to do more than peruse them. I read this particular one through. It was nice, had some good pointers on communication, and seemed to be the kind of thing that would leave a positive impression with most readers. My next thought was rather judgmental: "This is quaint, but it really isn't going to bring many people into the Church. Why waste the Church's money on such stuff?"

Then there came a very simple but effective chastisement to my narrow mind. It occurred to me that there just might be someone somewhere who would be prompted, after reading the insert, to inquire after the Church and its teachings. More important, maybe someone would be helped by the piece. Maybe some father or mother, some son or daughter, would take counsel and take heart from what was written. Oh, they may not join the Church, but what if the insert actually helped their family, resulted in greater harmony, moved their home a little closer to heaven? Wouldn't that make it all worth it? I sensed a broadening of my views through that experience and again, an awareness that the God and Father of us all will give unto us line upon line, precept upon precept, according to our ability and willingness to receive.

"ALL THAT HE SEETH FIT THAT THEY SHOULD HAVE"

One only has to wrestle personally with a wandering child or loved one, or feel the pain of someone else who does, to realize that we do not cease to love the straying or the ignorant. And surely he who is the embodiment of love and mercy does not cease to love those of his children who do not enjoy the fulness of gospel bless-ings in their lives. Our Father in heaven surely will do all that is appropriate dur-ing our mortal probation to inspire, lift, edify, and encourage individuals, families, communities, and nations. It was to Nephi that the Lord Jehovah spoke on this mat-ter: "Know ye not that there are more nations than one? Know ye not that I, the Lord your God, have created all men, and that I remember those who are upon the isles of the sea; and that I rule in the heavens above and in the earth beneath; and that *I bring forth my word unto the children of men, yea, even upon all the nations of the earth?* . . . For behold, I shall speak unto the Jews and they shall write it; and I shall also speak unto the Nephites and they shall write it; and I shall also speak unto the other tribes of the house of Israel, which I have led away, and they shall write it; and *I shall also speak unto all nations of the earth and they shall write it*" (2 Nephi 29:7, 12; emphasis added).

Alma explained that "the Lord doth grant unto all nations, of their own nation and tongue, to teach his word, yea, in wisdom, all that he seeth fit they should have" (Alma 29:8). One body of people may be prepared for the fulness of light and knowledge; another body will be prepared only for a glimmer of that ray of truth. God suits his blessings according to the present readiness of the children of men. Elder B. H. Roberts offered the following counsel on this principle: "While the Church of Jesus Christ of Latter-day Saints is established for the instruction of men; and is one of God's instrumentalities for the making known the truth, yet he is not limited to that institution for such purposes, neither in time nor place. God raises up wise men . . . of their own tongue and nationality, speaking to them through means that they can comprehend; not always giving a fulness of truth such as may be found in the fulness of the gospel of Jesus Christ; but always giving that meas-ure of truth that the people are prepared to receive. Mormonism holds, then, that all the great teachers are servants of God, among all nations and in all ages. They are inspired men, appointed to instruct God's children according to the conditions in the midst of which he finds them. . . . Wherever God finds a soul sufficiently enlightened and pure, one with whom his Spirit can communicate, lo! he makes of him a teacher of men. While the path of sensuality and darkness may be that which most men tread, a few . . . have been led along the upward path; a few in all coun-tries and generations have been wisdom seekers, or seekers of God. They have been so because the Divine Word of Wisdom has looked upon them, choosing them for the knowledge and service of himself."[7]

It is but reasonable, therefore, that elements of truth, pieces of a much larger mosaic, should be found throughout the world in varying cultures and among diverse religious groups. Further, as the world has passed through phases of apostasy and restoration, relics of revealed doctrine remain, albeit in some cases in altered or even convoluted forms. Persons lacking spiritual insight and the faith that derives from a knowledge of Christ's eternal plan of salvation may tend to cast doubt on the true gospel; may point to legends and traditions of creation epics or flood stories that presumably predate the Pentateuch; may eagerly note similarities between ordinances of the temple and practices in pagan cultures; and may thereby suggest that Christianity has but copied from the more ancient sources.

President Joseph F. Smith had much to say to those who seek to upstage Christianity. Jesus Christ, he taught, "being the fountain of truth, is no imitator. He taught the truth first; it was his before it was given to man." Further, "When I read books that are scattered . . . through the world, throwing discredit upon words and teachings and doctrines of the Lord Jesus Christ, saying that some of the ideas Jesus uttered, truths that he promulgated, have been enunciated before by the ancient philosophers among the heathen nations of the world, I want to tell you that there is not a heathen philosopher that ever lived in all the world from the beginning, that had a truth or enunciated a principle of God's truth that did not receive it from the fountain head, from God himself. . . .

"Let it be remembered that Christ was with the Father from the beginning, that the gospel of truth and light existed from the beginning, and is from everlasting to everlasting. The Father, Son, and Holy Ghost, as one God, are the fountain of truth. . . . If we find truth in broken fragments through the ages, it may be set down as an incontrovertible fact that it originated at the fountain, and was given to philosophers, inventors, patriots, reformers, and prophets by the inspiration of God. It came from him through his Son Jesus Christ and the Holy Ghost, in the first place, and from no other source. It is eternal.

" . . . Men are mere repeaters of what he has taught them. He has voiced no thought originating with man. The teachings of Jesus did not begin with his incarnation; for, like truth, he is eternal. He not only inspired the ancients, from the beginning, but when he came to earth he reiterated eternal, original truth, and added gloriously to the revelations men had uttered. When he returned to the Father, he still took, and does take, an interest in his children and people, by revealing to them new truths, and by inspiring their actions; and, as men grow in the knowledge of God, they shall become more and more like him unto the perfect day, when his knowledge shall cover the earth as the waters cover the deep."[8]

REMNANTS OF THE FAITH

Knowing what we know concerning God our Father—that he is a personal being; that he has a body of flesh and bones as tangible as our own; that he is an exalted and gloried being; that he was once a man and dwelt on an earth; and knowing that this knowledge was had by many of the ancients—should we be surprised to find legends and myths concerning gods who have divine power but human attributes and passions? Knowing that Adam and Seth and Enos and Cainan and Mahalaleel and others of the antedeluvians spoke of the coming of the Messiah, and that the Messiah would come to earth as a man but be possessed of the powers of a God, is it not likely that they also knew that he would be born of a virgin? Should we be surprised to find pagan traditions of virgin births and divine humans?

Adam heard the divine voice saying: "I am God; I made the world, and *men before they were in the flesh*" (Moses 6:51). That is, men and women in the earliest ages knew of a first estate, a premortal existence. Therefore, is it any wonder that several religious traditions are wedded to an idea of past lives? Inasmuch as the doctrines of rebirth, regeneration, resurrection, and the immortality of the soul were taught to Adam and his posterity, why should we flinch when we discover the misshapen doctrines of reincarnation, transmigration of souls, and rebirth in such traditions as Hinduism, Jainism, and Sikhism, or when we encounter a people like the ancient Egyptians who are obsessed not with death (as some suppose), but with life after death?

Of particular interest to Latter-day Saints is the resemblance between what goes on in our own temples and things that transpire in non-LDS sacred structures. In many cases those resemblances may originate with earnest truth seekers who act without authority, even as did Pharaoh, great-grandson of Noah. Pharaoh, "being a righteous man, established his kingdom and judged his people wisely and justly all his days, seeking earnestly to imitate that order established by the fathers in the first generations, in the days of the first patriarchal reign, even in the reign of Adam, and also of Noah, his father" (Abraham 1:26–27).

Hugh Nibley has long studied such parallels. He wrote: "Latter-day Saints believe that their temple ordinances are as old as the human race and represent a primordial revealed religion that has passed through alternate phases of apostasy and restoration which have left the world littered with the scattered fragments of the original structure, some more and some less recognizable, but all badly damaged and out of proper context. . . .

" . . . There are countless parallels, many of them very instructive, among the customs and religions of mankind, to what the Mormons do. But there is a world of difference between Ginzberg's *Legends of the Jews* and the book of Isaiah, or between the Infancy Gospels and the real Gospels, no matter how many points of contact one may detect between them. The LDS endowment was not built up of elements brought together by chance, custom, or long research; it is a single, perfectly consistent organic whole, conveying its message without the aid of rationalizing, spiritualizing, allegorizing, or moralizing interpretations.

"But what about the Egyptian rites? What are they to us? They are a parody, an imitation, but as such not to be despised. For all the great age and consistency of their rites and teachings, which certainly command respect, the Egyptians did not have the real thing, and they knew it. . . .

"The Mormon endowment . . . is frankly a model, a presentation in figurative terms. As such it is flexible and adjustable; for example, it may be presented in more languages than one and in more than one medium of communication. But since it does not attempt to be a picture of reality, but only a model or analog to show how things work, setting forth the pattern of man's life on earth with its fundamental whys and wherefores, it does not need to be changed or adapted greatly through the years; it is a remarkably stable model, which makes its comparison with other forms and traditions, including the more ancient ones, quite valid and instructive."[9]

And what is true of sacred practices and beliefs throughout the ancient non-Christian world is also true in today's modern Christian world. We know there was a great apostasy following the deaths of the meridian Apostles and that plain and precious truths and priesthood authority were lost. We know that God began the restoration of truths and powers through Joseph Smith and will continue to do so into and through the Millennium. But because Protestants or Catholics do not possess the authority to act in the name of God does not mean they have no truth or that any scriptural interpretation from them is automatically incorrect or corrupt. As noted earlier, elements of enlightenment, remnants of truth, and aspects of the faith of the Saints of ancient dispensations may be found in modern Christianity. The Lord loves his children, all of them, and he delights to "honor those who serve [him] in righteousness and in truth unto the end" (D&C 76:5).

CONCLUSION

There are good people in the world, men and women who love God, who are earnestly striving to be true to the standards of decency and integrity they have been taught. Indeed, everyone has access to some measure of light and truth from the Almighty. President Brigham Young thus declared that there has never been "a man or woman upon the face of the earth, from the days of Adam to this day, who has not been enlightened, instructed, and taught by the revelations of Jesus Christ."[10] The prophets teach that if people will be true to the light within them—the light of Christ—they will be led to the higher light of the Holy Ghost found in the covenant gospel, presumably either in this life or in the life to come. "And the Spirit giveth light to every man that cometh into the world; and the Spirit enlighteneth every man through the world, that hearkeneth to the voice of the Spirit" (D&C 84:46).[11]

In fact, is it not possible that one reason so many parallels and resemblances exist between the fulness of the gospel and the various approximations of the full truth is because men and women are responding to those "spirit memories" of the past, those things we once knew but now seem just out of conscious awareness? "All those salient truths," President Joseph F. Smith observed, "which come home so forcibly to the head and heart seem but the awakening of the memories of the spirit. Can we know anything here that we did not know before we came?"[12] Is this not why so many who join the Church recognize in the teachings of the missionaries things that they feel they have always known, things, interestingly enough, that are not necessarily to be found in their former religious profession? We generally refer to those who come into the Church as *converts,* implying that they turned from another belief to embrace the testimony of the Restoration. While that happens, in most instances those who are baptized tell us, essentially, "Everything the missionaries told me I already believed!" In fact, that which we call a conversion is very often the *awakening* of a distant memory, an echo from the past. "People ask me why I left my old church," the convert says. "I tell them it was not a matter of leaving my old church so much as it was a matter of coming home."

And so, in summary: Christ's gospel is eternal. It was delivered to earth's inhabitants in the beginning. It has been preached through the ages by Christian prophets who knew their Lord and sought to be true to divine covenants and ordinances. In The Church of Jesus Christ of Latter-day Saints we attend to sacred matters, matters that are ancient and eternal, matters that were discussed and foreordained from before the foundations of the world, matters that will prepare this earth to abide the coming of the King of kings. What the Latter-day Saints believe is what the former-day Saints believed. The covenants we make and the ordinances we perform thereby link us to the past and point us to a glorious future. God loves all men and women and is eager to enlighten them in whatever ways he can. We rejoice in our Father and God, and we rejoice in the knowledge that we are all part of the royal family. Like Nephi of old, we glory in our Jesus, for he has redeemed our souls from hell (see 2 Nephi 33:6).

In 1978 the First Presidency of the Church stated clearly and powerfully the position of the Latter-day Saints in the larger religious world: "Based upon ancient and modern revelation, The Church of Jesus Christ of Latter-day Saints gladly teaches and declares the Christian doctrine that all men and women are brothers and sisters, not only by blood relationship from common mortal progenitors, but also as literal spirit children of an Eternal Father.

"The great religious leaders of the world such as Mohammed, Confucius, and the Reformers, as well as philosophers including Socrates, Plato, and others, received a portion of God's light. Moral truths were given to them by God to enlighten whole nations and to bring a higher level of understanding to individuals.

"The Hebrew prophets prepared the way for the coming of Jesus Christ, the promised Messiah, who should provide salvation for all mankind who believe in the gospel.

"Consistent with these truths, we believe that God has given and will give to all peoples sufficient knowledge to help them on their way to eternal salvation, either in this life or in the life to come.

"We also declare that the gospel of Jesus Christ, restored to his Church in our day, provides the only way to a mortal life of happiness and a fulness of joy forever. For those who have not received this gospel, the opportunity will come to them in the life hereafter if not in this life.

"Our message therefore is one of special love and concern for the eternal welfare of all men and women, regardless of religious belief, race, or nationality, knowing that we are truly brothers and sisters because we are the sons and daughters of the same Eternal Father."[13]

Notes

From "The Eternal Gospel," *Ensign*, July 1996, 48–56.

1. *Promised Messiah*, 4–5.
2. *Teachings of the Prophet Joseph Smith*, 59–60.
3. Ibid., 264.
4. Ibid., 168.
5. Ibid., 308.
6. *Doctrines of Salvation*, 1:156; emphasis in original.
7. B. H. Roberts, *Defense of the Faith and the Saints*, 2 vols. (Salt Lake City: Deseret News Press, 1907), 1:512–13.
8. *Gospel Doctrine*, 30, 395, 398–400; see also *Journal of Discourses*, 15:325.
9. Hugh Nibley, *The Message of the Joseph Smith Papyri: An Egyptian Endowment* (Salt Lake City: Deseret Book Co., 1975), xii–xiii.

10. Brigham Young, in *Journal of Discourses,* 2:139.
11. See also D&C 84:47–48; *Gospel Doctrine,* 67–68; Bruce R. McConkie, *A New Witness for the Articles of Faith* (Salt Lake City: Deseret Book Co., 1985), 260–61.
12. *Gospel Doctrine,* 13.
13. Statement of the First Presidency, 15 February 1978.

THE MAN ADAM

F ew persons in all eternity have been more directly involved in the plan of salvation—the creation, fall and ultimate redemption of the children of God— than the man Adam. His ministry among the sons and daughters of earth stretches from the distant past of premortality to the distant future of resurrection, judgment, and beyond. As Michael, the archangel, he led the forces of God against the armies of Lucifer in the War in Heaven. Under the direction of Elohim and Jehovah, he assisted in the creation of the earth. After taking physical bodies, Adam and Eve brought mortality into being through partaking of the fruit of the tree of knowledge of good and evil; with the fall of our first parents came blood and posterity and pro- bation and death, as well as the need for redemption through a Savior, a "last Adam" (see 1 Corinthians 15:45). To Adam the gospel was first preached. Upon Adam the priesthood was first bestowed. From Adam and Eve the message of the gospel of salvation went forth to all the world. Following his death, which occurred almost a millennium after he entered mortality, Adam's watchcare over his poster- ity continued. Revelations have come and angels have ministered under his direc- tion. Priesthoods have been conferred and keys delivered at his behest.

BEFORE THE WORLD WAS

Adam's role in the eternal plan of God begins in our first estate. There he was known as Michael, literally one "who is like God." Indeed, "By his diligence and obedience there, as one of the spirit sons of God, he attained a stature and power second only to that of Christ, the Firstborn. None of all the billions of our Father's children equalled him in intelligence and might, save Jesus only."[1] He was "called and prepared from the foundation of the world according to the foreknowledge of God" (Alma 13:3) to perform his labors on earth. Michael stood with Jehovah in defense of the plan of the Father, the plan of salvation, this in opposition to the amendatory offering of Lucifer, a son of the morning. "The contention in heaven was," Joseph Smith explained, that "Jesus said there would be certain souls that would not be saved; and the devil said he could save them all, and laid his plans before the grand council, who gave their vote in favor of Jesus Christ. So the devil rose up in rebellion against God, and was cast down, with all who put up their heads for him."[2] Or, as the Revelator saw in vision, "There was war in heaven; Michael and his angels fought against the dragon; and the dragon and his angels fought against Michael; and the dragon prevailed not against Michael. . . . Neither was there place found in heaven for the great dragon, who was cast out; that old serpent called the devil, and also called Satan, which deceiveth the whole world; he was cast out into the earth; and his angels were cast out with him" (JST, Revelation 12:6–8).

Michael was directly involved in the preparation of the physical world in which he and his posterity would undergo a mortal probation. Elder Bruce R. McConkie has written: "Christ and Mary, Adam and Eve, Abraham and Sarah, and a host of mighty men and equally glorious women comprised that group of 'the noble and great ones,' to whom the Lord Jesus said: 'We will go down, for there is space there, and we will take of these materials, and we will make an earth whereon these may dwell' (Abraham 3:22–24; emphasis added). This we know: Christ, under the Father, is the Creator; Michael, his companion and associate, presided over much of the creative work; and with them, as Abraham saw, were many of the noble and great ones."[3] The Prophet Joseph Smith thus taught that "the Priesthood was first given to Adam; he obtained the First Presidency, and held the keys of it from generation to generation. *He obtained it in the Creation, before the world was formed, as in Genesis 1:26, 27, 28.*"[4]

IN EDEN

It is appropriate when it came time to initiate our second estate that God our Father should call upon Michael to tabernacle the flesh as earth's first inhabitant. In providing a genealogy of Jesus, the Gospel writer spoke of Cainan, who was "the son of Enos, which was the son of Seth, which was the son of Adam, which was the son of God" (Luke 3:38). In the Joseph Smith Translation of Genesis we read of the line of great patriarchs from Adam to Enoch. "And this is the genealogy of the sons of Adam, who was the son of God, with whom God himself conversed" (JST, Genesis 6:23; see also Moses 6:22). Adam—his very name means "man" or "mankind." Adam—his very title implies the first man of all men, which are many (Moses 1:34).

In the morn of creation, Adam, Eve, and all forms of life existed in a paradisiacal condition. All things were physical. They were *spiritual* in the sense that they were not mortal, not subject to death (see 1 Corinthians 15:44; Alma 11:45; D&C 88:27).[5] In the Garden of Eden, Adam and Eve walked and talked with God. Adam was made "lord or governor of all things on earth, and at the same time [enjoyed] communion and intercourse with his Maker, without a vail to separate between."[6] Our first parents would have remained in this state indefinitely had not circumstances changed (see 2 Nephi 2:22; Moses 3:9). Those circumstances did change as a result of Adam and Eve's partaking of the forbidden fruit.

The Latter-day Saint view of the scenes in Eden is remarkably optimistic when compared to traditional Christian views. We believe that Adam and Eve went into the Garden of Eden to fall, that their actions helped "to open the way of the world,"[7] and that the Fall was as much a part of the foreordained plan of the Father as was the very Atonement. "Adam did only what he had to do," President Joseph Fielding Smith said. "He partook of that fruit for one good reason, and that was to open the door to bring you and me and everyone else into this world, for Adam and Eve could have remained in the Garden of Eden; they could have been there to this day, if Eve hadn't done something."[8] Because the Fall is one of the three pillars of eternity (with the Creation and the Atonement), and because mortality, death, human experience, sin, and thus the need for redemption grow out of the Fall, we look upon what Adam and Eve did with appreciation rather than disdain. "The fall had a twofold direction—downward, yet forward. It brought man into the world and set his feet upon progression's highway."[9] As Enoch declared: "Because that Adam fell, we are" (Moses 6:48; see also 2 Nephi 2:25).

OUT OF EDEN

In addition, the Fall opened the door to sin and death. This life became a probationary estate, a time for men and women to prepare to meet God (see 2 Nephi 2:21; Alma 12:24; 34:32; 42:4). With the Fall came also a veil of separation between God and mankind; mortals "were shut out from his presence" (Moses 5:4).

After being cast from the Garden of Eden, Adam and his posterity were taught the gospel by the ministry of angels, by the voice of God, and through the power of the Holy Ghost (see Moses 5:1–8, 58). The veil separating Adam from the immediate presence of the Eternal Father did not, however, remove Adam's memory of life in Eden. As Joseph Smith clarified, Adam's transgression "did not deprive him of the previous knowledge with which he was endowed relative to the existence and glory of his Creator. . . . Though he was cast out from the garden of Eden, his knowledge of the existence of God was not lost, neither did God cease to manifest his will unto him."[10] President John Taylor asked: "How did Adam get his information of the things of God?" He then answered: "He got it through the gospel of Jesus Christ. . . . *God came to him in the garden and talked with him . . . and he was the first man upon this earth that had the gospel and the holy priesthood;* and if he had it not, he could not have known anything about God or his revelations."[11]

The Latter-day Saints stand alone in the religious world in certifying that Christ's gospel is eternal—that Christian prophets have taught Christian doctrine and administered Christian ordinances since the dawn of time.[12] Adam was earth's first Christian. He exercised faith in the redemption of Christ, was baptized in water, received the gift of the Holy Ghost, was "quickened in the inner man," and was received into the order of the Son of God (Moses 6:64–67). Further, Adam and Eve entered into the new and everlasting covenant of marriage and thus placed themselves on that pathway that leads to life eternal.[13] "Father Adam was called of God," President Wilford Woodruff explained, "and ordained to the fulness of the Melchizedek Priesthood—ordained to the highest office and gift of God to man on the earth."[14]

Adam and Eve taught their children and their grandchildren the gospel, as they had received the same from the lips of God and angels. Some of their posterity rejected the light of heaven, "loved Satan more than God," and thus turned away from the truth. Our first parents mourned over the choices of their loved ones (see Moses 5:13, 18, 27, 28), but their mourning was not as those who have no hope. Thus "Adam and Eve, his wife, ceased not to call upon God" (Moses 5:16). Three years prior to his death, Adam gathered his righteous posterity together in the valley of Adam-ondi-Ahman (the place where he and Eve had settled after their expulsion from Eden[15]). Seven generations of faithful patriarchs with their families met to receive prophetic counsel at the feet of him who had come to be known as the "Ancient of Days." There he bestowed upon them his last blessing. In describing a vision he had of this sacred occasion, the Prophet Joseph said: "I saw Adam in the valley of Adam-ondi-Ahman. He called together his children and blessed them with a patriarchal blessing. The Lord appeared in their midst, and he (Adam) blessed them all, and foretold what should befall them to the latest generation. This is why Adam blessed his posterity; he wanted to bring them into the presence of God."[16]

Adam was lord over the earth for his own day, but he also stands as earth's presiding high priest, the man who, under Christ, holds the keys of authority for the blessing of mankind and the perpetuation of righteousness in the earth. "The keys have to be brought from heaven whenever the Gospel is sent. When they are revealed from heaven, it is by Adam's authority."[17] On another occasion, the Prophet added that Adam was "the first to hold the spiritual blessings, to whom was made known the plan of ordinances for the salvation of his posterity unto the end, and to whom Christ was first revealed, and through whom Christ has been revealed from heaven, and will continue to be revealed from henceforth. Adam holds the keys of the dispensation of the fullness of times; i.e., the dispensation of all the times have been and will be revealed through him from the beginning to Christ, and from Christ to the end of the dispensations that are to be revealed."[18] A modern revelation thus states that Jehovah has "appointed Michael your prince, and established his feet, and set him upon high, and given unto him the keys of salvation under the counsel and direction of the Holy One, who is without beginning of days or end of life" (D&C 78:16).

After Death

The Ancient of Days lived some 930 years on this earth (see Moses 6:12). His death fulfilled the divine decree that in the day he ate of the forbidden fruit—in this case, meaning the day or time as measured according to the Lord—he would surely die (see Moses 3:17; Abraham 5:13). At death Adam entered the postmortal world of spirits and became a part of that abode of the righteous known as paradise (see 2 Nephi 9:13; Alma 40:12; Moroni 10:34). His must have been a glorious reunion with holy beings as he passed from time into eternity. There he ministered and labored among his faithful descendants for some three thousand years. The Prophet Joseph Smith explained that Adam "presides over the spirits of all men,"[19] and so his ministry and administrative responsibilities would have continued beyond death's door.

Just as the War in Heaven continues, in a sense, into our own time, even so Adam's efforts to thwart and oppose Satan, the son of the morning, have continued since Adam's mortal death. In the context of counseling the Saints to avoid speaking evil of responsible persons, Jude, the brother of our Lord, observed that

"Michael the archangel, when contending with the devil he disputed about the body of Moses, durst not bring against him a railing accusation, but said, The Lord rebuke thee" (Jude 1:9). This appears to be a reference to a rather obscure pseudepigraphic work known as the Assumption of Moses. We know that Moses was translated. It appears that Satan, as lord of the material world, sought Moses' death in order to gain control over his body, so that Moses "would not have a tangible body in which to come—along with Elijah, who also was taken up without tasting death—to confer the keys of the priesthood upon Peter, James, and John" on the Mount of Transfiguration.[20] In our own day Michael, on the banks of the Susquehanna River, detected "the devil when he appeared as an angel of light" (D&C 128:20). We wonder how many other occasions there may have been in earth's history when Michael the archangel has stood to rebuke and set the bounds of Lucifer the archdeceiver.

There is one other occasion in which Michael as a disembodied spirit may have played a particularly significant role in the plan of our Father. Luke records that on the night of Atonement, following the Last Supper, Jesus bowed in awful alienation and grief in the Garden of Gethsemane beneath the load of the world's sins. He uttered his soul-cry: "Father, if thou be willing, remove this cup from me: nevertheless not my will, but thine, be done. And there appeared an angel unto him from heaven, strengthening him" (Luke 22:42–43). An angel sent from the courts of glory. An angel sent to assist, to support, to sustain the sinless Son of Man in the apogee of his greatest agony. "The angelic ministrant is not named," Elder Bruce R. McConkie has written. "If we might indulge in speculation, we would suggest that the angel who came into this second Eden was the same person who dwelt in the first Eden. At least *Adam, who is Michael, the archangel—the head of the whole heavenly hierarchy of angelic ministrants—seems the logical one to give aid and comfort to his Lord on such a solemn occasion.* Adam fell, and Christ redeemed men from the fall; theirs was a joint enterprise, both parts of which were essential for the salvation of the Father's children."[21]

President Joseph F. Smith, who was privileged to glimpse in vision the world of the disembodied at the time Jesus entered therein, wrote: "Among the great and mighty ones who were assembled in this vast congregation of the righteous were Father Adam, the Ancient of Days and father of all, and our glorious Mother Eve, with many of her faithful daughters who had lived through the ages and worshiped the true and living God" (D&C 138:38–39). Adam and Eve were among that group who "waited and conversed, rejoicing in the hour of their deliverance from the chains of death." When the Lord of Life appeared, he taught and organized his righteous forces and empowered them to take the message of salvation to the wicked, "the ungodly and the unrepentant." The Master ministered to his own "and gave them power to come forth, after his resurrection from the dead, to enter into his Father's kingdom, there to be crowned with immortality and eternal life" (D&C 138:18, 20, 51).

We do not know at what point in time Adam came forth in the first resurrection unto celestial glory, whether, like many of his prophetic colleagues, at the time of Christ's rise from the tomb (see D&C 133:54–55), or whether he remained in the spirit world for a season to oversee or participate in the work of redemption for the dead. That Adam did eventually rise to godhood, to sit with his famous descendants—Abraham, Isaac, and Jacob (see D&C 132:37)—and that he shall come forth to dwell in the everlasting burnings associated with celestial glory (see D&C 137:5), is abundantly clear from latter-day revelation. Following his resurrection, "Adam's base of operation would be from wherever such righteous resurrected beings go to await the time when this earth will become celestialized and become their eternal home. Again, we should remember that Adam's priesthood keys go with him—from the premortal world, through his mortal ministry, into the post-earth spirit world, and into the resurrection."[22]

IN THE FUTURE

In what would be, without modern revelation, a rather mysterious passage in the book of Daniel, reference is made to an unusual gathering of people. "I saw in the night visions," Daniel wrote, "and, behold, one like the Son of man came with the clouds of heaven, and came to the Ancient of days, and they brought him near before him. And there was given him dominion, and glory, and a kingdom, that all people, nations, and languages should serve him: his dominion is an everlasting dominion, which shall not pass away, and his kingdom that which shall not be destroyed" (Daniel 7:13–14). Latter-day revelation informs us that the location of this gathering is Daviess County, Missouri, in that area we have come to know as Adam-ondi-Ahman (see D&C 116), the same place where Adam met and counseled with and prophesied to his numerous posterity three years before his death. Of this council, a meeting that will be a preliminary appearance of the Savior (prior to his coming in glory), the Prophet Joseph Smith said: "Daniel in his seventh chapter speaks of the Ancient of Days; he means the oldest man, our Father Adam, Michael, he will call his children together and hold a council with them to prepare them for the coming of the Son of Man. He (Adam) is the father of the human family, and presides over the spirits of all men, and all that have had the keys must stand before him in this grand council. . . . The Son of Man stands before him, and there is given him glory and dominion. Adam delivers up his stewardship to Christ, that which was delivered to him as holding the keys of the universe, but retains his standing as head of the human family."[23]

President Joseph Fielding Smith offered the following explanation: "This gathering of the children of Adam, where the thousands, and the tens of thousands are assembled in the judgment, will be one of the greatest events this troubled earth has ever seen. At this conference, or council, all who have held keys of dispensations will render a report of their stewardship. Adam will do likewise, and then he will surrender to Christ all authority. Then Adam will be confirmed in his calling as the prince over his posterity and will be officially installed and crowned eternally in this presiding calling. Then Christ will be received as King of kings, and Lord of lords. We do not know how long a time this gathering will be in session, or how many sessions may be held at this grand council. It is sufficient to know that it is a gathering of the Priesthood of God from the beginning of this earth down to the present, in which reports will be made and all who have been given dispensations (talents) will declare their keys and ministry and make report of their stewardship according to the parable [see Matthew 25:14–30]. Judgment will be rendered unto them for this is a gathering of the righteous, those who have held and who hold keys of authority in the Kingdom of God upon this earth. . . . This will precede the great day of destruction of the wicked and will be the preparation for the Millennial Reign."[24]

When the Lord Jesus returns in triumphant glory to initiate the "end of the world, or the destruction of the wicked" (Joseph Smith—Matthew 1:4), the first resurrection, which began with the resurrection of Christ, will resume. Here again Michael-Adam will play a significant role. "Before the earth shall pass away, Michael, mine archangel, shall sound his trump, and then shall all the dead awake, for their graves shall be opened, and they shall come forth" (D&C 29:26). In discussing the nature of the keys restored to earth by various angels, Elder Bruce R. McConkie noted that "the holy priesthood will be used in eternity as well as in time. It is not only the power and authority to save men here and now; it is also the power by which the worlds were made and by which all things are. It also could well be that *Adam, who brought mortality and death into the world, was also permitted to restore the power that brings immortality and life to his descendants.* Christ, of course, in the ultimate sense holds the keys of the resurrection and of raising souls in immortality, but, as we also know, it is his practice to operate through his servants, and righteous persons will, in due course, participate in calling their loved ones forth in the resurrection."[25] At the end of the earth—meaning at the end of the Millennium (see D&C 88:101; Joseph Smith—Matthew 1:55)—the final great battle between good and evil, known as the "battle of the great God" (D&C 88:114) or the battle of Gog and Magog,[26] will take place. And once again, the mighty Michael, the eternal captain of Jehovah, will come face to face with his nefarious foe, Satan. "And the devil and his armies shall be cast away into their own place, that they shall not have power over the saints any more at all. For Michael shall fight their battles, and shall overcome him who seeketh the throne of him who sitteth upon the throne, even the Lamb. This is the glory of God, and the sanctified; and they shall not any more see death" (D&C 88:114–16). Michael's final victory is in preparation for the celestialization of the earth.

CONCLUSION

All too often Adam's place and role in the plan of salvation have been misunderstood. To many in the religious world he is an enigma, to others a myth. Some despise him for his actions in Eden. The praise he receives from some others takes the strange form of adoration and even worship. But to misunderstand Adam is to misunderstand our own identity, as well as our relationship to the Lord and his plan. The gospel light has shone forth, and modern seers have made known great and marvelous things pertaining to the past and the future (see Mosiah 8:17); people need not wander in darkness as to who they are, whose they are, and what they may become. Searching the revelations and attuning ourselves to the living oracles in our own day will prepare us for a time when further light and knowledge concerning the Adamic dispensation will be given (see D&C 107:57), a time when the faithful will know "things which have passed, and hidden things which no man knew, things of the earth, by which it was made, and the purpose and the end thereof—things most precious" (D&C 101:33–34). A knowledge of the origin and destiny of man—as typified in the life and labors of our father Adam—this is the legacy of the Latter-day Saints.

Notes

From "The Man Adam," *Ensign,* January 1994, 8–15.

1. Bruce R. McConkie, *Mormon Doctrine,* 2d ed. (Salt Lake City: Bookcraft, 1966), 16.
2. *Teachings of the Prophet Joseph Smith,* 357.
3. Bruce R. McConkie, "Eve and the Fall," in *Woman* (Salt Lake City: Deseret Book Co., 1979), 59.

4. *Teachings of the Prophet Joseph Smith,* 157; emphasis added.

5. See also *Doctrines of Salvation,* 1:75–78.

6. *Lectures on Faith,* 2:12.

7. *Teachings of the Prophet Joseph Smith,* 12.

8. Joseph Fielding Smith, in Conference Report, October 1967, 121.

9. Matthias F. Cowley and Orson F. Whitney, *Cowley and Whitney on Doctrine,* comp. Forace Green (Salt Lake City: Bookcraft, 1963), 287.

10. *Lectures on Faith,* 2:19, 20.

11. John Taylor, *The Gospel Kingdom,* comp. G. Homer Durham (Salt Lake City: Bookcraft, 1964), 91; emphasis added.

12. See *Teachings of the Prophet Joseph Smith,* 59–60, 168, 264.

13. See *History of the Church,* 2:320; see also McConkie, *Mormon Doctrine,* 118.

14. *Discourses of Wilford Woodruff,* comp. G. Homer Durham (Salt Lake City: Bookcraft, 1946), 64; see also *Doctrines of Salvation* 3:81; Ezra Taft Benson, "What I Hope You Will Teach Your Children about the Temple," *Ensign,* August 1985, 8–9.

15. See John Taylor, *The Mediation and Atonement* (Salt Lake City: Deseret News Press, 1882), 69; Matthias Cowley, *Wilford Woodruff* (Salt Lake City: Bookcraft, 1964), 481, 545–46.

16. *Teachings of the Prophet Joseph Smith,* 158–59; see also D&C 107:53–57.

17. *Teachings of the Prophet Joseph Smith,* 157.

18. Ibid., 167–68.

19. Ibid., 157.

20. *Doctrinal New Testament Commentary,* 3:423.

21. *Mortal Messiah,* 4:125; emphasis added; see also Bruce R. McConkie in Conference Report, April 1985, 10.

22. Larry E. Dahl, "Adam's Role from the Fall to the End—and Beyond," in Joseph F. McConkie and Robert L. Millet, eds., *The Man Adam* (Salt Lake City: Bookcraft, 1990), 121.

23. *Teachings of the Prophet Joseph Smith,* 157.

24. Joseph Fielding Smith, *The Progress of Man* (Salt Lake City: Deseret Book Co., 1964), 481–82; see also McConkie, *Millennial Messiah,* 578–88.

25. *Millennial Messiah,* 119–20; emphasis added.

26. See *Teachings of the Prophet Joseph Smith,* 280.

THE REGENERATION
OF FALLEN MAN

In a revelation given to the Prophet Joseph Smith, the Book of Mormon is described as "a record of a fallen people" (D&C 20:9). It is certainly a narrative history of the rise and fall of two great civilizations, a sobering chronicle of how pride and secret combinations usher nations into destruction. It is also an ever-present reminder that without divine assistance and the regenerating powers of the atonement of Christ, men and women remain forevermore lost and fallen creatures. "Why is it so vital," Elder William R. Bradford asked, "that we have a record of a fallen people? Why would such a record merit the trial and suffering of those who have sacrificed to bring forth this book, even to the constant and direct intervention of God Almighty?" Elder Bradford then answered: "I submit to you that no one, regardless of race or creed, can ever understand the role of and the need for a savior and a redeemer unless he first knows from what he needs to be saved or redeemed. No person, regardless of his religion or tradition, can understand victory over death and the terms upon which his salvation depends unless he understands the doctrine of fallen man."[1]

Or, as he stated on another occasion, "The Book of Mormon contains the record of a fallen people. It outlines how man got into a condition which subjects him to death and separation from God. The Book of Mormon also contains the fulness of the gospel of Jesus Christ. It outlines for us in perfect clarity what has been done for us and what we must do ourselves to overcome our fallen condition and return to the presence of God. . . . The Book of Mormon holds out to us a fulness of what we must be saved from. It gives us a complete understanding of the role of, and the need for, a savior. It is another testament of Jesus Christ."[2] The plight and the promise, the malady and the medication, the Fall and the Atonement—this is the burden of the Book of Mormon.

THE FALL AND ITS EFFECTS

The Latter-day Saint view of the Fall is remarkably optimistic. We believe that Adam and Eve went into the Garden of Eden to fall, that what they did had the approbation of the Gods and thus is termed a transgression and not a sin, and that their Fall was as much a part of the foreordained plan of the Father as was the very Atonement. We believe in the words of the Prophet Joseph Smith, that "Adam was made to open the way of the world,"[3] that the Fall was a move downward but forward in the eternal scheme of things, and that it "brought man into the world and set his feet upon progression's highway."[4] We do not believe, like John Calvin, that men and women are, by virtue of the Fall, depraved creatures. We do not believe, like Martin Luther, that men and women are so inclined to evil that they do not even have the capacity to choose good on their own. We do not believe, with much of the Christian world, that because of the Fall little children are subject to an "original sin."

Sometimes as Latter-day Saints we get a little nervous about teaching the Fall, fretting perhaps that we might be misunderstood as being accepting of a belief in universal human depravity. It is true that all men and women are the literal spirit sons and daughters of a divine and exalted Father and that we have the capacity to become as He is.[5] It is wondrous indeed to contemplate the majesty of President Lorenzo Snow's doctrinal teachings:

> *As Abra'm, Isaac, Jacob, too,*
> *First babes, then men—to gods they grew.*
> *As man now is, our God once was;*
> *As now God is, so man may be—*
> *Which doth unfold man's destiny.*[6]

Having said all of that, having distanced ourselves from traditional Protestant and Catholic thought regarding the impact of Adam and Eve's transgression, I hasten to add that there was a fall and that the Fall does indeed take a measured toll on all mankind. It is real, and its effects cannot be ignored or its pull on the human heart mitigated by enlightened conversation. One's *capacity* to become as God is one thing, while his or her *inclination* to sin is quite another. It is only as men and women overcome many of the effects of the Fall through the atoning blood and ransoming power of Jesus Christ that they place themselves on the path to godhood.

I also add here that to fail to teach the Fall is to lessen the impact of the Atonement. President Ezra Taft Benson observed: "Just as a man does not really desire food until he is hungry, so he does not desire the salvation of Christ until he knows why he needs Christ. No one adequately and properly knows why he needs Christ until he understands and accepts the doctrine of the Fall and its effect upon all mankind."[7] The Fall and the Atonement are a package deal; one brings the other into existence, and I am not aware of any discussion of the Atonement in the Book of Mormon that is not accompanied, either directly or by implication, with a discussion of the Fall. We do not appreciate and treasure the medicine until we appreciate the seriousness of the malady. One cannot look earnestly and longingly to the Redeemer if he or she does not sense the need for redemption. Jesus came to earth to do more than offer sage advice. He is not merely a benevolent consultant. He is our Savior. He came to save us.

The following represent but a few of the principles that may be derived from the Book of Mormon regarding the effects of the Fall and of the nature of fallen humanity:

1. *All mankind are lost and fallen.* In what seems to be the very first reference in the Book of Mormon to the Fall, Nephi taught that "six hundred years from the time that my father left Jerusalem, a prophet would the Lord God raise up among the Jews—even a Messiah, or, in other words, a Savior of the world. And he also spake concerning the prophets, how great a number had testified of these things, concerning this Messiah, of whom he had spoken, or this Redeemer of the world. Wherefore, all mankind were in a lost and in a fallen state, and ever would be save they should rely on this Redeemer" (1 Nephi 10:4–6; see also Alma 42:6). I am fascinated with the two words so descriptive of mortals—*lost* and *fallen.* Truly as Isaiah declared (and as Abinadi quoted), "All we, like sheep, have gone astray; we have turned every one to his own way" (Mosiah 14:6; see also Isaiah 53:6). The Good Shepherd thus comes on a search and rescue mission after all of his lost sheep. He who never took a moral detour or a backward step thus reaches out and reaches down to lift us up. We are lost in the sense that we have wandered from a more exalted sphere; in the sense that we do not know our way home without a guide; in the sense that we are alienated from God and separated from things of righteousness. We are fallen in the sense that we have chosen, like our Exemplar, to condescend and enter a telestial tenement; in the sense that our eternal spirit, a spark of divinity struck from the fires of God's eternal blaze, has taken up its

temporary abode in a tabernacle of clay; in the sense that we must be lifted up, quickened, and resuscitated spiritually if we are to return to the glorious place from whence we came.

Men and women are lost and fallen in that they are subject to spiritual death, the separation from God (see Alma 42:7, 9), the separation from things of righteousness (see Alma 12:16, 32; 40:26). Alma explained to Corianton that after partaking of the forbidden fruit, our first parents were "cut off from the tree of life" and thereby "became lost forever, yea, they became fallen man. And now, ye see by this that our first parents were cut off both temporally and spiritually from the presence of the Lord; and thus we see they became subjects to follow after their own will." Alma pointed out that inasmuch as "the fall had brought upon all mankind a spiritual death as well as a temporal, that is, they were cut off from the presence of the Lord, it was expedient that mankind should be reclaimed from this spiritual death. Therefore, as they had become carnal, sensual, and devilish, by nature, this probationary state became a state for them to prepare; it became a preparatory state" (Alma 42:6–10).

2. *We inherit a fallen nature through conception.* God spoke to father Adam in the dawn of history: "Inasmuch as thy children are *conceived in sin,* even so when they begin to grow up, sin conceiveth in their hearts, and they taste the bitter, that they may know to prize the good" (Moses 6:55; emphasis added). In one sense, to be conceived in sin is to be conceived into a world of sin, to come forth into a telestial sphere, a state in which sin predominates. But there is more to it than that. Conception becomes the vehicle, the means whereby a fallen nature—mortality, what the scriptures call "the flesh"—is transmitted to the posterity of Adam and Eve. In short, to say that we are not responsible for the fall of Adam and Eve is not to say that we are unaffected by it. To say that we do not inherit an original sin through the Fall is not to say that we do not inherit a fallen nature and thus the capacity to sin. Fallenness and mortality are inherited. They come to us as a natural consequence of the second estate.

Lehi explained to Jacob that following the Fall "the days of the children of men were prolonged, according to the will of God, that they might repent while in the flesh; wherefore, their state became a state of probation, and their time was lengthened, according to the commandments which the Lord God gave unto the children of men. For he gave commandment that all men must repent; for *he showed unto all men that they were lost, because of the transgression of their parents*" (2 Nephi 2:21; emphasis added). Abinadi likewise explained to the priests of Noah that yielding to Lucifer's temptation in the Garden of Eden "was the cause of [Adam and

Eve's] fall; which [fall] was the cause of all mankind becoming carnal, sensual, devilish, knowing evil from good, subjecting themselves to the devil. Thus all mankind were lost; and behold, they would have been endlessly lost were it not that God redeemed his people from their lost and fallen state." At this point in reading the passage, we might be tempted to breathe a sigh of relief and rejoice in the fact that the Fall is already taken care of because Jesus suffered and died. Unfortunately, Abinadi continues, and in so doing he points out that the fallen nature is not just something we descend into through personal sin, but something out of which we must be extracted through divine regenerating powers. "But remember," he said, "that *he that persists in his own carnal nature, and goes on in the ways of sin and rebellion against God, remaineth in his fallen state and the devil hath all power over him.* Therefore, he is as though there was no redemption made, being an enemy to God; and also is the devil an enemy to God" (Mosiah 16:3–5; emphasis added).

Elder Bruce R. McConkie wrote: "Adam fell. We know that this fall came because of transgression, and that Adam broke the law of God, became mortal, and was thus subject to sin and disease and all the ills of mortality. We know that the effects of his fall passed upon all his posterity; all inherited a fallen state, a state of mortality, a state in which temporal and spiritual death prevail. In this state all men sin. All are lost. All are fallen. All are cut off from the presence of God. All have become carnal, sensual, and devilish by nature. Such a way of life is inherent in this mortal existence."[8] Similarly, President Brigham Young noted that a critical and doubting disposition concerning the work of the Lord "arises from the power of evil that is so prevalent upon the face of the whole earth. It was given to you by your father and mother; it was mingled with your conception in the womb, and it has ripened in your flesh, in your blood, and in your bones, so that it has become riveted in your very nature."[9] On another occasion he explained: "There are no persons without evil passions to embitter their lives. Mankind are revengeful, passionate, hateful, and devilish in their dispositions. This we inherit through the fall, and the grace of God is designed to enable us to overcome it."[10]

3. *One may be faithful and pure-hearted and yet still be buffeted by the pulls of a fallen world.* Another way of stating this principle is that there is a difference between the natural man (which we will discuss shortly) and the spiritual man who is taunted by the natural world in which he lives. Perhaps there is no better illustration in scripture than Nephi, son of Lehi. Here was a man who was obedient and submissive, a man who was led and empowered by the Spirit of Almighty God. "My soul delighteth in the things of the Lord," he wrote, "and my heart pondereth

continually upon the things which I have seen and heard." Now note the following words, spoken by a man who was surely as pure and virtuous as anyone we know: "Neverthcless, notwithstanding the great goodness of the Lord, in showing me his great and marvelous works, my heart exclaimeth: O wretched man that I am! Yea, my heart sorroweth because of my flesh; my soul grieveth because of mine iniquities. I am encompassed about, because of the temptations and the sins which do so easily beset me. And when I desire to rejoice, my heart groaneth because of my sins" (2 Nephi 4:16–19).

The people of Benjamin were described by their great king as "a diligent people in keeping the commandments of the Lord" (Mosiah 1:11). We would suppose they were members of the Church of Jesus Christ, followers of our Lord and Savior, people who had come out of the world by covenant. Benjamin delivered to his people one of the most significant addresses in all the Book of Mormon. He announced his own retirement and his son Mosiah as his successor; gave an accounting for his reign and ministry; encouraged the people to serve one another and thereby serve God; and counseled them (in the words of an angel) to put off the natural man and put on Christ through the Atonement. The people were electrified by the power of the message. Benjamin "cast his eyes round about on the multitude, and behold they had fallen to the earth, for the fear of the Lord had come upon them." And then this unusual insight: "And *they had viewed themselves in their own carnal state, even less than the dust of the earth*" (Mosiah 4:1–2; emphasis added). They then cried unto the Lord for forgiveness and deliverance. Interesting, isn't it? A noble people, a diligent people who view themselves in their own carnal state.

In Moroni's abridgment of the Jaredite record, we discover that the brother of Jared has encountered two major problems in his efforts to construct eight seaworthy vessels to transport his people to the promised land—air and light. We presume that the problem of how to ventilate the vessels was architecturally beyond the brother of Jared, for the Lord simply told him how to do it. But in regard to the light, Jehovah essentially asked: "Well, what would you have me to do?" This implies that God expected Moriancumr to do some homework. The Jaredite leader went to the top of Mount Shelem with sixteen transparent stones, eager to have the Lord touch them and thereby light their barges. He presented the stones to the Lord and prayed: "O Lord, thou hast said that we must be encompassed about by the floods. Now behold, O Lord, and do not be angry with thy servant because of his weakness before thee; for we know that thou art holy and dwellest in the heavens, and that *we are unworthy before thee; because of the fall our natures have become evil continually*" (Ether 3:2; emphasis added). He then called upon God for divine assistance.

We can grow in spiritual graces to the point wherein we have no more disposition to do evil but to do good continually (see Mosiah 5:2) and wherein we cannot look upon sin save it be with abhorrence (see Alma 13:12; see also 2 Nephi 9:49; Jacob 2:5). We can, like Nephi, delight in the things of the Lord (see 2 Nephi 4:16). But as long as we dwell in the flesh we shall be subject to the pulls of a fallen world. "Will sin be perfectly destroyed?" President Brigham Young asked. "No, it will not, for it is not so designed in the economy of heaven. . . . Do not suppose that we shall ever in the flesh be free from temptations to sin. Some suppose that they can in the flesh be sanctified body and spirit and become so pure that they will never again feel the effects of the power of the adversary of truth. Were it possible for a person to attain to this degree of perfection in the flesh, he could not die neither remain in a world where sin predominates. . . . I think we shall more or less feel the effects of sin so long as we live, and finally have to pass the ordeals of death."[11]

4. *Little children are innocent by virtue of the Atonement, not by nature.* Joseph Smith's teachings concerning the innocence and salvation of little children—drawn from the Book of Mormon, his inspired translation of the Bible, and the revelations we now have in the Doctrine and Covenants—came as a refreshing breeze amidst the arid and sweltering winds of doctrinal corruption and confusion. But even in the restored Church there is some confusion on this matter. We ask: Are little children innocent? The answer is a resounding yes. But that question is not really a debated issue. We all know that little children are innocent. The more difficult point is: Why are little children innocent? Two possibilities suggest themselves. First, there are those who believe little children are innocent because they are that way by nature. They are pure and holy and decent and good and unselfish and solicitous and benevolent and submissive, just by virtue of the fact that they are little children. I don't know about you, but I have not reared any of those types! The answer in the Book of Mormon and in modern revelation is that little children are innocent as one of the unconditional blessings of the Atonement, because Jesus Christ decreed them so.

Benjamin, in citing the message of an angel, declared that "even if it were possible that little children could sin they could not be saved," meaning, presumably, if there had been no Atonement; "but I say unto you they are blessed; for behold, *as in Adam, or by nature, they fall, even so the blood of Christ atoneth for their sins*" (Mosiah 3:16; emphasis added). Mormon taught similarly that little children are innocent, "even from the foundation of the world," and that "all little children are alive in Christ, and also all they that are without the law. For the power of redemption cometh on all them that have no law" (Moroni 8:12, 22). Modern revelation attests that "little children are redeemed from the foundation of the world through mine Only Begotten" (D&C 29:46), and that "little children are holy, being sanctified through the atonement of Jesus Christ" (D&C 74:7; see also JST, Matthew 18:11; 19:13). We are thus encouraged to become as little children, not only in the sense of becoming submissive, meek, humble, patient, and full of love (see Mosiah 3:19), but also in the sense of becoming innocent through the atoning blood of Christ (see Moroni 8:10).

5. *The natural man is an enemy to God and to all righteousness.* "There is a natural birth, and there is a spiritual birth," Elder Bruce R. McConkie has written. "The natural birth is to die as pertaining to premortal life, to leave the heavenly realms where all spirits dwell in the Divine Presence, and to begin a new life, a mortal life, a life here on earth. *The natural birth creates a natural man, and the natural man is an enemy to God. In his fallen state he is carnal, sensual, and devilish by nature. Appetites and passions govern his life and he is alive—acutely so— to all that is evil and wicked in the world.*"[12] The angel explained to Benjamin that "men drink damnation to their own souls except they humble themselves and become as little children, and believe that salvation was, and is, and is to come, in and through the atoning blood of Christ, the Lord Omnipotent. For the natural man is an enemy to God, and has been from the fall of Adam, and will be, forever and ever, unless he yields to the enticings of the Holy Spirit, and putteth off the natural man and becometh a saint through the atonement of Christ the Lord" (Mosiah 3:18–19).

The natural man is an enemy to God in that he (or she) is operating on another agenda than God's; is doing everything in his or her power to bring to pass their own whims and wishes; in general, has placed his or her will above that of the Captain of our soul. President Brigham Young taught that "the natural man is at enmity with God. That fallen nature in every one is naturally opposed, inherently, through the fall, to God and to His Kingdom, and wants nothing to do with them."[13] Such persons are thereby operating at cross purposes to the Father's plan for the salvation and redemption of his children and thus prove to be their own worst enemy as well. "All men that are in a state of nature," Alma observed, "or I would say, in a carnal state, are in the gall of bitterness and in the bonds of iniquity; they are without God in the world, and they have gone contrary to the nature of God; therefore, they are in a state contrary to the nature of happiness" (Alma 41:11).

The Apostle Paul wrote to the Corinthian Saints that "the natural man receiveth not the things of the Spirit of God: for they are foolishness unto him: neither can he know them, because they are spiritually discerned" (1 Corinthians 2:14). In the process of rejoicing in God, Ammon spoke of the gratitude he felt for the fact that he and his brothers had not been cast off forever for going about to destroy the Church of God. "Behold, he did not exercise his justice upon us, but in his great mercy hath brought us over that everlasting gulf of death and misery, even to the salvation of our souls. And now behold, my brethren, what natural man is there that knoweth these things? I say unto you, there is none that knoweth these things, save it be the penitent" (Alma 26:20–21). President Young stated that "the natural man (or as we now use the language, the fallen or sinful man) receiveth not the things of the Spirit of God. . . . In no other way can the things of God be understood. Men who are destitute of the influence of the Holy Ghost, or the Spirit of God, cannot understand the things of God; they may read them, but to them they are shrouded in darkness."[14]

REDEMPTION FROM THE FALL

We have spoken of the malady and now we turn to the cure. We have spoken of the bad news of the Fall and now turn to the good news, the glad tidings, of the Atonement.

Some years ago I sat with my counselors in a bishopric meeting. The session was drawing to a close because sacrament meeting would be starting in just ten minutes. A knock came at the door as we were making our way out of the office into the foyer. A young woman from my ward asked if she could visit with me for a moment. I indicated to her that we could chat for a bit, but that sacrament meeting would be starting soon. She assured me that we would be together for only a minute or two. After we had been seated for a few seconds, she said: "Bishop, I need to confess a sin." I was startled with the suddenness of the statement, but, managing to hold my composure, I offered the following: "Well, that could take some time, couldn't it? Shall we meet after the block of meetings today?" She quickly responded: "Oh no! This will just take a second."

I nodded and asked her to go ahead, and she proceeded to describe in some detail a very serious moral transgression in which she had been involved. It was now about one minute before the meetings were to start, and so I tried again: "Why don't we get together after priesthood and Relief Society meetings." She then staggered me with, "Well, I don't know why we would need to, unless it would be helpful to you, or something." I indicated that such a meeting might prove beneficial to both of us. She agreed to return. Three hours later, and after we had exchanged a few pleasantries, I asked her, "How do you feel about what has happened?" She responded, "Just fine." I must have shown my perplexity, because she added: "For a number of hours I felt bad about what had happened, but it's okay now because I've repented."

I couldn't ask her the question fast enough: "What do you mean when you say that you have repented?" (She had explained to me earlier that the transgression had taken place on Friday night, and it was now Sunday afternoon). At that point, she reached into her purse, rearranged a few items, and retrieved a yellow sheet of legal-size paper. Pointing one by one to various headings that began with an *R,* she said, "I've done this, and this, and this, and this, and finally I've confessed to you. I've repented."

"It seems to me that you've skipped an *R,* that your list is missing something," I said. A startled but persistent look was in her eyes, and I noted a slight impatience with me as she said, "No, that can't be. I have everything listed here!"

"The *R* you're missing," I responded, "is *Redeemer.* You have no place for Christ on your list. I mean, what does Jesus Christ have to do with your transgression? What does what happened in Gethsemane and on Calvary two thousand years ago have to do with what happened to you two nights ago?"

She answered: "Jesus died for me. He died for my sins."

To almost every question I asked thereafter she gave a perfect answer—at least, a perfectly correct answer. She had been well trained, and her answers reflected an awareness of the doctrines associated with repentance. But the answers were all totally cerebral, straight from memory and mind—not from the heart. She obviously saw no real tie between her own ungodly actions and the infinite actions of a God. We spent a few hours together that day and many days thereafter—searching the scriptures, praying together, and counseling over the way back to the strait and narrow path. We talked often and intently about Jesus Christ. She came in time to know the correct answers—by feeling, that is, from the heart.

Since that time, I have formulated my own brief list of R's, those that tend to point my mind and rivet my affections to Jesus the Messiah. There is nothing sacred about this list (how many, what order, etc.) except that they direct my own heart to sacred things.

1. *Resolving* to come unto Christ. Some years ago it was not uncommon to see bumper stickers and placards that read simply "Jesus is the answer." As we suggested earlier, answers are always much more appreciated when we know the question. As was the case anciently in Alma's dealings with the Zoramites, so it is

today—the great question is whether there is a Christ and what role he does or should serve in our lives (see Alma 34:5).

Those who labor tirelessly to lighten burdens or alleviate human suffering, but at the same time deny the fact that Jesus Christ is God or that there is no need for a Savior in this enlightened age, cannot have the lasting impact on society that they could have through drawing upon those spiritual forces that center in the Lord Omnipotent. Those in our day who focus endlessly on the moral teachings of Jesus but who downplay the divine Sonship miss the mark dramatically. For some persons, Jesus stands as the preeminent example of kindness, the ultimate illustration of social and interpersonal graciousness and morality. A favorite text for this group is the Sermon on the Mount, while their highest aspiration is the call to live the Golden Rule. A Roman Catholic philosopher has observed: "According to the theological liberal, [the Sermon on the Mount] is the essence of Christianity, and Christ is the best of human teachers and examples. . . . Christianity is essentially ethics. What's missing here?" he asks. "Simply, the essence of Christianity, which is *not* the Sermon on the Mount. When Christianity was proclaimed throughout the world, the proclamation *(kerygma)* was not 'Love your enemies!' but 'Christ is risen!' This was not a new *ideal* but a new *event,* that God became man, died, and rose for our salvation. Christianity is first of all not ideal but real, an event, news, the gospel, the 'good news.' The essence of Christianity is not Christianity; the essence of Christianity is Christ."[15]

We come unto Christ not alone to be taught but to be transformed. He is not only our Example but also our Change Agent and our Benefactor. Jesus is not only a convenient resource; he is the vital and indispensible element in our quest for happiness here and eternal reward hereafter. There is no hope and no possibility of reconciliation with the Father except by and through the Savior.

Enos wrestled with his sins until he heard the voice of God declaring, "Enos, thy sins are forgiven thee, and thou shalt be blessed." "Lord, how is it done?" Enos asked. The Lord answered: "Because of thy faith in Christ, whom thou hast never before heard nor seen. . . . Wherefore, go to, thy faith hath made thee whole" (Enos 1:5–8). In the apogee of his agony—confronted and tortured spiritually through the medium of memory—Alma the younger reported: "And it came to pass that as I was thus racked with torment, while I was harrowed up by the memory of my many sins, behold, I remembered also to have heard my father prophesy unto the people concerning the coming of one Jesus Christ, a Son of God, to atone for the sins of the world. Now, as my mind caught hold upon this thought, I cried within my heart: O Jesus, thou Son of God, have mercy on me, who am in the gall of bitterness, and am encircled about by the everlasting chains of death. And now, behold, when I thought this, I could remember my pains no more; yea, I was harrowed up by the memory of my sins no more. And oh, what joy, and what marvelous light I did behold; yea, my soul was filled with joy as exceeding as was my pain!" (Alma 36:17–20). Indeed, Jesus Christ is the Source of Solace. Jesus Christ is the Prince of Peace.

A grand key to coming unto Christ is acknowledging the goodness and omnipotence of Christ. It consists of yielding our hearts unto him (see Helaman 3:35), submitting to his wisdom and omniscience. It is an unconditional surrender, an unqualified sacrifice of self on the altar of Christ. It is to hearken to the counsel of Amaleki: "And now . . . , I would that ye should come unto Christ, who is the Holy One of Israel, and partake of his salvation, and the power of his redemption. Yea, *come unto him, and offer your whole souls as an offering unto him*" (Omni 1:26). "Men and women who turn their lives over to God," President Ezra Taft Benson stated, "will discover that He can make a lot more out of their lives than they can. He will deepen their joys, expand their vision, quicken their minds, strengthen their muscles, lift their spirits, multiply their blessings, increase their opportunities, comfort their souls, raise up friends, and pour out peace."[16]

2. Being *reconciled* to God through Christ. As indicated above, the Fall brought changes to the earth and all forms of life on earth, changes both cosmic and personal. In the spiritual realm, men and women began life in a new sphere, a new state, a new kind of being. Whereas in Eden, Adam and Eve had enjoyed the blessings of a terrestrial, immortal condition in which things were not subject to death, now on a fallen telestial earth all things began their steady decline toward dissolution. From modern revelation "we learn man's situation at his first creation, the knowledge with which he was endowed, and the high and exalted station in which he was placed—lord or governor of all things on earth, and at the same time enjoying communion . . . with his Maker, without a veil to separate between."[17] Following the Fall, however, Adam and Eve "heard the voice of the Lord from the way toward the Garden of Eden, speaking unto them, and they saw him not; for they were shut out from his presence" (Moses 5:4; see also D&C 29:41).

The Atonement is that divine act of mercy and grace and condescension by which our Father and God opens the door to reunion. In and through Adam we partake of mortality and death. In and through Christ our Mediator and Intercessor, we partake of immortality and the abundant life. By means of the Atonement we are reconciled to the Father. By means of the Atonement, the finite is reconciled to the Infinite, the incomplete to the Complete, the unfinished to the Finished, the imperfect to the Perfect. Jacob pleaded: "Wherefore, . . . reconcile yourselves to the will of God, and not to the will of the devil and the flesh; and remember, after ye are reconciled unto God, that it is only in and through the grace of God that ye are saved" (2 Nephi 10:24). The Atonement, as an act of grace, demonstrates the love of the Father for his children. Jesus Christ, who lived a sinless and perfect life, claims of the Father "his rights of mercy which he hath upon the children of men" (Moroni 7:27). Jacob also reminded his people and us: "Wherefore, . . . seek not to counsel the Lord, but to take counsel from his hand. For behold, ye yourselves know that he counseleth in wisdom, and in justice, and in great mercy, over all his works. Wherefore, . . . be reconciled unto him through the atonement of Christ, his Only Begotten Son, and ye may obtain a resurrection, according to the power of the resurrection which is in Christ, and be presented as the first-fruits of Christ unto God" (Jacob 4:10–11).

3. Being *renewed* in Christ. The Book of Mormon is a powerful invitation to come unto Christ and be changed. Indeed, one who chooses Christ chooses to be changed. The plan of salvation is not just a program bent on making bad men good and good men better; in addition, it is a system of salvation that seeks to renovate society and transform the whole of humankind. The gospel of Jesus Christ is intended to make of earth a heaven and of man a god.

Those who are dead to the things of the Spirit must be quickened, made alive, or born again in order to enter the realm of divine experience. This is not optional but required. Elder Bruce R. McConkie has written: "The spiritual birth comes after the natural birth. It is to die as pertaining to worldliness and carnality and to become a new creature by the power of the Spirit. It is to begin a new life, a life in which we bridle our passions and control our appetites, a life of righteousness, a spiritual life. Whereas we were in a deep abyss of darkness, now we are alive in Christ and bask in the shining rays of his everlasting light. Such is the new birth, the second birth, the birth into the household of Christ."[18] The new birth is the means by which "the dark veil of unbelief" is removed from our minds and by which the "light of the glory of God" infuses joy into our souls (Alma 19:6). It is the process by which we "lay aside every sin, which easily doth beset [us], which doth bind [us] down to destruction" (Alma 7:15). It is the only way whereby we can receive the image of Christ in our countenances (see Alma 5:14).

The renewal of which we speak is a conversion from worldliness to saintliness, from being lured by the lurid to being enticed by holiness. It comes to us by virtue of the cleansing blood of Jesus and through the medium of the Holy Ghost, who is the Sanctifier. After hearing a powerful address, the people of Benjamin "cried with one voice, saying: Yea, we believe all the words which thou hast spoken unto us; and also, we know of their surety and truth, because of *the Spirit of the Lord Omnipotent, which has wrought a mighty change in us, or in our hearts, that we have no more disposition to do evil, but to do good continually*" (Mosiah 5:2; emphasis added; see also Alma 19:33). This conversion experience was real. It was borne of the Spirit. It was of God. Surely as time passed and as they grew into that meaningful spiritual union with Christ of which the prophets speak, there would be little in the world to recommend itself to them, for their desires were to please the Almighty and enjoy his approbation. We do not suppose, however, that the people of Benjamin never sinned again; this would be impossible in this fallen sphere. No, they sinned and made mistakes thereafter, *but they had no desires to do so.* And, thanks be to God, we shall not only be judged by our works but also by the desires of our hearts (see Alma 41:3; D&C 137:9).

The testimony of Alma the younger is vital. Having lain immobile for three days and three nights and having come face to face with the heinous nature of his sins, he awoke to a new life. Alma "stood up and began to speak unto them, bidding them to be of good comfort: for, said he, I have repented of my sins, and have been redeemed of the Lord; behold I am born of the Spirit. And the Lord said unto me: Marvel not that all mankind, yea, men and women, all nations, kindreds, tongues, and people, must be born again; yea, born of God, *changed from their carnal and fallen state, to a state of righteousness, being redeemed of God,* becoming his sons and daughters; *and thus they become new creatures;* and unless they do this, they can in nowise inherit the kingdom of God" (Mosiah 27:23–26; emphasis added).

President Ezra Taft Benson noted that "we must be careful, as we seek to become more and more godlike, that we do not become discouraged and lose hope. Becoming Christlike is a lifetime pursuit and very often involves growth and change that is slow, almost imperceptible." Then, after mentioning the sudden spiritual transformations of such notables as Alma the younger, Paul, Enos, and King Lamoni, he added: "We must be cautious as we discuss these remarkable examples. *Though they are real and powerful, they are the exception more than the rule.* For every Paul, for every Enos, and for every King Lamoni, there are hundreds and thousands of people who find the process of repentance much more subtle, much more imperceptible. Day by day they move closer to the Lord, little realizing they are building a godlike life. They live quiet lives of goodness, service, and commitment. They are like the Lamanites, who the Lord said, 'were baptized with fire and with the Holy Ghost, and they knew it not' (3 Nephi 9:20)."[19]

4. Being *reinstated* in the Family of God. The Fall not only distances us from righteousness but also alienates us from the family of God. We come into this fallen world nameless and familyless. The Atonement therefore provides the means not only for forgiveness of sins but also of reinstatement in the royal family. Benjamin acknowledged this marvelous truth when he commended his people for their willingness to renew their baptismal covenant and come again unto Christ. "And now, *because of the covenant which ye have made ye shall be called the children of Christ, his sons, and his daughters; for behold, this day he hath spiritually begotten you;* for ye say that your hearts are changed through faith on his name; therefore, *ye are born of him and have become his sons and his daughters.* And under this head ye are made free, and there is no other head whereby ye can be made free. There is no other name given whereby salvation cometh; therefore, I would that ye should take upon you the name of Christ, all you that have entered into the covenant with God that ye should be obedient unto the end of your lives" (Mosiah 5:7–8; emphasis added; see also 27:25).

Just as the newborn in our mortal world automatically enters into a family relationship through birth, even so the new birth, the birth of the Spirit, becomes an avenue of life within the family of the Lord Jesus Christ. Christ is thus the Father of our awakening into newness of life, the Father of our resurrection, the Father of our salvation. We take his name upon us and seek to be worthy of that holy name. As members of his family we are expected to know who we are and act accordingly— to keep his commandments with fidelity and devotion and to take seriously our divine birthright as Christians. Thus we, as the seed of Christ, hearken unto the word of the prophets, look to Jesus our Lord for redemption, and publish peace after the manner of our Prince of Peace (see Mosiah 15:11–18). He is the Shepherd and we are the sheep of his fold. "Behold, I say unto you, that the good shepherd doth call you; yea, and in his own name he doth call you, which is the name of Christ; and if ye will not hearken unto the voice of the good shepherd, to the name by which ye are called, behold, ye are not the sheep of the good shepherd" (Alma 5:38).

5. *Relying* on the merits and mercy of Christ. The Book of Mormon teaches that we are saved by merit, but not by our own merit. "*Since man had fallen,*" Aaron explained to the father of Lamoni, "*he could not merit anything of himself; but the sufferings and death of Christ atone for their sins, through faith and repentance, and so forth*" (Alma 22:14; emphasis added). This requires a bit of explanation. Of course we are expected to receive the ordinances of salvation, work faithfully in the kingdom, perform acts of Christian service, and endure faithfully to

the end. Of course we are expected to do the works of righteousness. These things are necessary—they evidence our covenant with Christ to follow him and keep his commandments. They are *necessary,* but they are not *sufficient.*

We are expected to do the best we can, to give our whole service to our Master and our whole heart and soul to the cause of righteousness in the earth. But in the end it will not be enough. We cannot, simply cannot, save ourselves. Our merits, no matter how godlike and consistent, will not qualify us for the highest heaven. Truly, as Lehi explained, "there is no flesh that can dwell in the presence of God, save it be through the merits, and mercy, and grace of the Holy Messiah" (2 Nephi 2:8). "Wherefore, I know that thou art redeemed," Lehi explained to his son Jacob. And why was he redeemed? Because of his faithfulness, his submissiveness, his willingness, like Nephi, to follow the counsel of his father? No, Jacob was redeemed "because of the righteousness of thy Redeemer" (2 Nephi 2:3).

The Prophet Abinadi delivered a scathing denunciation of Noah and his priests, particularly of the manner in which they feigned allegiance to the Law of Moses but failed to live in harmony with its moral precepts. Further, he corrected their false impression that salvation could come by the Law alone. "I say unto you," he declared, "that it is expedient that ye should keep the law of Moses as yet; but I say unto you, that the time shall come when it shall no more be expedient to keep the law of Moses, and moreover, I say unto you, that salvation doth not come by the law alone; and were it not for the atonement, which God himself shall make for the sins and iniquities of his people, that they must unavoidably perish, notwithstanding the law of Moses" (Mosiah 13:27–28). Elder Bruce R. McConkie, in an address to students at Brigham Young University in 1984, suggested a latter-day application of Abinadi's words:

"Suppose we have the scriptures, the gospel, the priesthood, the Church, the ordinances, the organization, even the keys of the kingdom—everything that now is down to the last jot and tittle—and yet there is no atonement of Christ. What then? Can we be saved? Will all our good works save us? Will we be rewarded for all our righteousness?

"Most assuredly we will not. We are not saved by works alone, no matter how good; we are saved because God sent his Son to shed his blood in Gethsemane and on Calvary that all through him might ransomed be. We are saved by the blood of Christ.

"To paraphrase Abinadi: 'Salvation doth not come by the church alone: and were it not for the atonement, given by the grace of God as a free gift, all men must unavoidably perish, and this notwithstanding the Church and all that appertains to it.'"[20]

The issue is not whether we are saved by works or by grace. Both are necessary. The real questions to be asked are: In whom do I trust? On whom do I rely? If I trust in my own works or rely on the labors of my own hands—no matter how noble they may be—I am propping my ladder against the wrong wall. If my confidence is in my capacity to "handle it myself," then my perspective is skewed and my hope is misplaced. Our reliance must be *wholly* upon the "merits of him who is mighty to save" (2 Nephi 31:19), *alone* upon "the merits of Christ, who [is] the author and the finisher of our faith" (Moroni 6:4). We are saved by the grace of Christ after all we can do (see 2 Nephi 25:23), meaning above and beyond all we can do. In the words of C. S. Lewis, those who come unto Christ learn that they cannot do it themselves but must "leave it to God." Lewis goes on to say: *"The sense in which a Christian leaves it to God is that he puts all his trust in Christ:* trusts that Christ will somehow share with him the perfect human obedience which He carried out from His birth to His crucifixion: that Christ will make the man more like Himself and, in a sense, make good his deficiencies. . . . And, in yet another sense, handing everything over to Christ does not, of course, mean that you stop trying. To trust Him means, of course, trying to do all that He says. There would be no sense in saying you trusted a person if you would not take his advice. Thus if you have really handed yourself over to Him, it must follow that *you are trying to obey Him. But trying in a new way, a less worried way."*[21]

6. *Retaining* a remission of sins. It is a marvelous thing to know that through the cleansing powers of the blood of Christ we may obtain a remission of sins and thus stand spotless before God. The promise of forgiveness is indeed a miracle, a wondrous act on the part of a merciful and all-loving God. We know we are forgiven as the Spirit of the Lord returns and as joy and peace of conscience fill our souls once more (see Mosiah 4:1–3). And yet we stand each day, as it were, precariously on the edge of a cliff: we are subject to subsequent sin. How can we, without trifling with repentance, remain pure? The Book of Mormon prophets provide the answer. They speak of remaining in a justified condition, of maintaining or retaining our spotless standing before God even though we make mistakes. Like the people of Benjamin, we may err after our covenant with the Master, but we have no desire to do so. That is, our heart, our affections, our desires have all been surrendered unto Christ, and we have no desire to stray from our binding covenant with him. As we endure to the end through living constantly in a state of repentance with an ever-present desire to be transformed in Christ, the Savior holds us guiltless (see 3 Nephi 27:16; see also D&C 4:2).

Benjamin explained two means by which the Saints are enabled to retain a remission of sins from day to day. First of all, he said: "As ye have come to the knowledge of the glory of God, or if ye have known of his goodness and have tasted of his love, and have received a remission of your sins, which causeth such exceedingly great joy in your souls, even so I would that ye should remember, and always retain in remembrance, the greatness of God, and your own nothingness, and his goodness and long-suffering towards you, unworthy creatures, and humble yourselves even in the depths of humility, calling on the name of the Lord daily, and standing steadfastly in the faith of that which is to come, which was spoken by the mouth of the angel.

"And behold, I say unto you that *if ye do this ye shall always rejoice, and be filled with the love of God, and always retain a remission of your sins;* and ye shall grow in the knowledge of the glory of him that created you, or in the knowledge of that which is just and true" (Mosiah 4:11–12; emphasis added; see also Moroni 7:42–44). Acknowledgement of God's greatness and goodness; recognition of our absolute ineptitude without divine assistance; surrender to the sobering verity that our spiritual condition is bankrupt without the Atonement—these are the preconditions for redemption in Christ, the means whereby we retain a remission of sins from day to day. Surely to the degree that we bow in humble reverence before the Lord Omnipotent and trust in his incomparable might, to that degree we open ourselves to the sweet enabling power we know as the grace of God. That power serves not only as a final spiritual boost into exaltation hereafter but also as a significant means for the renovation of our character and personality in this life, the power behind the process wherein we become partakers of the divine nature (see 2 Peter 1:4) and evidence the fruit of the Spirit (see Galatians 5:22–25).

The second means of retaining a remission of sins is set forth by King Benjamin after his lengthy plea with the people of God to look to the care of the needy. "And now, for the sake of these things which I have spoken unto you—that is, *for the sake of retaining a remission of your sins from day to day, that ye may walk guiltless before God—I would that ye should impart of your substance to the poor, every man according to that which he hath,* such as feeding the hungry, clothing the naked, visiting the sick and administering to their relief, both spiritually and temporally, according to their wants" (Mosiah 4:26; emphasis added). Perhaps it is the case that these two matters are really one; that is, the more I look to the Lord, humble myself before him, freely acknowledge his goodness and grace, and strive to be like him, the more I am prone to look to the welfare of my brothers and sisters about me. Being filled with the love of God results in meaningful and lasting service to the children of God.

Mormon spoke of a time in the Nephite church's history when the pride and wickedness of the members proved to be "a great stumbling block to those who did not belong to the church; and thus the church began to fail in its progress." On the other hand, "others were *abasing themselves, succoring those who stood in need of their succor,* such as imparting their substance to the poor and the needy, feeding the hungry, and suffering all manner of afflictions, for Christ's sake, who should come according to the spirit of prophecy; *looking forward to that day, thus retaining a remission of their sins;* being filled with great joy because of the resurrection of the dead, according to the will and power and deliverance of Jesus Christ from the bands of death" (Alma 4:10, 13–14; emphasis added).

CONCLUSION

We might go on and on in listing different R's of regeneration in Christ. But I desire to close this chapter by *rejoicing* in Christ. Jacob surely sang the song of redeeming love (see Alma 5:26) when he gloried in the wisdom, goodness, greatness, justice, mercy, and holiness of our God (see 2 Nephi 9:8, 10, 17, 19, 20). Ammon boasted, not in his own strength but in the infinite power of his Lord: "Yea, I know that I am nothing; as to my strength I am weak; therefore I will not boast of myself, but I will boast of my God, for in his strength I can do all things" (Alma 26:12).

I rejoice in the great plan of happiness and in the satisfaction that comes from the knowledge that God does indeed have a plan and that there is purpose in all we experience in this life. I rejoice in the fact that Adam fell that we might be (see 2 Nephi 2:25) and that because of that fall all of us enter into mortality to undertake the second phase of our eternal journey. I rejoice in the Fall, for it brought forth the Atonement, the means whereby our hearts might be cleansed and our souls transformed and prepared to dwell with Christ and our Eternal Father.

I know of the malady we call the fallen condition and of the heartache that comes to us as we yield to the flesh. I also know of the consummate peace that comes as we strive to put off the natural man through the Atonement and yield to the enticings of the Holy Spirit. Thus "we talk of Christ, . . . we preach of Christ, we prophesy of Christ, . . . that our children may know to what source they may look for a remission of their sins" (2 Nephi 25:26). Like Nephi, "I glory in plainness; I glory in truth; I glory in my Jesus, for he hath redeemed my soul from hell" (2 Nephi 33:6). Of that supernal truth I testify. For that good news, those glad tidings, I am immeasurably grateful.

Notes

From *Nurturing Faith Through the Book of Mormon, The 24th Annual Sidney B. Sperry Symposium* (Salt Lake City: Deseret Book Co., 1995), 119–48.

1. William R. Bradford, "Message Sublime," in *Brigham Young University 1982–83 Fireside and Devotional Speeches* (Provo: Brigham Young University, 1983), 156.
2. William R. Bradford, in Conference Report, October 1983, 100–101.
3. *Teachings of the Prophet Joseph Smith,* 12.
4. Matthias Cowley and Orson F. Whitney, *Cowley and Whitney on Doctrine,* comp. Forace Green (Salt Lake City: Bookcraft, 1963), 287.
5. See *Teachings of the Prophet Joseph Smith,* 346–48; *Lectures on Faith,* 5:3.
6. Lorenzo Snow's poem, written 11 June 1892, was published in the *Improvement Era,* June 1919, 660.
7. Ezra Taft Benson, *A Witness and a Warning* (Salt Lake City: Deseret Book Co., 1988), 33.
8. *Promised Messiah,* 244.
9. Brigham Young, in *Journal of Discourses,* 2:134.
10. Ibid., 8:160.
11. Ibid., 10:173.
12. Bruce R. McConkie, *A New Witness for the Articles of Faith* (Salt Lake City: Deseret Book Co., 1985), 282; emphasis added.
13. Brigham Young, in *Journal of Discourses,* 12:323.
14. Ibid., 9:330.
15. Peter Kreeft, *Back to Virtue* (San Francisco: Ignatius Press, 1992), 83.
16. Ezra Taft Benson, *Teachings of Ezra Taft Benson* (Salt Lake City: Bookcraft, 1988), 361.
17. *Lectures on Faith,* 2:12.
18. McConkie, *A New Witness for the Articles of Faith,* 282.
19. Ezra Taft Benson, "A Mighty Change of Heart," *Ensign,* October 1989, 2–5; emphasis added.
20. Bruce R. McConkie, "What Think Ye of Salvation By Grace?" in *Brigham Young University 1983–84 Fireside and Devotional Speeches* (Provo: Brigham Young University, 1984), 48.
21. C. S. Lewis, *Mere Christianity* (New York: Macmillan, 1952), 128–29; emphasis added.

THE MINISTRY
OF THE HOLY GHOST

John the Beloved has delivered to us—in his Gospel, epistles, and Apocalypse—
an apostolic witness, a penetrating testimony of his Lord and Savior. John identified himself as "the one that Jesus loved," and that love of the Lord permeates his
writings. Indeed, there is a spirit that broods over the works of the Beloved
Disciple, a spirit that attests to its essential truthfulness and especially to the reality
of its central character, Jesus the Christ. John was a witness of the risen Lord, one
who saw and heard and touched (see 1 John 1:1). He knew by the physical senses,
and he knew by an inward sense—a sense more real and powerful than anything
earthly—that the Word, the supreme messenger of salvation, had come and dwelt
among men in the flesh (see John 1:1; D&C 93:8).

A person could profitably devote a lifetime to the study of John's writings and,
with each reading, come away refreshed, renewed, and infused with light and truth
and added understanding. There is so much that might be said. In this chapter I
would like to focus my attention on the work of the Holy Ghost, as set forth in the
Gospel and epistles of John. Although the Holy Ghost is a vital figure in each of
the other Gospels and writings of the New Testament, there is a reason why the
fourth Gospel is often called the "spiritual Gospel," and the central themes of the
Gospel of John, many of which attend to the work of the Holy Ghost, carry over
consistently into his epistles.

The Light of Christ

The four Gospels are particularly plain in setting forth the true nature of God and the various labors of the members of the Godhead. Indeed, one has to become involved in a stretching series of doctrinal maneuvers in order to derive the concept of Trinity or of a triune God in the New Testament. The simplest reading of the text reveals the supremacy of God the Eternal Father, the divine Sonship of Jesus of Nazareth, and the mission of the Holy Ghost to make known the persons and will of the Father and the Son.

But Latter-day Saints are not limited by what is in the text of the New Testament. Through modern revelation we come to perceive and appreciate precious truths that have been lost to the religious world, insights that bring clarity and conviction to the study of the Bible. The Prophet Joseph Smith explained: "I have always declared God to be a distinct personage, Jesus Christ a separate and distinct personage from God the Father, and that the Holy Ghost was a distinct personage and a spirit; and these three constitute three distinct personages and three Gods."[1]

The "marvelous flood of light" we know as the Restoration first establishes the essential truthfulness of the Bible (1 Nephi 13:39–40; Mormon 7:9; D&C 20:11) and then makes known the mysteries of God, those revealed doctrines associated with the nature and kind of Beings we worship.

John wrote: "This then is the message which we have heard of [Christ], and declare unto you, that God is light, and in him is no darkness at all" (1 John 1:5). We do not travel far in our study of the Gospel of John before we read that Jesus Christ is "the true Light, which lighteth every man that cometh into the world" (John 1:9). Because Jehovah was the foreordained Redeemer and Savior of worlds (D&C 76:22–24; Moses 1:32–35), the Lamb slain from the foundation of the world (Revelation 5:6; 13:8; Moses 7:47), the Father's plan became his by adoption; the gospel of God (Romans 1:1–3) thus became known as the gospel of Jesus Christ. Likewise, because Elohim has invested his Beloved Son with his own attributes and powers (Mosiah 15:3; D&C 93:4), because the "Father of lights" (James 1:17) has ordained that Christ is to be the Light of lights, the Light of the world, those powers of life and light that we know as the power of God have come to be known as the light of Christ or Spirit of Jesus Christ.

Though there is but passing reference to the light of Christ in the New Testament, the scriptures of the Restoration abound in detail, assisting us immeasurably to understand how and in what manner the light of Christ lights every man and woman born into mortality. We come to know, first of all, that that light is a manifestation of the glory of God, a divine influence that fills the immensity of space, and the means whereby God, a corporeal being who can only be in one place at a time, is omnipresent. Elder Charles W. Penrose declared that "this spirit which pervades all things . . . is the light and life of all things, by which our heavenly Father operates, by which He is omnipotent, never had a beginning and never will have an end. It is the light of truth; it is the spirit of intelligence."[2]

The light of Christ has both *natural* and *redemptive* functions. Elder Parley P. Pratt explained: "It is, in its less refined existence, the physical light that reflects from the sun, moon, and stars, and other substances, and, by reflection on the eye, makes visible the truths of the outward world. It is also in its higher degrees the intellectual light of our inward and spiritual organs, by which we reason, discern, judge, compare, comprehend, and remember the subjects within our reach. Its inspiration constitutes instinct in animal life, reason in man, and vision in the prophets, and is continually flowing from the Godhead throughout all his creations."[3] The Holy Ghost is a male spirit personage. As an individual spirit personage, he, like the Father, can be in only one place at a time, and thus he utilizes and draws upon the light of Christ to communicate sacred truths and to dispense spiritual gifts to myriad beings separated in time and space (see Moroni 10:17).[4]

And so the same power that makes it possible for us to see with our physical eyes also makes it possible for us to see with spiritual eyes (see D&C 88:6–13). Discernment—the innate capacity to distinguish good from evil and the relevant from the irrelevant—also comes through this Spirit of Jesus Christ (see Moroni 7:12–19). Further, those who are true to this Spirit within them—including their conscience and thus the canons of right and wrong and decency in society—will be led, either in this life or the next, to the higher light of the Holy Ghost that comes through the covenant gospel (see D&C 84:44–53).

Elder Bruce R. McConkie has written: "The light of Christ (also called the Spirit of Christ and the Spirit of the Lord) is a light, a power, and an influence that proceeds forth from the presence of God to fill the immensity of space. . . . It is the agency of God's power and the law by which all things are governed. It is also the agency used by the Holy Ghost to manifest truth and dispense spiritual gifts to many people at one and the same time. For instance, it is as though the Holy Ghost, who is a personage of spirit, was broadcasting all truth throughout the whole universe all the time, using the light of Christ as the agency by which the message is delivered. But only those who attune their souls to the Holy Spirit receive the available revelation. It is in this way that the person of the Holy Ghost makes his influence felt in the heart of every righteous person at one and the same time."[5]

THE FATHER, SON, AND HOLY GHOST

By inheritance as well as by perfect obedience, Jesus Christ was entitled to a fulness of the Spirit. Jesus spoke often of his divine inheritance. "Therefore doth my Father love me," John recorded, quoting the Savior, "because I lay down my life, that I might take it again. No man taketh it from me, but I lay it down of myself. I have power to lay it down, and I have power to take it again. This commandment have I received of my Father" (John 10:17–18). Herein is the fundamental truth to be believed if we are to accept the divine Sonship of Christ. Jesus was the son of Mary, a mortal woman, and from her inherited mortality, including the capacity to die. Jesus was the son of God, an immortal resurrected being, and from him inherited the capacity to rise up from the dead in resurrected immortality. In a discourse on the redemption of the Messiah, Lehi emphasized how vital it is to make these truths known "unto the inhabitants of the earth, that they may know that there is no flesh that can dwell in the presence of God, save it be through the merits, and mercy, and grace of the Holy Messiah, *who layeth down his life according to the flesh, and taketh it again by the power of the Spirit,* that he may bring to pass the resurrection of the dead, being the first that should rise" (2 Nephi 2:8; emphasis added). The Savior thus had "power given unto him from the Father" (Helaman 5:11; Mormon 7:5) to do what he was sent to earth to do.

Though the fulness of the glory of the Father would not be Christ's until after the resurrection (see Matthew 28:18; D&C 93:16–17),[6] Jesus lived and moved and had his being in the Spirit of God, "for God giveth him not the Spirit by measure, for he dwelleth in him, even the fulness" (JST, John 3:34). It was this fulness that enabled and empowered the lowly Nazarene to resist evil, dismiss Satan from his life, and enjoy constant communion with the Father. "Where is the man that is free from vanity?" Joseph Smith asked. "None ever were perfect but Jesus; and why was He perfect? Because He was the Son of God, and had the fullness of the Spirit, and greater power than any man."[7] In speaking of becoming perfect in this life, Elder Bruce R. McConkie observed: "We have to become perfect to be saved in the celestial kingdom. But nobody becomes perfect in this life. Only the Lord Jesus attained that state, and *he had an advantage that none of us has. He was the Son of God, and he came into this life with a spiritual capacity and a talent and an inheritance that exceeded beyond all comprehension what any of the rest of us was born with.*"[8]

The Latter-day Saints teach, and the New Testament affirms, that the Beloved Son was in fact subordinate to his Father in mortality. Jesus came to carry out the will of the Father (see John 4:34). He explained: "I seek not mine own will, but the will of the Father which hath sent me" (John 5:30; see also 6:38–40). In addition, the scriptures attest that Elohim had power, knowledge, glory, and dominion that Jesus did not have at the time. Truly, "the Son can do nothing of himself, but what he seeth the Father do" (John 5:19). Even what the Son spoke was what the Father desired to be spoken. "For I have not spoken of myself; but the Father which sent me, he gave me a commandment, what I should say, and what I should speak. And I know that his commandment is life everlasting: whatsoever I speak therefore, even as the Father said unto me, so I speak" (John 12:49–50). How much more plainly could the Lord speak concerning his subordinate position than when he said, "If ye loved me, ye would rejoice, because I said, I go unto the Father: for my Father is greater than I" (John 14:28)?

On the other hand, the Father and the Son enjoyed much more than what we might call closeness; theirs was a divine indwelling relationship. Because he kept the law of God, Jesus was in the Father, and the Father was in Jesus (see John 14:10, 20; 17:21; 1 John 3:24). Though they were two separate and distinct beings, they were one—infinitely more one than separate. Their transcendent unity but epitomizes what ought to exist between God and all of his children. That is to say, we are under commission to seek the Spirit of God, to strive to be one with the Gods, to be, as the Prophet Joseph explained, "agreed as one,"[9] to have, as Paul wrote, "the mind of Christ" (1 Corinthians 2:16). "Hereby know we that we dwell in him, and he in us, because he hath given us of his Spirit" (1 John 4:13). We thus gain the mind of Christ as Christ gained the mind of the Father—through the power of the Spirit.

The Holy Ghost, as the third member of the Godhead, is the minister of the Father and the Son. The Godhead does not consist, as some suppose, of a Supreme Being who operates with the assistance of his two counselors, the Son and the Holy Ghost. Rather, Christ sends the Comforter (see John 15:26; 16:7). That Comforter is not an independent Being in the sense of speaking his own mind and delivering a completely original message. Jesus taught: "When he, the Spirit of truth, is come, he will guide you into all truth: for he shall not speak of himself; but whatsoever he shall hear [presumably, from the Father and the Son], that shall he speak: and he will shew you things to come. He shall glorify me: for he shall receive of mine, and shall shew it unto you" (John 16:13–14). The three separate members of the Godhead are one—they bear the same witness and teach the same truths (see 1 John 5:7).

For reasons that are not completely clear in the New Testament, the full powers and gifts of the Holy Ghost were not given in the Old World meridian Church until the day of Pentecost. "He that believeth on me," Jesus stated, "as the Scripture hath said, out of his belly shall flow rivers of living water. (But this spake he of the Spirit, which they that believe on him should receive; for the Holy Ghost was promised unto them who believe, after that Jesus was glorified)" (JST, John 7:38–39). While the Bridegroom was present with his disciples in the flesh, he was their Comforter, their Revelator, their Testator. He was their Life and Light, their source of power and might. "Hence, as long as Jesus was with the disciples in person, there was not the full need for them to have the constant companionship of the Spirit that there would be after Jesus left."[10] But because of the vital role that Spirit would play thereafter in the growth, development, and expansion of the early Christian Church, Jesus said: "It is expedient for you that I go away: for if I go not away, the Comforter will not come unto you; but if I depart, I will send him unto you" (John 16:7).

Though Jesus loved those among whom he ministered—indeed, the love of the Father and the Son underlies the work of redemption (see John 3:16–17; 1 Nephi 11:22, 25; D&C 34:1–3)—he was neither controlled by men's views nor deterred by their ridicule, taunts, or rejection. "I receive not honour from men," the Master said simply (John 5:41). His sense of worth derived not from the fickle plaudits of myopic mortals, but from the approbation of heaven. "He that sent me is with me: the Father hath not left me alone; for I do always those things that please him" (John 8:29). That constant closeness is what empowered the Savior to act in quiet confidence and assurance in behalf of his Father. A knowledge of such consummate intimacy also highlights the profound sense of loss, the awful alienation which the Son of Man experienced when in the garden and on the cross he tread the winepress alone, "even the wine-press of the fierceness of the wrath of Almighty God" (D&C 76:107).

Jesus explained to the woman at the well at Samaria: "Ye [the Samaritans] worship ye know not what: we [the Jews] know what we worship: for salvation is of the Jews." The true God had been revealed through the prophets of Israel, and salvation comes only to those who worship that divine Being. The Master continued: "But the hour cometh, and now is, when the true worshippers shall worship the Father in spirit and in truth: for the Father seeketh such to worship him. God is a

Spirit: and they that worship him must worship him in spirit and in truth" (John 4:22–24). As you know, these verses, particularly the reference to God being a spirit, have been used often against the Latter-day Saints by those offended with our doctrine of the corporeality of the Father. An alteration in the Prophet Joseph Smith's inspired translation of the Bible suggests a problem with this verse, whether textual tampering had taken place or meaning and clarity had simply been lost through the years. In the JST we find that "true worshippers shall worship the Father in spirit and in truth; for the Father seeketh such to worship him. For unto such hath God promised his Spirit. And they who worship him, must worship in spirit and in truth" (JST, John 4:25–26).

But even if we were not blessed with this prophetic insight, we could discern that the present rendering of the verse and the typical interpretation are incorrect. "*There is a sense,*" Elder McConkie has written, "*in which it might be said, without impropriety, that God is a Spirit.* He is most assuredly not a spirit in the sense in which the [Christian] creeds speak. . . . But when it is remembered that a spirit is a personage, an entity, a living personality whose body is made of more pure and refined substance than the temporal bodies of men; and when it is remembered that such spirits live in preexistence, come to earth to gain temporary physical bodies, are separated from those bodies by the natural death, with the assurance that eventually body and spirit will be inseparably connected again in resurrected immortality; and when it is remembered, further, that God himself is an exalted, perfected, glorified, resurrected Man; then it might truly be said that God is a spirit. He is a Spirit Personage, a Personage with a body of flesh and bones. (D&C 130:22.) He is a Spirit in the same sense that all men are spirits [see D&C 93:33], and in the sense that all men eventually will have resurrected or spiritual bodies as contrasted with their present natural or mortal bodies. (1 Cor. 15:42–50; D&C 88:25–28.)"[11]

Rather than "God is a spirit," a better reading from the Greek is "God is spirit" (New King James Version; New International Version; New Revised English Bible; New Revised Standard Version). Raymond Brown has written concerning this verse: "God gives the Spirit. (We find three great equations in the Fourth Gospel and First John: 'God is spirit'; 'God is light'; 'God is love.' These are not definitions of God's essence, but refer to God's relation to people. He gives them the Spirit; he loves them; he gives them his Son, their light). And the Spirit enables them to worship the Father."[12]

The New Birth

John records that there came to Jesus by night a man named Nicodemus, a "ruler of the Jews," presumably a member of the Sanhedrin, a man who was "a master in Israel," meaning a master teacher or acknowledged scholar among the Jews. He and others had been impressed with the miracles of Jesus. He said: "Rabbi, we know that thou art a teacher come from God: for no man can do these miracles that thou doest, except God be with him." It was as though Jesus then desired to do two things: (1) to point out to Nicodemus that more was required of him than a verbal recognition of Jesus as a miracle worker; and (2) to anticipate the question that must have lurked in the shadows of Nicodemus's mind but that went unasked: "What must I do to inherit eternal life?" Jesus answered: "Except a man be born again, he cannot see the kingdom of God" (John 3:1–3).

This was no new idea, no novel conception revealed for the first time, for the doctrine of rebirth was as old as the world. God spoke to Adam and Eve: "I give unto you a commandment, to teach these things freely unto your children, saying: That by reason of transgression cometh the fall, which fall bringeth death, and inasmuch as ye were born into the world by water, and blood, and the spirit, which I have made, and so became of dust a living soul, even so *ye must be born again into the kingdom of heaven, of water, and of the Spirit, and be cleansed by blood, even the blood of mine Only Begotten; that ye might be sanctified from all sin, and enjoy the words of eternal life in this world, and eternal life in the world to come, even immortal glory*" (Moses 6:58–59; emphasis added).

Jeremiah had spoken of a time when the Lord would again propose a covenant to his covenant people, when He would "put [his] law in their inward parts, and write it in their hearts," and that Jehovah would truly be their God and Israel would be his people (Jeremiah 31:31–34). Likewise, the Lord had spoken through Ezekiel: "Then will I sprinkle clean water upon you, and ye shall be clean: from all your filthiness, and from all your idols, will I cleanse you. A new heart also will I give you, and a new spirit will I put within you: and I will take away the stony heart out of your flesh, and I will give you an heart of flesh" (Ezekiel 36:25–26). Even in the Book of Jubilees, an apocryphal work, the concept of a new birth was to be found: "But after this they will return to me in all uprighteousness and with all of their heart and soul. And I shall cut off the foreskin of their heart and the foreskin of the heart of their descendants. And I shall create for them a holy spirit, and I shall purify them so that they will not turn away from following me from that day and forever. And their souls will cleave to me and to all my commandments. And they will do my commandments. And I shall be a father to them, and they will be sons to me" (Jubilees 1:23–25).

Nicodemus either did not understand what Jesus was teaching, or he sought to prolong an otherwise interesting discussion, for he asked: "How can a man be born when he is old? can he enter the second time into his mother's womb, and be born?" (John 3:4). According to President Marion G. Romney, Nicodemus "did not know who Jesus was. All he could see in the Son of God was a great teacher. This was all he could be expected to see, however, because he based his knowledge of who Jesus was upon what he had seen and heard of the Master's miracles. . . . Although Nicodemus was wise in the things of the world, he could not understand this simple statement of truth."[13] Jesus continued: "Except a man be born of water and of the Spirit, he cannot enter into the kingdom of God" (John 3:5).

The Christian world is largely divided over this matter of the new birth. A large segment of Christianity today believes that being born again consists of having a personal spiritual experience with Jesus. A large segment of Christianity believes that being born again consists of receiving the sacraments (ordinances) of the church. And where are the Latter-day Saints? Where do we stand on this vital issue? Is it enough to receive the revelation that God lives, that Jesus is the Christ? Or is it sufficient to receive the proper ordinances? The Prophet Joseph Smith stated simply but powerfully that "being born again, comes by the Spirit of God through ordinances."[14] Brother Joseph explained on another occasion that it is one thing to *see* the kingdom of God and another to *enter* into that kingdom. One must have "a change of heart" to see the kingdom; that is, he or she must be awakened spiritually to recognize the truth, recognize that the Church of Jesus Christ is the custodian of the truth and of the required ordinances, and recognize that the fulness of salvation is to be had through acceptance of those principles and ordinances. Further, the Prophet taught, a person must "subscribe the articles of adoption"—the first principles and ordinances of the gospel—in order to enter into the kingdom.[15] True conversion includes acting upon the revealed witness and submitting to those divine statutes that make it possible for us to be born again and thereby adopted into the family of the Lord Jesus Christ.

Daniel Tyler heard the Prophet Joseph explain that the birth spoken of in John 3:3—the birth to see—"was not the gift of the Holy Ghost, which was promised after baptism, but was a portion of the spirit, which attended the preaching of the gospel by the elders of the Church. The people wondered why they had not previously understood the plain declarations of scripture, as explained by the elders, as they had read them hundreds of times. When they read the Bible [now] it was a new book to them. This was being born again, to see the Kingdom of God. They were not in it, but could see it from the outside, which they could not do until the Spirit of the Lord took the vail from before their eyes. It was a change of heart, but not of state; they were converted, but were yet in their sins. Although Cornelius [Acts 10] had seen an holy angel, and on the preaching of Peter the Holy Ghost was poured out upon him and his household, they were only born again to *see* the Kingdom of God. Had they not been baptized afterwards they would not have been saved."[16]

Although the new birth is made possible through the atoning blood of our Lord and Savior, the Holy Ghost is vital in bringing about change. The Holy Ghost is a revelator, a comforter, a teacher, a sanctifier, a sealer. Elder Parley P. Pratt wrote that the Spirit "quickens all the intellectual faculties, increases, enlarges, expands, and purifies all the natural passions and affections, and adapts them, by the gift of wisdom, to their lawful use. It inspires, develops, cultivates, and matures all the fine-toned sympathies, joys, tastes, kindred feelings, and affections of our nature. It inspires virtue, kindness, goodness, tenderness, gentleness, and charity. It develops beauty of person, form, and features. It tends to health, vigor, animation, and social feeling. It invigorates all the faculties of the physical and intellectual man. It strengthens and gives tone to the nerves. In short, it is, as it were, marrow to the bone, joy to the heart, light to the eyes, music to the ears, and life to the whole being."[17]

There are some things that cannot be taught by mortals, some lessons that can only be learned through close association with God and his Spirit. Of Christ's young manhood the holy word attests: "And he served under his father, and he spake not as other men, neither could he be taught; for he needed not that any man should teach him" (JST, Matthew 3:25). It was certainly not the case that young Jesus was resistant to instruction or that he did not in fact learn a great deal from his parents and teachers; rather, there were eternal verities that could be learned only by entering the realm of divine experience. And so with us. The anointing or unction of the Holy Ghost that comes through the birth of the Spirit places us in a position to acquire new feelings, new insights, new perspectives that no mortal instructor could ever convey to us (see 1 John 2:20, 27). Those who are born of the Spirit begin to embody the "fruit of the Spirit," the patience, longsuffering, gentleness, kindness, meekness, joy, and pure love of Christ that characterize the true sons and daughters of the Lord Jesus Christ (see Galatians 5:22–25; Moroni 7:47–48). Truly, "we know that we have passed from death unto life, because we love the brethren"

(1 John 3:14). "Beloved, let us love one another," John wrote, "for love is of God; and every one that loveth is born of God, and knoweth God" (1 John 4:7).

"Whosoever is born of God," John the Beloved declared, "doth not commit sin; for his [Christ's] seed remaineth in him: and he cannot sin, because he is born of God" (1 John 3:9; see also v. 6; 1 John 5:18). This is a troublesome passage, perhaps because I have had the privilege of associating with wonderful people in my life, holy people, men and women of faith who have given their all to God and His work; but they are not perfect, at least they are not perfect in the sense that we generally think about the term—they are not free from sin. To some degree at least, I have been born of the Spirit, have tasted of the sweet fruits of rebirth, have had my mind and heart expanded by the powers of the Holy Ghost, have had my witness of this work deepened and solidified. But I painfully and honestly admit that I am not free from sin. There is nothing I desire more than to be free from sin, nothing I long for more than to be holy before God. But I am not there yet.

The Prophet Joseph altered this verse as follows: "Whosoever is born of God *doth not continue in sin; for the Spirit of God remaineth in him;* and *he cannot continue in sin, because he is born of God,* having received that holy Spirit of promise" (JST, 1 John 3:9; emphasis added). One who has walked in the light comes to treasure the light. Should he or she step into the darkness momentarily, they are repulsed by the darkness and yearn to return, as soon as possible, to the light. "The new birth results in new behavior. Sin and the child of God are incompatible. They may occasionally meet; they cannot live together in harmony."[18] That is, those who have been born of the Spirit learn to repent quickly, to confess and forsake their misdeeds, to move on. Obviously serious sins require more time, but many of our transgressions may be faced head on and dispensed with in no time at all. Thus the Prophet Joseph Smith prayed in the Kirtland Temple: "And when thy people transgress, any of them, *they may speedily repent and return unto thee, and find favor in thy sight,* and be restored to the blessings which thou hast ordained to be poured out upon those who shall reverence thee in thy house" (D&C 109:21).

Our challenge is to learn to *abide in Christ.* Jesus taught in the fifteenth chapter of John that he is the vine and we are the branches. We tend to get ourselves in trouble sometimes when we see ourselves as the *producers* of fruit. We are at best the *bearers* of fruit. In that sense, may I suggest that we do all we can do by way of living a good life but remember that it is not difficult to live the Christian life. It is impossible! At least it is impossible by ourselves. It is only as the Lord assists us in that endeavor that we are able to bring to pass great things. An Evangelical minister noted: "If you do not learn to abide in Christ, you will never have a marriage

characterized by love, joy, and peace. You will never have the self-control necessary to consistently overcome temptation. And you will always be an emotional
hostage of your circumstances. Why? Because apart from abiding in Christ, you
can do nothing. . . .

"Jesus makes a clear delineation between the vine and the branch. The two are
not the same. He is the vine; we are the branches. The two are joined, but not one.
The common denominator in nature is the sap. The sap is the life of the vine and its
branches. Cut off the flow of the sap to the branch, and it slowly withers and dies.
As the branch draws its life from the vine, so we draw life from Christ. To abide in
Christ is to draw upon His life."[19]

The Promise of Eternal Life

It was in the Last Supper that the Savior delivered some of the most profound
teachings of his ministry concerning the work of the Holy Ghost in leading souls to
salvation. Jesus had been with his disciples for three years, had taught them,
empowered them, and prepared them for what was to come. He had been their
Tutor, their Comforter. "If ye love me," he taught his chosen followers, "keep my
commandments. And I will pray the Father, and *he shall give you another
Comforter,* that he may abide with you for ever; even the Spirit of truth; whom the
world cannot receive, because it seeth him not, neither knoweth him: but ye know
him; for he dwelleth with you, and shall be in you" (John 14:15–17; emphasis
added). The word *another* literally implies "another of the same kind," that is
"someone, like Jesus Himself who will take His place and do His work."[20] The
Greek word translated in the King James Version as Comforter is *paraclete,* literally
"one called to stand along side of." Other meanings include "a friend, especially a
legal friend."[21] The word refers to "a counselor who supports a defendant at a trial.
The Spirit, then, will be a great defender of the disciples."[22] Thus other translations
render the passage as "another Helper" (New King James Version), "another
Counselor" (New International Version), and even "another Advocate" (New
Revised Standard Version; see also the Revised English Bible). While ultimately
Christ is our Advocate with the Father (see D&C 45:3–5), the Savior has sent his
Spirit to convict us of sin, convince us of the truth, and direct us toward righteous-
ness (see John 16:8–11). The paraclete was "any person who helped someone in
trouble with the law. The Spirit will always stand by Christ's people."[23] The Holy
Ghost, "one called alongside to help" would be that member of the Godhead who
"encourages and exhorts" the Saints.[24]

This other Helper or Advocate, the Holy Ghost, is called the First Comforter. He is the First Comforter in the sense that his sacred influence is preparatory, fundamental, and foundational to all spiritual growth; by means of the powers of the Spirit, men and women gain the witness of the divinity of Jesus Christ and come to know the things of eternity (see 1 Corinthians 12:3). One cannot enjoy the blessings of the Second Comforter without having first received and cultivated the gifts of the First Comforter. The Savior later added: "These things have I spoken unto you, being yet present with you. But the Comforter, which is the Holy Ghost, whom the Father will send in my name, he shall teach you all things, and bring all things to your remembrance, whatsoever I have said unto you" (John 14:25–26). In the opening verses of the majestic revelation we know as the Olive Leaf (D&C 88), Jesus informed the early Saints that "the alms of your prayers have come up into the ears of the Lord of Sabaoth, and are recorded in the book of the names of the sanctified, even them of the celestial world. Wherefore, I now send upon you another Comforter, even upon you my friends, that it may abide in your hearts, even the Holy Spirit of promise; which other Comforter is the same that I promised unto my disciples, as is recorded in the testimony of John" (D&C 88:2–3).

The Holy Spirit of Promise is, of course, the Holy Ghost, the Holy Spirit promised the Saints.[25] The Lord continued: "This Comforter is the promise which I give unto you of eternal life, even the glory of the celestial kingdom" (D&C 88:4). It is by that Holy Spirit of Promise that the Saints of the Most High receive what the Apostle Paul called the "earnest of our inheritance" (Ephesians 1:13–14; see also 2 Corinthians 1:21–22; 5:5), by which they come to know that their lives are in order, that they are on course and in covenant, that they are "in Christ" and thus in line for eternal life. It is through that Holy Spirit of Promise that the people of God receive their reward, "even peace in this world, and eternal life in the world to come" (D&C 59:23). Elder Marion G. Romney observed that "the fulness of eternal life is not attainable in mortality, but the peace which is its harbinger and which comes as a result of making one's calling and election sure is attainable in this life."[26] That peace, unlike anything the world has to offer (see John 14:27), a peace that "passeth all understanding" (Philippians 4:7), comes through the Spirit.

We quoted the Savior earlier concerning the Comforter: "He shall teach you all things, and bring all things to your remembrance, whatsoever I have said unto you" (John 14:26). In a sermon delivered in 1839, the Prophet Joseph Smith paraphrased the Lord as follows: The Holy Ghost "shall bring all things to remembrance, whatsoever things I have said unto you. *He shall teach you until ye come to me and my Father.*"[27] This statement implies that the Holy Ghost is given to the

Saints to mature them, motivate them, empower and prepare them to eventually come into the presence of God. Perhaps this is what is intended in the Prophet Joseph's words in the dedicatory prayer of the Kirtland Temple: "And do thou grant, Holy Father, that all those who shall worship in this house may be taught words of wisdom out of the best books, and that they may seek learning even by study, and also by faith, as thou hast said; and *that they may grow up in thee, and receive a fulness of the Holy Ghost*" (D&C 109:14–15; emphasis added).

Thus the Lord said to his disciples at the Last Supper: "I will not leave you comfortless"—or, more properly, "I will not leave you orphans"—"I will come to you" (John 14:18). To be orphaned is to be left alone, comfortless, without the Spirit, without familial ties that foster warmth and security. Jesus continued: "He that hath my commandments, and keepeth them, he it is that loveth me: and he that loveth me shall be loved of my Father, and I will love him, and will manifest myself to him. . . . If a man love me, he will keep my words: and my Father will love him, and we will come unto him, and make our abode with him" (John 14:18, 21, 23). The Prophet Joseph Smith explained that after a person has been baptized and receives the gift of the Holy Ghost, which is the First Comforter; after they continue to hunger and thirst after righteousness and covenant to remain true and faithful no matter what is required of them; they will eventually make their calling and election sure. That is, they will receive the assurance of eternal life. The Prophet went on to say that if they then continue faithful—for continual striving and an additional measure of faith is required—they may qualify for the highest of revelations in this life: the privilege of seeing the face of the Lord.[28] This unspeakable blessing, the scriptures attest, comes to us according to the Lord's timetable, for he knows best our capacity to bear sacred things. "Therefore, sanctify yourselves that your minds become single to God, and the days will come that you shall see him; for he will unveil his face unto you, and it shall be in his own time, and in his own way, and according to his own will" (D&C 88:68).

Elder Bruce R. McConkie has written: "It is the privilege of all those who have made their calling and election sure to see God; to talk with him face to face; to commune with him on a personal basis from time to time. These are the ones upon whom the Lord sends the Second Comforter. Their inheritance of exaltation and eternal life is assured, and so it becomes with them here and now in this life as it will be with all exalted beings in the life to come. They become the friends of God and converse with him on a friendly basis as one man speaks to another. . . .

"There are, of course, those whose callings and election have been made sure who have never exercised the faith nor exhibited the righteousness which would enable them to commune with the Lord on the promised basis. There are even those who neither believe nor know that it is possible to see the Lord in this day, and they therefore are without the personal incentive that would urge them onward in the pursuit of this consummation so devoutly desired by those with spiritual insight."[29]

Truly, those who are "in Christ" become "new creatures" of the Holy Ghost (2 Corinthians 5:17). It is by the power of the Spirit that we come to know the Lord. "And this is life eternal," the Master explained just prior to departing the Upper Room for Gethsemane, "that they might know thee the only true God, and Jesus Christ, whom thou hast sent" (John 17:3). Note the following testimony of John: "We know that we are of God, and the whole world lieth in wickedness. And we know that the Son of God is come, and hath given us an understanding, that we may know him that is true, and we are in him that is true, even in his Son Jesus Christ. This is the true God, and eternal life" (1 John 5:19–20). As expanded in modern revelation: "Verily, verily, I say unto you, except ye abide my law ye cannot attain to this glory. For strait is the gate, and narrow the way that leadeth unto the exaltation and continuation of the lives, and few there be that find it, because ye receive me not in the world neither do ye know me. But if ye receive me in the world, then shall ye know me, and shall receive your exaltation; that where I am ye shall be also. This is eternal lives—to know the only wise and true God, and Jesus Christ, whom he hath sent. I am he. Receive ye, therefore, my law" (D&C 132:21–24). Or, as the Prophet Joseph Smith explained: "Make your calling and election sure. Go on from grace to grace until you obtain a promise from God for yourselves that you shall have eternal life. This is eternal life—to know God and his Son Jesus Christ. It is to be sealed up unto eternal life and obtain a promise for our posterity."[30]

CONCLUSION

Joseph Smith, the Prophet of the Restoration, explained that "everlasting covenant was made between three personages before the organization of this earth, and relates to their dispensation of things to men on the earth; these personages, according to Abraham's record, are called God the first, the Creator; God the second, the Redeemer; and God the third, the witness or Testator."[31] Clearly we owe everything to our Heavenly Father who created us. In addition, our everlasting gratitude must always be offered to our Lord and Savior who was sent to earth on a search and rescue mission—to retrieve the wandering sheep and to redeem us from death and hell and endless torment. Had there been no atonement, no amount of labor on our part could ever, worlds without end, compensate for the loss. Truly, as Jesus proclaimed at the Last Supper, without him we can do nothing (see John 15:1–5). And finally, one of the priceless blessings extended to the Saints is the gift of the Holy Ghost, a sacred endowment of power, a supernal privilege of enjoying companionship with a member of the Eternal Godhead. Thanks be to God that that Spirit, about which the world knows precious little (see John 14:17), is sent to quicken, inspire, teach, testify, reprove, sanctify, comfort, and seal.

We cannot, simply cannot face the challenges of life and triumph over the flesh without divine assistance. And so we worship and we pray, we labor and we trust in the merits and mercy of the Holy Messiah. And we rejoice in the reality that the Holy Ghost is given to prepare us for association with God and holy beings hereafter. "Man's natural powers are unequal to this task," Elder B. H. Roberts pointed out; "so, I believe, all will testify who have made the experiment. Mankind stand in some need of a strength superior to any they possess of themselves, to accomplish this work of rendering pure our fallen nature. Such strength, such power, such a sanctifying grace is conferred on man in being born of the Spirit—in receiving the Holy Ghost. Such, in the main, is its office, its work."[32]

Notes

From an address given at the 27th Annual Sidney B. Sperry Symposium, Brigham Young University, Provo, Utah, 19 September 1998.

1. *Teachings of the Prophet Joseph Smith,* 370.
2. Charles W. Penrose, in *Journal of Discourses,* 26:23.
3. Parley P. Pratt, *Key to the Science of Theology,* 1978 ed. (Salt Lake City: Deseret Book Co., 1978), 25.
4. See *Doctrines of Salvation,* 1:54; see also Bruce R. McConkie, *A New Witness for the Articles of Faith* (Salt Lake City: Deseret Book Co., 1985), 258.
5. McConkie, *A New Witness for the Articles of Faith,* 70.
6. See *Doctrines of Salvation,* 2:269; Bruce R. McConkie, *Mormon Doctrine,* 2d ed. (Salt Lake City: Bookcraft, 1966), 333.
7. *Teachings of the Prophet Joseph Smith,* 187–88.
8. Bruce R. McConkie, "Jesus Christ and Him Crucified," *1976 Devotional Speeches of the Year* (Provo: BYU Publications, 1976), 399; emphasis added.
9. *Teachings of the Prophet Joseph Smith,* 372.
10. *Doctrinal New Testament Commentary,* 1:753.
11. *Doctrinal New Testament Commentary,* 1:153; emphasis in original.
12. Raymond E. Brown, *The Gospel and Epistles of John, A Concise Commentary* (Collegeville, Minn.: The Liturgical Press, 1988), 37; see also Raymond E. Brown, *The Gospel According to John,* 2 vols., volumes 29 and 29A in the Anchor Bible Series (New York: Doubleday, 1966), 1:172; F. F. Bruce, *The Gospel of John* (Grand Rapids, Mich.: Eerdmans, 1983), 110–11.
13. Marion G. Romney, in Conference Report, October 1981, 18–19.
14. *Teachings of the Prophet Joseph Smith,* 162.
15. Ibid., 328.

16. Daniel Tyler, "Recollections of the Prophet Joseph Smith," *Juvenile Instructor* 27 (1 February 1892): 93–94.

17. Parley P. Pratt, *Key to the Science of Theology,* 61.

18. John Stott, *Authentic Christianity from the Writings of John Stott,* ed. Timothy Dudley-Smith (Downers Grove, Ill.: InterVarsity Press, 1995), 207.

19. Charles Stanley, *The Wonderful, Spirit-Filled Life* (Nashville: Thomas Nelson Publishers, 1992), 64.

20. *The MacArthur Study Bible,* ed. John MacArthur (Nashville: Word, 1997), 1614.

21. Leon Morris, *The Gospel According to John* (Grand Rapids, Mich.: Eerdmans, 1971), 649.

22. Brown, *Gospel and Epistles of John,* 76.

23. *The New International Version Study Bible,* ed. Kenneth Barker (Grand Rapids, Mich.: Zondervan, 1985), 1625.

24. *MacArthur Study Bible,* 1614.

25. See *Doctrines of Salvation,* 1:55.

26. Marion G. Romney, in Conference Report, October 1965, 20.

27. *Words of Joseph Smith,* 14–15; emphasis added; punctuation corrected.

28. See *Teachings of the Prophet Joseph Smith,* 150–51.

29. *Promised Messiah,* 584, 586.

30. *Words of Joseph Smith,* 334; spelling and punctuation corrected.

31. *Teachings of the Prophet Joseph Smith,* 190.

32. B. H. Roberts, *The Gospel: An Exposition of Its First Principles and Man's Relationship to Deity* (Salt Lake City: Deseret Book Co., 1966), 170.

Chapter 17

THE DOCTRINE OF FAITH

The Book of Mormon is a singular scriptural record. It is a gift of God, given to the people of our dispensation, to bear witness of the divine Sonship of Christ and to restore plain and precious truths that have been taken away or kept back from the Bible (see 1 Nephi 13:20–42).

Faith is the complete trust, confidence in, and reliance upon the merits, mercy, and grace of Jesus Christ for salvation. It is a gift of the Spirit (see Moroni 10:11), a divine endowment that affirms to the human heart the identity and redemptive mission of the Savior. Though one might speak of faith in a broad sense as the underlying reason why people live and move and go about their daily activities, the faith of which the scriptures speak, especially the Book of Mormon, is faith in the Lord Jesus Christ.

THE NEED FOR FAITH

The fall of Adam and Eve, though an essential part of the eternal plan of the Father (see 2 Nephi 2:25; Moses 6:48), brought dramatic changes to man and to all forms of life on earth. Because of the Fall, man is alienated from the Father and from things of righteousness; he is subject to spiritual death (see Alma 12:16, 32; 42:9). As Aaron taught the father of King Lamoni, "since man had fallen he could not merit anything of himself" (Alma 22:14). No matter how noble his own efforts to overcome spiritual death, to love and serve others, or to keep the commandments of God, man will forevermore fall short of the divine standard. His works, though acceptable to God, will always be insufficient to save him (see 2 Nephi 25:23).

In short, had there been no means of bridging the chasm between sinful man and a sinless God, nothing that man could do would make up for the loss. Thus there is a need for an atonement, a means of reconciling finite man with an infinite Deity, of repairing the breech between earth and the heavens. Man cannot save himself or rely upon his own merits. Truly, by the works of the law no flesh is justified (see 2 Nephi 2:5). Because "all have sinned, and come short of the glory of God" (Romans 3:23), man cannot be justified—pronounced innocent or free from sin—by law or by works. Man's only option is to be justified by faith, to lean upon one who did in fact keep the law of God perfectly. It is only through the name of Jesus Christ—meaning his power or authority, his atoning mission and work—that salvation comes to the children of men (see 2 Nephi 9:24; Mosiah 3:17; 26:22; Alma 22:13; Helaman 14:13; Acts 4:12). In the words of Amulek, the atonement of Christ "bringeth about means unto men that they may have faith unto repentance" (Alma 34:15).

ELEMENTS OF FAITH

God the Father is the ultimate object of our worship (see 2 Nephi 25:16; Jacob 4:5; D&C 18:40; 20:19; JST, John 4:25–26). Jesus worshiped the Father, and so must we. Our faith is therefore in the Father, just as it is in the Son. To have faith in the Son of God is to have faith in God, and so it is that many references in the Book of Mormon to faith or belief or trust or reliance mention God as often as they do Christ. Thus "as Christ is the way to the Father, faith centers in him and in his redeeming sacrifice and goes thereby to the Father, who is the Creator."[1]

The Apostle Paul wrote that "faith is the substance ["assurance," according to the JST] of things hoped for, the evidence [or proof] of things not seen" (Hebrews 11:1). Our faith must be in something substantial, something of worth. "All belief is founded on evidence," Elder Orson Pratt explained. "A true faith is founded on true evidence; a false faith on false evidence. And in no case can a man have faith, either true or false, unless it is the result of true or false evidence. The greater the evidence, the greater will be the faith resulting from that evidence."[2] Korihor had every reason to have faith in God; as Alma pointed out, he had evidence from the prophets and the scriptures, as well as the order of the cosmos (Alma 30:44; see also D&C 88:45–47). But he chose not to receive and incorporate those evidences into the construction of his house of faith, and he thereby laid the foundation for his own demise. Near the end of the Nephite saga, Mormon prayed with all his heart for the deliverance of his people, but his prayers were "without faith, because of the hardness of their hearts" (Mormon 3:12). That is, Mormon was unable to exercise faith in their behalf because his people offered no evidence of repentance whatsoever.

Alma declared to the Zoramites that to have faith is "not to have a perfect knowledge of things; therefore if ye have faith ye hope for things which are not seen, which are true" (Alma 32:21; see also Ether 12:6; Hebrews 11:1). Sincerity and devotion to a cause are not sufficient; saving faith can only be exercised in that which is true. Thus no matter how committed the Zoramites were to their unusual liturgy atop the Rameumptom (see Alma 31), their false beliefs concerning God could not result in faith unto life and salvation. Their refusal to believe in the coming condescension of God the Son precluded salvation, no matter how consistently they cried out to their deity in their weekly ritual.

We see also from this passage that faith is intimately connected with hope: to have true faith in Christ is to have hope in Christ. When we come to know who Jesus is, how great and marvelous are his powers and his knowledge, and the nature of his sacrificial offering—when we gain faith in Christ—then we gain a hope in Christ. No one can attain unto faith except he shall then have hope. We need not speak of faith as something one either has in its fulness or does not have. Gaining faith is a process. And so it is with hope. Individuals like the Zoramites begin with the simple hope that there is a Savior (see Alma 32:27). On the other end of the continuum are those who know their Lord, have treasured up his word, and have been valiant in their witness. Their hope is for eternal life, for exaltation in the celestial kingdom.

"And what is it that ye shall hope for?" Mormon asked. "Behold I say unto you that ye shall have hope through the atonement of Christ and the power of his resurrection, to be raised unto life eternal, and this because of your faith in him according to the promise. Wherefore, if a man have faith he must needs have hope; for without faith there cannot be any hope" (Moroni 7:41–42). The disciple of Christ has hope, not in the worldly sense (wishing or yearning), but rather in the sense of anticipation, expectation, and assurance that through the Divine Redeemer he will be saved in the highest heaven. He is motivated and directed, not by self-confidence, but by his confidence or hope in Christ.

BELIEF, TRUST, AND RELIANCE

In the scriptures, there is no distinction made between true faith and true belief; belief is a synonym for faith. To have faith in Christ is to believe in Christ, to "believe that he is, and that he created all things, both in heaven and in earth; [to] believe that he has all wisdom, and all power, both in heaven and in earth" (Mosiah 4:9). The Nephite prophets labored diligently to invite their people "to believe in Christ, and to be reconciled to God" (2 Nephi 25:23), "for the Lord covenanteth with none save it be with them that repent and believe in his Son, who is the Holy One of Israel" (2 Nephi 30:2). The Nephites were called upon to "believe in Christ, and view his death, and suffer his cross and bear the shame of the world" (Jacob 1:8). Truly, "whosoever shall believe on the Son of God, the same shall have everlasting life" (Helaman 14:8). In summarizing the first principles and ordinances of the gospel, Mormon wrote: "And if it so be that ye believe in Christ, and are baptized, first with water, then with fire and with the Holy Ghost, following the example of our Savior, . . . it shall be well with you in the day of judgment" (Mormon 7:10).

Trust and reliance are likewise synonyms for faith. To have faith in Christ is to trust in him, to rely completely upon him. The Lord Jesus extends his arm of mercy towards those who trust in him (see Mosiah 29:20). Those who come unto Christ trust in his arm, meaning his power, rather than the arm of flesh (see 2 Nephi 4:34), for "whosoever putteth his trust in him the same shall be lifted up at the last day" (Mosiah 23:22). Of the two thousand stripling warriors, Helaman noted: "Now this was the faith of these of whom I have spoken; they are young, and their minds are firm, and they do put their trust in God continually" (Alma 57:27). Nephi explained that the Saints of God were able to come unto Christ through "relying wholly upon the merits of him who is mighty to save" (2 Nephi 31:19). Moroni likewise wrote that people are nourished by the good word of God, "to keep them in the right way, . . . relying alone upon the merits of Christ, who was the author and the finisher of their faith" (Moroni 6:4). Jacob added the sobering conclusion to the matter: only those who have "perfect faith in the Holy One of Israel"—meaning, presumably, a wholehearted belief in, a complete trust in, and a total reliance upon his redeeming blood—can be saved in the kingdom of God (see 2 Nephi 9:23). Again, because we cannot save ourselves, our absolute dependence cannot be in ourselves, no matter how impressive our accomplishments, but in Him who bought us with his blood. Like Jacob, we are redeemed "because of the righteousness of [our] Redeemer" (2 Nephi 2:3).

A PRINCIPLE OF POWER

Faith is more than a tenet, more than a doctrine. It was the Prophet Joseph Smith who taught that faith is a principle of power, the power by which gods and men bring to pass divine purposes.[3] When the former-day Saints, especially those in the Book of Mormon, operated by faith, they operated according to the mind and will of God.[4] Faith is not merely the power of suggestion, the power of positive thinking. The faithful, though filled with hope in Christ, are not just more optimistic than the world. People do not exercise faith by wishing and willing something to be. Men and women operate by faith when they first seek to know the mind of God on a matter and then proceed confidently; they first obtain their "errand from the Lord" (Jacob 1:17) and then move forward with a quiet but dynamic assurance that God will work his wonders through them.

For example, Nephi was "led by the Spirit, not knowing beforehand the things which [he] should do" (1 Nephi 4:6). He could move into otherwise frightening circumstances, including life-threatening situations, without knowing the details of his assignment. Why? Because he knew what was most important; though he did not know the how, he knew *why* he was to proceed. Nephi knew what God wanted him to do, and so his confidence was centered in God. Nephi demonstrated faith in going and doing the things that God had commanded, knowing in his heart that he would not be asked to do so unless the Almighty would open the way (see 1 Nephi 3:7).

Abinadi evidenced his faith in the Savior when he sealed his messianic witness with his life's blood (Mosiah 11:20–17:20), just as Zenos (Helaman 8:19) and Zenock (Alma 33:15–17) had done many years before. Ammon, Aaron, Omner, and Himni exercised their faith in the redemption of Christ, volunteered for missionary service, and were able to be instruments in the hands of God in leading many thousands of Lamanites to the covenant gospel (Mosiah 28:1–9; Alma 17–23). Alma and Amulek were delivered from captivity through their faith (Alma 14:28; Ether 12:13), while Nephi and Lehi, sons of Helaman, both men of profound faith and spiritual maturity (Helaman 3:21; 11:19), participated in the spiritual rebirth of a large number of Lamanites (Helaman 5; Ether 12:14). Because of the faith of the Brother of Jared, he was able to remove a mountain. In addition, the Brother of Jared "could not be kept from beholding within the veil" (Ether 3:19); indeed, "the Lord could not withhold anything from him, for he knew that the Lord could show him all things" (Ether 3:26; see also Ether 12:20, 30).

FRUITS OF FAITH

There are numerous fruits of faith, attitudes and actions that derive from believing, trusting, and relying upon Christ. We have already mentioned hope. First of all, it is through faith that forgiveness comes, by which the soul is cleansed and sanctified (1 Nephi 12:10–11), and by which people are made alive in Christ (2 Nephi 25:25). Faith leads to joy and peace of conscience (Mosiah 4:3; Helaman 5:47). It is by faith that men and women undergo a mighty change of heart through the gospel covenant (Mosiah 5:7; Alma 5:12). People are made whole through their faith in Christ, through their reliance upon One they have never before seen or heard (Enos 1:8).

Faith and patience result in deliverance (1 Nephi 1:20; 7:17; Mosiah 24:16; Alma 14:26–28). Jacob encouraged his people to "look unto God with firmness of mind, and pray unto him with exceeding faith, and he will console you in your afflictions, and he will plead your cause, and send down justice upon those who seek your destruction" (Jacob 3:1). Helaman wrote how "the Lord our God did visit us with assurances that he would deliver us; yea, insomuch that he did speak peace to our souls, and did grant unto us great faith, and did cause us that we should hope for our deliverance in him" (Alma 58:11). So often the One in whom we trust does not remove the burden from our backs; rather, he lifts and lightens the burdens, so that we do not feel them (see Mosiah 24:11–14). Through faith, deliverance comes not only from physical bondage but also from temptation and from Satan's grasp. Alma instructed his son Helaman to teach the people "to humble themselves and to be meek and lowly in heart; teach them to withstand every temptation of the devil, with their faith on the Lord Jesus Christ" (Alma 37:33).

Further, true faith always manifests itself in faithfulness, in sustained obedience and endurance to the end (see 1 Nephi 7:12; Alma 44:4; 48:15). The Risen Lord declared that "no unclean thing can enter into [God's] kingdom; therefore nothing entereth into his rest save it be those who have washed their garments in my blood, because of their faith, and the repentance of all their sins, and their faithfulness unto the end" (3 Nephi 27:19). Ammon pointed out that "he that repenteth and exerciseth faith, and bringeth forth good works, and prayeth continually without ceasing—unto such it is given to know the mysteries of God" (Alma 26:22).

Spiritual gifts, signs, and wonders are also fruits of faith in Christ (2 Nephi 26:13; 27:23). Jesus announced to the Nephites that signs "follow them that believe" (Mormon 9:22–24). Mormon explained that "it is by faith that miracles are wrought; and it is by faith that angels appear and minister unto men" (Moroni 7:37; see also Mosiah 8:18; 3 Nephi 19:35). Before listing the various gifts of the Spirit, Moroni exhorted his readers to "deny not the power of God; for he worketh by power, according to the faith of the children of men, the same today and tomorrow, and forever" (Moroni 10:7).

FAITH AND KNOWLEDGE

Some have supposed that faith and knowledge are on opposite ends of a continuum, that once a person has knowledge he no longer has or needs faith. Actually, faith and knowledge build upon one another. A certain degree of knowledge is necessary in order to exercise faith, even "a particle of faith" (Alma 32:27). Then, after one has begun to develop faith, new and added knowledge comes—new feelings and desires, new insights, new perspectives. There is a sense in which one might speak, as Alma did to the Zoramites, of one's faith being replaced by knowledge whenever a testimony of a particular principle has been obtained (see Alma 32:34; Ether 3:19). In reality, however, faith has not disappeared but instead been added upon.

Faith is a principle of power and thus a divine attribute possessed by God in perfection; God is the embodiment of faith, just as he is the embodiment of love and justice and judgment and mercy.[5] And so mortals are not working toward that day when they will no longer live and act by faith, but rather toward that day, beyond the resurrection, when they operate by perfect faith. "In the eternal sense," Elder Bruce R. McConkie has written, "because faith is the power of God himself, it embraces within its fold a knowledge of all things. This measure of faith, the faith by which the worlds are and were created and which sustains and upholds all things, is found only among resurrected persons. It is the faith of saved beings."[6]

GROWING IN FAITH

Thus the people of God work and labor and sacrifice and serve in order to build their faith and thus expand the power of God in their lives. The Book of Mormon teaches clearly how faith comes and thus how it develops and is perfected. First of all, faith comes as one encounters the word of God, whether the spoken or written word. "Faith comes by hearing the word of God," Joseph Smith taught, "through the testimony of the servants of God; that testimony is always attended by the spirit of prophecy and revelation."[7] Nephi read the words of Isaiah to his people in order that he "might more fully persuade them to believe in the Lord their Redeemer" (1 Nephi 19:23).

Alma called upon the Zoramites to plant the word in their hearts—to ponder upon and pray over the idea that Christ should come to earth and offer salvation to all men (see Alma 32:26–31; 33:14–23; 34:4–5). In this famous sermon on faith (see Alma 32–33), Alma described the process by which the faithless develop in time the saving faith in Christ that leads to life eternal. That process entailed belief, action, and spiritual confirmation or witness. One begins through demonstrating a willingness to experiment upon the idea of a Savior, to plant that idea in his heart. He then performs the actions appropriate to spiritual investigation, such as prayer, scripture study, association with the people of God, and meaningful service to fellowman. He then gains a confirmation, the peaceful but powerful assurance that the word is good, that in fact Jesus is the Christ and Redeemer of the world and that salvation comes through him. There also follows the corollary change of nature that flows from faith in the Lord. The believer begins over time to embody and exemplify Christlike attributes, for "every seed bringeth forth unto its own likeness" (Alma 32:31). This process of assurance and validation continues throughout one's life.

Mormon spoke of a time when the Nephites "did fast and pray oft, and did wax stronger and stronger in their humility, and firmer and firmer in the faith of Christ, unto the filling their souls with joy and consolation, yea, even to the purifying and the sanctification of their hearts, which sanctification cometh because of their yielding their hearts unto God" (Helaman 3:35). Aminadab taught that faith comes as people repent and cry unto God, so that "the cloud of darkness [is] removed from overshadowing you" (Helaman 5:41). Further, Moroni set forth the mighty truth found also in the New Testament, the doctrine that we gain faith and come to *know* as we *do* (see John 7:16–17). He confirmed that "faith is things which are hoped for and not seen; wherefore, dispute not because ye see not, for ye receive no witness until after the trial of your faith" (Ether 12:6). President Harold B. Lee taught that we must be willing to "walk to the edge of the light, and perhaps a few steps into the darkness, and you will find that the light will appear and move ahead of you."[8]

The final great fruit of faith is eternal life. In the first estate man walked by sight and by faith. Those who were valiant in the premortal existence demonstrated "exceeding faith and good works" there and were foreordained and foreappointed to significant assignments here (Alma 13:1–6). In this life man walks by faith (see 2 Corinthians 5:7). That is, he proceeds through life with the Spirit-given assurance that his actions are approved of God and will result in the salvation of his soul. To see with an "eye of faith" (Alma 5:15; 32:40) is thus to act according to the witness of the Spirit, to act as though one had seen and thus had perfect knowledge. The Saints of God view things with an eye of faith in this life, until one day, because of their faithful endurance, they see "with their eyes the things which they had beheld with an eye of faith" (Ether 12:19).

"The very nature of the kind of life [God] lives is eternal life, and thus eternal life consists in living and being as he is. In other words, eternal life is to gain the power of God, which power is faith, and thus to be able to do what he does and to live as he lives. And the great and eternal plan of salvation that he has ordained and established consists of those laws, ordinances, and powers whereby faith is acquired and perfected until it is possessed in the same degree and to the same extent that it exists in Deity. Faith will thus dwell independently in every person who gains eternal life."[9]

CONCLUSION

The Prophet Joseph Smith taught that "when men begin to live by faith they begin to draw near to God; and when faith is perfected they are like him; and because he is saved they are saved also; for they will be in the same situation he is in, because they have come to him; and when he appears they shall be like him, for they will see him as he is."[10] In this sense, the plan of salvation is "a system of faith—it begins with faith, and continues by faith; and every blessing which is obtained in relation to it is the effect of faith, whether it pertains to this life or that which is to come. To this all the revelations of God bear witness."[11]

I feel a great surge of gratitude for the revelations of the Restoration, particularly the Book of Mormon. The Bible chronicles acts of faith and deeds of wonder in both the Old and New Testaments, and there are a few places wherein the principle of faith is discussed. But it is to the Book of Mormon that we turn if we are serious about gaining faith like the ancients. In the Book of Mormon we have restored to us, first of all, the knowledge of the God of miracles, the God of revelation, the God of the ancients. Having established these fundamental truths, all other doctrinal matters are then revealed in their pristine purity and fitted into place in the grand scheme of restoration. We learn from the Book of Mormon what faith is, the object upon which it rests, and the fruits that flow from it. The Book of Mormon is not just a book about faith. It is a book that describes the process of faith, illustrates that process, and invites us, by the power of the Holy Ghost, to be active participants, first, in the acquisition of faith unto life and salvation, and, second, in the dissemination and perpetuation of faith throughout the earth.

Alma taught that if we will nourish the word—especially the proposition concerning the redemptive reality of Jesus the Christ—that the fruits of faith will be forthcoming in our lives, that the seed of faith in Christ "shall take root; and behold it shall be a tree springing up unto everlasting life. And because of your diligence and your faith and your patience with the word in nourishing it, that it may take root in you, behold, by and by ye shall pluck the fruit thereof, which is most precious, which is sweet above all that is sweet, and which is white above all that is white, yea, and pure above all that is pure; and ye shall feast upon this fruit even until ye are filled, that ye hunger not, neither shall ye thirst" (Alma 32:41–42).

Notes

From an address delivered at the Twenty-eighth Annual Sidney B. Sperry Symposium, Brigham Young University, Provo, Utah, November 1999.

1. Bruce R. McConkie, *A New Witness for the Articles of Faith* (Salt Lake City: Deseret Book Co., 1985), 185.
2. Orson Pratt, *Orson Pratt's Works* (Salt Lake City: Deseret News Press, 1945), 48.
3. See *Lectures on Faith,* 1:13–17; 7:2; compare Hebrews 11:3.
4. See McConkie, *A New Witness for the Articles of Faith,* 167, 191–92, 206.
5. See *Lectures on Faith,* 1:15–17; 7:2.
6. McConkie, *A New Witness for the Articles of Faith,* 209.
7. *Teachings of the Prophet Joseph Smith,* 148.
8. Harold B. Lee, as quoted in Boyd K. Packer, *The Holy Temple* (Salt Lake City: Bookcraft, 1980), 184.
9. McConkie, *A New Witness for the Articles of Faith,* 169.
10. *Lectures on Faith,* 7:8.
11. Ibid., 7:17.

Chapter   18

FAITH: A PRINCIPLE OF POWER

The revelations and teachings of Joseph Smith and the truths made known through modern prophets testify that faith is a principle of power and is a moving cause of all action in both the temporal and spiritual spheres. Further, faith is a system of salvation by which men and women can grow into a meaningful spiritual union with the Lord and eventually qualify to go where Gods and angels are.

FAITH BASED ON EVIDENCE

Faith is based on evidence. "All belief is founded on evidence," Elder Orson Pratt wrote. "The greater the evidence, the greater will be the faith resulting from that evidence."[1] The Apostle Paul thus observed that "faith is the assurance of things hoped for, *the evidence of things not seen*" (JST, Hebrews 11:1; emphasis added). Individuals who reflect seriously on the purpose of life, who consider meaningfully the nature and order of the cosmos, upon what might be termed *external* evidence—these often come to sense the reality of a divine Creator behind the creation. "All things denote there is a God," Alma testified to Korihor; "yea, even the earth, and all things that are upon the face of it, yea, and its motion, yea, and also all the planets which move in their regular form do witness that there is a Supreme Creator" (Alma 30:44; see also D&C 88:45–47).

There is also what we might call *internal* evidence, the quiet but pervasive assurance that comes to the human heart, by and through the Holy Spirit. It is an evidence less visible but more certain, an evidence that establishes spiritual realities. Elder Pratt explained: "The gift of the Holy Ghost was given to me; and when it was shed forth upon me, it gave me a testimony concerning the truth of this work that no man can ever take from me. . . . And while I am speaking upon the subject, let me say that *the gift and power of the Holy Ghost given to an individual is the greatest evidence that he can receive concerning God, godliness, and the kingdom of heaven set up upon the earth. There is no evidence equal to it.*"[2] President Brigham Young likewise spoke of the influence of this kind of evidence that comes by the power of the word: "If all the talent, tact, wisdom, and refinement of the world had been sent to me with the Book of Mormon, and had declared, in the most exalted of earthly eloquence, the truth of it, . . . they would have been to me like the smoke which arises only to vanish away. But when I saw a man without eloquence, or talents for public speaking, who could only say, 'I know, by the power of the Holy Ghost, that the Book of Mormon is true, that Joseph Smith is a prophet of the Lord,' the Holy Ghost proceeding from that individual illuminated my understanding, and light, glory, and immortality were before me. I was encircled by them, filled with them, and I knew for myself that the testimony of the man was true."[3]

PREREQUISITES FOR FAITH

The Prophet Joseph Smith taught that three things are essentially necessary for any rational and intelligent being to exercise faith in God unto life and salvation: (1) the idea that God actually exists; (2) a correct idea of his character, perfections, and attributes; and (3) an actual knowledge that the course of life one is pursuing is according to the will of God.[4] It is axiomatic that unless we have the idea in our minds that there is a God, we simply cannot exercise faith in him. As we have seen, that idea comes through the presentation of the word, through the power of human testimony, though the declaration of one who knows. Thus "from the time [the knowledge of God] was first communicated, it was retained in the minds of righteous men, who taught not only their own posterity but the world."[5] The Prophet explained that "faith comes by hearing the word of God, through the testimony of the servants of God; that testimony is always attended by the spirit of prophecy and revelation."[6]

Faith unto life and salvation cannot be exercised in that which is untrue (see Alma 32:21). Thus Joseph Smith instructed that one cannot gain faith or power if he or she is not possessed of a correct knowledge of God. No matter one's commitment to a god of wood or stone, no matter one's sincerity in bowing down before the winds or the thunder, the faith of which the scriptures speak—faith to move mountains, heal the sick, raise the dead, and come into the presence of God—is found only in the hearts of those who have come to know the true and living God, to know his nature and his character. The scriptures set forth clearly and unmistakably that the God we worship possesses all of the divine attributes—such qualities as knowledge, power, love, justice, judgment, and mercy—in perfection. That is, our God is not and cannot be deficient in any particular attribute. Otherwise, his children could not have the faith or confidence that would motivate them to call upon him, trust in him, and serve him at all hazards.

In regard to God's omniscience, for example, the Prophet explained that "without the knowledge of all things, God would not be able to save any portion of his creatures; for it is by reason of the knowledge which he has of all things, from the beginning to the end, that enables him to give that understanding to his creatures by which they are made partakers of eternal life; and if it were not for the idea existing in the minds of men that God had all knowledge it would be impossible for them to exercise faith in him." Similarly, if there were any question in people's minds concerning God's justice, "they would be filled with fear and doubt lest the judge of all the earth would not do right, and thus fear or doubt, existing in the mind, would preclude the possibility of the exercise of faith in him for life and salvation."[7]

The first two prerequisites for faith mentioned above pertain to Deity; if we are to grow in faith in a manner that would allow us to navigate a safe course to eternal life, we must know certain things about God. The third prerequisite requires us to know something *about ourselves;* that is, in order to have faith or confidence in God, we must know that our lives are pleasing to him, that the course we are pursuing is according to the will of heaven. This kind of faith is inextricably tied to spirituality, for as President David O. McKay observed, "Spirituality is the consciousness of victory over self, and of communion with the Infinite."[8] This is a type of self-confidence that transcends dramatically what the world has come to know as self-esteem. It is the peaceful and sacred and soul-satisfying assurance that our lives are acceptable to our Father in Heaven. The Prophet Joseph Smith went on to teach that such a knowledge could be had only through being willing to sacrifice all things. Indeed, it is only as we honestly and completely submit to the will of the Lord; only as we are willing to part with all earthly things, including our own lives if necessary; only as we "count all things but loss for the excellency of the knowledge of Christ Jesus" (Philippians 3:8) that we will be in a position to lay hold on eternal life. In this sense we become truly free only through an unconditional surrender to the Lord.

The Church of Jesus Christ of Latter-day Saints makes tremendous demands (in terms of time, talents, and means) on each of its members, for, as the Prophet observed, "*a religion that does not require the sacrifice of all things never has power sufficient to produce the faith necessary unto life and salvation;* for, from the first existence of man, the faith necessary unto the enjoyment of life and salvation never could be obtained without the sacrifice of all earthly things."[9] It was Abraham's willingness to sacrifice Isaac, his beloved child of promise, that laid the foundation for his faith unto life and salvation. God knew Abraham, but, as President Hugh B. Brown wisely pointed out, "Abraham needed to learn something about Abraham."[10]

In the same spirit, after the Lord had sealed Joseph Smith unto eternal life He said: "Behold, I have seen your sacrifices, and will forgive all your sins; I have seen your sacrifices in obedience to that which I have told you. Go, therefore, and I make a way for your escape, as I accepted the offering of Abraham of his son Isaac" (D&C 132:49–50). Elder B. H. Roberts explained that through meeting these three prerequisites for faith, men and women may grow "from righteousness to righteousness, until the heavens will be opened to them and they will hold communion with the Church of the First Born, with Jesus Christ, and with God the Father, and thus will they make their calling and election sure—through faith ripening into knowledge."[11]

LIVING AND WORKING BY FAITH

Persons with faith are faithful persons. They are dependable. They are trustworthy. Truly, we cannot exercise saving faith unless we are striving to be obedient to the commandments of God and are thus in a position to have the approval of God. Joseph Smith taught that "when a man works by faith he works by mental exertion instead of physical force."[12] But this is not the mental exertion associated only with intellect, nor is it the power of positive thinking. Rather, it is the subduing of self, the bending of the whole soul, and the molding of the personal will that enable the faithful to know the mind and will of the Almighty, to gain "the mind of Christ" (1 Corinthians 2:16).

In commenting upon the Prophet's discussion of working by faith, Elder Bruce R. McConkie wrote: "*Working by faith is not the mere speaking of a few well-chosen words;* anyone with the power of speech could have commanded the rotting corpse of Lazarus to come forth, but only one whose power was greater than death could bring life again to the brother of Mary and Martha. *Nor is working by faith merely a mental desire, however strong, that some eventuality should occur.* There may be those whose mental powers and thought processes are greater than any of the saints, but only persons who are in tune with the Infinite can exercise the spiritual forces and powers that come from him." To say this another way, we work by faith when we come to know and carry out the will of the Lord. Elder McConkie continued: "*Faith cannot be exercised contrary to the order of heaven or contrary to the will and purposes of him whose power it is. Men work by faith when they are in tune with the Spirit and when what they seek to do by mental exertion and by the spoken word is the mind and will of the Lord.*"[13]

Salvation is the ultimate fruit of faith, for salvation consists of being with and like Jesus Christ, who is the prototype of saved beings. Those who wish to be saved must thereby seek to become as Christ is. "When men begin to live by faith they begin to draw near to God; and when faith is perfected they are like him; and because he is saved they are saved also."[14] In this light the plan of salvation becomes "a system of faith—it begins with faith, and continues by faith; and every blessing which is obtained in relation to it is the effect of faith, whether it pertains to this life or that which is to come."[15]

In a day of spreading disbelief; in a time when people are ensnared by the ephemeral and the fleeting and thus less focused on the significant and the eternal, we are wont to cry out like one man did to Jesus in the meridian of time: "Lord, I believe; help thou mine unbelief" (Mark 9:24). Indeed, there are few problems in our generation that could not be rectified through a return to gospel fundamentals, a resurgence of that faith and hope had and enjoyed by the ancients. And it is the testimony of the Latter-day Saints that the Lord has restored to earth the ancient system of salvation, the everlasting plan of happiness that will bring to those who accept it peace and joy in this world and eternal reward and glory in the world to come. Truly, the gospel has been restored "that every man might speak in the name of God the Lord, even the Savior of the world; *that faith also might increase in the earth*" (D&C 1:20–21; emphasis added). This is the legacy of the Latter-day Saints, the burden and the blessing available to all who seek to come unto Christ and be saved.

Notes

From "Through Faith, Mankind Can Grow into Spiritual Reunion with the Lord," *Church News*, 25 December 1993, 3–4.

1. Orson Pratt, *Orson Pratt's Works* (Salt Lake City: Deseret News Press, 1945), 48.

2. Orson Pratt, in *Journal of Discourses,* 7:178; emphasis added.

3. Brigham Young, in *Journal of Discourses,* 1:90.

4. See *Lectures on Faith,* 3:2–5.

5. Ibid., 2:44.

6. *Teachings of the Prophet Joseph Smith,* 148; see also Romans 10:17.

7. *Lectures on Faith,* 4:11, 12.

8. David O. McKay, *Gospel Ideals* (Salt Lake City: Deseret Book Co., 1976), 390.

9. *Lectures on Faith,* 6:7; emphasis added.

10. Hugh B. Brown, as quoted in Truman G. Madsen, *The Highest in Us* (Salt Lake City: Bookcraft, 1978), 49.

11. B. H. Roberts, *The Gospel: An Exposition of Its First Principles and Man's Relationship to Deity* (Salt Lake City: Deseret Book Co., 1966), 111.

12. *Lectures on Faith,* 7:3.

13. Bruce R. McConkie, *A New Witness for the Articles of Faith* (Salt Lake City: Deseret Book Co., 1985), 191–92; emphasis added.

14. *Lectures on Faith,* 7:8; see also 6:11; 7:9.

15. Ibid., 7:17.

THE NATURE OF GOD
IN THE LECTURES ON FAITH

Not long before his death, Elder Bruce R. McConkie of the Quorum of the Twelve wrote the following concerning the fifth lecture on faith:

"Using the holy scriptures as the recorded source of the knowledge of God, knowing what the Lord has revealed to them of old in visions and by the power of the Spirit, and writing as guided by that same Spirit, Joseph Smith and the early brethren of this dispensation prepared a creedal statement on the Godhead. It is without question the most excellent summary of revealed and eternal truth relative to the Godhead that is now extant in mortal language. In it is set forth the mystery of Godliness; that is, it sets forth the personalities, missions, and ministries of those holy beings who comprise the supreme presidency of the universe. To spiritually illiterate persons, it may seem hard and confusing; to those whose souls are aflame with heavenly light, it is a nearly perfect summary of those things which must be believed to gain salvation."[1]

After many years of concentrated study of the Lectures on Faith, and particularly lecture 5, I have come to appreciate Elder McConkie's assessment; I believe the doctrines taught therein to be true and the concepts presented—though difficult and in some cases seemingly at odds with more traditional discussions of God and the Godhead—to be deep, penetrating, and, when fully grasped, soul inspiring. I believe them to be in harmony with other doctrines found in the standard works and the teachings of living apostles and prophets.

Because the Prophet was not at liberty to reveal all he knew, we are under solemn obligation to read, study, teach, and take seriously that which God *did* see fit to make known to the Latter-day Saints through him. Because Joseph Smith was given the mind of Deity, and because he was given the unique power and authorization of "expounding all scriptures" (see D&C 24:5, 9) unto the people of this dispensation, it is both fitting and proper that as we search and prayerfully consider matters pertaining to the Godhead, we give solemn and ponderous thought to insights provided by "the choice seer" of the last days.

GOD AND THE GODHEAD: SOME PRELIMINARY OBSERVATIONS

First of all, it is important to note that there is no distinction made in the lectures between faith in God the Father and faith in his Son, Jesus Christ. This is as it should be, for faith in one is faith in the other. "Christ and his Father are one," wrote Elder McConkie.

"They possess the same powers, are of the same character, embody the same attributes, and stand as beacons to all others with reference to the same eternal perfections. The words and acts of one are the words and acts of the other. The Father was in Christ manifesting himself to the world. Hence, faith in the Son is faith in the Father. And as Christ is the way to the Father, faith centers in him and in his redeeming sacrifice and goes thereby to the Father, who is the Creator."[2]

Secondly, a careful study of all of the lectures reveals a profoundly deep concept of God. These teachings relative to God—despite some claims to the contrary—are neither primitive nor Protestant. We are made privy to a divine Being who is omnipotent, omniscient, and omnipresent:[3] he has all power, all knowledge, and is, by the power of his Spirit, everywhere present. At the same time, we are given insights into a Being who can be approached, a God who communicates freely with his people and reveals himself to those who, like Enoch, the brother of Jared, and Moses, seek after him with diligence and faithfulness.[4] Most profoundly, we come face to face with the reality later taught in the King Follett Sermon—that men and women can mature spiritually to the point where they can become even as their exalted Sire.[5] As indicated, these lectures are not primitive: they contain doctrinal pronouncements and allusions that would normally be associated with the mature Joseph Smith in Nauvoo. These lectures are not Protestant: indeed, we learn of a truly infinite Being—a totally independent Being[6] who possesses every godly attribute in perfection.[7] But in no way do we encounter the utterly transcendent Deity of the creeds. God's infinity does not preclude either his immediacy or his intimacy.

THE FATHER: A PERSONAGE OF SPIRIT

"There are two personages," Joseph Smith explained, "who constitute the great, matchless, governing, and supreme power over all things, by whom all things were created and made. . . . They are the Father and the Son."[8] The Father and the Son are indeed the central members of the heavenly hierarchy, but as the Prophet later observed in the same lecture, the Holy Spirit is also a vital part of this eternal presidency. "These three are one," he stated; "or, in other words, these three constitute the great, matchless, governing, and supreme power over all things, by whom all things were created and made. And these three constitute the Godhead and are one."[9]

Again quoting from the Prophet: "They are the Father and the Son—*the Father being a personage of spirit, glory, and power, possessing all perfection and fulness, the Son,* who was in the bosom of the Father, [is] *a personage of tabernacle.*"[10] This is a perplexing passage, perhaps one of the two most enigmatic passages of lecture 5,[11] a segment of the lecture that seems to have resulted in confusion on the part of members and may have contributed eventually to the deletion of the Lectures on Faith from the Doctrine and Covenants in 1921. The problem lies in the fact that the Prophet appears to be teaching that God the Father is a "personage of spirit" while Jesus is "a personage of tabernacle." The latter concept is, of course, no problem. It is the notion of the Father as a personage of spirit that is unsettling. Let us consider some possible explanations for this statement.

We cannot avoid the possible conclusion that Joseph Smith simply did not understand the corporeal or physical nature of God at the time the Lectures on Faith were delivered in the winter of 1834–35. His knowledge of things—like that of all men and women—was often incremental, and his development in understanding was thereby accomplished in "line upon line" fashion. When he left the grove of trees in 1820, Joseph Smith Jr. did not have the doctrinal grasp or spiritual maturity that he would have when he died a martyr's death in Carthage some twenty-four years later. As a result of the First Vision, Joseph knew that the heavens were no longer sealed; that Satan was more than myth or metaphor; and that the Father and Son were separate and distinct personages. There is no mention in any of his known accounts of the First Vision of the fact that God has a body of flesh and bones.[12] The earliest reference in a sermon by Joseph Smith on the corporeality of God seems to be 5 January 1841. On that occasion William Clayton recorded the Prophet as saying: "That which is without body or parts is nothing. There is no other God in heaven but that God who has flesh and bones."[13] Six weeks later "Joseph said concerning the Godhead [that] it was not as many imagined—three heads and but one body; he said the three were separate bodies."[14] On 9 March 1841 he spoke of the ministries of Jesus as the Mediator and the Holy Ghost as the Witness or Testator. He then declared that "the Son had a Tabernacle and so had the Father."[15] Finally, it was on 2 April 1843 in Ramus, Illinois, that Joseph the Prophet delivered instructions on this matter that are the basis for D&C 130:22–23: "The Father has a body of flesh and bones as tangible as man's; the Son also; but the Holy Ghost . . . is a personage of Spirit."[16]

A second possibility is that Joseph Smith did indeed understand that God has a body but that the passage in lecture 5 under consideration has simply been misunderstood. If so, what could the phrase mean? To begin with, we should note that the complete expression is not "a personage of spirit," but rather "a personage of *spirit, glory,* and *power.*" This may well be intended more as a description of God's divine nature—a statement regarding his exalted and glorified status—than of his physical being. The word *spirit*—as used, for example, in Moses 1—is a synonym for glory or power: his Spirit is his glory. Thus the account indicates that after a marvelous vision "the *presence* of God withdrew from Moses, that his *glory* was not upon Moses" (v. 9; emphasis added). When Satan came tempting and taunting, the Lawgiver found that he was still possessed of sufficient spiritual power and discernment to distinguish between the true God of glory and the "god of this world" (v. 20; see also 2 Corinthians 4:4). "Blessed be the name of my God," Moses exulted, "for *his Spirit* hath not altogether withdrawn from me" (Moses 1:15; emphasis added). To speak of the spirit, glory, and power of the Father is to speak of his greatness, of his omnipotence, of his majesty. Thus it is that later in this lecture the Prophet says, "The Father and the Son possessing the same mind, the same wisdom, glory, power, and fulness—filling all in all; *the Son being filled with the fulness of the mind, glory, and power; or, in other words, the spirit, glory, and power, of the Father,* possessing all knowledge and glory."[17] Please note that the phrase "spirit, glory, and power" is used here to describe that which makes the Son one with the Father—the attributes of Godhood. Note the equation of spirit with *light* in the following verse from the Doctrine and Covenants: "For the word of the Lord is truth, and whatsoever is truth is light, and whatsoever is light is Spirit, even the Spirit of Jesus Christ" (D&C 84:45).

Elder Bruce R. McConkie has suggested that the phrase "a personage of spirit" has reference to God's *spiritual* nature—the fact that he is a resurrected and immortal being and as such is not subject to death—i.e., he has a spiritual body. "They are the two personages who came to Joseph Smith in the spring of 1820," he explained. He also wrote:

"They are exalted men. Each is a personage of spirit; each is a personage of tabernacle. Both of them have bodies, tangible bodies of flesh and bones. They are resurrected beings. Words, with their finite connotations, cannot fully describe them. A personage of tabernacle, as here used, is one whose body and spirit are inseparably connected and for whom there can be no death. A personage of spirit, as here used and as distinguished from the spirit children of the Father, is a resurrected personage. Resurrected bodies, as contrasted with mortal bodies, are in fact spiritual bodies."[18]

It is interesting to read the catechism following lecture 5. In response to the question, "What is the Father?" the answer is given: "He is a personage of glory and of power." Note the rather obvious omission of any reference to the Father as *a personage of spirit*. I suggest that there is no reference to his being a personage of spirit because to say such is repetitious; we have already established that he is a personage of power and glory, which in the mind of Joseph Smith was perhaps the same as saying that he is a personage of spirit. It is also worth noting in the catechism that in the scriptures cited to establish the Father as a personage of power and glory, all of them speak of his attributes and his exaltation. Noticeably absent is John 4:24—the one passage from the Bible that might have been used to establish clearly that God is a spirit. "God is a spirit," the King James Version has Jesus explaining, "and they that worship him must worship him in spirit and in truth." But of course Joseph Smith would not cite this passage from the King James Bible, since he had previously learned by revelation—some time between November 1831 and 16 February 1832[19]—that this verse was a mistranslation. The inspired translation reads as follows: "And the hour cometh, and now is, when the true worshippers shall worship the Father in spirit and in truth; for the Father seeketh such to worship him. For unto such hath God promised his Spirit. And they who worship him, must worship in spirit and in truth" (JST, John 4:25–26). One cannot help but wonder whether the inspired translation did not have some impact on the Prophet's thought regarding the nature of God; that is to say, if he did not know of the corporeality of God at the time of the First Vision, did he know it by the time he had translated these verses in John?[20]

I am indebted to Professor Milton Backman for bringing to light an important document—a description of Mormonism by a Protestant clergyman in Ohio. Truman Coe, a Presbyterian minister who had for four years lived among the Saints in Kirtland, published the following regarding the Mormons in the 11 August 1836

Ohio Observer: "They contend that the God worshipped by the Presbyterians and all other sectarians is no better than a wooden god. *They believe that the true God is a material being, composed of body and parts;* and that when the Creator formed Adam in his own image, he made him about the size and shape of God himself."[21] If a non-Mormon had observed as early as 1836 that the Latter-day Saints were teaching that God has a body, it is certainly not inconceivable that such things were known by Joseph Smith a year or so earlier at the time of the School of the Elders. It is interesting to note that in D&C 93:33 the Lord states that "man is spirit." This would appear to be a reference to man's eternal nature, certainly not an allusion to his physical person.

The Son: A Personage of Tabernacle

Jesus Christ the Son is described in lecture 5 as having been "in the bosom of the Father . . . a personage of tabernacle, made or fashioned like unto man, being in the form and likeness of man, or rather man was formed after his likeness and in his image. He is also the express image and likeness of the personage of the Father, possessing all the fulness of the Father, or the same fulness with the Father."[22] The section of this lecture dealing with Christ is a statement of the Incarnation, a reaffirmation of what the Book of Mormon prophets knew as "the condescension of God" (see 1 Nephi 11; Mosiah 3:1–11; 7:26–28). He who had been in the bosom of the Father—who had been the Lord God Omnipotent, the Holy One of Israel, and the God of Abraham, Isaac, and Jacob—came to earth; he chose to "descend from his throne divine"[23] to accomplish his mission of mercy. The Son is called a "personage of tabernacle" here because his assignment on earth pertained to the redemption and regeneration of the flesh. Thus Elohim is designated as the Father, a being of spirit, glory, and power, while Jesus Christ is called the Son, "because of the flesh."[24] These words are in harmony with the doctrines of the condescension of God in the Book of Mormon. Abinadi thus prophesied that because Jesus the Messiah would dwell "in the flesh he shall be called the Son of God" (Mosiah 15:2). King Limhi explained to Ammon concerning Abinadi:

"And because he said unto them that Christ was the God, the Father of all things, and said that he should take upon him the image of man, and it should be the image after which man was created in the beginning; or in other words, he said that man was created after the image of God, and that God should come down among the children of men, and take upon him flesh and blood, and go forth upon the face of the earth—and now, because he said this, they did put him to death" (Mosiah 7:27–28).

The language of lecture 5 regarding the relationship of the Father to the Son is also highly reminiscent of the language of section 93 of the Doctrine and Covenants. In this revelation, for example, Christ explained that he is called "the Father because [Elohim] gave me of his fulness, and *the Son because I was in the world and made flesh my tabernacle,* and dwelt among the sons of men" (D&C 93:4; emphasis added). Further, in regard to the divine indwelling relationship that exists between the Father and the Son—the manner in which in the resurrection the fulness of the glory of the Father came to be centered in the Son—the revelation continues with an excerpt from the record of John. It is stated that Christ was called the Son of God "because he received not of the fulness at the first," but that in the resurrection "he received a fulness of the glory of the Father; and he received all power, both in heaven and on earth, and the glory of the Father was with him, for he dwelt in him" (D&C 93:14, 16–17).

The divine Sonship of Christ—the fact that Jesus possessed the powers of immortality while he dwelt in the flesh—is also affirmed in lecture 5. Jesus "descended in suffering below that which man can suffer; or, in other words, he suffered greater sufferings and was exposed to more powerful contradictions than any man can be."[25] The conclusion: Jesus of Nazareth was more than man, for the full act of propitiation required a god (see Mosiah 3:7, 9; Alma 34:11). Our Lord is "he that ascended up on high, as also he descended below all things, in that he comprehended all things, that he might be in all and through all things, the light of truth" (D&C 88:6). In the words of Paul, "he that descended is the same also that ascended up far above all heavens, that he might fill all things" (Ephesians 4:10). How is it that Christ "was exposed to more powerful contradictions than any man can be"? Simply stated, the ministry of Messiah was a life filled with irony. During the hours of atonement, for example, he who had remained sinless became, as it were, the great sinner. In the language of Paul, God the Father "made him to be sin for us, who knew no sin" (2 Corinthians 5:21). To the Galatian Saints, Paul taught that "Christ hath redeemed us from the curse of the law, being made a curse for us" (Galatians 3:13). He who deserved least of all to suffer suffered the most—more than mortal mind can fathom. He who had brought life—the more abundant life (see John 10:10)—subjected himself to the powers of death and darkness.

Notwithstanding all the sufferings and the infinite opposition faced by the Infinite One, the Prophet testified that the Savior "kept the law of God and remained without sin, showing thereby that it is in the power of man to keep the law and remain also without sin. And also that by him a righteous judgment might come upon all flesh, that all who walk not in the law of God may justly be condemned by the law and have no excuse for their sins."[26] Jesus never took a backward step or a moral detour. He "was in all points tempted like as we are, yet without sin" (Hebrews 4:15; see also 1 Peter 2:22). As the Sinless One, he is thus the perfect Prototype,[27] the standard against which all others are judged. The standard of perfection is fixed. It is in place. It is irrevocable. Because God himself is the embodiment of "truth, justice, judgment, mercy, and an infinity of fulness, from everlasting to everlasting" (D&C 109:77), he could not expect less from his children. What is possible, however, is not always probable. Though the standard is set and the example a matter of history, the Prophet recognized that ultimate perfection is a matter toward which men and women reach even beyond this life.[28] "Where is the man that is free from vanity?" Joseph Smith asked on a subsequent occasion. "None ever were perfect but Jesus," he taught, "and why was he perfect? because he was the Son of God, and had the fulness of the Spirit, and greater power than any man."[29] Similarly, Elder Bruce R. McConkie declared in an address at Brigham Young University:

"We have to become perfect to be saved in the celestial kingdom. But nobody becomes perfect in this life. Only the Lord Jesus attained that state, and he had an advantage that none of us has. He was the Son of God, and he came into this life with a spiritual capacity and a talent and an inheritance that exceeded beyond all comprehension what any of the rest of us was born with. Our revelations say that he was like unto God in the premortal life and he was, under the Father, the creator of worlds without number. That Holy Being was the Holy One of Israel anciently and he was the Sinless One in mortality. He lived a perfect life, and he set an ideal example. This shows that we can strive and go forward toward that goal, but no other mortal—not the greatest prophets nor the mightiest apostles nor any of the righteous saints of any of the ages—has ever been perfect, but we must become perfect to gain a celestial inheritance. As it is with being born again, and as it is with sanctifying our souls, so becoming perfect in Christ is a process."[30]

Christ is "the way, the truth, and the life" (John 14:6). To the Nephites he said: "I am the law, and the light. Look unto me, and endure to the end, and ye shall live" (3 Nephi 15:9).

The Holy Spirit: The Mind of the Father and Son

Though the Prophet began the fifth lecture by stating that the Father and Son were the supreme power over all things, he also observed that the Holy Spirit is the third member of the eternal presidency and that these three—the Father, Son, and Holy Spirit—"constitute the great, matchless, governing, and supreme power over all things, by whom all things were created and made. And these three constitute the Godhead and are one."[31] It is true, as some have pointed out, that the Prophet did not refer in lecture 5 to the Holy Spirit as a *personage.* As we will discuss later, what Joseph Smith knew and taught and what the Saints understood may be two different matters. One of the earliest references to the personage status of the Holy Spirit in the documents now available to us is from a sermon delivered some six years later, on 9 March 1841, a portion of which I cited earlier. In speaking of the separate functions of the members of the Godhead, Joseph Smith explained that "the Son had a tabernacle and so had the Father, but the Holy Ghost is a personage of spirit without tabernacle."[32] The most famous statement in Latter-day Saint theology regarding the mission of the Spirit is that recorded by Willard Richards in Ramus, Illinois:

"The Father has a body of flesh and bones as tangible as man's; the Son also. But the Holy Ghost is a personage of spirit. And a person cannot have the personage of the Holy Ghost in his heart. He may receive the gift of the Holy Ghost; it may descend upon him but not tarry with him."[33]

On 11 June 1843 Wilford Woodruff recorded the following remarks by the Prophet:

"There is much said concerning God [and] the Godhead. And the scripture says there are Gods many and Lords many. The teachers of the day say that the Father is God, the Son is God, and the Holy Ghost is God and that they are all in one body and one God. Jesus says or prays that those that the Father had given him out of the world might be made one in us as we are one, but if they were to be stuffed into one person that would make a great God. If I were to testify that the world was wrong on this point it would be true. Peter says that Jesus Christ sat on the right hand of God. *Any person that has seen the heavens opened knows that there are three personages in the heavens holding the keys of power.*"[34]

Finally, perhaps the most explicit statement as to the role and mission of the Holy Ghost is recorded by George Laub. According to Brother Laub, Joseph Smith taught on 16 June 1844 that God, Christ, and the Holy Ghost are separate persons but that they "all agree in one or the self same thing. But the Holy Ghost is yet a spiritual body and waiting to take to himself a body as the Savior did, or as God did, or the Gods before them took bodies."[35]

The matter in lecture 5 is complicated somewhat by the unusual manner in which the Prophet describes the work of the Spirit. Jesus Christ is said to have "received a fulness of the glory of the Father, *possessing the same mind with the Father, which mind is the Holy Spirit* that bears record of the Father and the Son."[36] Not only is the Holy Spirit not accorded personage status in this reference, but he seems to be relegated to some type of mystical connecting link between the other two members of the Godhead. The Son is said to be "filled with the fulness of the *mind,* glory, and power, or in other words, the *spirit,* glory, and power of the Father." The Son is "filled with the fulness of the *mind* of the Father, or . . . the *Spirit* of the Father, which Spirit is shed forth upon all who believe on his name and keep his commandments."[37] It appears to me that the difficulty here is heightened by the lack of distinction between what we would call the light of Christ and the Holy Ghost. Joseph Smith is speaking in the broadest of terms and simply refers to the Holy Spirit as the mind of God. "It is true," stated President Charles W. Penrose, "that the Holy Spirit conveys the mind of God; that is, I am speaking now of this universal spirit which is the life and the light of all things, which is in and through and round about all things, and God says he made the world by the power of that spirit. That is his agent; but the personage, the Comforter, which Jesus Christ said he would send when he went away, that was a personage of the Trinity."[38] Elder Bruce R. McConkie likewise wrote that the Savior "possesses the same mind with the Father, knowing and believing and speaking and doing as though he were the Father. This mind is theirs by the power of the Holy Ghost. That is, the Holy Ghost, who is a personage of spirit (a spirit man!), using the light of Christ, can give the same mind to all men, whether mortal or immortal. The saints who are true and faithful in all things have, as Paul said, 'the mind of Christ' (1 Corinthians 2:16), which means also that they have the mind of the Father."[39]

It would not be difficult to suppose that at the time the Lectures on Faith were delivered, the Prophet Joseph Smith had not yet learned of the personage status of the Holy Ghost and thus made no doctrinal distinction between the Spirit's person and powers. There is, however, one major difficulty with drawing such a conclusion. Joseph Smith stated just eleven days before his death: "I have always [taught]," Thomas Bullock reported Joseph Smith as saying, "in all congregations when I have preached, it has been the plurality of Gods. It has been preached fifteen years. I have always declared God to be a distinct personage, Jesus Christ a separate and distinct personage from God the Father. The Holy Ghost was a distinct personage and or spirit, and these three constitute three distinct personages and three Gods."[40]

Rather than contradicting the Prophet—rather than concluding that Joseph did not preach something when he said he had—I choose to believe, with Elders

Penrose and McConkie, that Joseph Smith did know the difference even though that difference is not clear in the records we have. Or it may have been that he thought it unnecessary to make that distinction every time he spoke because he had made it before. As we shall discuss shortly, there was, no doubt, a significant chasm between what the Prophet knew and what the Saints knew, as well as between what the Prophet knew and what he taught.

BECOMING HEIRS OF THE HEAVENLY KINGDOM

In lecture 5 Joseph Smith lifted our vision of man's eternal possibilities. Simply stated, he taught at this early date that man may become even as God. He instructed the School of the Elders that the Saints "who keep [the Lord's] commandments shall grow from grace to grace and become heirs of the heavenly kingdom, and joint-heirs with Jesus Christ. They will possess the same mind, being transformed into the same image or likeness, even the express image of him who fills all in all, being filled with the fulness of his glory and becoming one in him, even as the Father, Son, and Holy Spirit are one."[41] We see reflected once again the doctrine of D&C 93, wherein Christ's pathway to godhood is laid out, and the Saints are taught *how* to worship and *what* to worship. The essence of true worship is emulation, the imitation of the works and labors of Christ.[42] Just as their Prototype received divine assistance from the Father as he gave of himself to his fellow men (i.e., he received "grace for grace"); just as Christ "received not of the fulness" of the glory of the Father at the first, but "continued from grace to grace"—grew line upon line, developed from one level of spiritual grace to a higher; and just as Christ received in the resurrection the fulness of the Father, so may all men and women follow such a path and grow in spiritual graces until they inherit all that the Father has (see D&C 93:12–20).

To say that men may possess "the same mind" as God, that they may be "transformed into [his] same image or likeness," or that they may partake "of the fulness of the Father and the Son through the Spirit,"[43] is to say that men may come unto God in more than metaphorical fashion. To be a "joint-heir with Christ" is to be a co-inheritor with him, to possess on equal standing with the Holder of the birthright.[44] Elder McConkie has emphasized that the fifth lecture on faith teaches "that we, as fallible, weak, mortal men—subject to all the ills, difficulties, and vicissitudes of life—have power to advance and progress and become like our exalted and eternal Father and his beloved Son." It thus sets forth "the same doctrine that concludes, 'As God now is, man may become.' This thing was announced, in principle, in the School of the Prophets and did not have to wait for a King Follett sermon, although, I suppose, the Saints did not fully grasp what was involved in this language initially."[45]

"Here then is Eternal Life," the Prophet would teach at the theological peak of his ministry, "to know the only wise and true God. You have got to learn how to be a God yourself and to be a king and priest to God, [the] same as all have done, by going from a small capacity to another, from grace to grace, until the resurrection, and sit in everlasting power as they who have gone before. . . . How consoling to the mourner when they are called to part with a wife, mother, father, daughter, relative, to know that although the earthly tabernacle shall be dissolved that they shall be heirs of God and joint-heirs of Jesus Christ, to inherit the same power . . . the same as those who are gone before."[46]

Again I am eager to affirm that the Lectures on Faith are not primitive; I do not see them as being out of harmony in any way with what Joseph the Prophet later taught; they are certainly not something beyond which he and the Church later evolved. All the Lectures on Faith, and lecture 5 in particular, contain much that is meaty, much that requires pondering and prayer and comparison and contemplation. They "were given to the saints and not the world, to enable the apostles, elders, and righteous people of the kingdom to fulfill the same plea made by the prophets of old—'Lord, Increase our faith.'"[47]

THE KNOWLEDGE OF GOD:
THE PROPHETS AND THE PEOPLE

"Brother Joseph," observed Wilford Woodruff, "used a great many methods of testing the integrity of men; and he taught a great many things which, in consequence of tradition, required prayer, faith, and a testimony from the Lord, before they could be believed by many of the Saints. His mind was opened by the visions of the Almighty, and the Lord taught him many things by vision and revelation that were never taught publicly in his days; for the people could not bear the flood of intelligence which God poured into his mind."[48]

Five months before his death, Joseph Smith lamented that "there has been a great difficulty in getting anything into the heads of this generation. It has been like splitting hemlock knots with a corn-dodger for a wedge, and a pumpkin for a beetle. Even the Saints are slow to understand.

"I have tried for a number of years to get the minds of the Saints prepared to receive the things of God; but we frequently see some of them, after suffering all they have for the work of God, will fly to pieces like glass as soon as anything comes that is contrary to their traditions: they cannot stand the fire at all. How many will be able to abide a celestial law, and go through and receive their exaltation, I am unable to say, as many are called, but few are chosen."[49]

We simply are unable to gauge how much the Prophet knew—how much God had revealed to him personally—using only the basis of what the Saints knew. It would be a serious historical error to suppose that because the average member of the Church did not understand the nature of the Godhead—did not know, for example, whether the Father had a corporeal body or whether the Holy Ghost was a personage—that Joseph the Prophet did not understand, and that the Lectures on Faith reflect that lack of understanding. This would also apply to some of the leaders of the Church, even some of the first apostles. The fact that the people did not fully grasp the intricacies of the doctrines is totally unrelated to what their leader was able to grasp and thus is unrelated to what he taught and what he intended to be understood. We must not be guilty of setting bounds for God or his prophet-leaders, proscribing them on the basis of our present view of things.

CONCLUSION

In my view, the Lectures on Faith have not received the positive attention they ought to have received by the Latter-day Saints. They were, in fact, acknowledged by the members in 1835 as the "doctrine of the Church of the Latter-day Saints" (1835 edition of the Doctrine and Coventants). I find the doctrine and scope of the lectures to be stimulating and the perspective to be harmonious with traditional theology of the twentieth-century Church. I find their contents, like the contents of the Book of Mormon, to be profound, even though they come from an early period in the Church's history. Truly, one of the flaws in the reasoning of some is an over-reliance upon a linear view of history, an acceptance of the principle that phenomena evolve from previously existing circumstances. Such is certainly not the case in all situations; many events or movements—and, without question, many doctrines—are more revolutionary than evolutionary. The Lectures on Faith are illustrative of this phenomenon: they come from a formative period of our history but make known truths that, when carefully studied and fully appreciated, would be considered consistent with teachings of the mature Joseph Smith and the Nauvoo Church. Whether Joseph Smith himself literally wrote every word in lecture 5 is immaterial to me; the lectures were at least in part written by the Prophet and wholly approved by him in preparation for their inclusion in the first edition of the Doctrine and Covenants.[50]

"In my own judgment," said President Joseph Fielding Smith, "these Lectures on Faith are of great value and should be studied. . . . They were not taken out of the Doctrine and Covenants because they contained false doctrine, and I consider them to be of extreme value in the study of the gospel of Jesus Christ."[51] Perhaps Elder McConkie voiced my own feelings best when he spoke of lecture 5 to a Brigham Young University audience in 1972. "In my own judgment," he said, "it is the most comprehensive, intelligent, inspired utterance that now exists . . . in one place defining, interpreting, expounding, announcing, and testifying what kind of being God is. It was written by the power of the Holy Ghost, by the spirit of inspiration. It is, in effect, eternal scripture; it is true."[52]

Notes

From an address delivered at a symposium on the Lectures on Faith, sponsored by the Religious Studies Center, Brigham Young University, Provo, Utah, March 1988.

1. Bruce R. McConkie, *A New Witness for the Articles of Faith* (Salt Lake City: Deseret Book Co., 1985), 72.
2. Ibid., 185.
3. I should distinguish here between a Latter-day Saint view of God's omnipotence, omniscience, and omnipresence, and that held by many in Catholicism or Protestantism. We do not believe in the utterly transcendent Being of the creeds, nor do we subscribe to the notion of a creation *ex nihilo*. God has all power but works within established parameters. "Whatever His wisdom indicates as necessary to be done God can and will do. The means through which He operates may not be of infinite capacity in themselves, but they are directed by an infinite power. A rational conception of His omnipotence is power to do all that He may will to do" (James E. Talmage, *Jesus the Christ* [Salt Lake City: The Church of Jesus Christ of Latter-day Saints, 1981], 44). Latter-day Saints attest to God's corporeality and thus his inability to be, in person at least, everywhere at the same time. He is able, however, through his Holy Spirit (also called the light of Christ) to be in and through all things.
4. See *Lectures on Faith*, 2:55.
5. See ibid., 5:2–3; 7:8–9, 16.
6. See ibid., 2:2.
7. See ibid., 3:12–24; 4:3–16, 19; 5:1.
8. Ibid., 5:2.
9. Ibid.
10. Ibid.; emphasis added.
11. The other troublesome passage deals with the role of the Holy Spirit as the "mind" of the other two members of the Godhead (*Lectures on Faith*, 5:2) and will be discussed below.
12. Milton V. Backman Jr., *Joseph Smith's First Vision*, 2d ed. (Salt Lake City: Deseret Book Co., 1980), 155–67.
13. *Words of Joseph Smith*, 60; punctuation and spelling corrected.
14. Ibid., 63.
15. Ibid., 64.
16. Ibid., 173.
17. *Lectures on Faith*, 5:2; emphasis added.

18. McConkie, *A New Witness for the Articles of Faith,* 72–73; see also Charles W. Penrose, Conference Report, April 1921, 9–17. 1 Corinthians 15:44; Alma 11:45; Doctrine and Covenants 88:27.

19. Robert J. Matthews, *"A Plainer Translation": Joseph Smith's Translation of the Bible, A History and Commentary* (Provo: Brigham Young University Press, 1975), 96.

20. At an even earlier date (November–December 1830), the Prophet's inspired translation of Genesis resulted in the following scripture: "In the day that God created man, (in the likeness of God made he him,) *in the image of his own body,* male and female created he them, and blessed them, and called their name Adam, in the day when they were created, and became living souls, in the land, upon the footstool of God" (JST, Genesis 6:9; emphasis added; see also Moses 6:8–9).

21. "Truman Coe's 1836 Description of Mormonism," as quoted in Backman, *Joseph Smith's First Vision,* 347, 354; emphasis added.

22. *Lectures on Faith,* 5:2.

23. *Hymns,* no. 193.

24. *Lectures on Faith,* 5:2.

25. Ibid.

26. Ibid.

27. Ibid., 7:9.

28. See *Words of Joseph Smith,* 345, 358.

29. Ibid., 72.

30. Bruce R. McConkie, "Jesus Christ and Him Crucified," *Devotional and Fireside Speeches of the Year, 1976* (Provo: Brigham Young University, 1977), 399–400.

31. *Lectures on Faith,* 5:2.

32. *Words of Joseph Smith,* 64.

33. Ibid., 173.

34. Ibid., 214; emphasis added; spelling and punctuation corrected.

35. Ibid., 382.

36. *Lectures on Faith,* 5:2; emphasis added.

37. Ibid.; emphasis added.

38. Charles W. Penrose, in Conference Report, April 1921, 16.

39. McConkie, *A New Witness for the Articles of Faith,* 75.

40. *Words of Joseph Smith,* 378.

41. *Lectures on Faith,* 5:2.

42. See *Promised Messiah,* 568–69.

43. *Lectures on Faith,* 5:2, 3.

44. Thus those who are entitled to membership in the "Church of the Firstborn" are not simply those who are members of the Lord's earthly church, but rather those who with Christ become joint-heirs to all the Father has; they are entitled to all of the blessings of the Firstborn and thus inherit them as though they were the firstborn. As such they are not just sons and daughters of Jesus Christ but sons and daughters of God, meaning the Father (see *Doctrinal New Testament Commentary,* 2:471–75; see also D&C 76:58).

45. Bruce R. McConkie, "The Lord God of Joseph Smith," *Devotional and Fireside Speeches of the Year, 1971–1972* (Provo: Brigham Young University Press, 1972), 5.

46. *Words of Joseph Smith,* 350.

47. Bruce R. McConkie, "Lord, Increase Our Faith," *Devotional and Fireside Speeches of the Year, 1967–1968* (Provo: Brigham Young University, 1968), 5.

48. Wilford Woodruff, in *Journal of Discourses,* 5:83–84.

49. *History of the Church,* 6:184–85.

50. See *History of the Church,* 2:180.

51. Joseph Fielding Smith, *Seek Ye Earnestly* (Salt Lake City: Deseret Book Co., 1970), 194.

52. Bruce R. McConkie, "The Lord God of Joseph Smith," 4.

THE REVELATION OF THE
DOCTRINE OF ZION

It must have been a mighty vision that filled the mind and heart of Joseph Smith the Seer when he announced: "I calculate to be one of the instruments of setting up the kingdom of [God envisioned by] Daniel by the word of the Lord, and I intend to lay a foundation that will revolutionize the whole world." And how was this to be realized? "It will not be by sword or gun that this kingdom will roll on," the Prophet said. "The power of truth is such that all nations will be under the necessity of obeying the gospel."[1]

Joseph Smith's vision of the kingdom of God was cosmic. It consisted of more than preaching and study and Sabbath services; it entailed the entire renovation of the order of things on earth, the transformation of man and the elevation of society. And at the heart of that sublime scene was the doctrine of Zion, a doctrine and a worldview that would shape the early Church and point the Saints of the last days toward the eschatological ideal. This chapter will focus on the idea of Zion as a people or community of believers, Zion as a specific place, and Zion as a state of being—the pure in heart.

THE DISCOVERY OF ZION

Joseph Smith seems to have first encountered the concept of Zion (in a sense other than the holy mount or holy city in Jerusalem) in his translation of the Book of Mormon. The Book of Mormon prophets spoke of Zion as a holy commonwealth, a *society* of the Saints, *a way of life* that was to be established or brought forth under God's direction; those who fought against it were to incur God's displeasure. The municipals "labor for the welfare of Zion" rather than for money. In addition, in the words of the resurrected Savior, Zion was identified as a specific *place* in the land of America, a land of promise and inheritance for the descendants of Joseph of old (see 1 Nephi 13:37; 2 Nephi 10:11–13; 26:29–31; 28:20–24; 3 Nephi 16:16–18).

Evidence suggests that a key moment in Church history in regard to the discovery of the concept of Zion came during the Prophet Joseph Smith's inspired translation of the King James Bible. By the time Sidney Rigdon joined the Prophet in December 1830 and became the principal scribe in the Bible translation, particulars concerning the patriarch Enoch and his ancient city of Zion were first made known. A King James text of three verses on Enoch and his people was expanded by revelation to more than one hundred verses, restoring knowledge concerning such things as the manner in which an entire society of antedeluvians was spiritually awakened and stimulated to transcendent righteousness; the means by which this ancient people, formerly bent upon selfishness and pride, had their souls changed, saw to the needs of the poor, and became "of one heart and one mind"; and how, through the application of such a divine philosophy, they were translated, taken from the earth into the bosom of God (see Moses 7). Enoch's Zion became the pattern, the scriptural prototype for the Latter-day Saints. In the months that followed, several revelations that we now have in the Doctrine and Covenants spoke of the ancient Zion of Enoch and also provided the broad framework whereby the Latter-day Saints, through the principles of consecration and stewardship, could lay the foundation for a modern society of Zion.

Among the earliest revelations given in this dispensation, now found in the Doctrine and Covenants, was the repeated command, "Now, as you have asked, behold, I say unto you, keep my commandments, and seek to bring forth and establish the cause of Zion" (D&C 6:6; see also 11:6; 12:6; 14:6). Zion thus came to be associated with the restored *Church* and the grander work of the Restoration, and the faithful could take heart in the midst of their troubles, for Zion was the city of God (see D&C 97:19). Indeed, in speaking of the sacred spot where the people of God congregated, the Lord said: "Behold, the land of Zion—I, the Lord, hold it in mine own hands" (D&C 63:25). Surely the King of Zion (see Moses 7:53) would deal mercifully with his subjects.

Zion As a Place

The idea that there was a specific location for the city of Zion within North and South America was made known very early. The Lord explained to Oliver Cowdery in his September 1830 call to preach among the Lamanites that "it is not revealed, and no man knoweth where the city Zion shall be built, but it shall be given hereafter." The Lord then added that the location "shall be on the borders by the Lamanites" (D&C 28:9). It was on 20 July 1831, just as the leaders of the Saints had begun to arrive in Missouri, that the word of the Lord came concerning the specific location of Zion. The Savior declared that the land of Missouri was "the land which I have appointed and consecrated for the gathering of the saints. Wherefore, this is the land of promise, and the place for the city of Zion. . . . The place which is now called Independence is the center place" (D&C 57:1–3).

Zion As an Ensign

Zion is spoken of in scripture as a banner or *ensign* around which a weary or beleaguered people may rally. It is also a *standard* against which the substance and quality of all things are to be evaluated. The Saints are expected to judge all things by a set of guidelines obtained from a source beyond that of unenlightened man. Note the language of the revelation: "Behold, I, the Lord, have made my church in these last days like unto a judge sitting on a hill, or in a high place, to judge the nations. For it shall come to pass that the inhabitants of Zion shall judge all things pertaining to Zion" (D&C 64:37–38). As an illustration of this principle, Elder Joseph Young explained that Joseph Smith the Prophet "recommended the Saints to cultivate as high a state of perfection in their musical harmonies as the standard of the faith which he had brought was superior to sectarian religion. To obtain this, he gave them to understand that the refinement of singing would depend upon the attainment of the Holy Spirit. . . . When these graces and refinements and all the kindred attractions are obtained that characterized the ancient Zion of Enoch, then the Zion of the last days will become beautiful, she will be hailed by the Saints from the four winds, who will gather to Zion with songs of everlasting joy."[2]

In addition, Zion was and is to be the focus, the convergence, and the concentration of all that is good, all that is ennobling, all that is instructive and inspirational. In Zion all things are to be gathered together in one in Christ (see Ephesians 1:10). In short, according to President Brigham Young, "every accomplishment, every polished grace, every useful attainment in mathematics, music, in all science and art belong to the Saints."[3] The Saints "rapidly collect the intelligence that is bestowed upon the nations," President Young said on another occasion, "for all this intelligence belongs to Zion."[4]

ZION AS THE PURE IN HEART

Zion is people, the people of God, those people who have come out of the world of Babylon into the marvelous light of Christ. In this vein the Lord encouraged his little flock: "Verily, thus saith the Lord, let Zion rejoice, for this is Zion—THE PURE IN HEART; therefore, let Zion rejoice, while all the wicked shall mourn" (D&C 97:21). Thus Zion is *a state of being,* a state of purity of heart that entitles one to be known as a member of the household of faith. President Brigham Young therefore spoke of the Saints having Zion in their hearts: "Unless the people live before the Lord in the obedience of His commandments," he said, "they cannot have Zion within them." Further, "As to the spirit of Zion, it is in the hearts of the Saints, of those who love and serve the Lord with all their might, mind, and strength."[5] On another occasion President Young affirmed: "Zion will be redeemed and built up, and the saints will rejoice. This is the land of Zion; and *who are Zion? The pure in heart are Zion; they have Zion within them.* Purify yourselves, sanctify the Lord God in your hearts, and have the Zion of God within you."[6] Finally, President Young asked: "*Where is Zion? Where the organization of the Church of God is. And may it dwell spiritually in every heart;* and may we so live as to always enjoy the Spirit of Zion."[7]

ZION AS THE PLACE OF GATHERING

Isaiah the prophet had spoken some seven hundred years before Christ of the "mountain of the Lord's house" being established in the tops of the mountains (Isaiah 2:2). In July 1840 Joseph Smith declared (in harmony with the Savior's teachings in the Book of Mormon—see 3 Nephi 16:16–18) that "the land of Zion consists of all North and South America, but that *any place where the Saints gather is Zion.*"[8] The latter part of this statement—that Zion represented more than a place or a single location but rather any locus of gathering—is significant. It broadens the notion of Zion to include areas around the world where the people of the covenant congregate. The Lord surely foresaw this larger vision of Zion when he said in the midst of the Missouri persecutions, "Zion shall not be moved out of her place, notwithstanding her children are scattered. They that remain, and are pure in heart, shall return, and come to their inheritances, they and their children, with songs of everlasting joy, to build up the waste places of Zion—and all these things that the prophets might be fulfilled. And, behold, there is none other place appointed than that which I have appointed; neither shall there be any other place appointed than that which I have appointed, for the work of the gathering of my saints—until the day cometh that there is found no more room for them; and then I have other places which I will appoint unto them, and *they shall be called stakes, for the curtains or the strength of Zion*" (D&C 101:17–21; emphasis added). In the dedicatory prayer of the Kirtland Temple, the Prophet pleaded in behalf of the Saints, "that they may come forth to Zion, or *to her stakes, the places of thine appointment,* with songs of everlasting joy" (D&C 109:39; emphasis added). The revelations are explicit in their pronouncement that safety and refuge are to be found in the stakes of Zion. "Arise and shine forth," the Lord implored, "that thy light may be a standard for the nations; and that the gathering together upon the land of Zion, *and upon her stakes,* may be for a defense, and for a refuge from the storm, and from wrath when it shall be poured out without mixture upon the whole earth" (D&C 115:5–6; emphasis added).

As to the future of Zion, the New Jerusalem, Elder Bruce R. McConkie has written: "The center place! Let Israel gather to the stakes of Zion in all nations. Let every land be a Zion to those appointed to dwell there. Let the fulness of the gospel be for all the saints in all nations. Let no blessing be denied them. Let temples arise wherein the fulness of the ordinances of the Lord's house may be administered. *But still there is a center place, a place where the chief temple shall stand, a place to which the Lord shall come, a place whence the law shall go forth to govern all the earth in that day when the Second David reigns personally upon the earth. And that center place is what men now call Independence in Jackson County, Missouri,* but which in a day to come will be the Zion of our God and the City of Holiness of his people. The site is selected; the place is known; the decree has gone forth; and the promised destiny is assured."[9]

At the same time that the Church will establish a significant presence in Independence, Missouri, and although Jackson County will become a gathering place, indeed the Center Place, yet there will always be, as suggested above, a need for the stakes of Zion throughout the earth far and wide, a need for the Saints to gather to their own lands and congregate with their own people. President Spencer W. Kimball explained: "Now, the gathering of Israel consists of joining the true

Church and . . . coming to a knowledge of the true God. . . . Any person, therefore, who has accepted the restored gospel, and who now seeks to worship the Lord in his own tongue and with the Saints in the nations where he lives, has complied with the law of the gathering of Israel and is heir to all of the blessings promised the saints in these last days."[10] In addition, President Kimball taught: "The First Presidency and the Twelve see great wisdom in the multiple Zions, many gathering places where the Saints within their own culture and nation can act as a leaven in the building of the kingdom—a kingdom which seeks no earthly rewards or treasures. Sometimes, inadvertently, we have given artificial encouragement to individuals to leave their native land and culture and, too often, this has meant the loss of the leaven that is so badly needed, and the individuals involved have sometimes regretted their migrations."[11]

In this spirit—the spirit of an expansive concept of Zion—it is wrong to suppose and misleading to suggest that all of the Saints from all over the world will in a future day gather physically to Missouri. Elder McConkie observed, "As we are aware, the building of the New Jerusalem lies in the future, at a time yet to be designated by revelation. There is no present call for the saints to purchase land or to live in Jackson County or in any place connected therewith. The revealed word relative to the gathering to Independence and its environs will come through the prophet of God on earth. When it does come—with the consequent return of the saints to that Zion which shall not be moved out of its place—that call will not be for the saints in general to assemble there. The return to Jackson County will be by delegates, as it were. Those whose services are needed there will assemble as appointed. The rest of Israel will remain in their appointed places. The Lord's house is a house of order, and faithful saints do as they are told and go at the bidding of their prophet, for his voice is the voice of the Lord."[12]

CONCLUSION

Like the true and living church of which we are a part, the concept of Zion has grown and expanded as we have been humble and teachable enough as a people to perceive the plans and purposes of the Almighty. Elder Erastus Snow pointed out in 1884 that when the early Saints "first heard the fullness of the Gospel preached by the first Elders, and read the revelations given through the Prophet Joseph Smith, our ideas of Zion were very limited. But as our minds began to grow and expand, why we began to look upon Zion as a great people, and the Stakes of Zion as numerous. . . . We ceased to set bounds to Zion and her Stakes."[13] Likewise, Elder

Joseph Young explained that many Saints of the nineteenth century—moved upon by the spirit of prophecy and revelation, such that future events appeared close at hand—misconstrued and miscalculated on a number of matters, including the time when the Saints should return to Missouri and redeem Zion. "The Holy Spirit brought many things close to their minds—they appeared right by, and hence many were deceived. . . . I knew that faith and the Holy Ghost brought the designs of Providence close by, and by that means we were enabled to scan them, . . . but we had not knowledge enough to digest and fully comprehend those things."[14] Indeed, as Joseph Smith himself explained: "The things of God are of deep import; and time, and experience, and careful and ponderous and solemn thoughts can only find them out."[15] And so it is in regard to the doctrine of Zion. Careful and ponderous and solemn thoughts—informed and inspired by the revelations of the Restoration, the words of living oracles, and the personal guidance of the Holy Spirit—can lead us to grasp and share the Prophet Joseph's vision of this holy enterprise.

Zion is a place. Zion is a people. Zion is a holy state of being. In the words of President Spencer W. Kimball, Zion is "the highest order of priesthood society."[16] It is the heritage of the Saints. "The building up of Zion," Joseph Smith taught, "is a cause that has interested the people of God in every age; it is a theme upon which prophets, priests and kings have dwelt with peculiar delight; they have looked forward with joyful anticipation to the day in which we live; and fired with heavenly and joyful anticipations they have sung and written and prophesied of this our day; but they died without the sight; we are the favored people that God has made choice of to bring about the Latter-day glory."[17] This is the destiny of those who endure faithfully to the end. In that sense, as Joseph Smith stated, "We ought to have the building up of Zion as our greatest object."[18]

Notes

From "The Revelation of the Doctrine of Zion," in *Regional Studies in Latter-day Saint Church History: Missouri* (Provo, Utah: Department of Church History and Doctrine, Brigham Young University, 1994), 233–40.

1. *Teachings of the Prophet Joseph Smith,* 366.
2. Joseph Young, in "Vocal Music," in *History of the Organization of the Seventies* (Salt Lake City: Deseret Steam Printing Establishment, 1878), 14–15.
3. Brigham Young, in *Journal of Discourses,* 10:224.
4. Ibid., 8:279.
5. Ibid., 2:253.
6. Ibid., 8:198; emphasis added.
7. Ibid., 8:205; emphasis added.
8. *Words of Joseph Smith,* 415; emphasis added; spelling and punctuation corrected.

9. Bruce R. McConkie, *A New Witness for the Articles of Faith* (Salt Lake City: Deseret Book Co., 1985), 595; emphasis added.

10. Spencer W. Kimball, *Teachings of Spencer W. Kimball,* ed. Edward L. Kimball (Salt Lake City: Bookcraft, 1982), 439.

11. Ibid., 440.

12. *Millennial Messiah,* 294.

13. Erastus Snow, in *Journal of Discourses,* 25:30–31.

14. Joseph Young, in *Journal of Discourses,* 9:230.

15. *Teachings of the Prophet Joseph Smith,* 137.

16. Spencer W. Kimball, in Conference Report, October 1977, 125.

17. *Teachings of the Prophet Joseph Smith,* 231.

18. Ibid., 160.

Chapter 21

BEYOND THE VEIL:
TWO LATTER-DAY REVELATIONS

W e will live to sense the significance of [the announcement of sections 137 and 138 being added to the Doctrine and Covenants]; we will tell our grandchildren and our great-grandchildren, and we will record in our diaries, that we were on the earth and remember when that took place,"[1] said Elder Boyd K. Packer of the Quorum of the Twelve Apostles.

Additions to the Doctrine and Covenants are rare. The presentation of sections 137 and 138 marks the only time since President Wilford Woodruff's 1890 manifesto was added that the Church has been given the opportunity to accept a new revelation as part of our standard works.

A closer look at how we got these revelations and what they say may help us understand why they are now included in the Doctrine and Covenants.

THE VISION OF THE
CELESTIAL KINGDOM (D&C 137)

The historical setting of Joseph Smith's vision of the celestial kingdom is both inspiring and informative. In 1833 the Lord reminded the Saints in Kirtland, Ohio, of his commandment to "build a house, in the which house I design to endow those whom I have chosen with power from on high" (D&C 95:8). After it was built, the Lord rewarded their sacrifices with a marvelous outpouring of light and truth. One Latter-day Saint historian has written concerning this eventful epoch in our history:

"During a fifteen-week period, extending from January 21 to May 1, 1836, probably more Latter-day Saints beheld visions and witnessed other unusual spiritual manifestations than during any other era in the history of the Church. There were reports of Saints' beholding heavenly beings at ten different meetings held during that time. At eight of these meetings, many reported seeing angels; and at five of the services, individuals testified that Jesus, the Savior, appeared. While the Saints were thus communing with heavenly hosts, many prophesied, some spoke in tongues, and others received the gift of interpretation of tongues."[2]

On Thursday evening, 21 January 1836, the Prophet and a number of Church leaders from Kirtland and Missouri gathered in the temple. After anointings and after all the presidency had laid their hands upon the Prophet's head and pronounced many glorious blessings and prophecies, a mighty vision burst upon the Prophet.[3]

"The heavens were opened upon us, and I beheld the celestial kingdom of God, and the glory thereof, whether in the body or out I cannot tell.

"I saw the transcendent beauty of the gate through which the heirs of that kingdom will enter, which was like unto circling flames of fire;

"Also the blazing throne of God, whereon was seated the Father and the Son.

"I saw the beautiful streets of that kingdom, which had the appearance of being paved with gold" (D&C 137:1–4).

This vision of the celestial kingdom was not unlike John the Revelator's vision of the holy city, the earth in its sanctified and celestial state: "The foundations of the wall of the city," writes John, "were garnished with all manner of precious stones." Further, "the street of the city was pure gold, as it were transparent glass" (Revelation 21:19, 21).

Joseph's account of the vision continues:

"I saw Father Adam and Abraham; and my father and my mother; my brother Alvin, that has long since slept;

"And marveled how it was that he had obtained an inheritance in that kingdom, seeing that he had departed this life before the Lord had set his hand to gather Israel the second time, and had not been baptized for the remission of sins" (vv. 5–6).

Joseph's vision was a glimpse into the future celestial realm; he saw his parents in the kingdom of the just, when in fact both were still living in 1836. Father Smith was, interestingly, in the same room with his son at the time the vision was received.

The Prophet also saw his brother Alvin. Alvin Smith was the firstborn of Joseph Sr. and Lucy Mack Smith. He had a pleasant and loving disposition, and he constantly sought opportunities to aid the family in their financial struggles. The

Prophet later described his oldest brother as one in whom there was no guile,[4] and as "a very handsome man, surpassed by none but Adam and Seth."[5]

Lucy Mack Smith writes that on the morning of 15 November 1823, "Alvin was taken very sick with the bilious colic." One physician hurried to the Smith home and administered calomel to Alvin. The dose of calomel "lodged in his stomach," and on the third day of sickness, Alvin realized that his time was short. As Alvin was dying, he asked that each of the Smith children come to his bedside for his parting counsel and final expression of love. According to Mother Smith's record, "When he came to Joseph, he said, 'I am now going to die, the distress which I suffer, and the feelings that I have, tell me my time is very short. I want you to be a good boy, and do everything that lies in your power to obtain the Record. [Joseph had been visited by Moroni less than three months before this time.] Be faithful in receiving instruction, and in keeping every commandment that is given you.'"[6]

Alvin died on 19 November 1823. Lucy Mack Smith writes of the pall of grief surrounding his passing: "Alvin was a youth of singular goodness of disposition—kind and amiable, so that lamentation and mourning filled the whole neighborhood in which he resided."[7]

Joseph wrote many years later: "I remember well the pangs of sorrow that swelled my youthful bosom and almost burst my tender heart when he died. He was the oldest and noblest of my father's family. . . . He lived without spot from the time he was a child. . . . He was one of the soberest of men, and when he died the angel of the Lord visited him in his last moments."[8]

Inasmuch as Alvin had died seven years before the organization of the Church and had not been baptized by proper authority, Joseph wondered during his vision how it was possible for his brother to have attained the highest heaven.

"Thus came the voice of the Lord unto me, saying: All who have died without a knowledge of this gospel, who would have received it if they had been permitted to tarry, shall be heirs of the celestial kingdom of God;

"Also all that shall die henceforth without a knowledge of it, who would have received it with all their hearts, shall be heirs of that kingdom;

"For I, the Lord, will judge all men according to their works, according to the desire of their hearts" (vv. 7–9).

Joseph learned that every person will have an opportunity—here or hereafter—to accept and apply the principles of the gospel of Jesus Christ. This vision reaffirmed that the Lord will judge men not only by their actions, but also by their attitudes—the desires of their hearts (see also Alma 41:3).

Another of the profoundly beautiful doctrines enunciated in the Vision of the Celestial Kingdom deals with the status of children who die. "And I also beheld that all children who die before they arrive at the years of accountability are saved in the celestial kingdom of heaven" (v. 10).

This affirmed what earlier prophets had taught. King Benjamin had learned from an angel that "the infant perisheth not that dieth in his infancy" (Mosiah 3:18). And after having described the nature of those who will come forth in the first resurrection, Abinadi said simply: "Little children also have eternal life" (Mosiah 15:25).

A revelation given to Joseph Smith in September 1830 had specified that "little children are redeemed from the foundation of the world through mine Only Begotten" (D&C 29:46; see also JST, Matthew 19:13–15). And Joseph taught in 1842 that "the Lord takes many away, even in infancy, that they may escape the envy of man, and the sorrows and evils of this present world; they were too pure, too lovely, to live on earth; therefore, if rightly considered, instead of mourning we have reason to rejoice as they are delivered from evil, and we shall soon have them again."[9] These children will come forth from the grave as they lie down—as children.[10] They will not be expected to face in their resurrected state the same challenges we face in our mortal state, but will go on to enjoy the highest and grandest blessings of exaltation associated with the everlasting continuation of the family unit.[11]

Four and one-half years after receiving the Vision of the Celestial Kingdom, Joseph the Prophet delivered his first public discourse on the subject of baptism for the dead. One man who was in attendance has left us the following account:

"I was present at a discourse that the prophet Joseph delivered on baptism for the dead 15 August 1840. He read the greater part of the 15th chapter of Corinthians and remarked that the Gospel of Jesus Christ brought glad tidings of great joy. . . . He also said the Apostle [Paul] was talking to a people who understood baptism for the dead, for it was practiced among them. He went on to say that people could now act for their friends who had departed this life, and that the plan of salvation was calculated to save all who were willing to obey the requirements of the law of God. He went on and made a very beautiful discourse."[12]

A month following this address, Joseph Smith Senior passed away. Just before his death, Father Smith requested that someone be baptized in behalf of his oldest son, Alvin. Hyrum Smith complied with his father's last wishes and was baptized by proxy for Alvin in 1840 and again in 1841.[13] Alvin received the endowment by proxy on 11 April 1877 and was sealed to his parents on 25 August 1897.[14]

THE VISION OF THE REDEMPTION OF THE DEAD (D&C 138)

The truths revealed initially to the Prophet Joseph Smith continued to be expanded "line upon line" after his death. The Lord revealed to the Prophet's nephew—Joseph F. Smith—additional insights into the manner in which the gospel is preached in the world of spirits.

During the last six months of his life, President Joseph F. Smith suffered from the effects of age and spent much time in his personal study in the Beehive House. He did, however, garner enough strength to attend general conference in October 1918. In the opening session, he arose to address the Saints, and with a voice filled with emotion said:

"I will not, I dare not, attempt to enter upon many things that are resting upon my mind this morning, and I shall postpone until some future time, the Lord be willing, my attempt to tell you some of the things that are in my mind, and that dwell in my heart. I have not lived alone these last five months. I have dwelt in the spirit of prayer, of supplication, of faith and of determination; and I have had my communication with the Spirit of the Lord continuously."[15]

According to his son, Joseph Fielding Smith, the President was here expressing in broad terms the fact that during the past six months he had been the recipient of numerous manifestations, some of which he shared with his son. He had received one of these manifestations, the Vision of the Redemption of the Dead, just the day before, on 3 October 1918, and recorded it immediately following the close of the conference.[16]

Joseph F. Smith's attention was drawn to the world beyond mortality by his frequent confrontation with death. His parents, Hyrum and Mary Fielding Smith, both died while he was a young man. Among his later trials were the deaths of many of his children. Joseph Fielding Smith has written: "When death invaded his home, as frequently it did, and his little ones were taken from him, he grieved with a broken heart and mourned, not as those mourn who live without hope, but for the loss of his 'precious jewels' dearer to him than life itself."[17]

Just a few months before President Smith received the Vision of the Redemption of the Dead, his oldest son, Hyrum Mack Smith, a member of the Council of the Twelve Apostles, died; he was only forty-five years of age. This was a particularly traumatic affliction for the President. Already in a weakened physical condition due to age, he suffered "one of the most severe blows that he was ever called upon to endure."[18]

However, during much of his life, the veil covering the postmortal life had been thin. As a young missionary in Hawaii, he had received a dream or vision that strengthened his faith and built his confidence. Through the years that followed, it helped him chart his course and gave him assurance that his labors were acceptable to the Lord and to his predecessors in the presidency of the Church. In the dream, young Joseph encountered his uncle, the Prophet Joseph, and was fortified in his desire to remain free from the taints of the world. In addition, he learned at an early age that the separation between mortality and immortality is subtle and that the Lord frequently permits an intermingling of the inhabitants of the two spheres.[19]

The last thirty months of Joseph F. Smith's life, April 1916 to October 1918, represent an era of particular spiritual enlightenment. During this time he delivered to the Church some of the most important and inspiring insights of this dispensation.

At the April 1916 general conference President Smith delivered a remarkable address entitled "In the Presence of the Divine." He spoke of the nearness of the world of spirits, and of the interest and concern the spirits have for us and our labors. He emphasized that those who labored so diligently in their mortal estate to establish the cause of Zion would not be denied the privilege of "looking down upon the results of their own labors" from their *post-mortal* estate. In fact, "they are as deeply interested in our welfare today, if not with greater capacity, with far more interest behind the veil, than they were in the flesh." Perhaps his keynote statement in this sermon is the following: "Sometimes the Lord expands our vision from this point of view and this side of the veil, that we feel and seem to realize that we can look beyond the thin veil which separates us from that other sphere."[20]

In June 1916 the First Presidency and the Twelve released a doctrinal exposition in pamphlet form entitled "The Father and the Son," to alleviate doctrinal misunderstandings concerning the nature of the Godhead, and specifically the role of Jesus Christ as "Father."[21]

President Joseph F. Smith delivered one of his most significant addresses—"Status of Children in the Resurrection"—at a temple fast meeting in February 1918. From it we gain not only an insight into the power and prophetic stature of one schooled and prepared in doctrine, but we are allowed also a brief glimpse into the heart of a noble father who, having lost little ones to death and having mourned their absence, rejoices in the sure knowledge that (1) children are immortal beings, spirits who continue to live and progress beyond the veil; and (2) as taught by the

Prophet Joseph Smith, children will come forth from the grave as they lie down— as children—and such persons will thereafter be nurtured and reared to physical maturity by worthy parents. "O how I have been blessed with these children," exulted President Smith, "and how happy I shall be to meet them on the other side!"[22]

Months later, on Thursday, 3 October 1918, President Smith, largely confined to his room because of illness, sat reading and meditating about the universal nature of the Atonement and about the Apostle Peter's allusions to Christ's postmortal ministry. The stage was set: preparation of a lifetime and preparation of the moment were recompensed with a heavenly endowment—the Vision of the Redemption of the Dead.

"As I pondered over these things which are written," President Smith wrote, "the eyes of my understanding were opened, and the Spirit of the Lord rested upon me, and I saw the hosts of the dead, both small and great" (D&C 138:11).

Joseph F. Smith saw in vision "an innumerable company of the spirits of the just," the righteous dead from the days of Adam to the meridian of time. In his vision, they were anxiously awaiting the advent of Christ into their dimension of life and were exuberant in their anticipation of an imminent resurrection (see vv. 12–17). Having consummated the atoning sacrifice on Golgotha, the Lord of the living and the dead passed in the twinkling of an eye into the world of the departed. The dead, having "looked upon the long absence of their spirits from their bodies as a bondage" (see v. 50; see also D&C 45:17), are, in a sense, in prison; even the righteous seek "deliverance" (see vv. 15, 18). Thus, the Master came to declare "liberty to the captives who had been faithful" (v. 18). As Peter had said, Christ went beyond the veil to preach "unto the spirits in prison" (1 Peter 3:19). Joseph Smith had taught: "Hades, Shaole, paradise, spirits in prison, are all one; it is a world of spirits."[23] And as Elder Bruce R. McConkie has explained, in this vision, "it is clearly set forth that the whole spirit world, and not only that portion desig- nated as hell, is considered to be a spirit prison."[24] However, Christ extended to the righteous spirits "power to come forth, after his resurrection from the dead, to enter into his Father's kingdom, there to be crowned with immortality and eternal life" (v. 51).

While pondering the question of how the Savior could have taught the gospel to so many in the spirit world in the brief period between his death and resurrec- tion, President Smith received what is a most significant doctrinal insight. He came to understand "that the Lord went not in person among the wicked and the disobe- dient" but rather "organized his forces and appointed messengers, clothed with power and authority" (vv. 29–30), that such representatives might carry the message of the gospel "unto whom he [the Lord] could not go personally, because of their rebellion and transgression" (v. 37). The chosen messengers carry the gospel message to those who had no opportunity in mortality to accept or reject the truth, and also to those who rejected the prophets on earth. These are taught the first principles and ordinances of the gospel (including the vicarious nature of the ordinances), in order that they might be judged and rewarded by the same divine standards as those who inhabit the world of mortals (see vv. 31–34).

The insight that Christ did not personally visit the disobedient is a doctrinal matter introduced to the Church for the first time in this vision, broadening our scope of understanding of the work within that sphere. However, this clarification confirmed what had been taught by Joseph Smith: the faithful in this life continue to teach and labor in the world of spirits in behalf of those who know not God (see v. 57). As recorded in George Laub's journal under the date 12 May 1844, the Prophet Joseph declared: "Now all those [who] die in the faith go to the prison of spirits to preach to the dead in body, but they are alive in the spirit, and those spirits preach to the spirits that they may live according to God in the Spirit, and men do minister for them in the flesh."[25] Joseph F. Smith had taught this doctrine previously;[26] here he became an eyewitness of it.

As the vision continues, President Smith perceived the identity of many of the noble and great from the beginning of time, including Adam, Seth, Noah, Abraham, Isaiah, the Nephite prophets before Christ, and many more. In addition, he recognized Mother Eve and many of her faithful daughters. President Smith had taught a number of years earlier that women minister to women in the spirit world, even as they do in holy places on earth.[27] Again, through this vision, he became an eyewitness of that fact.

Having laid before us his remarkable vision—"a complete and comprehensive confirmation of the established doctrine of the Church where salvation for the dead is concerned"[28]—President Smith concluded his singular doctrinal contribution with his testimony: "Thus was the vision of the redemption of the dead revealed to me, and I bear record, and I know that this record is true, through the blessing of our Lord and Savior, Jesus Christ, even so. Amen" (v. 60).

The vision was presented to the First Presidency, the Twelve, and the Presiding Patriarch in a council meeting on Thursday, 31 October 1918. Because of his weakened condition, the President was not able to be in attendance but asked his son, Joseph Fielding Smith, to read the revelation to the gathered General Authorities.

Elder James Talmage recorded the following in his personal journal: "By united action the Council of the Twelve, with the Counselors in the First Presidency, and the Presiding Patriarch accepted and endorsed the revelation as the word of the Lord."[29]

President Smith's physical condition worsened during the first weeks of November 1918, and he died November 19. At the next general conference Elder Talmage delivered a touching and appropriate tribute to the President: "Where is he now?

"He was permitted shortly before his passing to have a glimpse into the hereafter, and to learn where he would soon be at work. He was a preacher of righteousness on earth, he is a preacher of righteousness today. He was a missionary from his boyhood up, and he is a missionary today amongst those who have not yet heard the gospel, though they have passed from mortality into the spirit world. I cannot conceive of him as otherwise than busily engaged in the work of the Master."[30]

CONCLUSION

Joseph Smith's vision of the celestial kingdom portrays a loving God who has indeed many mansions prepared. Joseph F. Smith's vision of the redemption of the dead sets forth with remarkable clarity the manner in which the Savior "declared liberty to the captives" in the meridian of time and also unfolds the pattern by which the doctrines of salvation continue to be made known in the world beyond the grave.

And so it is that the work of redemption goes forward on both sides of the veil. "Because of this," Peter taught the Saints, "is the gospel preached to them who are dead, that they might be judged according to men in the flesh, but live in the spirit according to the will of God" (JST, 1 Peter 4:6).

Notes

From "Beyond the Veil: Two Latter-day Revelations," *Ensign,* October 1985, 9–13.

1. Boyd K. Packer, "Teach the Scriptures," in *Charge to Religious Educators,* 2d ed. (Salt Lake City: The Church of Jesus Christ of Latter-day Saints, 1982), 21.
2. Milton V. Backman Jr., *The Heavens Resound: A History of the Latter-day Saints in Ohio* (Salt Lake City: Deseret Book Co., 1983), 285.
3. See *History of the Church,* 2:379–80.
4. Ibid., 5:126.
5. Ibid., 5:247.
6. Lucy Mack Smith, *History of Joseph Smith,* ed. Preston Nibley (Salt Lake City: Bookcraft, 1958), 87.
7. Ibid., 88.

8. *History of the Church,* 5:126–27.

9. Ibid., 4:553.

10. See ibid., 4:555–56.

11. See Bruce R. McConkie, "The Salvation of Little Children," *Ensign,* April 1977, 5–6.

12. See *Words of Joseph Smith,* 49; see also *History of the Church,* 4:231.

13. See "Nauvoo Baptisms for the Dead," Book A, LDS Church Genealogical Society Archives, Salt Lake City, Utah, 145, 149.

14. From Joseph Smith Sr. family group sheet, LDS Church Genealogical Society Archives, Salt Lake City, Utah.

15. Joseph F. Smith, in Conference Report, October 1918, 2.

16. See Joseph Fielding Smith, *The Life of Joseph F. Smith* (Salt Lake City: Deseret Book Co., 1969), 466.

17. Ibid., 455.

18. Ibid., 473–74.

19. See ibid., 445–47.

20. Joseph F. Smith, in Conference Report, April 1916, 1–8.

21. See *Messages of the First Presidency,* 5:23–34.

22. Ibid., 5:90–98.

23. *History of the Church,* 5:425

24. Bruce R. McConkie, "A New Commandment: Save Thyself and Thy Kindred," *Ensign,* August 1976, 11.

25. *Words of Joseph Smith,* 370; spelling and punctuation corrected.

26. See *Gospel Doctrine,* 134–35, 460–61.

27. Ibid., 461.

28. Bruce R. McConkie, "A New Commandment," 11.

29. James E. Talmage Journal, LDS Church Archives, Salt Lake City, Utah, under date of 31 October 1918.

30. James E. Talmage, in Conference Report, June 1919, 60.

FAMILIES

Chapter   22

THE HOUSE OF ISRAEL:
FROM EVERLASTING TO EVERLASTING

Several years ago I was startled by a question from a bright young woman in a rather large introductory Book of Mormon class. We were about two-thirds of the way through the second half of the Book of Mormon. She said, essentially, "Brother Millet, you continue to use a phrase that I don't understand. Maybe others in the class have the same problem. You keep referring to 'the house of Israel.' What do you mean?" For a full ten seconds I stood in wonder. It never occurred to me that at this point in the two-semester course I needed to define and describe something so fundamental. I made a brief explanation during the period and asked her to see me after class. I discovered that she was an "A" student, had been reared in a family who were active in the Church, had completed four years of seminary, and had an excellent knowledge of the gospel.

A year later in a large class for returned missionaries that featured the teachings of the Book of Mormon, a young man raised his hand during the middle of our discussion of the Savior's teachings in 3 Nephi concerning the destiny of Israel. He asked: "Brother Millet, I don't mean to be disrespectful or irreverent in any way, but I need to know: What difference does it make if I am of the house of Israel? Why does it matter that my patriarchal blessing specifies that I am of the tribe of Ephraim?" During this same class period, I asked the class: "How many of you feel that you are adopted into the house of Israel?" Of the eighty members of the class, perhaps sixty raised their hands, evidencing their own misunderstandings concerning patriarchal declarations of lineage.

These instances, and others that might be cited, illustrate what I sense to be a particular problem among many Latter-day Saints as this century draws to a close and as we draw nearer to the time when the Holy One of Israel will return to reign over his covenant people. I sense frequently among young and old a lack of covenant-consciousness, not necessarily in regard to the covenants and ordinances required for salvation, but rather a lack of appropriate kinship and identity with ancient Israel and with the fathers—Abraham, Isaac, and Jacob—and the responsibilities we have inherited from them.

In our democratic and egalitarian society—in a time when equality and brotherhood are all-important—I fear that we are losing a feel for what it means to be a covenant people, what it means to be a chosen people. Too many, even among the Latter-day Saints, cry out that such sentiments are parochial and primitive, that they lead to exclusivism and racism. Others contend that to emphasize Israel's chosen status is to denigrate and degrade others not designated as Israel.

I am convinced that many years of careful and prayerful study of scripture—particularly the Old Testament and the Book of Mormon—will not only bring people to understand in their minds the origins and destiny of the descendants of Jacob, but will also cause them to know in their hearts what it means to come to earth through a chosen lineage and what God would have them do to be a light to the world, particularly to so many who are in spiritual darkness. I feel that the words of the Lord to ancient Israel should be received by modern Israel with sobriety and humility, but they *must* be received and believed if we are to realize our potential to become a holy people and a royal priesthood. Jehovah spoke millennia ago of "Israel, whom I have chosen" (Isaiah 44:1), and assured the Israelites that "you only have I known of all the families of the earth" (Amos 3:2; see also Isaiah 45:4). This chapter will deal with the house of Israel—its place and mission on the earth; how and why God has chosen them; and what things lie ahead for the people that God delights to call his "peculiar treasure." The subject is vast and obviously worthy of volumes, but I will attempt to be brief and thus touch lightly upon what I perceive to be crucial elements in understanding Israel's past, present, and future.

Israel in Premortality

Zenos's allegory of the olive tree draws to a close as the millennial day witnesses the gathering of Israel in great numbers by the chosen servants and as the Gentiles join with Israel to constitute one royal family. "And thus they labored, with all diligence, according to the commandments of the Lord of the vineyard, even until the bad had been cast away out of the vineyard, and the Lord had preserved unto himself that the trees had become again the natural fruit; and they became like unto one body; and the fruits were equal; and *the Lord of the vineyard had preserved unto himself the natural fruit, which was most precious unto him from the beginning"* (Jacob 5:74; emphasis added). I believe this to be a reference to Jehovah's love and tender regard for Israel, which stretches beyond her mortal origins and sojournings and reaches back to the premortal day wherein certain souls qualified for a select status.

Following our birth as spirits, being endowed with agency, each of the spirit sons and daughters of God grew and developed and progressed according to his or her desires for truth and righteousness. "Being subject to law and having their agency," Elder Bruce R. McConkie has written, "all the spirits of men, while yet in the Eternal Presence, developed aptitudes, talents, capacities, and abilities of every sort, kind, and degree. During the long expanse of life that then was, an infinite variety of talents and abilities came into being. As the ages rolled, no two spirits remained alike. . . . Abraham and Moses and all of the prophets sought and obtained the talent for spirituality. Mary and Eve were two of the greatest spirit daughters of the Father. The whole house of Israel, known and segregated out from their fellows, was inclined toward spiritual things."[1] Perhaps the greatest foreordination—based on premortal faithfulness—is foreordination to lineage and family: certain individuals come to earth through a designated channel, through a lineage that entitles them to remarkable blessings, but also through a lineage that carries with it burdens and responsibilities. As a people, therefore, we enjoy what my colleague Brent Top calls "a type of collective foreordination—a selection of spirits to form an entire favored group or lineage." Yet, he adds, "although it is a collective foreordination it is nonetheless based on individual premortal faithfulness and spiritual capacity."[2] In the words of Elder Melvin J. Ballard, Israel is "a group of souls tested, tried, and proven before they were born into the world. . . . Through this lineage were to come the true and tried souls that had demonstrated their righteousness in the spirit world before they came here."[3]

"Remember the days of old," Moses counseled his people, "consider the years of many generations: ask thy father, and he will shew thee; thy elders, and they will tell thee. When the most High divided to the nations their inheritance, when he separated the sons of Adam, he set the bounds of the people *according to the number of the children of Israel.* For the Lord's portion is his people; Jacob is the lot of his inheritance" (Deuteronomy 32:7–9; emphasis added). In speaking to the Athenians, the Apostle Paul declared: "God that made the world and all things therein, . . . hath made of one blood all nations of men for to dwell on all the face of the earth, and *hath determined the times before appointed, and the bounds of their habitation"* (Acts 17:24, 26; emphasis added). President Harold B. Lee explained that "those born to the lineage of Jacob, who was later to be called Israel, and his posterity, who were known as the children of Israel, were born into the most illustrious lineage of any of those who came upon the earth as mortal beings. All these rewards were seemingly promised, or foreordained, before the world was. Surely these matters must have been determined by the kind of lives we had lived in that premortal spirit world. Some may question these assumptions, but at the same time they will accept without any question the belief that each one of us will be judged when we leave this earth according to his or her deeds during our lives here in mortality. Isn't it just as reasonable to believe that what we have received here in this earth [life] was given to each of us according to the merits of our conduct before we came here?"[4]

It thus appears that the declaration of lineage by patriarchs is as much a statement as to *who and what we were* as it is who we are now and what we may become. There are those, of course, who believe otherwise, those who propose that premortality has little or nothing to do with mortality, that there is no tie between faithfulness there and lineage and station here; to believe in any other way, they contend, is racist and exclusivistic. Despite the cleverness of the posture and the egalitarian-sounding nature of such a perspective, it is my firm belief that such views are doctrinally defenseless and even potentially hazardous. If there is no relationship between the first estate and the second, why, as President Lee might ask, should I believe that there is any relationship between what I do here and what I will receive hereafter? Our task as parents and teachers and students of the gospel is not simply to win friends and influence people through avoiding, watering down, or in some cases even denying what are "hard sayings" or difficult doctrines. Truth is not established by consensus or by popularity.

Who are we, then? President Lee answered: "You are all the sons and daughters of God. Your spirits were created and lived as organized intelligences before the world was. You have been blessed to have a physical body because of your obedience to certain commandments in that premortal state. You are now born into a family to which you have come, into the nations through which you have come, as a reward for the kind of lives you lived before you came here and at a time in the world's history, as the Apostle Paul taught the men of Athens and as the Lord revealed to Moses, determined by the faithfulness of each of those who lived before this world was created."[5]

And yet coming to earth through a peculiar lineage would involve much more than boasting of a blessing; it would entail bearing a burden. "Once we know who we are," Elder Russell M. Nelson said, "and the royal lineage of which we are a part, our actions and directions in life will be more appropriate to our inheritance."[6] Years ago, a wise man wrote of the burdens of chosenness and of why it is that God selected a particular people as his own. "A man will rise and demand," he suggested, "'By what right does God choose one race or people above another?'

"I like that form of the question. It is much better than asking by what right God degrades one people beneath another, although that is implied. God's grading is always upward. If he raises up a nation, it is that other nations may be raised up through its ministry. If he exalts a great man, an apostle of liberty or science or faith, it is that He might raise a degraded people to a better condition. The divine selection is not [alone] a prize, a compliment paid to the man or the race—it is a burden imposed. To appoint a Chosen people is not a pandering to the racial vanity of a 'superior people,' it is a yoke bound upon the necks of those who are chosen for a special service.

"In short, God 'hath made [Israel] great for what He is going to make [Israel] do.'"[7]

ISRAEL IN MORTALITY: THE SCATTERING AND GATHERING

Those of Israel who follow the light of Christ in this life will be led to the higher light of the Holy Ghost and will come to know the Lord. In time they will come to know of their noble heritage and of the royal blood that flows through their veins. They come to earth with a predisposition to receive the truth, with an inner attraction to the message of the gospel. "My sheep hear my voice," the Master said, "and I know them, and they follow me" (John 10:27). Those chosen to come to the earth through the favored lineage "are especially endowed at birth with spiritual talents. It is easier for them to believe the gospel than it is for the generality of mankind. Every living soul comes into this world with sufficient talent to believe and be saved, but the Lord's sheep, as a reward for their devotion when they dwelt in his presence, enjoy greater spiritual endowments than their fellows," wrote Elder Bruce R. McConkie.[8]

"The blood of Israel has flowed in the veins of the children of men," Wilford Woodruff declared, "mixed among the Gentile nations, and when they have heard the sound of the Gospel of Christ it has been like vivid lightening to them; it has opened their understandings, enlarged their minds, and enabled them to see the things of God. They have been born of the Spirit, and then they could behold the kingdom of God."⁹

And yet *chosenness* implies a succession of choices. Those who became Israel before the world was, those who were *called* in that pristine existence, must exercise wisdom and prudence and discernment in this life, before they become truly *chosen* to enjoy the privilege of ruling and reigning in the house of Israel forever. It was of such that Alma spoke when he declared that there were many who were foreordained to receive transcendent privileges, but who—because in mortality they choose to "reject the Spirit of God on account of the hardness of their hearts and blindness of their minds"—do not enjoy "as great privilege as their brethren" (Alma 13:4). The scriptures thus teach that "there are many called, but few are chosen" (D&C 121:34). "This suggests," President Harold B. Lee explained, "that even though we have our free agency here, there are many who were foreordained before the world was, to a greater state than they have prepared themselves for here. Even though they might have been among the noble and great, from among whom the Father declared he would make his chosen leaders, they may fail of that calling here in mortality."¹⁰ And so the vivid and harsh reality is that lineage and ancestry alone do not qualify one for a divine family inheritance. To use Paul's language, "they are not all Israel, which are of Israel: neither, because they are the seed of Abraham, are they all children" (Romans 9:6–7). In fact, as Nephi reminded us, only those who receive the gospel and commit themselves by obedience and continued faithfulness to the Mediator of that covenant are really covenant people. "As many of the Gentiles as will repent are the covenant people of the Lord," he said; "and as many of the Jews as will not repent shall be cast off; for the Lord covenanteth with none save it be with them that repent and believe in his Son, who is the Holy One of Israel" (2 Nephi 30:2).

Both the Old Testament and the Book of Mormon—and it is particularly in the latter volume that we see the pattern clearly—set forth in consistent detail the reasons why over the generations Israel has been scattered and how it is they are to be gathered. Speaking on behalf of Jehovah, Moses warned ancient Israel that if they should reject their God they would be scattered among the nations, dispersed among the Gentiles. "If thou wilt not hearken unto the voice of the Lord thy God," he said, "to observe to do all his commandments and his statutes which I command thee this day . . . [you will be] removed into all the kingdoms of the earth. . . . And ye shall be plucked from off the land whither thou goest to possess it. And the Lord shall scatter thee among all people, from the one end of the earth even unto the other; and there thou shalt serve other gods, which neither thou nor thy fathers have known" (Deuteronomy 28:15, 25, 63–64). The Lord spoke in a similar vein through Jeremiah more than half a millennium later: "Because your fathers have forsaken me, saith the Lord, and have walked after other gods, and have served them, and have worshipped them, and have forsaken me, and have not kept my law; and ye have done worse than your fathers; . . . therefore will I cast you out of this land into a land that ye know not, . . . where I will not shew you favour" (Jeremiah 16:11–13). The people of God became scattered—alienated from Jehovah and the ways of righteousness; lost as to their identity as covenant representatives; and displaced from the lands set aside for their inheritance—because they forsook the God of Abraham, Isaac, and Jacob and partook of the worship and ways of unholy men.

Though Israel is generally scattered because of her apostasy, we should also point out that the Lord scatters certain branches of his chosen people to the nethermost parts of the earth in order to accomplish his purposes—to spread the blood and influence of Abraham throughout the globe. Through this means, all the families of the earth with be blessed eventually—either through being of the blood of Abraham themselves, or through being ministered unto by the blood of Abraham—with the right to the gospel, the priesthood, and eternal life (see Abraham 2:8–11).

On the other hand, the *gathering* of Israel is accomplished through repentance and turning to the Lord. Individuals were gathered in ancient days when they aligned themselves with the people of God, with those who practiced the religion of Jehovah and received the ordinances of salvation. They were gathered when they gained a sense of tribal identity, when they came to know who they were and whose they were. They were gathered when they congregated with the former-day Saints, when they settled on those lands that were designated as promised lands—lands set apart as sacred sites for people of promise. The hope of the chosen people from Adam to Isaac, and the longing of the house of Israel from Joseph to Malachi, was to be reunited with their God and to enjoy fellowship with those of the household of faith. "But now thus saith the Lord that created thee, O Jacob," Isaiah recorded, "and he that formed thee, O Israel, Fear not: for I have redeemed thee, I have called thee by thy name; thou art mine.

"When thou passest through the waters, I will be with thee: and through the rivers, they shall not overflow thee; when thou walkest through the fire, thou shalt not be burned; neither shall the flame kindle upon thee.

"For I am the Lord thy God, the Holy One of Israel, thy Saviour . . .

"Since thou wast precious in my sight, thou hast been honourable, and I have loved thee: therefore will I give men for thee, and people for thy life.

"Fear not: for I am with thee: I will bring thy seed from the east, and gather thee from the west; I will say to the north, Give up; and to the south, Keep not back: bring my sons from far, and my daughters from the ends of the earth" (Isaiah 43:1–6).

"Ye shall be gathered one by one, O ye children of Israel" (Isaiah 27:12), Isaiah declared. The call to the dispersed of Israel has been and ever will be the same: "Turn, O backsliding children, saith the Lord," through Jeremiah; "for I am married unto you: and I will take you one of a city, and two of a family, and I will bring you to Zion" (Jeremiah 3:14). That is to say, gathering is accomplished through individual conversion, through faith and repentance and baptism and confirmation, through—as we shall see shortly—the receipt of and obedience to the ordinances of the holy temple.

Indeed, the Old Testament and Book of Mormon prophets longed for the day when the scattered remnants of Israel—those lost as to their identity and lost as to their relationship with the true Messiah and his church and kingdom—would be a part of a work that would cause all former gatherings to pale into insignificance. "Therefore, behold," Jeremiah recorded, "the days come, saith the Lord, that it shall no more be said, The Lord liveth, that brought up the children of Israel out of the land of Egypt; but, The Lord liveth, that brought up the children of Israel from the land of the north, and from all the lands whither he had driven them." And how is such a phenomenal gathering to be accomplished? Jehovah answers: "Behold, I will send for many fishers, saith the Lord, and they shall fish them; and after will I send for many hunters, and they shall hunt them from every mountain, and from every hill, and out of the holes of the rocks" (Jeremiah 16:14–16). That is, through the great missionary work of the Church, the elders and sisters—the Lord's legal administrators in the great proselyting program—seek and teach and baptize and thereby gather the strangers home.

And so people are gathered into the fold of God through learning the doctrine of Christ and subscribing to the principles and ordinances of his gospel. They learn through scripture and through patriarchal and prophetic pronouncement of their kinship with—or in rare instances today, of their adoption into—the house of Israel. The crowning tie to Israel, however, comes only by the worthy reception of the blessings of the temple, through being endowed and sealed into the holy order of God (see D&C 131:1–4). "What was the [ultimate] object," Joseph Smith asked, "of gathering the Jews, or the people of God, in any age of the world?" He then answered: "The main object was to build unto the Lord a house whereby He could reveal unto His people the ordinances of His house and the glories of His kingdom, and teach the people the way of salvation; for there are certain ordinances and principles that, when they are taught and practiced, must be done in a place or house built for that purpose."[11]

"Missionary work," Elder Russell M. Nelson observed, "is only the beginning" to the blessings of Abraham, Isaac, and Jacob. "The fulfillment, the consummation, of these blessings comes as those who have entered the waters of baptism perfect their lives to the point that they may enter the holy temple. Receiving an endowment there seals members of the Church to the Abrahamic Covenant."[12]

JOSEPH SMITH: A MODERN ABRAHAM

In September of 1823 the angel Moroni appeared to the Prophet Joseph Smith. "This messenger proclaimed himself," Joseph wrote to John Wentworth, "to be an angel of God, sent to bring the joyful tidings that the covenant which God made with ancient Israel was at hand to be fulfilled, that the preparatory work for the second coming of the Messiah was speedily to commence; that the time was at hand for the Gospel in all its fulness to be preached in power, unto all nations that a people might be prepared for the Millennial reign. I was informed that I was chosen to be an instrument in the hands of God to bring about some of His purposes in this glorious dispensation."[13] Joseph of old prophesied of his latter-day namesake that he would be a "choice seer," one who would be raised up by God to bring the people of the last days to the knowledge of the covenants which God had made with the ancient fathers (see 2 Nephi 3:7; 1 Nephi 13:26). The name *Joseph* is a blessed and significant name. Whether taken from the Hebrew word *Yasaf,* which means "to add," or from the word *Asaph,* meaning "to gather," one senses that the latter-day Seer was destined to perform a monumental labor in regard to the fulfillment of the Abrahamic covenant in the final dispensation.

Joseph Smith was a descendant of Abraham. By lineage he had a right to the priesthood, the gospel, and eternal life (see Abraham 2:8–11). In a revelation received on 6 December 1832, the Savior said: "Thus saith the Lord unto you, with whom the priesthood hath continued through the lineage of your fathers—for ye are lawful heirs, according to the flesh, and have been hid from the world with Christ in God—therefore your life and the priesthood have remained, and must needs remain through you and your lineage until the restoration of all things spoken by the mouths of all the holy prophets since the world began" (D&C 86:8–10). "It was decreed in the counsels of eternity," President Brigham Young stated, "long before the foundations of the earth were laid, that he [Joseph Smith] should be the man, in the last dispensation of this world, to bring forth the word of God to the people, and receive the fulness of the keys and power of the Priesthood of the Son of God. The Lord had his eye upon him, and upon his father, and upon his father's fathers, and upon their progenitors clear back to Abraham, and from Abraham to the flood, from the flood to Enoch, and from Enoch to Adam. He has watched that family and that blood as it has circulated from its fountain to the birth of that man."[14]

President Young declared on another occasion: "You have heard Joseph say that the people did not know him; he had his eyes on the relation to blood-relations. Some have supposed that he meant spirit, but it was the blood-relation. This is it that he referred to. His descent to Joseph that was sold into Egypt was direct, and the blood was pure in him. That is why the Lord chose him and we are pure when this blood-strain from Ephraim comes down pure. The decrees of the Almighty will be exalted—that blood which was in him was pure and he had the sole right and lawful power, as he was the legal heir to the blood that has been on the earth and has come down through a pure lineage. The union of various ancestors kept that blood pure. There is a great deal the people do not understand, and many of the Latter-day Saints have to learn all about it."[15]

What is true in regard to the Prophet's lineage, his right to the priesthood and the gospel, and his duty in regard to the salvation of the world is equally true for other members of the Lord's church. The Lord spoke of his Latter-day Saints as "a remnant of Jacob, and those who are heirs according to the covenant" (D&C 52:2). "Awake, awake; put on thy strength, O Zion," Isaiah recorded; "put on thy beautiful garments, O Jerusalem, the holy city" (Isaiah 52:1). A modern revelation provides our finest commentary on this passage and explains that Jehovah "had reference to those whom God should call in the last days, who should hold the power of priesthood to bring again Zion, and the redemption of Israel; and to put on her strength is to put on the authority of the priesthood, which she, Zion, has a right to by lineage; and to return to that power which she had lost" (D&C 113:8). The Lord also encouraged Israel through Isaiah to shake herself from the dust and loose herself from the bands about her neck (see Isaiah 52:2). That is, "the scattered remnants are exhorted to return to the Lord from whence they have fallen; which if they do, the promise of the Lord is that he will speak to them, or give them revelation." In so doing, Israel rids herself of "the curses of God upon her," her "scattered condition among the Gentiles" (D&C 113:10).

Joseph Smith became a "father of the faithful" to those of this dispensation, the means by which the chosen lineage could be identified, gathered, organized as family units, and sealed forevermore into the house of Israel to their God. The

Patriarch in the days of the early Church, Joseph Smith Sr., blessed his son as follows: "A marvelous work and a wonder has the Lord wrought by thy hand, even that which shall prepare the way for the remnants of his people to come in among the Gentiles, with their fulness, as the tribes of Israel are restored. I bless thee with the blessings of thy Fathers Abraham, Isaac and Jacob; and even the blessings of thy father Joseph, the son of Jacob. Behold, he looked after his posterity in the last days, when they should be scattered and driven by the Gentiles."[16]

On 3 April 1836 Moses, Elias, and Elijah appeared in the Kirtland Temple and restored priesthood keys of inestimable worth, keys that formalized much of the labor which had been under way since the organization of the Church (see D&C 110). Moses restored the keys of the gathering of Israel, including the right of presidency and directing powers needed to gather the ten lost tribes. Elias committed unto Joseph and Oliver the dispensation of the gospel of Abraham, making it possible that through those first elders all generations after them would be blessed. That is, Elias restored the keys necessary to organize eternal family units in the patriarchal order through the new and everlasting covenant of marriage. Elijah restored the keys necessary to bind and seal those family units for eternity, as well as the power to legitimize all priesthood ordinances and give them efficacy, virtue, and force in and after the resurrection.[17] Thus through the coming of Elijah and his prophetic colleagues in Kirtland, the promises made to the fathers—the promises of the gospel, the priesthood, and the possibility of eternal life granted to Abraham, Isaac, and Jacob—are planted in our hearts, the hearts of the children (see D&C 2). More specifically, because of what took place through Joseph Smith in Kirtland in 1836, the desire of our hearts to have all the blessings enjoyed by the ancients can be realized. And because of the spirit of Elijah, which moves upon the faithful, there comes also a desire to make those same blessings available for our more immediate fathers through family history and vicarious temple ordinances.

Through Joseph Smith the blessings of Abraham, Isaac, and Jacob are available to all who will join the Church and prove worthy of the blessings of the temple. Jehovah's plea through Isaiah that the people of the covenant become a light to the nations, that they might be his "salvation unto the end of the earth" (Isaiah 49:6) is thus realized through the restoration of the gospel. Thereby, as the Prophet himself declared, "the election of the promised seed still continues, and in the last days they shall have the priesthood restored unto them, and they shall be 'saviors on Mount Zion.'"[18] Because Joseph Smith was the head of this dispensation and its modern Abraham, Brigham Young could appropriately say of his predecessor, "Joseph is a father to Ephraim and to all Israel in these last days."[19] In a revelation given to President John Taylor on 22 June 1882, the Lord spoke of the Prophet Joseph: "Behold, I raised up my servant Joseph Smith to introduce my Gospel, and to build up my Church and establish my Kingdom on the earth. . . . He was called and ordained to this office before the world was. He was called by me, and empowered by me, and sustained by me to introduce and establish my Church and Kingdom upon the earth; and to be a Prophet, Seer, and Revelator to my Church and Kingdom; and to be a King and Ruler over Israel."[20]

The Lord has repeatedly affirmed the special status of the Prophet Joseph: "As I said unto Abraham concerning the kindreds of the earth, even so I say unto my servant Joseph: In thee and in thy seed shall the kindred of the earth be blessed" (D&C 124:58). Further: "Abraham received promises concerning his seed, and of the fruit of his loins—from whose loins ye are, namely, my servant Joseph—which were to continue so long as they were in the world; and as touching Abraham and his seed, out of the world they should continue; both in the world and out of the world should they continue as innumerable as the stars; or, if ye were to count the sand upon the seashore ye could not number them. This promise is yours also, because ye are of Abraham" (D&C 132:30–31).

THE MILLENNIAL GATHERING OF ISRAEL

Both the Old Testament and the Book of Mormon attest to the fact that a significant part of the drama we know as the gathering of Israel will be millennial, will be brought to pass after the second coming of Jesus Christ. Between now and then we shall see marvelous things on the earth in regard to the people of Israel coming unto their Lord and King and thereafter unto the lands of their inheritance. We have witnessed already the phenomenal gathering of many thousands of the seed of Lehi (of the tribe of Joseph) into the Church, and this is but the beginning. We have stood in awe as descendants of Jacob around the globe have been found, identified, taught, and converted to the faith of their fathers, and yet we have seen but the tip of the iceberg. Our missionaries shall soon enter into lands wherein pockets of Israelites will be baptized and confirmed and where patriarchs shall declare lineage through such tribes as Issachar, Zebulun, Gad, Asher, and Naphtali.

A major conversion of the Jews will take place near the time of the coming of the Lord in glory. "And it shall come to pass in that day," Jehovah said through Zechariah, "that I will seek to destroy all the nations that come against Jerusalem. And I will pour upon the house of David, and upon the inhabitants of Jerusalem, the spirit of grace and of supplications: and they shall look upon me whom they have pierced, and they shall mourn for him, as one mourneth for his only son, and shall be in bitterness for him, as one that is in bitterness for his firstborn. . . . And one shall say unto him, What are these wounds in thine hands? Then he shall answer, Those with which I was wounded in the house of my friends" (Zechariah 12:9–10; 13:6). A modern revelation provides a more detailed description of this poignant moment in our Lord's dealings with his own. Having set his foot on the Mount of Olives and the mountain having cleaved in twain, "then shall the Jews look upon me," the Lord prophesies, "and say: What are these wounds in thine hands and in thy feet? Then shall they know that I am the Lord; for I will say unto them: These wounds are the wounds with which I was wounded in the house of my friends. I am he who was lifted up. I am Jesus that was crucified. I am the Son of God. And then shall they weep because of their iniquities; then shall they lament because they persecuted their king" (D&C 45:51–53). Prior to this time, Jews from around the globe will already have investigated the message of the Restoration, entered into the covenant gospel, and come home to the God of Abraham, Isaac, and Jacob. They will not only have come to acknowledge Jesus as an honorable prophet-teacher, but will confess him as Lord and God, as Messiah. Their garments will have been "washed in the blood of the Lamb" (Ether 13:11). But at the time the Master appears at Olivet, the conversion of a nation will begin. "That is to say," writes Elder McConkie, "the Jews 'shall begin to believe in Christ' [2 Nephi 30:7] before he comes the second time. Some of them will accept the gospel and forsake the traditions of their fathers; a few will find in Jesus the fulfillment of their Messianic hopes; but their nation as a whole, their people as the distinct body that they now are in all nations, the Jews as a unit shall not, at that time, accept the word of truth. But a beginning will be made; a foundation will be laid; and then Christ will come and usher in the millennial year of his redeemed."[21]

In 721 B.C., the Assyrians under Shalmanezer took the ten northern tribes captive. According to tradition, these Israelites escaped as they were being taken northward and scattered themselves throughout different parts of the earth. They were never again heard of and came thereafter to be known as the "lost tribes." Nephi explained to his brothers early in the Book of Mormon story that "the house of Israel, sooner or later, will be scattered upon all the face of the earth, and also among all nations. And behold, there are many"—note that he is here making reference to the ten northern tribes—"who are already lost from the knowledge of those who are at Jerusalem. Yea, the more part of all the tribes have been led away; and they are scattered to and fro upon the isles of the sea; and whither they are none of us knoweth, save that we know that they have been led away" (1 Nephi 22:3–4).

Nephi's use of the word *lost* is most interesting. The tribes are lost "from the knowledge of those who are at Jerusalem." Let me here refer to a statement by President George Q. Cannon made in 1890. After having quoted at length from 2 Nephi 30 regarding the final gathering of Israel from among the nations, President Cannon said: "This prediction plainly foreshadows that which is now taking place, and which has been taking place for some years. 'As many of the Gentiles as will repent,' the prophet says, 'are the covenant people of the Lord.' By virtue of this promise which God has made, we are His covenant people. Though of Gentile descent, and numbered among the Gentile nations, by and through our obedience to the Gospel of the Son of God we become incorporated, so to speak, among His covenant people and are numbered with them. We say frequently that we are descendants of the house of Israel. This is undoubtedly true. . . . Our ancestors were of the house of Israel but they mingled with the Gentiles and became lost, that is, they became lost so far as being recognized as of the house of Israel, and the blood of our forefathers was mingled with the blood of the Gentile nations. We have been gathered out from those nations by the preaching of the gospel of the Son of God. The Lord has made precious promises unto us that every blessing, and every gift, and every power necessary for salvation and for exaltation to His Kingdom shall be given unto us in common with those who are more particularly known as the covenant people of the Lord."[22]

Mormon teaches that in the last days all of the twelve tribes will come to Christ through accepting the Book of Mormon and the restored gospel (see Mormon 3:17–22). Will such persons gather into the true church from the north? Yes. And they shall also come, as the scriptures attest, from the south and the east and the west (see Isaiah 43:5–6; 3 Nephi 20:13). In fact, it just may be that the idea of gathering from "the lands of the north" may simply be a reference to a return from all parts of the earth. For example, Jehovah, speaking through Zechariah, called forth to his chosen but scattered people: "Come! Come! Flee from the land of the north, declares the Lord, for I have scattered you to the four winds of heaven" (NIV, Zechariah 2:6).

As we have indicated, the work of the Father—the work of gathering Israel into the fold—though begun in the early nineteenth century, will continue into and through the Millennium. That is to say, the missionary effort begun in our time will accelerate at a pace that we cannot now comprehend. This is why the Book of Mormon speaks of the work of the Father "commencing" during the Millennium. In the millennial day "shall the power of heaven come down among them; and I also will be in the midst," the resurrected Lord stated. "And then shall the work of the

Father commence at that day, even when this gospel shall be preached among the remnant of this people. Verily I say unto you, at that day shall the work of the Father commence among all the dispersed of my people, yea, even the tribes which have been lost, which the Father hath led away out of Jerusalem" (3 Nephi 21:25–26; see also 2 Nephi 30:7–15).

We are prone to speak of there being no death during the thousand years. Let us be more precise. The Saints shall live to the age of a tree, the age of one hundred (see Isaiah 65:20; D&C 43:32; 63:51; 101:30–31), before they are changed in the twinkling of an eye from mortality to resurrected immortality. On the other hand, and presumably in speaking of terrestrial persons, Joseph Smith said: "There will be wicked men on the earth during the thousand years. The heathen nations who will not come up to worship will be visited with the judgments of God, and must eventually be destroyed from the earth."[23]

"There will be need for the preaching of the gospel after the millennium is brought in," President Joseph Fielding Smith explained, "until all men are either converted or pass away. In the course of the thousand years all men will either come into the Church, or kingdom of God, or they will die and pass away."[24] Or, as Elder McConkie has described this process: "There will be many churches on earth when the Millennium begins. False worship will continue among those whose desires are good, 'who are honorable men of the earth,' but who have been 'blinded by the craftiness of men.' (D&C 76:75.) Plagues will rest upon them until they repent and believe the gospel or are destroyed, as the Prophet said. It follows that missionary work will continue into the Millennium until all who remain are converted. Then 'the earth shall be full of the knowledge of the Lord as the waters cover the sea.' (Isaiah 11:9.) Then every living soul on earth will belong to The Church of Jesus Christ of Latter-day Saints."[25]

In that glorious era of peace and righteousness, the dispersed of Israel shall receive the message of the Restoration, read and believe the Book of Mormon, traverse the highway of righteousness (see Isaiah 35:8) into the true Church, and take their place beside their kinsmen in the household of faith. The revelation declares that "their enemies shall become a prey unto them" (D&C 133:28). That is, the enemies of Israel—the wicked and carnal elements of a fallen world—will have been destroyed by the glory and power of the Second Coming. "For the time speedily cometh," Nephi prophesied, "that the Lord God shall cause a great division among the people, and the wicked will he destroy; and he will spare his people, yea, even if it so be that he must destroy the wicked by fire" (2 Nephi 30:10; see also 1 Nephi 22:17). There will have been "an entire separation of the righteous and the wicked";

the enemies of the chosen people will be no more, because the Lord will have sent forth his angels "to pluck out the wicked and cast them into unquenchable fire" (D&C 63:54). Truly, "such of the gathering of Israel as has come to pass so far is but the gleam of a star that soon will be hidden by the splendor of the sun in full blaze; truly, the magnitude and grandeur and glory of the gathering is yet to be."[26]

One of the most graphic prophetic statements about Israel in the Millennium is contained in the writings of Zenos, one of the prophets of the brass plates. In speaking of what appears to be the millennial day, Zenos taught:

"And there began to be the natural fruit again in the vineyard; and the natural branches began to grow and thrive exceedingly; and the wild branches began to be plucked off and to be cast away; and they did keep the root and the top thereof equal, according to the strength thereof.

"And thus they labored, with all diligence, according to the commandments of the Lord of the vineyard, even until the bad had been cast away out of the vineyard, and the Lord had preserved unto himself that the trees had become again the natural fruit; and they became like unto one body; and the fruits were equal; and the Lord of the vineyard had preserved unto himself the natural fruit, which was most precious unto him from the beginning" (Jacob 5:73–74).

In that glorious day, the promise of God to his chosen seed will be well on the way to fulfillment. Paul's words, spoken in the meridian of time, will then have particular application and fulfillment. "As many of you as have been baptized into Christ," he observed, "have put on Christ. There is neither Jew nor Greek, there is neither bond nor free, there is neither male nor female: for ye are all one in Christ Jesus. And if ye be Christ's, then are ye Abraham's seed, and heirs according to the promise" (Galatians 3:27–29). All those who come unto Christ, who is the Holy One of Israel, shall, under Christ, rule and reign in the house of Israel forever. In the millennial day the Lord Jehovah will reign personally upon the earth (Articles of Faith 1:10). More specifically, "Christ and the resurrected Saints will reign over the earth during the thousand years. They will not probably dwell upon the earth, but will visit it when they please, or when it is necessary to govern it."[27] In that day he shall preside as King of kings and Lord of lords: Israel's Good Shepherd shall be with them and minister to them in everlasting splendor.

The blossoming and ultimate fulfillment of the everlasting covenant restored through Joseph Smith shall be millennial. The principles and ordinances of the gospel, the "articles of adoption"[28] by which men and women are received into the royal family and given a rightful place in the house of Israel, shall continue during the thousand years. "During the Millennium," as Elder Bruce R. McConkie has written, "children will be named and blessed by the elders of the kingdom. When those of the rising generation arrive at the years of accountability, they will be baptized in water and of the Spirit by legal administrators appointed so to act. Priesthood will be conferred upon young and old, and they will be ordained to offices therein as the needs of the ministry and their own salvation require. At the appropriate time each person will receive his patriarchal blessing, we suppose from the natural patriarch who presides in his family, as it was in Adamic days and as it was when Jacob blessed his sons. The saints will receive their endowments in the temples of the Lord, and they will receive the blessings of celestial marriage at their holy altars. And all the faithful will have their callings and elections made sure and will be sealed up unto that eternal life which will come to them when they reach the age of a tree."[29]

"Behold," Jeremiah wrote, "the days come, saith the Lord, that I will make a new covenant with the house of Israel, and with the house of Judah.

"Not according to the covenant that I made with their fathers in the day that I took them by the hand to bring them out of the land of Egypt; which my covenant they brake, although I was an husband unto them, saith the Lord:

"But this shall be the covenant that I will make with the house of Israel; After those days, saith the Lord, I will put my law in their inward parts, and write it in their hearts; and will be their God, and they shall be my people.

"And they shall teach no more every man his neighbour, and every man his brother, saying, Know the Lord: for they shall all know me, from the least of them unto the greatest of them, saith the Lord: for I will forgive their iniquity, and I will remember their sin no more" (Jeremiah 31:31–34).

"How is this to be done?" Joseph Smith asked. "It is to be done by this sealing power, and the other Comforter spoken of, which will be manifest by revelation."[30]

CONCLUSION

"When the Lord shall come," a modern revelation explains, "he shall reveal all things—things which have passed, and hidden things which no man knew, things of the earth, by which it was made, and the purpose and the end thereof—things most precious, things that are above, and things that are beneath, things that are in the earth, and upon the earth, and in heaven" (D&C 101:32–34). When the Lion of the tribe of Judah finally unseals the scrolls which contain "the revealed will, mysteries, and the works of God," even "the hidden things of his economy concerning this earth during the seven thousand years of its continuance, or its temporal existence" (D&C 77:6; see also Revelation 5:1), surely we shall one and all come to know of his peculiar dealings with Israel, of the strange but masterful manner in which he has moved upon and through his covenant people in mysterious ways his wonders to perform.

In 1882 Elder Erastus Snow delivered one of the most penetrating discourses on the role and mission of Israel that I know of. In speaking of those who come to the earth as descendants of Abraham, he said: "The Lord has sent those noble spirits into the world to perform a special work, and appointed their times; and they have always fulfilled the mission given them, and their future glory and exaltation is secured unto them; and that is what I understand by the doctrine of election spoken of by the Apostle Paul and other sacred writers." Such persons, Elder Snow continued, "were called and chosen and elected of God to perform a certain work at a certain time in the world's history and in due time he fitted them for that work.

"Their blood has permeated European society, and it coursed in the veins of the early colonists of America. And when the books shall be opened and the lineage of all men is known, it will be found that they have been first and foremost in everything noble among men in the various nations in breaking off the shackles of kingcraft and priestcraft and oppression of every kind, and the foremost among men in upholding and maintaining the principles of liberty and freedom upon this continent and establishing a representative government, and thus preparing the way for the coming forth of the fullness of the everlasting Gospel. And it is the foremost of those spirits whom the Lord has prepared to receive the Gospel when it was presented to them, and who did not wait for the Elders to hunt them from the hills and corners of the earth, but they were hunting for the Elders, impelled by a spirit which then they could not understand; and for this reason were they among the first Elders of the Church; they and the fathers having been watched over from the days that God promised those blessings upon Isaac and Jacob and Joseph and Ephraim. And these are they that will be found in the front ranks of all that is noble in their day and time, and who will be found among those whose efforts are directed in establishing upon the earth those heaven-born principles which tend directly to blessing and salvation, to ameliorating the condition of their fellow-men, and elevating them in the scale of their being; and among those who receive the fullness of the Everlasting Gospel, and the keys of Priesthood in the last days, through whom God determined to gather up again unto himself a peculiar people, a holy nation, a pure seed that shall stand upon Mount Zion as saviors."[31]

And so we say in summary, as Mormon said to the latter-day descendants of

Lehi: "Know ye that ye are of the house of Israel" (Mormon 7:2). Or as Jesus explained to the Nephites: "Ye are the children of the prophets; and ye are of the house of Israel; and ye are of the covenant which the Father made with your fathers, saying unto Abraham: And in thy seed shall all the kindreds of the earth be blessed" (3 Nephi 20:25). Our patriarchal blessings specify literal blood descent; and because of our connection to father Abraham, and through the call and ministry of a modern Abraham and the keys and powers delivered to him, ours is the right to the gospel, the priesthood, and the glories of eternal life. We need not misunderstand this matter and should not confuse ancestry with adoption.[32] Nor should those who are not directly descended from Israel who join the Church feel in any way less than chosen. Chosenness is a status based upon the choice to follow the Lord and associate with his people, and entrance into the true Church qualifies a person for the blessings of Ephraim as though he or she had been born a child of Abraham. Our duty is to walk with fidelity and humility and be worthy of the name and lineage that is ours. By so doing we shall help to bring to pass the foreordained purposes of God for us and our families. It can then be said of us as it was of Abraham: "I know him, that he will command his children and his household after him, and they shall keep the way of the Lord, to do justice and judgment" (Genesis 18:19).

"I am reminded," President Harold B. Lee said in his last address to BYU students, "of the old court jester who was supposed to entertain his king with interesting stories and antics. He looked at the king who was lolling on his throne, a drunken, filthy rascal; [he] doffed his cap and bells, and said with a mock gesture of obeisance, 'O king, be loyal to the royal within you.'"[33] Such is our opportunity and our great challenge, our glory or our condemnation.

Notes

From Richard D. Draper, ed., *A Witness of Jesus Christ: The 1989 Sperry Symposium on the Old Testament* (Salt Lake City: Deseret Book Co., 1990), 178–99.

1. *Mortal Messiah*, 1:23.
2. Brent L. Top, *The Life Before* (Salt Lake City: Bookcraft, 1988), 144.
3. Melvin J. Ballard, "The Three Degrees of Glory," in *Melvin J. Ballard: Crusader for Righteousness* (Salt Lake City: Bookcraft, 1966), 218–19.
4. Harold B. Lee, in Conference Report, October 1973, 7–8.
5. Ibid., 7.
6. Russell M. Nelson, "Thanks for the Covenant," *1988–89 BYU Speeches* (Provo, Utah: Brigham Young University Publications, 1989), 59.
7. W. J. Cameron, "Is There a Chosen People?" in James H. Anderson, *God's Covenant Race* (Salt Lake City: Deseret News Press, 1938), 300–302.

8. Bruce R. McConkie, *A New Witness for the Articles of Faith* (Salt Lake City: Deseret Book Co., 1985), 34.

9. Wilford Woodruff, in *Journal of Discourses,* 15:11.

10. Harold B. Lee, in Conference Report, October 1973, 7.

11. *Teachings of the Prophet Joseph Smith,* 307–8.

12. Nelson, "Thanks for the Covenant," 59.

13. *History of the Church,* 4:536–37.

14. Brigham Young, in *Journal of Discourses,* 7:289–90.

15. Brigham Young, as quoted in *Utah Genealogical and Historical Magazine,* 11 (July 1920): 107.

16. Joseph Smith Sr., as quoted in Joseph F. McConkie, *His Name Shall Be Joseph* (Salt Lake City: Hawkes Publishing, 1980), 103.

17. See *Teachings of the Prophet Joseph Smith,* 172.

18. Ibid., 189.

19. Brigham Young, in Journal History of The Church of Jesus Christ of Latter-day Saints, LDS Church Archives, Salt Lake City, Utah, under date of 9 April 1837.

20. Fred E. Collier, ed., *Unpublished Revelations of the Prophets and Presidents of The Church of Jesus Christ of Latter-day Saints* (Salt Lake City: Collier's Publishing Co., 1979), 1:133.

21. *Millennial Messiah,* 228–29.

22. George Q. Cannon, address delivered at the Tabernacle in Salt Lake City on 12 January 1890, in George Q. Cannon, *Collected Discourses,* comp. Brian H. Stuy (n.p.: BHS Publishing, 1988), 2:2–3.

23. *Teachings of the Prophet Joseph Smith,* 268–69; see also Zechariah 14.

24. *Doctrines of Salvation,* 1:86.

25. *Millennial Messiah,* 652.

26. Ibid., 196.

27. *Teachings of the Prophet Joseph Smith,* 268.

28. See *Teachings of the Prophet Joseph Smith,* 328; Orson Pratt, *Orson Pratt's Works* (Salt Lake City: Parker Pratt Robison, 1965), 46–48.

29. *Millennial Messiah,* 673–74.

30. *Teachings of the Prophet Joseph Smith,* 149.

31. Erastus Snow, in *Journal of Discourses,* 23:185–87.

32. For an excellent treatment of the literal nature of our descent from Israel—as taught specifically in the Doctrine and Covenants—see Monte S. Nyman, "The Second Gathering of the Literal Seed," in *Doctrines for Exaltation: The 1989 Sperry Symposium on the Doctrine and Covenants* (Salt Lake City: Deseret Book Co., 1989), 186–200.

33. Harold B. Lee, "Be Loyal to the Royal within You," *1973 Speeches of the Year* (Provo: Brigham Young University Press, 1974), 100.

RESTORING THE PATRIARCHAL ORDER

M uch has been said in the last two decades about patriarchy, a good portion of which has been negative. For many, patriarchy has come to be associated with male domination, chauvinism, sexism, and discrimination. Indeed, we should not expect that something so very important in the great plan of happiness as the patriarchal order should come forth without opposition, whether in terms of abuse, distortion, or misunderstanding. In this chapter, we will speak of the patriarchal order—of its origins, purpose, and restoration through the Prophet Joseph Smith. We will consider what it is, what it is not, and what it shall yet be. In doing so, we will lean heavily upon prophetic declarations—perhaps more so than would normally be the case—in order to establish doctrine and clarify what may be rather sensitive issues.

ORIGINS

The patriarchal order is an order of the Melchizedek Priesthood; it is, in fact, the new and everlasting covenant of marriage, an order entered into by men and women whenever they are married in the temple by one having proper sealing authority. The patriarchal order was established by God and predates mortal institutions. Our God is also our Father, our Father in heaven. He is a man, a glorified, resurrected man, a Man of Holiness (see Moses 6:57). The Prophet Joseph Smith taught that God was once a mortal, that he dwelt on an earth, worked out his salvation, and inherited the fulness of light and knowledge and power. "God himself was once as we are now," Joseph declared, "and is an exalted man, and sits enthroned in yonder heavens! That is the great secret. If the veil were rent today, and the great God who holds this world in its orbit, and who upholds all worlds and all things by his power, was to make himself visible—I say, if you were to see him today, you would see him like a man in form—like yourselves in all the person, image, and very form as a man; for Adam was created in the very fashion, image and likeness of God, and received instruction from, and walked, talked and conversed with him, as one man talks and communes with another."[1]

President Brigham Young explained: "After men have got their exaltations and their crowns—have become Gods, even the sons of God—are made Kings of kings and Lords of lords, they have the power then of propagating their species in spirit; and that is the first of their operations with regard to organizing a world."[2] We know that "man, as a spirit, was begotten and born of heavenly parents, and reared to maturity in the eternal mansions of the Father, prior to coming upon the earth in a temporal body to undergo an experience in mortality."[3] Thus God lives in the family unit. Indeed, godhood is defined in terms of (1) inheriting, possessing, and receiving a fulness of glory; and (2) the continuation of the family unit into eternity (see D&C 132:19–20). In the premortal existence—our first estate—we lived under the patriarchal order, the family order. It was an order consisting of Father, Mother, and children, an order presided over by our Parents and directed by love, kindness, gentleness, and godly persuasion. We are thus children of God, members of the royal family. Our souls are eternally attuned and acclimated to family things, and thus our greatest happiness (and therefore our greatest sorrows) are associated with the family.

Adam is described in modern revelation as "the son of God, with whom God, himself, conversed" (Moses 6:22; see also Luke 3:38). Adam and Eve were created "in the image of the Gods" (Abraham 4:27). The Prophet Joseph Smith taught that Adam and Eve were married in the Garden of Eden.[4] We know that they were taught the gospel by angels, by the voice of God, and by the power of the Holy Ghost (see Moses 5:1–8, 58). They were baptized, received the gift of the Holy Ghost, and enjoyed the quickening and renovating powers of the Spirit in their lives. "The priesthood was first given to Adam," the Prophet Joseph explained; "he obtained the First Presidency, and held the keys of it from generation to generation."[5] We would also assume that Adam and Eve participated in sacred ordinances associated with the perpetuation of the family. Adam "heard a voice out of heaven, saying: Thou art baptized with fire, and with the Holy Ghost. This is the record of the Father, and the Son, from henceforth and forever; and thou art after the order of him who was without beginning of days or end of years, from all eternity to all eternity. Behold, thou art one in me, a son of God; and thus may all become my sons" (Moses 6:66–68).

Adam and Eve were born again and became, through the Atonement, a son and daughter of Christ. But there was more. They became, through the powers of the holy priesthood and the ordinances associated therewith, a son and daughter of God, meaning the Father.[6] In referring to the experience of our first parents, President Joseph Fielding Smith wrote: "To Adam, after he was driven from the Garden of Eden, the plan of salvation was revealed, and upon him the fulness of the priesthood was conferred."[7]

President Ezra Taft Benson, in an address delivered at the Logan Temple centennial in May 1984, said: "The temple is a sacred place, and the ordinances in the temple are of a sacred character. Because of its sacredness we are sometimes reluctant to say anything about the temple to our children and grandchildren.

"As a consequence, many do not develop a real desire to go to the temple, or when they go there, they do so without much background to prepare them for the obligations and covenants they enter into. I believe a proper understanding or background will immeasurably help prepare our youth for the temple. This understanding, I believe, will foster within them a desire to seek their priesthood blessings just as Abraham sought his.

"When our Heavenly Father placed Adam and Eve on this earth, He did so with the purpose in mind of teaching them how to regain His presence. Our Father promised a Savior to redeem them from their fallen condition. He gave to them the plan of salvation and told them to teach their children faith in Jesus Christ and repentance. Further, Adam and his posterity were commanded by God to be baptized, to receive the Holy Ghost, and to enter into the order of the Son of God.

"To enter into the order of the Son of God is the equivalent today of entering into the fulness of the Melchizedek Priesthood, which is only received in the house of the Lord. Because Adam and Eve had complied with these requirements, God said to them, 'Thou art after the order of him who was without beginning of days or end of years, from all eternity to all eternity' (Moses 6:67)."[8] Jehovah spoke to the Ancient of Days: "I have set thee to be at the head; a multitude of nations shall come of thee, and thou art a prince over them forever" (D&C 107:55). Truly, as John Taylor proclaimed, "Adam was the natural father of his posterity, who were his family and over whom he presided as patriarch, prophet, priest, and king."[9]

Having overcome spiritual death through gospel regeneration, Adam and Eve sought to introduce their offspring to the realm of divine experience. As given to us in modern revelation (and as recorded originally in the book of Enoch), we learn that three years prior to his death, Adam gathered together his numerous posterity—some seven generations of people—in the valley of Adam-ondi-Ahman, bestowed upon them his last blessing, and "predicted whatsoever should befall his posterity unto the latest generation" (D&C 107:53–56). Adam blessed his posterity, the Prophet Joseph explained, because "he wanted to bring them into the presence of God."[10] President Benson asked: "How did Adam bring his descendants into the presence of the Lord? The answer: Adam and his descendants entered into the priesthood order of God. Today we would say they went to the House of the Lord and received their blessings. The order of priesthood spoken of in the scriptures is sometimes referred to as the patriarchal order because it came down from father to son. But this order is otherwise described in modern revelation as an order of family government where a man and woman enter into a covenant with God—just as did Adam and Eve—to be sealed for eternity, to have posterity, and to do the will and work of God throughout their mortality."[11]

Both Adam and Eve, as a partnership, rejoiced in the Fall and the Atonement, exulted in the opportunities for growth and refinement the great plan of happiness provided for them and their posterity. "Adam blessed God and was filled, and began to prophesy concerning all the families of the earth, saying: Blessed be the name of God, for because of my transgression my eyes are opened, and in this life I shall have joy, and again in the flesh I shall see God. And Eve, his wife, heard all these things and was glad, saying: Were it not for our transgression we never should have had seed, and never should have known good and evil, and the joy of our redemption, and the eternal life which God giveth unto all the obedient" (Moses 5:10–11). Modern revelation affirms that Eve and her husband continued to lift their voices in testimony in the postmortal spirit world after their mortal death (see D&C 138:38–39).[12]

THE PATRIARCHAL ORDER ANCIENTLY

From the days of Adam, the Melchizedek Priesthood was administered under the patriarchal order. Elder Bruce R. McConkie has written: "Adam, our father, the first man, is the presiding high priest over the earth for all ages. The government the Lord gave him was patriarchal, and from the expulsion from Eden to the cleansing of the earth by water in the day of Noah, the righteous portion of mankind were blessed and governed by a patriarchal theocracy.

"This theocratic system, patterned after the order and system that prevailed in heaven, was the government of God. He himself though dwelling in heaven, was the Lawgiver, Judge, and King. He gave direction in all things both civil and ecclesiastical; there was no separation of church and state as we know it. All governmental affairs were directed, controlled, and regulated from on high. The Lord's legal administrators on earth served by virtue of their callings and ordinations in the Holy Priesthood and as they were guided by the power of the Holy Ghost."[13]

Elder Erastus Snow further noted that "Adam was the first man appointed of God as the ruler of the earth; to him it was said, thou shalt have dominion over the earth and over the things therein. And as he began to multiply and replenish the earth, and as his children and their families increased in the land, there was a right of dominion given; it was called the birth-right, and it belongs to the first-born of the sons. And this seems to have been an order existing in the heavens even before Adam. For it is written of Jesus, the Lamb of God, that he was the first-born of many brethren. Moreover, his rights of dominion as the first-born continued with him because he loved righteousness and hated iniquity."[14]

And so it was that Seth, Enos, Cainaan, Mahalaleel, Jared, Enoch, Methuselah, Lamech, and Noah presided over the kingdom of God during their respective times on earth. From Noah to Abraham, an additional ten generations, righteous men were called upon to officiate in the Lord's theocratic system. They were high priests. They were presiding patriarchs. Others held the priesthood, but these men held the keys, the directing power over the affairs of God on earth.[15] It was a family order, an order of family government presided over by a father and a mother. Yes, in the ultimate sense, the father was responsible and accountable for the family. "Of necessity," the revelations affirm, "there are presidents, or presiding officers" within God's program (D&C 107:21). Knowing what we know, however, about the Lord's system of priesthood government, we must assume that in ancient times husbands and wives counseled together on the government of the family. It was called the patriarchal order because the law of primogeniture was in effect and the blessings of the priesthood and the birthright descended from father to oldest worthy son. As President Joseph Fielding Smith stated, "It is true that the patriarchal priesthood was handed down from father to son, and that the keys of it belonged to the oldest son by right of primogeniture; but notwithstanding this, all of the faithful men who obtained the priesthood had this patriarchal office from the days of Adam down to the days of Moses. This order of the priesthood was the one conferred upon these ancient prophets and teachers, whether they were the first-born or the last-born, if they were faithful."[16]

Few details are given in the Bible or the Book of Mormon concerning the lives or contributions of the great matriarchs. The scriptural records were kept by men and focused on certain fundamental doctrinal messages or precepts. But it is important for us to know that both Adam and Eve called on the name of the Lord, heard the voice of the Lord, received commandments to offer animal sacrifices, and obeyed the will of the Almighty (see Moses 5:1–8). "Adam held the priesthood," Elder Russell M. Nelson observed, "and Eve served in matriarchal partnership with the patriarchal priesthood."[17] Adam did not receive the fulness of the blessings of the priesthood alone, nor will any man; Eve was by his side as an intelligent, contributing, and equal partner. Again, the patriarchal order is celestial marriage, the new and everlasting covenant of marriage (see D&C 131:1–4). Abraham, Isaac, and Jacob may have qualified for exaltation in the highest heaven, but they did not so achieve on their own; they stand now, with their eternal companions, not as angels but as gods and goddesses (see D&C 132:37). The patriarchal order is a partnership.

Let us take a few illustrations from scripture to point up the vital place of woman in the patriarchal order. The revelation on marriage explains that "Abraham received all things, whatsoever he received, by revelation and commandment, by my word, saith the Lord" (D&C 132:29). And how was it done? That Abraham and Sarah counseled together on important matters, and that the Lord often made his will known through Sarah, is clear from the Old Testament. "Now Sarai Abram's wife bare him no children: and she had an handmaid, an Egyptian, whose name was Hagar. And Sarai said unto Abram, Behold now, the Lord hath restrained me from bearing: I pray thee, go in unto my maid; it may be that I may obtain children by her. And Abram hearkened to the voice of Sarai" (Genesis 16:1–2). Later in the story when Sarah insists that Hagar and Ishmael depart, Abraham is hurt and hesitant. "And God said unto Abraham, Let it not be grievous in thy sight because of the lad, and because of thy bondwoman; in all that Sarah hath said unto thee, hearken unto her voice; for in Isaac shall thy seed be called" (Genesis 21:12).

In Genesis 25 we find the story of Isaac and Rebekah. Elder McConkie has stated: "I think Rebekah is one of the greatest patterns in all the revelations of what a woman can do to influence a family in righteousness." After having quoted several verses that speak of the twins struggling within Rebekah's womb, Elder McConkie continued: "Now note it well. She did not say, 'Isaac, will you inquire of the Lord. You are the patriarch; you are the head of the house,' which he was. She went to inquire of the Lord, and she gained the answer: 'And the Lord said unto her [the woman], Two nations are in thy womb, and two manner of people shall be separated from thy bowels; and the one people shall be stronger than the other people; and the elder shall serve the younger.' (Gen. 25:23.) That is to say, 'To you,

Rebekah, I, the Lord, reveal the destiny of nations that are to be born which are yet in your womb.'"[18]

The Old Testament is a stunningly human record, a chronicle of men and women who wrestled with the challenges of mortality. We are told that Isaac loved Esau, while his wife Rebekah loved Jacob, meaning, presumably, that the father and mother of the family had their favorites. We read further that Esau despised and sold his birthright (see Genesis 25:29–34) and chose to marry outside the covenant (see Genesis 26:34–35). In Genesis 27 we are told that Isaac the patriarch had grown old and was losing his eyesight. For reasons that are unclear—and we look forward one day to having the full account—Isaac intended to deliver his first blessing, the birthright, to Esau, in spite of the latter's disobedience and disloyalty. Rebekah interceded and coaxed Jacob into a bit of intrigue, which seems to some readers to border on dishonesty, in an effort to have the birthright go to the worthy son. Erastus Snow explained: "From the story that is told of Rebekah helping her son Jacob to get the first blessing from his father Isaac, on purpose to secure the birthright from his brother Esau, many would be inclined to think that deceit, dishonesty and unrighteous means were employed to secure it, and they perhaps wonder why it should be so. This was really not the case; it is only made to appear so in the eyes of those who do not understand the dealings of God with man, and the workings of the Holy Spirit to bring about His purposes. . . . The Lord therefore saw fit to take [the birthright] from [Esau], and the mother was moved upon to help the younger son to bring about the purpose of the Lord, in securing to himself the blessing through the legitimate channel of the Priesthood. And as you know, the father was induced to bless him and confirm this blessing upon him."[19]

If we might be so bold, we might suggest that on this occasion Isaac was not as much in tune with the workings of the Spirit and the mind of God as was Rebekah, and that it took her inspired intervention to bring about the purposes of the Lord. This admission in no way minimizes the greatness and importance of Isaac, one who, as we have noted above, has ascended the throne of godhood. It does point up, nonetheless, that the patriarchal order is a family order, a partnership, a joint stewardship. "It is an eternal principle—the man and the woman are not alone: neither is the man without the woman, nor the woman without the man in the Lord. Women are appointed, Rebekah-like, to be guides and lights in righteousness in the family unit, and to engineer and arrange so that things are done in the way that will result in the salvation of more of our Father's children."[20]

The patriarchal order continued in the Old World until the days of Moses, when the children of Israel proved unworthy of the higher priesthood and unwilling to receive its highest privilege—entering the presence of Jehovah (see Exodus 20:19; D&C 84:19–27). When Moses was translated and taken from the midst of ancient Israel, the keys of the Melchizedek Priesthood—including the right to pass that divine authority from father to son—were taken also. The fulness of the everlasting gospel, including the blessings of the holy order of God, were taken. The preparatory gospel, with its governing priesthood, the Aaronic Priesthood, was then given to the people (see JST, Exodus 34:1–2; JST, Deuteronomy 10:1–2).

There were, of course, people living on the earth after this time who held the Melchizedek Priesthood—including the sons of Aaron, the seventy elders of Israel, and the prophets who were called thereafter—but the keys, the right of presidency, including the right to confer the higher priesthood, were taken from the generality of the people. "All Priesthood is Melchizedek," Joseph Smith taught, "but there are different portions or degrees of it. That portion which brought Moses to speak with God face to face was taken away; but that which brought the ministry of angels remained. All the prophets had the Melchizedek Priesthood and were ordained by God himself."[21] That is, prophets after Moses like Elijah, Isaiah, Jeremiah, Ezekiel, and Lehi were called by God and received the Melchizedek Priesthood and its keys by special dispensation. We are instructed in a modern revelation that Nathan and "others of the prophets who had the keys of this [sealing] power" officiated in sacred saving ordinances (D&C 132:39) in Old Testament times after the Melchizedek Priesthood was taken from the body of ancient Israel.

It was not until the mortal ministry of Christ that the keys of the higher priesthood were once again delivered more universally to men on earth.[22] Jesus bestowed apostolic authority upon his chosen Twelve, and they were thereby empowered to bind on earth and bind in heaven, to seal on earth and seal in heaven (see Matthew 16:19; 18:18). Modern revelation and modern prophets affirm that in addition to receiving the keys of the kingdom from Moses, Elijah, and other heavenly messengers on the Mount of Transfiguration, the chief apostles also received their temple endowment and perhaps even the more sure word of prophecy (see Matthew 17:1–9; 2 Peter 1:16–19).[23]

It would appear, therefore, that the powers of the priesthood necessary to perform eternal marriage—that is, to establish the patriarchal order—were on earth during the Savior's ministry. Joseph Smith taught: "If a man gets a fulness of the priesthood of God he has to get it in the same way that Jesus Christ obtained it, and that was by keeping all the commandments and obeying all the ordinances of the house of the Lord."[24] Following his resurrection, the risen Lord "shewed himself alive after his passion by many infallible proofs, being seen of them forty days, and speaking of the things pertaining to the kingdom of God" (Acts 1:3). Though scripture is relatively silent, New Testament apocryphal writings ("forty-day literature") abound in teachings on washings and ritual cleansings, holy garments, new names, sacred marriages, etc.[25] We know that the Master organized his church, but that with the death of the apostles the keys of the kingdom were taken. And thus for seventeen centuries the world was without sufficient power and understanding to comprehend the glory of the priesthood and the ordinance of eternal marriage.

THE PATRIARCHAL ORDER RESTORED

The restoration of the patriarchal order of the Melchizedek Priesthood would be an essential part of the restitution of all things (see Acts 3:21). The dispensation of the fulness of times was destined to be a day of consummation, an age in which all things would be brought to fruition, a time when everything would be gathered together in one, in Christ (see Ephesians 1:10). All of the rivers of dispensations past were destined to flow into the ocean of our final dispensation. It was necessary that "a whole and complete and perfect union, and welding together of dispensations, and keys, and powers, and glories should take place, and be revealed from the days of Adam even to the present time. And not only this, but those things which never have been revealed from the foundation of the world, but have been kept hid from the wise and prudent, shall be revealed unto babes and sucklings in this, the dispensation of the fulness of times" (D&C 128:18).

Hosts of angels came to Joseph Smith from the courts of glory, "all declaring their dispensation, their rights, their keys, their honors, their majesty and glory, and the power of their priesthood; giving line upon line, precept upon precept; here a little, and there a little; giving us consolation by holding forth that which is to come, confirming our hope!" (D&C 128:21). Aaronic and Melchizedek Priesthoods were restored in 1829, and the Church was organized in 1830. The first high priests were called in June of 1831, the First Presidency was organized in 1832, and the Quorum of the Twelve Apostles and the Seventy were called in 1835.

In April of 1836 Moses restored the keys to gather Israel, to bring people into the Church and kingdom through missionary work. Elias restored the keys associated with the patriarchal order, the power to organize the Saints into eternal families through the covenant and ordinance of eternal marriage. And Elijah restored the keys associated with the fulness of the priesthood, the powers necessary to bind families and seal them up unto eternal life. The ordinances associated with the ministry and bestowal of keys by Moses, Elias, and Elijah (culminating in temples of the Lord) are the capstone blessings of the gospel and the consummation of the Father's work: they provide purpose and perspective for all other gospel principles and ordinances (see D&C 110:11–16).[26]

And so with the coming of heavenly messengers to the Kirtland Temple, the ancient order of things was restored to earth. The order in which Adam and Eve, Abraham and Sarah, Isaac and Rebekah were a part, even those keys and powers and rights are once again available to men and women. The Prophet Joseph once spoke of "Patriarchal authority." He said: "Go to and finish the temple, and God will fill it with power, and you will then receive more knowledge concerning this priesthood."[27] Elder Bruce R. McConkie taught: "I went to the temple, and I took my wife with me, and we kneeled at the altar. There on that occasion we entered, the two of us, into an 'order of the priesthood.' When we did it, we had sealed upon us, on a conditional basis, every blessing that God promised Father Abraham—the blessings of exaltation and eternal increase. The name of that order of priesthood, which is patriarchal in nature, because Abraham was a natural patriarch to his posterity, is the New and Everlasting Covenant of marriage."[28]

DISTORTIONS AND MISUNDERSTANDINGS

It would be highly unusual for an institution as significant as the patriarchal order to go unnoticed by Satan or unattacked by those who either misunderstand its place in the Lord's scheme of things or who have been misled. The following represent but a few of the many ways in which this divine program has been abused, misused, or misunderstood:

1. *Equating priesthood with male administration.* In the ultimate sense, the priesthood is the power of God by which the worlds were made, by which all things are held in check in this and myriad universes, and the power by which human souls are regenerated, renewed, resurrected, redeemed, and glorified. In addition, the priesthood is the power and authority of God, delegated to man on earth, to act in all things for the salvation of men and women. It is not a person, nor a group of people. It is a power, God's power. Men and women alike do themselves a great disservice when they equate priesthood with men or with male administration. Elder James E. Faust explained: "Many people do not understand our belief that God has wisely established a guiding authority for the most important institutions in the world. This guiding authority is called the priesthood. The priesthood is held in trust to be used to bless all of God's children. Priesthood is not gender; it is blessings from God for all at the hands of the servants He has designated."[29]

Men and women are equal before God. Both are equally necessary to the fulfillment of the Eternal Father's plan for our redemption and happiness. And yet there are presiding officers in all divinely appointed organizations, including the family. The husband and father is appointed to lead the family as our Lord and Savior Jesus Christ leads his Church (see Ephesians 5:22–29). In modern revelation we learn that the Twelve Apostles form a quorum equal in authority and power to the First Presidency, and at the same time the Twelve serve under the direction of the Presidency. Thus equality among individuals (marriage partners) or organizations (the Church) does not preclude the necessity for a presiding officer.

We do not know why God has chosen to bestow the priesthood upon worthy men, but we do know that women are entitled to every blessing of the priesthood, including the fulness of the priesthood, the power to become queens and priestesses before God in the patriarchal order. When we reject or rebel against the patriarchal order, we rebel not against men or maleness or masculinity but against eternal marriage, against eternal lives, against God and godhood. Without the priesthood and the ordinances thereof, neither men nor women can enjoy the powers of godliness (see D&C 84:21) and thus achieve their highest potential.

2. *Assuming too much for men.* A young woman came to me as her priesthood leader many years ago. She indicated that a young man in her ward had approached her, declared that an angel had come to him, and instructed him to marry her. The angel, he added, was her brother, who had passed away two or three years earlier. She asked what she should do. I inquired: "Have you prayed about this? What has the Lord said to you?" She stated rather matter-of-factly that she had not prayed about it. I asked why. "He holds the priesthood," she responded, "and so I trust his judgment." I replied that revelation is not gender specific and that something this important demanded at least a confirmation of the Spirit to her.

All of us, men and women, are expected to become gospel scholars, to learn the gospel and to live the gospel. The right to know the will of the Lord—as well as the right to enjoy the gifts of the Spirit—is freely available to all who have been baptized, received the gift of the Holy Ghost, and lived worthy of that supernal gift. I am not aware of anything in the revelations or the teachings of latter-day prophets that suggests that men who hold the priesthood have any kind of superior intelligence, greater spiritual standing, or exclusive right to the mind of God. Women may know in the same way that men may know. This is as true for single women (either those who preside over families or those who have not yet begun a family of their own) as it is for married women. In fact, in recent years the Brethren have emphasized more than once the importance of priesthood leaders seeking the counsel of the women of the Church, not just to be polite or considerate but to draw upon the wisdom and perspective of those who contribute equally with men to the growth of the kingdom.[30]

3. Unrighteous dominion. The Church or ecclesiastical order is a hierarchical system with one person presiding at the head of the respective organization. In the ward, for example, although there are many important duties to be performed and several vital positions of authority, one man, the bishop, presides. He may seek counsel (and should do so regularly) and discuss his feelings with others, but he must eventually make decisions and move the work along. The family or patriarchal order is a partnership, with father and mother counseling together, in conjunction with the children, toward the resolution of family challenges and difficulties.

The Church and the home are both divine institutions, and their modes of government are inspired. But attempting to apply one system of government to the other institution may lead to serious problems. For example, the family is not hierarchical in nature, even though it is presided over by the father. The Church is not a partnership, although people in the ward must work together in love and harmony. The bishop and Relief Society president really are not the father and mother of the ward. And a father in the home must not govern the family as though he were a despot or even a personnel manager at the head of a complex organization.

Too many men have assumed that their position as the head of the home entitled them to some kind of dictatorial following, that the patriarchal order allowed them to rule wife and children by virtue of their divine appointment as supreme officer over the family. This perception is false. It is damning. Unfortunately, too many women have entered into family living with a misperception and have therefore submitted themselves in ignorance to a man who is in reality dishonoring the priesthood he holds and thereby forfeiting the powers of the priesthood (see D&C 121:37). President Gordon B. Hinckley has stated: "Some men who are evidently unable to gain respect by the goodness of their lives use as justification for their actions the statement that Eve was told that Adam should rule over her. How much sadness, how much tragedy, how much heartbreak has been caused through centuries of time by weak men who have used that as a scriptural warrant for atrocious behavior! They do not recognize that the same account indicates that Eve was given as a helpmeet to Adam. The facts are that they stood side by side in the garden. They were expelled from the garden together, and they worked together side by side in gaining their bread by the sweat of their brows."[31]

President Howard W. Hunter likewise instructed the men of the Church: "A man who holds the priesthood accepts his wife as a partner in the leadership of the home and family with full knowledge of and full participation in all decisions relating thereto. Of necessity there must be in the Church and in the home a presiding officer (see D&C 107:21). By divine appointment, the responsibility to preside in the home rests upon the priesthood holder (see Moses 4:22). The Lord intended that the wife be a helpmeet for man (meet means equal)—that is, a companion equal and necessary in full partnership. Presiding in righteousness necessitates a shared responsibility between husband and wife; together you act with knowledge and participation in all family matters. For a man to operate independently of or without regard to the feelings and counsel of his wife in governing the family is to exercise unrighteous dominion."[32]

The word of the Master through the Prophet Joseph Smith is clear on this matter: "No power or influence can or ought to be maintained by virtue of the priesthood" (D&C 121:41). One does not coerce individuals to follow him by virtue of the priesthood. One does not demand obedience by virtue of the priesthood. One certainly does not abuse family members, physically or verbally, by virtue of the priesthood. Power and influence come through righteous leadership, through persuasion, long-suffering, gentleness, meekness, love unfeigned, kindness, pure knowledge, and charity (see D&C 121:41–45).

4. *Attacks on men in general.* To be sure, men have not always been the most sensitive and considerate of creatures. This is true in the Church, as it is in the world. Some have been abusive, domineering, aloof, and almost uncaring in regard to the feelings and sentiments of loved ones. It is no wonder that women should grow weary of unrighteous dominion or should demand equality in terms of wages or opportunities. And to the degree that revolt has focused our attention more readily on the inequities and legislation has improved somewhat the conditions in society, so much the better. What is disheartening is to see male machismo replaced by female machismo; to witness harshness, roughness, and insensitivity becoming more and more characteristic of some females in society; to stand by helplessly as we substitute in some quarters female authoritarianism for male authoritarianism.

I am particularly troubled by the growing sentiment that men are unnecessary to a happy society. David Blankenhorn has written in his book, *Fatherless America:* "Fatherlessness is the most harmful demographic trend of this generation. It is the leading cause of declining child well-being in our society. It is also the engine driving our most urgent social problems, from crime to adolescent pregnancy to child sexual abuse to domestic violence against women. Yet, despite its scale and social consequences, fatherlessness is a problem that is frequently ignored or denied." Blankenhorn goes on to say: "If you were an alien from another planet, curious about human fathers but confined to the Current Periodical section of a leading university library, what would you conclude about fatherhood in late twentieth-century America?

"The basic answer is clear. Today's expert story of fatherhood largely assumes that fatherhood is superfluous. More precisely, our elite culture has now fully incorporated into its prevailing family narrative the idea that fatherhood, as a distinctive social role for men, is either unnecessary or undesirable.

"An essential claim of the script is that there are not—and ought not to be— any key parental tasks that belong essentially and primarily to fathers. In this view, society no longer requires, or can afford to recognize, any meaningful difference between norms of fatherhood and norms of parenthood."[33]

What an insidious development—to have a segment of our population declare that not only is patriarchy antiquated in our modern and enlightened age but also that men and masculinity are no longer desirable or necessary in the perpetuation of the family in society. Elder James E. Faust noted more than two decades ago: "There are some voices in our society who would demean some of the attributes of masculinity. A few of these are women who mistakenly believe that they build their own feminine causes by tearing down the image of manhood. This has serious social overtones, because a primary problem in the insecurity of both sons and daughters can be the diminution of the role of the father image."[34]

More recently, Elder Faust taught: "It is useless to debate which parent is most important. No one would doubt that a mother's influence is paramount with newborns and in the first years of a child's life. The father's influence increases as the child grows older. However, each parent is necessary at various times in a child's development. Both fathers and mothers do many intrinsically different things for their children. Both mothers and fathers are equipped to nurture children, but their approaches are different. Mothers seem to take a dominant role in preparing children to live within their families, present and future. Fathers seem best equipped to prepare children to function in the environment outside the family. . . .

"In my opinion, members of the Church have the most effective cure for our decaying family life. It is for men, women, and children to honor and respect the divine roles of both fathers and mothers in the home. In so doing, mutual respect and appreciation among the members of the Church will be fostered by the righteousness found there."[35]

The prophets have spoken over the generations about the importance of each of us—men and women—understanding our assignments, accepting and magnifying our eternal and God-given roles, and contributing jointly to the establishment of Zion. As Elder Neal A. Maxwell pointed out, "righteousness is not a matter of role, nor goodness a matter of gender. In the work of the kingdom, men and women are not without each other, but do not envy each other, lest by reversals and renunciations of role we make a wasteland of both womanhood and manhood."[36] President Spencer W. Kimball similarly declared that in his wisdom and mercy, "our Father made men and women dependent on each other for the full flowering of their potential. Because their natures are somewhat different, they can complement each other; because they are in many ways alike, they can understand each other. Let neither envy the other for their differences; let both discern what is superficial and what is beautifully basic in those differences, and act accordingly."[37]

5. *Apostate cults.* There is one final distortion that is worthy of brief mention. There are those, most of whom have been cut off from the Church, who claim scriptural or divine sanction (through secret ordinances or ordinations) for polygamous relationships on the basis that they are participating in what they call the patriarchal order. On the whole, they have chosen to reject the counsel of living prophets and thus forfeit the rights of membership in the living church. Stated simply, the Lord does not work that way! Nephi explained that the Lord God does not work in darkness (see 2 Nephi 26:23). In 1933 the First Presidency of the Church wrote: "Any ceremony pretending to bind man and woman together beyond the period of mortal life, which is not solemnized by one who has been commissioned and authorized by the man who holds the keys of authority to bind upon earth with a covenant which will be binding in heaven, is of no efficacy or force when people are out of the world. . . .

"We do not wish to pass judgment upon or evaluate the motives of our fellow men—that is for the Lord to do—but we unqualifiedly say, as it is our right and duty to say, that the doctrines these persons [who claim some special authority to practice plural marriage] preach and the practices they follow, are born of the Evil One and are contrary to the revealed will and word of the Lord. We call upon them to repent and to forsake their false doctrines and evil practices. Unless they do so the Lord will not hold them guiltless. . . .

"Celestial marriage—that is, marriage for time and eternity—and polygamous or plural marriage are not synonymous terms. Monogamous marriages for time and eternity, solemnized in our temples in accordance with the word of the Lord and the laws of the Church, are Celestial marriages."[38]

CONCLUSION

The family is the most important unit in time and in eternity. The Church exists to assist individuals and families in their quest to gain exaltation and eternal life. "Our very concept of heaven itself," President Hugh B. Brown stated, "is the projection of the home into eternity. Salvation, then, is essentially a family affair, and full participation in the plan of salvation can be had only in family units."[39] Indeed, the development of a celestial home is the object and design of all we do in the Church.

Today the family is under attack. And how could the Arch Deceiver more powerfully dismantle the family than to dismember it, to pull it apart, or to pit male against female, to confuse or to convolute? Beverly Campbell stated: "If he (Satan) can make men and women see one another, not as empowering partners, but as individuals who are of unequal worth or as competitors, seeking gifts the other has, he can cause great pain and anguish. He can distort the concepts of deity, spiritual powers, and the priesthood and thereby distort our response to each other.

"As men and women we need to recognize and validate the primary and many roles of women as well as those of men. We should strive to see that opportunities are provided and that equity abounds. . . .

"Satan knows that celestial (eternal) marriage is a basic principle on which all eternal promises hinge, and that its destruction is the only way whereby he can further frustrate the purpose of the Father."[40]

The patriarchal order of the Melchizedek Priesthood predates this mortal estate. Each of us is a spirit child of heavenly Parents and was nurtured in the family unit long before we were born into earth life. As children of Abraham, Isaac, and Jacob, we come to earth with a spiritual predisposition to recognize and receive the truth,[41] and, if we will be true to our innermost longings and desires, with an inclination to establish our own eternal family unit. After we have been baptized and received the gift of the Holy Ghost, it is our duty as children of the covenant to qualify ourselves for the blessings of the holy temple. In that holy house we are truly gathered to Christ[42] and endowed with power from on high; thereafter we may enter into that order of the Melchizedek Priesthood we know as the patriarchal order, also known as the new and everlasting covenant of marriage. And it is through fidelity and devotion to the ordinances and covenants of the house of the Lord that men and women qualify to become the sons and daughters of God. Through the mercy and grace of the Holy Messiah, we become by adoption the sons and daughters of Jesus Christ. Then, as we prove faithful to temple covenants, we eventually become "gods, even the sons [and daughters] of God" (D&C 76:58). These are they who are members of the Church of the Firstborn (see D&C 76:54, 94), who become joint heirs with Christ to all that the Father has (see Romans 8:14–18), who are then entitled to the blessings of the Firstborn, the blessings of the birthright.

The Apostle Paul taught that the man is not without the woman, neither is the woman without the man in the Lord (see 1 Corinthians 11:11). The patriarchal order of the priesthood is not an institution whereby men are exalted or where women are required to assume some lower station or powerless position. It is, rather, a divine system of family government. When entered into worthily and when the parties so live as to enjoy the companionship of the Holy Ghost, power in the priesthood is enjoyed by all concerned—husband, wife, and children—and peace, mutual respect, and individual and family growth are the order of the day. Such a family is thus a little bit of heaven on earth, inasmuch as the earthly family becomes thereby a reflection, a reminiscence, and an extension of the heavenly family.

Having spoken at length concerning the ministry of the ancients, the scripture attests: "Now this same Priesthood, which was in the beginning, shall be in the end of the world also" (Moses 6:7). That is to say, what was true for the former-day Saints is true for the Latter-day Saints. What inspired and motivated them can and should entice us to continued goodness in the household of faith. The patriarchal order that existed in the premortal world and that governed among the early people of God on earth has been restored through modern prophets and made available to all men and women who prove worthy of the blessings of the temple. It will prepare us here and now for life on a celestialized earth. "And that same sociality which exists among us here will exist among us there, only it will be coupled with eternal glory, which glory we do not now enjoy" (D&C 130:2). In the words of a modern apostle: "This is the priesthood which we hold. It will bless us as it blessed Melchizedek and Abraham. The priesthood of Almighty God is here."[43]

Notes

From an address delivered at the Family Expo Conference, Brigham Young University, Provo, Utah, 6 April 1998.

1. *Teachings of the Prophet Joseph Smith*, 345.
2. Brigham Young, in *Journal of Discourses*, 6:275.
3. *Messages of the First Presidency*, 4:205.
4. See *History of the Church*, 2:320.

5. Ibid.

6. See *Doctrinal New Testament Commentary,* 2:474.

7. *Doctrines of Salvation,* 3:81; see also Wilford Woodruff, *Discourses of Wilford Woodruff* (Salt Lake City: Bookcraft, 1969), 64.

8. Ezra Taft Benson, "What I Hope You Will Teach Your Children about the Temple," *Ensign,* August 1985, 8.

9. John Taylor, in *Times and Seasons,* 6:921–22, June 1, 1845.

10. *Teachings of the Prophet Joseph Smith,* 159.

11. Benson, "What I Hope You Will Teach Your Children about the Temple," 9.

12. See also *Gospel Doctrine,* 461.

13. Bruce R. McConkie, *A New Witness for the Articles of Faith* (Salt Lake City: Deseret Book Co., 1985), 35.

14. Erastus Snow, in *Journal of Discourses,* 21:369.

15. See Joseph Fielding Smith, *The Way to Perfection* (Salt Lake City: Deseret Book Co., 1970), 72–73.

16. Joseph Fielding Smith, *Answers to Gospel Questions,* 5 vols. (Salt Lake City: Deseret Book Co., 1957–66), 2:174; see also *Doctrines of Salvation,* 3:104.

17. Russell M. Nelson, *The Power within Us* (Salt Lake City: Deseret Book Co., 1988), 109.

18. Bruce R. McConkie, "Our Sisters from the Beginning," *Ensign,* January 1979, 62.

19. Erastus Snow, in *Journal of Discourses,* 21:370–71.

20. McConkie, "Our Sisters from the Beginning," 63.

21. *Teachings of the Prophet Joseph Smith,* 180–81; compare Joseph Fielding Smith, *Doctrines of Salvation,* 3:78; Bruce R. McConkie, *Promised Messiah,* 412; see also a statement by John Taylor, cited in *Words of Joseph Smith,* 82–83.

22. See *Teachings of the Prophet Joseph Smith,* 274.

23. See Joseph Fielding Smith, *Doctrines of Salvation,* 2:165; Bruce R. McConkie, *Doctrinal New Testament Commentary,* 1:400.

24. *Teachings of the Prophet Joseph Smith,* 308.

25. See Hugh Nibley, *Mormonism and Early Christianity,* ed. Todd M. Compton and Stephen D. Ricks (Salt Lake City: Deseret Book Co. and FARMS, 1987), 10–44.

26. See *Teachings of the Prophet Joseph Smith,* 172, 337–38; Joseph Fielding Smith, *Doctrines of Salvation,* 2:115–28.

27. *Teachings of the Prophet Joseph Smith,* 323.

28. Bruce R. McConkie, "The Eternal Family Concept," devotional address at the Second Annual Priesthood Genealogical Research Seminar, Brigham Young University, Provo, Utah, 23 June 1967; see also Bruce R. McConkie, in Conference Report, October 1977, 50.

29. James E. Faust, in Conference Report, April 1993, 45.

30. See M. Russell Ballard, in Conference Report, October 1993, 103; April 1994, 31–34.

31. Gordon B. Hinckley, in Conference Report, October 1991, 72.

32. Howard W. Hunter, in Conference Report, October 1994, 68.

33. David Blankenhorn, *Fatherless America* (New York: HarperCollins, 1996), 1, 67.

34. James E. Faust, in Conference Report, October 1973, 18.

35. James E. Faust, in Conference Report, April 1993, 44–45, 47.

36. Neal A. Maxwell, in Conference Report, April 1978, 13.

37. Spencer W. Kimball, "Relief Society—Its Promise and Potential," *Ensign,* March 1976, 5.

38. *Messages of the First Presidency,* 5:319, 329.

39. Hugh B. Brown, in Conference Report, October 1966, 103.

40. Beverly Campbell, "Mother Eve, Mentor for Today's Woman: A Heritage of Honor," address given at the eleventh annual conference of Collegium Aesculapium, Salt Lake City, Utah, 2 April 1993.

41. See *Teachings of the Prophet Joseph Smith*, 149–50; McConkie, *A New Witness for the Articles of Faith*, 38–39.
42. See *Teachings of the Prophet Joseph Smith*, 307–8.
43. Bruce R. McConkie, in Conference Report, October 1977, 35.

STANDING IN HOLY PLACES—
AS INDIVIDUALS AND FAMILIES

I like to think of the home as a sanctuary. A sanctuary is a holy place, a place where sacred things are felt and experienced, a place where men and women, boys and girls are linked to the divine and thus reacquainted with those tender and sweet associations we once knew. A sanctuary is also a defense, a refuge, a covert from the storms that descend upon all of us, whether in the form of temptation or false and degrading beliefs and practices. The disciples of Christ are commanded to stand in holy places and be not moved, "until the day of the Lord come; for behold, it cometh quickly, saith the Lord" (D&C 87:8; see also 45:32).

FOUNDATIONAL TRUTHS

I want to state unequivocally that I believe in God. I know that he lives, that he listens, that he longs for us to live in such a manner as to gain peace and happiness, both individually and as families. I know that he has a plan for his sons and daughters, that life is meant to be lived in harmony with that divine system of salvation, and that misery and unhappiness are the inevitable results of seeking to do things in our own way. I know that Jesus of Nazareth is the Son of God, the Savior and Redeemer of humankind, the One sent of the Father to bind up the brokenhearted and liberate the captives (see Isaiah 61:1). I have the perfect assurance that that upon which Christ places his hand, whether distraught individuals or dysfunctional families, will be healed and re-created.

I am also bold to testify of the enemy of righteousness, even Satan or Lucifer, the father of all lies. He is real. I know this from personal experience. He is an actual being from the unseen world who wields great power in this generation. He is, in reality, the god of this world (see 2 Corinthians 4:4). From the beginning, he and his minions have sought to deceive and blind men and women, to lead them captive at his will, even as many as would not hearken unto the voice of God (see Moses 4:4). In the words of Elder Dallin H. Oaks, "although Satan and his followers have lost their opportunity to have a physical body, they are permitted to use their spirit powers to try to frustrate God's plan. . . . *Satan's most strenuous opposition is directed at whatever is most important to the Father's plan. Satan seeks to discredit the Savior and divine authority, to nullify the effects of the Atonement,* to counterfeit revelation, to lead people away from the truth, to contradict individual accountability, *to confuse gender, to undermine marriage, and to discourage child-bearing* (especially by parents who will raise children in righteousness)."[1]

These are fundamental truths. They are essential to an understanding of individuals and of families. They are basic to any efforts to rectify the wrongs of society and minister to the wounded and scarred souls all about us. We ignore them at our peril. Most of our efforts to deal with social-emotional problems, to provide therapeutic remediation—independent of those absolute truths concerning God, Christ, Satan, and the eternal nature of men and women—will be at best deficient and at worse perverse. I assure you that such an attitude is neither naive nor ill-informed. I agree with C. S. Lewis, who observed that once we begin to mature spiritually, we realize that everything that really needs to be done in our souls can be done only by God.[2]

Elder Jeffrey R. Holland has said: "*We need to turn to God. We need to reaffirm our faith, and we need to reassert our hope. Where necessary we need to repent, and certainly we need to pray. It is the absence of spiritual fidelity that has led us to moral disarray in the twilight of the twentieth century.* We have sown the wind of religious skepticism, and we are reaping the whirlwind of existential despair.

"Without religious faith," Elder Holland continued, "*without recognizing the reality and necessity of spiritual life, the world makes no sense, and a nonsense world is a place of horror.* Only if the world has meaning at a spiritual level is it possible for human beings to keep going, to keep trying."[3]

If in fact the religious dimension to human personality or the spiritual indices underlying the success of the family are not something with which we feel we can deal, then I suggest that the Latter-day Saints have nothing to offer the world in this field. To teach and practice solely according to the canons of the behavioral sciences, without the clarifying and illuminating lenses of the Restoration, is to live beneath our privileges and to wander at dusk when we could walk in the light of the noonday sun. "I see no justification," President Marion G. Romney stated, "for us who have the clear light of the revealed Gospel of Christ, to spend our lives stumbling around through the mists following the uncertain glimmer of a flickering candle lighted by the wisdom of men. It seems to me that we should devote our energies to spreading the true light, and leave the mists to those who do not claim to see that light."[4]

THE STORMS THAT RAGE

Every person builds a house of faith. We do so knowingly or unknowingly. And every builder soon learns that a good building with a bad foundation is worse than useless; it is dangerous. I wish to mention certain ideologies, certain trends in our society to which I feel the doors of our hearts and our homes must be forever closed if we expect to enjoy the approbation of heaven. Then we will consider some simple principles of truth and righteousness upon which we must build our lives if we are to stand in holy places and be not moved.

1. *An obsession with self.* Everyone wants to be at peace, to feel good inside, to have a positive outlook on life. Everyone wants to find contentment in their labors and a feeling of satisfaction in their accomplishments. But there are limits here; we can become obsessed with *me, my* will, *my* wishes, *my* happiness, and *my* well-being. "The most basic truths of our [Christian] faith," one Protestant theologian has observed, "have fallen victim to [a] self-centered theology. Many modern-day evangelists have reduced the gospel message to little more than a formula by which people can live a happy and more fulfilling life. Sin is now defined by how it affects man, not how it dishonors God. Salvation is often presented as a means of receiving what Christ offers without obeying what He commands. The focus has shifted from God's glory to man's benefit. The gospel of persevering faith has given way to a kind of religious hedonism. Jesus, contemporary theology implies, is your ticket to avoiding all of life's pains and experiencing all of life's pleasures."[5]

We live in a day when the religious solutions to problems and questions, if they are given any credence at all, are among the least and last considered. With the growth of the behavioral sciences during the last century, we have witnessed repeated efforts to identify causes and label solutions that are independent of Jesus Christ and the discipleship to which he has called us. It is noteworthy that as the number of psychological and sociological explanations provided for misconduct or distress enlarges, as the complexity of the explanation for the problem increases, spiritual indices and roots of the behavior begin to be disregarded or to be ignored entirely.

We are reminded continually of what a tense and stress-filled world we live in. The complexity of life and the competition to not only stay afloat but also get ahead have resulted in a host of psycho-physiological disorders, maladies that would have been unknown to our forebears. Many people preoccupy themselves needlessly with self-inspections; they are compulsively taking their own emotional or spiritual temperatures to assure that they are happy or stable or "together" or worthy. Others spend a lifetime (and too often a fortune) seeking to love themselves or to "find themselves."

2. *An eagerness to take offense.* I have feelings just like the next person. I have been insulted, belittled, put down in front of others. I know what it feels like to be misunderstood, to have my motives or my intentions questioned. In other words, I know what it feels like to be offended. On the one hand, you and I need to be more sensitive, more cautious with people's feelings. We need to do all in our power to keep from excluding others, to keep from making people feel left out. We need to show respect and dignity to individuals, regardless of their color, their personal beliefs, their religion, or their gender. We are human beings, sons and daughters of God first and foremost; these things we share with every other mortal. God loves us all, and, as the scriptures affirm, he is no respecter of persons (see Acts 10:34).

There is, of course, another side to this story. In order to live in harmony, we must become the kind of people who are not constantly looking to take offense. Each of us could easily waste our lives striving to make our associates offenders for a word. Many times a day we could take offense with the way we are spoken to (or not spoken to), the way we are introduced, the way someone mispronounces our name, or the way we feel we are ignored or overlooked. Our society's inability to be fully Christian has led to a staggering increase in the number of court cases. We have become a litigious people, a nation that thinks first of justice and later (if at all) of reconciliation or even forgiveness.[6] Our tendency to look for and take offense has made it extremely difficult to function in society, even to the point where individuals are frightened to speak, anxious about saying anything, for fear that their language or their approach may not be "politically correct." One of the ironies of our day is that an overmuch dose of multiculturalism and an exaggerated emphasis on diversity can create a type of ethnicity that will in time contribute to the segregation and disunity of our society. Such separatism "nourishes prejudices, magnifies differences and stirs antagonisms."[7]

3. *False teachings about men and women.* Both men and women in the last three decades have bought into ideas and worldviews that are destructive of individuals and families. Many men, for example, have been told that they must be stoic, stern, and macho. They have been instructed to guard their feelings, hide their emotions, and maintain a cool exterior. Some have imbibed the poisonous notion that the great indicator of success in life is to be found outside the home, to be ascertained in terms of portfolios, chrome, real estate, business contacts, or academic degrees. Some have become so ensnared by their work—that which is intended, at best, to be a means to an end—that they have abrogated their responsibilities toward home and children. Some have given way to carnal urges, learned to relabel sin as psychology, and tragically surrendered to that great lie we have come to know as the "midlife crisis." Far too many men in the Church have missed the mark in leading their families, have taken license from what they would call the patriarchal order of government, and have become tyrannical and dictatorial in their leadership of the home. Truly, the vicious but versatile father of lies rages in the hearts of some while he pacifies others (see 2 Nephi 28:20–21).

There can be no question but that women have been the object of abuse and indignity for centuries, and that even today many women—in and out of the Church—live under circumstances that range from the uncomfortable to the intolerable. Men have too often been cruel and uncaring, insensitive to women—their needs, their desires, and their voices. In that sense the effort on the part of women to reassert their value and their critical place in society has been needed. Sadly, however, many women have turned to brands of radical feminism that have brought more heartache than help. "What is so frustrating," one woman has written, "looking back on all this, is how unnecessary and destructive it all was. American women in the fifties needed feminism, real feminism, feminism that would embrace both its career women and its career mothers. . . . A real feminism would have affirmed them both, searched for ways to allow each to be more secure and more valued in what she had chosen to do. Instead, the false feminism we got declared war on mothers. . . ."

She continues: "Thus it was that in the wake of the defeat of the ERA and the growth of the prolife movement, many feminist organizations, especially the National Organization for Women, woke up to 'family issues.' I would like to say that was a hopeful sign. The Lord only knows, we need some constructive thinking about family issues.

"All indications, however, are that nothing much has changed, except the rhetoric. Not a single one of the major mainstream feminist organizations is willing to consider marriage and motherhood as anything but a problem. Not one of them is interested in helping women who want to make that choice pursue it in dignity. Everyone wants to make that choice a near or total impossibility. Being 'just a housewife' still gets you no respect, especially from feminists. . . . *For a movement dedicated so stridently to choice, they are remarkably selective in the choices they are willing to allow other women to make.*

" . . . It's no wonder that the new woman of the nineties has no self-respect. You cannot devalue motherhood without devaluing everything else women do. *You cannot declare the primary work of most women throughout most of history to be beneath serious consideration without sending women the covert message that it is really women who are beneath serious consideration.*

"*You cannot train a whole generation of women in contempt for their mothers without training them in contempt for themselves. . . .*"

And then comes the following pointed and painful conclusion: "The New Woman of the nineties didn't need a society full of sexist men to make her believe she was worth nothing. She had the new wave of American feminism to do it for them."[8]

In general we could say that men and women, in and out of the Church, have been sold a bill of goods. They have been taunted by and titillated with views concerning man, woman, priesthood, and family that are at odds with the revealed word and thus with things as they really are and as they really will be. Confusion and conflict have ensued, and a few have forsaken the faith because they chose to give heed to seductive voices. No person, not here or in eternity, can be happy or find real fulfillment who revolts against the divinely established role and calling he or she was given before the foundations of this earth were laid.

4. *An erosion of moral absolutes.* One Christian writer has observed: "If the stability of buildings depends largely upon their foundations, so does the stability of human lives. The search for personal security is a primal instinct, but many fail to find it today. Old familiar landmarks are being obliterated. Moral absolutes which were once thought to be eternal are being abandoned."[9] The modern mind has yielded to what has become known as the "poison of subjectivism," the idea "that morality is manmade, private, subjective, a matter of feeling, a subdivision of psychology. 'I feel' replaces 'I believe.'"[10] In recent years we have sown the wind and now reap the whirlwind as far as standards of behavior are concerned. People clamor for rights and recognition in society while few speak of our moral responsibilities to society. We permit and even promote lewdness and perversion in the name of openness and acceptance. In the 1960s we heard much of the "new

morality," of "situational ethics," and of the fact that "all things are relative." Lectures and discussions and seminars abounded, while masses of people, young and old, chose to "march to a different drummer," to chart their own course, to "do their own thing," to re-create God in their own image. In the sixties people discoursed much on these things. Today, while we speak much less about these notions, many people now embody them.

The erosion of moral absolutes is highly correlated with what we consume in terms of literature, movies, music, and entertainment of many kinds. Young people in our day need not search out alleys and backstreets to become involved in the lurid and the obscene; they need only pay the box office price or flip the television channel. As movie critic Michael Medved has written, "Hollywood's crisis is, at its very core, a crisis of values. It's not 'mediocrity and escapism' that leave audiences cold, but sleaze and self-indulgence. What troubles people about the popular culture isn't the competence with which it's shaped, but the messages it sends, the view of the world it transmits." Continuing, Medved stated: "Hollywood no longer reflects—or even respects—the values of most American families. On many of the important issues in contemporary life, popular entertainment seems to go out of its way to challenge conventional notions of decency."[11] Likewise, "a survey of influential television writers and executives in Hollywood has shown that they are far less religious than the general public and 'diverge sharply from traditional values' on such issues as abortion, homosexual rights and extramarital sex."[12]

Some young Latter-day Saints discover inconsistency in the values purported by their parents; the mom and dad who would never allow the children to view this or that movie or video have little or no hesitation in doing so themselves. Surely no person interested in spiritual things could believe that what is morally taboo for the youth is fully acceptable for their elders. "One might well wonder," Elder Richard L. Evans warned, "about the term 'adult entertainment.' Could it be that something unclean or immoral which is not fit for children is wholesome for adults? Is 'adult evil' acceptable? How consistent is it to have a double standard?"[13] We should not be surprised if we find that our children or grandchildren wander about in a type of moral malaise. One philosopher has noted that "if a child's moral growth does not keep pace with his physical growth, there may soon be no child. Could this explain why the most common age for suicide today is adolescence? The human race is now in its adolescence and standing on the edge of a cliff."[14]

5. *A failure to hearken to prophetic counsel.* Too often the Saints have treated lightly prophetic counsel—the words of those called as apostles and prophets—on how to solve social and emotional problems, as well as how to strengthen marriages

and families. Sometimes we have not prepared ourselves to be taught by the Lord through his servants. And sometimes, sadly enough, we ignore or reject the living oracles because their instruction comes in conflict with our own training, background, or orientation. This is perilous. It places us in a position to lose light and deny ourselves and those we serve consummate spiritual privileges. To the Prophet Joseph Smith, the Lord said (and these words are particularly appropriate to our discussion): "Verily I say unto you, the keys of this kingdom shall never be taken from you, while thou art in the world, neither in the world to come; nevertheless, through you shall the oracles be given to another, yea, even unto the church." And now note this warning: "And *all they who receive the oracles of God, let them beware how they hold them lest they are accounted as a light thing, and are brought under condemnation thereby, and stumble and fall when the storms descend, and the winds blow, and the rains descend, and beat upon their house"* (D&C 90:3–5; emphasis added).

A SURE FOUNDATION

It is easy for us to be cynical, to step back and take potshots at America or the larger world. And it is often the case that those who cry doom and despair the loudest seldom offer remedies for a society that suffers from a sickness of the soul. I do not believe the way ahead will be easy, but I do sense keenly that most of the answers to life's most troublesome questions are simpler than we think. These answers call for a retrenchment, a return to our spiritual and moral moorings, a return to virtue, a return to the faith of our fathers and mothers.

1. *Losing ourselves.* "I receive not honour from men," Jesus said (John 5:41). By today's standards, therefore, Jesus must have wrestled incessantly with a miserably low self-esteem! In fact, his sense of personal worth seemed to be inextricably tied to his commitment to his mission and his complete submission to the will of his Father. Jesus went about doing good. His eye was single to the glory of God. His compassion for others often overrode his personal desires, even his need for rest (see JST, Mark 7:22–23). Note the focus of our Lord's life and labors:

"I seek not mine own will, but the will of the Father which hath sent me" (John 5:30).

"I came down from heaven, not to do mine own will, but the will of him that sent me" (John 6:38).

"My doctrine is not mine, but his that sent me" (John 7:16).

"He that sent me is with me: the Father hath not left me alone; for I do always those things that please him" (John 8:29).

"I and my Father are one" (John 10:30).

As President Ezra Taft Benson has explained, a wholesome view of self is "best established by a close relationship with God."[15] Surely a more significant undertaking than discovering ourselves is coming to know God and gaining his approval. The journey of self-discovery, the quest for self-esteem—these are elusive and man-made, far more fascinating than fruitful. We can feel and become all that we were intended to feel and be, but it will come about in the Lord's own way, through laboring in his cause, serving others, and seeking through him to become a new creature in Christ. The Savior's commission to "love thy neighbour as thyself" (Matthew 19:19) has little to do with loving oneself; it has much to do with loving others as one would desire to be loved, to fulfill the Golden Rule (see Matthew 7:12; 3 Nephi 14:12). There is no divine directive to spend time developing self-love or becoming obsessed with self-esteem. Rather, one of the solemn ironies of existence is the principle found in the words of the Master: "Whosoever will save his life in this world, shall lose it in the world to come. And *whosoever will lose his life in this world, for my sake, shall find it in the world to come*" (JST, Matthew 16:27–28; emphasis added).

As C.S. Lewis has suggested, "until you have given up your self to Him you will not have a real self. . . . The very first step [in giving up one's self] is to try to forget about the self altogether. Your real, new self (which is Christ's and also yours, and yours just because it is His) will not come as long as you are looking for it. It will come when you are looking for [Christ]."[16] Or, as another writer expressed it: "When we turn away from and reject self and turn unto Jesus, the very first thing that he gives to us is a new, lofty personal identity in him. *No longer must we 'find ourselves' in the various means of identification offered by this world. No longer do we need other people to bolster our flagging sense of self-worth. Our endless quest to be somebody and to gain power, influence, fame, and fortune comes to an end. The identity that God gives us in Christ Jesus lifts us far higher than anything this world can offer.*"[17]

Alma's counsel to Helaman to "look to God and live" (Alma 37:47) has as much to do with our sense of personal security as it does with our ultimate salvation. It is to Christ that we look. From him we receive strength. In him is found peace and quietude of soul. As Bruce Hafen has written: "When we place our confidence in God rather than in ourselves, our need for self-esteem takes care of itself. . . . The heart of it all is not *self*-confidence. It is confidence in *him,* and in his power to make us into creatures far beyond the reach of what our goal-setting and goal-achieving can ultimately accomplish in the process of becoming as he is."[18]

2. *Refusing to take offense.* One of the crying needs of our day is for us, every one of us, to take responsibility for our lives, face challenges with maturity and patience, and refuse to yield to the spirit of victimization. As long as we continue to point to others and to circumstances as the source of our problems, we will never enjoy the peace of mind that comes from Christ, a peace that transcends anything the world has to offer (see John 14:27). The answer is not to take offense, strike back, litigate, or harbor resentment. The answer, more often than not, is to forgive and forget, to "leave it alone."

I have come to know that we need not be offended, that one of the most important signs of spiritual growth is a refusal to take offense. We need not be angry or bitter or insulted. We need not make our sister or our brother an offender for a word. It really is not too difficult to look at a person's heart, to try to understand what they meant to do rather than what they did, or what they meant to say rather than what they said. Sometimes this entails simply looking the other way and assuming the best. Sometimes it requires forgiveness. President Gordon B. Hinckley pointed out that there is no virtue more needed in our day than forgiving and forgetting. "There are those who would look upon this," he said, "as a sign of weakness. Is it? I submit that it takes neither strength nor intelligence to brood in anger over wrongs suffered, to go through life with a spirit of vindictiveness, to dissipate one's abilities in planning retribution. There is no peace in the nursing of a grudge."[19] In addition, as Elder Boyd K. Packer has taught, "some frustrations we must endure without really solving the problem. *Some things that ought to be put in order are not put in order because we cannot control them. Things we cannot solve, we must survive.*"[20]

It may well be that forgiveness is one of the most difficult labors of the disciple, but one that makes us more like the Merciful One than anything else we might do. The German theologian Dietrich Bonhoeffer observed: "While it is true that only the sufferings of Christ are a means of atonement, yet since he has suffered for and borne the sins of the whole world and shares with his disciples the fruits of his [sufferings], the Christian also has to undergo temptation; he too has to bear the sins of others; he too must bear their shame and be driven like a scapegoat from the gate of the city. . . . My brother's burden which I must bear is not only his outward lot, his natural characteristics and gifts, but quite literally his sin. And the only way to bear that sin is by forgiving it in the power of the cross of Christ in which I now share."[21] To truly forgive others—especially those who have inflicted pain on us—is in a very real way to take up our cross, to become "a Christ-figure," one who, as Bruce and Marie Hafen have written, is willing "to absorb a terrible trauma of the spirit" in order to "help the sinner."[22]

As we observed earlier, whatever Christ puts his hand upon is healed. That is true of homes as well as hearts. Most of us will require a special endowment of spiritual strength, and in some cases a spiritual transformation, in order to put things behind us. But I bear witness that there is a Balm in Gilead, a healing Balm not of this world, a soothing and sanctifying Balm that works mighty changes in the hearts and minds of those who put their trust in the Great Physician.

3. *Accepting absolute truths.* While in the true and living church (see D&C 1:30) specific policies or programs may change from time to time, certain truths and practices are set, fixed, and immutable. They may not be altered by time or opinion. They are eternal absolutes. "God, our Heavenly Father—Elohim—lives," President Spencer W. Kimball testified some years ago. "That is an absolute truth. All . . . of the children of men on the earth might be ignorant of him and his attributes and his powers, but he still lives. All the people on the earth might deny him and disbelieve, but he lives in spite of them. . . . In short, opinion alone has no power in the matter of an absolute truth. . . . The watchmaker in Switzerland, with materials at hand, made the watch that was found in the sand in a California desert. The people who found the watch had never been to Switzerland, nor seen the watchmaker, nor seen the watch made. The watchmaker still existed, no matter the extent of their ignorance or experience. If the watch had a tongue, it might even lie and say, 'There is no watchmaker.' That would not alter the truth."[23]

Without absolute truths, without set and established principles and practices within our personal and social experience, life would have little meaning, and, in fact, there would be few things on which we could depend with certainty. President Rex Lee explained to BYU students that "there is nothing more important for each of you to do than build a firm, personal testimony that there are in this life some absolutes, things that never change, regardless of time, place, or circumstances. They are eternal truths, eternal principles, and . . . they are and ever will be the same yesterday, today, and forever."[24]

No matter the regularity of society's chants or the decibels of special interest groups' demands, some things are forever proper and right, and some things are eternally wrong. Popular vote or consensus are not the means of ascertaining truth. We turn instead to the scriptures, to revelation, to those called and anointed to make known to the Church and the world the mind and voice and will of the Lord. President Kimball taught that "right and wrong, righteousness and sin, are not dependent upon men's interpretations, conventions and attitudes. Social acceptance does not change the status of an act, making wrong into right." And then, as a very timely illustration, he noted: "If all the people in the world were to accept homosexuality, as it seems to have been accepted in Sodom and Gomorrah, the practice would still be deep, dark sin."[25] President Kimball also testified: "The world may have its norm; the Church has a different one. . . . The world may countenance premarital sex experiences, but the Lord and his Church condemn in no uncertain terms any and every sex relationship outside of marriage, and even indecent and uncontrolled ones within marriage. And so, though many self-styled authorities justify these practices as a normal release, the Church condemns them."[26]

4. *Receiving the Lord's servants.* There are at least two sources of spiritual power. One is personal righteousness, the power that comes from diligent study and work and discipline, the inspiration and revelation that come as a result of fasting and prayer and service. There is also a power associated with loyalty to the Lord's anointed servants. God has called and empowered prophets to lead us, revelators to dispense saving truths, and seers to discern and prepare us for the challenges and storms that are on the horizon. "A seer can know of things which are past, and also of things which are to come, and by them shall all things be revealed, or, rather, shall secret things be made manifest, and hidden things shall come to light" (Mosiah 8:17). Those we sustain as seers are endowed with divine power to see things "afar off" (D&C 101:54), things that are "not visible to the natural eye" (Moses 6:36). Threats to the family, threats to the stability of personal life and society, threats to the foundations of our nation and world—these are the things an omniscient God makes known to his chosen servants, almost always many years before the storm arrives. The wisest among us learn to prepare ourselves and our homes against the assault when things are calm and dry and sunny. As President J. Reuben Clark Jr. pointed out over forty years ago, "We do not lack a prophet; what we lack is a listening ear by the people and a determination to live as God has commanded."[27] Acceptance of the Lord's servants is a sure sign of the depth of our commitment to him and his plan; as President Harold B. Lee testified so often, a man or woman is not fully converted until they see the power of God resting upon the leaders of this Church, and that witness goes down into their hearts like fire.[28]

CONCLUSION

It has occurred to me many times in the last several years that one of the most important gifts to be sought for and acquired in this complex age is the gift of discernment—not alone the capacity to distinguish good from evil, as important as that is, but also the ability to discern what matters from what doesn't matter quite so much. I shudder at the possibility that I might finish my life and then have the Lord explain to me that I had spent my time laboring largely in secondary causes.

Indeed, one of the signs of the times, one of the evidences that all is not well in this world, is that so many of our priorities seem to be perverted. "The fight to stop nuclear power is far more trendy than the fight to save the nuclear family; reducing the level of pollution seems to be a higher priority than reducing the level of teenage promiscuity."[29] As George Will lamented: "America today is capable of terrific intolerance about smoking or toxic waste that threatens trout. But only a deeply confused society is more concerned about protecting lungs than minds, trout than black women."[30] Elder Boyd K. Packer warned: "As we test the *moral* environment, we find the *pollution* index is spiraling upward. . . . God grant that we will come to our senses and protect our moral environment from this mist of darkness which deepens day by day. The fate of all humanity hangs precariously in the balance."[31]

C. S. Lewis, in his masterwork, *The Screwtape Letters,* has one of the archdevils, Screwtape, giving instruction to his nephew, Wormwood, about how to deceive those who have become Christians: "The real trouble about the set your patient is living in is that it is *merely* Christian. They all have individual interests, of course, but the bond remains mere Christianity. What we want, if men become Christians at all, is to keep them in the state of mind I call 'Christianity And.' You know—Christianity and the Crisis, Christianity and the New Psychology, Christianity and the New Order, Christianity and Faith Healing, Christianity and Psychical Research, Christianity and Vegetarianism, Christianity and Spelling Reform. If they must be Christians, let them at least be Christians with a difference. Substitute for the faith itself some Fashion with a Christian colouring. Work on their horror of the Same Old Thing."[32]

The devil doesn't need to persuade us to steal or lie or commit adultery. You and I need merely undersell, understate, and thus underestimate the powers, appropriateness, and relevance of the gospel. One challenge we face in a world that is expanding dramatically in regard to information, discovery, and technology is to hold fast to that which is fundamental, to rivet ourselves to the simple. In many cases new discoveries have paved and will yet pave the way to the amelioration of human suffering and the removal of so many of life's struggles. But there are some things that never change, some problems whose resolution is brought to pass only through divine intervention. The Apostle Paul taught us that in Christ "dwelleth all the fulness of the Godhead bodily. And *ye are complete in him,* which is the head of all principality and power" (Colossians 2:9–10; emphasis added).

I wish to reaffirm that the hope of the world lies in the person and powers of Jesus Christ, who is the Hope of the Ages. He is the "Wonderful Counselor" (Isaiah 9:6).[33] I am very much aware that certain kinds of mental or social-emotional problems result from a chemical imbalance, and that others may require intensive therapy. But I have studied and worked in the fields associated with individual and family therapy enough to know that we are foolish to suppose that we can bring about lasting change in human personalities or family relationships solely through the theories and philosophies of men and women, even men and women of good will. The blood of Christ, the transforming power of his love, the Spirit of God, and the blessings of the holy priesthood—these are remarkably therapeutic and must not be taken lightly, lest we place ourselves under condemnation (see D&C 84:54–61). In the words of a modern prophet, Ezra Taft Benson, "the Lord works from the inside out. The world works from the outside in. The world would take people out of the slums. Christ takes the slums out of people, and then they take themselves out of the slums. *The world would mold men by changing their environment. Christ changes men, who then change their environment. The world would shape human behavior, but Christ can change human nature.* . . . Yes, Christ changes men, and changed men can change the world."[34]

There are, as latter-day prophets have declared, many tight places through which the people of the covenant will be required to pass in the days ahead. Peace and protection and progress will be ours as we stand in holy places—as individuals and families—as we learn to be selective, as we sift and sort through the sordid and even the subsidiary. Some things simply matter more than others. The family is the most important unit in time and in eternity, and the home is the most sacred of all the holy places in which we are privileged to stand. Of this eternal institution, the Lord might well say, as he did to Moses: "Put off thy shoes from off thy feet, for the place whereon thou standest is holy ground" (Exodus 3:5).

Notes

From an address delivered at the BYU Family Expo, Brigham Young University, Provo, Utah, 4 April 1994.

1. Dallin H. Oaks, in Conference Report, October 1993, 97; emphasis added.
2. See C. S. Lewis, *Mere Christianity* (New York: Macmillan, 1952), 165.
3. Jeffrey R. Holland, in Conference Report, October 1993, 16; emphasis added.
4. Marion G. Romney, "The Price of Peace," BYU devotional address, 1 March 1955, 10.
5. John MacArthur Jr., *Our Sufficiency in Christ* (Dallas: Word Publishing, 1991), 154–55.
6. See Dallin H. Oaks, *The Lord's Way* (Salt Lake City: Deseret Book Co., 1991), 157–58.
7. Arthur M. Schlesinger Jr., *The Disuniting of America* (New York: W. W. Norton & Co., 1992), 17.
8. Orania Papazoglou, "Despising Our Mothers, Despising Ourselves," *First Things,* January 1992, 16, 18–19; emphasis added.

9. John Stott, *Life in Christ* (Wheaton, Ill.: Tyndale House, 1991), 22.

10. Peter Kreeft, *Back to Virtue* (San Francisco: Ignatius Press, 1992), 26.

11. Michael Medved, *Hollywood vs. America* (New York: HarperCollins Publishers, 1992), 10.

12. John Dart, in *Los Angeles Times,* 19 February 1983, section 2, 5; as quoted by Gordon B. Hinckley, in Conference Report, October 1983, 67.

13. Richard L. Evans, in Conference Report, April 1969, 74.

14. Kreeft, *Back to Virtue,* 20.

15. Ezra Taft Benson, in Conference Report, April 1986, 5.

16. Lewis, *Mere Christianity,* 190.

17. Don Matzat, *Christ Esteem* (Eugene, Ore.: Harvest House, 1990), 87; emphasis added.

18. Bruce C. Hafen, *The Broken Heart* (Salt Lake City: Deseret Book Co., 1989), 120; emphasis in original.

19. Gordon B. Hinckley, "Of You It Is Required to Forgive," *Ensign,* June 1991, 2, 4.

20. Boyd K. Packer, in Conference Report, October 1987, 20; emphasis added.

21. Dietrich Bonhoeffer, *The Cost of Discipleship* (New York: Macmillan, 1967), 79–80.

22. Bruce C. and Marie K. Hafen, *The Belonging Heart* (Salt Lake City: Deseret Book Co., 1994), 123.

23. Spencer W. Kimball, "Absolute Truth," *1977 BYU Fireside and Devotional Speeches of the Year* (Provo: Brigham Young University Publications, 1977), 138.

24. Rex E. Lee, "Things That Change and Things That Don't," *1991–92 BYU Fireside and Devotional Speeches of the Year* (Provo: Brigham Young University Publications, 1992), 54.

25. Spencer W. Kimball, *The Miracle of Forgiveness* (Salt Lake City: Bookcraft, 1969), 79.

26. Spencer W. Kimball, *Faith Precedes the Miracle* (Salt Lake City: Deseret Book Co., 1974), 175.

27. J. Reuben Clark Jr., in Conference Report, October 1948, 80.

28. See Harold B. Lee, "Be Loyal to the Royal within You," *1973 BYU Fireside and Devotional Speeches of the Year* (Provo: Brigham Young University Publications, 1973), 90.

29. Medved, *Hollywood vs. America,* 340.

30. George Will, "America's Slide into the Sewer," *Newsweek,* 30 July 1990, 64.

31. Boyd K. Packer, in Conference Report, April 1992, 91, 95; emphasis in original.

32. C. S. Lewis, *The Screwtape Letters* (New York: Touchstone, 1996), 115–16; emphasis in original.

33. See Donald W. Parry, Jay A. Parry, and Tina M. Peterson, *Understanding Isaiah* (Salt Lake City: Deseret Book Co., 1998), 96.

34. Ezra Taft Benson, in Conference Report, October 1985, 5; emphasis added.

A DIVINE DETERRENT
TO CREEPING RELATIVISM

The Apostle Paul prophesied of our day, and many of the elements of that prophecy are pathetically present in today's newspapers. "This know also," he wrote, "that in the last days perilous times shall come. For men shall be lovers of their own selves, covetous, boasters, proud, blasphemers, disobedient to parents, unthankful, unholy, without natural affection, trucebreakers, false accusers, incontinent, fierce, despisers of those that are good, traitors, heady, highminded, lovers of pleasures more than lovers of God; having a form of godliness, but denying the power thereof: from such turn away." Perhaps as an indication of the source of the problem in our day, Paul concluded that such souls would be "ever learning, and never able to come to the knowledge of the truth" (2 Timothy 3:1–5, 7).

We live in the day of an information explosion, a time when raw knowledge is being processed and disseminated far faster than we can incorporate or inculcate. But we also live in a time of moral erosion, indicating clearly that our decency has not kept pace with our discoveries. As a world, and more particularly as a nation, we have drifted from our moral moorings, strayed from the faith of our fathers. That the decline in society is due to a moral decay is perhaps obvious to most of us. I desire, however, to take a step beyond that premise. I suggest that the lack of scriptural or theological literacy and the subsequent lack of doctrinal depth are at the heart of our problem. Very often what we believe and know affect what we do. I suggest that when men and women comprehend the great plan of happiness—the plan of salvation, the gospel—many begin to see themselves within that plan as a part of God's program. They then begin to govern their actions accordingly.

THE EROSION

I would like now to discuss some key factors that have contributed to our doctrinal desensitization and thereby our moral decline. We could choose any number of things that have hacked away at the roots of our religious heritage, but I will focus on four: (1) the trivialization of religion; (2) the loss of a moral sense; (3) a denial of personal responsibility; and (4) emphasizing ethics over doctrine. In subsequent sections of this chapter, we will consider some solutions to our problem.

1. *The trivialization of religion.* Whereas a hundred years ago religion was central to the outlook of most Americans, we have in the last three decades become prey to a growing secularism, a world view that seeks to make sense of life without reference to God or the divine. If there is no real purpose to life, no God, no system of salvation, no hope of a life beyond the grave, and no divine parameters by which to distinguish right from wrong—in short, if anything goes—then eventually everything goes.

In the early 1960s a strange and to some a frightful sound was heard throughout the academic world of religious studies—the cry that "God is dead." Protestant, Roman Catholic, and even Jewish theologians spoke often of Godless theologies, Christless christs, and Christian atheism, phrases that at first blush seem meaningless and absurd. The essence of their rhetorical requiem was that God had died in the hearts of men and women, that "God [had] passed out of our existence and become a dead entity for us because we crowded him out of our consciousness in creating and worshipping idols of our own ethnic likenesses."[1] How strikingly similar are the words of the Lord concerning the state of things at the time of Joseph Smith's call: "They seek not the Lord to establish his righteousness, but every man walketh in his own way, and after the image of his own god, whose image is in the likeness of the world, and whose substance is that of an idol, which waxeth old and shall perish in Babylon, even Babylon the great, which shall fall" (D&C 1:16).

The Death of God Movement, though not necessarily characteristic of the rank and file of the religious world (or even typical of the views or feelings of the average priest, minister, or rabbi), nevertheless symbolized a growing uneasiness in society, a loss of confidence in religious life, and a gradual distancing from religious values and time-honored traditions. Though the pendulum would yet swing to the religious right during the 1970s with the rise of the Charismatic Movement and Christian Fundamentalism, yet the age of existential anguish—of moral malaise, cynicism, skepticism, and doubt—would take its terrible toll.

In recent times, where religion has not been rejected outright, it has been either ignored or in many cases trivialized. As Professor Stephen L. Carter has pointed out, "one sees a trend in our political and legal cultures toward treating religious beliefs as arbitrary and unimportant, a trend supported by a rhetoric that implies that there is something wrong with religious devotion. More and more, our culture seems to take the position that believing deeply in the tenets of one's faith represents a kind of mystical irrationality, something that thoughtful, public-spirited American citizens would do better to avoid. . . . The consistent message of modern American society is that whenever the demands of one's religion conflict with what one has to do to get ahead, one is expected to ignore the religious demands and act . . . well . . . *rationally.*" Carter points out that "one good way to end a conversation—or start an argument—is to tell a group of well-educated professionals that you hold a political position (preferably a controversial one, such as being against abortion or pornography) because it is required by your understanding of God's will. In the unlikely event that anyone hangs around to talk with you about it, the chances are that you will be challenged on the ground that you are intent on imposing your religious beliefs on other people. And in contemporary political and legal culture, nothing is worse."[2]

2. *The loss of a moral sense.* Certain problems arise whenever people either deny or ignore absolute truths. One Protestant writer has stated: "I believe that one of the prime reasons this generation is setting new records for dishonesty, disrespect, sexual promiscuity, violence, suicide, and other pathologies, is because they have lost their moral underpinnings; their foundational belief in morality and truth has been eroded. . . . At one time, our society, by and large, explained the universe, humanity, and the purpose of life from the Judeo-Christian tradition: a belief that truth existed, and everyone could know and understand it. A clear understanding of what was right and wrong gave society a moral standard by which to measure crime and punishment, business ethics, community values, character, and social conduct. . . .

"That has changed dramatically, however. Our children are being raised in a society that has largely rejected the notions of truth and morality, a society that has somewhere lost the ability to decide what is true and what is right. Truth has become a matter of taste; morality has been replaced by individual preference."[3]

"If modern man has taken seriously the main intellectual currents of the last century or so," Professor James Wilson has written, "he would have found himself confronted by the need to make moral choices when the very possibility of making such choices had been denied. God is dead or silent, reason suspect or defective, nature meaningless or hostile. As a result, man is adrift on an uncharted sea, left to find his moral bearings with no compass and no pole star, and so able to do little more than utter personal preferences, bow to historical necessity, or accept social conventions." Further, "if the moral sense is the result of nothing more significant than a cultural or historical throw of the dice, then it will occur to some people . . . that they are free to do whatever they can get away with by practicing indulgent self-absorption or embracing an angry ideology."[4]

In the 1960s—hand in hand with the Death of God Movement—a second movement began to take shape, one that has had its flowering in our own time. It was known as Situation Ethics or Ethical Relativism. Inspired by the writings of Bishop John A. T. Robinson and Professor Joseph Fletcher, this movement proposed that any moral system is too shallow to provide answers to all situations and that every man and woman must decide what is right. It was a time when all were told to open themselves to the "new morality." "The sanctions of Sinai have lost their terrors, and people no longer accept the authority of Jesus even as a great moral teacher. Robbed of its supranatural supports, men find it difficult to take seriously a code of living that confessedly depended on them."[5] Many of you will remember how common it was to hear young people spout off with, "It's all relative," or the even more common dictum, "There are no absolutes" (a pretty absolute statement, it seems to me!). Though we hear fewer chants and may notice fewer crusades for ethical relativism at the end of this decade, the die is cast, and what was once parlor conversation or even college colloquy is now applied theology.

We seem to be caught in a vicious cycle. Knowing and sensing the things of God tend to prevent (or at least slow down) profligate wickedness. We cannot, however, come to know the things of God while we are sinning, for the Spirit of Truth will have difficulty penetrating the barriers we have erected through disobedience. Thus the need to declare repentance, to set forth the great plan of happiness, to teach of things eternal and of the need to bring our lives and our lifestyles into harmony with the mind and will of the Almighty. We cannot, simply cannot—as a people and a Church—be guilty of moving the standards, shifting the anchors, or diluting the doctrine (especially the hard doctrine) in order to enhance our public image. Indeed, if those called to be the salt of the earth—those who have come out of the world by covenant (see D&C 101:39–40)—lose their savor, either by mixture or by contamination, wherewith shall the world be salted or the people be saved?

3. *A denial of personal responsibility.* The growth of the behavioral sciences in the last century has been phenomenal. Humankind seems at least as eager to

understand the behavior and motivation of men and women as they are to understand light waves and black holes and the mysteries of DNA. The application of scientific principles to the study of human behavior—in an effort to formalize and objectify that study—has resulted in the superimposition of a cause-effect model on man and woman. Though it may be healthy and in some cases helpful to search for root causes, the cause-effect, stimulus-response model for understanding man will forevermore yield deficient and perhaps even perverse results, so long as we ignore the role of moral agency in that process. I say that, not only in regard to behaviorism, but also any other system—humanistic or Freudian—that attempts to define the cause of human behavior solely in terms of inner mechanisms, self-actualization, id or ego functions, or even genetic predisposition.

Our fascination with causes ancillary to human agency has led us to paint ourselves into a corner in today's world. "Whereas in the late nineteenth century," James Wilson has written, "crime rates seem to have decreased during periods of economic growth, in the last few decades they have often increased during such periods. Over the course of the last hundred years the world has experienced a shift from an era in which crime chiefly responded to material circumstances to one in which it responds to cultural ones. That shift has many causes, but one is the collapse in the legitimacy of what once was respectfully called middle-class morality but today is sneeringly referred to as 'middle-class values.'

"The moral relativism of the modern age," Wilson continues, "has probably contributed to the increase in crime rates, especially the increases that occur during prosperous times. It has done so by replacing the belief in personal responsibility with the notion of social causation and by supplying to those marginal persons at risk for crime a justification for doing what they might have done anyway."[6] Add to this movement the gradual attack our society has made on guilt—the inner monitor by which we sense within ourselves that we have violated the laws of God or the norms of society—and we find ourselves in a precarious position. "That kind of thinking," one Protestant theologian has observed, "has all but driven words like *sin, repentance, contrition, atonement,* and *redemption* out of public discourse. If no one is supposed to feel guilty, how could anyone be a sinner? Modern culture has the answer: people are *victims.* Victims are not responsible for what they do; they are casualties of what happens to them. So every human failing must be described in terms of how the perpetrator has been victimized."[7]

To be sure, there are real victims in society—abused children or spouses, persons who suffer at the hands of racism or sexism—and they deserve our empathy, our support, and our zealous defense against such tragedies. My specific concern is with men and women who do wrong, who knowingly violate the laws of decency and morality, and then seek refuge behind the growing wall of victimization. For example, "a man who was shot and paralyzed while committing a burglary in New York recovered damages from the store owner who shot him. His attorney told a jury the man was first of all a victim of society, driven to crime by economic disadvantages. Now, the lawyer said, he is a victim of the insensitivity of the man who shot him. Because of that man's callous disregard of the thief's plight as a victim, the poor criminal will be confined to a wheelchair for the rest of his life. He deserves some redress. The jury agreed. The store owner paid a large settlement. Several months later, the same man, still in his wheelchair, was arrested while committing another armed robbery.

"Bernard McCummings parlayed a similar victimism into wealth. After mugging and brutally beating an elderly New York man in the subway, McCummings was shot while fleeing the scene. Permanently paralyzed, he sued and won $4.8 million in compensation from the New York Transit Authority. The man he mugged, a cancer patient, is still paying doctor bills. McCummings, the mugger—whom the courts deemed the greater victim—is now a multimillionaire.

"In two separate cases in England, a barmaid who stabbed another woman to death in a barroom brawl, and a woman who angrily drove her car into her lover were both acquitted of murder after they claimed acute pre-menstrual syndrome (PMS) addled their thinking and caused them to act in ways they could not control. Both received therapy rather than punishment.

"A San Francisco city supervisor claimed he murdered a fellow supervisor and Mayor George Mascone because too much junk food—especially Hostess Twinkies—made him act irrationally. Thus the famous 'Twinkie' defense was born. A lenient jury bought the line and produced a verdict of voluntary manslaughter rather than murder. They ruled that the junk food resulted in 'diminished mental capacity,' which mitigated the killer's guilt. He was out of prison before the mayor's next term would have been complete."[8] In the words of one author, what we have here is "a formula for social gridlock: the irresistible search for someone or something to blame colliding with the unmovable unwillingness to accept responsibility. Now enshrined in law and jurisprudence, victimism is reshaping the fabric of society, including employment policies, criminal justice, education, urban politics, and, in an increasingly Orwellian emphasis on 'sensitivity' in language. A community of interdependent citizens has been displaced by a society of resentful, competing, and self-interested individuals who have dressed their private annoyances in the garb of victimism."[9]

4. *Emphasizing ethics over doctrine.* In the absence of the real thing—the fulness of the gospel—there are many ideas and movements that seek to occupy center stage.

For many, the doctrine of Christ has been replaced by the ethics of Jesus. Those who insist that ethics must be discussed or taught or enforced point toward the declining moral standards of our day, the increase of drug abuse or teenage pregnancy, the prevalence of our inhumanity to each other. They contend that if Christianity is to make a difference in the world, we must find ways to transform ethereal theology into religious practice in a decaying society. They thus promote a social gospel, a relevant religion. The problem with a social gospel is that it is inherently and forevermore deficient as far as engaging the real problems of human beings. It almost always focuses on symptoms rather than causes. Ethics is not the essence of the gospel. Ethics is not necessarily righteousness. The very word *ethics* has come to connote socially acceptable standards based on current consensus, as opposed to absolute truths based on God's eternal laws. Ethics is too often to virtue and righteousness what theology is to religion—a pale and wimpy substitute. Indeed, ethics without that virtue that comes through the cleansing powers of the Redeemer is like religion without God, at least the true and living God.

IT'S ALL ABSOLUTE

Let us begin with the certain assurance that we cannot solve spiritual maladies through temporal solutions. Our problem in the world today is a detachment from morality, and morality cannot, in the long run, be severed from religion. *Religion* is a most interesting word. It means literally "to tie back to." It is related to the word ligament, that which ties the bone to the muscle. Religion is thus that which ties us back to God and to sacred things. To define morality in terms of utility (what works) or in terms of consensus (what most people believe) is to fall short of what was, is, and is to be (see D&C 93:24).

As we noted in an earlier chapter, some things are. They just are. Neither congressional decisions nor popular opinion changes absolute truth. All the people in the world but the Latter-day Saints may decide that abortion is humane, homosexuality is merely an alternative lifestyle, and assisted suicide is compassionate, but that does not change the fact that these matters are sinful and wrong and contrary to the great plan of the eternal God. They cannot bring happiness. They cannot result in peace. Every religious body on the globe except the Latter-day Saints may conclude that God is a spirit, that he is uninvolved in our daily doings, and that men and women will prosper according to their genius and not through the divine assistance of a Savior. But such sentiments do not matter a snap of the finger in the eternal scheme of things, for what God is, does, and accomplishes among his children—through the mediation of his Beloved Son—is in the realm of absolute truths. These things we know from scripture, from modern prophets, and by personal revelation.

"We know instinctively," one Christian writer has observed, "that some things are right and some things are wrong. Let [a young woman] discover, for example, that her soccer shoes were stolen from her school locker and she'll feel wronged. She would not argue that the thief is entitled to his opinion of right and wrong; she would appeal to an objective sense of justice because she would claim that she had suffered an injustice. In so doing, of course, she would appeal to a moral law that she believes everyone—not just herself—ought to follow."[10] That is to say, while many who yearn to speak of ethical relativism or situational ethics do so from their philosophical perch above the real world, those same persons expect others to treat them according to a model of truth and morality that reflects a more objective and absolute way of knowing what is right or wrong. If it is true that "there are no atheists in foxholes," then it is also true that "there are no relativists who expect to be treated relatively."[11]

THE FOUNDATION FOR ETHICS

"It is one thing," Elder Bruce R. McConkie has written, "to teach ethical principles, quite another to proclaim the great doctrinal verities, which are the foundation of true Christianity and out of which eternal salvation comes. True it is that salvation is limited to those in whose souls the ethical principles abound, but true it is also that Christian ethics, in the full and saving sense, automatically become a part of the lives of those who first believe Christian doctrines." In summary, "it is only when gospel ethics are tied to gospel doctrines that they rest on a sure and enduring foundation and gain full operation in the lives of the saints."[12]

The Latter-day Saints are occasionally criticized for expending so much of the resources of the Church on missionary work or the construction of temples. Some indicate that the institutional Church should be more involved in leading or officially supporting this or that crusade, in laboring for this or that social cause. "Where is your charity?" they ask. "Of what avail are your noble theological principles?" they inquire. I agree with Bruce Hafen, who pointed out that "the ultimate purpose of the gospel of Jesus Christ is to cause the sons and daughters of God to become as Christ is. Those who see religious purpose only in terms of ethical service in the relationship between man and fellowmen may miss that divinely ordained possibility. It is quite possible to render charitable—even 'Christian'—service without developing deeply ingrained and permanent Christlike character. Paul understood this when he warned against giving all one's goods to feed the poor without charity. . . . *While religious philosophies whose highest aim is social relevance may do much good, they will not ultimately lead people to achieve the highest religious purpose, which is to become as God and Christ are.*"[13]

The Master warned of what would happen if we seek to be his but are not built upon his gospel. If our effort "be not built upon my gospel," he said, "and is built upon the works of men, or upon the works of the devil, verily I say unto you they have joy in their works for a season, and by and by the end cometh, and they are hewn down and cast into the fire, from whence there is no return" (3 Nephi 27:11). The works of the devil obviously pertain to carnality and devilishness, what Paul called "the works of the flesh"—such sins as adultery, fornication, idolatry, witchcraft, hatred, strife, and heresy (Galatians 5:19–21). They bring pleasure and telestial titillation for a season, but they result inevitably in shrinkage of the soul, followed in time by bitter loneliness and that awful alienation from things of lasting worth. Indeed, "their works do follow them, for it is because of their works that they are hewn down" (3 Nephi 27:12).

God's work and glory is to bring to pass the immortality and eternal life of man (see Moses 1:39). Our most noble work will be accomplished and our greatest glory and joy will come to the degree that we are similarly occupied with this overarching objective. The "works of men" may refer to what we know as honorable endeavors, worthwhile efforts to improve man and society, but labors whose focus are not truly on the Lord or his work and glory. Political agendas, ethical concerns, and environmental issues, all works of men, are good and proper, and we should be involved in them to the degree that our time and circumstances allow. Noble enterprises bring a measure of personal satisfaction. Too often, however, the works of men bring glory to men. More often than not, the works of men hack away at the leaves of the inconsequential while ignoring the spiritual roots of attitudes and behavior.

The poignant message of the Savior is that happiness, meaning lasting joy, comes only to those who are built upon his gospel and whose works are really the Lord's works. So many people, as C. S. Lewis observed, seek to "invent some sort of happiness for themselves outside God, apart from God. And out of that hopeless attempt has come nearly all that we call human history—money, poverty, ambition, war, prostitution, classes, empires, slavery—the long terrible story of man trying to find something other than God which will make him happy.

"The reason why it can never succeed is this. . . . *God designed the human machine to run on Himself. He Himself is the fuel our spirits were designed to burn, or the food our spirits were designed to feed on. There is no other. That is why it is just no good asking God to make us happy in our own way without bothering about religion. God cannot give us a happiness and peace apart from Himself,* because it is not there. There is no such thing."[14] Similarly, Elder Neal A. Maxwell pointed out that "mankind has not had much success in keeping the second commandment by loving our neighbors as ourselves, without also keeping the first great commandment, loving God with all of our heart, might, mind, and strength. *Try as mankind may to achieve the brotherhood of man without the Fatherhood of God, it is cosmetic and does not last!*"[15]

GETTING BACK TO THE SOURCE

Let me propose what might be a rather typical discussion between an LDS parent and child:

Father: "Billy, is it wrong to steal?"

Son: "Yeah, Dad, it's wrong to steal."

Father: "Why is it wrong?"

Son: "Because you taught us that it's wrong."

Father: "That's right, son, we did. But why did we teach you that?"

Son: "Because the Church teaches us that it's not right to steal."

Father: "Right again. But why does the Church teach that?"

(Then there is a long pause.)

Son: "I don't know, Dad. Is it because Heavenly Father doesn't want us to steal?"

Father: "You're absolutely right, Billy. Heavenly Father does not want us to steal. Why doesn't he want us to steal?"

(This time there is a longer and even more uncomfortable pause.)

Son: "I don't really know, Dad."

This fictional encounter highlights a problem we face in teaching one another (and especially our children) the principles of morality and decency. Notice that the *precept* of "Thou shalt not steal" is pretty clear in this young man's mind. He has been taught the commandments and is able to articulate what he understands. A little less clear is that which underlies the precept, namely the *principle,* in this case the principle of honesty. Our young man knows what has been forbidden (to steal), and he senses that the major reasons it is forbidden is because his parents, his Church, and his Heavenly Father have condemned it. But beneath the principle is the *person* of God. A vital part of the great plan of happiness is the kind of Being we worship. Fundamental to the purpose of life and the hope for glory hereafter is the knowledge that has been revealed concerning God—his character, his perfections, his relationship to us, and, most important to this discussion, the knowledge that we can become as he is.

To complete our conversation:

Father: "Billy, we are commanded not to steal [the *precept*] because the Lord wants his people to be honest [the *principle*]. He wants us to be honest because he is a God of truth [the *person*]. We are sent to earth to strive as best we can to become as he is. Only as we become a people of truth can we ever hope to be like our Heavenly Father."

It is one thing to teach that honesty is the best policy (utility) or to teach that it is best to be honest because most people in society expect us to deal respectfully and responsibly with one another (consensus). Both utility and consensus have done much in the past to maintain some semblance of order in our world. But with changing times and the erosion of time-honored values, many look about hopelessly for a more solid and enduring foundation. That foundation is doctrinal; it is the foundation of faith and theology. Our children deserve answers to the hard question of *why*. And the only lasting and satisfying answer to why we do what we do or why we do not do other things is to be found in the great plan of happiness, in the understanding of God and man, in the clear statement of our eternal possibilities here and hereafter.

As a priesthood leader, I have had occasion to listen as young people confess major moral transgressions. I have asked about why the violation of the law of chastity is so serious. I have been interested as they have spoken of disappointing their parents, postponing temple marriage or missions, bearing children out of wedlock, and contracting deadly diseases—all of which, from the perspective of utility or consensus, are darned good reasons to stay morally clean. But there is more to it, much more, and it is that added light and added knowledge that come from our divinely given doctrine to which we turn for the greatest preventative medicine against serious sin.

I learned something very valuable many years ago when my wife and I timidly approached the much-dreaded but needed conversation about the facts of life with our oldest child. We sweated and we stewed for weeks. We read. We debated. We prepared charts and graphs and pictures of the human reproductive system; we went into the conversation with several books under our arms. We had also prayed earnestly for inspiration. We dove into the presentation and discovered to our surprise that it was going in a direction that neither my wife nor I had anticipated. For about an hour we spoke of the plan of salvation—of who we are, where we came from, why we are here, and where we are going when we die. We spoke of physical bodies and experiences and Satan and opposition and relationships and families and children and temples and covenants and ordinances and sealing powers. The Spirit of the Lord was present, and so we learned a great deal from what we said. I think my daughter did also. At the end of that most unusual hour, I asked: "Now, sweetheart, do you understand why it is so very important to stay morally clean?" She nodded.

It was not until many years later that I sensed the significance of a passage of scripture, one that President Boyd K. Packer has emphasized again and again. Speaking of the ancients, Alma said: "God gave unto them commandments, *after having made known unto them the plan of redemption*" (Alma 12:32; emphasis added). From the knowledge of the person of God, as well as the doctrines and principles that follow, come the precepts. President Packer explained to Church Educational System personnel: "Young people wonder 'why?'—Why are we commanded *to do* some things, and why are we commanded *not* to do other things? A knowledge of the plan of happiness, even in outline form, can give young minds a 'why.'

"A parent once angrily scolded a child for a serious mistake, saying, 'Why on earth did you do such a thing?' The child answered, 'If I'd had a 'why,' I wouldn't have done it.'

"Providing your students [or, we might add, our children] with a collection of unrelated truths will hurt as much as it helps. Provide a basic feeling for the whole plan, even with just a few details, and it will help them ever so much more. Let them know what it's all about, then they will have the 'why.'

"Most of the difficult questions we face in the Church right now, and we could list them—abortion and all the rest of them, all of the challenges of who holds the priesthood and who does not—cannot be answered without some knowledge of the plan as a background. . . .

"You will not be with your students or your own children at the time of their temptations. At those dangerous moments they must depend on their own resources. If they can locate themselves within the framework of the gospel plan, they will be immensely strengthened.

"The plan is worthy of repetition over and over again. Then the purpose of life, the reality of the Redeemer, and the reason for the commandments will stay with them.

"Their gospel study, their life experiences, will add to an ever-growing witness of the Christ, of the Atonement, of the restoration of the gospel."[16]

Having said all this, I hasten to add that even with a knowledge of the great plan of happiness before them, men and women, boys and girls may choose to walk in the ways of the world and thus settle for less than what they could be. But I have a conviction that the proper teaching of the Father's plan will do much to hold on to those who are children of the covenant and heirs to the promises made to Abraham, Isaac, and Jacob. We will speak of the power of the covenant and the binding nature of temple blessings in a subsequent chapter.

CONCLUSION

Let me conclude where I began—with the sobering prophecy of the Apostle Paul. You recall that he warned of such sins in the last days as pride, blasphemy, disrespect for parents, ingratitude, dishonesty, immorality, and perversion. Finally, he spoke of persons who are "ever learning, and never able to come to the knowledge of the truth" (2 Timothy 3:1–7). The visible disarray in our world is but symptomatic of the invisible decay, an evidence that our moral foundation is under attack. And should we be surprised? The Psalmist warned that "the wicked bend their bow; lo, they make ready their arrow upon the string, that they may privily shoot at the upright in heart, to destroy their foundation" (JST, Psalm 11:2).

Indeed, the Latter-day Saints boldly proclaim that "the knowledge of the truth" of which Paul wrote constitutes the sure foundation upon which true believers must build their houses of faith. It is worth noting that the Apostle Paul did not leave us without comfort or recourse. Later in that same chapter, he wrote to Timothy: "For evil men and seducers shall wax worse and worse, deceiving, and being deceived. But continue thou in the things which thou hast learned and hast been assured of, knowing of whom thou hast learned them; and that from a child *thou hast known the holy scriptures, which are able to make thee wise unto salvation through faith which is in Christ Jesus.* And all Scripture given by inspiration of God, is profitable for doctrine, for reproof, for correction, for instruction in righteousness; that the man of God may be perfect, thoroughly furnished unto all good works" (JST, 2 Timothy 3:13–17; emphasis added).

The scriptures. The word of God. The living oracles. The doctrines of salvation—these are the means by which we come to know the *precepts,* the *principles,* and the *person* of God. They set forth what we must and must not do, as well as who we are and what we may become. Thus President Packer explained: "True doctrine, understood, changes attitudes and behavior. The study of the doctrines of the gospel will improve behavior quicker than a study of behavior will improve behavior. . . . That is why we stress so forcefully the study of the doctrines of the gospel."[17] There is a power, a supernal power that flows from us when we teach the great plan of happiness. There is peace, consummate peace that comes into our lives when we erect our divine domiciles on the foundation of doctrine and faith. Therein is our safety. Therein is our hope.

Notes

From an address delivered at the Family Expo Conference, Brigham Young University, Provo, Utah, 3 April 1995.

1. Gabriel Vahanian, as quoted in Jackson Lee Ice and John J. Carey, eds., *The Death of God Debate* (Philadelphia: Westminster Press, 1967), 16.
2. Stephen L. Carter, *The Culture of Disbelief: How American Law and Politics Trivialize Religious Devotion* (New York: HarperCollins Publishers, Inc., 1993), 6–7, 13, 23; emphasis in original.
3. Josh McDowell and Bob Hostetler, *Right from Wrong* (Dallas: Word Publishing, 1994), 12–13.
4. James Wilson, *The Moral Sense* (New York: Macmillan, Inc., 1993), 5, 9.
5. John A. T. Robinson, *Honest to God* (Philadelphia: The Westminster Press, 1963), 109; see also Joseph Fletcher, *Situation Ethics: The New Morality* (Philadelphia: The Westminster Press, 1966), chapters 1 and 2.
6. Wilson, *Moral Sense,* 10.
7. John F. MacArthur, Jr., *The Vanishing Conscience* (Dallas: Word Publishing, 1994), 21; emphasis in original.
8. Ibid., 22–23.
9. Charles Sykes, *A Nation of Victims* (New York: St. Martin's Press, 1992), 15.
10. McDowell, *Right from Wrong,* 78.
11. Ibid.
12. *A New Witness for the Articles of Faith,* 699–700.
13. Bruce C. Hafen, *The Broken Heart* (Salt Lake City: Deseret Book Co., 1989), 196–97; emphasis added.
14. C. S. Lewis, *Mere Christianity* (New York: Macmillan, 1952), 53–54; emphasis added.
15. Neal A. Maxwell, "This Is a Special Institution," inaugural address at BYU–Hawaii, Laie, Hawaii; as quoted in *Profile Magazine,* December 1994, 9; emphasis added.
16. Boyd K. Packer, "The Great Plan of Happiness," Seventeenth Annual Church Educational System Religious Educators' Symposium, Provo, Utah, 10 August 1993, 3.
17. Boyd K. Packer, in Conference Report, October 1986, 20.

THE ABUNDANT LIFE

ON BEING CHRISTIAN

I was born and reared in the southern states and attended Louisiana State University for two years. Those two years were perhaps the loneliest time of my life. In spite of what many have said, for me the 1960s were a lousy time to grow up. By the time I had graduated from high school, the Beatles and British music had taken the world by storm. The other type of music that survived the revolution was folk music, where everyone sang or chanted about the economy, the Vietnam War, and nuclear holocaust. Really depressing stuff! Many of the movies dealt with social issues, and few had happy endings. It was a time of revolution, and everyone seemed to be in search of a cause, a crusade of some type. Marches and sit-ins and protests abounded. In addition, I was a part of the "baby boom" generation that arrived at the college campus before we were ready to be received. Institutions of higher learning literally did not have the resources to meet the needs of the flood of young people who hit the campus. Consequently, many universities set up a type of selection process, a means whereby only the most serious and dedicated of students would make it through the first year. For example, we were told that of the 4,300 freshmen who entered with me in the fall of 1965 at LSU, only about 1,800 continued as sophomores. Freshman biology and freshman English were the designated "flunkout" courses. To be honest, although I was very happy in high school, I did not enjoy my first years of college. I felt very much alone.

After my mission I transferred to Brigham Young University and fell in love with the Provo community and with BYU. For someone who as a boy had gotten no closer to the Salt Lake Temple than an Articles of Faith card, there was something special about being so near the headquarters of the Church. Every Tuesday there was a devotional on the campus, and almost always one of the General Authorities of the Church was the speaker. I loved each of those devotionals; I still have copies of the addresses in my files. I thrilled at the idea of having prayer in some of my classes. I can't explain it, but there was something strange and unusual, something marvelous about being on a large university campus among thousands of people who believed basically the same things about life that I did.

My earliest class was an 8:00 A.M. Monday-Wednesday-Friday class titled "An Introduction to Philosophy." The instructor was excellent; he was warm and accommodating and patient with us as students. About three weeks into the semester, I approached him on a matter we had covered during the hour. "What can I do for you?" he asked. I posed my question. He looked at his watch. Memories of disinterested and discourteous teachers from other places flooded back into my mind, and my heart began to beat a little faster. I fully expected him to say: "I'm a busy man. Don't bother me at times other than my office hours!" Instead, he asked: "What are you doing this hour? Do you have a class?" I answered that I was free for two hours. "Come on," he said, as he began to leave the classroom, "walk with me to the Wilkinson Center (the Student Union)—I'll buy you something to drink, and we'll talk about it." It was a tender and important moment for me, one that comes back frequently when I'm busy, tired, and being summoned by a troubled student. It was a simple act of courtesy and concern; it was a quiet, Christian deed, and it made all the difference in the world to me. I felt at home, at peace on campus, and my grades showed it.

The spirit of that little incident over thirty years ago drives what I feel today. I speak of being Christian, followers of him who has taught us to reach out, lift up, and embrace those who need us. The incident epitomizes for me what can exist among people, how men and women, how Latter-day Saints and non-Latter-day Saints can live together in love and harmony.

ON BEING A TRUE CHRISTIAN

Maybe it would be helpful, to begin with, to suggest what being Christian is *not*. It is easy to become caught up in many of the trappings of Christendom, to become enamored with so much of what so many feel to be Christian activity. For example, a Christian is not necessarily one who is so nice, so sweet, so Milquetoast, that people trample over him or her. Jesus was not a doormat, and he certainly did not call his disciples to be doormats. He has asked us to be patient, to avoid confrontations and disputations where such is possible, but he never asked us to roll over and play dead while others take advantage of us.

Nor is a Christian necessarily one who is so broad-minded, so eager to celebrate diversity, so tolerant, so pluralistic that he or she cannot hold to principle or embrace the full truth. Elder Dallin H. Oaks explained that "other strengths that can be used for our downfall are the gifts of love and tolerance. Clearly, these are great virtues. Love is an ultimate quality, and tolerance is its handmaiden. Love and tolerance are pluralistic, and that is their strength, but it is also the source of their potential weakness. Love and tolerance are incomplete unless they are accompanied by a concern for truth and a commitment to the unity God has commanded of his servants. Carried to an undisciplined excess," Elder Oaks continued, "love and tolerance can produce an indifference to truth and justice and opposition to unity. What makes mankind 'free' from death and sin is not merely love but love accompanied by truth. 'And ye shall know the truth, and the truth shall make you free' (John 8:32). And *the test of whether we are the Lord's is not just love and tolerance but unity.* 'If ye are not one,' the risen Lord said, 'ye are not mine' (D&C 38:27)."[1]

A Christian is not necessarily one who champions every cause and leads every crusade. In fact, one of the great needs of this age is for persons possessed of the Spirit of God to be discerning, not alone in knowing good from evil, but also in sensing what things matter more than others. In a word, with so very many pressing needs, so very many enterprises that beckon for a leader or for followers, it is essential that we spend our days laboring in primary causes. Only four months after the Watergate scandal had become public, Elder Bruce R. McConkie spoke in general conference: "In view of all that prevails in the world," he said, "it might be easy to center our attention on negative or evil things, or to dissipate our energies on causes and enterprises of doubtful worth and questionable productivity.

"I am fully aware of the divine decree to be actively engaged in a good cause; of the fact that every true principle which works for the freedom and blessing of mankind has the Lord's approval; of the need to sustain and support those who espouse proper causes and advocate true principles—all of which things we also should do in the best and most beneficial way we can. The issue, I think, is not *what* we should do but *how* we should do it; and I maintain that the most beneficial and productive thing which Latter-day Saints can do to strengthen every good and proper cause is to live and teach the principles of the everlasting gospel."[2]

The problem with the "social gospel movement," the effort to take Christendom into society and make of Christian theology a relevant religion, is that such an enterprise is, and will be forevermore, deficient. Permanent change is in Christ the Person, not in programs. Christ can have impact on society only to the degree that he is allowed to have impact on individual souls. One Evangelical writer, John Stott, has beautifully described the importance of extending the full blessings of Christianity to those who are in need: "If a vagrant comes to us in dire need, down and out, in rags and tatters, and sick, even starving, it will be good to give him a bath and a change of clothing, but not enough. For he is ill and under-nourished. So, in addition, he needs food and hospital treatment. Similarly, we come to Christ down and out, in the rags and tatters of our sin, spiritually sick and starving. In Christ we are at once made welcome and accepted, and given a bath and a change of clothes. God sees us as righteous in Christ. This is our new status. So he puts his Spirit within us to give us new life and health, and he feeds us with his word until we grow strong and vigorous. There are no half-measures with him."[3]

In the truest sense, one is a Christian when he or she fully believes that Jesus of Nazareth was and is the Son of God, the Savior and Redeemer, the Christ or Anointed One. A Christian is one who knows by the witness of the Holy Spirit that Christ is God, that he laid down his life by the power of the flesh and took it up again by the power of the Spirit. A Christian is one who calls upon the Father in the name of the Son for forgiveness, forsakes sin and indecency, and yearns to qualify for that new life that comes through redemption and renovation of the soul. A Christian is one whose commitment to Christ is such that he or she strives daily to become as Christ is, to acquire that nature and to embody those spiritual attributes and qualities that flow from him in whom all fulness and perfection dwell. A Christian, in other words, is not just one who does good deeds, as important as that is. It is one who accepts the doctrine of Christ, takes the name of Christ, and seeks thereafter to do the works of Christ. Goodness and decency and compassion are the natural by-products, the fruits that readily manifest themselves in the lives of those who have truly made Jesus their Lord and Master.

On Giving and Taking Offense

In 1977 my family and I moved to the South where I was to assume the direction of the institute of religion adjacent to the university there. I was asked to replace a man who had become an institution—both among his students and the members of the stake in which he served. He had become one of the most beloved of teachers I have ever known. A few days after our arrival, it became very clear that taking his place would not be easy. A student stopped by my office and, with a frightened look in his eye, asked: "Where's Brother Jensen?" I answered that he had moved from the area. "Moved from the area? Well, who's going to take his place?" I meekly admitted that I would try to do so. "Oh, terrific," he answered. The overall reception was not exactly cold, but rather a bit guarded. For three weeks students came into the place asking about Brother Jensen, some mourning his departure, others observing sadly that they had enjoyed institute very much up until now.

My wife, Shauna, and I were asked to speak in sacrament meeting in our new ward. We did so, and I thought it went fairly well. After "Amen" was said, I noticed a man from the congregation walking very quickly to the stand. He reached out his right hand, shook mine and said: "Hello. My name is Alex Campbell. My family was very, very close to the Jensens. I would like to say that you will never replace Brother Jensen as a speaker or a teacher, but we will try to love you anyway." I waited for him to smile, supposing that he was teasing or being sarcastic. He did not smile, but simply left the stand and returned to his family. The member of the bishopric conducting the meeting hastened to my side and explained how, indeed, the two families had become very close. When my wife and I got home, I remember going to the bedroom, lying on the bed, and crying. I said to her: "Why won't they at least give me a chance?" For a day or two, I am ashamed to admit, I had unkind feelings toward Alex Campbell. He was the straw that had broken the camel's back. It is important that you understand that my family and I came to love that part of the country more than any place we had lived, and, ironically, Alex became one of my dearest and closest friends.

To show you that Alex didn't change a great deal even after we became quite close, I relate the following. About six months after we had moved from the area, Alex and his family came to visit us during the Christmas season in our new home. I opened the door to welcome them and Brother Campbell looked into our home. His opening words were: "I've never cared for artificial Christmas trees!" I came to love him like a brother (and still do), not because all of his comments to me or mine were complimentary, nor because his style or taste or manner was just like mine. No, once I knew his heart, once I knew who he was and how much he cared, I felt no reason to take offense. I knew he had no desire to give offense, and so I chose to love him in spite of himself.

A few years after I had joined the faculty at BYU I had an experience that caused me much pain at the time. A man came to my office and indicated that he had heard that Joseph McConkie and I had published a book on life after death. I nodded. He then said: "I wonder if I might borrow a copy for a few days to see if it's something I might want to buy." I was a bit startled by the request but sheepishly complied and provided a copy of the book for him. Three days later he dropped by, slid the book across the desk, and said: "I've looked it over and decided that I don't want to buy it!" To say that I was hurt would be the grossest of understatements. Most of all I was shocked. And, of course, hurt. But I add quickly that over time this person and I developed a warm relationship.

I have feelings just like the next person. I have been insulted, belittled, put down in front of others. I know what it feels like to be misunderstood, to have my motives or my intentions questioned. In other words, I know what it feels like to be offended. On the one hand, you and I need to be more sensitive, more cautious with people's feelings. God loves us all, and, as the scriptures affirm, he is no respecter of persons. Christians do not shun others whose religious or political views are different than their own, any more than the Lord Jesus Christ would shun people. The Prophet Joseph Smith taught that "there is a love from God that should be exercised toward those of our faith, who walk uprightly, which is peculiar to itself, but it is without prejudice; *it also gives scope to the mind, which enables us to conduct ourselves with greater liberality towards all that are not of our faith, than what they exercise towards one another*. These principles approximate nearer to the mind of God, because [they are] like God, or Godlike."[4]

There is, of course, another side to this story. In order to live in harmony, we must become the kind of people who are not constantly looking to take offense. Each of us could easily waste our lives striving to make our associates offenders for a word. I have come to know that we need not be offended, that one of the most important signs of spiritual growth is a refusal to take offense. We need not be angry or bitter or insulted. We need not make our sister or our brother an offender for a word. It really is not too difficult to look at a person's heart, to try to understand what they meant to do rather than what they did, or what they meant to say rather than what they said. Sometimes this entails simply looking the other way and assuming the best. Sometimes it requires forgiveness.

ON BEING A FRIEND TO ALL

Jesus ate and drank with sinners. He occasionally companied with those who were considered to be on the lower crust of society. He befriended the underdog and was kind to the castoff. Because there was no insecurity within him, because he was guided always by the knowledge of who he was and whose he was, he felt no need to put on airs, manage appearances, or be socially selective. When someone spoke to Jesus, surely they had his full attention.

It is so easy for those of us who aspire to Christian discipleship to be driven by what others think, to allow our conversation and our conduct to be determined by less-than-noble motives. It is so simple to be drawn into duplicity, to become obsessed with whose opinion matters and whose company would bring the most mortal medals. But the lowly Nazarene calls us to a higher righteousness. He bids us to follow where he has led, to become a friend to all. I know what it feels like to be conversing with someone, only to have that conversation interrupted by a man or woman of greater social stature. I know what it feels like for the person with whom I was conversing to then ignore or shun me, to turn his attention to the one who seems to matter most at the moment. I also have been in the presence of persons whose hearts are unconcerned with society's pecking order, men and women who love people, not position. The former category of persons are those who tend to distinguish people in terms of rank and place in society; theirs is a degrading and demoralizing perspective and influence. On the other hand, those who have risen above the temptation to exclude or divide or distinguish in terms of getting ahead make a significant difference in the world.

On Being Inconvenienced

The call to follow Christ is a call to inconvenience. Some things simply take time. They take effort. Doing for others generally entails putting on hold what I had planned to do for myself. In the seventh chapter of Mark we read the following: "And from thence [Jesus] arose, and went into the borders of Tyre and Sidon, and entered into an house, and would have no man know it: but he could not be hid." The account continues by explaining that a certain woman found Jesus and pleaded with him to heal her daughter (Mark 7:24–26). Our Lord appears to be tired, weary, in need of rest and peace and solitude. The Joseph Smith Translation of this passage is most instructive: "And from thence he arose, and went into the borders of Tyre and Sidon, and entered into a house, and would that no man should come into him. *But he could not deny them; for he had compassion upon all men*" (JST, Mark 7:22–23; emphasis added). It is inconceivable that the Redeemer of the world couldn't hide himself if he wanted to. He is the God of the universe and has power over the elements. It is unthinkable that he could not conceal himself in some way, *except* that his compassion for his brothers and sisters would not allow him to do so. Our Savior was willing to be inconvenienced. And so must we be, if we are to become as he is. Such inconvenience may take many forms, some quite simple, others more dramatic. We may offer to assist a fellow member of the Church who is struggling with a particular principle; sincerely befriend a non-Latter-day Saint, even if he or she has no intention whatsoever of joining the LDS Church; or take the time to visit and cheer up someone who is homesick, lonely, or depressed.

Sometimes all we can do is wish we could help (see Mosiah 4:24). At least that's a start. Elder Boyd K. Packer told of an experience he had while in the military. Having been stationed for a time in Japan, Elder Packer explained, "I boarded a train in Osaka for Yokohama and a ship that would take me home. . . . Many tears were shed as we bade one another farewell.

"It was a very chilly night. The railroad station, what there was left of it, was very cold. Starving children were sleeping in the corners. That was a common sight in Japan in those days. The fortunate ones had a newspaper or a few old rags to fend off the cold.

"On that train I slept restlessly. The berths were too short anyway. In the bleak, chilly hours of the dawn, the train stopped at a station along the way. I heard a tapping on the window and raised the blind. There on the platform stood a little boy tapping on the window with a tin can. I knew he was one of the orphans and a beggar; the tin can was the symbol of their suffering. Sometimes they carried a spoon as well, as if to say, 'I am hungry; feed me.'

"He might have been six or seven years old. His little body was thin with starvation. He had on a thin, ragged shirt-like kimono, nothing else. His head was shingled with scabs. One side of his jaw was swollen—perhaps from an abscessed tooth. Around his head he had tied a filthy rag with a knot on top of his head—a pathetic gesture of treatment.

"When I saw him and he saw that I was awake, he waved his can. He was begging. In pity, I thought, 'How can I help him?' Then I remembered. I had money, Japanese money. I quickly groped for my clothing and found some yen notes in my pocket. I tried to open the window, but it was stuck. I slipped on my trousers and hurried to the end of the car. He stood outside expectantly. As I pushed at the resistant door, the train pulled away from the station. Through the dirty windows I could see him, holding that rusty tin can, with the dirty rag around his swollen jaw.

"There I stood, an officer from a conquering army, heading home to a family and a future. There I stood, half-dressed, clutching some money which he had seen, but which I could not get to him. I wanted to help him, but couldn't. The only comfort I draw is that I did want to help him.

"Perhaps I was scarred by that experience," Elder Packer concludes. "If so, it is a battle scar, a worthy one, for which I bear no shame. It reminds me of my duty."[5]

In January 1982 at Washington's National Airport, Air Florida's flight 90 to Tampa crashed into the Fourteenth Street Bridge and slid into the Potomac River with seventy-four passengers aboard. One reporter explained: "For a moment, there was silence, and then pandemonium. Commuters watched helplessly as the plane quickly sank. . . . A few passengers bobbed to the surface; some clung numbly to pieces of debris while others screamed desperately for help. Scattered across the ice were pieces of green upholstery, twisted chunks of metal, luggage, a tennis racket, a child's shoe. . . .

"Within minutes, sirens began to wail as fire trucks, ambulances and police cars rushed to the scene. A U.S. Park Police helicopter hovered overhead to pluck survivors out of the water. Six were clinging to the plane's tail. Dangling a life preserving ring to them, the chopper began ferrying them to shore. One woman had injured her right arm, so [the] pilot . . . lowered the copter until its skids touched the water; his partner [then leaped out and] scooped her up in his arms. Then [a young woman] grabbed the preserver, but as she was being helped out of the . . . river by [a] fellow passenger . . . she lost her grip. . . . A clerk for the Congressional Budget Office who was watching from the shore plunged into the water and dragged her to land. But the most notable act of heroism was performed by [another] of the passengers, a balding man in his early 50s. Each time the ring was lowered, he grabbed it and passed it along to a comrade; when the helicopter finally returned to pick him up, he had disappeared beneath the ice."[6]

In that same issue of *Time,* another writer described the unknown man in the water: "His selflessness [is] one reason the story held national attention; his anonymity another. The fact that he [has gone] unidentified invests him with a universal character. For a while he was Everyman, and thus proof (as if one needed it) that no man is ordinary.

"Still, he could never have imagined such a capacity in himself. Only minutes before his character was tested, he was sitting in the ordinary plane among the ordinary passengers, dutifully listening to the stewardess telling him to fasten his seat belt and saying something about the 'no smoking sign.' So our man relaxed with the others, some of whom would owe their lives to him. Perhaps he started to read, or to doze, or to regret some harsh remark made in the office that morning. Then suddenly he knew that the trip would not be ordinary. Like every other person on that flight, he was desperate to live, which makes his final act so stunning.

"For at some moment in the water he must have realized that he would not live if he continued to hand over the rope and ring to others. He *had* to know it, no matter how gradual the effect of the cold. In his judgment he had no choice. When the helicopter took off with what was to be the last survivor, he watched everything in [his] world move away from him, and he deliberately let it [go]. . . .

"The odd thing is that we do not . . . really believe that the man in the water lost his fight.

" . . . He could not [like nature], make ice storms, or freeze the water until it froze the blood. But he could hand life over to a stranger, and that is a power of nature too. The man in the water pitted himself against an implacable, impersonal enemy; he fought it with charity; and he [won]."[7]

CONCLUSION

The Savior expects us to do our part to assure that all we do in the Church is imbued with the religion of Jesus Christ. President Hugh B. Brown observed that "religion has too often spent a large proportion of its effort on doings apart from the real business of life. One of life's problems is to establish a deep understanding of man's relationship to his fellow men. . . . Every man's religion should have practical issue," he continued, "not merely emotional responsiveness which delights in hearing the gospel but lacks diligence in living it. *We must remember that religion is action, not diction.* Let us pray that God will deliver us from our dullness of conscience, from a feeble sense of duty, from thoughtless disregard of others, and from all halfheartedness in our work."[8] People really matter. They matter more than anything. God is in the people business (see Moses 1:39), and we should be too. The story is told that Julia Ward Howe expressed a concern to a senator on one occasion. "I am in need of help for a very special person," she said. "Julia, I am so busy," the man answered, "I can no longer concern myself with individuals." Her reply is so very pertinent to our day: "That's remarkable," she came back. "Even God hasn't reached that stage yet."[9]

Is there someone out there who needs me? Do I know of someone who could use a friend, who would come alive to an unassigned or unexpected phone call or visit? Do I treat those not of my faith with dignity, respect, and consideration, attempting earnestly never to exclude them or make them feel uncomfortable? "It is a serious thing," C. S. Lewis has written, "to live in a society of possible gods and goddesses, to remember that the dullest and most uninteresting person you talk to may one day be a creature which, if you saw it now, you would be strongly tempted to worship. . . . There are no *ordinary* people. You have never talked to a mere mortal. Nations, cultures, arts, civilization—these are mortal, and their life is to ours as the life of a gnat. But it is immortals whom we joke with, work with, marry, snub, and exploit."[10]

At the convocation for the College of Education at Brigham Young University in the summer of 1992, one of the students shared with her fellow graduates, and the others present, a touching story about an experience she had with a young Native American boy. He had been stereotyped by previous teachers as incorrigible, as a serious problem. She felt impelled to reach out and help. She knew the family situation was difficult and thought that if she visited his home she might find some clue as to how to reach him. The experience stunned and sobered her. She found poverty, neglect, addiction—everything that is negative and destructive seemed to be present. Her heart ached for the boy; his situation made her despondent. As she poured her heart out in prayer to the Lord she found herself asking, "Have you forgotten this boy?" Then the answer came, quietly and reassuringly: "No, that is why I sent you."

So very often the Almighty answers people's prayers—the prayers of the lonely, the downtrodden, the hungry, the bitter—through other people, through those sensitive souls who open themselves to inspiration and are willing to be inconvenienced. There are joys, supernal joys, that unfold in our lives as we learn to love others as we would desire to be loved. As we come to do so, we come unto him who is the embodiment of love. And in so doing, we become truly Christian.

Notes

From an address given to BYU faculty and students, Provo, Utah, 14 January 1993.

1. Dallin H. Oaks, "Our Strengths Can Become Our Downfall," *Brigham Young University 1991–92 Devotional and Fireside Speeches* (Provo: Brigham Young University Publications, 1992), 14; emphasis added.
2. Bruce R. McConkie, in Conference Report, October 1973, 55; emphasis in original.
3. John Stott, *Life in Christ* (Wheaton, Ill.: Tyndale House, 1991), 44.
4. *Teachings of the Prophet Joseph Smith,* 147; emphasis added.
5. Boyd K. Packer, *Let Not Your Heart Be Troubled* (Salt Lake City: Bookcraft, 1991), 35–36.
6. James Kelly, "We're Not Going to Make It," *Time,* 25 January 1982, 16–17.
7. Roger Rosenblatt, "The Man in the Water," *Time,* 25 January 1982, 86.
8. Hugh B. Brown, *Vision and Valor* (Salt Lake City: Bookcraft, 1971), 48, 50; emphasis added.
9. Richard L. Evans, *Richard Evans' Quote Book* (Salt Lake City: Publisher's Press, 1971), 165.
10. C. S. Lewis, *The Weight of Glory* (New York: Macmillan, 1949), 14–15; emphasis in original.

LATTER-DAY SAINT CHRISTIANITY

F ew things are needed more in this complex world than understanding. Unfortunately, religious discussions too often devolve into debates or wars of words as a result of defensiveness over this or that theological issue. On the other hand, I have been involved in some truly remarkable conversations during the last several years, sharing and comparing and contrasting the vexations of the soul that took place between people who honestly wanted to know about the other person's faith and way of life. Christian dialogue is vital if we are to come to that understanding out of which can derive meaningful engagement of the pressing problems that face us as we enter the twenty-first century.

THE CHRISTIAN DEFINITION

Latter-day Saints claim to be Christians on the basis of their doctrine, their defined relationship to Christ, and their practice or way of life. One reason why C. S. Lewis is so well received by Latter-day Saints—and so often quoted—is because of his broad and inclusive vision of Christianity. We resonate with Lewis's words: "It is not for us to say who, in the deepest sense, is or is not close to the spirit of Christ. We do not see into men's hearts. We cannot judge, and are indeed forbidden to judge. It would be wicked arrogance for us to say that any man is, or is not, a Christian in this refined sense. . . . When a man who accepts the Christian doctrine lives unworthily of it, it is much clearer to say he is a bad Christian than to say he is not a Christian."[1]

Several years ago, Professor Stephen Robinson and I were contacted by the LDS Church Public Affairs Office and asked if we would be willing to participate in an interview with representatives of the Southern Baptist Convention (SBC). We were informed that they were preparing a video presentation on The Church of Jesus Christ of Latter-day Saints, in preparation for an upcoming SBC conference in Salt Lake City in June of 1998. My interview—which consisted basically of my response to a series of questions—lasted for about an hour and a half. We covered much ground, including the role of prophets, our views concerning the Bible, the person and nature of God the Father, and our teachings on Jesus Christ. For at least twenty or thirty minutes I described our understanding of the Atonement and of the necessity of the mercy and grace of Christ. When the Baptists' videotape *The Mormon Puzzle* was released about a year later, I felt that it portrayed quite accurately, for the most part, our fundamental beliefs and, of course, the differences between LDS and Baptist beliefs. One part was, however, particularly troublesome to me: the narrator stated that the Latter-day Saints do not believe in salvation by the grace of Christ.

Several months later, Stephen and I were invited to Kansas City to meet once again with representatives of the SBC. They were eager to know our feelings concerning the movie. We commented that it was nice that Mormons had been allowed to express themselves. But I also voiced my disappointment in what was said about our lack of belief in grace. I said, essentially, "If you want to say that the Latter-day Saints have an *unusual* view of grace, or a *deficient* view of grace, or a *false* view of grace, we can live with that, for we obviously have differences on what constitutes grace. But to say that we have *no* view of grace is a serious misrepresentation that confuses and misleads people." This episode highlights what I believe to be an important issue in meaningful dialogue: people ought to be allowed to express their views, and we ought to believe them. We don't have to agree with their beliefs, but it accomplishes precious little to ask a person what he believes and then to ignore his observations or to respond, as the interviewer did to me—at least ten times—"Yes, but you don't *really* believe that." After hearing that phrase repeatedly, I said: "You know, I don't mean to be defensive or unkind, but I'm an expert on what I believe. I have no reason to be dishonest with you. Don't you think it would be extremely unwise for me to state on film that the Latter-day Saints believe this or that when in fact we believe something else?"

I have reflected on those experiences for some time now. That visit of the Southern Baptists provided at least twenty opportunities for me to clarify to newspaper reporters, radio or television personalities, or magazine editors what we really believe. Having done this a few times, therefore, let me state what I believe our position is in regard to Christianity. In short, Latter-day Saints believe in Christ. That is:

We believe Jesus is the Son of God, the Only Begotten Son in the flesh.

We believe the accounts of Jesus' life and ministry recorded in Matthew, Mark, Luke, and John in the New Testament to be historical and thus truthful. For us the Jesus of history is indeed the Christ of faith.

We believe that he was born of a virgin, Mary, in Bethlehem of Judea in what has come to be known as the meridian of time, the central point in salvation history. From his mother Mary, Jesus inherited mortality, the capacity to feel the pains and frustrations and ills of this world, including the capacity to die.

We believe Jesus is the Son of God the Father and as such inherited powers of godhood and divinity from his Father, including immortality, the capacity to live forever and to make those same attributes and powers available to others.

We believe Jesus performed miracles, including granting sight to the blind, hearing to the deaf, life to those who had died, and forgiveness to those steeped in sin. We believe the New Testament accounts of healings and nature miracles and the cleansing of human souls to be authentic and real.

We believe Jesus taught his gospel—the glad tidings or good news that salvation had come to earth through him—in order that people might more clearly understand their relationship to God and their responsibility to one another.

We believe Jesus conferred divine authority upon others and organized a church. The Church of Jesus Christ was established, as the Apostle Paul later wrote, for the perfecting of the Saints and for the unity of the faith (see Ephesians 4:11–14).

We believe that Jesus' teachings and his own matchless and perfect life provide a pattern for men and women to live by and the only way to find true happiness and fulfillment in this life.

We believe that Jesus understood clearly who he was and that he made it sufficiently clear to others. He was condemned and tried for what the Jews called blasphemy and for what the Romans considered treason.

We believe Jesus suffered in the Garden of Gethsemane and that he submitted to a cruel death on the cross of Calvary, all as a willing sacrifice, a substitutionary atonement for our sins. We believe that offering is made efficacious as we exercise faith and trust in him; repent of our sins; are baptized by immersion as a symbol of our acceptance of his death, burial, and rise to newness of life; and receive the gift of the Holy Ghost (see Acts 2:37–38; 3 Nephi 27:19–20).

We believe that true Christian discipleship consists in continuing in his word (see John 8:31–32) through faithful obedience to his commandments. We do not believe that we can either overcome the flesh or gain eternal reward through our own unaided efforts. We must work to our limit and then rely upon his merits, mercy, and grace to see us through the struggles of life and into life eternal (see 2 Nephi 2:8; 31:19; Moroni 6:4).

We believe that our discipleship ought to be evident in the way we live our lives, that those who have come unto Christ by covenant should manifest the "fruit of the Spirit" (Galatians 5:22–25; Alma 7:23–24) and thus be Christlike in their dealings with others.

Obviously I could go on and on in setting forth what we believe, in articulating the ways in which the Latter-day Saint tradition defines itself as Christian. But suffice it to say that we consider ourselves to be Christian in that we claim that Jesus Christ is the head of our church and the central figure in the doctrine and practice of the LDS faith and way of life.

President Gordon B. Hinckley stated: "Are we Christians? Of course we are! No one can honestly deny that. We may be somewhat different from the traditional pattern of Christianity. But no one believes more literally in the redemption wrought by the Lord Jesus Christ. No one believes more fundamentally that He was the Son of God, that He died for the sins of mankind, that He rose from the grave, and that He is the living resurrected Son of the living Father.

"All of our doctrine, all of our religious practice stems from that one basic doctrinal position: 'We believe in God, the Eternal Father, and in His Son, Jesus Christ, and in the Holy Ghost.' This is the first article of our faith, and all else flows therefrom."[2]

RELATING TO OTHER CHRISTIAN GROUPS

President Hinckley has also noted: "There are some of other faiths who do not regard us as Christians. That is not important. How we regard ourselves is what is important. We acknowledge without hesitation that there are differences between us. Were this not so there would have been no need for a restoration of the gospel."[3] This statement highlights one of the challenges Latter-day Saints face in the religious world: people deny that we are Christian. Having read others' views on the matter and having discussed this for hundreds of hours, my conclusion is that the LDS Church is said to be a non-Christian organization for the following reasons:

The Church of Jesus Christ of Latter-day Saints is not in the historical

Christian tradition. That is to say, we are neither Catholic nor Protestant and thus cannot trace our roots historically, in an unbroken fashion, through the Reformation and back in time to the first-century Christian church. Implied in this criticism is the fact that Latter-day Saints believe in an apostasy, a loss of precious truths and divine authority from the church Jesus organized. Thus the Latter-day Saints reject the doctrine of the Trinity and the theological formulations of the church councils through the centuries.

The Mormons do not believe in the sufficiency or inerrancy of the Bible. They believe in modern revelation, modern prophets, and thus modern scripture.

The Mormons have unusual doctrines that distance them from traditional Christians (nature of God, nature of the creation, the need for temples and temple ordinances, the deification of man, etc.).

Again, we could list other reasons why certain groups do not acknowledge the Latter-day Saints as Christian, but these three seem to distil the concerns most effectively.

Our belief in an apostasy of the primitive church is of course directly tied to our belief in the need for a complete *restoration* of the gospel. We are neither Protestant nor Catholic, but rather a restored church. Thus when someone asks a Latter-day Saint to justify or "prove" this or that Latter-day Saint doctrine or prac-tice from the Bible, the most honest response might be something like this: "We do not establish our doctrine from the Bible alone. Ours is an independent revelation. We know what we know and do what we do as a result of modern and continuing revelation delivered to Joseph Smith and his prophetic successors."

Occasionally we hear certain Latter-day Saint teachings described as *unbiblical* or of a particular doctrine being *contradictory* to the Bible. The Bible is one of the books within our canon or standard works, and thus our doctrines and practices are in harmony with the Bible. There are times, of course, when latter-day revelation provides clarification or enhancement of the intended meaning in the Bible. But addition to the canon is not the same as rejection of the canon. Supplementation is not the same as contradiction. All of the prophets, including the Savior himself, were sent to bring new light and knowledge to the world; in many cases, new scrip-ture came as a result of their ministry. That new scripture did not invalidate what went before, nor did it close the door to subsequent revelation.

A belief in the need for a restoration (as well as our position, so understand-ably unpopular among many, that ours is the "only true church") does not mean that we do not acknowledge truth and goodness in individuals and organizations throughout the earth, but rather that through Joseph Smith God chose to restore the *fulness* of the everlasting gospel with its doctrine, priesthood authority, and church organization. And so on the one hand, there are many things about which fruitful dialogue can and should go on, including the testimony and teachings of Jesus contained in the four Gospels and the other books of the New Testament.

In early August of 1997, my colleague Brent Top and I traveled to another part of the country to meet with a well-known Evangelical theologian, author, pastor, and teacher who is also host of a radio broadcast that is heard throughout the nation. Brent and I had read several of this man's books and had enjoyed his preaching over the years. Let me explain that as a part of an outreach effort to better understand those of other faiths (and to assist them to understand us a little better), we have visited such institutions as Notre Dame, Baylor, Catholic University, and Wheaton College. We met the minister and then attended his church on both Sunday morning and Sunday evening, and in both meetings were impressed with his expository preaching style.

The next day we met for lunch and then had a wonderful, two-hour doctrinal discussion. I explained that we had no set agenda and were not exactly sure why we had chosen to visit him, except that we had admired his writings and wanted to meet him. I think we added that we had several questions we would like to pose in order to better understand Evangelical theology. I mentioned that I oversaw the teaching of religion of almost thirty thousand young people at Brigham Young University and that I felt it would be wise for me to be able to articulate properly and accurately the beliefs of our brothers and sisters of other faiths. I hoped, as well, that they might make the effort to understand our beliefs so as not to misrepresent what we teach.

I should add, at the first, that the pastor was absolutely stunned that two Latter-day Saint religion professors would visit him, but he was even more perplexed that we had read his books and enjoyed them! I took it a step farther: I indicated to him that although there were some doctrinal chasms between us, I had quoted him in quite a few of my own books. We began our discussion of one of his books and shared our feelings, as he had stated so forcefully in his work, that true faith always manifests itself in faithfulness and that too many people who claim Christian discipleship betray their lack of conversion to the Savior by their worldliness.

Early in our conversation he said something like, "Look, anyone knows there are big differences between us. But I don't want to focus on those differences. Let's talk about Christ." We then discussed faith in Christ, justification by faith, baptism, sanctification, salvation, heaven, hell, agency and predestination, premortal existence, and a number of other fascinating topics. We compared and contrasted, we asked questions, and we answered questions. In thinking back on what was one of the most productive and worthwhile learning experiences of our lives, I recognize that the one thing that characterized our discussion, and the one thing that made the biggest difference, was the mood that existed there—a mood of openness, candor, and a general lack of defensiveness. We knew what we believed, and we were all committed to our own religious tradition. No one was trying to convert the other, but rather instead we were making an effort to understand one another. To be sure, we would have loved to have left the area after having attended his baptism, but that wasn't why we organized the visit, nor did we have any pretension to anything so bold. Likewise, the minister said to us, "Well, guys, obviously I would love to bring you around to my way of thinking, but it's nice to better understand you." This experience says something to me about what can happen when men and women of good will come together in an attitude of openness and in a sincere effort to better understand and be understood.

More recently my colleague Andrew Skinner and I visited Wheaton College in Illinois on two different occasions. The first trip was simply an opportunity to get to know some of the religion faculty there, to visit religion and history classes, and to become acquainted with the personnel and the resources at the Wade Center, which houses the largest collection of C. S. Lewis materials in the world. We learned of an upcoming conference on Lewis and requested information. A call for papers was sent to me, and I made a proposal. The organizing committee accepted and explained that they would be delighted to have me come. Our hosts stated that the Latter-day Saint perspective on Lewis would add a valuable dimension to the conference.

My paper provided an LDS perspective on the theology of C. S. Lewis (one of the later chapters in this volume), dealing mostly with why Lewis's thinking is so well received among the Mormons. Professor Skinner and I had an unforgettable experience there and came away richly blessed for the association, the conversations, and the exchange. Again, everyone there, faculty and students alike, knew of our religious differences, but no one seemed eager (at least in the public settings) to label us as cultists or to suggest that we had some malicious purpose or ulterior motive for being there. The questions from students and faculty were courteous, thoughtful, and contributive to meaningful dialogue.

IMPLICATIONS FOR DIALOGUE

There is a very real sense in which the Latter-day Saints are a part of the larger "body of Christ," the Christian community, whether certain groups feel comfortable with acknowledging our Christianity or not. Given the challenges we face in our society—fatherless homes, child and spouse abuse, divorce, poverty, spreading crime and delinquency, spiritual wickedness in high places—it seems so foolish for men and women who claim to believe in the same Lord and Savior, whose hearts and lives have been surrendered to that Savior, to allow doctrinal differences to prevent them from working together. Okay, you believe in a triune God, that the Almighty is a spirit, and that he created all things *ex nihilo*. I believe that God is an exalted Man, that he is a separate and distinct personage from the Son and the Holy Ghost. She believes that the Sabbath should be observed on Saturday, while her neighbor does not believe in blood transfusions. This one speaks in tongues, that one spends much of his time leading marches against social injustice, while a third believes that little children should be baptized. One good Baptist is a strict Calvinist, while another tends to take freedom of the will seriously. And so on, and so on.

Do we agree on the problems in our world? Do we agree on the fact that most all of these ills have moral or spiritual roots? President Ezra Taft Benson once quoted Beverly Nichols: "You do change human nature, your own human nature, if you surrender it to Christ. Human nature can be changed here and now. Human nature has been changed in the past. Human nature must be changed on an enormous scale in the future, unless the world is to be drowned in its own blood. And only Christ can change it."[4] Do we, as believers in the divinity of Jesus of Nazareth, believe this? Elder Howard W. Hunter once remarked that "whatever Jesus lays his hands upon lives. If Jesus lays his hands upon a marriage, it lives. If he is allowed to lay his hands on the family, it lives."[5] Does this have implications for broken homes, broken covenants, and broken hearts in a world strangled by relativism?

What I am asking is this: in the spirit of Christian brotherhood and sisterhood, is it not possible to lay aside theological differences long enough to address the staggering social issues in our troubled world? My recent interactions with men and women of various faiths have had a profound impact on me; they have broadened my horizons dramatically and reminded me—a sobering reminder we all need once in a while—that we are all sons and daughters of the same Eternal Father. We may never resolve our differences on the Godhead or the Trinity, on the spiritual or corporeal nature of Deity, or on the sufficiency of the Bible, but we can agree that salvation is in Christ; that the ultimate transformation of society will come only through the application of Christian solutions to pressing moral issues; and that the regeneration of individual hearts and souls is foundational to the restoration of virtue in our communities and nations. One need not surrender cherished religious values or doctrines in order to be a better neighbor, a more caring citizen, a more involved municipal.

In addition, we can have lively and provocative discussions on our differences, and such interactions need not be threatening, offensive, or damaging to our relationships. What we cannot afford to do, if we are to communicate and cooperate, is to misrepresent one another or ascribe ulterior motives. Such measures are divisive and do not partake of that Spirit of Christ that strengthens, binds, and reinforces.

CONCLUSION

President Gordon B. Hinckley said of the Latter-day Saints: "We want to be good neighbors; we want to be good friends. We feel we can differ theologically with people without being disagreeable in any sense. We hope they feel the same way toward us. We have many friends and many associations with people who are not of our faith, with whom we deal constantly, and we have a wonderful relationship. It disturbs me when I hear about any antagonisms. . . . I don't think they are necessary. I hope that we can overcome them."[6]

In conclusion, it seems appropriate to share some personal feelings. I believe with all my heart in God and in his Son, Jesus Christ. I am committed to the doctrine and practices of The Church of Jesus Christ of Latter-day Saints; indeed, I have never been more committed to my own religious tradition than I am right now. At the same time, I have never been more liberal in my views—in the proper sense of that word *liberal,* meaning open, receptive—in regard to people of other faiths, especially Christian faiths. To some extent I am motivated in this direction by the following statement in the Book of Mormon: "For behold, the Spirit of Christ is given to every man, that he may know good from evil; wherefore, I show unto you the way to judge; for every thing which inviteth to do good, and to persuade to believe in Christ, is sent forth by the power and gift of Christ; wherefore ye may know with a perfect knowledge it is of God" (Moroni 7:16).

It is my conviction that God loves us, one and all, for I believe he is our Father in heaven and that he has tender regard for us. I also feel strongly that, in spite of growing wickedness, men and women throughout the earth are being led to greater light and knowledge, to the gradual realization of their own fallen nature and thus of their need for spiritual transformation. C. S. Lewis once stated that there are people "who are slowly becoming Christians though they do not yet call themselves so. There are people who do not accept the full Christian doctrine about Christ but who are so strongly attracted by Him that they are His in a much deeper sense than they themselves understand." Lewis went on to speak of people "who are being led by God's secret influence to concentrate on those parts of their religion which are in agreement with Christianity, and who thus belong to Christ without knowing it."[7]

That God's Holy Spirit will bring to consummation his works and designs on this planet, in order that the ancient Christian supplication—"Thy kingdom come. Thy will be done in earth, as it is in heaven" (Matthew 6:10)—may thereby be granted, is my sincere prayer.

Notes

From an address delivered at the Conference on Christian Dialogue, Utah Valley State College, Orem, Utah, 29 October 1998.

1. C. S. Lewis, *Mere Christianity* (New York: Touchstone, 1996), 10–11.
2. Gordon B. Hinckley, "Excerpts from Recent Addresses of President Gordon B. Hinckley," *Ensign*, February 1998, 73.
3. Gordon B. Hinckley, in Conference Report, April 1998, 13.
4. Ezra Taft Benson, in Conference Report, October 1985, 5.
5. Howard W. Hunter, in Conference Report, October 1979, 93.
6. Gordon B. Hinckley, in interview with Phil Riesen, KUTV Television, Salt Lake City, 12 May 1995; as quoted in Sheri L. Dew, *Go Forward with Faith: The Biography of Gordon B. Hinckley* (Salt Lake City: Deseret Book Co., 1996), 576.
7. Lewis, *Mere Christianity,* 178.

A CALL TO HOLINESS

We are Latter-day Saints. As members of the Lord's restored church, we are striving to become holy. Let's begin with a definition. To be *holy* is to be consecrated, dedicated, devoted, devout, pure, just, good, godly.[1] As the 1828 Webster's Dictionary states, "We call a man holy, when his heart is conformed in some degree to the image of God, and his life is regulated by the divine precepts." Please note, then, that a holy person is one who lives a life that is patterned after the Savior, where divine precepts both motivate and monitor one's conduct.

We live in a day that militates against holiness, when time-honored values are ridiculed and when those who stand up for basic morality are considered marginal in society. It is, in fact, the day of Satan's power, wherein evil is called good and good is defined as evil, where darkness is labeled as light and light is considered to be darkness (see Isaiah 5:20). Because society's slouch toward Gomorrah will persist, it is impossible for us to ascertain moral truth in the world and dangerous for us to follow current and future trends. That is to say, we take our cues from society at our peril. Where, then, in a world afflicted with creeping relativism, do we turn for standards? A few years ago President Gordon B. Hinckley cited a study conducted on the moral values of producers, directors, and writers in Hollywood and television. The study indicated that these persons are "far less religious than the general public and 'diverge sharply from traditional values' on such issues as abortion, homosexual rights and extramarital sex. . . . This group has had a major role in shaping the shows whose themes and stars have become staples in our popular culture."[2]

Again, where do we look for moral and spiritual constants? We look to the scriptures, to the prophets. We sustain fifteen men as prophets, seers, and revelators. They are prophets in that they have the testimony of Jesus (see Revelation 19:10; D&C 46:13) and stand as special witnesses of the name of Christ in all the world (see D&C 107:23). They are revelators in the sense that they are called to stand as covenant spokesmen, charged to learn the will of God concerning the people of the covenant and then make it known. They are seers in the sense that they see things not visible to the natural eye, troublesome and disturbing things afar off, things about which we need to be forewarned (see D&C 101:54; Moses 6:36). The children sing it best: "Follow the prophet; he knows the way."[3] I plead with us, therefore, to look to the prophets, to listen to them, to read their words in the most recent conference issue of the *Ensign,* to make their teachings our walk and talk.

EXCESSIVE TOLERANCE AND MISPLACED LOYALTY

I have a grave concern with spiritual desensitization, with the effort by Satan to dull our sensitivities to sin and to confuse our consciences. As the poet Wordsworth wisely observed, "The world is too much with us."[4] There are too many things that an earlier generation would have spurned and rejected as deadly to their souls that we have allowed to become part of our world. Some of this has happened as a result of what I call excessive tolerance or misplaced loyalty. Let me illustrate. Several years ago one of my students asked if she could visit with me after class. She had been with me for two semesters of Book of Mormon, and she was, frankly, a delight to have in class. The light of the gospel radiated from her countenance. She came in to tell me good-bye. I said, "Well, I'll see you next year, won't I?" She shook her head and said, "No, I won't be coming back to BYU." I asked why. She said: "Brother Millet, I'm tired. No, it's more than that—I'm worn out. I haven't slept for almost a year now." Was she tired of studying? I asked. Wouldn't a summer break do the trick? No, that wasn't it. She explained that her roommates, all returned missionaries, had their boyfriends over each night until the early morning hours. More specifically, there was never a place for her to sleep, inasmuch as two of her roommates had their male companions in bed with them every night.

I was stunned. Shocked. Sickened. "Well, why didn't you tell someone? Why didn't you mention it to the landlord or the bishop?" Her answer was very revealing, and it also highlights a significant problem that many in this generation face.

She said: "But wouldn't that be judging them?" We then had a long, long discussion about what it meant to judge righteous judgment.

I explained to her that you and I, as men and women seeking to be holy, are under obligation to make judgments each day of our lives. We must decide whether we will spend time with some people, in particular places, doing certain things. Such decisions, very much a part of making our way through the mists of darkness, are vital; our hope for eternal life depends upon our making wise judgments.

In our day, it seems as though the most serious flaw a person can have is to be intolerant. One would rather be immoral, unclean, degenerate. But whatever you do, don't dare to be intolerant. Now, to be sure, we must be Christian, must be understanding, must be loving and concerned. But such virtues must never cloud the issue of what is right and what is wrong, what is good and what is evil. We must not, as Elder Dallin H. Oaks pointed out to BYU students, allow our strengths to become our weaknesses.[5] We must not allow our tendency to be tolerant to become the very means by which vice becomes acceptable and even encouraged. If we do not stand up for some things, we will fall for most anything.

To be aware of sins and indiscretions all about us and to refuse to report these things is to be dishonest and dishonorable. It is, in a sense, to condone and even enable sin. Further, please do not misunderstand the principle of loyalty. I am under no obligation, even as a caring friend, to be loyal to an associate or a roommate or a coworker who is guilty of gross dishonesty or of violating the standards of the Church or the community in which we live. My primary loyalty is to God, his Son Jesus Christ, and the leaders of the Church. Can we not see the inconsistency of attempting to be loyal to someone who is being disloyal to divine precepts or established standards of decency?

SAFEGUARDING OUR THOUGHTS

President Boyd K. Packer declared: "Years ago I put up signs in my mind. They are very clearly printed and simply read: No Trespassing. No dumping allowed. On occasions it has been necessary to show them very plainly to others.

"I do not want anything coming into my mind that does not have some useful purpose or some value that makes it worth keeping. I have enough trouble keeping the weeds down that sprout there on their own without permitting someone else to clutter my mind with things that do not edify.

"I've hauled a few of these away in my lifetime. Occasionally I've tossed these thoughts back over the fence where they came from, when it could be done in a friendly manner.

"I've had to evict some thoughts a hundred times before they would stay out. I have never been successful until I have put something edifying in their place."[6]

Happy is the man or woman whose thoughts are clean and pure. We must do all in our power to control what goes into our minds. Let us use wisdom and discernment in what movies we attend, what videos we watch, what sitcoms we become addicted to. If for no other reason than pure obedience, we should avoid R-rated movies and any others (no matter their rating) that wink at immorality or parade excessive violence. We must not gauge our viewing according to what the box office says. Very often, in fact, box office success should serve as a caution light. Remember the words of the Savior: "Enter ye in at the strait gate: for wide is the gate, and broad is the way, that leadeth to destruction, and many there be which go in thereat: because strait is the gate, and narrow is the way, which leadeth unto life, and few there be that find it" (Matthew 7:13–14).

We must give careful attention to the music we consume, the pictures that surround us, and what we view on the internet. Thoughts are seedbeds of action. Some years ago President Dallin H. Oaks said to BYU students: "We are surrounded by the promotional literature of illicit sexual relations on the printed page and on the screen. For your own good, avoid it. Pornographic or erotic stories are worse than filthy or polluted food. The body has defenses to rid itself of unwholesome food, but the brain won't vomit back filth. Once recorded it will always remain subject to recall, flashing its perverted images across your mind, and drawing you away from the wholesome things in life."[7]

There is another matter that prevents many of us from enjoying the Spirit of the Lord in our lives as we might: the tendency to live on the edge, to play percentages with God, to tempt fate and to place ourselves in circumstances that can contribute to our spiritual undoing. There are those who want to see how far they can go without going all the way; those who want to drive the vehicle as close to the edge of the cliff as possible with no intention whatever of falling; those who cunningly creep up on the flame with no intention of ever being burned; those who want to enjoy all the privileges of Babylon but at the same time keep their citizenship in Zion intact. I promise you that there is no lasting happiness in such approaches to life, but rather a type of moral or spiritual schizophrenia. Too many people want to be good, but not too good; others want to be bad, but not too bad. Some want to serve the Lord without offending the Devil. As my colleague Brent Top once observed, one cannot "dance and dine in the great and spacious building" and still hold on to the iron rod; clinging to the iron rod requires both hands, as well as both heart and soul.[8] James taught that "a double minded man is unstable in all his ways" (James 1:8). We would do well to stay as far away from sin and compromise as we can, to not only avoid evil but also the very appearance of evil (see 1 Thessalonians 5:22). Prevention is far, far better than redemption.

A Peculiar People

The Apostle Peter wrote to the primitive Saints scattered abroad: "Ye are a chosen generation, a royal priesthood, an holy nation, a peculiar people; that ye should shew forth the praises of him who hath called you out of darkness into his marvellous light" (1 Peter 2:9). Yes, the Saints of the Most High are called upon to be a peculiar people. "We are not freaks," Elder Bruce R. McConkie pointed out, "but normal, wholesome people who enjoy life. We work and play, engage in sports, mingle with other people, go to parties, and enjoy festive occasions. But we are, nonetheless, peculiar in the eyes of worldly people. We are a breed set apart. We are different from the world because we do not ape the practices and follow the fashions of worldly and carnal people. We glory in the things which set us apart by ourselves, and we hope and pray that we may maintain and increase the differences."[9]

We ought to search out, be sensitive to, and applaud the good that is in our society. There is much that is sweet and uplifting and edifying. But if we are to qualify to go where God and angels are, we must see to it that the distance between us and worldliness is increasing day by day. This will come to pass as our minds and hearts are transformed by the Spirit of God, as we come to see what we ought to see, hear what we ought to hear, and feel what we ought to feel. If we live in such a way that the Holy Ghost can dwell in us, then over time our desires are educated, our judgment is refined, our conscience is sharpened. In speaking of the former-day Saints, Alma observed that they "were sanctified, and their garments were washed white through the blood of the Lamb." Now note what follows: "Now they, after being sanctified by the Holy Ghost, having their garments made white, being pure and spotless before God, could not look upon sin save it were with abhorrence; and there were many, exceedingly great many, who were made pure and entered into the rest of the Lord their God" (Alma 13:11–12).

The Holy Ghost is a Revelator as well as a Comforter. And the Holy Ghost is a Sanctifier, the means by which waywardness and rebellion and stubbornness, along with sin and iniquity and vice, are burned out of our souls as though by fire. That sanctifying or cleansing influence can be ours as we make up our minds to do things the way the Lord would have us do them. Too many people in today's world want to go to their graves singing, "I did it my way." As C. S. Lewis once remarked, there are only two kinds of people in this world: those who say to God in this life, "Thy will be done," and those to whom God says, in the life to come, "Thy will be done."[10] In that spirit, Mormon explained concerning a group of Saints living in about 40 B.C.: "They did fast and pray oft, and did wax stronger and stronger in their humility, and firmer and firmer in the faith of Christ, unto the filling their souls with joy and consolation, yea, even to the purifying and the sanctification of their hearts, which sanctification cometh because of their yielding their hearts unto God" (Helaman 3:35).

A peculiar people is a *purchased* people. That is, we are not our own; we have been bought with a price (see 1 Corinthians 6:19–20), even "the precious blood of Christ, as of a lamb without blemish and without spot" (1 Peter 1:19). We believe that we are saved by the merits and mercy and grace of the Holy Messiah (see 2 Nephi 2:8), but we do not believe in "cheap grace." What cost God the Father everything, even the life blood of his Only Begotten Son, cannot be treated as "a thing of naught" (1 Nephi 19:9). We are a people of covenant. We have made supernal promises, some of us in holy places, to stand as lights to a world desperately in need of direction and focus. We are under solemn obligation to be the salt of the earth (see D&C 101:39–40), to bring out the best in the world, to preserve the world from decay and destruction. It is important to remember that salt does not lose its savor or influence with age; salt loses its savor through mixture and contamination.

THE WAY BACK

Perhaps there are some among us who are carrying heavy burdens, even the burdens of sin. Satan would whisper lies to us. He would suggest that serious sins are between you and God, that you can work it out by yourself. He would try to convince some that it's too late, that they have gone too far, that the way back is too difficult. I bear my witness that these are lies, lies spawned in the infernal pits by the Father of Lies himself. He would have you to be miserable like unto himself (see 2 Nephi 2:18). We must never surrender ourselves to such rubbish. There is a way back. It will not be easy, but it is possible. Our priesthood leaders hold the keys that will assist in lifting the heavy weight from the heart. Our Savior suits his tender mercies according to our varying and specific needs (see D&C 46:15), and he who knows us best will direct our priesthood leader in exactly how best to bless our lives.

That 1828 Webster's Dictionary that I mentioned earlier provides one additional definition of the word *holy*. To be holy is to be whole, complete, fully formed, finished. In other words, to be holy is to be *perfect* in the scriptural sense. No man nor woman can of themselves ever, worlds without end, become perfect in this life in the sense that they no longer make mistakes, no longer take a backward step. But we can become perfect in Christ. Our Divine Redeemer is complete, while I am incomplete. As I come unto him, we (the Lord and I) are complete. He is whole while I am partial. Together we are whole and complete. He is finished while I am unfinished. Together we are finished. And he is perfect while I am oh, so imperfect. Together, in covenant, we are perfect. Covenant union with Christ allows him to share with me and transfer to my spiritual account his riches and his righteousness. Thus it is that the faithful learn to rely alone upon the merits of Christ, "who [is] the author and the finisher of their faith" (Moroni 6:4). Thus it is that the revelations declare concerning those who inherit the celestial kingdom: "These are they whose names are written in heaven, where God and Christ are the judge of all. These are they who are just men [and women] made perfect through Jesus the mediator of the new covenant, who wrought out this perfect atonement through the shedding of his own blood" (D&C 76:68–69; see also Moroni 10:32).

<hr>

CONCLUSION

I know that God, our Heavenly Father, lives. He is the Man of Holiness (see Moses 6:57).

I desire with all the strength I have within me to become a holy man, to qualify one day to go where he is. I desire the same for you. Peter wrote: "As he which hath called you is holy, so be ye holy in all manner of conversation," meaning in conduct as well as in speech. "Because it is written, Be ye holy; for I am holy" (1 Peter 1:15–16; see also Leviticus 11:44).

I know that Jesus Christ lives, that he is the Son of God and our only hope for reconciliation with the Man of Holiness. It is only through applying his atoning blood and putting off the natural man that we become a holy people (see Mosiah 3:19). Truly, there is power, power in the blood, even the blood of Christ (see Leviticus 17:11). I know that the Holy Ghost, the third member of the Godhead, is a revelator and a sanctifier. By his influence we come to know the truthfulness of the restored gospel and the reality of personal redemption in Christ. While it is by virtue of the blood of Christ that we are purified, the Spirit is the agent, the sanctifying medium by which we come unto Christ and are made holy.

I know that Joseph Smith was a prophet of God, the Choice Seer (see 2 Nephi 3:7) raised up by the Almighty to stand as the head of this final dispensation. And I know that this Church of Jesus Christ of Latter-day Saints is, in the language of the revelations, the only true and living church on the face of the whole earth (see D&C 1:30). As now constituted, with apostles and prophets at its head, it is in the line of its duty and is preparing a people for the second coming of the Son of Man.

God grant that we, the people of the covenant, will be wise in the days of our probation; that we will put away the foolishness of the flesh and put out of our lives those things that have no place among a people concerned with holiness. I pray that we will do so, that we may in time see the face of the Lord with pleasure and hear those tender words of welcome, "Come unto me, ye blessed, there is a place prepared for you in the mansions of my Father" (Enos 1:27).

Notes

From an address delivered at the BYU Fourteenth Stake Conference, Provo, Utah, 25 October 1998.

1. See *Random House College Dictionary,* rev. ed. (New York: Random House, 1988), s.v. "holy."
2. *Teachings of Gordon B. Hinckley* (Salt Lake City: Deseret Book Co., 1997), 461–62.
3. "Follow the Prophet," *Children's Songbook* (Salt Lake City: The Church of Jesus Christ of Latter-day Saints, 1989), 111.
4. William Wordsworth, as cited in Jack M. Lyon et al., *Best-Loved Poems of the LDS People* (Salt Lake City: Deseret Book Co., 1996), 305.
5. Dallin H. Oaks, "Our Strengths Can Become Our Downfall," *1991–92 Brigham Young University Speeches* (Provo: Brigham Young University Publications, 1992), 107–15.
6. Boyd K. Packer, *"That All May Be Edified"* (Salt Lake City: Bookcraft, 1982), 65.
7. Dallin H. Oaks, as quoted by N. Eldon Tanner, in Conference Report, October 1973, 124.
8. Brent L. Top, "The Blessings of Repentance and the Rewards for Righteousness," in *Why Say No When the World Says Yes,* comp. Randal A. Wright (Salt Lake City: Deseret Book Co., 1993), 189.
9. Bruce R. McConkie, "The Ten Commandments of a Peculiar People," *1975 BYU Speeches of the Year* (Provo: Brigham Young University Publications, 1975), 28.
10. C. S. Lewis, *The Great Divorce* (New York: Touchstone, 1996), 72.

DEALING WITH
DIFFICULT QUESTIONS

Ponder for a moment upon what God has revealed in these last days. Through Joseph Smith and his successors, the Lord Almighty has seen fit to make known the answers to some of life's most perplexing questions: Where did I come from? Why am I here? Where am I going when I leave here? As Latter-day Saints we are able to talk intelligently about doctrinal matters that are completely mysterious to those outside the faith, some matters that must sound like the gibberish of alien tongues to those who have not received the gift of the Holy Ghost. The nature of God, life in a premortal and postmortal existence, the continuation of the family unit into eternity—these and a myriad of other topics are but illustrative of the unspeakable knowledge and intelligence that have been poured out upon the heads of the Lord's people in this final gospel dispensation. These great truths are unique to our church; they are a part of our heritage and constitute the doctrinal reservoir that helps to make of the Latter-day Saints "a peculiar people" (see 1 Peter 2:9). We have so much.

In fact, we're spoiled! We have the answers to so many questions, the solutions to so many of the world's vexing issues, the only meaningful suggestion for peace in a troubled world, peace here and hereafter. In fact, we have so many answers to so many religious questions that some of us expect to have them all. And it's downright unsettling when we happen upon some dilemma for which no answer is forthcoming, something that is at best unclear or at worst unrevealed. It is the nature of mankind to seek for closure, to strive to fill in the blanks. That is as it should be. Our souls reach out for answers. We are eternal creatures living in a mortal world, spiritual beings undergoing a temporal experience. The veil of forgetfulness purposely and purposefully denies us access to many things we once knew, many parts of a rather intricate and complex puzzle. Even with all that has been delivered by prophets and apostles, by wise men and women, and by the spirit of inspiration, there are and will be questions. Difficult questions. Nagging questions that are troublesome and at times seemingly unanswerable.

It is important to note that there is no evil in having questions, no harm in wondering and asking and inquiring. No person, Latter-day Saint or otherwise, ought to feel guilty because he or she has questions. Such is perfectly normal, a part of the plan. If we already possessed the solutions to all the traumas and the formulae for all the paradoxes, there would be little purpose and certainly little fulfillment to be had in this second estate. Success in life and, as we shall discuss at some length in this chapter, spiritual maturity depend not upon whether we have questions but rather with how we deal with them. Whatever the nature of our queries, there are both counterproductive and productive, both fruitful and unfruitful means of engaging them. We shall in this chapter consider some examples of each.

SOME COUNTERPRODUCTIVE APPROACHES

There are several approaches to solving our doctrinal or historical problems that do not prove to be extremely helpful. Indeed, they are and will always be hazardous to our spiritual health. Some years ago my family and I moved from a part of the country we had come to love dearly. I was asked to assume a new assignment in the Church Educational System that required a relocation. We had been in our new home for only a few weeks when I received a telephone call late one Sunday evening. The woman on the other end of the line was deeply distraught. "Brother Millet," she said. "This is Sister Johnson." "Yes, Sister Johnson," I responded. "How are you and the family?" I had known the Johnson family quite well. Brother Johnson had been a member of the bishopric in their ward (Sister Johnson had served in the presidencies of both the Primary and Relief Society) while I had served as a member of the stake presidency in that area. I had been in their home several times, had enjoyed dinners and social gatherings with them, had known of their dedicated Church service, and believed them to be one of the most settled and secure Latter-day Saint families anywhere. They had joined the Church after having been found and taught by the missionaries some ten years earlier. They were themselves extremely missionary-minded and had been instrumental in leading several families to baptism. But there was obvious pain in Sister Johnson's voice. I tried to be positive and asked: "What can I do for you?" "I desperately need your help," she said. "My husband is about to leave the Church."

Her statement nearly took my breath. "Leave the Church?" I asked. "What do you mean?" She went on to explain that her husband's brother, a man of another faith who had opposed their baptism, had for several months been sending rather bitter anti-Mormon propaganda through the mail. She mentioned that at first her husband had ignored the stuff, but that after a few weeks he began perusing it out of sheer curiosity. "I began to notice a gradual change in Bill," she stated. She pointed out that he became argumentative and uncooperative at church, touchy and ill at ease at home, and just plain unsettled in his demeanor. "He has a lot of questions, Brother Millet," she added, "and I'm afraid if he doesn't get them answered pretty soon we'll lose him." "How can I help?" I inquired. "He wants to talk with you," Sister Johnson came back. "Good," I said, "put him on the line." "Oh, no," she said, "he wants to meet with you in person." I expressed to her that such a meeting would be perfectly fine with me, but that we were now some ten or twelve hours driving distance from one another. I suggested that if this was the only way to deal with his concerns, if his concerns could not be addressed by someone in their area, then we should set a time when we might get together. "He's already on his way," she then observed. "He left a couple of hours ago. Would you please meet with him? He'll be at the institute by nine o'clock tomorrow morning." I was a bit startled but quickly assured Sister Johnson that I would be more than happy to meet with him and do what I could.

Brother Johnson wasn't the only one who didn't sleep that night. I tossed and turned through the night, arose several times, and retired to the living room to pray for guidance. The morning came faster than I had wished, and my stomach churned as I contemplated what the meeting might entail. Sister Johnson was quite accurate in her prediction: her husband arrived a little after nine o'clock. She was also quite accurate in her description of her husband's condition. He had a fallen countenance, a dark look in his eyes, and in general a rather gloomy appearance; this simply was not the man I had known before. He had lost the Spirit and was in many ways like a broken man, like a person who had lost his innocence, indeed had lost his way. We knelt and prayed together and I pleaded with the Lord to dispel the spirit of gloom and doubt and endow us with the spirit of light and understanding. The answer to that prayer came eventually, but only after a long and difficult struggle. As is so often the case, Brother Johnson had been confronted with scores of questions on authority, on the Church's claim to being Christian, on temple rites, on doctrinal teachings of specific Church leaders, on changes in scripture or Church practice, etc., etc. An endless list. We took the time to respond to every issue, to suggest an answer if such was possible. In some cases, the answer was simply a call for faith, an invitation to pray or repray about whether Joseph Smith was a prophet of God, whether his successors have worn the same mantle of authority, and whether the Church is divinely led today. I sensed, however, that there was something deeper, something beneath the surface issues that he was raising, something that was festering and eating away at his soul like a cancer. It took me almost eight hours to discover what that something was.

To make an already long story shorter, let me simply say that when Brother and Sister Johnson were first taught the gospel and introduced to the Book of Mormon, one of the missionaries—no doubt well-meaning but shortsighted—had said something like, "Now, Brother and Sister Johnson, the Book of Mormon is true. It came from God to Joseph Smith. And you can know for yourselves that it is true by praying about it. But, the fact is, there are so many archaeological evidences of its truthfulness, these days it almost isn't necessary to pray about it!" The statement sounded convincing enough. Brother Johnson bought into that line of reasoning and—shortsighted on his part—never took occasion to pray with real intent about the Book of Mormon. When anti-Mormon materials suggested that there were not as many external evidences of the Nephite or Jaredite civilizations as he had been told previously, his whole world collapsed. If the Book of Mormon wasn't true, he reasoned, then Joseph Smith was not a prophet. If Joseph Smith was not a prophet . . . and so on. One fatal step led to another. And now he was ready to throw it all away, unfortunately because his testimony was not substantive, his doctrinal foundation was weak and shifting. And he had been unwilling to exercise sufficient faith and patience to resee and refocus upon the things that really count, in this case the message or content of the Book of Mormon.

It was almost a relief to finally get down to the core issue. I explained to him that we were now up against the wall of faith and that the only issue to be decided was whether or not he was willing to pay the price to know the truth. I asked some hard questions: Did you ever know that this work is true? What was your witness based on? What has this doubting and this vexation of the soul done to your wife and children? Does the bitter spirit you have felt during the last few months come from God? And then I asked: "Are you willing to throw it all away, to jettison all that is good and ennobling because your foundation was deficient?" He paused, reflected again with me on the painful and poignant strugglings he had undergone, but then added that he wanted more than anything to feel once more what he had felt ten years earlier. I stressed to him the need for staying with simple and solid doctrinal matters, particularly in regard to the Book of Mormon and the Restoration, for focusing upon the things of greatest worth, for following the same course of study and pondering and prayer that he had followed during his initial investigation of the Church. I challenged him never to yield to the temptation to "jump ship" when he encountered things he didn't understand, especially when there were so many things he *did* understand and know. It was a sweet experience to watch the light of faith and trust come back into his countenance and into his life.

I have taken the time to detail this experience because it highlights the tragic reality that too often people are prone to "jump ship," to forsake family and friends and faith—to give it all up—because there is an unanswered question or an unresolved dilemma. (It also points up graphically that our spiritual lives must be built upon the proper foundations if we are to be steady in our discipleship and mature in our faith. We shall discuss this at more length in a later chapter.)

Let me briefly refer to a different experience. Several years ago I became acquainted with a lovely young family who joined the Church—a mother, father, and two children. From all appearances theirs was a perfect conversion; they were people who loved the Church, were eager to jump in with both feet and anxious to share their newfound way of life with others. Sister Brown was quickly absorbed into the Primary, while Brother Brown found friends among the members of the elders quorum. It was after they had been in the Church for well over a year that Brother Brown came to see me at my office one day. He expressed his love for the Church as well as the thrill he felt at seeing his family deeply rooted in Mormonism. It was then that he shared with me something that I never would have supposed—that he did not really have a witness of Joseph Smith's prophetic calling. He said, in essence: "Bob, I love the gospel with all my heart. I know that this is the true church. There's no question in my mind about it. This is what I want for my family, now and always. But I have a problem, one that won't seem to go away. I just don't know that Joseph Smith was a prophet."

He then expressed how silly such a thing must sound to me, that is, to accept and embrace the revelation and at the same time be unable to accept and acknowledge the revelator. He said, in essence, "I've prayed and prayed and prayed for a testimony of Joseph Smith, but I still can't say that I know he was called of God. I sincerely believe that he was a great and good man and that in the purest sense he was inspired of God. But I just don't know for sure that he was a prophet. What do I do?" This was a bit unusual to me. From all I could discern, there was no duplicity, no cynicism, no skepticism, only simple and pure uncertainty; he wanted so badly to know, but he didn't know. We worked together on this problem for years. We read books on Joseph Smith, we fasted together, we prayed together. In all that time, Brother Brown remained true and faithful. He labored in many of the auxiliaries of the Church and for a time served as an elders quorum president. He and his family were active in the Church and involved in every way that could be expected of them. Our families became quite close, and we often spent time talking about life and its challenges, about the central place of the gospel in our lives, and about where we would be if we were not members of the Church.

In time we moved from the area. It was several years later that I received a telephone call from Brother Brown. "Bob," he said excitedly, "I have something to tell you. I have a testimony of Joseph Smith. These feelings have been growing within me for several months now, but I can finally stand and say that I know. I know!" I wept with him as we talked about the peace of mind he had gained, as we discussed this most recent phase of his lengthy but steady conversion. It had taken almost eight years for him to come to know, but in the interim he had done all that was expected of him. I have a witness as to how much the Lord loves Brother Brown and all the other Brother Browns who have the spiritual stamina and moral courage to hang on, to hold to the rod, even when they are not absolutely certain as to the destination of the path they traverse. Surely this is what the Savior meant when he counseled us: "Search diligently, pray always, and be believing, and all things shall work together for your good, if ye walk uprightly and remember the covenant wherewith ye have covenanted one with another" (D&C 90:24).

Another example of a counterproductive approach to obtaining answers is going to the wrong people for help. A man and his wife whom I knew quite well joined the Church in the southern part of the United States. After a year's involvement with the Church, they traveled to Washington, D. C., to receive the blessings of the temple. On returning home, the father felt there were several unanswered questions he had about the temple, and so he contacted his former Protestant minister and arranged for a meeting. The minister was of course more than willing to oblige him and especially eager to give answers to his queries regarding Mormon temples. As one might suppose, the family ceased association with the Latter-day Saints within a matter of weeks and returned to their former church. Simply stated, one does not go to Caiaphas or Pilate to learn about Jesus. He goes to Peter, James, or John, those who knew the Master intimately well. One does not go to the enemies of Joseph Smith or the critics of the present Church if he or she sincerely wants to gain understanding concerning the faith. Wisdom would suggest that one does not take his doubts to a known doubter and expect to receive peace of mind.

Each of us is under obligation to search and ponder upon the issues ourselves, to do our best to learn by study and by faith the answers to our concerns (see D&C 9:7–9). Every member of this church has a direct channel to our Heavenly Father; there is no one between us and God. Every person who has been baptized and confirmed has a right to the companionship and guidance of the Holy Ghost, the Comforter, even that Spirit of Truth which knows all things (see D&C 42:17; Moses 6:61). In addition, members of a given ward can readily take their concerns to their priesthood leaders—their branch president or bishop. If the bishop does not know the answer to the question, he can inquire of the stake president. If the stake president is unable to address the concern and feels it advisable to do so, he may inquire of the General Authorities of the Church. As indicated earlier, people ought to feel free to ask their questions. If an answer is to be had, it can be obtained through proper channels.

There is a temptation, when we are troubled by a particular matter, to spend inordinate amounts of time researching it. Some things have just not been revealed, and thus to devote ourselves endlessly to the discovery of what in essence is the undiscoverable (at least for now) is counterproductive. It's almost a waste of time, especially when our efforts could be so much more profitably expended in studying upon and reinforcing the things that *have* been given by God. There is a remarkable phenomenon to which we ought to pay particular attention, one to which I can bear especial witness. It might be stated thus: Constant review of basic principles constantly brings increased spiritual insight. "Those who preach by the power of the Holy Ghost," Elder Bruce R. McConkie explained, "use the scriptures as their basic source of knowledge and doctrine. They begin with what the Lord has before revealed to other inspired men. But *it is the practice of the Lord to give added knowledge to those upon whose hearts the true meaning and intents of the scriptures have been impressed.* Many great doctrinal revelations come to those who preach from the scriptures. When they are in tune with the Infinite, *the Lord lets them know, first, the full and complete meaning of the scriptures they are expounding, and then he ofttimes expands their views so that new truths flood in upon them, and they learn added things* that those who do not follow such a course can never know."[1]

Stated differently, we reduce the realm of the unknown, not by wandering in it, but rather by delighting in and expanding our knowledge of that which God has already revealed. It is a soul-satisfying experience to be reading topic A and then to have our minds caught away to consider topic B. Indeed, serious, consistent, prayerful consideration and reflection upon the *institutional* revelations (the standard works and the words of the living oracles) result in *individual* revelations, including—where the Lord senses it is appropriate and we are ready to receive the same—the answers to our more difficult questions. Those answers may come as a specific response to a specific concern, or they may come in the form of a comforting and peaceful assurance that all is well, that God is in his heaven, that the work in which we are engaged is true, that specifics will be made known in the Lord's due time. Either way, answers do come. They really do, but only as we go to the right source.

Some people trip over a false assumption whenever they encounter hard doctrine or tough issues or whenever they uncover something that they consider to be a painful discovery. After they have searched and looked and sifted and sorted through all they can find, after they have made what they believe to be their best effort to solve the problem, they conclude that because they do not understand, then no one else does either. That's quite a presumptuous conclusion, but it is, nevertheless, a surprisingly common one. Humility would demand a different stance. Meekness would force us to acknowledge that there just might be someone either brighter or more experienced than ourselves, or maybe even someone who has struggled with this issue before. Common sense would suggest that the odds are against absolute originality in regard to our specific concern. And even if it is possible that we have indeed unearthed something no other mortal has ever encountered, still there are good and wise people in our midst who have been blessed with the gifts of the Spirit—with discernment, with revelation, with wisdom and judgment—to assist us in putting all things in proper perspective.

Unfortunately, some members of the Church do not learn this lesson and thus wander in the morass of dwindling unbelief. Having yielded themselves to the spirit of skepticism, having become thereby an easy prey to those who proselyte others to share their doubts, some members of the Church begin to read, as President Joseph F. Smith warned, by the lamp of their own conceit, to interpret what they know and experience by rules of their own contriving.[2] If not checked by repentance and sincere submission, such persons can lose their faith and thus their vision. When a person refuses to exercise faith—to have a hope in that which is unseen but true (see Alma 32:21)—he thereby denies himself access to the spiritual world, another realm of reality entirely. His vision of things is at best deficient; he does not see things "as they really are" (see Jacob 4:13; compare D&C 93:24). Such a view of reality precludes one's apprehension of the unseen and his desire to grasp the unknown. In time there is no place in such a person's tightly enclosed epistemological system for such matters as spirit and revelation and prophecy. The doubter—the one whose faith centers in that which may be seen and heard and felt through natural means only—errs grossly through generalizing beyond his own experiences. What he has not experienced, he assumes no one else can. Because he does not know, no one knows (see Alma 30:48); because he is past feeling, surely no one else has felt; because he lacks internal evidence concerning the things of God, unquestionably the evidence amassed by every believing soul is either insufficient or naively misinterpreted. Those who dare not believe dare not allow others to believe.

A related tendency by some is to parade their doubts, to suppose that by "coming out of the closet" with an announcement of all things that trouble them, they will somehow either feel better about their difficulties or identify and join hands with others who similarly struggle. As we have suggested already, one need not suffer alone. There is help available, within fairly easy reach. To be quite direct, however, precious little good comes from "hanging out our dirty wash," from making public proclamations about one's inner anxieties—little good to the individual and little good to groups of people. Such things merely feed doubt and perpetuate it. Elder Neal A. Maxwell asked: "Why are a few members, who somewhat resemble the ancient Athenians, so eager to hear some new doubt or criticism? (See Acts 17:21.) Just as some weak members slip across a state line to gamble, a few go out of their way to have their doubts titillated. Instead of nourishing their faith, they are gambling 'offshore' with their fragile faith. To the question 'Will ye also go away?' these few would reply, 'Oh no, we merely want a weekend pass in order to go to a casino for critics or a clubhouse for cloak holders.' Such easily diverted members are not disciples but fair-weather followers. Instead," Elder Maxwell concluded, "true disciples are rightly described as steadfast and immovable, pressing forward with 'a perfect brightness of hope' (2 Nephi 31:20; see also D&C 49:23)."[3]

Again, one of the signs of our spiritual maturity is how we handle difficult issues or controversial matters. A Latter-day Saint may have a genuine difference of opinion from one or more leaders of the Church, or may not agree with a particular doctrine or practice of the Church. These may be matters with which he or she labors for many years before a resolution is forthcoming. But for the loyal and devoted Saint they are private struggles of the soul, never intended to become public crusades. To proceed otherwise—to promote differing views, to publish differences with the Church, to sensationalize what we feel to be error or misdeed in the Church—is to border on personal apostasy. "We could conceive of a man," President George Q. Cannon observed, "honestly differing in opinion from the Authorities of the Church and yet not be an apostate; but *we could not conceive of a man publishing those differences of opinion and seeking by arguments, sophistry and special pleading to enforce them upon the people to produce division and strife and to place the acts and counsels of the Authorities of the Church, if possible, in a wrong light and not be an apostate,* for such conduct was apostasy as we understood the term. We further said that *while a man might honestly differ in opinion from the Authorities through a want of understanding, he had to be exceedingly careful how he acted in relation to such differences, or the adversary would take advantage of him, and he would soon become imbued with the spirit of apostasy* and be found fighting against God and the authority which He had placed here to govern His Church."[4]

SOME PRODUCTIVE APPROACHES

Questions will arise in each of our individual spheres, at least as long as we are learning and growing and seeking to understand what life is about. With some questions we may simply be able to ask ourselves: "Does this really matter? Is this issue important enough to worry myself about? Is it worth the effort?" We only have so much time and energy in this life; we would do well to ignore, where possible, the unimportant, to avoid getting caught up, as someone has suggested, in the thick of thin things! As a professor of religion at Brigham Young University, it has been fascinating (and sometimes a bit discouraging) to find what some students grapple with. This one just has to know the exact size of Kolob. That one won't rest until he has calculated the precise dimensions of the celestial city seen by John the Revelator. Others wrestle with the present resting place of the Ark of the Covenant or Joseph Smith's seer stone. "There is so much to learn," Elder Bruce R. McConkie has written in an open letter to honest truth seekers, "about the great eternal verities which shape our destiny that it seems a shame to turn our attention everlastingly to the minutiae and insignificant things. So often questions like this are asked: 'I know it is not essential to my salvation, but I would really like to know how many angels can dance on the head of a pin and if it makes any difference whether the pin is made of brass or bronze?' There is such a thing as getting so tied up with little fly specks on the great canvas which depicts the whole plan of salvation that we lose sight of what the life and the light and the glory of eternal reward are all about (see, for example, Matthew 23:23–25). There is such a thing as virtually useless knowledge, the acquisition of which won't make one iota of difference to the destiny of the kingdom or the salvation of its subjects."[5]

In teaching some of my religion classes, I have occasionally said that it is as important to know *what we do not know* as it is to know what we know. Further, to quarrel and dispute over the unknown and the unrevealed is fruitless and absolutely unnecessary. In that spirit, it is fundamentally necessary for us occasionally to say, "I don't know!" Part of our spiritual maturity is reflected in our ability to deal with ambiguity, to handle uncertainty. President Joseph F. Smith wisely pointed out that "the religion of the heart, the unaffected and simple communion which we should hold with God, is the highest safeguard of the Latter-day Saints. It is no discredit to our intelligence or to our integrity to say frankly in the face of a hundred speculative questions, 'I do not know.'"[6] And yet our focus need not be upon the unknown; rather, we can emphasize what we *do* know. This is the pattern found in scripture, the pattern whereby a prophet says, in essence, "I don't know this, but let me tell you what I do know." An angel asked Nephi: "Knowest thou the condescension of God?" Now note the young prophet's response: "I know that he loveth his children; nevertheless, I do not know the meaning of all things" (1 Nephi 11:16–17). Alma, in discoursing on the coming of the Messiah to the people of Gideon, said: "Behold, I do not say that he will come among us at the time of his dwelling in his mortal tabernacle; for behold, the Spirit hath not said unto me that this should be the case. *Now as to this thing I do not know; but this much I do know,* that the Lord God hath power to do all things which are according to his word" (Alma 7:8, emphasis added). Later in the Nephite story Alma, in counseling his errant son Corianton, spoke concerning life after death. He indicated that he did not know the particulars, the details concerning the time of the resurrection. "There is a time appointed unto men that they shall rise from the dead; and there is a space between the time of death and the resurrection. And now, concerning this space of time, what becometh of the souls of men is the thing which I have inquired diligently of the Lord to know; and *this is the thing of which I do know*" (Alma 40:8–9; emphasis added).

Though it may be obvious at this point, one cannot be lazy or lethargic in his or her quest to find answers to difficult questions. There is an effort required in the spiritual realm, at least as extensive an effort as that associated with finding solutions in the world of physical phenomena. "It is a paradox," Elder John A. Widtsoe noted, "that men will gladly devote time every day for many years to learn a science or an art; yet will expect to win a knowledge of the gospel, which comprehends all sciences and arts, through perfunctory glances at books or occasional listening to sermons. The gospel should be studied more intensively than any school or college subject. They who pass opinion on the gospel without having given it intimate and careful study are not lovers of truth, and their opinions are worthless."[7] It is one thing to know that the gospel is true and another to know the gospel. And we certainly cannot expect to gain answers to some of the more difficult doctrinal matters, for example, save we pay the price in appropriate study and investigation.

It is one thing to be ignorant of a matter. It is quite another to allow that ignorance to be transformed into a type of festering spiritual sore that robs one of peace and shakes the foundations of one's faith. Though the following is a rather lengthy quotation, I feel it is an excellent statement on the matter of doubt. Elder Widtsoe explained: "Doubt usually means uncertainty. You doubt the presence of gold in the ore, though there are yellow flakes in it; or that the man is a thief, though stolen goods are found in his possession; or that a principle of the gospel is correctly interpreted by the speaker. What you really mean is that the evidence in your possession is insufficient to convince you that there is gold in the ore, or that the man is a thief, or that the gospel principle has been explained correctly. Doubt arises from lack of evidence.

"Intelligent people cannot long endure such doubt. It must be resolved. Proof must be secured of the presence of gold in the ore, or of the dishonesty of the man, or of the correctness of the doctrinal exposition. Consequently, we set about to remove doubt by gathering information and making tests concerning the subject in question. Doubt, then, becomes converted into inquiry or investigation.

"After proper inquiries, using all the powers at our command, the truth concerning the subject becomes known, or it remains unknown to be unraveled perhaps at some future time. The weight of evidence is on one side or the other. Doubt is removed. Doubt, therefore, can be and should be only a temporary condition. Certainly, a question cannot forever be suspended between heaven and earth; it is either answered or unanswered. As the results of an inquiry appear, doubt must flee. . . .

"The strong man is not afraid to say, 'I do not know'; the weak man simpers and answers, 'I doubt.' Doubt, unless transmuted into inquiry, has no value or worth in the world. Of itself it has never lifted a brick, driven a nail, or turned a furrow. To take pride in being a doubter, without earnestly seeking to remove the doubt, is to reveal shallowness of thought and purpose. . . .

"Doubt of the right kind—that is, honest questioning—leads to faith. Such doubt impels men to inquiry which always opens the door to truth. The scientist in his laboratory, the explorer in distant parts, the prayerful man upon his knees—these and all inquirers like them find truth. They learn that some things are known, others are not. They cease to doubt. They settle down with the knowledge they possess to make the forces of nature do their bidding, knowing well that they will be victorious; and that more knowledge will come to them, if sought, to yield new power.

"On the other hand, the stagnant doubter, one content with himself, unwilling to make the effort, to pay the price of discovery, inevitably reaches unbelief and miry darkness. His doubts grow like poisonous mushrooms in the dim shadows of his mental and spiritual chambers. At last, blind like the mole in his burrow, he usually substitutes ridicule for reason, and indolence for labor. The simplest truth is worth the sum of all such doubts. He joins the unhappy army of doubters who, weakened by their doubts, have at all periods of human history allowed others, men of faith, to move the world into increasing light."[8]

There are many things we will need to wait on, many questions we will encounter whose answers will definitely not be forthcoming right away. Some things we need to be willing to "put on a shelf." We continue our searching, our prayer, our discussions, but we wait patiently upon the Lord. I, like many others, do not understand for the present all the things that took place in the history of our Church or all the doctrines preached by leaders of the Church. But my confidence and my trust in Joseph Smith and his successors is implicit. We simply do not have the whole story yet. Joseph and Brigham and John and Wilford are not here to fill in the gaps in our knowledge, nor are the rank-and-file members of the Church from bygone days available for oral interviews and clarifications. We must do all that we can in the present to reconstruct the past, to write and understand the story of the Latter-day Saints. But we must be patient, avoiding the temptation to attribute improper motivation or to jump prematurely to conclusions; we need to give the leaders of the Church the benefit of the doubt. The Lord will vindicate the words and works of his anointed servants in time. Of this I have no doubt. In the meantime, we must receive their words, as the revelation declares, "in all patience and faith" (D&C 21:5).

While serving as a missionary in the Eastern States, my senior companion and I entered a town in New Jersey and began a systematic program of door-to-door contacting. We had not worked in the area for many days before it became obvious that the local Protestant ministers had prepared their parishioners for our coming. At almost every door we would be greeted with, "Oh, you must be the Mormons. Here, we have something for you." They would then hand us an anti-Mormon tract. We collected literally hundreds of these pamphlets and stacked them in the corner of our apartment. Curiosity eventually got the best of us, and both of us decided to peruse some of the material. There were many things we read that were disturbing, but I remember most of all an issue regarding the LDS view of the Godhead that caused me extreme uneasiness. My companion was no less disturbed than I. Day after day we went about our task of knocking on doors, being rejected and rebuffed, and expanding our collection of anti-Mormon propaganda. When I had reached the point of spiritual discomfort where I couldn't stand the tension any longer, I said to my companion at lunch: "Elder Henderson, what if the Church isn't true?" I expected him to be startled by such a question. He was not. He responded: "I've been wondering the same thing." Now I *was* startled. He was my senior companion, my leader, my example. "What if the Baptist Church is right?" I asked. "What if the Catholics have had priesthood authority all along?" "I don't know what to say," he replied. It was a depressing time for both of us.

I can still remember how very intense and focused my prayers were during those difficult days. I pleaded with God to give me an answer, to give me a feeling, to give me something! I lifted my voice heavenward constantly—on my knees whenever I had occasion and in my heart all through the day. For over two weeks we struggled. I had concluded—though I had not expressed this to my companion—that unless some resolution to my soul-searching came soon, I would go home. I felt then that I just couldn't be a hypocrite, that I couldn't bear testimony of something I didn't know was true. (If I had only understood the principle that a testimony is strengthened through the bearing of it, I could have gone on.) The questions I had in regard to the Godhead were eating me alive. I was confused, ashamed, and terribly uncomfortable. One afternoon as we came home for lunch I sat in the easy chair in the small living room in the apartment. I propped my feet up, sat back, let out a sigh, and for some reason picked up a copy of the pamphlet, "Joseph Smith Tells His Own Story." I opened the brochure and began reading. I was not five lines into the Prophet's opening statement before I was absolutely wrapped in a feeling of warmth and comfort that I had never known, almost as though someone had covered me with a type of spiritual blanket. Though I heard no words, the feelings that came to me seemed to voice the following: "Of course this work is true. You know it is true. And now, as to your question, be patient. You'll understand soon enough." This was all I needed for the time being. It was inspiration. It was perspective. I shared my newfound faith with Elder Henderson, he felt a similar spirit of comfort, and we went about our task with more courage in our conviction. The difficult matter had been put on a shelf. The answer to my question, by the way, did come in time. Within a year I was blessed with a companion who thoroughly understood the issue and helped me to see an aspect of the gospel that to me had previously been a mystery.

I have no hesitation in acknowledging that I have placed many things on a shelf over the last thirty years. A number of those items have come down from the shelf as information and inspiration have brought light and understanding where darkness and uncertainty had been. Some matters will probably stay on the shelf until that glorious millennial day when the God of heaven makes known those things "which have passed, and hidden things which no man knew, things of the earth, by which it was made, and the purpose and the end thereof—things most precious, things that are above, and things that are beneath, things that are in the earth, and upon the earth, and in heaven" (D&C 101:32–34).

There is a final suggestion that we might consider in regard to finding answers to difficult questions. It is a bit more painful, requires a strict honesty on our part, a willingness to reflect and introspect. "Search your hearts," was Joseph Smith's challenge and invitation, "and see if you are like God. I have searched mine," he added, "and feel to repent of all my sins."[9] Some things are kept from us because we are not prepared, spiritually ready, to receive them. Some things we cannot comprehend because our souls are not attuned to the Infinite, because we are in sin. Sometimes our willful submission to sin points up our unbelief, and unbelief frequently leads to misunderstanding or lack of understanding (see Mosiah 26:1–3). There is an incident in the Book of Mormon that symbolizes our dilemma and at the same time prescribes a means of recovery. Nephi and Lehi, sons of Helaman, taught the gospel to the Lamanites with great power and persuasion. A multitude of people watched with much interest as Nephi and Lehi, held as prisoners up to this time, were "encircled about as if by fire." The earth shook, a cloud of darkness overshadowed the people, and "an awful solemn fear came upon them." A voice was heard: "Repent ye, repent ye, and seek no more to destroy my servants whom I have sent unto you to declare good tidings." This voice was heard three times. Aminadab, a Nephite by birth, sensed what needed to be done to dispel the darkness. Now note: "*You must repent,* and cry unto the voice, even until ye shall have faith in Christ . . . ; *and when ye shall do this, the cloud of darkness shall be removed from overshadowing you*" (Helaman 5:21–41; emphasis added). And so it is with each of us. As we call on the Lord in secret and solemn prayer, express to him our willingness to forsake our sins and follow his Son in truth and righteousness, and live in such a manner thereafter that we evidence the sincerity of our covenant, we will once again walk in the light; the film of facade, the dimming and damning influences of duplicity and double-mindedness, and the painful and poignant pull of pride will have been removed. It will be as if a cloud of spiritual darkness will have been blown away by the winds of faith and trust in our Redeemer. We then can begin to see things as they really are. We can be at peace.

Notes

From an address delivered at Brigham Young University Education Week and Know Your Religion series, 1989–91.

1. *Promised Messiah,* 515–16; emphasis added.
2. See *Gospel Doctrine,* 373.
3. Neal A. Maxwell, in Conference Report, October 1988, 40.
4. George Q. Cannon, *Gospel Truth,* comp. Jerreld L. Newquist, 2 vols. in 1 (Salt Lake City: Deseret Book Co., 1987), 493.
5. Bruce R. McConkie, *Doctrines of the Restoration,* ed. Mark L. McConkie (Salt Lake City: Bookcraft, 1989), 232.
6. *Gospel Doctrine,* 9.
7. John A. Widtsoe, *Evidences and Reconciliations,* arr. G. Homer Durham (Salt Lake City: Bookcraft, 1987), 16–17.
8. Ibid., 31–32.
9. *Teachings of the Prophet Joseph Smith,* 216.

PURSUING A SANE AND BALANCED COURSE

One of the signs of our spiritual maturity is steadiness, our capacity to navigate the strait and narrow path in a stable and fairly consistent manner, to work with zeal but patient maturity, to stay in the mainstream of the Church. God does not expect us to work ourselves into spiritual, emotional, or physical oblivion, nor does he desire that the members of the true church be truer than true. There is little virtue in excess, even in gospel excess. In fact, as members of the Church exceed the bounds of propriety and go beyond the established mark, they open themselves to deception and ultimately to destruction. Imbalance leads to instability. If Satan cannot cause us to lie or steal or smoke or be immoral, it just may be that he will cause our strength—our zeal for goodness and righteousness—to become our weakness. He will encourage excess, for surely any virtue, when taken to the extreme, becomes a vice.

EXCESSIVE ZEAL AND GOSPEL HOBBIES

A friend of mine shared the following experience. More than forty years ago he and his wife became acquainted with an older couple in their ward. This couple were about as devoted to the Church as people could be. The wife had been raised in the Church, while her husband had come in contact with the missionaries and been baptized while in the military. Like most of us, this couple had had their ups and downs in the faith, had struggled with a commandment here and there, but had managed to put much of the foolishness of youth behind them. In their eagerness to "make up" for all the times they may have disappointed the Lord, they determined upon a course to do everything they could to live the laws of the gospel with perfectness. They would leave no stone unturned, no *i* undotted. If the Lord through his Church asked for ten percent of their income as a tithing, they would pay fifteen percent. If Church members were asked to fast once per month, they would fast once per week. If most people studied the scriptures an hour per day, they would search and ponder and pray over holy writ for two hours. And so on and so on.

My friend mentioned one other aspect of this couple's zeal—their observance of the Word of Wisdom. They not only abstained from alcohol, tobacco, tea, coffee, and harmful drugs, they felt it was important to avoid white bread, as well as chocolate. They insisted that their children also follow such a course, which brought no end to frustration and contention in the home. What had in the beginning been merely a simple effort to demonstrate their willingness to keep all the commandments became, in time, an arduous task, a burdensome and uncomfortable labor. Resentment grew in the hearts of the children. Neighbors felt uncomfortable around them. In the area of Word of Wisdom observance, what had begun as a matter of health became a matter of "religious" fanaticism; the children (and the neighbors) were taught to avoid chocolate with at least as much enthusiasm as the Saints had been taught to avoid sexual immorality. Subtle suggestions to comply with this "higher law" were soon transformed into divine directives. Persons who chose to observe the commandments in a more traditional way were viewed as lacking in valiance. The couple withdrew into themselves and away from others who did not share their zeal. It was only a matter of time before Satan capitalized on their imbalance and led them to the brink of spiritual destruction. Only through the love, patience, and vigilance of priesthood leaders, loved ones, and friends were they delivered from their error and enabled to begin the slow and painful return to the true strait and narrow path.

We all know that we would be better off physically if we avoided chocolate, or at least if we ate it in moderation. But this is not the issue. In this case, and in too many others, persons who determine upon a course which will take them beyond the expected, above the required, inevitably begin to expect the same of others. It becomes a "religious" principle, one to which persons are proselyted. The overzealous tend to judge others by their own standard. I have known persons who are so completely committed to family history and temple work that they constantly badger and criticize others who are not in a position to do as much as they are. Obviously such work is a vital part of our ministry as Latter-day Saints; we neglect it at the peril of our eternal salvation. I also know, as Elder Dallin H. Oaks has pointed out, that there is a time and a season for all things, that a person's specific contributions to the kingdom are and must be private consecrations, between the individual and God. This is why the leaders of the Church have discouraged quotas and pre-established goals for temple work. "Our efforts to promote temple and family history work," Elder Oaks has noted, "should be such as to accomplish the work of the Lord, not to impose guilt on his children. Members of this Church have many individual circumstances—age, health, education, place of residence, family responsibilities, financial circumstances, accessibility to sources for individual or library research, and many others. If we encourage members in this work without taking these individual circumstances into account, we may do more to impose guilt than to further the work. . . . There are many different things our members can do to help in the redeeming of the dead, in temple and family history work. Some involve callings. All are expressions of devotion and discipleship. All present opportunities for sacrifice and service."[1]

One could take a simple observance such as fasting or praying and soon find, with just the slightest amount of extra zeal, that these wonderful principles, given for the blessing and benefit of mankind, can contribute to error. I spoke once to a temple president who described what had happened over the years in the temple in which he and his wife had served. He said that there was a particular room set aside as a prayer room, a place where patrons of the temple could retire for pondering and meditation, where they could go to seek inspiration or guidance on personal matters. For the longest time, he said, the room served a useful purpose: it reminded the patrons that temples were places of learning and revelation, holy edifices where we go to attend to sacred matters for the living as well as the dead. In time, however, the room became such a popular spot that long lines were often seen winding their way around the celestial room, where hosts of people stood awaiting their turn. "Brother Millet," the president observed, "sometimes people went into the room and we simply couldn't get them out. Some of them," he added, "would pray themselves into a frenzy, until we had to pack them out unconscious!"

What we are describing here is a phenomenon known as "gospel hobbies," the tendency to take a good thing and run it into the ground. We are speaking of the evils of excess, even in noble and worthwhile causes. Gospel hobbies lead to imbalance. To instability. To distraction. To misperception. They are dangerous and should be avoided as we would any other sin. President Joseph F. Smith said: "We frequently look about us and see people who incline to extremes, who are fanatical. We may be sure that this class of people do not understand the gospel. They have forgotten, if they ever knew, that it is very unwise to take a fragment of truth and treat it as if it were the whole thing."[2] To ride a gospel hobby is to participate in and perpetuate fanaticism. Harsh words, but true ones. On another occasion President Smith taught: "Brethren and sisters, don't have hobbies. Hobbies are dangerous in the Church of Christ. They are dangerous because they give undue prominence to certain principles or ideas to the detriment and dwarfing of others just as important, just as binding, just as saving as the favored doctrines or commandments.

"Hobbies give to those who encourage them a false aspect of the gospel of the Redeemer; they distort and place out of harmony its principles and teachings. The point of view is unnatural. Every principle and practice revealed from God is essential to man's salvation, and to place any one of them unduly in front, hiding and dimming all others is unwise and dangerous; it jeopardizes our salvation, for it darkens our minds and beclouds our understandings. . . .

"We have noticed this difficulty: that Saints with hobbies are prone to judge and condemn their brethren and sisters who are not so zealous in the one particular direction of their pet theory as they are. . . . There is another phase of this difficulty—the man with a hobby is apt to assume an 'I am holier than thou' position, to feel puffed up and conceited, and to look with distrust, if with no severer feeling, on his brethren and sisters who do not so perfectly live that one particular law."[3] In other words, an emphasis upon excellence in gospel living—as manifest in gospel hobbies—can result in pride, the father of all other sins. President Harold B. Lee explained that "at . . . times people who pride themselves on their strict observance of the rules and ordinances and ceremonies of the Church are led astray by false spirits, who exercise an influence so imitative of that which proceeds from a divine source that even these persons, who think they are the 'very elect,' find it difficult to discern the essential difference."[4] True excellence in gospel living—compliance with the established laws and ordinances in a quiet and patient manner—results in humility, in greater reliance upon God, and a broadening love and acceptance of one's fellow man. There is a principle here: what I am doing in the name of goodness ought to bring me closer to those I love and serve, ought to turn my heart toward people, rather than causing me to turn my nose up in judgmental scorn and rejection. The greatest man to walk the earth, the only fully perfect human being, looked with tenderness and compassion upon those whose ways and actions were less than perfect. He is the Exemplar.

Elder Bruce R. McConkie has similarly written: "It is . . . my experience that people who ride gospel hobbies, who try to qualify themselves as experts in some specialized field, who try to make the whole plan of salvation revolve around some field of particular interest to them—it is my experience that such persons are usually spiritually immature and spiritually unstable. This includes those who devote themselves—as though by divine appointment—to setting forth the signs of the times; or, to expounding about the Second Coming; or, to a faddist interpretation of the Word of Wisdom; or, to a twisted emphasis on temple work or any other doctrine or practice. The Jews of Jesus' day made themselves hobbyists and extremists in the field of Sabbath observance, and it colored and blackened their whole way of worship. *We would do well to have a sane, rounded, and balanced approach to the whole gospel and all of its doctrines.*"[5]

Not unrelated to excessive zeal and overmuch righteousness is the tendency by some to attempt to force spiritual things. What would we think of a father who said to his fourteen-year-old son: "Larry, if you really love me you will be tall. I have been short all my life. I love basketball and have always wanted to be a star forward on a successful team. But it's never worked out. If you love me, if you have any respect for me as your father, you will grow to be six foot eight." Strange, isn't it? In fact, such a request would be cruel and unkind, especially given the fact that Larry has little control over how tall he will be. He can eat the right foods, train and work out, and do everything within his power to be big and strong, but he cannot control how tall he will be. In a way, it's just the same with spiritual growth. We cannot program it. We cannot specify and delineate and produce. We cannot prepare formulae and plans that will result in specific spiritual phenomena. We cannot say with certitude that if a man or woman does X and Y and Z that a dream or vision will be forthcoming; that if he or she does A or B or C consistently, they will be able to prophesy or speak in tongues. We can prepare the soil, if you will; we can provide a setting for development. But that is all. We must exercise patience and trust in the Lord and his purposes.

I knew one man who claimed that he would be perfect by the age of thirty. He set out on a deliberate program, organized his goals according to a ten-year, five-year, one-year, monthly, weekly, and daily plan. He pushed and pulled and stretched and reached spiritually, as much so as any person I have known. But he was not perfect at thirty. You cannot force spiritual things. I am acquainted with a woman who announced to several of our friends that she would make her calling and election sure by the time she was fifty years old. She has been faithful in the Church. She has long since passed the age of fifty and is terribly discouraged because the goal of her existence, so far as she knows, has not been realized. You cannot force spiritual things. Endless prayers, lengthy scripture vigils, excessive fasting—all of these, though at first well-intended, may come to be more a curse than a blessing. Gospel growth must come slowly, steadily, gradually. Elder Boyd K. Packer has warned: "Such words as *compel, coerce, constrain, pressure, demand* do not describe our privileges with the Spirit. You can no more force the Spirit to respond than you can force a bean to sprout, or an egg to hatch before its time. You can create a climate to foster growth; you can nourish, and protect; but you cannot force or compel: You must await the growth. Do not be impatient to gain great spiritual knowledge. Let it grow, help it grow; but do not force it, or you will open the way to be misled."[6]

For years I wrestled with the meaning of the parable of the ten virgins, as contained in the twenty-fifth chapter of Matthew. The scene seemed so wrong, the message so counter to all that the Master taught. Why couldn't the wise virgins just break down and share their oil? If each one just contributed a little, I reasoned, perhaps everyone, or at least some of the "foolish" ones, could make it to the wedding to meet the Bridegroom. And then an experience taught me the answer to my query. While I was serving as a priesthood leader, a husband and wife came to see me. They were both distressed about the state of their marriage and family; things seemed to be coming apart in their lives. "How can I help?" I asked. "We need more spirituality in our home," the wife answered. I asked a few questions. "How often do you pray as a family?" They answered that their schedules precluded any kind of family prayer. "Have you been able to hold family home evening?" "Bill and I bowl on Monday nights," was the response. "Do you ever take occasion to read the scriptures as a family or as individuals?" The answer from the husband: "Reading hurts my eyes." "Well, then, how can I help you?" I asked. Again came the reply: "We want the Spirit in our lives."

It was as though they were saying to me, "Brother Millet, could you reach down into your heart and loan us five years of daily prayer, ten years of regular scripture study, and fifteen years of family spiritual activities?" I couldn't do it. I realized dramatically that there are simply some things that we cannot share. I also came to appreciate that, like the small oil lamps of the Middle East that require a careful and methodical and slow effort to fill, so in our own lives we need to build our reservoirs of faith and spiritual experience gradually and consistently. Consistent gospel growth—that was the answer. A colleague of mine drew my attention to these words of President Spencer W. Kimball: "The foolish asked the others to share their oil, but spiritual preparedness cannot be shared in an instant. . . . This was not selfishness or unkindness. The kind of oil that is needed to illuminate the way and light up the darkness is not shareable. . . . In our lives the oil of preparedness is accumulated drop by drop in righteous living."[7]

Finally, in our eagerness to prepare and do all that is required, we must be careful that our personal expectations, though rigorous, are realistic. Zion of old became a society of the pure in heart "in process of time" (Moses 7:21), and, with but few exceptions, members of the Church become Saints of the Most High in similar fashion. Except for a limited number of cases that are so miraculous they are written up in scripture, being born again is a process; we are born again gradually, from one level of spiritual grace to a higher. Almost always people are sanctified—made clean and holy and pure through the blood of Christ by the medium of the Holy Ghost—in gradual, line-upon-line fashion. Thus ultimate perfection and salvation are processes. One of the great challenges we face in our quest for spiritual maturity is to balance a type of divine discontent, a constant yearning for improvement and growth, with what Nephi called a "perfect brightness of hope" (2 Nephi 31:20), the assurance born of the Spirit that although we are not perfect—we have much sanctification and perfection ahead of us—we have a hope in Christ, a quiet confidence that in and through him we shall in time overcome all things and go on to eternal life.

MORMON GNOSTICISM

Alexander the Great's empire, as a political entity, did not long survive his death in 323 B.C. But the cultural empire he founded lasted for nearly one thousand years, until the rise of Islam and the Arab conquests in the seventh century A.D. Greek or Hellenistic influence was profound—upon the Roman empire, upon the world of Judaism, and, unfortunately, upon the early Christian Church. As Zenos had declared in prophetic vision, the grafting of branches from the "wild olive tree" (Gentile influence) resulted in a season of strength for the Church (see Jacob 5:17). But it was only a matter of time before the doctrines of the prophets and the ideas of the philosophers came in conflict; those with eyes to see were aware that attempts to merge the revelations of the temple of God with the doctrines of Plato would be abortive to the true Christian faith. Ecumenism would lead to shared impotence. And so it did.

In the first few centuries of the Christian era there grew up a movement which came to be known as Gnosticism. The word *gnosis* connoted knowledge, not a general kind of knowledge, but rather a special, saving knowledge. The Gnostics were a group who claimed to be possessors of the esoteric teachings of Jesus, the supposedly sacred and secret messages reserved only for those who sought to rise above the mundane and liberate themselves from the fetters of ignorance and a confining physical world. They decried and defied, for the most part, what they believed to be a stifling and restrictive priesthood hierarchy of the orthodox church. Salvation was an individual experience that came through spiritual illumination of the mysteries of godliness. Theirs was an emphasis upon the damning nature of this fallen world (and the physical body) and the supernal treasures to be had through transcending our condition here and ascending to pure spirit. Some of the Gnostics, known as Docetists (from a Greek word meaning "appears" or "seems"), went so far as to claim that Jesus did not really come to earth with a corporeal body, but—since the body was something to be shunned and overcome—it only appeared that he had a physical tabernacle. (It is interesting, therefore, to consider the significance of John's teachings in 1 John 4:1–3 and 2 John 1:7.) We have heard much over the years about the impact of Roman persecution on the early Christian Church, but in reality the death knell for Christianity came through hellenization—the mingling of Greek philosophy with the scriptures and teachings of the earliest Christian Church. There was lost in and through the perpetuation of this hybrid heresy the true knowledge of God, of man, and of the purpose of life. The great apostasy followed.

In the times of restitution we have not been without our own little Gnostic groups. There was Hiram Page, who sought to reveal things about Zion (see D&C 28); Mrs. Hubble, who claimed to be receiving divine direction for the Saints (see D&C 43); some who spoke of secret commissions and ordinations under the hands of Joseph Smith; and others today who make much of special callings or unusual insights. We have watched with much interest and pain as a surprising number of the Lord's people are lured away by voices that beckon for their attention. Some charismatic figures boldly declare that only those properly trained or with the right credentials can interpret scripture or lead the way. Some speak openly of visions, dreams, or revelations that entitle them to turn the Church in a direction different than its present course. Frequently we hear from some well-meaning Saints that we must reinstitute the united order or bring back this idea or that practice. Where is our safety? How can we know who to follow?

The prophets have been especially vocal in their warnings against such movements. As we begin to mature in our citizenship in the kingdom, we find ourselves less attracted to such things, less enamored by the strange, the sensational, or the exotic; rather, we become more prone to focus upon and delight in the fundamental principles and doctrines of the gospel, more prone to teach and act with simplicity, more prone to stress the things the Lord's servants stress. We take seriously the scriptural charge to say "none other things than that which the prophets and apostles have written, and that which is taught [us] by the Comforter through the prayer of faith" (D&C 52:9; see also verse 36). We begin to realize that there are no secret doctrines, no private ways of life, nothing that the General Authorities believe or practice that is not readily accessible to every member of the Church. Elder Boyd K. Packer spoke of the problem of claims to special ordination. "There have been too many names presented," he stated, "too many sustaining votes taken, too many ordinations and settings apart performed before too many witnesses; there have been too many records kept, too many certificates prepared, and too many pictures published in too many places for anyone to be deceived as to who holds proper authority. Claims of special revelation or secret authority from the Lord or from the Brethren are false on the face of them and really utter nonsense! The Lord never operated that way; these things were not done in a corner (see Acts 26:26); there is light on every official call and every authorized ordination, and it has always been that way."[8]

Safety and security in the midst of a babble of voices (even some voices from Latter-day Saints) are to be found in following the Brethren, in giving heed to the counsel and direction we receive from our leaders at the general conferences of the Church and in the official organs and publications of the Church. As members of the true church, we really ought to read and know and teach from the conference addresses as much as we do from the standard works. I know from personal experience of the remarkable spiritual presence that accompanies our teaching and our presentations as we cite or quote the Brethren. We thus evidence our respect and appreciation for the words of the living oracles. When we are loyal to this principle, we would never seek to run before our file leaders, to suggest that the Saints should do this or that when in fact those responsible for guiding the destiny of the Church and kingdom have not so spoken. President Joseph F. Smith observed that "no man possessing a correct understanding of the spirit of the gospel and of the authority and law of the Holy Priesthood will attempt for a moment to run before his file leader or to do anything that is not strictly in harmony with his wish and the authority that belongs to him. The moment a man in a subordinate position begins to usurp the authority of his leader, that moment he is out of his place, and proves by his conduct that he does not comprehend his duty, that he is not acting in the line of his calling, and is a dangerous character."[9]

A vital part of maturing in the faith is coming to acknowledge the position of those called to lead us, on both a general and local level. Few people would go astray, would find themselves in apostasy or in the center of controversy, if they simply sought and followed the counsel of their Church leaders. People are not necessarily called to positions of responsibility because they are the most qualified, the most talented, or the most gifted gospel scholars. Our challenge is to sustain— that is, give our full loyalty and support to—people who are often less than perfect, even people that we might feel to be less capable than ourselves. "Here is a lesson for all of us in this Church," President David O. McKay said. "Let us . . . recognize the local authority. The bishop may be a humble man. Some of you may think you are superior to him, and you may be, but he is given authority direct from our Father in heaven. You recognize it. Seek his advice, the advice of your stake president. If they cannot answer your difficulties or your problems, they will write to the General Authorities and get the advice needed. Recognition of authority is an important principle."[10]

Indeed, those who, through pride or an elevated sense of self-worth, feel to ignore or reject the counsel of bishops or stake presidents will lose the Spirit of the Lord and be left to themselves. It is a small thing to take counsel from a local leader, but it is vital to our eternal welfare. In fact, as the scriptures attest, it is by small means that great things are brought to pass (see 1 Nephi 16:29; Alma 37:6–7; D&C 64:33). "You can put it down in your little black book," Elder Boyd K. Packer taught, "that if you will not be loyal in the small things, you will not be loyal in the large things. If you will not respond to the so-called insignificant or menial tasks which need to be performed in the Church and Kingdom, there will be no opportunity for service in the so-called greater challenges. A man who says he will sustain the President of the Church or the General Authorities, but cannot sustain his own bishop, is deceiving himself. The man who will not sustain the bishop of his ward and the president of his stake will not sustain the President of the Church."[11] We must never forget that the organization of the Church—the officers and teachers and the manuals and other helps—have been provided "for the perfecting of the saints, for the work of the ministry, for the edifying of the body of Christ"—meaning, of course, the members of the Church. "Till we all come in the unity of the faith, and of the knowledge of the Son of God, unto a perfect [fully formed, mature] man, unto the measure of the stature of the fulness of Christ: *that we henceforth be no more children, tossed to and fro, and carried about with every wind of doctrine, and by the sleight of men, and cunning craftiness, whereby they lie in wait to deceive;* but speaking the truth in love, may *grow up into him in all things, which is the head, even Christ*" (Ephesians 4:11–15; emphasis added).

There are ways of knowing the truth, of discerning the veracity and fruitfulness of a doctrine or a point of view. Joseph Smith pointed out that nothing is a greater injury to the children of men than to be under the influence of a false spirit when we suppose we have the Spirit of God.[12] If someone comes to us claiming a special appointment, special knowledge which is not available to most members, special training and abilities which entitle him or her to interpret scripture or clarify doctrine beyond what has been given by the authorized servants of God, we might ask the following:

1. *Is the person claiming a divine communication or insight acting within the bounds of his or her respective assignment?* The Lord's house is a house of order, not of confusion (see D&C 132:8). Chaos would ensue rather quickly if every person could receive revelations for every other person in the Church, irrespective of stewardship. Joseph Smith the Prophet taught that it is contrary to the economy of God for people to receive revelation for those higher in authority than themselves.[13] He also explained that it is the "privilege of any officer in this Church to obtain revelations so far as [it] relates to his particular calling and duty in the Church."[14] Through the generations people have repeatedly insisted that they have received direction for the Church regarding its financial status, its placement of temples, its meetings or schedule, and its doctrinal positions on this or that topic. No matter the genuineness or sincerity of the supposed recipients, the directives are not of God. The Lord simply does not work that way. There is order. There are proper channels.

2. *Is the recipient of the communication worthy to receive the same?* Though we may not always be in a position to judge another's worthiness, we are generally pretty good judges of our own. The revelations indicate that the works of God are brought to pass through those who are clean, who have been purified from the sins of the world (see 3 Nephi 8:1; D&C 50:28). If I have received what I believe to be a revelation from God, then it is perfectly appropriate for me to ask (and it would be well if I asked with sincerity and humility) whether I was in spiritual condition to receive such a matter from God. While I was serving as a priesthood leader several years ago, a young man came to visit with me on numerous occasions about what he believed to be revelations from God. He told me of visions and angelic appearances, of specific messages about his life. Such would be well within the bounds of propriety, except for one thing: the young man was also guilty of gross violations of the law of chastity, so much so that his membership was at stake. Without attempting to be cruel or unkind, allowing that no one of us is perfect, we must attend to the principle that God will generally not work through polluted channels. In fact, President Harold B. Lee pointed out: "We get our answers from the source of the power we list to obey. If we're following the ways of the devil, we'll get

answers from the devil. If we're keeping the commandments of God, we'll get our answers from God."[15]

3. *Is the communication in harmony with the teachings in the standard works and those of the living oracles?* When people claim to have received word that they should join a polygamous cult or participate in a demonic practice or be disloyal or disobedient to the government, one wonders how they can justify their position. When others indicate that they have been directed by the Lord to lie or cheat or steal or be immoral, one wonders how such actions can square with the teachings of the Church. Often individuals claim that their case is an exception to the rule. We would do well as a people to stay within the rules and avoid the exceptions, especially when such exceptions stand in violation of the law and order of the kingdom of God. Those still convinced that what they are commanded to do is of God would then do well to counsel with their priesthood leaders and then follow that counsel emphatically. On the other hand, there are certain groups of people who contend that the Church should be doing this or that, so as to be in harmony with such and such a scripture. We only need remind ourselves that ours is a living constitution, a living Church (see D&C 1:30), and that the principle on which the government of heaven is conducted is, as Joseph Smith testified, "revelation adapted to the circumstances in which the children of the kingdom are placed."[16] Wise counsel for the Saints was given by Elder Bruce R. McConkie when he said: "The proper course for all of us is to stay in the mainstream of the Church. This is the Lord's Church, and it is led by the spirit of inspiration, and *the practice of the Church constitutes the interpretation of the scripture.*"[17]

4. *Does the communication edify or instruct? Is it consistent with the dignity that should attend something which comes from the Almighty?* While I was teaching seminary many years ago, I spoke often to the students of the need to remain open to the Spirit and prepared to receive its quiet promptings. After class one day a young lady asked if she could visit with me. She explained that on the previous night she had had a wonderful experience that she wanted to share. Not knowing the nature of the experience, I invited her to proceed. She mentioned that her parents had left her alone at home for the evening while they had gone to dinner. While sitting in the living room listening to music, she indicated that the Spirit came upon her and said: "Get up. Run into your room." She did so. This voice then said: "Get under the bed," which she did. It then said: "Get out from under the bed and run outside into the back yard," which she did. Then: "Hide behind the wood pile." She explained that she stayed behind the wood pile for a while, until she was ordered around, back and forth, from one place to another in her family's rather large back

yard. This lasted for about half an hour. The young woman turned to me and with much emotion said: "Isn't it wonderful how the Spirit can work with us?" I smiled and nodded. I am in no position to judge whether her experience was genuine or not; perhaps there was some reason why the Lord would have a fifteen-year-old rushing about at 8:00 P.M. at night in the back yard. But I doubt it. I rather suppose that she was responding to whatever thought came into her mind that evening. The Prophet taught that God's revelations communicate something of worth to us. He also pointed out that there is a certain dignity and decorum that are associated with divine communications.[18]

5. *Does the communication build our faith and strengthen our commitment?* There is a litmus test that can be applied, a vital criterion which must be met if a supposed revelation is from God. We ask such questions as the following: Does this communication build my faith in Joseph Smith and the Restoration? Do I feel more motivated to serve faithfully in the Church and kingdom? Do I have confidence in the Lord's anointed servants today and in the destiny of the Church? God does not and will not work against himself; he will not confuse his people by having them believe or do things that would in any way weaken their hold on the iron rod. Those who suggest that the present Church is not progressive enough, that it needs to move faster toward this or that social or political or moral end, act outside the bounds of propriety. They are walking on shaky ground. As Joseph Smith stated: "That man who rises up to condemn others, finding fault with the Church, saying that they are out of the way, while he himself is righteous, then know assuredly, that that man is on the high road to apostasy; and if he does not repent, will apostatize, as God lives."[19]

PRINCIPLES THAT PRESERVE

The scriptures set forth certain principles which, if we are sensitive to their implications, will keep us on course and thus assist us in our quest for spiritual maturity. In his response to Satan's temptation to use divine powers for personal gain, the Savior answered: "It is written, Man shall not live by bread alone, but by every word that proceedeth out of the mouth of God" (Matthew 4:4; compare D&C 84:44). *Every* word. Not every other word, not those words that are most acceptable and pleasing, not those words that support my own peculiar views. Every word. Members of the Church would seldom become embroiled in doctrinal disputes, controversial dialogues, or gospel hobbies if they truly sought to live by every word that has come from the Lord, the scriptures, and the servants of God.

To live by every word of God also implies the need to read and study widely, to be seeking for at least as much breadth in our gospel scholarship as we have depth, to seek to have the big picture. It has been wisely said that the greatest commentary on the scriptures is the scriptures themselves.

In preaching to his American Hebrews, the resurrected Lord delivered the doctrine of Christ, the need for all men and women to have faith, repent, be reborn, and to endure faithfully to the end. He then declared: "Verily, verily, I say unto you, that this is my doctrine, and whoso buildeth upon this buildeth upon my rock, and the gates of hell shall not prevail against them. And *whoso shall declare more or less than this, and establish it for my doctrine, the same cometh of evil, and is not built upon my rock; but he buildeth upon a sandy foundation,* and the gates of hell stand open to receive such when the floods come and the winds beat upon them" (3 Nephi 11:39–40; emphasis added). In a modern revelation, the Lord spoke of bringing forth the Book of Mormon, another testament of Jesus Christ, in order that he might establish his gospel to put down contention and disputation. "Behold, this is my doctrine—whosoever repenteth and cometh unto me, the same is my church. *Whosoever declareth more or less than this, the same is not of me, but is against me;* therefore he is not of my church" (D&C 10:67–68; emphasis added). We need to live the gospel in such a way that we seek neither to add to nor take away from that which comes by and through the appointed channels of revelation for the Church.

This is not unrelated to the indictment sounded by Jacob against the ancient Jews. "The Jews were a stiffnecked people," he stated; "and *they despised the words of plainness,* and killed the prophets, and *sought for things that they could not understand.* Wherefore, because of their blindness, which *blindness came by looking beyond the mark,* they must needs fall; for God hath taken away his plainness from them, and delivered unto them many things which they cannot understand, because they desired it. And because they desired it God hath done it, that they may stumble" (Jacob 4:14; emphasis added). What a fascinating situation! A people despised, or perhaps spurned or little appreciated, the words of plainness. They sought things that they could not understand, perhaps meaning that they pushed themselves well beyond what had been revealed and thus what men and women could appropriately grasp. They became blind by "looking beyond the mark." That is, they missed the point! They missed the main message! In the case of the Jews, they looked beyond the mark when Christ was the mark. They focused on the minutiae of the commentary on the Law, when Christ was the message of the Law. They confused means with ends, tokens with covenants, ritual with religion.

Elder Dean L. Larsen offered the following insights into this unusual scriptural passage: "Jacob speaks of people who placed themselves in serious jeopardy in spiritual things because they were unwilling to accept simple, basic principles of truth. They entertained and intrigued themselves with 'things that they could not understand' (Jacob 4:14). They were apparently afflicted with a pseudosophistication and a snobbishness that gave them a false sense of superiority over those who came among them with the Lord's words of plainness. They went beyond the mark of wisdom and prudence, and obviously failed to stay within the circle of fundamental gospel truths, which provide a basis for faith. They must have reveled in speculative and theoretical matters that obscured for them the fundamental spiritual truths."[20] We begin the process of spiritual maturity as we come to treasure up the word of the Lord, a sure means of avoiding deception (see Joseph Smith–Matthew 1:37); as we find satisfaction and great delight in poring over and discussing the fundamental doctrines of the gospel; and as we wait upon the Lord to make us into new creatures and to reveal his purposes, all in his own time, and in his own way, and according to his own will (see D&C 88:67–68).

In summary, it may be well to state again that this is the Lord's church; he is at the helm. Revelation for the guidance of the Church as a whole will come through the ministry of those called as prophets, seers, and revelators (see D&C 21:4–6; 28:2; 43:3–6; 90:3–5). If it were the church of a man, then perhaps we might be justified in fretting and stewing over the status or directions of the Church. But it is in good hands. Though individuals may lose the Spirit and fall away, there will never again be an apostasy of the Church. In 1905 the First Presidency (Presidents Joseph F. Smith, John R. Winder, and Anthon H. Lund) issued a statement entitled "One Mighty and Strong." Let me conclude things in this chapter by quoting a portion of the final two paragraphs of this important document:

"In conclusion, we would say that the Latter-day Saints by this time, should be so well settled in the conviction that God has established his Church in the earth for the last time, to remain, and no more to be thrown down, or destroyed; and that God's house is a house of order, of law, of regularity, that erratic disturbers of that order of men of restless temperament, who, through ignorance and egotism become vain babblers, yet make great pretensions to prophetic powers and other spiritual graces and gifts, ought not to have any influence with them, nor ought the Saints to be disturbed in their spirit by such characters and their theories. The Church of Christ is with the Saints. It has committed to it the law of God for its own government and perpetuation. It possesses every means for the correction of every wrong or abuse or error which may from time to time arise, and that without anarchy, or even revolution; it can do it by processes of evolution—by development, by an increase of knowledge, wisdom, patience and charity.

"The presiding quorums of the Church will always be composed of such men, they will be chosen in such manner, that the Saints can be assured that solid wisdom, righteousness, and conscientious adherence to duty, will characterize the policy of those who are entrusted with the administration of the affairs of the Church."[21]

Notes

From an address delivered at Brigham Young University Education Week and Know Your Religion series, 1989–91.

1. Dallin H. Oaks, "Family History: In Wisdom and Order," *Ensign,* June 1989, 6–7.
2. *Gospel Doctrine,* 122.
3. Ibid., 116–17.
4. Harold B. Lee, "To the Defenders of the Faith," *Improvement Era,* June 1970, 63–64.
5. Bruce R. McConkie, *Doctrines of the Restoration,* ed. Mark L. McConkie (Salt Lake City: Bookcraft, 1989), 232; emphasis added.
6. Boyd K. Packer, *"That All May Be Edified"* (Salt Lake City: Bookcraft, 1982), 338.
7. Spencer W. Kimball, *Faith Precedes the Miracle* (Salt Lake City: Deseret Book Co., 1974), 255–56.
8. Boyd K. Packer, in Conference Report, April 1985, 43.
9. *Gospel Doctrine,* 185.
10. David O. McKay, in Conference Report, October 1965, 105.
11. Boyd K. Packer, *Follow the Brethren,* 1965 BYU Speeches (Provo, Utah: Brigham Young University Publications, 1965), 4–5.
12. See *Teachings of the Prophet Joseph Smith,* 205.
13. See ibid., 21.
14. Ibid., 111.
15. Harold B. Lee, *Stand Ye in Holy Places* (Salt Lake City: Deseret Book Co., 1974), 138.
16. *Teachings of the Prophet Joseph Smith,* 256.
17. McConkie, *Doctrines of the Restoration,* 66; emphasis added.
18. See *Teachings of the Prophet Joseph Smith,* 203–4, 209.
19. Ibid., 156–57.
20. Dean L. Larsen, in Conference Report, October 1987, 12.
21. *Messages of the First Presidency,* 4:120.

THE POWER OF
PURE TESTIMONY

We are engaged in the work of the Lord. This is his church. It administers his gospel and teaches his doctrine. It bears his priesthood and performs his ordinances. These are facts. They are true. A knowledge of such things, an inner certitude, we call a testimony. We cannot long progress in the kingdom without a witness of this work, without a testimony. It is a testimony of the Savior, of his gospel, and of the Restoration, which must be at the foundation of all we do. In fact, a knowledge of such things motivates us and impels us to faithfulness in the face of opposition; such an assurance helps us know why we do what we do.

A testimony is fundamental to our spiritual maturity. It is absolutely necessary to our spiritual preservation in a world whose discordant voices beckon us to loosen our hold on the rod of iron. President Heber C. Kimball issued a prophetic warning that should lead to sober thinking among Latter-day Saints. "We think we are secure here in the chambers of the everlasting hills," he said, "where we can close those few doors of the canyons against mobs and persecutors, the wicked and the vile, who have always beset us with violence and robbery, but I want to say to you, my brethren, the time is coming when we will be mixed up in these now peaceful valleys to that extent that it will be difficult to tell the face of a Saint from the face of an enemy to the people of God. Then, brethren, look out for the great sieve, for there will be a great sifting time, and many will fall; for I say unto you there is a test, a Test, a TEST coming, and who will be able to stand? . . .

"Let me say to you, that many of you will see the time when you will have all the trouble, trial and persecution that you can stand, and plenty of opportunities to show that you are true to God and his work. *This Church has before it many close places through which it will have to pass before the work of God is crowned with victory. To meet the difficulties that are coming, it will be necessary for you to have a knowledge of the truth of this work for yourselves. The difficulties will be of such a character that the man or woman who does not possess this personal knowledge or witness will fall. If you have not got the testimony, live right and call upon the Lord and cease not till you obtain it.* If you do not you will not stand.

"Remember these sayings, for many of you will live to see them fulfilled. *The time will come when no man nor woman will be able to endure on borrowed light. Each will have to be guided by the light within himself. If you do not have it, how can you stand?*"[1]

ACQUIRING THE WITNESS

To *bear* a testimony has at least two meanings. It means, first of all, to *possess* one, in the sense that a person bears his armor or his priesthood. Secondly, to bear a testimony is to *express* or convey or declare it to others. We shall speak of the first sense of bearing a testimony in this section and discuss the manner in which a testimony is proclaimed in a subsequent section. It is true that it generally takes months and years and decades to develop the kind of spiritual conviction that proves to be the anchor to life and the safeguard against the trials spoken of above by President Heber C. Kimball. On the other hand, there are some things we have always known. Many things that we come to know here we knew clearly in our premortal existence before we came here. Thus the recognition of truth, the awareness of a verity, the sensitivity to significant doctrines—such things are, as President Joseph F. Smith taught so powerfully, "but the awakening of the memories of the spirit. Can we know anything here that we did not know before we came? Are not the means of knowledge in the first estate equal to those of this?"[2] As my colleague, Joseph F. McConkie, and I have written elsewhere, "We traditionally describe those who are born outside the Church and who subsequently join it as converts, implying that they turned from another belief to embrace the testimony of the Restoration. In fact, this is rarely the case. In most instances, those who have joined the Church tell us: 'There was no conversion. Everything the missionaries told me I already believed!' That which we call conversion may more aptly be described as an awakening, a distant memory, or an echo from the past. 'People ask me why I left my old church,' the so-called convert said. 'I tell them it was not a matter of my leaving my old church, but rather a matter of my coming home.'"[3]

Though a bit tangential, let me relate an experience that teaches that all people—member and nonmember alike—are entitled to the light of Christ, or stated another way, the personal testimony of right and wrong. Many years ago I was asked to work with a woman who was reported to be having some serious psychological problems. I learned in my first visit with her that she had been raised in the Jewish faith, that for many years she was serious about her beliefs, a devoted Reformed Jew. It took about two or three visits to get to the meat of the matter. She admitted to having been unfaithful to her husband and essentially was insisting that I assist her to feel more comfortable with her infidelity. I indicated that I could not. She said: "Why not? I'm paying you to help me!" I answered that I simply could not help anyone go against their sense of values, their inner sense of right and wrong. She responded: "Oh no, you don't understand. I'm no longer a religious person. I'm no longer a practicing Jew. I don't believe anymore." I responded that this matter had nothing to do with religion. It had everything to do with being true to ourselves. She looked puzzled.

"You have been untrue to yourself," I said. "You know it, and there's no way to escape from that reality." "I tell you that I'm not religious anymore," she responded. "I don't have all those religious hang-ups I once had." I spent the next hour or so trying to help her get in touch with her own feelings, to hearken to the light within her. Finally I asked: "What are you feeling deep down, in your heart of hearts?" She paused a very long time and then replied: "I know I have done wrong. It's wrong, wrong, wrong! Help me do what's right." She knew, not just because she had been taught by men and women in this life, but because she had been taught by the light of Christ within. I came away from that experience with an appreciation for the fact that all persons are entitled to know things, sweet and sacred things, and that they mature in spiritual things as they give heed to the light they already have.

Spiritual things are known. They are *known.* We need not apologize for things we know by the power of the Spirit, for they are as real as (if not more so than) the things we perceive in the physical world by means of the five senses. When I served as a bishop several years ago there was a man who worked as my executive secretary and who I came to know and love over time. He and his family had joined the Church just a few years earlier. They were great people. My friend Larry would stand in every testimony meeting and, without fail, say something like this: "I want to bear testimony that I . . . (long pause) . . . *believe* that this is the true Church. I want to say also that I really do . . . (pause) . . . *believe* that Joseph Smith is a prophet and that the Church is divinely led today." I listened month after month to his testimony. It was a sweet and touching expression. When I knew him quite well, and when the moment was right, I asked: "Larry, when you bear your testimony, why don't you just break down and say 'I *know*'?" He turned to me and gave me a strange look. "I couldn't do that," he responded, "because I haven't seen God. I wasn't personally present in the Sacred Grove in 1820. I'm not in the council meetings of the leadership of the Church today. I just couldn't say I *know*, because that wouldn't be true. For now I have to say that I *believe*."

We had a long and very productive chat. I showed him from scripture that spiritual things are known, not because they are seen with the physical eyes or felt with our hands or even heard with our ears, but because they are seen and felt and experienced with eyes and ears of faith. Indeed, believing is seeing. As Elder Boyd K. Packer has explained: "These delicate, refined spiritual communications are not seen with our eyes nor heard with our ears. And even though it is described as a voice, it is a voice that one feels more than one hears."[4] I explained to Larry that spiritual realities make their way into our consciousness and our memory and our view of life in quiet but certain ways. They may be spiritual, but they are real. "O then, is not this real?" Alma asked concerning the beginnings of testimony. "I say unto you, Yea, because it is light; and whatsoever is light, is good, because it is discernible" (Alma 32:35). Alma had seen angels. He had seen the Lord. But his testimony had come in softer, quieter, less dramatic ways (just as does ours). "Do ye not suppose that *I know* of these things [of Christ and his gospel] myself [that is, above and beyond what his prophetic predecessors had affirmed]? . . . Behold, I say unto you they are made known unto me by the Holy Spirit of God. Behold, I have fasted and prayed many days that I might *know* these things of myself. And now *I do know* of myself that they are true; for *the Lord God hath made them manifest unto me by his Holy Spirit;* and this is the spirit of revelation which is in me" (Alma 5:45–46; emphasis added). "*I know with a witness that is more powerful than sight,*" President Harold B. Lee said to Brigham Young University students just three months before his death. "Sometime, if the Spirit prompts me, I may feel free to tell you more, but may I say to you that *I know as though I had seen,* that He lives, that He is real, that God the Father and his Son are living realities, personalities with bodies, parts, and passions—glorified beings. If you believe that, then you are safe. If you don't believe it, then struggle for that witness, and all will be well with you."[5]

Paul taught that faith comes through hearing the word of God (see Romans 10:17). Joseph Smith added: "Faith comes by hearing the word of God, through the testimony of the servants of God; that testimony is always attended by the Spirit of prophecy and revelation."[6] We begin with the light of Christ within us, which quietly points out right from wrong and which assists us in discerning the ways of the Lord from the ways of the world. Our faith and our testimony then begin to grow as we hear the gospel declared by one who knows, by one who has a personal witness, by one who has had experience with the Spirit of the Lord. We often begin our spiritual development by relying on and trusting in the witness of others. On more than one occasion, I heard Elder Harold B. Lee say to groups of missionaries: "Elders and sisters, if the time comes when you are shaken, when you wonder or doubt, when you don't know for sure, then lean on my witness, because I do know." I leaned on the testimony of my mother and father. When I was in the depths of despair and shaken to the core over anti-Mormon material one of the things to which I held tenaciously was the witness of my parents. More specifically, I knew that my dad knew. He was a good man. I knew that. He wouldn't believe in something or commit himself to it if it were false. I knew that. And so I leaned on his faith until I acquired a witness of my own. In fact, the revelations affirm that "to some it is given by the Holy Ghost to know that Jesus Christ is the Son of God, and that he was crucified for the sins of the world. To others it is given to believe on their words, that they also might have eternal life if they continue faithful" (D&C 46:13–14). Like Alma, those who pray and search and read and study and inquire—those who follow the course of gaining a witness—come in time to know, to know as surely as they know they live. It is the promise of God to all. He is no respecter of persons. He knows and he wants all his children to know as he knows. Truly, as Moroni explained, it is by the power of the Holy Ghost that we may *know* the truth of all things (see Moroni 10:5).

DECLARING THE WITNESS

One of the struggles that my companion and I had while we were wrestling with our testimonies was our inability, as we supposed, to bear testimony of something about which we were not certain. Is such proper? Is it not hypocritical? Elder Packer addressed himself to this question. "It is not unusual," he observed, "to have a missionary say, 'How can I bear testimony until I get one? How can I testify that God lives, that Jesus is the Christ and that the gospel is true? If I do not have such a testimony would that not be dishonest?'

"Oh, if I could teach you this one principle! A testimony is to be *found* in the *bearing* of it. Somewhere in your quest for spiritual knowledge, there is that 'leap of faith,' as the philosophers call it. It is the moment when you have gone to the edge of the light and step into the darkness to discover that the way is lighted ahead for just a footstep or two. The spirit of man, as the scripture says, indeed is the candle of the Lord.

"It is one thing to receive a witness from what you have read or what another has said; and that is a necessary beginning. It is quite another to have the Spirit confirm to you in your bosom that what *you* have testified is true. Can you not see that it will be supplied as you share it? As you give that which you have, there is a replacement, with increase!"[7]

I have been interested over the years in the manner in which testimonies are borne. Let me share an experience which, though painful, started me on a course that greatly aided my comprehension of what it means to bear witness of the truth. While serving in a stake presidency a number of years ago, I had the responsibility for the youth programs of the stake. One year I worked closely with the stake Young Men and Young Women presidents in the planning of a youth conference. Because the young people of the stake were so spread out, because they saw one another so seldom, we wanted this two-day conference to be just right, to combine the elements of sociality and spirituality in such a way as to really make a difference in the lives of the youth. All of the events of Saturday morning and evening (including a dance) had gone so well. And now we wanted more than anything for the testimony meeting, held early Sunday morning, to be the highlight of the conference. Special musical numbers were arranged. The setting was prepared. I asked that the Young Men and Young Women presidents stand at the first of the meeting and bear brief, heartfelt testimonies, to set the tone of the meeting and to model what we hoped would come to pass.

There was a brief pause after the Young Women president had expressed her testimony. Then the youth became involved. A young lady from one of the distant branches spoke: "I want to stand and bear my testimony. I want to tell Laura (a young woman to whom she pointed) how much I love her. I want her to know how much she means to me." The speaker was very emotional, but managed to spend about ten minutes telling stories about herself and Laura. She closed. At that point Laura stood up, came to the pulpit, and said: "I want to bear my testimony. I want to tell Stephanie how much I love her." She cried and cried, told stories about how the two of them had romped and played as little children, and about how close they were. Before she sat down she added: "Oh, I also need to tell Bill what a difference he has made in my life. He's been a wonderful friend to Stephanie and me. We love you, Bill." As we might guess, Stephanie was followed by Bill, who was followed by the person about whom Bill spoke, and so on for about forty-five minutes. This approach to things was broken suddenly by one young lady striding up to the stand and with much confidence saying: "I've been thinking about this meeting for some time, wondering what I should speak about, and so I went to my mom and asked her what I should say. My mother suggested that I tell you what her Catholic priest taught her: 'Every time we sin, we drive the crown of thorns deeper into the skull of Jesus.'" She then encouraged us as a congregation to avoid sin. At this point the stake president, who sat two chairs from me, let out with a quiet groan that indicated his disappointment with the meeting. But frankly, things had been going fine when I consider where they would head for the next little while! A young man from one of the local wards came up to the pulpit carrying a folder. He opened the folder, took out several legal-size sheets of paper, and began: "My talk today is on the sacrament." This person then delivered an eleven-minute sermon on the importance of the sacrament of the Lord's Supper, on the need for being worthy to take the bread and water each Sunday morning, and on the meaning of taking upon us the name of Christ. It was really quite good.

At about the midpoint of the meeting, a young man came to the stand and took charge for about twenty-five minutes: he began by telling a few jokes, told a number of sad stories, and then (having elicited both laughter and tears) said: "Hey, I'm pretty good at this. I think I'll be an entertainer!" The congregation roared. At least most of them did. The stake president groaned again. (He slipped me a note that said simply: "This meeting is a disaster." I nodded to him my agreement of his assessment.) I sweated. The Young Women president wept. The Young Men president sighed. I wasn't sure what to do, whether to close the meeting, cast out the strange spirit there, or simply get up and explain what was wrong. The stake leaders, all of us, knew that this was a sensitive time, that feelings were delicate, that persons are easily hurt or their efforts easily stifled. So we did nothing. We sat. And we sat. Painfully, we sat.

After about two hours, a young man came to the pulpit, a boy we didn't recognize. He was extremely nervous, so much so that he dared not even lift his head to look at the congregation. He stammered: "My friends or, uh . . . brothers and sisters, I . . . uh . . . would like to . . . uh . . . share some of my feelings. I am not a Mormon, not a member of your church, and so I don't really know how to bear testimony." The stake president, one of the most Christlike men I have ever known, whispered gently: "He should relax. He's in great company!" The young man continued: "The missionaries have been teaching my family about your church for a couple of weeks now. I just wanted to let you know that I really believe in God. I feel a lot of love for Jesus, who died for me. Something inside me tells me that what the missionaries have said about Joseph Smith and the Book of Mormon and the Mormon Church is true. I'm happy that in a short time we will be baptized. Thank you for being so nice to me." Then he sat down. Here was a testimony, a real testimony, and it came from the person in the group who was not a member of the Church!

The meeting did finally come to an end. Mercifully, after almost three hours, it came to an end. I sat in despair. So did the other stake leaders. The stake president looked at me, shook his head in disbelief, and sighed. He then left. I turned to the stake youth leaders and said: "I'm too depressed to talk about it now. Could we meet this Wednesday evening in my office?" They agreed that we would face the music then. It was clear from the looks on their faces on Wednesday that they had spent a great deal of time in ponderous and solemn thought. So had I. Interestingly enough, each of us had had occasion on Sunday to return to our own wards and participate in the monthly fast and testimony meeting. And so I asked: "Is this a youth problem?" The Young Women president quickly spoke up: "No, it's a Church problem." She continued: "The kids do basically the same things the adults do. Perhaps the grown-ups are a bit more dignified and formal about it." The Young Men president nodded in agreement. I indicated that those were my feelings as well. We sat for a long time that night, asking questions like: What's supposed to happen in a testimony meeting? What is appropriate and what is inappropriate? Are there some expressions that are perfectly right and good in one setting but not quite right for a testimony meeting? Why was the spirit of the youth meeting so strange? Why did so many of the youth feel it was inspirational? Are we the ones who are out of it, insensitive to what we ought to feel? And so on. It was a sober occasion for the three of us, a vexation of the soul, painful searching after truth. We felt the need thereafter to express our concerns to the stake president and to suggest that a message be prepared and delivered by him (or whomever he recommended) on the matter of acquiring and bearing testimony, a message for the whole stake member- ship. As a stake presidency we first instructed the bishops and high council, turning to the scriptures and the words of living apostles and prophets for our pattern. We stressed the need for being delicate and sensitive, for never indicating that there was one "approved" way of bearing witness, a "proper" approach to sharing one's testimony. Rather, we strove to speak in terms of correct principles. I think some good came from the whole thing.

Seldom in my life have I spent as much time in serious reflection on a matter as I did in the weeks and months that followed that youth testimony meeting. Seldom in my life have I pondered and searched to understand the meaning and purpose of a meeting. I thought back of a thousand testimony meetings I had attended, and of the unusual things that had taken place there. I thought of my Sunday School teacher when I was twelve, a lovely young woman who loved the Lord and lived his gospel. It showed. I distinctly remember that every month in fast and testimony meeting she would stand up and say: "I'd like to read a message from the *Improvement Era.*" She would then read an article to the congregation. I thought it was what she was supposed to do, perhaps her Church assignment or something! She did that month after month, year after year. I thought back of a middle-aged woman standing up in testimony meeting and, with fire in her eyes and voice, saying to all of us: "You hypocrites! You phonies! You claim to be Christians. That's a joke!" She went on to tear apart the ward for not being more helpful in fellowshipping her non-LDS husband. I reflected on a man standing up in testimony meeting and startling us with the following: "As many of you know, I teach the fourteen-year-olds in Sunday School. I wasn't able to finish my lesson in time today, and so I'd like to do that now, if it's okay with the rest of you." He then took about fifteen minutes to complete his Sunday School lesson.

A few years ago in one of my Book of Mormon classes at Brigham Young University, after I had finished a discussion of Alma 4:19 and of the matter of bearing pure testimony, a student spoke to me after class. He said: "Brother Millet, I wanted so badly to bear my testimony in yesterday's fast meeting in my BYU ward, but I knew that I didn't have anything original to say. I didn't have a special message to deliver." This experience highlights a problem we sometimes see in the Church: the assumption that one has to deliver a message, preach a sermon, or make some original contribution to the meeting. The Church's general handbook of instructions simply indicates that members of the Church are to be invited to bear brief, heartfelt testimonies and, where appropriate, share faith-promoting experiences. There really is no need for the members of the Church to worry one tenth of a second about coming up with something to say, about leaving the congregation with a lasting message, about giving a talk. I frequently ask returned missionaries the following questions: "Did you ever have any inspirational testimony meetings on your mission?" They inevitably respond: "Oh, yes. We had some great ones!" I continue: "I'll bet they were spiritual feasts because every elder or sister said something different. Right?" "Not usually," they answer. "I'll bet they were unusual spiritual experiences because each missionary came with a prepared sermon, delivered it effectively, and set the other missionaries back on their heels with the power of their oratory. Right?" "Not really," they respond. "Well then, what did the missionaries say as part of their expressions?" After a few moments' reflection, the returned missionary relates that most of the elders and sisters said about the same thing—they bore testimony of God, of Jesus as the Christ, of Joseph Smith and the Book of Mormon, and of the guiding hand of the Lord in the Church today. Very little original stuff. But powerful. There's a lesson there.

As I understand it, the purpose of a testimony meeting is for the bearing of personal testimony. Expressions of gratitude and love, so much a part of the lives of followers of the Christ, should take a backseat to the bearing of testimonies if in fact the meeting has been set aside for the bearing of testimonies. Letting others know how thankful we are for our blessings, as well as how much we love the Lord and one another—these expressions can and should accompany our testimony, but we are asked primarily to stand and bear witness of what we know to be true. President Spencer W. Kimball counseled a group of young people gathered in a testimony meeting: "*Do not exhort each other; that is not a testimony. Do not tell others how to live. Just tell how you feel inside. That is the testimony. The moment you begin preaching to others, your testimony ended. Just tell us how you feel,* what your mind and heart and every fiber of your body tells you."[8] On another occasion, President Kimball said to a similar group: "Now, you are going to give your testimonies this afternoon. I hope that you'll just open your hearts and let us look inside . . . will you? Just open them up wide and turn on the lights and let us see your hearts, . . . how you feel. *A testimony is not an exhortation; a testimony is not a sermon; none of you are here to exhort the rest. You are here to bear your own witness.* It is amazing what you can say in thirty seconds by way of testimony, or in sixty seconds, or one hundred and twenty, or two hundred and forty, or whatever time you are given, if you confine yourselves to testimony. We'd like to know how you feel."[9]

I've thought back many times of the amount of emotion that was evident in the youth testimony meeting. I've been troubled over the years that too often our youth (and, unfortunately, some of our more experienced members) are prone to confuse sentimentality with spirituality, tears with testimony. Let me illustrate. One Mutual night as I came out of my bishop's office, I noticed that the Laurel class was huddled in the hall in the midst of what seemed to be quite a fascinating discussion. They appeared to be talking about one of the young women in their class who had during the last year slipped into inactivity in the Church. I heard one of the girls say, with some fervor: "Well, I can tell you this much—she doesn't have much of a testimony." One of the others challenged her: "How can you say that? How do you know?" The first replied: "Well, you think about it for a minute. I've seen her bear her testimony many times, and I've never seen her cry once!" There was a pause, a moment of reflection on the part of twelve young ladies, and then a rather visible concurrence. Most of them nodded in agreement and said: "She's right about that." I was flabbergasted. Many years ago I taught several classes of eleventh graders in seminary. My fourth period class was a remarkable group. During the first part of the year, however, I noticed something a bit unusual. Day after day for about three weeks I noticed that every devotional (to start the class and set the spiritual tone) involved some kind of death story. Somebody was dying or giving their life or blood or something. I pulled the class president aside after the third week and asked: "Fred, what's the deal with the devotionals?" He didn't follow me. "I mean, why all the morbid stories in our devotionals? Why are we so hung up with death?" Fred responded verbally in a polite manner, but the look on his face betrayed the fact that my question had totally mystified him. "Brother Millet," he came right back, "how else are we going to get the kids to cry?" I said, "Oh, I understand." I didn't follow up on the conversation at the time, but felt it was best to wait until I had thought through my response.

There's no question that when we have a genuine spiritual experience we may be touched emotionally. Tears come easily for some of us, and there should never be the slightest embarrassment about such a thing. And yet we do ourselves and our youth a tremendous disservice if we begin to believe that an emotional experience is always a spiritual experience. Tears may come, but they should never be manipulated or elicited or sought for. In the classroom, for example, there is plenty for the gospel teacher to do by way of study, prayer, preparation, organization, and presentation; he or she must not seek to usurp the role of the Holy Ghost. He is the Comforter. He is the Revelator. He is the Converter. He is, in reality, the Teacher. We strive to be an instrument. We may seek and pray for an outpouring of the Spirit, but we must never attempt to manufacture the same. President Howard W. Hunter, in speaking to Church Educational System personnel, said: "In one of the most basic revelations of this dispensation, the Lord said, 'And the Spirit shall be given unto you by the prayer of faith; and if ye receive not the Spirit ye shall not teach' (D&C 42:14).

"I take this verse to mean not only that we *should not* teach without the Spirit, but also that we really *cannot* teach without it. Learning of spiritual things simply cannot take place without the instructional and confirming presence of the Spirit of the Lord. . . .

"Let me offer a word of caution on this subject. I think if we are not careful as professional teachers working in the classroom every day, we may begin to try to counterfeit the true influence of the Spirit of the Lord by unworthy and manipulative means. I get concerned when it appears that strong emotion or free-flowing tears are equated with the presence of the Spirit. Certainly the Spirit of the Lord can bring strong emotional feelings, including tears, but that outward manifestation ought not be confused with the presence of the Spirit itself.

"I have watched a great many of my brethren over the years and we have shared some rare and unspeakable spiritual experiences together. Those experiences have all been different, each special in its own way, and such sacred moments may or may not be accompanied by tears. Very often they are, but sometimes they are accompanied by total silence. Other times they are accompanied by joy. Always they are accompanied by a great manifestation of the truth, of revelation to the heart.

"Give your students gospel truth powerfully taught; that is the way to give them a spiritual experience. Let it come naturally and as it will, perhaps with the shedding of tears, but perhaps not. If what you say is the truth, and you say it purely and with honest conviction, those students will feel the spirit of the truth being taught them and will recognize that inspiration and revelation has come into their hearts. That is how we build faith. That is how we strengthen testimonies—with the power of the word of God taught in purity and with conviction."[10]

Though President Hunter's remarks were directed primarily to full-time religious educators, the principles he enunciates certainly apply in our discussion of the bearing of pure testimony. There is something remarkable that takes place when the Latter-day Saints bear pure testimony. There is a spiritual presence that accompanies such expressions that can be felt in no other way, and there are outcomes that attest to the power and validity of doing so. Because of the growing waywardness of his people, Alma the younger determined to leave the office of chief judge or governor and devote himself to the work of the ministry. Of this occasion, Mormon wrote: "And this he did that he himself might go forth among his people, or among the people of Nephi, that he might preach the word of God unto them, to stir them up in remembrance of their duty, and that he might pull down, by the word of God, all the pride and craftiness and all the contentions which were among his people, *seeing no way that he might reclaim them save it were in bearing down in pure testimony against them*" (Alma 4:19; emphasis added).

There is, on the other hand, something missing when the Latter-day Saints fail to bear pure testimony. Something is lost. Elder Boyd K. Packer spoke of a time when he presided over the New England Mission. "We held a series of zone conferences," he wrote, "to improve the spirituality of the mission. Rather than schedule instruction on the mechanics of missionary work, we determined to have a testimony meeting. In the last conference, in the testimony of one of the humble elders, I found the answer to the problem. There was something different about the brief testimony of this frightened new elder. He stood for less than a minute, yet I learned from his expression what it was that was missing.

"The testimonies we'd heard from all the other missionaries went something like this: 'I'm grateful to be in the mission field. I've learned a lot from it. I have a fine companion. I've learned a lot from him. I'm grateful for my parents. We had an interesting experience last week. We were out knocking on doors and . . . ' Then the missionary would relate an experience. His conclusion would be something like this: 'I'm grateful to be in the mission field. I have a testimony of the gospel.' And he would conclude 'in the name of Jesus Christ. Amen.'

"This young elder was different somehow. Anxious not to spend an extra second on his feet, he said simply, in hurried, frightened words, 'I know that God lives. I know that Jesus is the Christ. I know that we have a prophet of God leading the Church. In the name of Jesus Christ. Amen.'

"This was a testimony. It was not just an experience nor an expression of gratitude. It was a declaration, a witness!

"Most of the elders had said 'I have a testimony,' but they had not declared it. This young elder had, in a very few words, delivered his testimony—direct, basic, and, as it turned out, powerful.

"I then knew what was wrong in the mission. We were telling stories, expressing gratitude, admitting that we had testimonies, but we were not bearing them."[11]

A WITNESS PROPERLY ROOTED

I was asked some years ago by a mission president to speak to his missionaries at a zone conference. We had a lovely gathering and a fine exchange of ideas. I was invited to stay for lunch and visit with the missionaries. I did a great deal of listening and learned much. One of the most interesting conversations revolved around a young couple who were being taught by the missionaries but who were not progressing. "They're golden people," one elder said, "ripe and ready for membership in the Church. They just won't commit to be baptized." Several suggestions were made by the missionaries listening in—fasting with them, having the bishop meet with them, intensifying the friendshipping effort, etc., to all of which the first elder said, "We've tried that." After a long pause, one elder spoke up: "Have you given them the Scrolls Discussion?" The first elder responded: "No, do you think this would be a good time for the Scrolls Discussion?" "Sounds like a perfect time to me," the second came back. Now I had never heard of the Scrolls Discussion. I was dying to know what it was so I blurted out: "What's the Scrolls Discussion?" The second elder looked quizzically at me and said: "Surely, Brother Millet, you've heard of the Scrolls Discussion?" I indicated that I had not. "The Scrolls Discussion," he said, "involves showing the people how the Dead Sea Scrolls prove the truthfulness of the Church!" I asked: "How do you do that?" "Well," he replied, "as you know, the Dead Sea Scrolls contain information about a group of Christians out in the deserts of Judea." I said: "No, they don't. The Dead Sea Scrolls were written by a group of hyperreligious Jews." He said: "Oh. I didn't know that." Then the elder followed up: "Well, you do know that they had three presiding high priests at the head of their church." I indicated that the leaders of their group were Aaronic priests, not Melchizedek. He went on: "Well, there's much doctrine within the Dead Sea Scrolls that proves our church to be true." I commented that the Scrolls were interesting historical documents but did very little for us doctrinally. This exchange went on for about ten minutes, the elder providing what he thought to be airtight "proofs" and me trying to gently let him know that most of what he understood about the Dead Sea Scrolls was simply untrue. I could see the frustration in his eyes. He breathed a sigh and then concluded the conversation with: "Well, I'll just say this—the Scrolls Discussion has always worked perfectly for me!" I thought then (and have since) about all the people who may have come into the Church as a result of what they learned in the famous Scrolls Discussion. I shuddered.

This is the Lord's church. It is built upon divine precepts and principles, founded on diamond truth and God-given authority. It needs no props. We need not stretch nor sensationalize nor intellectualize the message of the Restoration in order to make it more palatable. It will stand on its own. Joseph Smith taught that truth cuts its own way.[12] Our witness of the truth—a sign of our spiritual maturity in the faith—must be grounded in substance, in true doctrine, in that which will endure the test of time. My friend who almost left the Church because his testimony was founded on archaeological evidences of the Book of Mormon had not paid a sufficient price to know by the power of the Holy Ghost that the Book of Mormon is the word of God; consequently, he was found wanting at the moment of trial. We may have a testimony of many things—of the programs and procedures and policies of the Restored Church—and yet not be settled in truth. There are some things which we must come to know, know with an assurance borne of the Spirit, if we are to endure the tests spoken of earlier in this chapter. We need to know that there is a God in heaven, that he is infinite and eternal, and that he is our Parent, the Father of the spirits of all men and women. We need to know that Jesus is the

Christ, that he is literally the Only Begotten Son of the Father in the flesh, and that salvation comes by and through him and in no other way. We need to know that Joseph Smith was and is a prophet of God, that he is a revealer of truth and a legal administrator, that knowledge and authority have been delivered to earth in this final gospel dispensation through his instrumentality. We need to know that the revelations and translations given through Joseph the Seer, especially the Book of Mormon, are true and from God, that they contain the mind and will and voice of the Almighty to those who live in this last age of the earth's history. Finally, we need to know that The Church of Jesus Christ of Latter-day Saints is, in the language of the revelation, the only true and living church on the face of the earth (see D&C 1:30), is the kingdom of God on earth. These things matter. They matter a great deal. Our testimonies will be intact and solid to the degree that they are grounded in these essential verities.

Though we may begin simply in the development of our witness, though at the first what we testify to be true may be based more upon feeling than knowledge, the Lord expects his servants to search and study and grow in understanding, to acquire a reason for the hope that is within them (see 1 Peter 3:15). Simply stated, the Spirit bears witness of truth, of substantive realities. "The sanctity of a true testimony," President Joseph F. Smith counseled the Church, "should inspire a thoughtful care as to its use. That testimony is not to be forced upon everybody, nor is it to be proclaimed at large from the housetop. It is not to be voiced merely to 'fill up the time' in a public meeting; far less to excuse or disguise the speaker's poverty of thought or ignorance of the truth he is called to expound. . . . Of those who speak in his name, the Lord requires humility, not ignorance."[13]

In this day we have been commanded to be true and loyal to the Restoration, to bear testimony of those things that have come by and through Joseph Smith (see D&C 31:4; 49:1–4). Indeed, the Lord has warned us as a people of the condemnation, scourge, and judgment—surely the lost spiritual privileges and opportunities—which rest upon the Church because of our near neglect of the Book of Mormon and modern revelations. The Savior has also instructed us as to how we may extricate ourselves from this spiritual plight: "I will forgive you of your sins with this commandment—that you remain steadfast in your minds in solemnity and the spirit of prayer, in bearing testimony to all the world of those things which are communicated unto you" (D&C 84:61). Occasionally we hear people complain that they hear too few testimonies of Christ and too many of Joseph Smith. To be sure, we worship the Father in the name of the Son; Christ our Lord is the way to the Father and his is the only name under heaven whereby man can be saved. And yet the dispensation head is the preeminent revealer of Christ to the world in his day. Thus to bear witness of Joseph Smith is to bear witness of Jesus Christ who sent him, in the same way that a testimony of Christ also implies clearly a testimony of the Eternal Father who sent Christ. I have observed that there is a power—an unusual spiritual endowment from that Lord we worship—associated with the bearing of a pure and fervent testimony of Joseph Smith and the Restoration. Such outpourings surely signify heaven's approbation.

President David O. McKay's father learned, as a young missionary, of the importance of bearing testimony of the Choice Seer. After laboring in a town in Scotland he had decided, because of persecution, to speak of Christ and Christian principles and to postpone for the time being his discussion of the Restoration. He thereafter experienced a gloom and darkness of soul that he had never known, a pall of bitterness so intense that he concluded either he would have it removed or he would leave his labors and return home. In pleading and sober prayer he called upon God for deliverance. The Spirit spoke: "Testify that Joseph Smith is a prophet of God." The darkness was lifted and Elder McKay's ministry continued.[14] In this same spirit, Elder Matthew Cowley, prior to leaving on his first mission, was given the following counsel from his father: "My boy, you will go out on that mission; you will study; you will try to prepare your sermons; and sometimes when you are called upon, you will think you are wonderfully prepared, but when you stand up, your mind will go completely blank."

Young Elder Cowley asked what he should do in such circumstances. "He said, 'You stand up there and with all the fervor of your soul, you bear witness that Joseph Smith was a prophet of the living God, and thoughts will flood into your mind and words to your mouth, to round out those thoughts in a facility of expression that will carry conviction to the heart of everyone who listens.' And so my mind, being mostly blank during my five years in the mission field, gave me the opportunity to bear testimony to the greatest event in the history of the world since the crucifixion of the Master."[15]

There is no way, given our limited perspective in this life, that we can measure the eternal impact of pure testimony. Perhaps only when we are able to look back on the whole of our existence, able to see things as they really are, from God Almighty's point of view, will we be able to sense and feel the powerful coalescence of circumstances, the divinely contrived orchestration of people and events. Perhaps then we will be in a position to measure just how much difference has been made by human testimony. Some testimonies shake the earth.

I remember very well the feeling of deep personal loss when I learned of the passing of President David O. McKay in January 1970. He had been the prophet of my youth, the only president of the Church I really remembered. I worried about my ability to shift allegiance and commitment to President Joseph Fielding Smith, his successor. I prayed and prayed to have the same witness as to President Smith's call that I had felt in regard to President McKay. By the time the April 1970 conference convened, I still had not received what was to me a sufficient confirmation that the will of the Lord had been done. Things changed dramatically for me, however, as I heard President Smith speak the following words at the close of the conference:

"I desire to say that no man of himself can lead this church. It is the Church of the Lord Jesus Christ; he is at the head. The Church bears his name, has his priesthood, administers his gospel, preaches his doctrine, and does his work.

"He chooses men and calls them to be instruments in his hands to accomplish his purposes, and he guides and directs them in their labors. But men are only instruments in the Lord's hands, and the honor and glory for all that his servants accomplish is and should be ascribed unto him forever. If this were the work of man, it would fail, but it is the work of the Lord, and he does not fail."[16] Something happened to me as a result of hearing that sweet but direct testimony, something that has affected my life permanently. I saw the power of God resting upon President Joseph Fielding Smith; that witness went down into my heart and burned like fire. It has happened in like manner on subsequent occasions as new prophets have been chosen and appointed. I remember also some two and a half years later when a new apostle was called at the time of the October 1972 conference, the occasion when President Harold B. Lee was sustained as the eleventh president of the Church. This new special witness declared: "As members of the church and kingdom of God on earth, we enjoy the gifts of the Spirit—those wonders and glories and miracles that a gracious and benevolent God always has bestowed on his faithful saints. The first of these gifts listed in our modern revelation on spiritual gifts is the gift of testimony, the gift of revelation, the gift of knowing of the truth and divinity of the work. This gift is elsewhere described as the testimony of Jesus, which is the spirit of prophecy. This is my gift. I know this work is true.

"I have a perfect knowledge that Jesus Christ is the Son of the living God and that he was crucified for the sins of the world. I know that Joseph Smith is a prophet of God through whose instrumentality the fulness of the everlasting gospel has been restored again in our day. And I know that this Church of Jesus Christ of Latter-day Saints is the kingdom of God on earth."[17] I was moved and strengthened by that witness in ways that I cannot explain. I knew, with a knowledge more powerful than sight, that he knew.

More than twelve years later that same apostle delivered his last testimony to the Church, one that has touched and will yet touch the hearts of millions of people across the globe. "And now," he affirmed, in speaking of the redemption of Christ, "as pertaining to this perfect atonement, wrought by the shedding of the blood of God—I testify that it took place in Gethsemane and at Golgotha, and as pertaining to Jesus Christ, I testify that he is the Son of the Living God and was crucified for the sins of the world. He is our Lord, our God, and our King. This I know of myself independent of any other person.

"I am one of his witnesses, and in a coming day I shall feel the nail marks in his hands and in his feet and shall wet his feet with my tears.

"But I shall not know any better then than I know now that he is God's Almighty Son, that he is our Savior and Redeemer, and that salvation comes in and through his atoning blood and in no other way."[18] Who among us that heard this final earthly apostolic witness of Elder Bruce R. McConkie will ever be the same? Indeed, the witness of the Brethren provides not only sustenance and support for our own developing testimonies, but they also stand as a pattern and a guide as to how the Lord expects his Saints to bear pure testimony.

As we develop in line-upon-line fashion, as we grow here a little and there a little in our appreciation for and witness of the work in which we are engaged, we are becoming steadfast and immovable. Like Jacob, son of Lehi, because of our experience with the Spirit of the Lord we will be unshaken in the faith when we encounter anti-Christs and the doctrine of devils (see Jacob 7:5). And like Enos, his son, because we will have heard the word of the Lord and will have come to treasure above all else those matters of eternal import, our faith will begin to be unshaken in the Lord (see Enos 1:11). We will have begun to mature in our convictions.

Notes

From an address delivered at Brigham Young University Education Week and Know Your Religion series, 1989–91.

1. Heber C. Kimball, as quoted in Orson F. Whitney, *Life of Heber C. Kimball,* 4th ed. (Salt Lake City: Bookcraft, 1973), 446, 449–50; emphasis added.
2. *Gospel Doctrine,* 13.
3. Joseph F. McConkie and Robert L. Millet, *The Holy Ghost* (Salt Lake City: Bookcraft, 1989), 45.
4. Boyd K. Packer, *"That All May Be Edified"* (Salt Lake City: Bookcraft, 1982), 335.
5. Harold B. Lee, "Be Loyal to the Royal within You," *1973 Brigham Young University Speeches of the Year* (Provo: Brigham Young University Publications, 1974), 103; emphasis added.

6. *Teachings of the Prophet Joseph Smith,* 148.

7. Packer, *"That All May Be Edified,"* 339–40; emphasis in original.

8. Spencer W. Kimball, *The Teachings of Spencer W. Kimball,* ed. Edward L. Kimball (Salt Lake City: Bookcraft, 1982), 138; emphasis added.

9. Spencer W. Kimball, unpublished address delivered in Los Angeles, California, 2 January 1969, 9, as cited in *Testimony,* comp. H. Stephen Stoker and Joseph C. Muren (Salt Lake City: Bookcraft, 1980), 139; emphasis added.

10. Howard W. Hunter, "Eternal Investments," address given to Church Educational System personnel, Salt Lake City, Utah, 10 February 1989, 3; emphasis in original.

11. Boyd K. Packer, *Teach Ye Diligently* (Salt Lake City: Deseret Book Co., 1975), 275.

12. See *Teachings of the Prophet Joseph Smith,* 313.

13. *Gospel Doctrine,* 205–6.

14. See David O. McKay, *Gospel Ideals* (Salt Lake City: Improvement Era, 1953), 21–22.

15. Matthew Cowley, *Matthew Cowley Speaks* (Salt Lake City: Deseret Book Co., 1971), 298–99.

16. Joseph Fielding Smith, in Conference Report, April 1970, 113.

17. Bruce R. McConkie, in Conference Report, October 1972, 21.

18. Bruce R. McConkie, in Conference Report, April 1985, 12.

ALMA, THE ANGEL, AND AUNT GLADYS

In the Book of Mormon we read of a tragic and poignant moment in the lives of King Mosiah and Alma. These two noble souls had given themselves to the gospel cause and laid their all on the altar of Christ. What might otherwise have been a joyful season in life was flawed by the disobedience and waywardness of their own sons: Alma the younger and the sons of Mosiah were among the unbelievers who had actually begun to fight against the Church of Christ and to lead others astray. Of Alma the younger, the account states: "He was a man of many words, and did speak much flattery to the people; therefore he led many of the people to do after the manner of his iniquities. And he became a great hinderment to the prosperity of the church of God; stealing away the hearts of the people; causing much dissension among the people; giving a chance for the enemy of God to exercise his power over them" (Mosiah 27:8–9). One can only imagine the grief and perhaps embarrassment that the king and president of the Church must have felt as they preached of the importance of love and fidelity to truth and the joys of family living.

Mormon writes that "as they were going about rebelling against God, behold, the angel of the Lord appeared unto them; and he descended as it were in a cloud; and he spake as it were with the voice of thunder, which caused the earth to shake upon which they stood." The angel said unto Alma: "Behold, the Lord hath heard the prayers of his people, and also the prayers of his servant, Alma, who is thy father; for he has prayed with much faith concerning thee that thou mightest be brought to the knowledge of the truth; therefore, for this purpose have I come to convince thee of the power and authority of God, that the prayers of his servants might be answered according to their faith" (Mosiah 27:11, 14).

Alma and the sons of Mosiah were stopped in their tracks, as it were, turned about and redirected. Alma underwent a major spiritual transformation, was born again—changed from a carnal and fallen state to a state of righteousness. The sons of Mosiah—Ammon, Aaron, Omner, and Himni—underwent a similar transformation (see Mosiah 28:3). Thereafter the foursome devoted themselves wholly to the work of the Lord and were directly involved in the conversion of thousands of souls to the gospel. Their conversion could not repair every damage and retrieve every apostate word. Indeed, as President Boyd K. Packer explained, "There are times you cannot mend that which you have broken. Perhaps the offense was long ago, or the injured refuse your penance. Perhaps the damage was so severe that you cannot fix it no matter how desperately you want to." However, he continued, "when your desire is firm and you are willing to pay the 'uttermost farthing,' the law of restitution is suspended. Your obligation is transferred to the Lord. He will settle your accounts."[1] And so it was that Alma and the sons of Mosiah transferred their burden to God and yielded themselves to the work of the Master. They "labored without ceasing, that [they] might bring souls unto repentance; that [they] might bring them to taste of the exceeding joy of which [they] did taste; that they might also be born of God, and be filled with the Holy Ghost" (Alma 36:24).

This conversion is a remarkable story, an inspiring narrative, one that spawns significant lessons for life, lessons that span the chasm of time. For example, one important lesson is that no one of us is beyond spiritual recovery, that "all are within the reach of pardoning mercy, who have not committed the unpardonable sin."[2] God can recognize goodness and potential within each of us, as he did with Saul of Tarsus, the infamous persecutor of the Christians. When Ananias hesitated to assist this enemy of the faith after Saul had been struck down on the road to Damascus, the Lord said boldly: "Go thy way: for he is a chosen vessel unto me, to bear my name before the Gentiles, and kings, and the children of Israel" (Acts 9:15).

Secondly, parents may find especial comfort in this story, particularly parents whose children have wandered from the fold. It is so very difficult to keep going, to do all the right things, to keep one's head up and one's courage intact—it is extremely tough to stay at the wheel when those we love the most forsake the faith and way of life to which we have consecrated ourselves. And yet the promise is extended to all of us that "the effectual fervent prayer of a righteous man availeth much" (James 5:16), and that both in time and eternity our God shall wipe away all tears (see Isaiah 25:8; Revelation 7:17; 21:4). Parents thus hope on, pray on, and trust in the power of the gospel covenant to restore, renew, and rekindle the flame of faith in the hearts of our children.

These are indeed soothing and settling thoughts. But there is an aspect of the story that may prove a bit unsettling for some, a dimension of this conversion experience that may cause us unrest. Some questions arise: Why would an angel come to Alma? Why should he be so privileged? Is that the way most of us are turned around? Where is the fairness in the system? Why should the bulk of humankind be asked to wait and yearn and suffer until something much less dramatic (if at all) comes to pass? And so forth.

I suppose if all rebellious souls were struck down by an angel who confirmed such matters as the reality of God, the truthfulness of the gospel, and the certainty of a life beyond, there would be little need for faith on anyone's part. If every time I was about to take a backward step or to stray from the strait and narrow, my effort were to be blocked by a caring but conspicuous ministering angel, I would never be left to myself to choose good over evil and therefore would never grow into that spiritual maturity that derives from overcoming the world.

Second, such appearances by angels might actually create the temptation to obtain a testimony by negative behavior rather than through quiet and consistent gospel living. Young people might, for example, become fascinated with the possibility of seeing an angel. And what would be required? Simply to misbehave. Since few among the faithful are accorded the privilege of seeing angels, it would seem a strange system of salvation that freely granted such a privilege to the wayward.

Third, it just might be the case that an appreciable number of people have indeed had an angelic ministration but have rejected the divine counsel and chosen to continue in their waywardness. We would undoubtedly be left without a record of such instances, except perhaps by believers who knew about them. Furthermore, the coming of an angel does not assure change. We know, for example, that Laman and Lemuel were chastened by an angel but that his words were ignored. "Ye are swift to do iniquity," Nephi said to his older brothers, "but slow to remember the Lord your God. *Ye have seen an angel, and he spake unto you; yea, ye have heard his voice from time to time; and he hath spoken unto you in a still small voice, but ye were past feeling, that ye could not feel his words;* wherefore, he has spoken unto you like unto the voice of thunder, which did cause the earth to shake as if it were to divide asunder" (1 Nephi 17:45; emphasis added).

Fourth, the Savior explained that those who reject the testimony of scripture and living prophets are no more prone to accept the testimony of angels. In the parable of the rich man and Lazarus, the rich man, now in the postmortal spirit world and sensing finally that he has sealed his doom by insulating himself from the pleadings of the needy on earth, begs thereafter that words of warning be sent to his living kindred. "Then he said, I pray thee therefore, father [Abraham], that thou wouldest send him [Lazarus, who is now in paradise] to my father's house: for I have five brethren; that he may testify unto them, lest they also come into this place of torment. Abraham saith unto him, They have Moses and the prophets; let them hear them. And he said, Nay, father Abraham: but if one went unto them from the dead, they will repent. And he said unto him, *If they hear not Moses and the prophets, neither will they be persuaded, though one rose from the dead*" (Luke 16:27–31; emphasis added).

Fifth, the Apostle Paul offered the following sobering counsel: "Let brotherly love continue. Be not forgetful to entertain strangers: for thereby some have entertained angels unawares" (Hebrews 13:1–2). That is to say, sometimes we are like the two disciples on the road to Emmaus—our eyes are holden or restrained (see Luke 24:16) so that we are not able to see who it is that walks among us, teaches us, lifts us up, and points or repoints us toward the abundant life. For that matter, is it not possible that unseen angels whisper or testify or warn in ways that we cannot now perceive but which will be obvious to us one day? In speaking of angels, Mormon affirmed that "the office of their ministry is to call men unto repentance, and to fulfil and to do the work of the covenants of the Father, which he hath made unto the children of men, to prepare the way among the children of men, by declaring the word of Christ unto the chosen vessels of the Lord, that they may bear testimony of him. And by so doing, the Lord God prepareth the way that the residue of men may have faith in Christ, that the Holy Ghost may have place in their hearts" (Moroni 7:31–32).

Finally, it should be remembered that the Lord, who can manifest his power in a variety of ways, is hardly limited to angelic ministrations or open visions. Many have had conversion experiences of spiritual impact and consequence equal to that of Alma and the sons of Mosiah, experiences that are the result of a coalescence of divinely contrived circumstances: life-changing experiences involving such things as a confrontation with death, an inspired sermon, a scriptural passage that seemed to leap off the page, or a caring and sensitive parent, relative, friend, or a concerned and persistent priesthood leader.

It was in fact while pondering upon the matter of this grand Book of Mormon conversion story several years ago that I was instructed through the medium of memory. At about the time I turned eighteen years of age, I was deeply involved in the activities and programs of the Church. I was a stake missionary, had memorized some of the missionary discussions and scriptures, and had been working along with the full-time missionaries at least a couple of nights per week. I was so excited about serving a full-time mission that I couldn't wait for the time to pass when my bishop (who was my dad) and I could begin the paperwork and interviews. All was well for several months, and then, without warning, my attitudes and my ideas began to change. I gradually began to think more and more about life at home, about friends and school, and about how long two years really was. In looking back now on that season of my life, there's no question but that Satan began to make subtle inroads into my character and my resolve to be a missionary.

I remember my father sitting down with me on a number of occasions at about the time of my nineteenth birthday and asking: "Well, son, shall we begin the process?" And I recall an answer that went something like: "Look, I really do want to do this, but I just don't feel prepared yet. I'm not quite ready." This happened at least three times. The last time my dad heard those words about my lack of readiness he gently and lovingly said, in effect, "Robert, this is your decision. It's something you need to do on your own. You need to pray sincerely about this. Your mom and I will never pressure or push you to go on a mission." And then he added this pertinent comment: "But let me say one more thing. You're as ready as anyone I know. If you wait until you are perfectly prepared to go, you will never go." His words meant something to me, mainly because I had such a deep respect for my father and for his example of commitment to the kingdom. But I didn't make any progress toward beginning the process.

A few days after my interview with Dad, there came a phone call for me. The person on the other end of the line said, "Is this you, Robert? This is Aunt Gladys. Do you have a few minutes?" I asked her if she wanted to speak with my mother, but she quickly fired back: "No, you're the one I want to talk to." I thought it was a little odd that she should call me in the middle of the day. But she was one of my favorite people in the world. Her daughter (my cousin Linda) and I had always been very close, and so Aunt Gladys was someone I dearly loved. There's one other thing that made her and my Uncle Junior special: they had been a significant influence in helping our family come back into full activity in the Church just after I was baptized. Uncle Junior had baptized me and my mother (who had been a Methodist) and had written my very first talk (which I memorized and delivered), a brief message on Joseph Smith's First Vision. It was clear from the way they lived and the things they valued that the gospel meant everything to them.

We carried on a light conversation for an hour and a half, discussing such varied topics as football and college and my love life. Though one side of me felt a little strange spending so much time on the phone with a mature adult, it was actually kind of fun. Then Gladys surprised me with this question: "Listen, Robert, there are some things I want to chat with you about. Do you have some time tomorrow?" I thought and searched and finally admitted that I had no plans. "Good," she said. "Why don't you come over and have lunch with me and we can spend the afternoon together." Again, I thought it sounded a bit strange, but I felt that no harm could come from it. I need to add that Aunt Gladys is one who is close to the Source, one who has lived in tune with the Spirit of the Lord. She always made me slightly nervous when she said something like, "I had a dream the other night . . ." or "I've been feeling lately as though I ought to . . ." or as she said to me when she called that day on the phone: "You've been on my mind a lot lately." Let me make it clear that there was nothing out of line, nothing inappropriate about her impressions, her feelings, and her dreams. They were from the Lord and we knew her well enough to know that. I suppose that my respect for her judgment and my awareness of her spirituality combined to cause me some nervousness about spending the afternoon with her. But I decided to do so anyway.

The next afternoon I found that the time slipped by rather quickly. There was an unusual spirit in her living room as we spoke, and my fears were banished by the feeling of love and peace I felt there. At the right moment, in a voice that shared her tender concern, she said, in essence: "Robert, I've been worried about you. I have known from the time that you were a tiny boy that you should serve a mission, and that your mission would chart the course for your life. I want you to know that your Uncle Junior and I love you, just as if you were one of our own children. Perhaps it is out of this love for you, and the deep affection I feel for your mom and dad, that I share with you some feelings I have had during the past few weeks. I feel that it's critical that you leave on a mission and that you leave soon. If you do not, I'm afraid you will never go." Though she didn't perhaps know it, I had heard similar words not long before from my father. But Aunt Gladys's words went down into my heart and burned like fire. I knew that I must serve a mission, and I knew that the time was short. The Lord needed me now. We embraced as I left and I thanked her for being in tune.

I left within weeks for the Eastern States Mission. And, as she predicted (and as I knew would be the case), my mission was a turning point in my life. I learned how to work hard, how to set and achieve goals, how to lead others, how to take setbacks and deal productively with adversity, how to love and cherish people, and how to acquire and cultivate the spirit of revelation. I learned what things matter most in life, how critical it is to have an eye single to the glory of God, and how to consecrate my heart to the gospel cause. Every major decision in my life thereafter—including what kind of person I should marry and how I would know when I found her—has to some degree been made by virtue of what I learned and what I experienced on a mission. Other than my temple marriage, which is the most significant event in my life, the choice to serve a mission is without exception the most far-reaching and influential decision I have ever made.

Over the last few years as I have rethought my experience with Aunt Gladys, it has become clear to me that although our Heavenly Father will force no man or woman to heaven, he *will* do everything he can to attract and entice us toward the fulness of gospel blessings. A zealous but misdirected Saul of Tarsus was redirected by the Lord Jesus himself. Alma's wayward course was interrupted by an angel, and his personal life and the Nephite narrative were never the same thereafter. God didn't choose to send an angel to me, but he did send Aunt Gladys, and my life has not been the same since. Alma may have had his angel, but I had Gladys. And for me at least, the turnaround was just as dramatic. I have come to appreciate President Spencer W. Kimball's insight that "God does notice us, and he watches over us. But it is usually through another mortal that he meets our needs."[3] I know that angels have ministered and do minister and will yet minister to men and women on earth, "so long as time shall last, or the earth shall stand, or there shall be one man on the face thereof to be saved" (Moroni 7:36). But I also rejoice in the knowledge that the Almighty, who knows all things from beginning to end, has brought to pass, does now bring to pass, and will yet bring to pass great and important things through the sensitive intervention of attentive and caring men and women.

Notes

From a lecture given to an adult religion class on the Book of Mormon, BYU Continuing Education, Provo, Utah, 1996.

1. Boyd K. Packer, in Conference Report, October 1995, 23.
2. *Teachings of the Prophet Joseph Smith,* 191.
3. Spencer W. Kimball, *Teachings of Spencer W. Kimball,* comp. Edward L. Kimball (Salt Lake City: Bookcraft, 1982), 252.

LEARNING THE SPIRIT
OF REVELATION

S alvation cannot come without revelation," Joseph Smith taught. "It is in vain for anyone to minister without it."¹ It should thus come as no surprise to Latter-day Saints to learn that when the time had fully arrived for the promised restitution of all things, when the glorious day of restoration had dawned, it was necessary for God to make known through Joseph Smith myriad pertinent truths. Not the least of these was the nature and scope of revelation itself—from whence it comes, the manner in which it is to be received, and how it is to be understood. Thus, numerous passages in the Doctrine and Covenants describe, some almost as a passing comment, what people must do to qualify for the gifts and guidance of that member of the Godhead known as the Revelator. "It remained for Joseph Smith to announce to a disbelieving world," one Latter-day Saint has written, "that that same God who spoke so freely in times past not only could, but had spoken again, and that the promise of James that any who sought the wisdom of heaven in faith still had claim upon it."²

THE LIGHT OF CHRIST AND THE HOLY GHOST

The Lord pulled back the veil, tore away the theological cobwebs of centuries of darkness and apostasy, and revealed to Joseph the Seer the nature and kind of being we worship. "The Father has a body of flesh and bones as tangible as man's," he explained; "the Son also; but the Holy Ghost has not a body of flesh and bones, but is a personage of spirit. Were it not so, the Holy Ghost could not dwell in us"

(D&C 130:22). The Prophet thus made clear that our God is an exalted man, a Man of Holiness, a resurrected, immortal being in whose image man is in reality created.[3] The *corporeal* or physical nature of the Almighty was thus made known once again through the one called and chosen in premortality to reveal God to man in the final dispensation of time.

Some of the revelations in the Doctrine and Covenants also do much toward explaining the *divine* nature of God. God is omnipotent: he has all power. He is omniscient: he has all knowledge. It is in the Doctrine and Covenants we learn that through his influence, that divine glory and power which emanates from him to fill the immensity of space, he is omnipresent: he is everywhere present at once. Inasmuch as God is a physical being, he cannot occupy more than one space at a time, but through his glory (called in the scriptures the light of Christ or the spirit of Jesus Christ) he is able to be in and through and round about all things:

"He that ascended up on high, as also he descended below all things, in that he comprehended all things, that he might be in all and through all things, the light of truth;

"Which truth shineth. This is the light of Christ. As also he is in the sun, and the light of the sun, and the power thereof by which it was made.

"As also he is in the moon, and is the light of the moon, and the power thereof by which it was made;

"As also the light of the stars, and the power thereof by which they were made;

"And the earth also, and the power thereof, even the earth upon which you stand.

"And the light which shineth, which giveth you light, is through him who enlighteneth your eyes, which is the same light that quickeneth your understandings;

"Which light proceedeth forth from the presence of God to fill the immensity of space—

"The light which is in all things, which giveth life to all things, which is the law by which all things are governed, even the power of God who sitteth upon his throne, who is in the bosom of eternity, who is in the midst of all things" (D&C 88:6–13).

This is a most remarkable revelation. Through it we become privy to the fact that the light of Christ is the governing principle in nature, the power by which the cosmos is held in check and by which order and organization exist. Elder Parley P. Pratt wrote that the light of Christ, "in its less refined existence," is "the physical light which reflects from the sun, moon, and stars." In its higher degrees, it serves as the means "by which we reason, discern, judge, compare, comprehend and remember the subjects within our reach. Its inspiration constitutes instinct in animal life, reason in man, vision in the Prophets, and is continually flowing from the Godhead throughout all his creations."[4] According to Elder Bruce R. McConkie, the light of Christ "defies description and is beyond mortal comprehension. . . . It has neither shape nor form nor personality. It is not an entity nor a person nor a personage. It has no agency, does not act independently, and exists not to act but to be acted upon. It is variously described as light and life and law and truth and power. . . . It is the power of God who sitteth upon his throne. It may be that it is also priesthood and faith and omnipotence, for these too are the power of God."[5]

The light of Christ is given to every man and woman at birth as a natural endowment; it is described as that spirit which "giveth light to every man that cometh into the world" (D&C 84:46; compare John 1:9; Moroni 7:16). It is a director, a moral monitor which is "innate, inborn, and intuitional in nature. Call it conscience, if you will; say that it is a divine inheritance from a Divine Parent; identify it as a spark of divinity sent by Deity to fire the soul with the flames of righteousness; . . . it has many names. But what counts is that it is real."[6] The revelations further attest that "every one that hearkeneth to the voice of the Spirit [the light of Christ] cometh unto God, even the Father. And the Father teacheth him of the covenant which he has renewed and confirmed upon you . . . for the sake of the whole world" (D&C 84:47–48). That is to say, if men and women in the world will respond to the quiet promptings and subtle whisperings of the light of Christ within them, they will be led, either in this life or the next, to that higher light of the Holy Ghost found only in the covenant gospel through membership in the Lord's church. President Joseph F. Smith explained that this light "strives with the children of men, and will continue to strive with them, until it brings them to a knowledge of the truth and the possession of the greater light and testimony of the Holy Ghost."[7] Elder McConkie has thus described the influence of the light of Christ and the ministry of the Holy Ghost as follows:

"The light of Christ (also called the Spirit of Christ and the Spirit of the Lord) is a light, a power, and an influence that . . . is everywhere present and accounts for the omnipresence of God. It is the agency of God's power and the law by which all things are governed. It is also the agency used by the Holy Ghost to manifest truth and dispense spiritual gifts to many people at one and the same time. For instance, it is as though the Holy Ghost, who is a personage of spirit, was broadcasting all truth throughout the whole universe all the time, using the light of Christ as the agency by which the message is delivered. But only those who attune their souls to the Holy Spirit receive the available revelation. It is in this way that the person of the Holy Ghost makes his influence felt in the heart of every righteous person at one and the same time."[8]

REVELATION FOR THE CHURCH

The Restored Church was less than six months old when difficulties regarding revelation were encountered. "Brother Hiram Page had in his possession a certain stone," Joseph Smith recorded, "by which he had obtained certain 'revelations' concerning the upbuilding of Zion, the order of the Church, etc., all of which were entirely at variance with the order of God's house, as laid down in the New Testament, as well as in our late revelations."[9] In describing this incident in Church history, Newel Knight observed that "even Oliver Cowdery and the Whitmer family had given heed to them. . . . Joseph was perplexed and scarcely knew how to meet this new exigency. That night I occupied the same room he did," Brother Knight continued, "and the greater part of the night was spent in prayer and supplication. After much labor with these brethren, they were convinced of their error, and confessed the same, renouncing [Page's] revelations as not being of God."[10] It was because of Page's claims to revelation for the Church that the Lord spoke through Joseph Smith to Oliver Cowdery, giving what we now know as section 28 of the Doctrine and Covenants:

"Behold, I say unto thee, Oliver, that it shall be given unto thee that thou shalt be heard by the church in all things whatsoever thou shalt teach them by the Comforter, concerning the revelations and commandments which I have given.

"But, behold, verily, verily, I say unto thee, no one shall be appointed to receive commandments and revelations in this church excepting my servant Joseph Smith, Jun., for he receiveth them even as Moses" (D&C 28:1–2).

Some five months later another episode provoked a similar oracle from the Lord. A Mrs. Hubble, presumably a recent convert to the Church, "professed to be a prophetess of the Lord and professed to have many revelations, and knew the Book of Mormon was true, and that she would become a teacher in the Church of Christ. She appeared to be very sanctimonious and deceived some who were not able to detect her in her hypocrisy: others however had the spirit of discernment, and her follies and abominations were made manifest."[11] Again in reply the Lord spoke of Joseph Smith as "him whom I have appointed unto you to receive commandments and revelations from my hand. And this ye shall know assuredly" the Savior reemphasized, "that there is none other appointed unto you to receive commandments and revelations until he be taken, if he abide in me." And then, in summarizing the course the Saints were to follow in that day and forevermore, the Master said: "And this shall be a law unto you, that ye receive not the teachings of any that shall come before you as revelations or commandments; and this I give unto you that you may not be deceived, that you may know they are not of me" (D&C 43:2–3, 5–6).

The principle is clear and the doctrine certain: only the president of the Church—the prophet, seer, and revelator for the Church—has the right to receive divine direction for the whole Church, for this is the person the Lord will inspire "to move the cause of Zion in mighty power for good" (D&C 21:7). "He alone," explained President J. Reuben Clark Jr., "has the right to receive revelations for the Church, either new or amendatory, or to give authoritative interpretations of scriptures that shall be binding on the Church, or change in any way the existing doctrines of the Church. He is God's sole mouthpiece on earth for The Church of Jesus Christ of Latter-day Saints, the only true Church. He alone may declare the mind and will of God to His people."[12] This principle and practice ensure orthodoxy in the Church and kingdom of God, an institution guided and led by him whose house is a house of order (see D&C 132:8).

RECEIVING PERSONAL REVELATION

"No man can receive the Holy Ghost," the Prophet explained, "without receiving revelations," for "the Holy Ghost is a revelator."[13] President Joseph F. Smith likewise taught that "every individual in the Church has just as much right to enjoy the spirit of revelation and the understanding from God which that spirit of revelation gives him, for his own good, as the bishop has to enable him to preside over his ward."[14] We thus find numerous instances in the Doctrine and Covenants—particularly in the early revelations to the Church—detailing such matters as how and in what manner God may choose to communicate with his people.

An important insight pertaining to the spirit of revelation came to Oliver Cowdery in April of 1829. Oliver, who desired to translate and thus do more than act as scribe to the Prophet in their work with the gold plates, was told: "Oliver Cowdery, verily, verily, I say unto you, that assuredly as the Lord liveth, who is your God and your Redeemer, even so surely shall you receive a knowledge of whatsoever things you shall ask in faith, with an honest heart. . . . Yea, behold, I will tell you in your mind and in your heart, by the Holy Ghost, which shall come upon you and which shall dwell in your heart. Now, behold, this is the spirit of revelation; behold, this is the spirit by which Moses brought the children of Israel through the Red Sea on dry ground" (D&C 8:1–3).[15] We note with much interest that revelation is to be given to the heart as well as to the mind, that the divine communication is to involve the feelings as well as the natural cognitive processes of man. In commenting upon these verses, Joseph F. McConkie has written:

"We observe that neither [Oliver] nor Joseph was to experience any suspension of their natural faculties in the process of obtaining revelation. Quite to the contrary, their hearts and minds were to be the very media through which the revelation came. Prophets are not hollow shells through which the voice of the Lord echoes, nor are they mechanical recording devices; prophets are men of passion, feeling, and intellect. One does not suspend agency, mind, or spirit in the service of God. It is . . . with heart, might, mind and strength that we have been asked to serve, and in nothing is this more apparent than the receiving of revelation. There is no mindless worship or service in the kingdom of heaven."[16]

In a sense, the mind and the heart serve as a system of witnesses, a means whereby one may not be deceived or misled to trust his eternal salvation to either the rational processes alone or to the feelings or emotions alone.

As to the workings of the Spirit of God, and as to the matter of things coming into the mind, let us here observe that almost always a revelation from God will be rational, will make sense, will be in harmony with the commonly accepted standards and ideals set down by God and prophets and the laws of the land. "In the Church," Elder Boyd K. Packer has pointed out, "we are not exempt from common sense. You can know to begin with that you won't be prompted from any righteous source to steal, to lie, to cheat, to join anyone in any kind of moral transgression."[17] Yes, God did command Abraham to sacrifice Isaac, and Nephi to slay Laban, but these were rare exceptions, and both Abraham and Nephi were prophets and seers: they knew the voice of the Lord implicitly and thus could converse with the Spirit, which had come to be a constant companion. The Lord will not reveal to an individual member of the Church anything that is out of harmony with law and order and good judgment, or in conflict with the order of the Church and the position of the leaders of the Church. Further, God will never call upon his people to perform an action which is unnatural or indecorous in the eyes of God and man.[18]

Enos, the son of Jacob, explained concerning his own spiritual odyssey: "I went to hunt beasts in the forests; and the words which I had often heard my father speak concerning eternal life, and the joy of the saints, sunk deep into my heart. And my soul hungered." After crying unto God "all the day long" in "mighty prayer," Enos declared that "there came a voice unto me, saying: Enos, thy sins are forgiven thee, and thou shalt be blessed." After Enos had learned that the remission of sins had come because of his faith in Jesus the Christ, after he had begun to feel a desire for the welfare of the Nephites, and after he had continued his struggle in the spirit, he recounted, "Behold, the voice of the Lord came into my mind again, saying: I will visit thy brethren according to their diligence in keeping my commandments" (Enos 1:3–5, 10). Joseph Smith also spoke of the manner in which the Spirit may act upon the mind: "A person may profit by noticing the first intimation of the spirit of revelation; for instance, when you feel pure intelligence flowing into you, it may give you sudden strokes of ideas, so that by noticing it, you may find it fulfilled the same day or soon; (i.e.) those things that were presented unto your minds by the Spirit of God, will come to pass; and thus by learning the Spirit of God and understanding it, you may grow into the principle of revelation, until you become perfect in Christ Jesus."[19]

The nature of the occasion, as well as the readiness and need of the recipient, dictates how a message from God may be communicated. Certain situations require a message that pierces to the very soul, and in some cases that voice, although still and small, makes "the bones to quake" while it makes manifest the mind of the Lord (D&C 85:6; see also Helaman 5:30; 3 Nephi 11:3). In speaking of how God makes known his will through the heart of man, Elder Packer said: "These delicate, refined spiritual communications are not seen with our eyes nor heard with our ears. And even though it is described as a voice, it is a voice that one feels more than he hears."[20] President Ezra Taft Benson similarly taught: "We hear the words of the Lord most often by a feeling. If we are humble and sensitive, the Lord will prompt us through our feelings. That is why spiritual promptings move us on occasion to great joy, sometimes to tears. . . . The Holy Ghost causes our feelings to be more tender. We feel more charitable and compassionate. We are calmer. We have a greater capacity to love. People want to be around us because our very countenances radiate the influence of the Spirit."[21] Thus it is that Nephi explained to his errant brothers that in spite of the visible manifestations they had received from a benevolent God, they had remained unmoved and unchanged, incorrigible because they were "past feeling" (1 Nephi 17:45). Thus it is that the Lord explained to Oliver Cowdery that after he had studied and pondered and drawn conclusions on his own, he would come to feel those things which were right and from God (see D&C 9:8).

One of the precious but often overlooked aspects of revelation through our feelings is peace. In one sense, to be at peace is to have received a meaningful revelation, to have the inner awareness that God is pleased with one's life and that the course one has charted is in harmony with the divine will (see D&C 59:23). In another sense, peace is a means by which the Lord responds to petitions and answers prayers. "Blessed art thou," the Lord said to Oliver Cowdery, "for what thou hast done; for thou hast inquired of me [concerning the truthfulness of the Restoration], and behold, as often as thou hast inquired thou hast received instruction of my Spirit. . . . Behold, thou knowest that thou hast inquired of me and I did enlighten thy mind; and now I tell thee these things that thou mayest know that thou hast been enlightened by the Spirit of truth." The Savior then continued with his instructions and an invitation: "Verily, verily, I say unto you, if you desire a further witness, cast your mind upon the night that you cried unto me in your heart, that you might know concerning the truth of these things." This is a reference to the occasion when, while residing in the Smith home, Oliver had inquired of the Lord concerning the truthfulness of the family's claims concerning Joseph Smith Jr. and the coming forth of the Book of Mormon. "Did I not speak peace to your mind concerning the matter?" the Lord asked. "What greater witness can you have than from God?" (D&C 6:14–15, 22–23).

The Doctrine and Covenants identifies and illustrates a number of ways revelation comes: through personal appearance of the Lord (D&C 110:1–10); through personal appearance of other heavenly messengers (D&C 110:11–15; 128:20); in vision (D&C 76; 137; 138); by the voice of God (D&C 128:21); through the Urim and Thummim (D&C 3, 6, 11, 14); and through the Holy Ghost speaking to our minds and hearts (D&C 8:2–3; 9:7–9). It would be a mistake for the Latter-day Saints to suppose that answers and confirmations come only in one way—as a burning in the bosom, for example. The Lord desires to communicate with his children and will choose the means that will most clearly and persuasively convey his holy words and his perfect will to those who seek him diligently. "If thou shalt ask," he stated as early as 1831, "thou shalt receive revelation upon revelation, knowledge upon knowledge, that thou mayest know the mysteries and peaceable things—that which bringeth joy, that which bringeth life eternal" (D&C 42:61).

TEACHING AND LEARNING BY THE SPIRIT: A FORM OF REVELATION

In a revelation called "the law of the Church," the Lord established the divine standard under which teachers of the gospel are to operate. "And the Spirit shall be given unto you by the prayer of faith; and if ye receive not the Spirit ye shall not teach" (D&C 42:14). This statement appears to be both a command and a prophecy. That is, the gospel teacher is told to seek for and to live worthy of the guidance and confirming power of that Spirit, which causes lessons to go down into the heart and burn like fire. In addition, the Lord affirms that which every teacher knows only too well—that if the Spirit of the Lord does not accompany the presentation of the message, then true spiritual communication, edification, and lasting learning will not take place.

Indeed, the teacher is under obligation to teach the gospel "by the Spirit, even the Comforter which was sent forth to teach the truth." In the language of our Lord, "He that is ordained of me and sent forth to preach the word of truth by the Comforter, in the Spirit of truth, doth he preach it by the Spirit of truth or some other way? And if it be by some other way it is not of God. And again, he that receiveth the word of truth, doth he receive it by the Spirit of truth or some other way? If it be some other way it is not of God" (D&C 50:14, 17–20). In offering commentary upon these verses, particularly upon other ways in which someone might seek to convey the word of truth, Elder Bruce R. McConkie observed: "If you teach the word of truth—now note, you're saying what is true, every thing you say is accurate and right—by some other way than the Spirit, it is not of God. Now what is the other way to teach than by the Spirit? Well, obviously, it is by the power of the intellect.

"Suppose I came here tonight and delivered a great message on teaching, and I did it by the power of the intellect without any of the Spirit of God attending. Suppose that every word that I said was true, no error whatever, but it was an intellectual presentation. This revelation says: 'If it be by some other way it is not of God' (D&C 50:18).

"That is, God did not present the message through me because I used the power of the intellect instead of the power of the Spirit. Intellectual things—reason and logic—can do some good, and they can prepare the way, and they can get the mind ready to receive the Spirit under certain circumstances. But conversion comes and the truth sinks into the hearts of people only when it is taught by the power of the Spirit."[22]

One of the early messages of this dispensation is that adequate preparation must precede the power that accompanies a gospel presentation. Hyrum Smith was instructed in May of 1829: "Behold, this is your work, to keep my commandments, yea, with all your might, mind and strength." And then the Lord, the Master Teacher, spoke of the prerequisites for spiritual power: "Seek not to declare my word, but first seek to obtain my word, and then shall your tongue be loosed; then, if you desire, you shall have my Spirit and my word, yea, the power of God unto the convincing of men. But now hold your peace; study my word which hath gone forth among the children of men [e.g., the Bible], and also study my word which shall come forth among the children of men, or that which is now translating [the Book of Mormon]" (D&C 11:20–22).

This directive is certainly in harmony with what we find in the Book of Mormon. Of the sons of Mosiah the Nephite record attests that "they had waxed strong in the knowledge of the truth; for they were men of a sound understanding and they had searched the scriptures diligently, that they might know the word of God. But this is not all; they had given themselves to much prayer, and fasting; therefore they had the spirit of prophecy, and the spirit of revelation, and when they taught, they taught with power and authority of God" (Alma 17:2–3). In emphasizing that the study of scripture is directly associated with the receipt of revelation, Elder Bruce R. McConkie explained to the regional representatives of the Church in 1982:

"Our tendency—it is an almost universal practice among most church leaders—is to get so involved with the operation of the institutional church that we never gain faith like the ancients, simply because we do not involve ourselves in the basic gospel matters that were the center of their lives.

"We are so wound up in programs and statistics and trends, in properties, lands, and mammon, and in achieving goals that will highlight the excellence of our work, that we 'have omitted the weightier matters of the law.' And as Jesus would have said: 'These [weightier things] ought ye to have done, and not to leave the other undone' (Matthew 23:23).

"Let us be reminded of the great basic verities upon which all church programs and all church organization rest.

"We are not saved by church programs as such, by church organizations alone, or even by the Church itself. It is the gospel that saves. The gospel is 'the power of God unto salvation' (Romans 1:16). . . .

"May I suggest, based on personal experience, that faith comes and revelations are received as a direct result of scriptural study.

"Paul says 'faith cometh by hearing' the word of God (Romans 10:17). Joseph Smith taught that to gain faith men must have a knowledge of the nature and kind of being God is; they must have a correct idea of his character, perfections, and attributes; and they must so live as to gain the assurance that their conduct is in harmony with the divine will.

"Faith is thus born of scriptural study. Those who study, ponder, and pray about the scriptures, seeking to understand their deep and hidden meanings, receive from time to time great outpourings of light and knowledge from the Holy Spirit. This is what happened to Joseph Smith and Sidney Rigdon when they received the vision of the degrees of glory.

"However talented men may be in administrative matters; however eloquent they may be in expressing their views; however learned they may be in worldly things—they will be denied the sweet whisperings of the Spirit that might have been theirs unless they pay the price of studying, pondering, and praying about the scriptures."[23]

As we note from the above comment, the revelations specify the curriculum of the gospel teacher—that which is to be taught. "And again, the elders, priests and teachers of this church shall teach the principles of my gospel, which are in the Bible and the Book of Mormon, in the which is the fulness of the gospel. And they shall observe the covenants and church articles to do them, and these shall be their teachings, as they shall be directed by the Spirit" (D&C 42:12–13).[24] In our standard works—which now include the Doctrine and Covenants and the Pearl of Great Price—when supplemented with the words of modern prophets and apostles, we have a standard that directs all that we should teach in the Church. These books of holy writ constitute the canon of scripture, the rule of faith and doctrine against which truth and error are to be measured. Those who teach the message of the Restoration are to say "none other things than that which the prophets and apostles have written, and that which is taught them by the Comforter through the prayer of faith" (D&C 52:9; see also verse 36; 80:4). In what is a marvelous recommendation for gospel teachers to see to it that they teach from the standard works,[25] Elder Bruce R. McConkie has also written that "those who preach by the power of the Holy Ghost use the scriptures as their basic source of knowledge and doctrine. They begin with what the Lord has before revealed to other inspired men. But it is the practice of the Lord to give added knowledge to those upon whose hearts the true meanings and intents of the scriptures have been impressed. Many great doctrinal revelations come to those who preach from the scriptures."[26]

TRYING THE SPIRITS

"Believe not every spirit," John the Beloved taught, "but try the spirits whether they are of God: because many false prophets are gone out into the world" (1 John 4:1). For those interested in spiritual things, for those intent on knowing the will of the Lord and doing it, such is an essential exercise, for "nothing is a greater injury to the children of men than to be under the influence of a false spirit when they think they have the Spirit of God."[27] It is but fitting, then, to attend to some of the instructions delivered through Joseph Smith to enable the Saints of the Most High to stay on that strait and narrow course which leads to life eternal.

In the early days of the Church, "a custom of admitting only members and earnest investigators to the sacrament meetings and other assemblies of the Church had become somewhat general" (preface to D&C section 46). In March of 1831 the Lord instructed the Saints:

"And again I say unto you, concerning your confirmation meetings, that if there be any that are not of the church, that are earnestly seeking after the kingdom, ye shall not cast them out.

"But ye are commanded in all things to ask of God, who giveth liberally; and that which the Spirit testifies unto you even so I would that ye should do in all holiness of heart, walking uprightly before me, considering the end of your salvation, doing all things with prayer and thanksgiving, that ye may not be seduced by evil spirits, or doctrines of devils, or the commandments of men; for some are of men, and others of devils.

"Wherefore, beware lest ye are deceived; and *that ye may not be deceived seek ye earnestly the best gifts,* always remembering for what they are given;

"For verily I say unto you, they are given for the benefit of those who love me and keep all my commandments, and him that seeketh so to do; that all may be benefited that seek or that ask of me, that ask and not for a sign that they may consume it upon their lusts.

"And again, verily I say unto you, I would that ye should always remember, and always retain in your minds what those gifts are, that are given unto the church" (D&C 46:6–10; emphasis added).

The revelation then enumerates the various gifts of the Spirit, including the knowledge that Jesus is the Christ, as well as the gift to believe on the faith of those who know; the differences of administration and the diversities of operations; the gifts of wisdom and of knowledge; faith to heal as well as to be healed; prophecy; discernment; tongues, and the interpretation of tongues (see D&C 46:13–25; see also 1 Corinthians 12; Moroni 10).

The gifts of the Spirit of God are given to the Saints to enable them to discern and perceive those manifestations, beliefs, voices, and persons which claim heaven as the source of their authority but in reality represent the views and vagaries of men or the damning doctrines of demons. Because of the Restoration, because keys and powers and priesthoods and authorities have been delivered to man once again, and because the power to confer and enjoy the gifts and manifestations of the Holy Ghost is among us, every man and woman who qualifies is able to speak in the name of God the Lord, even the Savior of the world (see D&C 1:20). Every person possessing the testimony of Jesus becomes a prophet (see Revelation 19:10) and is thereby able to discern and dispel that which is not of the Light. Further, since "the spirits of the prophets are subject to the prophets" (1 Corinthians 14:32), it is appropriate and right and orderly that "unto the bishop of the church, and unto such as God shall appoint and ordain to watch over the church and to be elders unto the church, are to have it given unto them to discern all those gifts lest there shall be any among you professing and yet be not of God" (D&C 46:27). "Not every spirit, or vision, or singing, is of God," the Prophet taught. "The devil is an orator; he is powerful. . . . The gift of discerning spirits will be given to the Presiding Elder. Pray for him that he may have this gift."[28] And thus it is that the revelations speak emphatically of the president of the Church, the presiding officer in the earthly kingdom, as he who is to "preside over the whole church, and to be like unto Moses—Behold, here is wisdom; yea, to be a seer, a revelator, a translator, and a prophet, having all the gifts of God which he [God] bestows upon the head of the church" (D&C 107:91–92).

The challenge of discerning when a teaching or a manifestation or revelation is from God was a significant challenge for the early Latter-day Saints, just as it is for us today. On the occasion when the first high priests of this dispensation were called and ordained (in June of 1831), some unusual spiritual displays were evident. A revelation given through Joseph Smith indicated a central guide, a standard, a pattern by which the Saints should judge that which is of God from that which is not. "And again," the Lord said, "I will give unto you a pattern in all things, that ye may not be deceived; for Satan is abroad in the land, and he goeth forth deceiving the nations—

"Wherefore he that prayeth, whose spirit is contrite, the same is accepted of me if he obey mine ordinances.

"He that speaketh, whose spirit is contrite, whose language is meek and edifieth, the same is of God if he obey mine ordinances.

"And again, he that trembleth under my power shall be made strong, and shall bring forth fruits of praise and wisdom, according to the revelations and truths which I have given you.

"And again, he that is overcome and bringeth not forth fruits, even according to this pattern, is not of me.

"Wherefore, by this pattern ye shall know the spirits in all cases under the whole heavens" (D&C 52:14–19).

Only those who obey the ordinances of God, his laws, commandments, and statutes, including the rites and ceremonies necessary for salvation (e.g., baptism and confirmation at the hands of an authorized servant of God), are accepted of him. In the true and saving sense, only those who have entered in at the strait gate bring forth fruits and works that originate with God and thus are to be received as his. "The whole world lieth in sin," the Savior explained, "and groaneth under darkness and under the bondage of sin. And by this you may know they are under the bondage of sin, because they come not unto me" (D&C 84:49–50). More specifically, the Lord remarked to Sidney Rigdon just after he had joined the Church that "there are none that doeth good except those who are ready to receive the fulness of my gospel, which I have sent forth unto this generation" (D&C 35:12). The light of Christ and the influence of the Holy Ghost[29] are available to all men and women; the people of the earth may thereby be led into all truth, the fulness of which is to be found in the "only true and living Church upon the face of the whole earth" (D&C 1:30). But the gift of the Holy Ghost and the gifts of the Holy Ghost are reserved for baptized members, those who have truly come unto Christ and who forsake the ways of the world.

CONCLUSION

"We believe all that God has revealed, all that He does now reveal, and we believe that He will yet reveal many great and important things pertaining to the Kingdom of God" (Articles of Faith 1:9). This statement of belief is as true of individuals as it is of the institutional Church. There are great and important things yet to be made known to those Latter-day Saints who search, ponder, and pray. The Lord is no respecter of persons. He does not simply bless office holders, nor does he endow with knowledge from on high only those called to direct the destiny of the Church. "God hath not revealed anything to Joseph," the Prophet himself observed, "but what he will make known unto the Twelve, and even the least Saint may know all things as fast as he is able to bear them."[30] In the words of a modern apostle, "we are entitled to revelation. I say that every member of the Church, independent and irrespective of any position that he may hold, is entitled to get revelation from the Holy Ghost; he is entitled to entertain angels; he is entitled to view the visions of eternity; and if we would like to go the full measure, he is entitled to see God the same way that any prophet in literal and actual reality has seen the face of Deity."[31]

Some time after Joseph Smith's death, he appeared to Brigham Young and gave specific and pointed instructions as to why the members of the Church must labor to acquire and keep the Spirit of the Lord. "Tell the people to be humble and faithful," Joseph Smith counseled his successor, "and be sure to keep the Spirit of the Lord and it will lead them right.

"Be careful and not turn away the small still voice; it will teach them what to do and where to go; it will yield the fruits of the kingdom. Tell the brethren to keep their hearts open to conviction, so that when the Holy Ghost comes to them, their hearts will be ready to receive it. They can tell the Spirit of the Lord from all other spirits; it will whisper peace and joy to their souls; it will take malice, hatred, strife and all evil from their hearts; and their whole desire will be to do good, bring forth righteousness and build up the kingdom of God. Tell the brethren if they will follow the Spirit of the Lord, they will go right. Be sure to tell the people to keep the Spirit of the Lord; and if they will, they will find themselves just as they were organized by our Father in Heaven before they came into the world. Our Father in Heaven organized the human family, but they are all disorganized and in great confusion.

"Joseph then showed me the pattern," President Young continued, "how they were in the beginning. This I cannot describe, but I saw it, and saw where the Priesthood had been taken from the earth and how it must be joined together, so that there would be a perfect chain from Father Adam to his latest posterity. Joseph again said, 'Tell the people to be sure to keep the Spirit of the Lord and follow it, and it will lead them just right.'"[32]

Growing into and learning the spirit of revelation is a central duty as well as a consummate privilege of those who belong to The Church of Jesus Christ of Latter-day Saints. God has spoken. He speaks now. He will yet speak. There is a crying need in this generation for more and better-attuned listening ears. And there is much need to understand how and in what manner the Lord communicates with his people. The Doctrine and Covenants is a marvelous collection of revelations—many and varied in type and kind, but all are sure and certain evidences of the reality that God is the same yesterday, today, and forever; that he who is infinite is ever ready to reveal himself and his will to those of us who are so very finite; that he is "merciful and gracious unto those who fear [him]" and delights to honor those who serve him "in righteousness and in truth." In his own words: "To them will I reveal all mysteries, yea, all the hidden mysteries of my kingdom from days of old, and for ages to come, will I make known unto them the good pleasure of my will concerning all things pertaining to my kingdom. Yea, even the wonders of eternity shall they know, and things to come will I show them, even the things of many generations" (D&C 76:5, 7–8).

This is the Lord's work and must be undertaken according to his holy will and in harmony with his grand and glorious purposes. "This latter-day work is spiritual," President Ezra Taft Benson has taught. "It takes spirituality to comprehend it, to love it, and to discern it. Therefore, we should seek the Spirit in all we do. That is our challenge."[33]

Notes

From an address delivered at Brigham Young University Education Week and Know Your Religion series, 1987–88.

1. *Teachings of the Prophet Joseph Smith,* 160.
2. Joseph Fielding McConkie, "The Principle of Revelation," in Robert L. Millet and Kent Jackson, eds., *Studies in Scripture, Volume 1: The Doctrine and Covenants* (Sandy, Ut.: Randall Book Co., 1984), 81.
3. For prophetic statements as to the corporeality of God prior to this statement in section 130, see *Words of Joseph Smith,* 60, 64. For a detailed discussion of Joseph Smith's teachings regarding God's physical nature, see Robert L. Millett, "The Supreme Power Over All Things: The Doctrine of the Godhead in the Lectures on Faith," in *The Lectures on Faith in Historical Perspective* (Provo: Religious Studies Center, Brigham Young University, 1990), 221–40.
4. Parley P. Pratt, *Key to the Science of Theology,* 1978 ed. (Salt Lake City: Deseret Book Co., 1978), 25.
5. Bruce R. McConkie, *A New Witness for the Articles of Faith* (Salt Lake City: Deseret Book Co., 1985), 257.
6. Ibid., 45.
7. *Gospel Doctrine,* 67–68.
8. McConkie, *A New Witness for the Articles of Faith,* 70.
9. *History of the Church,* 1:109–10.
10. From Newel Knight Journal, LDS Church Archives, Salt Lake City, Utah, as quoted in Lyndon W. Cook, *The Revelations of the Prophet Joseph Smith* (Salt Lake City: Deseret Book Co., 1985), 39–40.
11. From F. Mark McKiernan and Roger D. Launius, eds., *An Early Latter-Day Saint History: The Book of John Whitmer, Kept by Commandment* (Independence, Mo.: Herald Publishing House, 1980), 42; spelling corrected. Joseph Smith's record of this event is given as follows: "Soon after the foregoing revelation [D&C 42] was received, a woman came making great pretensions of revealing commandments, laws and other curious matters" (*History of the Church,* 1:154).
12. J. Reuben Clark Jr., "When Are the Writings and Sermons of Church Leaders Entitled to the Claim of Being Scripture?" address delivered to seminary and institute teachers at Brigham Young University, Provo, Utah, 7 July 1954; in J. Reuben Clark Jr., *J. Reuben Clark: Selected Papers,* ed. David H. Yarn Jr. (Provo: Brigham Young University Press, 1984), 101. It is true that all of the elders of the Church, when moved upon by the power of the Holy Ghost, have the right to speak forth scripture—the will, mind, word, and voice of the Lord (see D&C 68:1–4). Yet, as Paul taught, "the spirits of the prophets are subject to the prophets" (1 Corinthians 14:32), and thus there is a head, a single prophet responsible for scripture being delivered or clarified or expanded for the entire Church.
13. *Teachings of the Prophet Joseph Smith,* 328.
14. Joseph F. Smith, in Conference Report, April 1912, 9–10; see also *Teachings of the Prophet Joseph Smith,* 111.

15. Moses was the head of a dispensation and thus a prophets' prophet. Of him the Lord Jehovah explained to Aaron and Miriam: "If there be a prophet among you, I the Lord will make myself known unto him in a vision, and will speak unto him in a dream. My servant Moses is not so, who is faithful in all mine house. With him will I speak mouth to mouth, even apparently, and not in dark speeches; and the similitude of the Lord shall he behold" (Numbers 12:6–8; see also Exodus 33:11). But the above verse indicates that Moses—like all prophets, and, for that matter, all men and women—walked most often and most surely by the kindly light and whisperings of the Spirit.

16. Joseph Fielding McConkie, "The Principle of Revelation," 83.

17. Boyd K. Packer, in Conference Report, October 1979, 29.

18. See *Teachings of the Prophet Joseph Smith,* 156–57, 209, 214. See also Marion G. Romney, in Conference Report, April 1942, 17–18.

19. *Teachings of the Prophet Joseph Smith,* 151.

20. "The Candle of the Lord," in Boyd K. Packer, *That All May Be Edified* (Salt Lake City: Bookcraft, 1982), 335; see also Conference Report, October 1979, 28; see also 1 Nephi 17:45.

21. Ezra Taft Benson, *Come unto Christ* (Salt Lake City: Deseret Book Co., 1983), 20.

22. Bruce R. McConkie, "The Foolishness of Teaching," address delivered to Church Educational System personnel (Salt Lake City: The Church of Jesus Christ of Latter-day Saints, 1981), 9.

23. Bruce R. McConkie, "Holy Writ: Published Anew," address delivered at a seminar for Regional Representatives, 2 April 1982, in *Doctrines of the Restoration,* ed. Mark L. McConkie (Salt Lake City: Bookcraft, 1989), 236–38.

24. The "articles and covenants" were specifically what we have today as sections 20 and 22 of the Doctrine and Covenants. See Richard O. Cowan, "How Our Doctrine and Covenants Came to Be," in Robert L. Millet and Larry E. Dahl, eds., *The Capstone of Our Religion* (Salt Lake City: Bookcraft, 1989), 1–16.

25. In 1938 President J. Reuben Clark Jr. emphasized to Church educators that "your chief interest, your essential and all but sole duty, is to teach the Gospel of the Lord Jesus Christ as that has been revealed in these latter days. You are to teach this Gospel using as your sources and authorities the Standard Works of the Church, and the words of those whom God has called to lead his people in these last days. You are not, whether high or low, to intrude into your work your own peculiar philosophy, no matter what its source or how pleasing or rational it seems to you to be. To do so would be to have as many different churches as we have seminaries—and that is chaos" (J. Reuben Clark Jr., "The Charted Course of the Church in Education," address delivered on 8 August 1938; in Clark, *J. Reuben Clark: Selected Papers,* 253).

26. *Promised Messiah,* 515–16.

27. See *Teachings of the Prophet Joseph Smith,* 205.

28. Ibid., 162.

29. Joseph Smith made a distinction between the Holy Ghost (i.e., the influence of the Holy Ghost) and the gift of the Holy Ghost. The former is the means, for example, by which an interested investigator of the faith comes to know the truth of the message of the Restoration (see Moroni 10:4–5). The latter—the gift of the Holy Ghost—comes only after baptism by proper authority at the hands of a legal administrator. See *Teachings of the Prophet Joseph Smith,* 199.

30. *Teachings of the Prophet Joseph Smith,* 149.

31. Bruce R. McConkie, "How to Get Personal Revelation," address delivered at a devotional assembly at Brigham Young University, 11 October 1966.

32. Journal History, 23 February 1847.

33. Ezra Taft Benson, *Come unto Christ* 23.

COMMUNION
WITH THE INFINITE

I have felt the need to discuss the matter of spirituality, the degree to which, as President David O. McKay stated, we have a "consciousness of victory over self" and enjoy "communion with the Infinite."[1] In this chapter I would like to discuss ways in which we can enjoy greater "communion with the Infinite" through refining and improving our prayer life, the way we communicate with God.

WHY WE PRAY

Why do we pray? First, we believe our Heavenly Father is a Man of Holiness (see Moses 6:57), a glorified and exalted being, to be sure, but a resurrected and redeemed man who is literally the father of our spirits. He knows us, one by one, and has infinite love and tender regard for each one of us. He has a physical body, parts, and passions. He feels. He yearns. He feels pain and sorrows for our struggles and our wanderings and, like his Beloved Son, is touched with the feeling of our infirmities (see Hebrews 4:15). He delights in our successes. He responds to petitions and pleadings. He is neither untouchable nor unapproachable. Thus our prayers allow us to express to God our needs, our challenges, our deepest feelings and desires, and to ask sincerely for his help. The more prayerful a man or a woman becomes, the more dependent he or she is upon God and thus the more trusting and reliant upon spiritual powers beyond the person's own. Prayer thus builds spiritual strength by pointing us beyond our limited resources to him who has all power. In short, we pray to better understand who we are and who God is. We pray to better understand what we can do on our own and what we can do only with divine assistance.

Second, prayer allows us to communicate with Deity, to open ourselves to conversation with divinity. If indeed the quality of a person's life is largely a product of the kinds of associations they enjoy, then we may rest assured that a man or woman who spends much time in prayer will in time blossom in personality and rise above pettiness, littleness of soul, and mortal jealousies and fears. We cannot have regular contact with influences that are degrading without being affected adversely, almost as though the words and deeds of the depraved become a part of us. On the other hand, a person who regularly calls upon God, pours out the soul in prayer, and yearns for genuine communion with Deity—such a person cannot help but be elevated and transformed by that association. The very powers of God, coming to us through his Holy Spirit, make us into men and women of purpose, of purity, and of power. In short, we pray in order to receive an infusion of power, to draw strength from an omnipotent Being.

> *Oh, may my soul commune with thee*
> *And find thy holy peace;*
> *From worldly care and pain of fear,*
> *Please bring me sweet release.*
> *Oh, bless me when I worship thee*
> *To keep my heart in tune,*
> *That I may hear thy still, small voice,*
> *And, Lord, with thee commune.*
>
> *Enfold me in thy quiet hour*
> *And gently guide my mind*
> *To seek thy will, to know thy ways,*
> *And thy sweet Spirit find.*
> *Lord, grant me thy abiding love*
> *And make my turmoil cease.*
> *Oh, may my soul commune with thee*
> *And find thy holy peace.*[2]

ROADBLOCKS TO COMMUNION

There are certain roadblocks or barriers to communion with the Infinite, things that get in the way and prevent us from enjoying the kind of closeness with our

Heavenly Father that we could have. We all could volunteer examples of such road-blocks. Let me suggest but a few.

1. Surely no roadblock could be more prevalent than distraction and preoccupation. Sometimes we don't pray well because our minds and hearts are focused on other things. We are too prone to think of prayer as something within the spiritual realm, and religion becomes just another department of life—alongside our social, economic, political, or intellectual lives—rather than a vital dimension of everyday living. Notice how hard it is sometimes to focus on the Savior during the passing of the sacrament. That's often because we haven't spent much time during the week focusing on the Savior. Communion with the Infinite requires discipline, and discipline requires prioritization. Obviously we need to chase darkness out of our lives (see D&C 50:25) if we are to draw close to God in prayer. But, in addition, when it is time to pray, we must put aside the things of the world, even good things, in order to engage the greatest good. We do not rush into the divine presence any more than we would rush into the office of the President of the Church or the president of the United States. It is often helpful, before we begin to pray, to slow down, stop what we're doing, sit quietly, listen to inspiring music, read several verses of scripture, ponder and reflect on things that matter most.

2. Another roadblock to an effective prayer life is duplicity or trying to lead two lives. James explained that "a double minded man is unstable in all his ways" (James 1:8). Thus we would suppose that a person who is worldly throughout the day would have great difficulty praying intently at night. Elder Howard W. Hunter observed: "Henry Ward Beecher once said: 'It is not well for a man to pray cream and live skim milk.' That was a century ago. There is now before us a danger that many may pray skim milk and live *that* not at all."[3] Just as our lives are only as good as our prayers, so our prayers are only as good as our lives. That is, the more faithful we become in keeping the Lord's commandments and putting first things first in our lives, the more we open the doors of communication with the heavens and the more comfortable we feel with holy things and holy beings.

3. One of our most common shortcomings is to say our prayers regularly but to do so without much thought, reflection, or devotion, except when we suppose that we really need God's help. Now you know and I know that we need his help every moment of every day of our lives. As King Benjamin pointed out to his people, God "is preserving you from day to day, by lending you breath, that ye may live and move and do according to your own will, and even supporting you from one moment to another" (Mosiah 2:21). Elder Hunter explained: "If prayer is only a spasmodic cry at the time of crisis, then it is utterly selfish, and we come to think of

God as a repairman or a service agency to help us only in our emergencies. We should remember the Most High day and night—always—not only at times when all other assistance has failed and we desperately need help. If there is any element in human life on which we have a record of miraculous success and inestimable worth to the human soul, it is prayerful, reverential, devout communication with our Heavenly Father."[4] One practice that I have found particularly meaningful—especially when I find myself reciting words instead of communing with God—is to devote myself to a prayer in which I ask the Lord for absolutely nothing but instead express sincere gratitude for all my blessings. This kind of prayer pays remarkable dividends and settles the soul like few other efforts.

4. Coach Vince Lombardi wisely remarked that fatigue makes cowards of us all. Fatigue also makes it extremely difficult to enjoy our prayers. Perhaps it is not always wise to make our prayers the last thing we do each day. It may be worth-while occasionally to have prayer well before going to bed while our mind and body are in a position to do more than utter a few well-worn but familiar phrases. There have been several times over the years when one of my children has talked me into watching a late movie with them, perhaps on a Friday night. Concerned that I would inevitably fall asleep either on the floor or on the couch, more than once I have gone into my bedroom, closed the door, and had a meaningful prayer *before* going downstairs to watch the movie.

PUBLIC PRAYER

It's a marvelous thing—although I am certain we do not think about it very much—to be called upon to offer prayer in a public meeting. It's an honor to address the Almighty God but an especial honor to be asked to do so in behalf of a group of fellow believers. We damage ourselves spiritually, rob ourselves of a small but significant opportunity to grow, when we refuse to pray. Some of us feel shy or afraid. Take heart, brothers and sisters, for we are all in this together. No one of us has all of the answers, and no one of us has so achieved spiritually that he or she is in a position to judge another's prayer, no matter how simple or halting it might be. Others may refuse to pray because they do not feel worthy to do so. With the exception of those who are under Church discipline and have thus been asked by priesthood leaders not to participate openly in public meetings, all are in a position to pray if called upon.

Nephi explained the source of the attitude of one who refuses to pray. "If ye would hearken unto the Spirit which teacheth a man to pray," he wrote, "ye would know that ye must pray; for the evil spirit teacheth not a man to pray, but teacheth him that he must not pray" (2 Nephi 32:8). The officers of the Church are charged to "visit the house of each member, and exhort them to pray vocally and in secret and attend to all family duties" (D&C 20:47; see also verse 51). Elsewhere the Savior instructs the Saints: "I command thee that thou shalt pray vocally as well as in thy heart; yea, before the world as well as in secret, in public as well as in private" (D&C 19:28; see also 23:6; 81:3).

There are some things we ought to keep in mind when we pray vocally. My father was fond of saying that we should "pray for the occasion." I think that means that we ought to consider why we are gathered together, what is needed most, and how we might best express those needs to our Father in Heaven. For one thing, public prayers, with perhaps the exception of temple dedicatory prayers, are and should be relatively short. There is an apocryphal story to the effect that Heber C. Kimball was famous for his extremely long prayers. It was said that some of his children—and he had many—would often sneak away during family prayer, play for a while, and then make it back in time to kneel before being discovered. One story has it that one of the boys sneaked away, lost track of time, realized what had happened, and then hurriedly made it back. Dad was still praying. The breathless and concerned young man let out a sigh of relief and whispered to one of his brothers that he had been afraid he had stayed away too long. The brother responded: "No, you're okay. Father hasn't even gotten to the ten tribes yet!"

Well, I suppose there are times when it is necessary to take more time in prayer than usual, but such is rarely the case in public meetings. My wife, Shauna, and I can still remember attending a missionary farewell almost thirty years ago. A man and his wife had been called to serve a full-time mission. A large number of people were called upon to speak (those were the days when sacrament meetings were an hour and a half long), but Grandpa was not asked to speak. He was, however, asked to offer the opening prayer. And Grandpa was not to be denied. I can still remember our two children, Angie and David, who were just learning to bow their little heads and keep their eyes closed for more than a snap, glancing up with a puzzled look in their eyes as the elderly gentleman spoke in great detail in his prayer of Christ, the different dimensions of the Atonement, and a variety of other doctrinal topics. That prayer lasted for seventeen minutes and seemed a bit out of place. Our prayers are not sermons; they are not public discourses. They are not addressed to the other Saints, but to God. Elder Francis M. Lyman taught: "It is not necessary to offer very long and tedious prayers, either at opening or closing. It is not only not pleasing to the Lord for us to use excess of words, but also it is not pleasing to the Latter-day

Saints. Two minutes will open any kind of meeting, and a half minute will close it."⁵

Two of the keys to meaningful prayer, even public prayer, are sincerity and simplicity. We have no one to impress, no one's judgment to fear. Our words are addressed to him who knows all things, including the desires of our hearts (see D&C 6:16). It is thus wise to speak the words that we really feel. In Shakespeare's play *Hamlet,* Claudius stopped praying because his heart was simply not in his prayers. He said: "My words fly up, my thoughts remain below; Words without thoughts never to heaven go."⁶ The Prophet Joseph Smith taught in regard to prayer: "Be plain and simple, and ask for what you want, just like you would go to a neighbor and say, 'I want to borrow your horse to go to the mill.' "⁷ As a part of his own prayer to God, Zenos exclaimed: "Yea, thou art merciful unto thy children when they cry unto thee, to be heard of thee and not of men, and thou wilt hear them" (Alma 33:8).

I hope as we are called upon to pray that we will slow down, take our time, and pray from our hearts. I am often pained as people hurry through a prayer as though it were a formality or even something that needed to be dispensed with as painlessly as possible. This is particularly true for the end of the prayer. I sincerely hope that we will close our prayers with the dignity and transcendent respect that we ought to have for the name of him who bought us with his blood, the Savior of all mankind. Sometimes people are so eager to be done with the prayer that they race through the name of Jesus Christ as though they were sprinting toward a finish line. I assure you that this is not pleasing to his Father, who is also our Father. I promise you that if you and I will pray sincerely, from our hearts, speaking our words soberly and distinctly—especially the concluding words, "in the name of Jesus Christ"—we will begin to feel a power and a sacred influence in our lives that attests that the Lord hears us and is pleased with us.

SERIOUS COMMUNION

One of the things most needed in our prayer lives is consistency and regularity. Some people find it helpful to pray often in the same place. One man I know set aside a special place in his home, a place which over the years came to be like unto a personal sacred grove. It seemed when he entered that room that he felt a hallowed presence. In fact, that is exactly what had happened over the years; because some of the most profound insights and some of the sweetest feelings and impressions had come to him in that room, it had come to represent almost a holy of holies within his home, which was his temple.

Almost forty years ago a man taught me something that has changed my life. He said simply: "When you get out of bed in the morning, never let your feet touch the floor first. Always let your knees touch first." I recommend that bit of practical wisdom to you, especially if you find it difficult to have a regular, meaningful morning prayer. I have been surprised at how many people who would never, ever consider going to bed without praying in the evening have not managed to develop a consistent pattern of prayer in the mornings. Perhaps my practical side comes through here, but I have thought that there are very few harmful or hazardous things that could happen to me between the time I lay my head on the pillow at night and the time I get up. But there are many challenges and temptations and decisions I must face throughout the day, and I need all the help I can get. Evening prayers are extremely important, and morning prayers are vital.

Two of my colleagues at BYU, Brent Top and Bruce Chadwick, tell me that their studies of morality and faithfulness in Latter-day Saint youth throughout the Church reveal some interesting things. Those LDS young people who remained steadfast and solid and straight in the midst of serious temptation were those whose parents had helped their children to somehow internalize the gospel, to make personal scripture study and especially personal prayer high priorities in their lives. The following are some comments from active Latter-day Saint young people who have made it through the challenges without losing their way, at least so far:

"I am so blessed now because my parents encouraged me to pray and read the scriptures on my own."

"My dad always reminds me, 'Say your prayers.' This reminds me that it is not enough to have family prayer. I must pray on my own."

"My parents taught me how important personal revelation is and how I could find answers in the scriptures and receive answers to my prayers."

"It was my parents' example that had the most effect on me. . . . They would give thoughts and advice, but they left it up to me. But they would always counsel me to turn to the Lord and find out his will. In doing this it helped me to start to have spiritual experiences in my own life."[8]

These comments affirm the promise of President Ezra Taft Benson, who said to the youth: "If you will earnestly seek guidance from your Heavenly Father, morning and evening, you will be given the strength to shun any temptation."[9] I think we all know that such a promise applies equally well to the rest of us.

Awake, ye Saints of God, awake!
Call on the Lord in mighty prayer
That he will Zion's bondage break
And bring to naught the tempter's snare.

Though Zion's foes have counseled deep,
Although they bind with fetters strong,
The God of Jacob does not sleep;
His vengeance will not slumber long.

With constant faith and fervent prayer,
With deep humility of soul,
With steadfast mind and heart, prepare
To see the eternal purpose roll.

Awake to righteousness; be one,
Or, saith the Lord, "Ye are not mine!"
Yea, like the Father and the Son,
Let all the Saints in unison join.[10]

WRESTLING WITH GOD

There are prayers and then there are prayers. Sometimes we need to pray with a light spirit and without heavy and deep need weighing upon us. At other times, we long for the kind of spiritual contact and association that demand our most strenuous and disciplined efforts. Jacob of old wrestled with an angel until the breaking of day and thus obtained a blessing from God (see Genesis 32:24–32). Hungering and thirsting after righteousness, Enos wrestled with the Lord in prayer all day and into the night, until the holy voice declared that his sins were forgiven (see Enos 1:1–8).

Even our Lord and Savior came to know something about prayer that he could not have known before his entrance into mortality. In the Garden of Gethsemane the Savior began to feel the loss of his Father's sustaining Spirit. "And being in an agony," Luke records, "he prayed more earnestly" (Luke 22:44). In writing of this singular occasion, Elder Bruce R. McConkie observed: "Now here is a marvelous thing. Note it well. The Son of God 'prayed more earnestly'! He who did all things well, whose every word was right, whose every emphasis was proper; he to whom the Father gave his Spirit without measure; he who was the only perfect being ever to walk the dusty paths of planet earth—the Son of God 'prayed more earnestly,' teaching us, his brethren [and sisters], that all prayers, his included, are not alike, and that a greater need calls forth more earnest and faith-filled pleadings before the throne of him to whom the prayers of the saints are a sweet savor."[11] Indeed, some thorns in the flesh call forth prayers of great intensity (see 2 Corinthians 12:7–10), supplications and pleading that are certainly out of the ordinary. Such vexations of the soul are not typical, not part of our daily prayer life. Just as it would be a mistake to suppose that Jacob or Enos wrestled with God in prayer every day, so you and I are not expected to involve ourselves with the same tenacity, to be involved in the same bending of the soul on a regular basis. But now and then in the eternal scheme of things, we must pass through the fire in order to come through life purified and refined and thus prepared to dwell one day in everlasting burnings with God and Christ and holy beings.

PRAYER IN SPIRIT

If we are willing to move beyond a casual relationship with God, willing to spend the time and exert the energy necessary to make of our prayer life something more than it is now, great things await us. For one thing, in time and with experience, our prayers can become more than petitions, as important as it is to petition the Lord. Our prayers can lead to our receiving instruction: they can be the means whereby God can reveal great and important things to us. The Apostle Paul taught us that "the Spirit also helpeth our infirmities: for we know not what we should pray for as we ought: but the Spirit itself maketh intercession for us with [strivings] which cannot be [expressed]."[12] That is to say, if we are quiet and attentive, the Spirit of the Lord can, on some occasions, lead us to pray for things that were not on our personal agenda, things deep down, things that pertain more to our eternal needs than our temporal wants. In such settings we find our words reaching beyond our thoughts, praying for people and circumstances and eventualities that will surprise us. President Marion G. Romney was fond of saying: "I can always tell when I have spoken by the power of the Holy Ghost, because I learn something from what I have said." And so it is with praying in Spirit.

"God sees things as they really are," Elder Neal A. Maxwell wrote, "and as they will become. We don't! In order to tap that precious perspective during our prayers, we must rely upon the promptings of the Holy Ghost. With access to that kind of knowledge, we would then pray for what we and others should have—*really* have. With the Spirit prompting us, we will not pray 'amiss.'

"With access to the Spirit, our circles of concern will expand. The mighty prayer of Enos began with understandable self-concern, moved outward to family, then to his enemies, and then outward to future generations."[13]

WILLING TO SUBMIT

In the first estate, the premortal world, the great Jehovah declared: "Father, thy will be done, and the glory be thine forever" (Moses 4:2). In Gethsemane, as the hours of atonement began, he said in prayer: "Not my will, but thine, be done" (Luke 22:42; see also Matthew 26:39; Mark 14:36). As he breathed his last breath on the accursed cross of Calvary, Jesus said, as the capstone to his incomparable life: "Father, it is finished, thy will is done." He then "yielded up the ghost" (JST, Matthew 27:54). That sacred submission—coupled with his divine inheritance from the Eternal Father—is what made him who he was. That sublime relinquishment of will enabled him to do what no other mortal could do. That quest to know the will of the Father and then follow it opened him to incomprehensible powers of God. There is a lasting lesson here for us. Spiritual maturity manifests itself in our prayers as we become more and more willing to submit, more and more anxious to learn and carry out the will of him who knows best what to do with us. Through divine grace and assistance (see D&C 109:44), we are enabled to see things as they really are, to realize what really matters, and to consecrate our whole souls toward the realization of God's great work and glory, "to bring to pass the immortality and eternal life of man" (Moses 1:39).

It is true that praying "Thy will be done" may entail submitting to difficult or challenging circumstances ahead. C. S. Lewis provides a slightly different approach to this scripture: " 'Thy will be done.' But a great deal of it is to be done by God's creatures; including me. The petition, then, is not merely that I may patiently suffer God's will but also that I may vigorously do it. I must be an agent as well as a patient. I am asking that I may be enabled to do it. . . .

"Taken this way, I find the words have a more regular daily application. For there isn't always—or we don't always have reason to suspect that there is—some great affliction looming in the near future, but there are always duties to be done; usually, for me, neglected duties to be caught up with. 'Thy will be *done*—by me—now' brings one back to brass tacks." Further, Lewis explained, "Thy will be done" may also imply a readiness on our part to receive and experience new and unanticipated blessings. "I know it sounds fantastic," he added, "but think it over. It seems to me that we often, almost sulkily, reject the good that God offers us because, at that moment, we expected some other good."[14] "Thy will be done" thus represents our petition that the Almighty work his wonders through us, that he soften our hearts to new ideas, new avenues of understanding, and open us to new paths and new doors of opportunity when it is best for us to move in another direction.

CONCLUSION

We kneel before God to show our reverence toward him. Where possible, we speak our prayers aloud. But many times in the day we are not in a position to kneel or to give voice to our yearnings or our feelings. And so it is that we have the commission to "pray always," to keep a prayer in our hearts, to speak to the Almighty in our mind. We pray for his direction and his strength in school, in our work, in our studies, in counseling with troubled friends or confused loved ones, and in our athletic endeavors. Amulek delivered this invitation: "Yea, cry unto him for mercy; for he is mighty to save. Yea, humble yourselves, and continue in prayer unto him. Cry unto him when ye are in your fields, yea, over all your flocks. Cry unto him in your houses, yea, over all your household, both morning, mid-day, and evening. Yea, cry unto him against the power of your enemies. Yea, cry unto him against the devil, who is an enemy to all righteousness. Cry unto him over the crops of your fields, that ye may prosper in them. Cry over the flocks of your fields, that they may increase. But this is not all; ye must pour out your souls in your closets, and your secret places, and in your wilderness. Yea, and when you do not cry unto the Lord, let your hearts be full, drawn out in prayer unto him continually for your welfare, and also for the welfare of those who are around you" (Alma 34:18–27).

Alma also implored: "Cry unto God for all thy support; yea, let all thy doings be unto the Lord, and whithersoever thou goest let it be in the Lord; yea, let all thy thoughts be directed unto the Lord; yea, let the affections of thy heart be placed upon the Lord forever. Counsel with the Lord in all thy doings, and he will direct thee for good; yea, when thou liest down at night lie down unto the Lord, that he may watch over you in your sleep; and when thou risest in the morning let thy heart be full of thanks unto God; and if ye do these things, ye shall be lifted up at the last day" (Alma 37:36–37).

Brothers and sisters, as President Boyd K. Packer pointed out some years ago, the moral pollution index in our society is rising.[15] Evil is on the loose. Satan is abroad in the land (see D&C 52:14); it is truly the day of his power. I do not consider myself any stronger than any other Latter-day Saint. I cannot resist the incessant pull of immorality nor escape the desensitization that follows naturally from larger doses of harshness, crudeness, and violence without the infusion of spiritual power that comes through communion with the Infinite. I would suggest that the same thing is true for each one of you. No one of us is invulnerable to satanic influences. No one of us is strong enough to confront the enemy alone.

I bear witness that prayer makes available that "balm of Gilead" that comes to us from God in heaven through his Holy Spirit. Peace and perspective come to us as we come unto him. I bear witness of the great irony that submission and surrender to the Almighty, in prayer and in practice, lead to dynamic individualism. I know that God our Father lives, that he knows us and hears our prayers. When we pray we are not speaking to a force in the universe but instead to the Father of our spirits. I know that each of us can refine and purify our lives through a greater attention to the regularity, intensity, and overall quality of our prayers. That we will more consistently pour out our souls in prayer as individuals and as families, that the Lord may pour out upon us a blessing hitherto unknown, is the earnest desire of my heart.

Notes

From an address delivered in the Sunset Heights Eighth Ward, Orem, Utah, 15 March 1998.

1. David O. McKay, *Gospel Ideals* (Salt Lake City: *Improvement Era*, 1954), 390.
2. *Hymns*, no. 123.
3. Howard W. Hunter, in Conference Report, October 1977, 79.
4. Ibid.
5. Francis M. Lyman, address delivered at MIA Conference, 5 June 1892, Salt Lake City, Utah; reprinted in *Improvement Era*, April 1947, 245.
6. William Shakespeare, *Hamlet,* act 3, scene 3.
7. Joseph Smith, as quoted in Hyrum and Helen Mae Andrus, comps., *They Knew the Prophet* (Salt Lake City: Bookcraft, 1974), 100.
8. Anonymous LDS youth, as quoted in Brent L. Top and Bruce A. Chadwick, *Rearing Righteous Youth of Zion* (Salt Lake City: Bookcraft, 1998), 89.
9. Ezra Taft Benson, "A Message to the Rising Generation," *Ensign,* November 1977, 32.
10. *Hymns*, no. 17.
11. Bruce R. McConkie, "Why the Lord Ordained Prayer," in *Prayer* (Salt Lake City: Deseret Book, 1978), 8.
12. Romans 8:26; see also *Teachings of the Prophet Joseph Smith*, 278. Compare 3 Nephi 19:24; D&C 46:30; 50:29–30; 63:65.
13. Neal A. Maxwell, "What Should We Pray For?" in *Prayer,* 45.
14. C. S. Lewis, *Letters to Malcolm, Chiefly on Prayer* (New York: Harcourt Brace & Co., 1992), 25–26.
15. Boyd K. Packer, in Conference Report, April 1992, 91.

HONORING HIS HOLY NAME

S everal years ago I sat with my oldest son in a large stadium at a professional baseball game in the eastern United States. We were thrilled to see some of the more famous players up close and excited to watch a well-played athletic contest. There was one thing, however, that clouded the evening for me—the language of some of the fans. It was only a matter of a half hour or so before the tension of the contest and the desire for a win brought forth a stream of profanities from some of the people behind us. For the next three hours, we were subjected to a variety of the coarse and the crude, including constant use of the Lord's name in the form of either cursing or exclamation. As we rode the subway back to our motel, I felt literally beaten down, deflated, even defiled. It was a painful experience.

In a world where upright, moral, God-fearing people would never conceive of murder, theft, or adultery, it is surprising how unthinkingly some take the sacred name of God in vain, dragging it through the gutter in flippant, profane, or unclean speech. Why is it that good people can be observant of the commandments from Sinai that pertain to interpersonal relationships but so careless with regard to the dignity and sanctity of the name and person of Deity? The answer, I think, is that violating the third commandment has as much to do with the way we live and the way we are as it does with the way we speak. It is tied to our eternal perspective— the way we think and act upon sacred things.

We cannot fully appreciate the seriousness of violating this commandment without understanding what it means for people to take the name of God upon themselves and then for them to speak and act and pray in the name of the Lord.

BEARING HIS NAME

The Fall of Adam and Eve, though it was an essential step toward mortality and a pillar of the plan of salvation, resulted in bringing all mankind into a fallen, telestial world. The spiritual death that we thus suffer represents an alienation from God and from the royal family. If not for the possibility of reconciliation with the family head through the Atonement, we would lose the right to bear the family name and the right to eternal life with our Father in Heaven.

Deliverance or redemption from spiritual death is made possible only through the labors of a God, one mightier than death, one upon whom justice has no claim. As the foreordained Messiah, Jesus Christ, our Savior, became the "author of eternal salvation unto all them that obey him" (Hebrews 5:9), Abinadi taught that "God himself shall come down among the children of men, and shall redeem his people. . . . I say unto you, that these are his seed, or they are the heirs of the kingdom of God" (Mosiah 15:1, 11). Thus Christ is the Father of salvation, of resurrection, of redemption. Those who have been born again—through faith, repentance, baptism, and the reception of the Holy Ghost—are adopted into his family. As sons and daughters of Christ (see Mosiah 5:7), they are obligated by covenant to live a life befitting the new and holy name they have taken upon themselves.

We are, then, of the family of the Most High, linked to him through the only One who could reconcile us with our Heavenly Father (see Romans 5:10). It should be expected of us (indeed, of all who profess to follow the Christ) that we speak the names of the Father and of the Son with dignity and respect.

ACTING IN HIS NAME

An angel explained to Adam nearly six millennia ago: "*Thou shalt do all that thou doest in the name of the Son,* and thou shalt repent and call upon God in the name of the Son forevermore" (Moses 5:8; emphasis added). This is a call to action for Adam and all of his posterity. We are to do *all* things in the name of the Son. We are to speak and act and worship and perform the labors of the kingdom and the labors of life in the name of the Son. Whenever the gospel has been on the earth, he has empowered others to act in his holy name, extending an investiture of his divine authority to chosen servants and recognizing the acts they perform by his word. Likewise, the everlasting gospel has been restored in our day "that every man might speak in the name of God the Lord, even the Savior of the world" (D&C

1:20). It is an awesome responsibility. We must seek to think and speak and act as though we were the One whose blessed name we bear, so that our words and acts may become his words and acts.

Our Savior came in his Father's name and in his own right, and he acted in all the majesty of his own divine calling. He healed the sick and forgave sins; in so doing he illustrated his power over both physical and spiritual maladies (see Matthew 9:1–5; Luke 5:23; with JST footnotes). He preached and prayed in ways that were clear to mortals (through the Spirit) and yet clearly divine (see 3 Nephi 17:13–17; 19:31–36). Jesus is Jehovah, and Jehovah is God, and God works miracles in his own right; he needs neither the name nor the power of another. In contrast, all those who are agents of the Lord act and operate and are authorized by the name above all other names that have been in mortality, the name of Jesus Christ (see Philipians 2:9). We may only serve him truly when we have truly taken his name upon us.

TAKING THE NAME OF GOD IN VAIN

How, then, do we become guilty of taking the name of God in vain, whether it be the name of the Father or of the Son?

Let us first define a few terms. The words that are used in Exodus 20:7 are highly significant. The King James Version has it: "Thou shalt not take the name of the Lord thy God in vain." The word translated "take" is from the Hebrew word *Nasah,* used in several related ways in the Old Testament—to lift or lift up, raise, bear or carry (as we carry a burden), and to take or carry away (unjustly). Thus we might speak of taking the name of God in the sense of lifting up or holding up the name, bearing the name of God as we would a standard or a banner, or taking away (from its proper context) the name of God. The word translated "vain" is from the Hebrew word *Shav,* meaning empty, worthless, meaningless, even waste and disorder. As one biblical scholar has observed, *vain* implies "emptiness—a wandering in shadows without substance, a life without the possibility of satisfaction."[1]

What, then, are some ways men and women take the name of God in vain?

1. *His children take his name in vain through profanity and vulgarity.* The most commonly understood violation is speaking the name of Deity in the context of cursing or profaning. It is interesting to note that the word *profane* (from the Latin *pro-* and *fanum*) means literally "outside the temple." What an insightful way to describe the profanation of the name of God: to take that which is most holy, remove it from its hallowed setting, and thrust it into an environment that is unholy

and unclean. Thus, alternate translations of this passage read as follows: "You must not make wrong use of the name of the Lord your God" (Revised English Bible); "You shall not make wrongful use of the name of the Lord your God" (New Revised Standard Version); "You shall not misuse the name of the Lord your God" (New International Version). President Gordon B. Hinckley has taught: "So serious was violation of this law considered in ancient Israel that blasphemy of the name of the Lord was regarded as a capital crime. . . .

"While that most serious of penalties [death] has long since ceased to be inflicted, the gravity of the sin has not changed."[2]

The increase of profanity and vulgarity in music, books, television, and movies serves as a commentary on our times. It seems likely that people's inhumanity to people is related to their neglect of sacred matters, that the growing harshness, crudeness, and insensitivity in society are correlated directly with denying, defying, or ignoring God. When we love the Lord, cherish his word, and humbly bow beneath his rod, we seek always to act and speak with deferential reverence toward Deity. On the other hand, one who knows not God and finds no personal value in worship or devotion cannot understand the true, deep meaning of *holy* and *holiness*. Such a person may have no sense of restraint in regard to speech, no hesitation to drag the sacred out of its context and thrust it into the profane.

In a modern revelation, the Lord cautioned:

"Wherefore, let all men beware how they take my name in their lips—

"For behold, verily I say, that *many there be who are under this condemnation, who use the name of the Lord, and use it in vain, having not authority. . . .*

"Remember that *that which cometh from above is sacred, and must be spoken with care, and by constraint of the Spirit;* and in this there is no condemnation" (D&C 63:61–62, 64; emphasis added).

The Lord is from above, as is his word (see D&C 63:59). When we speak of him or take his name, we should do so with the deepest reverence. To do otherwise is to take or hold up or raise up his holy name before others without serious thought, without appropriate reflection—in other words, in vain.

Elder Dallin H. Oaks has explained that "we take the name of the Lord in vain when we use his name without authority. This obviously occurs when the sacred names of God the Father and his Son, Jesus Christ, are used in what is called profanity: in hateful cursings, in angry denunciations, or as marks of punctuation in common discourse." On the other hand, Elder Oaks added, "The names of the Father and the Son are used with authority when we reverently teach and testify of them, when we pray, and when we perform the sacred ordinances of the priesthood."[3]

2. His children take his name in vain through the breaking of oaths and covenants. To ancient Israel the Lord said: "Ye shall not swear by my name falsely, neither shalt thou profane the name of thy God: I am the Lord" (Leviticus 19:12). The Jewish Publication Society translation of Exodus 20:7 is: "You shall not swear falsely by the name of the Lord your God." One commentator has written of the third commandment: "This prohibition applies strictly to perjury or false swearing, the breaking of a promise or contract that has been sealed with an oath in the name of God. He will not allow His name to be associated with any act of falsehood or treachery. His name must not be taken in vain, i.e., lightly or heedlessly."[4]

Anciently an oath was a means of impressing the necessity of truth and integrity upon parties to an agreement or upon witnesses in an investigation. The legal procedure involving an oath was fortified by holy words and sacred acts and sealed by invocation of the name of Deity. To break such an oath was indeed a very serious matter and was not to go unpunished (see Ezekiel 17:12–19). But in time people began to abuse their oaths, to swear in a manner that was unholy, inappropriate, or that would allow for loopholes.

Jesus called his followers to a greater accountability: "Swear not at all; neither by heaven; for it is God's throne:

"Nor by the earth; for it is his footstool: neither by Jerusalem; for it is the city of the great King.

"Neither shalt thou swear by thy head, because thou canst not make one hair white or black.

"But let your communication be, Yea, yea; Nay, nay: for whatsoever is more than these cometh of evil" (Matthew 5:34–37). His was a call to his disciples to let their word be their bond in righteousness. *Yes* as a part of a legal or interpersonal arrangement should mean *yes,* and *no* must mean *no.* Personal honor and integrity are at stake.

Covenants are two-way promises between us and our God. All gospel covenants and ordinances are administered and entered into in the name of Jesus Christ; nothing can be done for the salvation of mankind in any other name or by any other authority. Thus, to willingly or knowingly violate our covenants made in his name is to take the name of the Lord in vain—to take lightly or treat as empty and meaningless our sacred and solemn obligations. God will not be mocked (see Galatians 6:7), nor will he suffer that his holy ordinances be mocked or treated capriciously or cavalierly.

Further, those who have entered into the covenants of the gospel are under sacred obligation to labor to build up the kingdom of God. To refuse callings outright, neglect our duties, or in general fail to do our part is to take the name of the Lord upon us and then fail to bear it honorably. "Hearken and hear, O ye my people, saith the Lord and your God, ye whom I delight to bless with the greatest of all blessings, ye that hear me; and *ye that hear me not will I curse, that have professed my name,* with the heaviest of all cursings" (D&C 41:1; emphasis added). The Lord has warned that in the last days "vengeance cometh speedily upon the inhabitants of the earth . . ."

"And upon my house shall it begin, and from my house shall it go forth, saith the Lord;

"*First among those among you, saith the Lord, who have professed to know my name and have not known me,* and have blasphemed against me in the midst of my house, saith the Lord" (D&C 112:24–26; emphasis added).

3. *His children take his name in vain through being flippant, sacrilegious, and irreverent.* The divine decree from Sinai "necessarily forbids all light and irreverent mention of God, or any of His attributes, and we may safely add to all these that every prayer, . . . etc., that is not accompanied with deep reverence and the genuine spirit of piety is here condemned also."[5]

Several years ago a young man who addressed our ward in sacrament meeting began by saying, in essence, "Brothers and sisters, it's great to be in your ward today. I am told that the best way to get a congregation with you is to liven them up with a few jokes." He related several humorous stories, including some inappropriate for the occasion. The congregation roared—or at least some of them did. Others wondered what was going on. After fifteen or twenty minutes, the young man looked at his watch and said, "Well, I'd better close now. I say all these things in the name of Jesus Christ, amen."

His address was amusing and entertaining, something that might have been fun under other circumstances. But we were in a sacrament meeting, a sacred worship service. There was something haunting about his closing words, "In the name of Jesus Christ." I had, of course, heard those very words thousands of times over the years. That day, however, I thought of all the times I had delivered talks or offered prayers in the name of Jesus Christ but had done so without much reflection upon whose name I had taken. I thought of occasions when I had spoken on topics of my own choosing but topics that may not have represented what the Lord wanted discussed. I thought of those times I had closed my prayers in a flash, zipping through the name of the Redeemer as though I were sprinting toward some finish line. I thought of the scores of times I had partaken of the emblems of the body and blood of the Savior with my mind focused on things alien to the spirit of the occasion.

It occurred to me then, and has many times since, that we need not be involved with profanity to be guilty of taking the name of the Lord our God in vain. We need merely to treat lightly, flippantly, and without serious thought the sobering charge we carry as members of his Church to speak and act in God's name.

To be guilty of taking God's name in vain is to participate in sacred ordinances lightly or unworthily, to pretend to faithfulness when our hearts or hands are unclean.

We are a happy people, and the joy and satisfaction that derive from living the gospel must not be kept a secret. On the other hand, Joseph Smith taught that "the things of God are of deep import; and time, and experience, and careful and ponderous and solemn thoughts can only find them out."[6]

PRAISE YE HIS NAME

We have the privilege of bearing the name of God honorably and righteously. When we do so, we walk in his light. "That which is of God is light; and he that receiveth light, and continueth in God, receiveth more light; and that light groweth brighter and brighter until the perfect day" (D&C 50:24). On the other hand, when we have covenanted to honor the name of God (see Exodus 20:2–6) and we do not do so, our minds will be darkened by our unbelief, and then the Lord has said that we are under condemnation, that a scourge and a judgment await (see D&C 84:54–59).

To be called upon to speak or act in the name of God is a sacred trust. It is deserving of solemn and ponderous thought. We would preach gospel doctrines more diligently and bear more fervent testimonies if we kept fixed in our minds the weighty fact that our words or our deeds can be the words and actions of our eternal Head. Our divine commission includes this sobering provision: "Wherefore, as ye are agents, ye are on the Lord's errand; and whatsoever ye do according to the will of the Lord is the Lord's business" (D&C 64:29). By contrast, if we speak or act or pray without seeking for inspiration, if we teach for doctrine the views and philosophies of men, if we approach spiritual opportunities lightly or carelessly, we are probably taking the name of God in vain.

President Spencer W. Kimball counseled: "It is not enough to refrain from profanity or blasphemy. We need to make important in our lives the name of the Lord. While we do not use the Lord's name lightly, we should not leave our friends or our neighbors or our children in any doubt as to where we stand. Let there be no doubt about our being followers of Jesus Christ."[7] Obedience to the third commandment has as much to do with the way we live and the way we are as it does with the way we speak.

It is our privilege to know him and, through him, our Father. We can rejoice in the revealed knowledge of our divine birthright and in the opportunity to take upon us the name of the Son. Our desires to acknowledge, recognize, and praise our Heavenly Father and our loving Savior should know no bounds.

Mortality offers the opportunity to be true to who and what we are by righteously taking upon us the name of God. At the same time, it offers the risk of losing our divine heritage if we take and use his name in vain. The Apostle Paul counseled the Corinthians: "Know ye not that ye are the temple of God, and that the Spirit of God dwelleth in you?

"If any man defile the temple of God, him shall God destroy; for the temple of God is holy, which temple ye are" (1 Corinthians 3:16–17; see also 6:19–20).

If we truly want to be as living temples of our God, we would do well to remember, in our thoughts and words and actions, the dedication that is inscribed on each of the sacred buildings we call temples: "Holiness to the Lord."

Notes

From "Honoring His Holy Name," *Ensign,* March 1994, 6–11.

1. Lawrence O. Richards, *Expository Dictionary of Bible Words* (Grand Rapids, Mich.: Zondervan, 1985), 608.
2. Gordon B. Hinckley, "Take Not the Name of God in Vain," *Ensign,* November 1987, 45.
3. Dallin H. Oaks, "Reverent and Clean," *Ensign,* May 1986, 49–50.
4. J. R. Dummelow, *A Commentary on the Holy Bible* (New York: Macmillan Publishing Co., 1936), 67.
5. Adam Clarke, *Commentary on the Holy Bible,* abridged by Ralph Earle (Grand Rapids, Mich.: Baker Book House, 1967), 126.
6. *Teachings of the Prophet Joseph Smith,* 137.
7. Spencer W. Kimball, "'Hold Fast to the Iron Rod,'"*Ensign,* November 1978, 6.

Chapter 36

REMEMBER THE SABBATH DAY

The observance of the Sabbath predates Sinai, for we learn from Moses that after the Gods had completed the paradisiacal creation of all things, the Lord "rested on the seventh day from all his work which he had made. And God blessed the seventh day, and sanctified it: because that in it he rested from all his work which God created and made" (Genesis 2:2–3; see also Moses 3:2–3). Interestingly, there is no mention in the Old Testament about the Sabbath or Sabbath observance during the times of Abraham, Isaac, and Jacob, but we would suppose, knowing the import of this statute, that the former-day Saints during patriarchal times did in fact honor the seventh day as a holy memorial. From the time of the exodus of the children of Israel from Egypt, the Sabbath commemorated the deliverance of the covenant people from bondage. "Keep the sabbath day to sanctify it, as the Lord thy God hath commanded thee. . . . And remember that thou wast a servant in the land of Egypt, and that the Lord thy God brought thee out thence through a mighty hand and by a stretched out arm: therefore the Lord thy God commanded thee to keep the sabbath day" (Deuteronomy 5:12, 15). This would mean, therefore, that the Sabbath was kept on a different day each year.

During the wilderness wanderings the Israelites were instructed to gather enough manna on the day prior to the Sabbath so that they would have sufficient. "And Moses said, Eat that to day: for to day is a sabbath unto the Lord: to day ye shall not find it in the field. Six days ye shall gather it; but on the seventh day, which is the sabbath, in it there shall be none" (Exodus 16:25–26). Indeed, the seriousness of the law of the Sabbath is illustrated in an instance in Numbers 15, in which "a man that gathered sticks upon the sabbath day" is stoned to death by the congregation of Israel (vv. 32–36).

Inasmuch as a proper observance of the Sabbath signals and symbolizes a worshipful attitude, it would seem to follow that during periods of waywardness the people of God would naturally cease to comply with this law. Thus Nehemiah's reform included a reinstitution of a strict Sabbath observance. "In those days saw I in Judah some treading wine presses on the sabbath, and bringing in sheaves, and lading asses. . . . Then I contended with the nobles of Judah, and said unto them, What evil thing is this that ye do, and profane the sabbath day? Did not your fathers thus, and did not our God bring all this evil upon us, and upon this city? yet ye bring more wrath upon Israel by profaning the sabbath. And it came to pass, that when the gates of Jerusalem began to be dark before the sabbath, I commanded that the gates should be shut, and charged that they should not be opened till after the sabbath: and some of my servants set I at the gates, that there should no burden be brought in on the sabbath day" (Nehemiah 13:15–19).

During the centuries preceding the coming of the Messiah, efforts to interpret the Law resulted in massive commentary, rules, and "traditions of the elders." No aspect of the Law became more burdensome and cumbersome than the law of the Sabbath. Endless lists and formulae pertaining to servile work, distances to be traveled, and in general what was and was not appropriate for the Sabbath—these things constituted an integral part of daily life among Jews in the first century. "We do not overstate our case," Elder Bruce R. McConkie has written, "when we say that the Jewish system of Sabbath observance that prevailed in the day of Jesus was ritualistic, degenerate, and almost unbelievably absurd, a system filled with fanatical restrictions."[1] In an effort to establish a sane perspective on the Sabbath day— to point up the spiritual inconsistency associated with so many innane restrictions— Jesus took occasion to lift and teach and heal and work miracles, to do good on the Sabbath, for all of which he was attacked by his enemies among the Jewish leaders. "Wherefore the Sabbath was given unto man for a day of rest," he taught, "and also that man should glorify God, and not that man should not eat; for the Son of Man made the Sabbath day, therefore the Son of Man is Lord also of the Sabbath" (JST, Mark 2:26–27). Following Jesus' mortal ministry, the members of the Church of Jesus Christ observed the first day of the week as the Sabbath day, the Lord's day, in remembrance of the Resurrection of the Master (see Acts 20:7; 1 Corinthians 16:2; Revelation 1:10).

Purposes of the Sabbath

Why would God stress so forcefully the proper observance of the Sabbath? Why would this be one of the Ten Commandments? Consider the following principles:

1. *Acquiring physical rest.* In a very practical way, the Sabbath was given to man to enable us to take a break, to rest our tired bodies, to renew ourselves physically. So many in our modern age work themselves to exhaustion, work long days (and some even into the night), in an effort to get ahead financially and get a jump on rising costs. Too often they choose to work on the Sabbath, only to face themselves in the mirror on Monday mornings unrested and unsatisfied. The body is the temple of God (see 1 Corinthians 3:16–17; 6:19), and we can do ourselves quite as much harm through overwork as we can by other more obvious forms of abuse.

2. *Acquiring spiritual rest.* Perhaps more important than our need for physical respite is our need for spiritual rest. Many of us face the world Monday through Saturday, face a hostile environment that tugs at our testimony and digs at our devotion. We engage a fallen world that weakens our resolve and entices us toward ungodliness. The Sabbath is fundamentally necessary in order to charge our batteries and empower our souls. President Brigham Young noted that "the Lord has planted within us a divinity; and that divine immortal spirit requires to be fed. Will earthly food answer for that purpose? No. It will only keep this body alive as long as the spirit stays within it." President Young also explained that "that divinity within us needs food from the Fountain from which it emanated."[2]

"It is a day of worship," President Joseph F. Smith declared, "a day in which the spiritual life of man may be enriched. *A day of indolence, a day of physical recuperation is too often a very different thing from the God-ordained day of rest. . . .* A proper observance of the duties and devotions of the Sabbath day will, by its change and its spiritual life, give the best rest that men can enjoy on the Sabbath day."[3]

It is essential for us to go to Church to participate in those sacraments or ordinances that provide a clear channel for divine power. "And that thou mayest more fully keep thyself unspotted from the world," Jehovah said in a modern revelation, "thou shalt go to the house of prayer and offer up thy sacraments upon my holy day; for verily this is a day appointed unto you to rest from your labors, and to pay thy devotions unto the Most High" (D&C 59:9–10). Partaking of the sacrament of the Lord's Supper enables us to renew sacred covenants—our promise to take the

Lord's name, to keep his commandments, to bear one another's burdens—and to renew the Lord's promise to us—that we can be forgiven and renewed in spirit, that we may always have his Spirit to be with us (see Moroni 4–5).

There is a grander sense in which proper Sabbath observance rests our souls. Too many of us depend on Church attendance and weekly association with the Saints to make all the difference in our spiritual lives; we suppose that one-day-a-week holiness is sufficient to make it through the mists of darkness. I am persuaded that the Sabbath serves us most powerfully when we have earnestly sought through the week to come unto Christ—through at least brief daily efforts at personal and family devotion. One of the reasons we often have such difficulty pondering on the Savior and his atoning sacrifice during the sacramental service is because we have not thought too much about such things Monday through Saturday. On the other hand, when members of the Church are striving to think and ponder and pray and search the scriptures during the week, then the Sabbath becomes a capstone to a well spent week. It is of such seven-day-a-week holiness that the Master speaks when he says: "Nevertheless thy vows shall be offered up in righteousness *on all days and at all times*" (D&C 59:11; emphasis added).

The scriptures often speak of *rest* in other ways as well. The Sabbath is a day of rest in the sense that it is a day wherein we seek to enter the "rest of the Lord," that is, "rest from doubt, from fear, from apprehension of danger, rest from religious turmoil of the world."[4] To rest on the Sabbath is also to move closer to that supernal day when we are permitted to enter God's presence (JST, Exodus 34:1–2) and receive the fulness of his glory (D&C 84:24). We thus rest here, in this life, in preparation for the ultimate rest hereafter. Mormon thus declared: "Wherefore, I would speak unto you that are of the church, that are the peaceable followers of Christ, and that have obtained a sufficient hope by which ye can enter into the rest of the Lord, from this time henceforth until ye shall rest with him in heaven" (Moroni 7:3).

3. *Demonstrating devotion to Deity.* As we have already suggested, the Sabbath allows us to focus, at least once per week, on matters of eternal import. We are all expected to cultivate the spirit of revelation and the spirit of Christian service every day of our lives, but the Sabbath provides us a unique opportunity to divorce ourselves from the cares of Babylon—making money, meeting deadlines, competing—and give our full time and attention to the establishment of Zion. On the Sabbath we teach our families the gospel, study the scriptures and the words of the living oracles, and in general delight in the things of the Spirit. To observe the Sabbath, President Spencer W. Kimball wrote, "One will be on his knees in prayer, preparing

lessons, studying the gospel, meditating, visiting the ill and distressed, sleeping, reading wholesome material, and attending all the meetings of that day to which he is expected."[5] President Harold B. Lee explained that "Sunday is more than a day of rest from the ordinary occupations of the week. It is not to be considered as merely a day of lazy indolence and idleness or for physical pleasures and indulgences. It is a feast day for your spirit bodies."[6]

Because the Lord established the Sabbath as a day of rest at the consummation of the Creation, it would be wise for us to reflect, on the Sabbath, on the goodness and omnipotence of our Creator, to ponder on the beauties and wonders about us. Because the Sabbath at one time in history commemorated the deliverance of ancient Israel from the hold of the Egyptians, it would be wise for us to reflect, on the Sabbath, on the power of the Almighty's arm to deliver us from ignorance and sin and death and eternal unhappiness. And because since the ministry of the Messiah the Sabbath has pointed us to his rise from death, it would be wise for us to reflect, on the Sabbath, on the infinite and eternal atoning sacrifice of Jesus the Christ. President David O. McKay observed: "Our Sabbath, the first day of the week, commemorates the greatest event in all history—Christ's resurrection, and his visit as a resurrected being to his assembled Apostles."[7] Elder Mark E. Petersen added that "our observance or nonobservance of the Sabbath is an unerring measure of our attitude toward the Lord personally and toward his suffering in Gethsemane, his death on the cross, and his resurrection from the dead. It is a sign of whether we are Christians in very deed, or whether our conversion is so shallow that commemoration of his atoning sacrifice means little or nothing to us."[8]

PROPHETIC COUNSEL

The leaders of the Church have made it abundantly clear that God expects a covenant people to be true to their covenants, including our ongoing promise to properly observe the Sabbath. We cannot expect to avoid the perils that await the ungodly if we are contributors to society's ungodliness and irreverence. Elder George Albert Smith declared the following in a much quieter and more reverent day than our own: "The Sabbath has become the play-day of this great nation, the day set apart by thousands to violate the commandment that God gave long, long ago, and I am persuaded that much of the sorrow and distress that is afflicting and will continue to inflict mankind is traceable to the fact that they have ignored his admonition to keep the Sabbath day holy."[9] President Spencer W. Kimball stated: "I again would urge upon all Saints everywhere a more strict observance of the

Sabbath day. The Lord's holy day is fast losing its sacred significance throughout the world, at least our world. More and more, man destroys the Sabbath's sacred purposes in pursuit of wealth, pleasure, recreation, and the worship of false and material gods."[10] Also: "Brethren and sisters, once again I call to our attention the fourth commandment given by the Lord to Moses on Mount Sinai. . . . Let us observe it strictly in our homes and in our families. Let us refrain from all unnecessary labors. Sunday is not a day for hunting and fishing, nor for swimming, picnicking, boating, or engaging in any other sports."[11]

President Benson taught: "I don't believe that it is possible to keep our spirituality on a high plane by spending our Sabbaths on the beach, on the golf course, in the mountains, or in our own homes reading newspapers and looking at television. When the Lord said, 'And that thou mayest more fully keep thyself unspotted from the world, thou shalt go to the house of prayer' (D&C 59:9), that is exactly what He meant. We must have spiritual food.

"Of course you can live a pretty good life out on the golf course on Sunday. But you don't build your spirituality. Probably you could worship the Lord out there, but the fact is you don't do it as you don't worship Him down on the beach. But if you go the house of the Lord you will worship Him. If you attend to your prayers in your home with your family you will worship Him. And your spirituality will be raised. The spiritual food which your body requires will be provided and you are much more apt to have this joy."[12]

Note the following counsel regarding purchases on the Sabbath:

"We note," President Kimball observed, "that in our Christian world in many places we still have business establishments open for business on the sacred Sabbath. We are sure the cure of this lies in ourselves, the buying public. Certainly the stores and business houses would not remain open if we, the people, failed to purchase from them. Will you all please reconsider this matter. Take it to your home evenings and discuss it with your children. It would be wonderful if every family determined that henceforth no Sabbath purchase would be made."[13]

"I wish I had the power," President Gordon B. Hinckley said, "to convert this whole Church to the observance of the Sabbath. I know our people would be more richly blessed of the Lord if they would walk in faithfulness in the observance of the Sabbath. . . . There isn't anybody in this Church who has to buy furniture on Sunday. There really isn't. There isn't anybody in this Church who has to buy a new automobile on Sunday, is there? No. There isn't anybody in this Church who, with a little care and planning, has to buy groceries on Sunday. . . . You don't need to make Sunday a day of merchandising. . . . I don't think we need to patronize the ordinary business merchants on the Sabbath day. Why do they stay open? To get customers. Who are those customers? Well, they are not all nonmembers of this Church. You know that and I know that."[14]

Note the counsel from President James E. Faust: "Over a lifetime of observation, it is clear to me that the farmer who observes the Sabbath day seems to get more done on his farm than he would if he worked seven days. The mechanic will be able to turn out more and better products in six days than in seven. The doctor, the lawyer, the dentist, the scientist will accomplish more by trying to rest on the Sabbath than if he tries to utilize every day of the week for his professional work. I would counsel all students, if they can, to arrange their schedules so that they do not study on the Sabbath. If students and other seekers after truth will do this, their minds will be quickened and the infinite Spirit will lead them to the verities they wish to learn. This is because God has hallowed his day and blessed it as a perpetual covenant of faithfulness."[15]

CONCLUSION

We live in a rapidly decaying world, in a society that is taking the most direct route to destruction. Because we cannot afford to partake of worldliness, we must seek to do all in our power to acquire and cultivate holiness. "Be ye holy," we have been told, "for I [the Lord] am holy" (1 Peter 1:16; see also Leviticus 11:44). More specifically, "Ye shall keep my sabbaths, and reverence my sanctuary: I am the Lord" (Leviticus 19:30). "But remember that on this, the Lord's day, thou shalt offer thine oblations and thy sacraments unto the Most High, confessing thy sins unto thy brethren, and before the Lord. And on this day thou shalt do none other thing, only let thy food be prepared with singleness of heart that thy fasting"—that is, our hungering and thirsting after righteousness—"may be perfect, or, in other words, that thy joy may be full. Verily, this is fasting and prayer, or in other words, rejoicing and prayer" (D&C 59:12–14).

One sign and witness to God and to all men and women that we are eager to keep ourselves unspotted from the vices of the world is our willingness to keep the Sabbath day holy. It is a token of holiness, a visible symbol of our desire to honor Jehovah, even he who established the Sabbath, "the very Eternal Father of heaven and of earth" (Alma 11:39). I have a conviction if we strive daily to draw near unto God—through brief but consistent scripture study, pondering, and prayer—that the Sabbath will indeed become the spiritual highlight and capstone of our week, the culmination of a diligent quest for holiness and peace. We thereby qualify for the cleansing and motivating power of the Holy Spirit in our lives and thus enter into the rest of the Lord. The Holy One becomes our God and we become his people, a people of covenant.

Notes

From *The Ten Commandments for Today,* ed. John G. Scott (Salt Lake City: Bookcraft, 1997), 67–77.

1. Bruce R. McConkie, *Mortal Messiah,* 1:201.
2. Brigham Young, in *Journal of Discourses,* 7:138.
3. Joseph F. Smith, *Gospel Doctrine,* 242; emphasis added.
4. Ibid., 58.
5. Spencer W. Kimball, *The Miracle of Forgiveness* (Salt Lake City: Bookcraft, 1969), 97.
6. Harold B. Lee, *Teachings of Harold B. Lee,* ed. Clyde J. Williams (Salt Lake City: Bookcraft, 1996), 210.
7. David O. McKay, *Gospel Ideals* (Salt Lake City: Improvement Era, 1953), 397–98.
8. Mark E. Petersen, in Conference Report, April 1975, 72.
9. George Albert Smith, in Conference Report, October 1935, 120.
10. Spencer W. Kimball, in Conference Report, October 1978, 5.
11. Spencer W. Kimball, in Conference Report, October 1979, 4.
12. Ezra Taft Benson, *Teachings of Ezra Taft Benson* (Salt Lake City: Bookcraft, 1988), 439.
13. Spencer W. Kimball, in Conference Report, October 1975, 6.
14. Gordon B. Hinckley, in Heber City–Springville Utah regional conference, priesthood leadership session, 13 May 1995; as quoted by Earl C. Tingey, in Conference Report, April 1996, 11–12.
15. James E. Faust, *Finding Light in a Dark World* (Salt Lake City: Deseret Book Co., 1995), 112.

FAITH AND SCHOLARSHIP

There has never been a time when there was a greater need for disciple-scholars, for persons of faith and intellect. Moral courage. Integrity. Priorities. These are principles of power, anchors that will enable us to make a difference in a world that has drifted from its moorings.

A HIERARCHY OF TRUTHS

I believe in study. I find great joy in reading broadly and expanding my mind on many subjects. I think we are expected to do that as much as our time and circumstances allow. It is good for men and women to specialize, to focus their attention and efforts on certain disciplines or fields of study, to master the disciplines, to become expert on what the great minds have discovered or uncovered. In short, it is good to be learned (see 2 Nephi 9:29). I am sincerely grateful for noble teachers, both Latter-day Saint and of other faiths, who have motivated me—set me on fire—in regard to the social and behavioral sciences, as well as the ancient world of the Bible. At the same time, I thank God for those great minds whose faith in the true, eternal, but unseen verities has inspired me to prioritize. I have come to know that although ours is a thoughtful faith, one that requires reason as well as revelation, it is often necessary to place our unanswered questions on a shelf, to suspend intellectual judgment while our findings from study manage to catch up with the feelings and impressions obtained from the Spirit of the Lord.

All truths are not of equal worth, nor are they acquired in the same way.

"Seeking learning by study," Elder Dallin H. Oaks observed, "we use the method of reason. Seeking learning by faith, we must rely on revelation. . . . Reason is a thinking process using facts and logic that can be communicated to another person and tested by objective (that is, measurable) criteria. Revelation is communication from God to man. It cannot be defined and tested like reason. Reason involves thinking and demonstrating. Revelation involves hearing or seeing or understanding or feeling. Reason is potentially public. Revelation is invariably personal."[1] Surely we are put here on the earth to learn as much as we can in the sciences, in the arts, in languages, in history and foreign culture, and so on. And, to the degree that we can master some of these fields, we are better able to present the truth understandably and appropriately to more and more people (see D&C 88:78–80).

I have a conviction, however, that some truths matter more than others. It is valuable to know of gravity or the laws of motion, but it is vital to know of the reality of a Redeemer. It is helpful to know the laws of thermodynamics, but it is essential to know how to repent and call upon God, in the name of his Son, for forgiveness. The idea that spiritual truths are of greater worth to our eternal welfare than the field to which we have dedicated our professional lives should not be threatening to anyone, nor should it cause us to be defensive about our own discipline. The perpetuation of eternal truth and the conversion of individual souls must be more important to us than the discovery or dissemination of this or that idea. We are children of God, Christians, Latter-day Saints, and devotees to disciplines, in that order. When we get things out of order we open ourselves to trouble; we begin the gradual dilution of our discipleship.

On the one hand, I am convinced that the restored gospel is robust enough to open itself to rigorous study and analysis. It is commendable when a member of the Church, when confronted by a challenging issue, responds with the simple statement of testimony. Every one of us will be in that position at one time or another. And yet there is a particular power associated with the bearing of testimony informed by adequate study, testimony that represents, in the words of the Apostle Peter, a *reason* for the *hope* within us (see 1 Peter 3:15). On the other hand, I refuse to allow my commitment to the faith to be held hostage to the latest fads and trends in the academic world. I cannot, for example, afford to postpone believing in Christ until New Testament scholars of many faiths come to a consensus on what Jesus really did and what he really said. I cannot allow my witness of the Book of Mormon to rest on archaeological evidences in North, Central, or South America, any more than I can prop my faith in the Book of Abraham on what a handful of Egyptologists make of the Joseph Smith papyri. More than forty years ago Hugh Nibley reminded us that "the words of the prophets cannot be held to the tentative and defective tests that men have devised for them. Science, philosophy, and common sense all have a right to their day in court. But the last word does not lie with them. Every time men in their wisdom have come forth with the last word, other words have promptly followed. The last word is a testimony of the gospel that comes only by direct revelation. Our Father in heaven speaks it, and if it were in perfect agreement with the science of today, it would surely be out of line with the science of tomorrow. Let us not, therefore, seek to hold God to the learned opinions of the moment when he speaks the language of eternity."[2]

FAITH IN A DAY OF UNBELIEF

There are few things more desperately needed in our day than faith—faith in the unseen, or as one astute observer of Christianity has noted, "faith that bridges the chasm between what our minds can know and what our souls aspire after."[3] Faith is not whimpering acquiescence, not timid and spineless hope for happiness or for pie in the sky in the great by and by. Faith is active. Faith is powerful. Faith is based on evidence, internal evidence, the kind of evidence that men and women acquire who search and pray and open themselves to the Infinite, who refuse to yield to cynicism or arrogance.

Though one need not be simpleminded to have faith, one may need to be simple in his or her approach to life and its challenges in order to enjoy the fruits of faith. How open are we today to simple belief? Just how believing are we? How would we respond to the miracles of days gone by? Malcolm Muggeridge has written: "In humanistic times like ours, a contemporary virgin—assuming there are any such—would regard a message from the Angel Gabriel that she might expect to give birth to a son to be called the Son of the Highest as ill-tidings of great sorrow and a slur on the local family-planning center. It is, in point of fact, extremely improbable, under existing conditions, that Jesus would have been permitted to be born at all. Mary's pregnancy, in poor circumstances, and with the father unknown, would have been an obvious case for abortion; and her talk of having conceived as a result of the intervention of the Holy Ghost would have pointed to the need for psychiatric treatment, and made the case for terminating her pregnancy even stronger. Thus our generation, needing a Saviour more, perhaps, than any that has ever existed, would be too humane to allow one to be born; too enlightened to permit the Light of the World to shine in a darkness that grows ever more oppressive."[4]

There is a sense in which faith requires us to act in the face of (what the world would consider to be) the absurd. Abraham was asked to put to death his beloved and long-awaited son Isaac, the one hope Abraham had of fulfilling the promise that his posterity would be as numberless as the sands upon the seashore or the stars in the heavens. Jehovah had spoken. Abraham had entered the realm of divine experience, knew the voice of the Lord, and knew that what he had encountered was real. Therefore, when the awful assignment came to offer up Isaac in sacrifice, he obeyed, even though, rationally speaking, there was no way the promises could thereafter be realized. But Abraham, the father of the faithful, had implicit trust in his God, "accounting that God was able to raise [Isaac] up, even from the dead" (Hebrews 11:19). Abraham knew God and he knew his purposes; the finite mind yielded to the Infinite, knowing fully that "whatever God requires is right, no matter what it is, although we may not see the reason thereof till long after the events transpire."[5] His leap of faith was prerequisite to his ascent to glory.

FAITH AND THE WILL OF GOD

I am surprised by the ways some of us often use the word *faith*. I hear a missionary in Vienna say: "Come on, Elder, where's your faith? Why, if we had the faith we could baptize this whole city!" I watch with some sorrow as well-meaning but insensitive souls explain to a grieving mother and father that if the family had sufficient faith, their fifteen-year-old daughter, who has struggled with multiple sclerosis for five years, would not be forced to suffer longer. Let us be clear on this matter: Faith is *not* the power of positive thinking. Faith is *not* the personal resolve that enables us to will some difficult situation into existence. Faith is *not* always the capacity to turn tragedy into celebration. Faith is a principle of power, of God's power. We do not generate faith on our own, for it is the gift of God (see Ephesians 2:8). We do not act ourselves into faith, for faith is a gift of the Spirit, given by God to suit his purposes and bless the body of Christ, the Church.

C. S. Lewis wisely remarked: "We must not encourage in ourselves or others any tendency to work up a subjective state which, if we succeeded, we should describe as 'faith,' with the idea that this will somehow insure the granting of our prayer. We have probably all done this as children. But the state of mind which desperate desire working on a strong imagination can manufacture is not faith in the Christian sense. It is a feat of psychological gymnastics."[6]

People act in faith when they act according to the will of God. To say that another way, I have sufficient faith to move Mount Timpanogos to the middle of Utah Lake only when I know that the Lord wants it moved! I have faith or power to touch the hearts of men and women with my testimony of the truth only when they are prepared and readied for the word. Even the Master could not perform miracles in the midst of a people steeped in spiritual indifference. "A prophet is not without honour," Jesus said in speaking of his own reception in Nazareth, "save in his own country, and in his own house. *And he did not many mighty works there because of their unbelief*" (Matthew 13:57–58; emphasis added). Similarly, the prophet-leader Mormon loved his people and poured out his soul in prayer in their behalf; "nevertheless, it was without faith, because of the hardness of their hearts" (Mormon 3:12). Someone watching from the sidelines, unaware of what faith really is, might have cried out: "Come on, Mormon, where's your faith?"

Again, acting by faith is acting according to the will of the Lord. I remember very well one warm June evening in Louisiana, only a few months after I had returned from my mission, sitting with my mom and dad, watching television. The phone rang, and my father and I were quickly summoned to the hospital to give a priesthood blessing to someone. A sixteen-year-old boy, a friend of my younger sister, had suddenly collapsed on the softball field and had been rushed to the hospital. He had been diagnosed as having a rare degenerative nerve disease, and my father was told that if something didn't happen soon he would die. We rushed to the hospital, took the elevator to the fifth floor, and hurried through the doors that opened to the waiting room. We were greeted by the weeping and sorrow of family members; the young man had died. We did our best to console them and then made our way home. As we walked in the back door my sister asked, "How is he?" I answered that her friend had passed away. She came right back with: "Well, why didn't you raise him from the dead?" Being the seasoned and experienced returned missionary that I was, having most all of the answers to life's questions, I stuttered for a second and then turned to my father: "Yeah, why didn't we raise him from the dead?" Dad's answer was kindly but firm. It was also extremely instructive: "Because the Spirit of the Lord didn't prompt us to do so," he said. In the years that followed, I came to know something about my dad's faith: he had been with his father when in fact the Spirit had prompted and the dead had been raised to life again. He knew when to move and when not to move. He had faith.

Let me share another story. Wilford Woodruff was traveling to Zion to assume his new assignment to the Quorum of the Twelve. On the journey his wife Phoebe was overcome with a high fever and lay upon the point of death. "I alighted at a house," Brother Woodruff wrote, "and carried my wife and her bed into it, with a determination to tarry there until she either recovered her health, or passed away. This was on Sunday morning, December 2nd.

"After getting my wife and things into the house and wood provided to keep up a fire, I employed my time in taking care of her. It looked as though she had but a short time to live.

"She called me to her bedside in the evening and said she felt as though a few moments more would end her existence in this life. She manifested great confidence in the cause she had embraced, and exhorted me to have confidence in God and keep his commandments.

"To all appearances, she was dying. I laid hands upon her and prayed for her, and she soon revived and slept some during the night.

"December 3rd found my wife very low. I spent the day taking care of her. . . . She seemed to be gradually sinking, and in the evening her spirit apparently left her body, and she was dead.

"The sisters gathered around her body, weeping, while I stood looking at her in sorrow. The spirit and power of God began to rest upon me until, for the first time during her sickness, faith filled my soul, although she lay before me as one dead.

"I had some oil that was consecrated for my anointing while in Kirtland. . . . I then bowed down before the Lord and prayed for the life of my companion, and I anointed her body with the oil in the name of the Lord. I laid my hands upon her, and in the name of Jesus Christ, I rebuked the power of death and the destroyer, and commanded the same to depart from her, and the spirit of life to enter her body.

"Her spirit returned to her body, and from that hour she was made whole; and we all felt to praise the name of God, and to trust in Him and to keep His commandments.

"While this operation was going on with me (as my wife related afterwards) her spirit left her body, and she saw her body lying upon the bed, and the sisters weeping. She looked at them and at me, and upon her babe, and while gazing upon this scene, two personages came into the room . . . , and told her they had come for her. . . . One of these messengers informed her that she could have her choice: she might go to rest in the spirit world, or, on one condition she could have the privilege of returning to her tabernacle and continuing her labors upon the earth. The condition was, if she felt that she could stand by her husband, and with him pass through all the cares, trials, tribulations and afflictions of life which he would be called to pass through for the gospel's sake unto the end. When she looked at the situation of her husband and child she said: 'Yes, I will do it!'

"At the moment that decision was made the power of faith rested upon me, and when I administered unto her, her spirit entered her tabernacle, and she saw the messengers [go out] the door."[7]

Joseph Smith taught that working by faith is working by the power of mental exertion rather than physical force.[8] I am persuaded that the mental exertion of which he spoke is not merely a cognitive exercise but rather a strenuous effort, a spiritual search to know the will of God and then the determination to accept and abide by that will. "Working by faith is not the mere speaking of a few well-chosen words," Elder Bruce R. McConkie has written; "anyone with the power of speech could have commanded the rotting corpse of Lazarus to come forth, but only one whose power was greater than death could bring life again to the brother of Mary and Martha. Nor is working by faith merely a mental desire, however strong, that some eventuality should occur. There may be those whose mental powers and thought processes are greater than any of the saints, but only persons who are in tune with the Infinite can exercise the spiritual forces and powers that come from him." In short, "faith cannot be exercised contrary to the order of heaven or contrary to the will and purposes of him whose power it is. *Men work by faith when they are in tune with the Spirit and when what they seek to do by mental exertion and by the spoken word is the mind and will of the Lord.*"[9]

The Lord asks us to move forward on the path of life on the basis of what has been made known through prophets. We cannot always see the end from the beginning. We cannot always act in the face of the observable or the demonstrable. In many cases, believing must precede seeing. Indeed, the revelations affirm that as we search diligently, pray always, and *be believing,* all things will work together for our good (see D&C 90:24). We are further counseled to doubt not because we see not, for we receive no witness until after the trial of our faith (see Ether 12:6). This is the nature of the leap of faith, a leap from the safe and the secure to the anticipated and the hoped for (see Alma 32:21). The disciples of Christ are not called upon to proceed wholly in the dark, to leap from the precipice without evidence of deliverance. Rather, we are asked to look through the eyes of faith (see Alma 5:15; 32:40; Ether 12:19), to rely upon the unseen, to trust in the quiet but persistent whisperings of the Spirit, to lean upon the prophetic promises. In the words of President Harold B. Lee, we must "learn to walk to the edge of the light, and perhaps a few steps into the darkness, and [we] will find that the light will appear and move ahead of [us]."[10]

THE DISCIPLINE OF FAITH

This kind of faith may be particularly difficult for one devoted to research and study, one dependent solely on external evidence; it requires that we put first things first, that we not judge the restored gospel—its history or doctrines—by the canons of our own discipline, but the other way around. That is, faithful scholarship does not, as some have naively supposed, entail hiding from the truth or hiding the truth, but rather viewing all things through the lenses of the Restoration. It is only then that we are able to see things as they really are and as they really will be (see Jacob 4:13; D&C 93:24). One of the challenges a serious student faces is to learn the strengths—and thus the limitations—of his or her own field of study, what it can teach us and what it cannot teach us. It just may be that faithful scholarship requires more, not less, mental discipline than scholarship involving the intellect alone. Faithful scholarship requires that we not live a divided or disjointed life, that we not be a psychologist or a historian or a chemist during the week and a Latter-day Saint on Sunday, but that we take the restored gospel seriously and incorporate it into all areas of worthwhile investigation. The Apostasy was long and broad and deep; it made its influence felt in the pure sciences, the social sciences, the arts, literature, and, of course, theology. The Restoration is destined to have an impact not alone in the explication of doctrine and the delivery of divine authority (as vital as those things are) but also in all areas of study. When disciplined minds and creative artists open themselves to the enlightening powers of the Holy Ghost and are imbued with the spirit and power of the restored gospel, learning and discovery and creativity reach beyond the paltry bounds of what has been done heretofore and open us to new vistas of understanding and expression.

Indeed, faith has its own type of discipline. Some things that are obvious to the faithful sound like the gibberish of alien tongues to the faithless. The discipline of faith, the concentrated and consecrated effort to become single to God, has its own reward, a reward that includes the expansion of the mind. Such persons come to be filled with light and are able in time to comprehend all things (see D&C 88:67). It is worth considering the words of a revelation given in Kirtland, Ohio. Having encouraged the Saints to call a solemn assembly, the Lord continued: "And as all have not faith, seek ye diligently and teach one another words of wisdom; . . . seek learning, even by study and also by faith" (D&C 88:118). We note that the counsel to seek learning out of the best books is prefaced by the negative clause "and as all *have not* faith . . ." One wonders whether the Master did not intend something like the following: Since all do not have sufficient faith—or, in the words of Elder B. H. Roberts, since they have not "matured in their religious convictions" to learn by any other means[11]—then they must seek learning by study, the use of the rational processes alone. In other words, if all *did* have the requisite faith, then what? Perhaps learning by studying from the best books would then be greatly enhanced by revelation. Honest truth seekers would learn things in this way that they could not know otherwise.

Could this be what Joseph Smith meant when he taught that "the best way to obtain truth and wisdom is not to ask it from books, but to go to God in prayer, and obtain divine teaching"?[12] It is surely in this same context that another of the Prophet's famous yet little-understood statements finds meaning: "Could you gaze into heaven five minutes," he declared, "you would know more than you would by reading all that ever was written on the subject" of life after death.[13] "I believe in study," President Marion G. Romney stated. "I believe that men learn much through study. As a matter of fact, it has been my observation that they learn little concerning things as they are, as they were, or as they are to come without study. *I also believe, however, and know, that learning by study is greatly accelerated by faith.*"[14]

President Harold B. Lee expressed the following to BYU students just weeks before his death: "The acquiring of knowledge by faith is no easy road to learning. It will demand strenuous effort and continual striving by faith. In short, learning by faith is no task for a lazy man. Someone has said, in effect, that 'such a process requires the bending of the whole soul, the calling up from the depths of the human mind and linking the person with God. The right connection must be formed; then only comes knowledge by faith, a kind of knowledge that goes beyond secular learning, that reaches into the realms of the unknown and makes those who follow that course great in the sight of the Lord.'"[15] On another occasion, President Lee taught that "learning by faith requires *the bending of the whole soul through worthy living to become attuned to the Holy Spirit of the Lord,* the calling up from the depths of one's own mental searching, and the linking of our own efforts to receive the true witness of the Spirit."[16]

Learning by faith requires that we be as rigorous in our pursuit of sacred things through the established channels—scriptures, living prophets, personal revelation—as we are in our research and study of secular things. Sometimes members of the Church dismiss outright or at least underestimate the power of the gospel message because they have not paid a sufficient price to plumb the depths of those things God has made known. Elder John A. Widtsoe thus stated that "it is a paradox that men will gladly devote time every day for many years to learn a science or an art; yet will expect to win a knowledge of the gospel, which comprehends all sciences and arts, through perfunctory glances at books or occasional listening to sermons. The gospel should be studied more intensively than any school or college subject. They who pass opinion on the gospel without having given it intimate and careful study are not lovers of truth, and their opinions are worthless."[17]

Learning by faith seems to entail something else as well. An episode in the Book of Mormon highlights a very important principle. "Now it came to pass," Mormon writes, "that there were many of the rising generation that could not understand the words of king Benjamin, being little children at the time he spake unto his people; and they did not believe the tradition of their fathers. They did not believe what had been said concerning the resurrection of the dead, neither did they believe concerning the coming of Christ." And now note this powerful statement: "And now *because of their unbelief they could not understand the word of God;* and their hearts were hardened" (Mosiah 26:1–3; emphasis added). Because of their unbelief—their refusal to believe, to accept the true but unseen, to surrender and yield to God—they denied themselves the right to understanding. One who approaches the reading of the Book of Mormon, for example, with a cynical eye is not likely to mine its doctrinal pearls or to gain a witness of its truthfulness; there must be a willful suspension of disbelief, an inclination to accept the truth when confronted with it, an openness to the possibility that something just might be true.

God doesn't ask us to be gullible or to obey blindly. "Of those who speak in his name," President Joseph F. Smith declared, "the Lord requires humility, not ignorance."[18] Neither ignorance nor blind obedience add strength to the kingdom. Instead, the Omniscient One simply asks of his Saints that they believe, that they be willing to trust in him, in his plan, and in those who direct the destiny of his church. Some knowledge may come by study, but intelligence or the glory of God requires diligence and obedience (see D&C 130:19). In a revelation to President Brigham Young, the Savior explained: "Let him that is ignorant learn wisdom by humbling himself and calling upon the Lord his God, that his eyes may be opened that he may see, and his ears opened that he may hear" (D&C 136:32).

CONCLUSION

I have learned a few things as I have learned a few things over the years. I thank God for the formal education I have received, for the privilege it is (and I count it such) to have received university training and to have earned bachelor's, masters, and doctoral degrees. Education has expanded my mind and opened conversations and doors for me. It has taught me what books to read, how to research a topic, and how to make my case or present my point of view more effectively. But the more I learn, the more I value the truths of salvation, those simple but profound verities that soothe and settle and sanctify human hearts. I appreciate knowing that the order of the cosmos points toward a Providential Hand; I am deeply grateful to know, by the power of the Holy Ghost, that there is a God and that he is our Father in Heaven. I appreciate knowing something about the social, political, and religious world into which Jesus of Nazareth was born; I am deeply grateful for the witness of the Spirit that he is indeed God's Almighty Son.

I appreciate knowing something about the social and intellectual climate of nineteenth-century America; I am grateful to have, burning within my soul, a testimony that the Father and the Son appeared to Joseph Smith in the spring of 1820, and that The Church of Jesus Christ of Latter-day Saints is truly the kingdom of God on earth. In short, the more I encounter men's approximations to what is, the more I treasure those absolute truths that make known "things as they really are, and . . . things as they really will be" (Jacob 4:13; compare D&C 93:24). In fact, the more we learn, the more we begin to realize what we do not know, the more we feel the need to consider ourselves "fools before God" (2 Nephi 9:42).

Those who choose to follow the Brethren, believe in and teach the scriptures, and be loyal to the Church—no matter the extent of their academic training or intellectual capacity—open themselves to ridicule from the cynic and the critic. Ultimately, doctrinal truth comes not through the explorations of scholars but through the revelations of God to apostles and prophets. And if such a position be labeled as narrow, parochial, or anti-intellectual, then so be it. I cast my lot with the prophets. I am one who sincerely believes that education need not be antithetical to conversion and commitment; it all depends on where one places his or her trust. "True religion," Elder Bruce R. McConkie testified, "deals with spiritual things. We do not come to a knowledge of God and his laws through intellectuality, or by research, or by reason. . . . In their sphere, education and intellectuality are devoutly to be desired. But when contrasted with spiritual endowments, they are of but slight and passing worth. From an eternal perspective what each of us needs is a Ph.D. in faith and righteousness. The things that will profit us everlastingly are not the power to reason, but the ability to receive revelation; not the truths learned by study, but the knowledge gained by faith; not what we know about the things of the world, but our knowledge of God and his laws."[19]

Notes

From an address to Kappa Omicron Nu, Brigham Young University, Provo, Utah, 2 April 1998.

1. Dallin H. Oaks, *The Lord's Way* (Salt Lake City: Deseret Book Co., 1991), 16–17; see also page 19.
2. Hugh Nibley, *The World and the Prophets* (Salt Lake City: Deseret Book Co. and FARMS, 1987), 134.
3. Malcolm Muggeridge, *Jesus: The Man Who Lives* (New York: Harper & Row, 1975), 20.
4. Ibid., 19–20.
5. *Teachings of the Prophet Joseph Smith,* 256.

6. C. S. Lewis, *Letters to Malcolm, Chiefly on Prayer* (New York: Harcourt, Brace & Co., 1964), 60.

7. Wilford Woodruff, in George Q. Cannon, *A String of Pearls* (Salt Lake City: Juvenile Instructor Office, 1882), 85.

8. *Lectures on Faith,* 7:3.

9. Bruce R. McConkie, *A New Witness for the Articles of Faith* (Salt Lake City: Deseret Book Co., 1985), 191–92; emphasis added.

10. In Boyd K. Packer, *The Holy Temple* (Salt Lake City: Bookcraft, 1980), 184.

11. B. H. Roberts, as quoted by Harold B. Lee in Conference Report, April 1968, 129.

12. *Teachings of the Prophet Joseph Smith,* 191.

13. Ibid., 324.

14. Marion G. Romney, *Learning for the Eternities* (Salt Lake City: Deseret Book Co., 1977), 7; emphasis added.

15. Harold B. Lee, "Be Loyal to the Royal within You," *1973 BYU Speeches of the Year* (Provo: BYU Publications, 1974), 91.

16. Harold B. Lee, in Conference Report, April 1971, 94; emphasis added.

17. John A. Widtsoe, *Evidences and Reconciliations* (Salt Lake City: Bookcraft, 1960), 16–17.

18. *Gospel Doctrine,* 206.

19. Bruce R. McConkie, in Conference Report, April 1971, 99.

THE THEOLOGY OF C. S. LEWIS:
A LATTER-DAY SAINT PERSPECTIVE

C. S. Lewis is widely read among the Latter-day Saints and has had a profound influence on the understanding of Christian doctrine among the members of the Church. I have personally been fascinated by his life and stimulated by his writings and teachings. In no way could I be identified as an expert on Lewis, but if passion for his theology and fond appreciation for his practical religion qualify one to write about him, then I am qualified. Terry Glaspey observed that "one of the surest reasons for Lewis's vast popular appeal was his belief that the ultimate truths of life are not hidden only in the minds of the learned, but what is really most important in life is accessible to all."[1] Lewis himself noted: "My only function as a Christian writer is to preach 'Mere Christianity' not *ad clerum* but *ad populum.* Any success that has been given me has, I believe, been due to my strict observance of those limits."[2] For this, the LDS people have admired him and, for the most part, embraced his teachings.

A LAY CHURCH AND THEOLOGICAL LITERACY

Although The Church of Jesus Christ of Latter-day Saints is a lay church and sermons in the main worship service on the Sabbath are usually delivered by members of the congregation, a visitor would notice how frequently the talks revolve around scripture and scriptural commentary, with insights frequently drawn from thinkers who represent other faiths. One writer for Salt Lake City's *Deseret News* found that C. S. Lewis in particular "had been quoted from the [Salt Lake]

Tabernacle podium [in the Church's semiannual general conference] almost twenty times in twenty years—more than Thomas Jefferson, Ralph Waldo Emerson, Winston Churchill, Pearl S. Buck—more than any other non-LDS author." He suggested that Lewis's common touch with uncommon ideas is what has endeared him to Mormons. As this writer put it, Lewis is "the one who leans over and speaks into our ear, the friend we can't help but take into our hearts."[3]

Perhaps a lay church like ours is more prone than other, more traditionally structured Christian churches to adopt and appropriate writings that seek to take otherwise esoteric tenets and reduce them to reachable and memorable concepts. Lewis appears to me to be far more practical than sacramental, far more prone to speak of personal engagement with divinity than to focus on ecclesiastical or liturgical matters. In addition, his popularity in Latter-day Saint culture, as with a broader Christian readership, is no doubt related to the fact that he does not come across as denominational or wedded to any particular religious persuasion. In his adherence to "mere Christianity," he is everyman's preacher, every woman's exegete. He is the thinking Christian's supreme apologist. "He was not a theological liberal, but neither did his views square with fundamentalism."[4]

One final reason why C. S. Lewis is so well received by Latter-day Saints is found in his broad and inclusive vision of Christianity. Mormons have taken their share of lumps in past decades, especially with the continuing growth of the Church, from those religious organizations who insist that Latter-day Saints are not Christian. That exclusion generally comes through an extremely narrow definition of Christianity, by misrepresentation of Mormonism, or over nonbiblical historical or doctrinal issues.[5] We resonate to Lewis's words: "It is not for us to say who, in the deepest sense, is or is not close to the spirit of Christ. We do not see into men's hearts. We cannot judge, and are indeed forbidden to judge. It would be wicked arrogance for us to say that any man is, or is not, a Christian in this refined sense. . . . When a man who accepts the Christian doctrine lives unworthily of it, it is much clearer to say he is a bad Christian than to say he is not a Christian."[6]

Of course, Clive Staples Lewis was not a Latter-day Saint, and I have no intention of contorting him into one. I cannot read his mind, nor can I always know assuredly what he meant by what he said. But then, neither can anyone else who reads him, unless they were intimately acquainted with him during his life. It is not even possible to say, "Well, Lewis must have meant this or that, inasmuch as he was an Anglican," or "Surely Jack intended to convey this or that idea, since he was a defender of the Christian faith." Why not? Because there are parts of Lewis's theology that defy rubric, that are not placed comfortably within any particular religious tradition.

This is, in fact, what makes him so very fascinating to me and other Latter-day Saints. For pages on end, Lewis's insights capture Christians of every denomination, and then—suddenly and without warning, in the next paragraph—he will make this person or that person extremely uncomfortable. This breadth, this inclusiveness, this freshness and distinctiveness—these are the things that endear Lewis to at least one Latter-day Saint. In the remainder of this chapter I will consider the following five doctrinal items from Lewis's teachings and comment on how they are viewed from an LDS perspective: (1) the true myth; (2) surprised by joy; (3) the nature of fallen man; (4) transformation in Christ; and (5) evil and suffering.

THE TRUE MYTH

One area of study that has seemed especially challenging to the faith of many young Christians proved, ironically, to be foundational to Lewis's acceptance of Christianity. Central to his conversion was his recognition of similarities between mythical patterns in cultures and belief systems throughout the world. The symbols of descent and renascence, the suffering and dying god, rebirth and resurrection are, in his words, "derived (through human imagination) from the facts of Nature, and the facts of Nature from her Creator." Lewis added that "the Death and Re-birth pattern is in her because it was first in Him."[7] Lewis called such phenomena "good dreams," archetypical occurrences all about us, those "queer stories scattered all through the heathen religions about a god who dies and comes to life again, and, by his death, has somehow given new life to men."[8] Whereas some challenge the uniqueness of Christianity because of the ubiquity of such myths, Lewis came to acknowledge Christianity as the "true myth," the myth that became history. That is, "Christians are not claiming that simply 'God' was incarnate in Jesus. They are claiming that the one true God is He whom the Jews worshipped as Jahweh, and that it is He who has descended."[9]

We as Latter-day Saints believe that a plan of salvation—a system of redemption in which God the Father would send his Beloved Son into the world as a Savior—was known to men and women from the beginning and that Christian prophets have taught what we call "Christ's eternal gospel" and have even administered Christian sacraments since the beginning of time.[10] In overview, Jesus is truly the "Lamb slain from the foundation of the world, as the apostles John and Peter declared" (1 Peter 1:19–20; Revelation 13:8; Moses 7:47). The atoning sacrifice is not only timely (for those of us who regularly need its cleansing powers) but *timeless*. Though the act of atonement would not take place until Jesus suffered in Gethsemane and on Golgotha in the meridian of time, earth's earliest inhabitants were taught from the beginning to call upon God in the name of his Beloved Son. Mormons take literally the words of the Apostle Peter that "to [Christ] give all the prophets witness" (Acts 10:43).

It is but reasonable in the LDS view, therefore, that remnants of truth, pieces of a much larger mosaic, should be found scattered throughout the world in varying cultures and among diverse religious groups, albeit in some cases in altered or even convoluted forms. Joseph F. Smith, sixth president of the Church, said of those who seek to upstage Christianity that Jesus Christ "is no imitator. He taught the truth first; it was his before it was given to man. . . . If we find truth in broken fragments through the ages, it may be set down as an incontrovertible fact that it originated at the fountain, and was given to philosophers, inventors, patriots, reformers, and prophets by the inspiration of God. It came from him through his Son Jesus Christ and the Holy Ghost, in the first place, and from no other source. It is eternal. . . . Men are mere repeaters of what he has taught them."[11]

And so as a Latter-day Saint I find Lewis's discussion of the true myth to be especially compelling. The "doctrine of death" of a god found throughout the world is, in Lewis's words, "an 'eternal gospel' revealed to men wherever men have sought, or endured, the truth: it is the very nerve of redemption, which anatomizing wisdom at all times and in all places lays bare; the unescapable knowledge which the Light that lighteneth every man presses down upon the minds of all who seriously question what the universe is 'about.' "[12]

SURPRISED BY JOY

Lewis frequently commented on another divine manifestation in life—the inner longings that men and women so often feel, a sense of divine homesickness, mysterious moments when we feel ill at ease or out of place in this life, not put off by the throes of mortality as much as by mortality itself. He noted that men and women were often "surprised by joy," startled by moments that matter, brief brushes with eternity. "All your life," Lewis pointed out, "an inattained ecstasy has hovered just beyond the grasp of your consciousness."[13] "If I find in myself a desire which no experience in this world can satisfy," he stated, "the most probable explanation is that I was made for another world. . . . I must keep alive in myself the desire for my true country, which I shall not find till after death; I must never let it get snowed under or turned aside; I must make it the main object of life to press on to that other country and to help others to do the same."[14]

Lewis is speaking, of course, of our longing for heaven and for heavenly things. Latter-day Saints identify with the sentiment because we have, like others, felt the same longings or homesickness. We look at the situation, however, from a slightly different perspective. Because Latter-day Saints believe in a premortal existence—of a life as spirits before we were born, a time wherein we were acquainted with God—we would agree with Wordsworth that "our birth is but a sleep and a forgetting."[15] These intimations of immortality also bespeak a memory of what once was, a longing for reunion, reacquaintance, renewal of association. For us, "homesickness" is not figurative but literal. Our souls pine for the home our bodies cannot remember. As early as 1883, one Church leader wrote: "Our knowledge of persons and things before we came here, combined with the divinity awakened within our souls through obedience to the gospel, powerfully affects, in my opinion, all our likes and dislikes, and guides our preferences in the course of this life, provided we give careful heed to the admonitions of the Spirit. All those salient truths which come home so forcibly to the head and heart seem but the awakening of the memories of the spirit."[16]

THE NATURE OF FALLEN MAN

As a Christian, C. S. Lewis believed in the reality and in the consequences of the Fall of Adam and Eve. Because of that Fall, death and sin and corruption and decay have entered into the world and encompass us here. Indeed, an acknowledgment of the Fall and of man's fallen nature is indispensable to an appreciation for the Atonement of Jesus Christ. "A recovery of the old sense of sin," Lewis observed, "is essential to Christianity. Christ takes it for granted that men are bad. Until we really feel this assumption of his to be true, though we are part of the world He came to save, we are not part of the audience to whom His words are addressed."[17] In fact, as men and women come unto Christ and surrender their old selves, they begin to recognize more and more their need for redemption and renovation. "When a man is getting better," Lewis said, "he understands more and more clearly the evil that is still left in him."[18]

So far as I can tell, however, Lewis did not believe that men and women are punished for what Adam and Eve did or that we individually "sinned in Adam," as the Christian church fathers declared.[19] Further, he taught that "the doctrine of Total Depravity—when the consequence is drawn that, since we are totally depraved, our idea of good is worth simply nothing—may thus turn Christianity into a form of devil-worship."[20] Having discussed the nature of the Fall and of fallen man, Lewis went on to say that he would have been misunderstood if anyone described his views "as a restatement of the doctrine of Total Depravity. I disbelieve that doctrine, partly on the logical ground that if our depravity were total we should not know ourselves to be depraved, and partly because experience shows us much goodness in human nature."[21] Nor did Lewis believe that the human body was to be spurned or despised. "I know some muddle-headed Christians have talked as if Christianity thought that sex, or the body, or pleasure, were bad in themselves. But they were wrong. Christianity is almost the only one of the great religions which thoroughly approves of the body—which believes that matter is good, that God Himself once took on a human body, that some kind of body is going to be given to us even in Heaven and is going to be an essential part of our happiness, our beauty, and our energy."[22]

Ezra Taft Benson, thirteenth president of The Church of Jesus Christ of Latter-day Saints, stated that "just as a man does not really desire food until he is hungry, so he does not desire the salvation of Christ until he knows why he needs Christ. No one adequately and properly knows why he needs Christ until he understands and accepts the doctrine of the Fall and its effect upon all mankind."[23] The Latter-day Saints thus view the Fall as a companion doctrine to the Atonement. If there had been no Fall, there would have been no Atonement, and thus the regeneration and glorification that come only through the cleansing power of Christ's blood could not have been extended to humankind.

Thus, for Latter-day Saints, partaking of the forbidden fruit in Eden brought about a "fortunate fall," one that opened the way to far more glorious blessings in eternity. As one early Church leader explained: "The fall had a twofold direction—downward, yet forward. It brought man into the world and set his feet upon progression's highway."[24] The Latter-day Saints teach that even though we are not responsible or accountable for the Fall of Adam and Eve, we are certainly affected by it—physically, mentally, emotionally, and spiritually. We agree wholeheartedly with Lewis that fallen man is "not simply an imperfect creature who needs improvement: he is a rebel who must lay down his arms."[25]

The Book of Mormon contains the clearest statements in LDS literature on the doctrine of the Fall and the plight of fallen man. Note the following passages:

"Wherefore, all mankind were in a lost and in a fallen state, and ever would be save they should rely on this Redeemer" (1 Nephi 10:6).

"Men drink damnation to their own souls except they humble themselves and become as little children, and believe that salvation was, and is, and is to come, in and through the atoning blood of Christ, the Lord Omnipotent.

"For the natural man is an enemy to God, and has been from the fall of Adam, and will be, forever and ever, unless he yields to the enticings of the Holy Spirit, and putteth off the natural man and becometh a saint through the atonement of Christ the Lord" (Mosiah 3:18–19).

"And since man had fallen he could not merit anything of himself; but the sufferings and death of Christ atone for their sins, through faith and repentance, and so forth" (Alma 22:14).

In addition, Lewis once stated that "to ask that God's love should be content with us as we are is to ask that God should cease to be God: because He is what He is, His love must, in the nature of things, be impeded and repelled by certain stains in our present character, and because He already loves us He must labour to make us lovable."[26] The Book of Mormon similarly teaches the self-contradiction of God's trying to save us in our sins rather than from our sins: "What, do ye suppose that mercy can rob justice? I say unto you, Nay; not one whit. If so, God would cease to be God" (Alma 42:25). As Brigham Young declared: "It requires all the atonement of Christ, the mercy of the Father, the pity of angels and the grace of the Lord Jesus Christ to be with us always, and then to do the very best we possibly can, to get rid of this sin within us."[27]

TRANSFORMATION IN CHRIST

There is so much that could be said in discussing Lewis's thoughts regarding the preeminent place of Jesus Christ. I have been stimulated over the years by Lewis's discussions of Christ's suffering and forsakenness in Gethsemane;[28] the nature of repentance and how it is that Christ's "advantage" allows him to "pay the debt";[29] and his provocative and memorable illustrations of how spiritual rebirth entails more than cosmetic or outward changes in behavior.[30] The following expression, which Lewis wrote in a letter in 1942, is deeply comforting to the Latter-day Saint while at the same time supportive of our emphasis on the need to "endure to the end": "No amount of falls will really undo us if we keep on picking ourselves up each time. We shall of course be very muddy and tattered children by the time we reach home. But the bathrooms are all ready, the towels put out, and the clean clothes in the airing cupboard. The only fatal thing is to lose one's temper and give it up. It is when we notice the dirt that God is most present in us: it is the very sign of His presence."[31]

C. S. Lewis boldly refused to accept the impotent position of Jesus as merely a great moral teacher. He is absolutely right: Jesus of Nazareth was either a God or a liar or madman.[32] "Only two views of this man are possible," he noted. "Either He was a raving lunatic of an unusually abominable type, or else He was, and is, precisely what He said. There is no middle way. If the records make the first hypothesis unacceptable, you must submit to the second. And if you do that, all else that is claimed by Christians becomes credible—that this Man, having been killed, was yet alive, and that His death, in some manner incomprehensible to human thought, has effected a real change in our relations to the 'awful' and 'righteous' Lord, and a change in our favour."[33]

Let me focus briefly on two aspects of Lewis's treatment of Christ's redemptive work that particularly appeal to Latter-day Saints: first, the balance between divine grace and human action; and second, the ultimate glorification of man in Christ. From my reading of Lewis, I conclude that although there was no question in his mind that salvation was in Christ and that the renovation of men and women's souls was the work of a God, that persons who chose to come unto Christ were expected to be more than grateful and passive observers of the changes taking place within them. "We profanely assume that divine and human action exclude one another like the actions of two fellow-creatures so that 'God did this' and 'I did this' cannot both be true of the same act except in the sense that each contributed a share." He continued: "In the end we must admit a two-way traffic at the junction. . . . We have nothing that we have not received; but part of what we have received is the power of being something more than receptacles."[34] As Lewis stated elsewhere, "Christians have often disputed as to whether what leads the Christian home is good actions, or faith in Christ. I have no right really to speak on such a difficult question, but it does seem to me like asking which blade in a pair of scissors is most necessary. . . . You see, we are now trying to understand, and to separate into water-tight compartments, what exactly God does and what man does when God and man are working together."[35]

Latter-day Saints have often been critical of those who emphasize salvation by grace alone, while we have often been criticized for a type of works-righteousness because we give work any significance at all. The Mormons believe that the gospel is, in fact, a gospel *covenant*. The Lord agrees to do for us what we could never do for ourselves—to forgive our sins, to lift our burdens, to renew our souls and re-create our nature, to raise us from the dead and qualify us for glory hereafter. Whereupon, we strive to do what we *can* do: have faith in Christ, repent of our sins, be baptized, love and serve one another, and do all in our power to put off the natural man and deny ourselves of ungodliness. In short, Latter-day Saints believe that more is required of men and women than a verbal expression of faith in the Lord, more than a confession with the lips that we have received Christ into our hearts. Without question, the power to save us, to change us, to renew our souls, is in Christ. True faith, however, always manifests itself in *faithfulness.* Thus, the real questions are not whether one is saved by grace or by works but rather, In whom do we trust? On whom do we rely? (see 1 Nephi 10:6; 2 Nephi 2:8; 31:19; Moroni 6:4).

As Latter-day Saints, we feel that few things would be more sinister than encouraging lip service to God while discouraging obedience and faithful discipleship. On the other hand, surely nothing could be more offensive to God than a smug self-assurance that comes from trusting in one's own works or relying upon one's own strength. What is perhaps the most well-known passage in LDS literature on this delicate matter is found in the Book of Mormon: "For we labor diligently to write, to persuade our children, and also our brethren, to believe in Christ, and to be reconciled to God; for we know that it is by grace that we are saved, after all we can do" (2 Nephi 25:23; see also 10:24; Alma 24:10–11). That is, above and beyond all we can do, we are saved by the grace of Christ; salvation is still the greatest of all the *gifts* of God (see D&C 6:13; 14:7). Further, the more we learn to trust the Lord and rely upon his merits and mercy, the less anxious we become about life here and hereafter. "Thus, if you have really handed yourself over to Him," Lewis wisely remarked, "it must follow that you are trying to obey Him. But trying in a new way, a less worried way."[36]

The second aspect of Christ's redeeming work found in Lewis's writing, which I want to treat briefly, concerns what God eventually intends to do with us. More specifically, let me turn to Lewis's teachings regarding our becoming like Christ. He wrote in *The Problem of Pain* that "we are, not metaphorically but in very truth, a Divine work of art, something that God is making, and therefore something with which He will not be satisfied until it has a certain character. Here again we come up against what I have called the 'intolerable compliment.'"[37]

From *Miracles:* "Christ, reascending from his great dive, is bringing up Human Nature with Him. Where He goes, it goes too. It will be made 'like him' (Philippians 3:21; 1 John 3:1–2)." Lewis went on to say that eventually those who are redeemed in Christ will have the power to perform miracles, just as Christ did. "Christ's isolation," he continued, "is not that of a prodigy but of a pioneer. He is the first of His kind; He will not be the last."[38]

From *A Grief Observed:* "Sometimes, Lord, one is tempted to say that if you wanted us to behave like the lilies of the field you might have given us an organization more like theirs. But that, I suppose, is just your grand experiment. Or no; not an experiment, for you have no need to find things out. Rather your grand enterprise. To make an organism which is also a spirit; to make that terrible oxymoron, a 'spiritual animal.' To take a poor primate, a beast with nerve-endings all over it, a creature with a stomach that wants to be filled, a breeding animal that wants its mate, and say, 'Now get on with it. Become a god.'"[39]

From *The Weight of Glory:* "It is a serious thing to live in a society of possible gods and goddesses, to remember that the dullest and most uninteresting person you can talk to may one day be a creature which, if you saw it now, you would be strongly tempted to worship. . . . There are no *ordinary* people. You have never talked to a mere mortal. Nations, cultures, arts, civilization—these are mortal, and their life is to ours as the life of a gnat. But it is immortals whom we joke with, work with, marry, snub, and exploit. . . . Next to the Blessed Sacrament itself, your neighbour is the holiest object presented to your senses."[40]

And from *Mere Christianity:* "Century by century God has guided nature up to the point of producing creatures which can (if they will) be taken right out of nature, turned into 'gods.'"[41]

Being changed in Christ "is not a change from being brainy men to brainier men: it is a change that goes off in a totally different direction—a change from being creatures of God to being sons of God."[42]

"Now the point in Christianity which gives us the greatest shock is the statement that by attaching ourselves to Christ, we can 'become Sons of God.' Aren't we Sons of God already? Surely the fatherhood of God is one of the main Christian ideas? Well, in a certain sense, no doubt we are sons of God already. I mean, God has brought us into existence and loves us and looks after us, and in that way is like a father. But when the Bible talks of our 'becoming' Sons of God, obviously it must mean something different. And that brings us up against the very centre of Theology. . . .

"We don't use the words *begetting* or *begotten* much in modern English, but everyone still knows what they mean. To beget is to become the father of: to create is to make. And the difference is this. When you beget, you beget something of the same kind as yourself. A man begets human babies, a beaver begets little beavers and a bird begets eggs which turn into little birds. But when you make, you make something of a different kind from yourself. A bird makes a nest, a beaver builds a dam, a man makes a wireless set. . . .

"Now that is the first thing to get clear. What God begets is God; just as what man begets is man. What God creates is not God; just as what man makes is not man. That is why men are not Sons of God in the sense that Christ is. They may be like God in certain ways, but they are not things of the same kind. They are more like statues or pictures of God. . . .

"And that is precisely what Christianity is about. The world is a great sculptor's shop. We are the statues and there is a rumour going round the shop that some of us are some day going to come to life."[43]

"We are not begotten by God, we are only made by Him: in our natural state we are not sons of God, only (so to speak) statues. . . . Now the whole offer which Christianity makes is this: that we can, if we let God have His way, come to share in the life of Christ. If we do, we shall then be sharing a life which was begotten, not made, which always has existed and always will exist. Christ is the Son of God. We shall love the Father as He does and the Holy Ghost will arise in us. He came to this world and became a man in order to spread to other men the kind of life He has."[44]

"The command *Be ye perfect* is not idealistic gas. Nor is it a command to do the impossible. He is going to make us into creatures that can obey that command. He said (in the Bible) that we were 'gods' and He is going to make good His words. If we let Him—for we can prevent Him if we choose—He will make the feeblest and filthiest of us into a god or goddess, a dazzling, radiant, immortal creature, pulsating all through with such energy and joy and wisdom and love as we cannot now imagine, a bright stainless mirror which reflects back to God perfectly (though, of course, on a smaller scale) His own boundless power and delight and goodness. The process will be long and in parts very painful; but that is what we are in for. Nothing less. He meant what He said."[45]

As Latter-day Saints, we perk up and listen carefully to this kind of discussion. One of the tenets of our faith is that human spirits were born sons and daughters of God before this life, and if they will be born again now, they can be empowered and transformed by Jesus Christ, becoming eventually as he is. Elder B. H. Roberts wrote: "The term 'father' carries with it the notion of generation, begetting from one's own person, springing from one's own nature, and partaking of one's own physical and mental qualities and perhaps likeness, but the term 'creator' does not necessarily convey that notion, since a created thing may be external to the nature of the being who created it; as, for example, when God created the heaven and the earth. In this case the heaven and the earth did not bear the image of God; nor was it made in his likeness, as the result was when God said, 'Let us make man in our image, and after our likeness.' So in relation to man; he begets a son or a daughter by act of generation; he is a father; and also, in a sense, a creator."[46]

We teach and believe that all men and women, like Christ, are made in the spiritual image and likeness of God (Genesis 1:27; Moses 2:27). Through Christ, our physical selves can also become begotten sons and daughters, and so Latter-day Saints feel it is neither robbery nor heresy for the children of God to aspire to be like their Heavenly Father (Matthew 5:48; Philippians 2:6). Transformation comes through the merits of Christ and his Atonement (1 John 5:4–5; Revelation 2:7, 11). Through faith we become heirs of God and joint-heirs with Christ, the natural Heir (Romans 8:17; Galatians 4:7), thus inheriting *all* things, just as Jesus inherits all things (1 Corinthians 3:21–23; Hebrews 1:2; Revelation 21:7). In that glorified state we will conform to the image of the Lord Jesus (Romans 8:29; 1 Corinthians 15:49; 2 Corinthians 3:18; 1 John 3:2), be made partakers of his divine nature (2 Peter 1:3–4), and become one with him and with the Father (John 17:21–23; Philippians 3:21).

Although Mormons teach that godhood comes through receiving eternal life in Christ, they do not believe anyone will ever, worlds without end, unseat or oust God the Eternal Father or his Only Begotten Son, Jesus Christ; those holy beings are and forever will be the Gods we worship.[47] Even though we believe in the ultimate deification of man, I am unaware of any authoritative statement in LDS literature, despite frequent claims of other faiths to the contrary, that suggests that we will ever worship any being other than God. We believe in "one God" in the sense that we love and serve one Godhead, one divine presidency, each of whom possesses all of the attributes of godhood.

EVIL AND SUFFERING

C. S. Lewis was an articulate voice in the centuries-old conversation regarding human suffering and the question of evil. If in fact people choose so poorly, and those choices make such tragic impact on others' lives as they do, why should God allow human agency or choice? Lewis answers that for one thing, "free will, though it makes evil possible, is also the only thing that makes possible any love or goodness or joy worth having. . . . Of course God knew what would happen if they used their freedom the wrong way: apparently He thought it worth the risk."[48] The inevitable pain and tragedy associated with allowing men and women—even debauched and vicious men and women—to exercise their moral agency was less than the evil of denying such agency and thereby reducing us to something less than human beings.[49]

For Lewis, suffering "is not good in itself. What is good in any painful experience is, for the sufferer, his submission to the will of God, and, for the spectators, the compassion aroused and the acts of mercy to which it leads."[50] Suffering is also God's way of getting our attention, Lewis taught, of focusing us on the things of greatest worth, and forcing us to assess the depth and substance of our faith; only then can we learn something about what we are made of and, like Abraham, discover what God already knows about our integrity.[51] "God whispers to us in our pleasures," Lewis pointed out, "speaks in our conscience, but shouts in our pains: it is His megaphone to rouse a deaf world."[52] Thus, God's love and goodness to us are eternal in nature and work for the ultimate perfection of our character. That love and goodness may not be readily perceived as kind, for often it is through suffering that the dross is burned out and the soul is refined and purified.

God is not just a "senile benevolence" who delights in everyone moving through life in serene, uninterrupted, fashion, void of challenges and absent of irony. Indeed, the Almighty has "paid us the intolerable compliment of loving us, in the deepest, most tragic, most inexorable sense."[53] The scriptures attest that Jesus learned obedience by the things which he suffered (see Hebrews 5:8) and that our Lord's personal engagement with temptation and suffering enabled him to be "touched with the feeling of our infirmities" (see Hebrews 4:15). Therefore "if tribulation is a necessary element in redemption, we must anticipate that it will never cease till God sees that world to be either redeemed or no further redeemable."[54]

Latter-day Saints believe that one of the major purposes of mortality is to learn to overcome, to put things into perspective, to keep our passions and desires within the bounds the Lord has set. Some of the greatest challenges to faith come in the form of pain, abuse, seemingly meaningless suffering, ironic tragedy, and man's inhumanity to man. It is a tenet of the gospel that pain and suffering are an essential part of God's plan, not something we seek out, to be sure, but a vital dimension of mortality. In the midst of enormous suffering in a miserable jail in Missouri, Joseph Smith wrote by way of inquiry: "O God, where art thou? And where is the pavilion that covereth thy hiding place? How long shall thy hand be stayed, and thine eye, yea thy pure eye, behold from the eternal heavens the wrongs of thy people and of thy servants, and thine ear be penetrated with their cries? Yea, O Lord, how long shall they suffer these wrongs and unlawful oppressions, before thine heart shall be softened toward them, and thy bowels be moved with compassion toward them?" Within moments he received the divine reply: "My son, peace be unto thy soul; thine adversity and thine afflictions shall be but a small moment. And then, if thou endure it well, God shall exalt thee on high; thou shalt triumph over all thy foes." And then, "Know thou, my son, that all these things shall give thee experience, and shall be for thy good. The Son of Man hath descended below them all. Art thou greater than he? Therefore, hold on thy way, and . . . fear not what man can do, for God shall be with you forever and ever" (D&C 121:1–3, 7–8; 122:7–9).

Like Lewis, Latter-day Saints believe that God is all-powerful, that he *could* prevent all suffering, stop all abuse, remove even the possibility of inhumanity, and erase all pain—but that he will not. In what may be one of the most important addresses on the place of human suffering in the development of an eternal character, President Spencer W. Kimball said:

"If all the sick for whom we pray were healed, if all the righteous were protected and the wicked destroyed, the whole program of the Father would be annulled and the basic principle of the gospel, free agency, would be ended. No man would have to live by faith. . . .

"Being human, we would expel from our lives physical pain and mental anguish and assure ourselves of continual ease and comfort, but if we were to close the doors upon sorrow and distress, we might be excluding our greatest friends and benefactors. Suffering can make saints of people as they learn patience, long-suffering, and self-mastery. The sufferings of our Savior were part of his education."[55]

I hasten to add that the believing Latter-day Saint is not ascetic. We do not seek out persecution nor glory in pain. "Life is an obstacle course," one LDS philosopher observed. "And sometimes it is a spook alley. . . . And some of our prayers [here in this life] are like the gambler's [request], 'Give me the money I made you promise not to give me if I asked for it.' What does a true friend do in such a case? God will honor our first request, to let us go through it; and He will provide you with . . . the way to make it bearable. More, to make it productive."[56]

There is one other dimension of the problem of evil and suffering in Lewis that deserves at least brief mention. It is what some Evangelical scholars have begun to call the "soteriological problem of evil." It may be stated simply as follows: If God is good, caring, and omniloving, how can he allow so many of his children to go to their graves without ever having heard of Jesus Christ, the only name under heaven whereby man can be saved (see Acts 4:12)? Some have chosen to take a rather restrictive view of the matter and have concluded that because God is all-wise and all-good and because no one really deserves to be saved anyway, we ought to be forever grateful that a few, relatively speaking, are saved. Others in a similar camp would simply reply that those who have never heard of Jesus were not elected to do so in the grand economy of God anyway. Still others would swing the pendulum toward a more inclusive position and thus open the door to a broader definition of "faith in God" or being in Christ.[57]

Lewis explained that "those who put themselves in [God's] hands will become perfect, as He is perfect—perfect in love, wisdom, joy, beauty, and immortality. The change will not be completed in this life, for death is an important part of the treatment."[58] On another occasion he remarked: "Here is another thing that used to puzzle me. Is it not frightfully unfair that this new life [in Christ] should be confined to people who have heard of Christ and been able to believe in Him? But the truth is God has not told us what His arrangements about the other people are. We do know that no man can be saved except through Christ; we do not know that only those who know Him can be saved through Him."[59]

Further, Lewis said: "There are people (a great many of them) who are slowly ceasing to be Christians but who still call themselves by that name: some of them are clergymen. There are other people who are slowly becoming Christians though they do not yet call themselves so. There are people who do not accept the full Christian doctrine about Christ but who are so strongly attracted by Him that they are His in a much deeper sense than they themselves understand. There are people in other religions who are being led by God's secret influence to concentrate on those parts of their religion which are in agreement with Christianity, and who thus belong to Christ without knowing it. . . . Many of the good Pagans long before Christ's birth may have been in this position."[60]

In the closing pages of *The Great Divorce,* there is a fascinating conversation between Lewis and George MacDonald. There Lewis is taught concerning Christ's descent into hell and is told, "There is no spirit in prison to Whom He did not preach." Lewis then asks: "And some hear him?" MacDonald answers: "Aye." Lewis follows up: "In your own books, . . . you were a Universalist. You talked as if all men would be saved. And St. Paul too." MacDonald then delivers a rather complex and difficult response, but one in which he seems to be saying, in essence, that everyone who desires to be saved will be saved. Although we speak rather categorically here of heaven and hell and formulate straightforward criteria for attaining each, from an eternal perspective, far more will be saved than we realize. Lewis did not attempt to correct MacDonald's doctrine for the reader.[61]

Latter-day Saints take very seriously the obligation to do missionary work throughout the world, in order that every person might be invited to come unto Christ in this manner. And what of those who have died without this opportunity? What of those who never heard Jesus preach? What of those in the first century who never had occasion to hear the testimony of Peter or Nathaniel or Paul? And what of those before or since that day, men and women throughout the earth who have died ignorant of the gospel of Jesus Christ? Are they damned forever by bad timing or poor transportation facilities?

Like Lewis, Latter-day Saints are inclusivists and hold out hope for the unevangelized without giving up the belief that Christ is the only way to salvation. As Latter-day Saints we feel that every person will have the opportunity, either in this life or the next, to receive the fulness of the gospel of Jesus Christ and enter into the everlasting covenant. We have been taught that between the time of Christ's death on the cross and his rise from the tomb, he went into the postmortal spirit world, preached his message and organized the faithful, in order that the message of truth might be made available to all who are willing to receive it (see 1 Peter 3:18–20; 4:6; D&C 138). But the sacraments or ordinances of the Church are earthly ordinances and must be performed on this side of the veil of death. Thus members of the Church go into holy temples, receive these ordinances, and then return frequently to perform them in behalf of those who have died without them. In short, Latter-day Saints are involved in what some Evangelicals have called "postmortem evangelism."[62]

CONCLUSION

My purpose in this chapter has been to explain why we as Latter-day Saints have such a fascination with C. S. Lewis. To put it simply, we admire and quote him frequently for one reason: he touches upon doctrinal matters that are at the heart of much of what we believe. We could certainly explore ideas about which members of the Church would take issue with Lewis—the nature of God, *ex nihilo* creation, the Nicene Trinity, and a few others. And there may also be things about Mormonism that would grind on Lewis, both in terms of doctrine and lifestyle. He once remarked in a letter, for example, that he strongly objected "to the tyrannic and unscriptural insolence of anything that calls itself a Church and makes teetotalism a condition of membership."[63] But again, that is not the purpose of this chapter. My whole point is that C. S. Lewis is an important religious figure throughout the Christian world, including that of the Latter-day Saints, and that his influence may be broader than many had even supposed. C. S. Lewis is a thinking man's theologian, a writer whose views are crisp and sharp and challenging; his presentation is neither syrupy nor sentimental on the one hand, nor tedious on the other. His discussions are both spiritually satisfying and intellectually enlarging. He himself once described his task and his achievement: "When I began, Christianity came before the great mass of my unbelieving fellow-countrymen either in the highly emotional form offered by revivalists or in the unintelligible language of highly cultured clergymen. Most men were reached by neither. My task was therefore simply that of a translator—one *turning Christian doctrine, or what he believed to be such, into the vernacular, into language that the unscholarly people would attend to and could understand.*"[64]

In short, as one Latter-day Saint has written, in tribute to this great Christian, "Lewis was able to deal with fundamentals without being fundamentalistic. He sought to revive Christian belief in the minds of men without being revivalistic. In this disposable age of paper plates and paper philosophies which are good for one use only, Lewis insisted that all things had to be tested spiritually, rationally, and experientially before an honest man could give allegiance to them. He believed that Christianity met every test."[65]

Notes

From an address at the Seventh Annual Wheaton Theology Conference, Wheaton College, Norton, Massachusetts, 16 April 1998.

1. Terry Glaspey, *Not a Tame Lion* (Nashville: Cumberland House, 1996), 160.
2. C. S. Lewis, *Christian Reunion and Other Essays,* ed. Walter Hooper (London: Collins Fount Paperbacks, 1990), 20; see also C. S. Lewis, *Mere Christianity* (New York: Touchstone, 1996), 6.
3. Jerry Johnston, "Ideally Speaking," *Deseret News,* 28 March 1998, E1.
4. Glaspey, *Not a Tame Lion,* introduction.
5. See Stephen E. Robinson, *Are Mormons Christians?* (Salt Lake City: Bookcraft, 1991); Craig L. Blomberg and Stephen E. Robinson, *How Wide the Divide?* (Downers Grove, Ill.: InterVarsity Press, 1997).
6. Lewis, *Mere Christianity,* 10–11.
7. C. S. Lewis, *Miracles: A Preliminary Study* (New York: Touchstone, 1996), 153; see also 148–57; 176, note 1; and C. S. Lewis, *The Problem of Pain* (New York: Touchstone, 1996), 22.
8. Lewis, *Mere Christianity,* 54.
9. Lewis, *Miracles,* 151.
10. See Robert L. Millet, "The Eternal Gospel," *Ensign,* July 1996, 48–56.
11. *Gospel Doctrine,* 31, 395, 398–400.
12. Lewis, *The Problem of Pain,* 92.
13. Ibid., 132.
14. Lewis, *Mere Christianity,* 121.
15. William W. Wordsworth, *Ode on Intimations of Immortality,* as quoted in Jack M. Lyon et al., *Best-Loved Poems of the LDS People* (Salt Lake City: Deseret Book Co., 1996), 62.
16. *Gospel Doctrine,* 12–13.
17. Lewis, *The Problem of Pain,* 51.
18. Lewis, *Mere Christianity,* 88; see also Lewis, *The Problem of Pain,* 60.
19. Lewis, *The Problem of Pain,* 62, 75–76.
20. Ibid., 33.
21. Ibid., 59.

22. Lewis, *Mere Christianity,* 92.
23. Ezra Taft Benson, *A Witness and a Warning* (Salt Lake City: Deseret Book Co., 1988), 33.
24. Orson F. Whitney and Matthias Cowley, *Cowley and Whitney on Doctrine,* comp. Forace Green (Salt Lake City: Bookcraft, 1963), 287.
25. Lewis, *Mere Christianity,* 59.
26. Lewis, *The Problem of Pain,* 43.
27. Brigham Young, in *Journal of Discourses,* 11:301.
28. See C. S. Lewis, *Letters to Malcolm: Chiefly on Prayer* (New York: Harcourt Brace & Co., 1992), 42, 44.
29. See Lewis, *Mere Christianity,* 59–61.
30. Ibid., 165–66, 169–70.
31. C. S. Lewis, *Letters of C. S. Lewis,* ed. W. H. Lewis; rev. and enlarged edition, edited by Walter Hooper (New York: Harcourt Brace & Co., 1993), 365.
32. See Lewis, *Mere Christianity,* 55–56; C. S. Lewis, *The Weight of Glory and Other Essays,* ed. Walter Hooper (New York: Touchstone, 1996), 105.
33. Lewis, *The Problem of Pain,* 21.
34. Lewis, *Letters to Malcolm,* 49–50.
35. Lewis, *Mere Christianity,* 131–32; see also Lewis, *Christian Reunion,* 18.
36. Lewis, *Mere Christianity,* 131.
37. Lewis, *The Problem of Pain,* 38.
38. Lewis, *Miracles,* 178.
39. Lewis, *A Grief Observed* (San Francisco: HarperCollins, 1989), 84–85.
40. Lewis, *The Weight of Glory,* 39–40; emphasis in original.
41. Lewis, *Mere Christianity,* 188.
42. Ibid., 186.
43. Ibid., 137–40.
44. Ibid., 153–54.
45. Ibid., 176.
46. B. H. Roberts, *The Seventy's Course in Theology, Fifth Year* (Salt Lake City: Deseret News Press, 1912), 47.
47. See Parley P. Pratt, *Key to Science of Theology,* 1978 ed. (Salt Lake City: Deseret Book Co., 1978), 22–23.
48. Lewis, *Mere Christianity,* 53.
49. See Lewis, *Miracles,* 234.
50. Lewis, *The Problem of Pain,* 98.
51. See Lewis, *A Grief Observed,* 34–35, 49–50; see also Lewis, *The Problem of Pain,* 90–91.
52. Lewis, *The Problem of Pain,* 83.
53. Ibid., 35–37.
54. Ibid., 102.
55. Spencer W. Kimball, *Faith Precedes the Miracle* (Salt Lake City: Deseret Book Co., 1972), 97–98.
56. Truman G. Madsen, "Human Anguish and Divine Love," *Four Essays on Love* (Provo: Communications Workshop, 1971), 59.
57. For a detailed treatment of this challenging issue, see John Sanders, *No Other Name: An Investigation into the Destiny of the Unevangelized* (Grand Rapids, Mich.: Eerdmans, 1992); John Sanders, ed., *What About Those Who Have Never Heard?* (Downers Grove, Ill.: InterVarsity Press, 1995); Dennis L. Okholm and Timothy R. Philips, eds., *Four Views on Salvation in a Pluralistic World* (Grand Rapids, Mich.: Zondervan, 1996); Clark Pinnock et al., *The Openness of God* (Downers Grove, Ill.: InterVarsity Press, 1994).
58. Lewis, *Mere Christianity,* 177.
59. Ibid., 65.
60. Ibid., 178.

61. C. S. Lewis, *The Great Divorce* (New York: Touchstone, 1996), 121–22.
62. See Gabriel Fackre, "Divine Perseverance," in Sanders, *What About Those Who Have Never Heard?* 71–95; Leonhard Goppelt, *A Commentary on 1 Peter,* ed. Ferdinand Hahn (Grand Rapids, Mich.: Eerdmans, 1993), 253–65.
63. Lewis, *Letters of C. S. Lewis,* 447.
64. C. S. Lewis, *God in the Dock: Essays on Theology and Ethics,* ed. Walter Hooper (Grand Rapids, Mich.: Eerdmans, 1970), 183; emphasis in original.
65. William Clayton Kimball, "The Christian Commitment: C. S. Lewis and the Defense of Doctrine," *Brigham Young University Studies,* 12, no. 2 (winter 1972): 208.

FEAR NOT

L ike Nephi of old, "I glory in my Jesus, for he hath redeemed my soul from hell" (2 Nephi 33:6). Like Ammon, son of Mosiah, I feel to rejoice in the Lord: "Yea, I know that I am nothing; as to my strength I am weak; therefore I will . . . boast of my God, for in his strength I can do all things" (Alma 26:12). I ask, as did Jacob, "Why not speak of the atonement of Christ?" (Jacob 4:12). Indeed, why not?

WHY BE FAITHFUL?

Let me pose to each one of us a few questions: Why do we serve? Why do we come to church? Why do we avoid R-rated movies and pornography? Why do we live the Word of Wisdom? Why do we avoid immorality in every form? There are many people in this Church who are in good standing and thus qualify for temple recommends. Why do they do what they do, and why do they avoid what they avoid? For many, the motivation to keep the commandments is fear—fear of rejection by friends or family, fear of being arrested or of contracting a life-threatening disease, fear of encountering disciplinary measures in the Church, or fear of having to face God one day.

To be sure, fear is not a bad motive. Sometimes there is nothing except "harshness, preaching and prophesying of wars, and contentions, and destructions, and continually reminding [us] of death, and the duration of eternity, and the judgments and the power of God, and all these things—stirring [us] up continually to keep [us] in the fear of the Lord" (Enos 1:23). Yes, sometimes the prophets and apostles and Church leaders must resort to speaking of such consequences to sin as endless torment and eternal damnation so "that it might work upon the hearts of the children of men" (D&C 19:6–7). It is better to be afraid of sin and to be frightened of the effects of wilful wandering than to sin or wander. To say this another way, once in a while, we simply need to have the word of the Lord shake us in our boots in order to remind us why we are here, who we are, and whose we are. In that sense, fear can and does serve a useful purpose in calling us to repentance.

I would suggest, however, that if fear is our only motive for faithfulness, we will eventually become weary and beaten down spiritually, or else we will begin to ignore the word of truth and turn a deaf ear to the invitation to change. Further, we will never come to know the Lord, trust the Lord, and enjoy a quiet confidence in the Lord unless we are motivated by other things. Let me illustrate by turning to the scriptures, to a message from one of the parables of Jesus.

THE TALENTS

Chapter 25 of Matthew contains what might be called three parables of preparation—the parable of the ten virgins, the parable of the talents, and the parable of the sheep and the goats. They all have something to say about how to prepare for the Second Coming of the Son of Man and the time of judgment. The parable of the ten virgins speaks essentially of the need for a consistent, ongoing program of spiritual growth and of the problem with trying to develop spirituality suddenly. The parable of the sheep and the goats teaches that those who are prepared to meet the Lord are those who have come to love and serve the people of the Lord, those whose hearts are drawn out in compassion to "the least" of our brothers and sisters.

It was only a few months ago, while sitting in an inspiring Gospel Doctrine class, that I saw something in the parable of the talents that I had never seen before. You know the story: the master travels into a far country and leaves differing talents—amounts of money, in this case—with three men. The assumption here is that the master expects them to build upon what they have received, to be productive and industrious with what they have been given. When he returns, he praises and rewards the man whose five talents have been doubled, as well as the one whose two talents have likewise been doubled.

"Then he which had received the one talent came and said, Lord, I knew thee that thou art an hard man, reaping where thou hast not sown, and gathering where thou hast not strawed: And I was afraid, and went and hid thy talent in the earth:

lo, there thou hast that is thine." The master was angry and responded: "Thou wicked and slothful servant, thou knewest that I reap where I sowed not, and gather where I have not strawed: Thou oughtest therefore to have put my money to the exchangers, and then at my coming I should have received mine own with usury. Take therefore the talent from him, and give it unto him which hath ten talents. For unto every one that hath shall be given, and he shall have abundance: but from him that hath not shall be taken away even that which he hath. And cast ye the unprofitable servant into outer darkness: there shall be weeping and gnashing of teeth" (Matthew 25:14–30).

Generally, when we speak of the meaning or interpretation of this parable we focus on the need for everyone to use their talents—their gifts, abilities, or even financial resources—wisely, and to become more profitable servants. We assume, I suppose rightly, that the master in this parable is God; that he has given to each one of us some things that we should enhance and improve in order to contribute to the building of the kingdom of God and the establishment of Zion; and that he will soon come again, at which point we will be required to stand before him and account for what we did with what we had. And perhaps this is just what the Savior wants us to understand in the parable of the talents.

I would like to draw our attention, however, to a less obvious aspect of the parable. Note that the unproductive steward saw his master as hard or strict, one who punishes and condemns.

I believe this perspective of the master—which is undoubtedly an ill-advised and inaccurate one—directly affected how the steward behaved. What we believe affects what we do. If I live my life in constant fear of God, in dread or unhealthy fear, then my actions will seldom if ever be done out of proper motives, such as love of God and a longing to serve my fellow man. Rather, I will approach each day with the kind of fear and trembling that leads to fretful and unproductive living.

We know that our God is almighty, that he has all power and that he can, as the scriptures attest, smite us with one glance of his all-searching eye. His is the power and prerogative to give life and take it. We are told that we should "fear God" and that the fear of the Lord is the beginning of wisdom (Psalm 11:10; Proverbs 1:7; 9:10). We are told that we should "work out [our] own salvation with fear and trembling" (Philippians 2:12). But almost always the word translated as *fear* may also be translated as *reverence*. That is, we should honor and respect and reverence our God. He is the Man of Holiness (see Moses 6:55), the God of all creation, the embodiment of every virtue and perfection. But he is also our Father in Heaven, the Father of our spirits, a kind and loving Parent who delights in our happiness and yearns to save us, one and all, with an everlasting salvation (see D&C 43:25).

If I might take a bit of license with the parable of the talents, I would suggest that while the Lord does indeed want us to be productive with what we have, he is in no way desirous of comparing us with others, nor is the quantity of the return of any special interest to him. I believe that if one of the servants in the parable had sincerely worked and labored to improve upon his talent but had in the end been unable to expand appreciably upon the original amount, the Lord would have accepted of his offering. Truly, "the Lord requireth the heart and a willing mind" (D&C 64:34). We are judged by the desires of the heart, as well as our works (see Alma 41:3: D&C 137:9).

In speaking of a little-known character in Church history, a man by the name of Oliver Granger—called to serve as the agent of the First Presidency in Kirtland as the Saints moved themselves to Missouri—the Lord said: "I remember my servant Oliver Granger; behold, verily I say unto him that his name shall be had in sacred remembrance from generation to generation, forever and ever, saith the Lord." And now note these tender and consoling words, words that teach us a great deal about the Being we worship: "Therefore, let him contend earnestly for the redemption of the First Presidency of my Church, saith the Lord; and *when he falls he shall rise again, for his sacrifice shall be more sacred unto me than his increase,* saith the Lord" (D&C 117:12–13; emphasis added).

In short, how we view the Lord affects how we live the gospel. If in every move we make we find ourselves looking over our shoulder to make certain that God isn't going to smite us should we fail or fall short, our offering will not be from the heart nor will the product of our labors be fruitful. And, frankly, it just won't be much fun to choose the right. Who wants to live that way? On the other hand, if we see our Heavenly Father and his Son, Jesus Christ, for who and what they are—as glorified, exalted beings whose whole purpose and work are to "bring to pass the immortality and eternal life of man" (Moses 1:39), and whose greatest desire is for all of us to inherit exaltation—then our hearts will be lighter, our actions will be motivated by love and acceptance, and our work will be profitable and enjoyable.

CHRIST'S LOVE FOR US

It is only in and through the Savior that we can be changed and renewed, made clean and free from guilt and shame, relieved of the anxiety and unhealthy dread associated with fearful living. As we properly confess our sins and forsake them, the blood of Christ is able to sanctify us from worldliness and from a stilted view of things. The more pure we become—and this purity comes only through Christ, by the power of the Holy Ghost—the more we are able to see things as they really are. When we continue in sin, we are unable to see things clearly; we see things as *we* are, not as they are in reality. But the power of the Atonement gives us a new heart and a new mind and new eyes with which to see things. We feel and think and perceive an entirely new realm of reality.

These blessings come to us through the mercy and love of the Lord Jesus Christ. But they do not come to us fully until we choose to repent, to turn away from our sins and to be transformed in our minds and our hearts (see Romans 12:1–3). In speaking of charity or the pure love of Christ, Mormon implored: "Wherefore, my beloved brethren [and sisters], pray unto the Father with all the energy of heart, that ye may be filled with this love, which he hath bestowed upon all who are true followers of his Son, Jesus Christ; that ye may become the sons [and daughters] of God; that when he shall appear we shall be like him, for we shall see him as he is; that we may have this hope; that we may be purified even as he is pure" (Moroni 7:48).

Generally when we speak of charity we speak of the love that we should and must demonstrate toward our brothers and sisters. But let us be clear in our minds that we will never be in a position to love purely and have a meaningful impact on the lives of others until we have experienced the pure love of Christ in our own hearts and minds. Elder Jeffrey R. Holland has written: "It is instructive to note that the charity or 'the pure love of Christ' we are to cherish can be interpreted two ways. One of its meanings is the kind of merciful, forgiving love Christ's disciples should have one for another. That is, all Christians should try to love as the Savior loved, showing pure, redeeming compassion for all. Unfortunately, few, if any, mortals have been entirely successful in this endeavor, but it is an invitation that all should try to meet.

"The greater definition of 'the pure love of Christ,' however, is not what we as Christians try but largely fail to demonstrate toward others but rather what Christ totally succeeded in demonstrating toward us. *True charity has been known only once. It is shown perfectly and purely in Christ's unfailing, ultimate, and atoning love for us.* It is Christ's love for us that 'suffereth long, and is kind, and envieth not.' It is his love for us that is not 'puffed up . . . , not easily provoked, thinketh no evil.' It is Christ's love for us that 'beareth all things, believeth all things, hopeth all things, endureth all things.' *It is as demonstrated in Christ that 'charity never faileth.' It is that charity—his pure love for us—without which we would be noth-ing, hopeless, of all men and women most miserable. Truly, those found possessed of the blessings of his love at the last day—the Atonement, the Resurrection, eternal life, eternal promise—surely it shall be well with them.*

"This does not in any way," Elder Holland continues, "minimize the com-mandment that we are to try to acquire this kind of love for one another. We should 'pray unto the Father with all the energy of heart that [we] may be filled with this love.' We should try to be more constant and unfailing, more longsuffering and kind, less envious and puffed up in our relationships with others. As Christ lived so should we live, and as Christ loved so should we love. But the 'pure love of Christ' Mormon spoke of is precisely that—Christ's love. *With that divine gift, that redeeming bestowal, we have everything; without it we have nothing and ultimately are nothing,* except in the end 'devils [and] angels to a devil.'

"Life has its share of fears and failures. Sometimes things fall short. Sometimes people fail us, or economies or businesses or governments fail us. But one thing in time or eternity does not fail us—the pure love of Christ."[1]

COMFORT IN THE COVENANT

I bear my testimony that there is a new life in Christ that enables and empow-ers us to live peacefully, peaceably, and comfortably, even as hell rages on all sides. The revelations declare that "he that looketh on a woman to lust after her, or if any shall commit adultery in their hearts, they shall not have the Spirit, but shall deny the faith *and shall fear*" (D&C 63:16; emphasis added). On the other hand, those who "let virtue garnish [their] thoughts unceasingly" feel confidence "in the pres-ence of God" (D&C 121:45). Fear. Confidence. Which do you want? Which of these appeals to you? Those who choose to live the gospel—to repent and submit to the will of the Lord, to deny themselves of all ungodliness (see Moroni 10:32)—enjoy that quiet and sublime confidence, that peace which passes all understanding (see Philippians 4:7). Truly, as John the Beloved wrote, "if our heart condemn us not, then have we confidence toward God" (1 John 3:21; see also 2:28; 5:14).

The Lord never intended for us to languish in guilt or to live in constant anxi-ety concerning whether or not we are pleasing a hard-to-please God. Each of us has within us a manifestation of the light of Christ or Spirit of Jesus Christ (see Moroni 7:16–19). It is the conscience, that inborn, inherent moral monitor that points us toward the right and warns us of the wrong. If we give heed to that light, we are led to higher light and knowledge (see D&C 84:46–48), as well as a deeper measure of joy and fulfillment. If we ignore or spurn the warnings of the light of Christ, we weaken our resistance to sin and distance ourselves from Deity. We then become oblivious to the light and resentful of those who possess it. And we fear. We feel tension and anxiety, frustration and noise within our souls. Isaiah wrote: "Peace, peace to him that is far off, and to him that is near, saith the Lord; and I will heal him. But the wicked are like the troubled sea, when it cannot rest, whose waters cast up mire and dirt. There is no peace, saith my God, to the wicked" (Isaiah 57:19–21; see also 48:22).

The Prophet Joseph Smith taught: "If you wish to go where God is, you must be like God, or possess the principles which God possesses, for if we are not drawing towards God in principle, we are going from Him and drawing towards the devil. . . . Search your hearts and see if you are like God. I have searched mine, and feel to repent of all my sins. . . . As far as we degenerate from God, we descend to the devil and lose knowledge, and without knowledge we cannot be saved, and while our hearts are filled with evil, and we are studying evil, there is no room in our hearts for good, or studying good. Is not God good? Then you be good; if He is faithful, then you be faithful."[2]

The gospel of Jesus Christ is in reality a gospel covenant. As a part of that covenant, we agree to do those things that we *can* do—to have faith, to repent, to be baptized and receive the gift of the Holy Ghost, and to endure faithfully to the end of our lives. On his part, the Lord agrees to do for us what we *cannot* do for ourselves—forgive our sins, cleanse and purify our hearts, empower us in our efforts to keep the commandments, raise us from the dead, and endow us with glory and honor hereafter.

Our Heavenly Father and his Son, Jesus Christ, are eager to do all in their power to welcome us back, to make us better and truer than we are now, and to bring into our lives that peace and assurance that we are on course. "No amount of falls will really undo us if we keep on picking ourselves up each time. We shall of course be very muddy and tattered children by the time we reach home. But the bathrooms are all ready, the towels put out, and the clean clothes in the airing cupboard. The only fatal thing is to lose one's temper and give it up. It is when we notice the dirt that God is most present in us: it is the very sign of His presence."[3]

The story is told of a woman who visited President Joseph Fielding Smith. She had been guilty of serious transgression but had fully repented and now just wanted to find her way. President Smith asked her to read to him from Genesis the story of the destruction of Sodom and Gomorrah and of Lot's wife being turned to a pillar of salt. He asked her what lesson was to be learned. She answered, essentially: "The message of that story is that God will destroy the wicked." "Not so," President Smith told this repentant woman. "The message for you is: 'Don't look back!'"[4]

I bear testimony that happiness cannot come through acquiring this world's toys or through yielding to the enticements of the great and spacious building; true happiness can come only through faithful observance of the Lord's commandments, through being loyal to the royal within us. "Therefore, fear not, little flock; do good; let earth and hell combine against you, for if ye are built upon my rock, they cannot prevail. . . . Look unto me in every thought; doubt not, fear not" (D&C 6:34, 36). Truly, "if [we] are prepared [we] shall not fear" (D&C 38:30).

Jesus Christ is the Promised Messiah, our Savior and Redeemer, and because of what he has done and is doing for us, we need not fear. The Gods of heaven have restored the everlasting gospel to earth in these last days through the instrumentality of a modern prophet, Joseph Smith, and all the powers and knowledge needed to exalt us in the highest heaven are vested in The Church of Jesus Christ of Latter-day Saints. Further, living apostles and prophets preside over this, the "only true and living church" on the face of the earth (D&C 1:30). Let us each choose to come unto Christ, partake of his healing and regenerating powers, and find joy and peace in this world and eternal life in the world to come. God grant that we may be true and faithful—true to who we are and faithful to Him whose we are.

Notes

From an address delivered at Brigham Young University Fourteenth Stake conference, Provo, Utah, 24 October 1999.

1. Jeffrey R. Holland, *Christ and the New Covenant* (Salt Lake City: Deseret Book Co., 1997), 336–37; emphasis added.
2. *Teachings of the Prophet Joseph Smith*, 216–17.
3. C. S. Lewis, *Letters of C. S. Lewis*, rev. ed., ed. Walter Hooper (New York: Harcourt Brace & Co., 1993), 365.
4. Joseph Fielding Smith, as quoted by Boyd K. Packer, "The Fountain of Life," fireside address at Brigham Young University, Provo, Utah, 29 March 1992.

AFTER ALL WE CAN DO

The matter of the grace of God, as mediated through Jesus the Christ, has for some time now seemed to "occupy my mind, and press itself upon my feelings" (D&C 128:1); in fact, for the past fifteen years the topic has nearly consumed me. I have not desired to become a crusader or to be a part of some new theological craze in the Church but have sought with real intent to better understand what it means to trust in and rely upon the merits and mercy and grace of the Holy Messiah (see 2 Nephi 2:8).

IN CONTEXT

I have felt for some time that the matter of the grace of Jesus Christ deserves more of our attention as Latter-day Saints, especially when it is such a central doctrine in the Book of Mormon and the New Testament. Perhaps some of us have been hesitant to perceive the truthfulness and eternal relevance of this doctrine because it brings us face to face with our own limitations. Perhaps we shy away from it because we sense that it may entail an alteration in our present way of viewing things. Whatever the cause, it just may be that we have not enjoyed the quiet but pervasive power that does come to those who acknowledge their weakness and turn to Him who has all power. I do believe, however, that there is wisdom in presenting this doctrinal message in context, in the way it is presented in scripture—the context of the Atonement. That is to say, grace is not a doctrine that stands alone; it is inextricably tied to several other matters and therefore makes sense and brings peace only when seen in that context.

Latter-day Saints have often been critical of those who emphasize salvation by grace alone, while we as a church have often been criticized for a type of works-righteousness. The gospel is in fact a gospel covenant—a two-way promise. The Lord agrees to do for us what we could never do for ourselves—to forgive our sins, to lift our burdens, to renew our souls and re-create our nature, to raise us from the dead and qualify us for glory hereafter. At the same time, we promise to do what we *can* do: receive the ordinances of salvation, love and serve one another (see Mosiah 18:8–10), and do all in our power to put off the natural man and deny ourselves of ungodliness (see Mosiah 3:19; Moroni 10:32). We believe that more is required of men and women than a verbal expression of faith in the Lord, more than a confession with the lips that we have received Christ into our hearts. The scriptures of the Restoration add perspective and balance to the majestic teachings of the Apostle Paul on the matter of salvation by grace. We know, without question, that the power to save us, to change us, to renew our souls, is in Christ. True faith, however, always manifests itself in *faithfulness.* Good works evidence our faith, our desire to remain in covenant with Christ. But these good works, though *necessary,* are not *sufficient.*

Too often we are prone to view grace as that increment of goodness, that final gift of God that will make up the difference and thereby boost us into the celestial kingdom, "after all we can do" (2 Nephi 25:23). To be sure, we will need a full measure of divine assistance to become celestial material. But the grace of God, through Jesus Christ our Lord, is available to us every hour of every day of our lives. "True grace," as one non-LDS writer has suggested, "is more than just a giant freebie, opening the door to heaven in the sweet by and by, but leaving us to wallow in sin in the bitter here and now. Grace is God presently at work in our lives."[1] The grace of God is a precious gift, an enabling power to face life with quiet courage, to do things we could never do on our own. The Great Physician does more than forgive sins. He ministers relief to the disconsolate, comfort to the bereaved, confidence to those who wrestle with infirmities and feelings of inadequacy, strength and peace to those who have been battered and scarred by the ironies of this life (see Isaiah 61:1–2; Alma 7:11–13).

Few things would be more sinister than encouraging lip service to God but discouraging obedience and faithful discipleship. On the other hand, surely nothing could be more offensive to God than a smug self-assurance that comes from trusting in one's own works or relying upon one's own strength. Understanding this sacred principle—the relationship between the grace of an infinite Being and the works of finite man—is not easy, but it is immensely rewarding.

WHO'S IN CONTROL?

I cannot speak for the Church. I am, however, an expert on my own feelings. I have come to know firsthand some of the despondency and guilt associated with falling short of my goals, of trying to do it all, of striving to make myself perfect. The Apostle Paul seems to have been addressing a similar problem in his day. He wrote: "Brethren, my heart's desire and prayer to God for Israel is, that they might be saved. For I bear them record that they have a zeal of God, but not according to knowledge. For they being ignorant of God's righteousness, and *going about to establish their own righteousness, have not submitted themselves unto the righteousness of God.* For Christ is the end of the law for righteousness to every one that believeth" (Romans 10:1–4; emphasis added).

I have been associated with many wonderful, caring people who struggle often with feelings of inadequacy, who hope against hope that one day—in some distant age in the future—in spite of their frailty in this sphere, they might qualify to go and feel comfortable where Gods and angels are. Since it is true that the gospel of Jesus Christ is intended to liberate us, to ease and lighten our burdens, to bring that comfort and rest found in no other way, why is it that some of us struggle at times? Why is it that once in a while we find ourselves simply going through the motions, doing our duty in the Church but finding little fulfillment and enjoyment in it?

I suspect that many Latter-day Saints will agree to the same faulty orientation I find occasionally in myself. My greatest frustrations seem to come as a result of my efforts to "handle it" myself or, in other words, my failure to trust in and rely on the Lord. Maybe it's our culture that contributes to our dilemma; maybe it's the constant chants of "You can do anything you put your mind to," or "You have unlimited possibilities and potential" that tend to focus our attention away from the powers of the Divine toward *our* abilities, *our* merits, and *our* contributions. I have come to know that the answer to our problems is not to be found alone in humanity, no matter how impressive our accomplishments. The solution to the soul's yearning for solace is not to be located in the programs of society per se. In a way, we almost need to work at cross purposes to social trends, to attune our ears to a quiet voice that beckons to us amidst the loud babble of competing voices. That quiet voice pleads with us simply to come unto Christ. The answer to individual hurt and personal pain is not to be found solely in congressional decisions or developments in personnel management, not in louder cries of victimization, but in and through Jesus Christ. The most pertinent crusade in which the Christian is involved is the quest for personal peace and the campaign for purity of heart, all of which come from Christ through the ordinances of the priesthood and by the power of the Holy Ghost. The scriptures teach plainly and persuasively that coming unto Christ entails a moment of decision. It is that poignant point in our progression wherein we realize that man-made solutions are in reality "broken cisterns, that can hold no water" (Jeremiah 2:13) and that only through yoking ourselves to the Master may we rid ourselves of the burdens of Babylon.

Few things in this life are exactly as they seem to be. We live in a time, for example, where everyone is told of the importance of being in control. We must be in charge. We must have access to and management over all the variables. We operate by plans and formulae and procedures. Lists and tables and charts abound. One of the harsh realities facing someone acclimated to this fallen world is that spiritual things are not programmable. We cannot require or demand or shape spiritual experience. The Spirit is in control, not us. The Lord through his Spirit works his marvelous wonders in his own time, in his own way, and according to his own will and purposes. To enter the realm of divine experience, therefore, is to enter a realm where we are not in complete control. We can seek to be worthy, strive to be in a position to be blessed, plead and pray for divine intervention, but we do not force the hand of the Almighty.

Though such matters as self-reliance and self-confidence may prove to be valuable in some of our dealings in this life, the reciprocal principles of submission, surrender, and having an eye single to the glory of God are essential if we are to acquire that enabling power described in scripture as the saving grace of Jesus Christ. It is as if the Lord inquires of us: "Do you want to be a possessor of all things such that all things are subject unto you?" We of course respond in the affirmative. He then says: "Good. Then submit to me. Yield your heart unto me." The Lord asks further: "Do you want to have victory over all things?" We nod. He follows up: "Then surrender to me. Unconditionally." Odd, isn't it? We incorporate the powers of divinity only through acknowledging our own inabilities, accepting our limitations, and realizing our weakness. We open ourselves to infinite strength only through accepting our finite condition. We in time gain control through being willing to relinquish control.

I am haunted by the words that Paul wrote in his second epistle to the Corinthians. As you know, Paul was, sadly, required to spend a significant amount of time defending his apostolic calling. Having been a zealous Pharisee and even a persecutor of the Christians before his conversion, and not having been one of the original witnesses of the Resurrection of Christ, he felt the need to testify to his detractors that his call had indeed come from God. In doing so with the Corinthian Saints, he went on to describe some of the marvelous spiritual experiences the Lord had given to him. "And lest I should be exalted above measure," Paul hastened to add, "through the abundance of the revelations, there was given to me a thorn in the flesh, the messenger of Satan to buffet me, lest I should be exalted above measure. For this thing I besought the Lord thrice, that it might depart from me. And [the Lord] said unto me, *My grace is sufficient for thee: for my strength is made perfect in weakness.*" Paul then remarks: "Most gladly therefore will I rather glory in my infirmities, that the power of Christ may rest upon me. Therefore I take pleasure in infirmities, in reproaches, in necessities, in persecutions, in distresses for Christ's sake: for *when I am weak, then am I strong*" (2 Corinthians 12:7–10; emphasis added).

No one really knows what Paul's "thorn in the flesh" was. Was it a lingering sickness, perhaps malaria, so common in Galatia? Was it a memory of his past, a hellish reminder of who he had been? Was it an evil spirit that dogged his steps and wearied him in his ministry? Perhaps one day we'll know. All we know for sure is that whatever it was, it kept Paul humble and forced him to his knees. His inabilities and his impotence in the face of this particular challenge were ever before him. I rather think that when Paul states that he "besought the Lord thrice" for the removal of the thorn, he is not describing merely three prayers but instead three seasons of prayer, extended periods of wrestling and laboring in the Spirit for a specific blessing that never came. Indeed, as he suggests, another kind of blessing came—a closeness, a sensitivity, an acquaintance with Deity, a sanctified strength that came through pain and suffering. It was up against the wall of faith, when shorn of self-assurance and naked in his extremity and his frightening finitude, that a mere mortal received that enabling power we know as the grace of Christ. As the Savior explained to Moroni, when we acknowledge and confess our weakness—not just our specific weaknesses, our individual sins, but our weakness, our mortal limitation—and submit unto him, we transform weakness into strength (see Ether 12:27).

As Jacob, son of Lehi, affirmed: "Wherefore, we search the prophets, and we have many revelations and the spirit of prophecy; and having all these witnesses we obtain a hope, and our faith becometh unshaken, insomuch that we truly can command in the name of Jesus and the very trees obey us, or the mountains, or the waves of the sea." Now note these words: "Nevertheless, *the Lord God showeth us our weakness that we may know that it is by his grace, and his great condescensions unto the children of men, that we have power to do these things"* (Jacob 4:6–7; emphasis added).

Too much of my own frustration over the years has come as a result of my refusal to let go and thus let God. Something—I suppose it is the natural man, the prideful self that automatically asserts its own agenda—drives me to want to do it myself. Oh, I believe in God, to be sure, that he loves me, that he sent his Son to earth to help me. All too often, however, my actions have betrayed my limited orientation, my vision of Christ as a type of spiritual adviser, a sort of celestial cheerleader who stands on the sidelines and whispers encouragement, but not the Lord God Omnipotent who came to earth to make men and women into new creatures through empowering them to do what they could never do for themselves.

In an eagerness to draw closer to Christ, some members of the Church have begun to cross a sacred line and go beyond that reverential barrier that must be observed by true followers of the Christ. They speak of Jesus as though he were their next door neighbor, their buddy or chum, their pal. This is not the way to intimacy with the Savior. Oddly enough, strangely enough, it is not through humanizing Jesus, through trying to make him one of the boys, that we draw close to him and incorporate his saving powers. It is, rather, through recognizing his godhood, his divinity, his unspeakable power. In short, the more I sense his greatness, his infinity, his capacity to transform the human soul, and my utter helplessness without him, the more I come unto him. Remember, it is through the recognition of our own nothingness and weakness that strength is derived (see Mosiah 2:20–21; 4:11–12, 26; Moses 1:10).

This is somewhat related to our tendency to speak of Jesus as our Elder Brother. He is, of course, our Elder Brother in that he was the firstborn spirit child of God in the premortal existence. But it is of interest to me that the Book of Mormon prophets never speak of Jehovah as our Elder Brother. Rather, he is the Almighty God, the Eternal Judge, the Holy One of Israel, the Holy Messiah, the Everlasting Father, the Father of heaven and of earth, the God of nature, the Supreme Being, the Keeper of the gate, the King of heaven, and the Lord God Omnipotent. Elder M. Russell Ballard explained: "We occasionally hear some members refer to Jesus as our Elder Brother, which is a true concept based on our understanding of the premortal life with our Father in Heaven. But like many points of gospel doctrine, that simple truth doesn't go far enough in terms of describing the Savior's role in our present lives and His great position as a member of the Godhead. Thus, some non-LDS Christians are uncomfortable with what they perceive as a secondary role for Christ in our theology. They feel that we view Jesus as a spiritual peer. They believe that we view Christ as an implementor, if you will, for God but that we don't view Him as God to us and to all mankind, which, of course, is counter to Biblical testimony about Christ's divinity. Let me help us understand, with clarity and testimony, our belief about Jesus Christ. We declare He is the King of Kings, Lord of Lords, the Creator, the Savior, the Captain of our salvation, the Bright and Morning Star. He has taught us that He is in all things, above all things, through all things and round about all things, that He is Alpha and Omega, the Lord of the universe, the first and the last relative to our salvation, and that His name is above every name and is in fact the only name under heaven by which we can be saved. . . .

". . . We can understand why some Latter-day Saints have tended to focus on Christ's Sonship as opposed to His Godhood. As members of earthly families, we can relate to Him as a child, as a Son, and as a Brother because we know how that feels. We can personalize that relationship because we ourselves are children, sons and daughters, brothers and sisters. For some it may be more difficult to relate to Him as a God. And so in an attempt to draw closer to Christ and to cultivate warm and personal feelings toward Him, some tend to humanize Him, sometimes at the expense of acknowledging His Divinity. So let us be very clear on this point: it is true that Jesus was our Elder Brother in the premortal life, but we believe that in this life it is crucial that we become 'born again' as His sons and daughters in the gospel covenant."[2]

Too many of my efforts and unfortunately too many of my prayers have been bent on succeeding—according to my own predetermined plan. Instead of opening myself to divine direction and incorporating the powers of heaven, I wanted to be able to look back on life and sing with gusto, "I did it my way!" Too little time was spent in sacred submission; on too few occasions did I say the words (and mean it!), "Thy will be done, O Lord, and not mine." Instead of praying to know my limits, to know when my offering was acceptable, I prayed for more drive and more willpower. I have since come to believe that "fallen man is not simply an imperfect creature who needs improvement: he is a rebel who must lay down his arms."[3] The saving and ironic truth is this: as we submit, we come to know his will. As we surrender, we come to gain his power. As we yield our hearts unto God, our affections and our feelings are sanctified by his grace. As President Ezra Taft Benson has taught, once we turn our lives over to the Lord, we discover that he can do far more with us than we could ever do with ourselves.[4]

IN WHOM DO I TRUST?

There is a passage in the Book of Mormon that can be rather frightening. Jacob explained: "And [Christ] commandeth all men that they must repent, and be baptized in his name, having perfect faith in the Holy One of Israel, or they cannot be saved in the kingdom of God" (2 Nephi 9:23). Perfect faith. *Perfect* faith! Who do you know who has perfect faith, at least as we tend to gauge perfection? I suggest that Jacob is here driving at a point that we are prone to miss—those who have perfect faith in the Holy One of Israel are those who have learned to trust in him completely, to trust in his purposes as well as his timetable. To come out of the world is to realize that we cannot place our trust in the world. "To come out of the world," President Stephen L Richards observed, "one must forsake the philosophy of the world, and to come into Zion one must adopt the philosophy of Zion. In my own thinking," he continued, "I have reduced the process to a simple formula: Forsake the philosophy of self-sufficiency, which is the philosophy of the world, and adopt the philosophy of faith, which is the philosophy of Christ. Substitute faith for self-assurance."[5]

If I trust completely (or perfectly) in Christ, then how much do I trust in myself? Answer: None. My works are necessary. My reception of the ordinances, the performance of my duties in the Church, acts of service and kindness—these are a part of my Christian covenantal obligation. They are the things I can strive to do. My good works are necessary, but they are not sufficient. I cannot work myself into celestial glory, and I cannot guarantee myself a place among the sanctified through my own unaided efforts. Therefore even though my own merits are essential to salvation, it is not by my own merits that I will ever make it. Rather, it is by and through the merits of Christ. This transcendent truth should create not feelings of futility but feelings of deep humility.

"Suppose we have the scriptures," Elder Bruce R. McConkie explained, "the gospel, the priesthood, the Church, the ordinances, the organization, even the keys of the kingdom—everything that now is, down to the last jot and tittle—and yet there is no atonement of Christ. What then? Can we be saved? Will all our good works save us? Will we be rewarded for all our righteousness?

"Most assuredly we will not. We are not saved by works alone, no matter how good; we are saved because God sent his Son to shed his blood in Gethsemane and on Calvary that all through him might ransomed be. We are saved by the blood of Christ (Acts 20:28; 1 Corinthians 6:20).

"To paraphrase Abinadi [see Mosiah 13:28], 'Salvation doth not come by the Church alone; and were it not for the atonement, given by the grace of God as a free gift, all men must unavoidably perish, and this notwithstanding the Church and all that appertains to it.' "[6] Or, as Elder Dallin H. Oaks observed: "Man unquestionably has impressive powers and can bring to pass great things by tireless efforts and indomitable will. But after all our obedience and good works, we cannot be saved from the effect of our sins without the grace extended by the atonement of Jesus Christ."[7]

Lehi addressed his son Jacob with these words: "Wherefore, I know that thou art redeemed. . . ." Why was he redeemed? Because he was such an obedient son? Because he had followed the direction of his older brother? Because he was sensitive and submissive and faithful? We know that he was all of that. But note Lehi's words: "Wherefore, I know that thou art redeemed, *because of the righteousness of thy Redeemer*" (2 Nephi 2:3; emphasis added). Jacob was bound for glory because of the goodness of Jesus! But didn't Jacob's goodness matter? Of course it did; Jacob's carefulness to live according to the commandments evidenced his commitment to the Lord and his desire to keep his part of the covenant. But as noble a son as Jacob was, he could never save himself. As a modern revelation attests, Christ pleads our cause before the Father on the basis of *his* suffering and death and perfection (see D&C 45:3–5). Imperfect people can only be redeemed by a perfect Being.

Nephi encouraged his readers to rely "wholly upon the merits of him who is mighty to save" (2 Nephi 31:19). Aaron explained that "since man had fallen he could not merit anything of himself; but the sufferings and death of Christ atone for their sins, through faith and repentance" (Alma 22:14). Moroni added that the Saints of God rely "alone upon the merits of Christ, who [is] the author and the finisher of [our] faith" (Moroni 6:4). We are indeed saved by merits but by the merits of our Redeemer. Truly, as someone has suggested, the word *grace* is an acronym for a glorious concept—"God's Riches At Christ's Expense."[8]

My confidence in God is essential. My confidence in myself is incidental, inextricably tied to my trust in God. As Elder Bruce Hafen has observed: "When we place our confidence in God rather than in ourselves, our need for self-esteem takes care of itself—not because of our manipulation of successful experiences but because our fundamental attitude allows us access to the only trustworthy source for knowing that the course of life we pursue is known to and accepted by God. It is not just the mistake-free, no-fault life that pleases God. He has deliberately placed us in a sphere where the most sharply focused purpose is to learn from our experience and to grow in both our desires and our understanding to be like him. Obviously that includes the greatest effort and integrity we can muster as we seek to do his will. But the heart of it all is not *self*-confidence. It is confidence in *him*, and in his power to make us into creatures far beyond the reach of what our goal setting and goal achieving can ultimately accomplish in the process of becoming as he is."[9]

There is, then, a life, a life in Christ, a new life in Christ that we cannot know or experience unless we yield to and appropriate his transforming powers and stop trying to do everything ourselves. In the spiritual realm, there is nothing weak about trusting, nothing passive about reliance. In one sense, as C. S. Lewis observed, "the road back to God is a road of moral effort, of trying harder and harder. But in another sense it is not trying that is ever going to bring us home. All this trying leads up to the vital moment at which you turn to God and say, 'You must do this, I can't.'" Such submission, Lewis adds, represents a significant change in our nature, "the change from being confident about our own efforts to the state in which we despair of doing anything for ourselves and leave it to God.

"I know the words 'leave it to God' can be misunderstood," Lewis continues. "The sense in which a Christian leaves it to God is that he puts all his trust in Christ: trusts that Christ will somehow share with him the perfect human obedience which he carried out from His birth to His crucifixion: that Christ will make the man [or woman] more like Himself and, in a sense, make good his [or her] deficiencies."[10]

GRACEFUL LIVING

We have dealt at some length with this marvelous theological concept, one that is at the core of Christianity. Our doctrine undergirds our religious life, for what we believe always informs and directs what we do. Now, knowing as we do that we are saved by grace, after all we can do (see 2 Nephi 25:23), how shall we then live? What does it mean to live by grace? Consider the following simple points:

1. It is unhealthy, inappropriate, and spiritually counterproductive to compare ourselves with others, whether in terms of perks and benefits and blessings or of crosses to be borne. None of us knows what goes on in the hidden parts of another's life, either the successes or the failures. We are told by the Savior to judge righteous judgment (see JST, Matthew 7:1); that includes a warning against judging ourselves too harshly as a result of what we *think* we know about others. Always remember that the Lord can do extraordinary things with very ordinary people, *if*

they will let him. President Joseph F. Smith explained that "to do well those things which God ordained to be the common lot of all mankind, is the truest greatness."[11]

2. Jesus warned about being unduly anxious or concerned about having enough food or clothing for the future (see 3 Nephi 13:25). That is good counsel about life in general; the disciples would do well to stop worrying and fretting so much about making the cut. The more we learn to trust the Lord and rely upon his merits and mercy, the less anxious we become about life here and hereafter. "Thus, if you have really handed yourself over to Him," C. S. Lewis remarked, "it must follow that you are trying to obey Him. But trying in a new way, a less worried way."[12]

3. The work of spiritual transformation is only partly our work. We will become holy people as we do our best to keep our covenants and then, as Moses said, "stand still, and see the salvation of the Lord" (Exodus 14:13).

4. The Lord God loves us and desires to save us with an everlasting salvation. There is no quota on the number of saved beings, no bell curve to determine our final standing in the royal grade books. We can make it. God knows that and desires for each one of us to know it as well. Lucifer would prefer, of course, that we think otherwise. Whereas the ultimate blessings of salvation do not come until the next life, there is a sense in which people in this life may enjoy the assurance of salvation and the peace that accompanies that knowledge (see D&C 59:23).

CONCLUSION

These principles have been in the scriptures all along. They have been a part of the restored gospel since the beginning and have been an integral part of the lives of those Latter-day Saints whose trust in the Lord was greater than their trust in other things. Living by grace is a way of life, an understanding, a perspective that comes to us as we come unto *him* who is the embodiment of peace and rest. Perhaps it is the complexity of life in a modern world that has driven many of us to our knees more frequently and caused us to search the scriptures with an earnestness born of pressing need. And perhaps it is our rediscovery of the Book of Mormon: Another Testament of Jesus Christ, that has led some of us to recognize through study what we have begun to know by faith. We sense more than ever the need to do our duty, to attend to our family and Church responsibilities, all as a part of keeping our covenant with Christ. That is, we come to know the value and necessity of good works. Those works come to be motivated by his Spirit and evidence our covenant. But we also seek for that balance, that critical and elusive balance in life that allows us to do our best without browbeating ourselves because of all we cannot do at the moment.

I know the Lord wants us to succeed and that he has every intention of bringing back as many of his children as is possible. Discouragement and despondency are not of the Lord. They are of Lucifer. The arch-deceiver would have us lose our balance, lose track of what matters most in life, and focus too much on the less significant. He would have us labor to exhaustion in secondary causes. We cannot do everything we are asked to do, at least not in a few weeks or months. There is great virtue in praying that the Lord will reveal to us our limits, let us know when enough is enough, when doubling or tripling our efforts will in reality be spiritually counterproductive.

Because we are human—because we are weak and mortal and tired—we will probably never reach the point in this life when we have done "all we can do." Too many of us misread 2 Nephi 25:23 and conclude that the Lord can assist us only *after,* meaning *following the time that,* we have done "all we can do." That is incorrect; he can and does help us all along the way. I think Nephi is trying to emphasize that no matter how much we do, it simply will not be enough to guarantee salvation without Christ's intervention. To paraphrase Nephi, *"Above and beyond* all we can do, it is by the grace of Christ that we are saved." And what is true of our ultimate salvation is true of our daily walk and talk, of our personality and our passions. Above and beyond all efforts at self-control, behavior modification, or reducing our sins to manageable categories, "everything which really needs to be done in our souls can only be done by God."[13]

There is yet another way to look at 2 Nephi 25:23. After the conversion of thousands of Lamanites by the sons of Mosiah, the brother of Lamoni, named Anti-Nephi-Lehi, counseled with his people, those, you remember, who had made a covenant not to take up weapons against their brethren in war. Let me repeat here a part of his sermon, much of which was an expression of gratitude for the goodness of God—for sending the Spirit, softening the hearts of the Lamanites, opening doors of communication between the Nephites and the Lamanites, and convicting the people of their sins. He continues: "And I also thank my God, yea, my great God, that he hath granted unto us that we might repent of these things, and also that he hath forgiven us of those our many sins and murders which we have committed, and taken away the guilt from our hearts, through the merits of his Son.

"And now behold, my brethren, since it has been *all that we could do,* (as we were the most lost of all mankind) *to repent of all our sins* and the many murders which we have committed, and to get God to take them away from our hearts, for *it was all we could do to repent sufficiently before God that he would take away our stain—*

"Now, my best beloved brethren, since God hath taken away our stains, and our swords have become bright, then let us stain our swords no more with the blood of our brethren" (Alma 24:8–12; emphasis added).

There is a very real sense in which "all we can do" is to come before the Lord in reverent humility, confess our weakness, and plead for his forgiveness, for his mercy and grace. It occurred to me recently that life is repentance, that progression and improvement and growth and maturity and refinement are all forms of repentance, and that the God-fearing live in a constant state of repentance. It is not intended that we exist in a constant state of fear or frustration or anxiety, but rather that we have desires for holiness and purity, longings to feel quiet confidence before God. Indeed, king Benjamin taught that those who regularly and consistently acknowledge the greatness of God and our own nothingness without him are able to retain a remission of sins from day to day (see Mosiah 4:11–12).

To push ourselves beyond what is appropriate is, in a strange sort of way, a statement that we fear we must do the job ourselves if we expect it to get done. I know we must do our duty in the Church and that the works of righteousness are necessary. What seems so very unnecessary is the type of pharisaical extremism and the subsequent negative feelings that too often characterize the efforts of some members of the Church. I have a conviction that God is unquestionably aware of us. He loves you and he loves me. This I know. He certainly wants us to improve, but he definitely does not want us to spend our days languishing in guilt. I reaffirm that the gospel of Jesus Christ is intended to liberate us, to lift and lighten our burdens. If it is not doing that in our personal lives, then perhaps our approach and understanding, our orientation—not necessarily the quantity of work to be done— may need some adjustment. Balance. Balance. That is the key. I have come to sense the need to balance a type of "divine discontent"—a healthy longing to improve— with what Nephi called a "perfect brightness of hope" (2 Nephi 31:20)—the Spirit-given assurance that in and through Jesus Christ we are going to make it.

I am very much aware that there are those among us who have been subjected to much pain and distress in their lives, to abuse, to neglect, and to the agonies of wanting more than anything to live a normal life and to feel normal feelings but have been unable to do so. I would say, first of all, that each one of us, whoever we are, wrestles with something. Perhaps it's things like my weight or height or complexion or baldness or I.Q. Perhaps it's stuff that passes in time like a phase. Perhaps it's the torture of watching helplessly as loved ones choose unwisely and thereby close doors of opportunity for themselves and foreclose future privileges. And then there are the terrible traumas in our life, those occasions when someone we love betrays our tender trust and deals a blow that strikes at the center of all we hold dear and all we value about ourselves.

I bear my witness of the fact that the day is coming when all the awful wrongs of this life will be righted. I bear witness that the God of justice will attend to all evil. And I certify, for I know this to be true, that those things that are beyond our power to control will be corrected, either here or hereafter. Many of us may come to enjoy the lifting, liberating powers of the Atonement in this life and all our losses will be made up before we pass from this sphere of existence. Perhaps some of us will wrestle all our days with our traumas, for he who orchestrates the events of our lives will surely fix the time of our release. I have a conviction that when a person passes through the veil of death, all those impediments and challenges and crosses that were beyond his or her power to control—abuse, neglect, immoral environment, weighty traditions, etc.—will be torn away like a film, and perfect peace will prevail in our hearts. "Some frustrations," President Boyd K. Packer taught, "we must endure without really solving the problem. Some things that ought to be put in order are not put in order because we cannot control them. Things we cannot solve, we must survive."[14]

Our Lord and Master seems to ask of us the impossible—to forgive those who have hurt us so dreadfully. Bruce and Marie Hafen have observed, "It seems fair to ask why the victims of abuse should be required to do anything to deserve the Lord's vast healing powers in such a case. Because abuse victims suffer so many of the same symptoms of guilt and estrangement from God as do willful transgressors, the irony that they should need to forgive those who have wronged them is almost overpowering.

"Still, there lurks between the lines of the scriptures on forgiveness a message of transcendent meaning—not only about abuse victims but about all of us, and about all of the Atonement."

The Hafens continue: "What are we doing when we are willing to absorb a terrible trauma of the spirit, caused not by our own doing but by one who claimed to love us—and we absorb the trauma even to help the sinner? That picture somehow has a familiar look—we've seen all this before. Of course, because this picture depicts the sacrifice of Jesus Christ: he took upon himself undeserved and unbearable burdens, heaped upon him by people who often said, and often believed, that they loved him. And he assumed that load not for any need of his, but only to help them.

"So to forgive—not just for abuse victims, but for each of us—is to be a Christ figure, a transitional point in the war between good and evil, stopping the current of evil by absorbing it in every pore, thereby protecting the innocent next generation and helping to enable the repentance and healing of those whose failures sent the jolts into our own systems."[15]

I know of the power that is in Christ, power not only to create the worlds and divide the seas but also to still the storms of the human heart, to right life's wrongs, to ease and eventually even remove the pain of scarred and beaten souls. There is no bitterness, no anger, no fear, no jealousy, no feeling of inadequacy that cannot be healed by the Great Physician. He is the Balm of Gilead. He is the One sent by the Father to "bind up the brokenhearted, to proclaim liberty to the captives, and the opening of the prison to them that are bound" (Isaiah 61:1). True followers of Christ learn to trust in him more, in the arm of flesh less. They learn to rely on him more, on manmade solutions less. They learn to surrender their burdens to him more. They learn to work to their limits and then be willing to seek that grace or enabling power that will make up the difference, that sacred power that makes all the difference!

As Moroni has instructed us on the last page of the Book of Mormon, when we come unto Christ and seek, all through our lives, to deny ourselves of ungodliness and give ourselves without let or hindrance to God, "then is his grace sufficient for you, that by his grace ye may be perfect in Christ"—that is, whole, complete, fully formed. "And if by the grace of God ye are perfect in Christ, ye can in nowise deny the power of God" (Moroni 10:32). Those who completely surrender and submit to the Almighty cannot deny—block, stop, or prevent—the power of God from coming into their lives. In short, to come unto the Savior is to come to life, to awaken to an entirely new realm of reality. Because of who Christ our Lord is and what he has done, there is no obstacle to peace and joy here or hereafter that is too great to face or overcome. Because of him, our minds can be at peace. Our souls may rest.

Notes

From an address delivered at the 1998 Brigham Young University Women's Conference, Provo, Utah, May 1998.

1. John F. MacArthur Jr., *Faith Works: The Gospel According to the Apostles* (Dallas: Word Publishing, 1993), 32.
2. M. Russell Ballard, "Building Bridges of Understanding," address delivered to the Logan Institute of Religion, Logan, Utah, 17 February 1998, typescript, 6–7.
3. C. S. Lewis, *Mere Christianity* (New York: Touchstone, 1996), 59.
4. See Ezra Taft Benson, *Teachings of Ezra Taft Benson* (Salt Lake City: Bookcraft, 1988), 361.
5. Stephen L Richards, *Where Is Wisdom?* (Salt Lake City: Deseret Book Co., 1955), 419.

6. Bruce R. McConkie, "What Think Ye of Salvation by Grace?" address given at Brigham Young University devotional, Provo, Utah, 10 January 1984; in Bruce R. McConkie, *Doctrines of the Restoration,* ed. Mark L. McConkie (Salt Lake City: Bookcraft, 1989), 76.

7. Dallin H. Oaks, in Conference Report, October 1988, 78.

8. MacArthur, *Faith Works,* 57.

9. Bruce C. Hafen, *The Broken Heart* (Salt Lake City: Deseret Book Co., 1989), 120; emphasis in original.

10. Lewis, *Mere Christianity,* 130.

11. Joseph F. Smith, *Gospel Doctrine,* 285.

12. Lewis, *Mere Christianity,* 131.

13. Ibid., 166.

14. Boyd K. Packer, in Conference Report, October 1987, 20.

15. Bruce C. and Marie K. Hafen, *The Belonging Heart* (Salt Lake City: Deseret Book Co., 1994), 122–23.

ARE YOU A
"SAVED" MORMON?

L et me reconstruct a rather familiar scene to most of us. We attempt to explain the message of the Restoration to a member of a Protestant church, only to have them remark, "Thank you, but I'm a saved Christian." We recoil or turn off or, I suppose in some cases, are tempted to argue with them about what they mean. Or we may respond as my father did so many times: "Yes, of course, you are saved from the grave." But that's obviously not what they meant. In like fashion, when a Protestant asks us: "Are you a saved Christian?" we are uncertain about how to respond. Generally, even if we do not voice our feelings, we feel the need to emphasize that one is not saved until he or she endures to the end of mortal life.

It is unfortunate that a topic like being saved carries with it so much emotional baggage (and thus so many barriers between us and others of our Father's children) that we are not in a position to communicate even our differences appropriately. Over the years as I have spoken openly with friends or colleagues from other faiths, I have come to appreciate a little better what they are saying. Some mean that they have received in their heart a witness that Jesus is the Christ; that the Savior has forgiven their sins and they are now willing to turn their lives over to him; and that they are now in a saved condition in regard to happiness here and eternal reward hereafter. I know there are people out there who feel that once they profess Jesus with their lips they are saved forevermore and that what they do thereafter with their lives in terms of goodness and morality is immaterial. Yes, there are such people, but I don't know many of them. Most of those Protestants who I grew up with and most of the ministers and theologians I have encountered since then really do see a very close tie between their saved condition and a righteous, God-fearing life. Those who are serious students of the New Testament understand the central message of the second chapter of James—that good works flow from the regenerate heart, that righteousness evidences true faith.

I want to begin this chapter with a clear statement of witness—that there was an Apostasy, a loss of plain and precious truths, a loss of priesthood authority. I know that God began the Restoration of truths and powers through Joseph Smith and will continue to do so into and through the Millennium. There's no question in my mind about any of that. But I want to suggest that because the Baptists or the Methodists or the Pentecostals do not possess the authority to act in the name of God does not mean that they have no truth or that any scriptural interpretation from them is automatically incorrect or corrupt. Though the fulness of the gospel is to be found in The Church of Jesus Christ of Latter-day Saints, remnants of truth, elements of enlightenment, and aspects of the original faith of the former-day Saints may be found in modern Christianity. More specifically, I would like to propose a sense in which Latter-day Saint theology encompasses the notion of being saved, here and now, in this life. Before doing so, I want to discuss several related concepts.

REDEMPTION

It is often the case that the scriptures may be understood on many levels. Words and phrases and doctrinal concepts may mean a number of things, depending upon the context, the audience, and the need at the time. For this reason, it is seldom wise to be overly zealous about exclusive definitions, singular interpretations, and formulas when it comes to comprehending holy writ. We have this principle illustrated in Moroni's recitation to Joseph Smith of the prophecy of Malachi concerning the coming of Elijah. In the midst of quoting numerous passages from the Old and New Testaments, Moroni quoted Malachi 4:5–6 quite differently from how it appears in the King James Version. Did this new rendition invalidate the old one? Are the renditions in our present Bibles inaccurate, or does Moroni's account simply represent another dimension of the prophecy? Knowing full well what Moroni had said in 1823, Joseph the Prophet, in an epistle to the Church in 1842, quoted the Malachi passage directly from the King James Version. "I might have rendered a plainer translation to this," he said, "but it is sufficiently plain to suit my purpose as it stands" (D&C 128:18).

In addition, many words have both present and ultimate meaning. For example, let us consider the word *redeem.* We all know that the ultimate form of redemption is salvation or exaltation in the highest degree of the celestial kingdom. Abinadi taught that Christ has redeemed us in that he has "granted salvation unto his people" (Mosiah 15:18). He spoke of the conditional aspect of redemption when he stated that "the Lord redeemeth none such that rebel against him and die in their sins . . . that have known the commandments of God, and would not keep them. . . . For salvation cometh to none such; for the Lord hath redeemed none such; yea, neither can the Lord redeem such" (Mosiah 15:26–27). In another vein, all men and women are redeemed in the sense that the spirit and the body of every mortal shall be inseparably joined. We know that "through the redemption which is made for [us] is brought to pass the redemption from the dead. And the spirit and the body are the soul of man. . . . And the redemption of the soul is through him that quickeneth all things" (D&C 88:14–15, 17).

Moroni testified that God had "created Adam, and by Adam came the fall of man. And because of the fall of man came Jesus Christ, even the Father and the Son; and because of Jesus Christ came the redemption of man. And because of the redemption of man, which came by Jesus Christ, they are brought back into the presence of the Lord." Now note Moroni's broad definition of redemption, one in which all men and women have part: "Yea, *this is wherein all men are redeemed, because the death of Christ bringeth to pass the resurrection, which bringeth to pass a redemption from an endless sleep,* from which sleep all men shall be awakened by the power of God when the trump shall sound; . . . and all shall stand before his bar, being redeemed and loosed from this eternal band of death, which death is temporal death" (Mormon 9:12–13; emphasis added; compare Helaman 14:17). Further, the sons of perdition are "the only ones who shall not be redeemed in the due time of the Lord, after the sufferings of his wrath" (D&C 76:38), meaning the only ones who shall be resurrected but not redeemed unto a kingdom of glory.

But what of our being redeemed in this life? Simply stated, forgiveness of sin entails redemption from sin. Christ came to redeem us from sin by virtue of his atoning blood, through the receipt of sacred ordinances, and by the medium of the Holy Spirit (see Alma 5:21; 9:27). Just prior to his death, father Lehi exulted: "The Lord hath redeemed my soul from hell; I have beheld his glory, and I am encircled about eternally in the arms of his love" (2 Nephi 1:15). That is, Lehi had been forgiven of his sins, had through the Atonement put off the natural man and put on Christ, and had come to know the supernal and sanctifying power of divine love. Christ came into the world, as Lehi explained to Jacob, to "redeem the children of men from the fall. And because that they are redeemed from the fall they have become free forever, knowing good from evil" (2 Nephi 2:26). Because of the knowledge and faith of the brother of Jared, he was redeemed from the Fall and brought back into the presence of Jehovah (see Ether 3:13). After three days of darkness and anguish of soul, Alma the younger declared: "I have repented of my sins, and have been redeemed of the Lord; behold I am born of the Spirit" (Mosiah 27:24). When men and women are born again; when they are changed from their carnal and fallen state to a state of righteousness; when they come alive and are quickened in regard to the spiritual realm—they are redeemed of the Lord, here, in this life. That redemption reaches also to those who die without law (see Moroni 8:22).

On the other hand, Amulek observed: "And [Christ] shall come into the world to redeem his people; and he shall take upon him the transgressions of those who believe on his name; and these are they that shall have eternal life, and salvation cometh to none else. Therefore the wicked remain as though there had been no redemption made, except it be the loosing of the bands of death" (Alma 11:40–41). In a like manner, Mormon taught that where faith is insufficient among the people to call down the signs and wonders of heaven, "they are as though there had been no redemption made" (Moroni 7:38). Truly, "only unto him that has faith unto repentance is brought about the great and eternal plan of redemption" (Alma 34:16; see also 42:13). The Savior cannot redeem his people in their sins, only from them (see Alma 11:34–37; Helaman 5:9–10).

JUSTIFICATION, SANCTIFICATION, AND SEALING

The scriptures are consistent in their declaration that "no unclean thing can enter into [God's] kingdom" (3 Nephi 27:19). In theory there are two ways by which men and women may inherit eternal life. The first is simply to live the law of God perfectly, to make no mistakes. To do so is to be justified—pronounced innocent, declared blameless—by works or by law. If we keep the commandments completely (including receiving the ordinances of salvation), never deviating from the strait and narrow path throughout our mortal lives, then we qualify for the blessings of the obedient. And yet we are very much aware of the terrible truth that all are unclean as a result of sin (see Romans 3:23). All of us have broken at least one of the laws of God, and we therefore disqualify ourselves for justification by law. Moral perfection may be a possibility, but it is certainly not a probability. Jesus alone trod that path. "Therefore," Paul observed, "by the deeds of the law"—

meaning the law of Moses, as well as any law of God—"there shall no flesh be justified in his sight" (Romans 3:20; see also 2 Nephi 2:5).

The second way to be justified is by faith; it is for the sinner to be pronounced clean or innocent through trusting in and relying upon the merits of him who answered the ends of the law (see Romans 10:4; 2 Nephi 2:6–7). Jesus owed no personal debt to justice; the Holy One thus claims of the Father "his rights of mercy which he hath upon the children of men" (Moroni 7:27). Because we are guilty of transgression, if there had been no Atonement of Christ, no amount of good deeds on our part, no nobility independent of divine intercession, could make up for the loss. Truly, "since man had fallen he could not merit anything of himself" (Alma 22:14). Thus He who loved us first (see 1 John 4:10, 19) reaches out to the lost and fallen, to the disinherited, and proposes a marriage. The Infinite One joins with the finite, the Finished with the unfinished, the Whole with the partial, in short, the Perfect with the imperfect. Through covenant with Christ and thus union with the Bridegroom, we place ourselves in a condition to become fully formed, whole, finished.

Now back to our story. In one sense—in the present, in the here and now—we are justified as our sins are forgiven. Whenever we repent or turn away from our evil ways (the Hebrew connotation); whenever we repent or change our thoughts, attitudes and desires (the Greek connotation), we are justified—pronounced clean and free from sin and the demands of divine justice. To be justified by God is to be made clean in spite of one's inability to repay the Master, to be made innocent in spite of one's lack of moral perfection. It is to be acquitted from sin through one's faith in Christ, faith which manifests itself in the works of righteousness (see Romans 2:6–7, 13; Galatians 5:6; Titus 3:8, 14). The Lord Jesus compensates for the chasm between man's simple strivings and God's immutable standards of perfection, between where a man really is and where he must eventually be. Justification is both a journey and a destination, a process as well as a condition. Sidney Sperry thus spoke of being justified as not only a matter of "acquittal" from guilt and sin but also of "being regarded as righteous in a future divine judgment." Brother Sperry noted that "a comparison may be made by reference to a man on an escalator. We anticipate that he will reach a given floor if he stays on the escalator. So a person will eventually be justified"—meaning, fully entitled to enter the Lord's presence—"but may be regarded as being so now, if he retains a remission of sins (Mosiah 4:26) and continually shows his faith in God."[1]

Another way of saying this is that when we come unto Christ by covenant, the Lord Jesus justifies or exonerates us in the here and now; he treats us now as if we were fully qualified to inherit eternal life. In process of time and as we remain "in Christ," meaning in covenant, his Spirit, the sanctifier, works and labors with our soul, ridding us of filth and dross, transforming our actions and our desires. In short, for now God justifies or ratifies our actions, and the way we know we are approved of God is that He sends forth his Spirit upon us. We enjoy the peaceful assurance that he is pleased with our offering (see D&C 59:23). In time and after we have been proven and tried, we are justified in the sense that our lives, covenants, and ordinances receive the ratifying and certifying approval of heaven.

The same principle holds for being sealed by the Holy Spirit of Promise. In one sense—in the present, in the here and now—a young couple can go into the temple to be married for eternity, and if they approach that sacred covenant and ordinance reverently and worthily, it could appropriately be said of them that their marriage has been sealed by the Holy Spirit of Promise. That is, the Holy Spirit of Promise, meaning the Holy Spirit promised to the Saints, the Holy Ghost, was present to manifest his approval and to place a type of ratifying seal upon what took place. That seal is maintained and made sure as the couple remain faithful to their covenants and endure to the end through dedicated service, through trust in and reliance upon Jesus Christ.[2] Our revelations thus speak of the candidates for exaltation as those who are "overcome by faith, and are sealed by the Holy Spirit of promise, which the Father sheds forth upon all those who are just and true" (D&C 76:53).

We are sanctified when the Holy Ghost cleanses and renews our souls. Whereas justification is a decreed change of *standing,* sanctification is a change of *state.* "Sanctification is the work of God," one theologian has written, "whereby he sets the believer apart from sin. Sanctification is a practical reality, not simply a legal declaration. Sanctification involves a change in the sinner's character, not just a new standing before God."[3] Also: "Justification frees us from the *guilt* of sin, sanctification from the *pollution* of sin. . . . God not only frees us from sin's penalty (justification), but He frees us from sin's tyranny as well (sanctification)."[4] Elder Orson Pratt wrote of this purifying process as follows: "Without the aid of the Holy Ghost, a person . . . would have but very little power to change his mind, at once, from its habituated course, and to walk in newness of life. Though his sins may have been cleansed away, yet so great is the force of habit, that he would, without being renewed by the Holy Ghost, be easily overcome, and contaminated by sin. Hence, it is infinitely important that the affections and desires should be, in a measure, changed and renewed, so as to cause him to hate that which he before loved, and to love that which he before hated: to thus renew the mind of man is the work of the Holy Ghost."[5]

What is true in regard to being justified is equally true in regard to being *sanctified*. We may in this life be sanctified in regard to certain sinful enticements. We may come to abhor sin (see Alma 13:12; compare 2 Nephi 9:49; Jacob 2:5), shake at its appearance (see 2 Nephi 4:31), and even have no more disposition to do evil (see Mosiah 5:2). But sanctification is a process, one that goes on minute by minute, day by day, and year by year. Of a chain smoker who had after baptism lost all desire for tobacco, it could appropriately be said that he had been sanctified in regard to that particular temptation. Of the divorced woman who had been abused by her former husband but who had through the intercession of divine powers had bitterness and vengeance burned out of her soul, it could rightly be said that she had been sanctified in regard to her feelings. Of the promiscuous man who had come unto Christ and forsaken his past life and who after conversion was no longer driven by lust, it could be said that he had been sanctified.

Sanctification comes in time to those who yield their hearts to God (see Helaman 3:35), to those whose minds are single to the glory of God (see D&C 88:67–68), to those who trust in and seek after the redeeming grace of him who calls his people to holiness. In one sense, we will never be completely freed from the pulls and tug of sin in this life. "Will sin be perfectly destroyed?" President Brigham Young asked. "No, it will not, for it is not so designed in the economy of heaven. . . . Do not suppose that we shall ever in the flesh be free from temptations to sin. Some suppose that they can in the flesh be sanctified body and spirit and become so pure that they will never again feel the effects of the power of the adversary of truth. Were it possible for a person to attain to this degree of perfection in the flesh, he could not die neither remain in a world where sin predominates. . . . I think we should more or less feel the effects of sin so long as we live, and finally have to pass the ordeals of death."[6] Sanctification may be a condition, but it is also a process. "Those who go to the celestial kingdom of heaven," Elder Bruce R. McConkie explained to BYU students in 1976, "have to be sanctified, meaning that they become clean and pure and spotless. They've had evil and sin and iniquity burned out of their souls as though by fire. . . . It is a process. Nobody is sanctified in an instant, suddenly. But if we keep the commandments and press forward with steadfastness after baptism, then degree by degree and step by step we sanctify our souls until that glorious day when we're qualified to go where God and angels are."[7]

The Rest of the Lord

In reading Alma 13 in context—as a part of a larger sermon—we begin to see that the idea of entering the rest of the Lord is a central theme. The word *rest* is mentioned in each of the final four verses of the preceding chapter. It is mentioned five times in chapter 13. It would appear that Alma is trying to point out that it is through the atoning blood of Christ and by the power of the holy priesthood that individuals and congregations are prepared and made ready to enter the rest of God. In one sense, a person enters the rest of God in the present, in the here and now, when he or she gains a testimony of the gospel and is brought out of worldly confusion into the peace and security that comes only from God. In this sense, the rest of God is "the spiritual rest and peace which are born from a settled conviction of the truth in the minds of [individuals]."[8] It is to know the peace of the Spirit, to enjoy the blessing of the Comforter. It is what Jesus promised to disciples when he said: "Come unto me, all ye that labour and are heavy laden, and I will give you rest" (Matthew 11:28).

Second, spirits enter the rest of God when they enter paradise, the abode of the righteous in the postmortal spirit world at the time of death (see Alma 40:11–12; 60:13). A third dimension of the rest of the Lord is that which follows the Resurrection and Judgment, as we enter the celestial kingdom and receive exaltation. It is interesting that Mormon, speaking to the members of the Church in his day, uses *rest* in at least two ways. "Wherefore," he said, "I would speak unto you that are of the church, that are the peaceable followers of Christ, and that have obtained a sufficient hope by which ye can enter into the rest of the Lord"—meaning here in mortality—"from this time henceforth until ye shall rest with him in heaven" (Moroni 7:3).

There is yet another sense in which the word *rest* is used in scripture, particularly in the Book of Mormon. This is also the sense in which a modern revelation uses the word:

"And this greater priesthood administereth the gospel and holdeth the key of the mysteries of the kingdom, even the key of the knowledge of God.

"Therefore, in the ordinances thereof, the power of godliness is manifest.

"And without the ordinances thereof, and the authority of the priesthood, the power of godliness is not manifest unto men in the flesh;

"For without this [the power of godliness] no man can see the face of God, even the Father, and live.

"Now this Moses plainly taught to the children of Israel in the wilderness, and sought diligently to sanctify his people that they might behold the face of God;

"But they hardened their hearts and could not endure his presence; therefore, the Lord in his wrath, for his anger was kindled against them, swore that they should not enter into his rest while in the wilderness, *which rest is the fulness of his glory.*

"Therefore, he took Moses out of their midst, and the Holy Priesthood also" (D&C 84:19–25; emphasis added).

This is a significant scriptural statement. Alma's invitation for the people of Ammonihah to enter into the rest of the Lord is built upon the notion that ancient Israel provoked God and proved unworthy of this blessing (see Alma 12:36–37). Moses desired to make available the highest privilege of the priesthood to Israel— the privilege of seeing the face of God, of coming directly into the divine presence. Of the Israelites, Jehovah said: "I have sworn in my wrath, that they shall not enter into my presence, *into my rest,* in the days of their pilgrimage" (JST, Exodus 34:2; emphasis added). Here the rest of the Lord is equated with being received into the personal presence of the Lord while the recipients are still mortal.

PERFECTION

Jesus' call to a higher righteousness, embodied in the Sermon on the Mount, contained the penetrating and poignant statute: "Ye are therefore commanded to be perfect, even as your Father who is in heaven is perfect" (JST, Matthew 5:50). Many months later that same Lord, now resurrected and glorified, commanded his Saints in the Western Hemisphere: "Therefore I would that ye should be perfect even as I, or your Father who is in heaven is perfect" (3 Nephi 12:48). The directive has been given, the standard set. Nothing short of the ideal can possibly suffice: a being of absolute perfection could ask nothing less of his people.

"*Finite perfection,*" Elder McConkie has written, "may be gained by the righteous saints in this life. It consists in living a God-fearing life of devotion to the truth, of walking in complete submission to the will of the Lord, and of putting first in one's life the things of the kingdom of God."[9] In one sense, to be perfect is to be complete, whole, mature, fully focused. Only Jesus of Nazareth maintained a perfect walk in this life in the sense that he navigated the strait and narrow without moral detour or transgression; he alone achieved moral perfection and completed mortality without flaw or error. But others have achieved perfection in the sense that they did all that was commanded them, in the sense that they gave themselves wholly to the accomplishment of the will of the Lord. The scriptural record attests that "Noah found grace in the eyes of the Lord; for Noah was a just man, and perfect in his generation; and he walked with God, as did also his three sons, Shem, Ham, and Japheth" (Moses 8:27; compare Genesis 6:9). The same is said of Seth, the son of Adam (see D&C 107:43). Further, "there was a man in the land of Uz, whose name was Job; and that man was perfect and upright, and one that feared God, and eschewed evil" (Job 1:1).

What do the scriptures mean when they speak of a person being "perfect in his generation"? President Brigham Young declared that "we all occupy diversified stations in the world and in the kingdom of God. Those who do right, and seek the glory of the Father in heaven, whether they can do little or much, if they do the very best they know how, they are perfect. . . . 'Be ye as perfect as ye can,' for that is all we can do tho it is written, 'Be ye perfect as your Father who is in heaven is perfect.' To be as perfect as we possibly can according to our knowledge is to be just as perfect as our Father in heaven is. He cannot be any more perfect than he knows how, any more than we. When we are doing as well as we know in the sphere and station which we occupy here we are justified. . . . We are as justified as the angels who are before the throne of God."[10]

"*Infinite perfection* is reserved for those who overcome all things and inherit the fulness of the Father in the mansions hereafter. It consists in gaining eternal life, the kind of life which God has in the highest heaven within the celestial world."[11] Though you and I cannot enjoy infinite perfection in the present, in the here and now, we can be perfect in the sense that we do the best we can and then rely wholly upon the merits and mercy of our Redeemer (see 2 Nephi 31:19; Moroni 6:4). That is, we can be "perfect in Christ" (Moroni 10:32). It is not that we must become sin-free in this life in order to be saved, though we ever press toward that glorious eventuality. Rather, it is expected that after we sin we return quickly to the light through godly sorrow and repentance. We become perfect in Christ in the sense that we yield to the will of Christ, become one with him through the Holy Spirit, and become whole, fully formed, and complete. In Stephen Robinson's words, "in the new covenant of faith, perfect innocence is still required, but it is required of the team or partnership of Christ-and-me, rather than of me alone. Because Christ and I are one in the gospel covenant, God accepts our combined total worthiness, and together Christ and I are perfectly worthy."[12]

SALVATION

Having dealt with several related concepts, let us finally turn our attention to the matter of being saved. We know, in the words of Joseph Smith, that to be saved is to be placed beyond the power of our enemies.[13] "Salvation consists in the glory, authority, majesty, power and dominion which Jehovah possesses and in nothing else; and no being can possess it but himself or one like him." To be saved is to be conformed into the image of Christ, to become like unto the Prototype of all saved beings.[14] There is obviously what might be called a limited dimension to salvation—meaning, salvation from the grave, salvation from physical death. All mortals will be resurrected and thus enjoy this aspect of salvation. With but few exceptions, however (for example, see D&C 76:43–44, 88; 132:17),[15] when the prophets speak of salvation they are referring to the highest of eternal rewards hereafter. Salvation is redemption, exaltation, eternal life, and eternal lives; each of these words means the same thing, but each lays stress on a particular aspect of the saved condition. And so in the ultimate meaning, to be saved is to qualify for exaltation in the celestial kingdom—to be endowed with a fulness of the glory of the Father and to enjoy a continuation of the family unit into eternity (see D&C 132:19).

But now to the question with which we began. Do Latter-day Saints believe that men and women may enjoy the benefits of salvation only in the world to come? Is there no sense in which we may be saved in the present, in the here and now? Though I quickly acknowledge that most scriptural references to salvation seem to point toward that which comes in the next life, we do have within our theology principles and doctrines that suggest a form of salvation in this life. Perhaps the most obvious illustration is when a member of the Church makes his or her calling and election sure to eternal life. As Joseph Smith taught, when we exercise saving faith and demonstrate our willingness to serve God at all hazards, we eventually, in this life or the next (see D&C 14:7; 50:5; 58:2), receive the assurance of eternal life.[16]

If the more sure word of prophecy comes to us in this life, our salvation is secure or, we might say, fairly secure. In fact, there is never a time in this life when faithful endurance to the end is not required. The scriptures teach that a man or woman may fall from grace and depart from the living God; that even the sanctified must take heed lest they fall (see D&C 20:30–34;124:124); that those who were once enlightened and have tasted the heavenly gift may fall away (see Hebrews 6:4–6); and that "if we sin willfully after that we have received the knowledge of the truth"—meaning, the knowledge that we are sealed to eternal life[17]—"there remaineth no more sacrifice for sins" (Hebrews 10:26).[18] The Prophet Joseph thus taught in regard to the debate in his own day between the Presbyterians and the Methodists—"once in grace, always in grace" versus "having grace today, falling from it, and being renewed to grace again": "They are both wrong. Truth takes a road between them both, for . . . according to the Scripture, if men have received the good word of God, and tasted of the powers of the world to come, if they shall fall away, it is impossible to renew them again, seeing they have crucified the Son of God afresh, and put Him to an open shame; so there is a possibility of falling away; you could not be renewed again, and the power of Elijah cannot seal against this sin, for this is a reserve made in the seals and power of the Priesthood."[19]

Those who have been sealed to eternal life are no doubt fully aware of the fact that they must stay faithful to the end, but even so they know assuredly that if they were to die suddenly, their salvation is secure. Thus they are saved, or, to put it another way, they are living in a saved condition. That may not be exactly what our Protestant brothers and sisters have in mind when they speak of being saved, but it's not far removed. Thus there is a condition or state you and I may attain unto in this mortal life in which salvation hereafter is promised here; the day of judgment has essentially been advanced.

But is there any way to know we are saved other than receiving the more sure word of prophecy? I think there is. That same Holy Spirit of Promise that searches the hearts of men and women, that ratifies and approves and seals ordinances and lives, that same Holy Spirit serves, as Paul indicates, as the "earnest of our inheritance" (Ephesians 1:14). The Lord's "earnest money" on us, his down payment, his indication to us that he will save us is the Holy Spirit. We know that we are on course when the Spirit is with us. We know that our lives are approved of God when the Spirit is with us. We know that we are in Christ, in covenant, when the Spirit is with us. And we know, I suggest, that we are saved when the Spirit is with us. If we live in such a way that we can take the sacrament worthily, hold and use a current temple recommend, and maintain the gift and gifts of the Spirit, then we are in the line of our duty; we are approved of the heavens; and if we were to die suddenly, we would go into paradise and eventually into the celestial kingdom.

The King James Version of 1 John 3:9 states: "Whosoever is born of God doth not commit sin." There is a problem here: you know and I know that those who have been born again are not free from sin. But they repent quickly (see D&C 109:21). They move rapidly from the darkness back into the light. As we have stated earlier, the God-fearing live always in a spirit of repentance. President Brigham Young made this important explanation regarding living in a constant state of worthiness: "I do not recollect that I have seen five minutes since I was baptized that I have not been ready to preach a funeral sermon, lay hands on the sick, or to pray in private or in public. I will tell you the secret of this. In all your business transactions, words, and communications, *if you commit an overt act, repent of that immediately, and call upon God to deliver you from evil and give you the light of His Spirit.* . . . *If I commit an overt act, the Lord knows the integrity of my heart, and, through sincere repentance, He forgives me.*"[20] Further: "When men truly and heartily repent, and make manifest to the heavens that their repentance is genuine by obedience to the requirements made known to them through the laws of the gospel, then are they entitled to the administration of salvation, and no power can withhold the good spirit from them."[21] The Joseph Smith Translation of the passage from 1 John reads as follows: "Whosoever is born of God *doth not continue in sin; for the Spirit of God remaineth in him; and he cannot continue in sin, because he is born of God, having received that Holy Spirit of promise"* (emphasis added).

A modern revelation attests: "But learn that he who doeth the works of righteousness shall receive his reward, even peace in this world, and eternal life in the world to come" (D&C 59:23). Indeed, we might ask ourselves the same question the Lord asked Oliver Cowdery: "What greater witness can you have than from God?" (D&C 6:23). Another way of saying this is to state that we are living in a saved condition to the extent that we are living in the light, living according to our spiritual privileges, living in harmony with the knowledge and the blessings we have received to that point. On 15 July 1860 President Brigham Young said:

"If a person with an honest heart, a broken, contrite, and pure spirit, in all fervency and honesty of soul, presents himself and says that he wishes to be baptized for the remission of his sins, and the ordinance is administered by one having authority, is that man saved? Yes, to that period of time. Should the Lord see proper to take him then from the earth, the man has believed and been baptized, and is a fit subject for heaven—a candidate for the kingdom of God in the celestial world, because he has repented and done all that was required of him at that hour. . . .

"*It is present salvation and the present influence of the Holy Ghost that we need every day to keep us on saving ground.* When an individual refuses to comply with the further requirements of heaven, then the sins he had formerly committed return upon his head; his former righteousness departs from him, and is not accounted to him for righteousness: but if he had continued in righteousness and obedience to the requirements of heaven, *he is saved all the time, through baptism, the laying on of hands, and obeying the commandments of the Lord* and all that is required of him by the heavens—the living oracles. He is saved now, next week, next year, and continually, and is prepared for the celestial kingdom of God whenever the time comes for him to inherit it.

"*I want present salvation.* I preach, comparatively, but little about the eternities and Gods, and their wonderful works in eternity; and do not tell who first made them, nor how they were made; for I know nothing about that. *Life is for us, and it is for us to receive it today, and not wait for the Millennium. Let us take a course to be saved today,* and, when evening comes, review the acts of the day, repent of our sins, if we have any to repent of, and say our prayers; then we can lie down and sleep in peace until the morning, arise with gratitude to God, commence the labors of another day, and strive to live the whole day to God and nobody else."[22]

CONCLUSION

I don't expect that many of us will adopt the terminology of many modern Christians or of those who believe they have been saved at the time they received Jesus into their heart. Nor do I think we should. But it certainly wouldn't hurt us to better understand them. In addition, I am concerned that far too many Latter-day Saints wrestle with feelings of inadequacy, struggle with hopelessness, and in general are much too anxious about their standing before God. Too many worry about qualifying for the celestial kingdom. It is important to keep the ultimate goal in our minds, but it seems so much more profitable to focus on fundamentals and on the here and now—staying in covenant, being true to our promises, cultivating the gift of the Holy Ghost. "I am in the hands of the Lord," President Brigham Young pointed out, "and never trouble myself about my salvation, or what the Lord will do with me hereafter."[23] As he said on another occasion, our work "is a work of the present. The salvation we are seeking is for the present, and sought correctly, it can be obtained, and be continually enjoyed. If it continues today, it is upon the same principle that it will continue tomorrow, the next day, the next week, or the next year, and, we might say, the next eternity."[24]

Though we must guard against all forms of pride or self-assurance, we must also avoid the kind of false modesty or doubt that is antithetical to faith; as Joseph Smith taught, doubt—certainly including a constant worry as to our standing before God or our capacity to go where Christ is—cannot co-exist with saving faith. Fear and doubt "preclude the possibility of the exercise of faith in [God] for life and salvation."[25] If indeed "happiness is the object and design of our existence,"[26] then happiness is something to be enjoyed in the present, in the here and now, not something reserved for the distant there and then. *"If we are saved,"* President Young declared, *"we are happy,* we are filled with light, glory, intelligence, and we pursue a course to enjoy the blessings that the Lord has in store for us. If we continue to pursue that course, it produces just the thing we want, that is, *to be saved at this present moment. And that will lay the foundation to be saved forever and forever, which will amount to an eternal salvation."*[27]

Living in a state of salvation does not entail an inordinate self-confidence but rather a hope in Christ. To hope in our modern world is to wish, to worry, to fret about some particular outcome. In the scriptures, however, hope is expectation, anticipation, and assurance. Faith in Christ, true faith, always gives rise to hope in Christ. "And what is it that ye shall hope for? Behold I say unto you that ye shall have hope through the atonement of Christ and the power of his resurrection, to be raised unto life eternal" (Moroni 7:41). To have faith in Christ is to have the assurance that as we rely wholly upon his merits and mercy and trust in his redeeming grace, we will make it (see 2 Nephi 31:19; Moroni 6:4). He will not only bridge the chasm between the ideal and the real and thus provide that final spiritual boost into eternal life, but he will also extend to us that marvelous enabling power so essential to daily living, a power that enables us to conquer weakness and acquire the divine nature. In short, living in a state of salvation is living in the quiet assurance that God is in his heaven, Christ is the Lord, and that the plan of redemption is real and in active operation in our personal lives. It is not to be totally free of weakness, but to proceed confidently in the Savior's promise that in him we shall find strength to overcome, as well as rest and peace, here and hereafter.

Notes

From an address to BYU Religious Education Faculty, 9 September 1994.

1 Sidney Sperry, *Paul's Life and Letters* (Salt Lake City: Bookcraft, 1955), 176.

2. See Bruce R. McConkie, *Mormon Doctrine,* 2d ed. (Salt Lake City: Bookcraft, 1966), 408; see also McConkie, *Doctrinal New Testament Commentary,* 3:333–36.

3. John F. MacArthur, *The Gospel According to Jesus* (Grand Rapids, Mich.: Zondervan, 1988), 198.

4. John F. MacArthur, *Faith Works: The Gospel According to the Apostles* (Dallas: Word Publishing, 1993), 109, 121; emphasis in original.

5. Orson Pratt, "The Holy Spirit," pamphlet (Liverpool: n.p., 1852).

6. Brigham Young, in *Journal of Discourses,* 10:173.

7. Bruce R. McConkie, "Jesus Christ and Him Crucified," *1976 Brigham Young University Fireside and Devotional Speeches of the Year* (Provo: Brigham Young University Publications, 1976), 399.

8. *Gospel Doctrine,* 58, 126.

9. McConkie, *Mormon Doctrine,* 567; emphasis in original.

10. Brigham Young, in *Deseret News Weekly,* 31 August 1854, 37.

11. McConkie, *Mormon Doctrine,* 567; emphasis in original.

12. Stephen E. Robinson, *Believing Christ* (Salt Lake City: Deseret Book Co., 1992), 43.

13. See *Teachings of the Prophet Joseph Smith,* 301, 305.

14. See *Lectures on Faith,* 7:9, 16.

15. See *Teachings of the Prophet Joseph Smith,* 12.

16. Ibid., 149–50.

17. *Doctrinal New Testament Commentary,* 3:191.

18. See also *Teachings of the Prophet Joseph Smith,* 128.

19. Ibid., 338–39.

20. Brigham Young, in *Journal of Discourses,* 12:103; emphasis added.

21. Ibid., 10:18.

22. Ibid., 8:124–25; emphasis added.

23. Ibid., 6:276.

24. Ibid., 1:131.

25. *Lectures on Faith,* 4:13; see also 3:20–21; 6:12.

26. *Teachings of the Prophet Joseph Smith,* 255.

27. Brigham Young, in *Journal of Discourses,* 1:131; emphasis added.

SECURING THE
CHILDREN THROUGH
THE COVENANT

There is power, consummate power, in the new and everlasting covenant. That power transcends our finite capacity to fully understand the infinite willingness of God—and his eternal plan—to save all of those who will be saved. We know so little. In a world that presses for fairness, we too often close our eyes to the tender mercies of a loving Savior. The Master demonstrates his infinite mercy, for example, by refusing to condemn those who were ignorant of the gospel message and its requirements (see 2 Nephi 9:25–26; Mosiah 3:11; Moroni 8:22; D&C 137:7–9), including little children who died before the age of accountability (see Mosiah 3:16; 15:25; Moroni 8:8–12, 22; D&C 29:46–47; 74:7; 137:10). He offers the sublime gift—eternal life—to those laborers who join the work in the vineyard in the eleventh hour, the same gift he offers to those who have labored the entire day (see Matthew 20:1–16).

EXPANDING OUR VISION AND OUR HOPE

The Prophet Joseph Smith called upon us to repent of littleness of soul and broaden our horizons. "It is the constitutional disposition of mankind to set up stakes and set bounds to the works and ways of the Almighty." And further, by way of warning, "I say to all those who are disposed to set up stakes for the Almighty, You will come short of the glory of God."[1] Earlier he had said: "Our heavenly Father is more liberal in His views, and boundless in His mercies and blessings, than we are ready to believe or receive."[2] He added that "inasmuch as the Lord

Almighty has preserved me until today, He will continue to preserve me, by the united faith and prayers of the Saints, until I have fully accomplished my mission in this life, and so firmly established *the dispensation of the fulness of the priesthood* in the last days, that all the powers of earth and hell can never prevail against it."[3]

In speaking at a funeral for Judge Elias Higbee on 13 August 1843, the Prophet stated: "Had I inspiration, revelation, and lungs to communicate what my soul has contemplated in times past, there is not a soul in this congregation but would go to their homes and shut their mouths in everlasting silence on religion till they had learned something. Why be so certain that you comprehend the things of God, when all things with you are so uncertain. You are welcome to all the knowledge and intelligence I can impart to you." After thus preparing us for what was to come, he continued: "That which hath been hid from before the foundation of the world is revealed to babes and sucklings in the last days. The world is reserved unto burning in the last days. *He shall send Elijah the prophet, and he shall reveal the covenants of the fathers in relation to the children, and the covenants of the children in relation to the fathers.*" He then referred to the four angels mentioned in Revelation 7, described in modern revelation as "four angels sent forth from God, to whom is given power over the four parts of the earth, to save life and to destroy; these are they who have the everlasting gospel to commit to every nation, kindred, tongue, and people; having power to shut up the heavens, *to seal up unto life,* or to cast down to the regions of darkness" (D&C 77:8; emphasis added). The Prophet then mentioned "four destroying angels holding power over the four quarters of the earth until the servants of God are sealed in their foreheads, which signifies sealing the blessing upon their heads, meaning the everlasting covenant, thereby making their calling and election sure. *When a seal is put upon the father and mother, it secures their posterity, so that they cannot be lost, but will be saved by virtue of the covenant of their father and mother.*"[4]

Howard and Martha Coray recorded that same sermon as follows: "God shall send unto them Elijah the prophet and he shall reveal unto them the covenants of the fathers with relation to the children and the covenants of the children in relation to the Fathers, *that they may have the privilege of entering into the same in order to effect their mutual salvation.*"[5] Franklin D. Richards recorded the Prophet's words in the following manner: "Judge Higbee would say that *covenants either there or here must be made in view of eternity. The covenant sealed on the foreheads of the parents secured the children from falling [and] that they shall all sit upon thrones as one with the godhead, joint heirs of God with Jesus Christ.*"[6]

What does this mean? To what degree can righteous parents, fathers and mothers who have entered into and kept sacred covenants, affect and effect the salvation of their posterity? President Brigham Young taught: "Let the father and mother, who are members of this Church and kingdom, take a righteous course, and strive with all their might never to do a wrong, but to do good all their lives; if they have one child or one hundred children, *if they conduct themselves towards them as they should, binding them to the Lord by their faith and prayers, I care not where those children go, they are bound up to their parents by an everlasting tie, and no power on earth or hell can separate them from their parents in eternity;* they will return again to the fountain from whence they sprang."[7] We think of the sufferings and pleadings of Alma the elder and his wife and remember the words of the angel to the wandering son: "Behold, the Lord hath heard the prayers of his people, and also the prayers of his servant, Alma, who is thy father; for he has prayed with much faith concerning thee that thou mightest be brought to the knowledge of the truth; therefore, for this purpose have I come to convince thee of the power and authority of God, that the prayers of his servants might be answered according to their faith" (Mosiah 27:14).

William Clayton's account of a funeral address by the Prophet Joseph contains the following: "When speaking of the passage 'I will send Elijah the prophet etc.,' he said it should read: 'And he shall turn the hearts of the children to the covenant made with their fathers.'"[8] We believe that those who are faithful in their first estate come to the earth with certain predispositions to receive and embrace the truth. The Prophet himself declared that those of the house of Israel who come into the Church do so with quiet receptivity to the Spirit of the Lord and an openness to pure intelligence.[9] Similarly, we have no difficulty speaking of the "spirit of Elijah" that reaches out, touches, directs, and impels individuals to search out their dead and perform the saving ordinances. Why should we have difficulty, then, in accepting the fact that the power of the covenant will reach out, touch, redirect, and impel the wandering sheep? Could it be that that power is indeed the same spirit of Elijah, the spirit that turns the hearts of the children to the covenant made with their fathers?

Elder Orson F. Whitney offered the following powerful commentary on Joseph Smith's words: "The Prophet Joseph Smith declared—and he never taught more comforting doctrine—that *the eternal sealings of faithful parents and the divine promises made to them for valiant service in the cause of truth, would save not only themselves but likewise their posterity. Though some of the sheep may wander, the eye of the shepherd is upon them, and sooner or later they will feel the tentacles of divine providence reaching out after them and drawing them back to the fold.*

Either in this life or in the life to come, they will return. They will have to pay their debt to justice; they will suffer for their sins; and may tread a thorny path; but if it leads them at last, like the penitent prodigal, to a loving and forgiving father's heart and home, the painful experience will not have been in vain. Pray for your careless and disobedient children; hold on to them with your faith. Hope on, trust on, till you see the salvation of God. . . .

"You parents of the wilful and the wayward: Don't give them up. Don't cast them off. *They are not utterly lost. The shepherd will find his sheep.* They were his before they were yours—long before he entrusted them to your care; and you cannot begin to love them as he loves them. *They have but strayed in ignorance from the Path of Right, and God is merciful to ignorance. Only the fulness of knowledge brings the fulness of accountability.* Our Heavenly Father is far more merciful, infinitely more charitable, than even the best of his servants, and the Everlasting Gospel is mightier in power to save than our narrow finite minds can comprehend."[10]

In our own day, Elder Boyd K. Packer has provided a comforting context and reaffirmation for the promise to faithful parents. In discussing the "moral pollution" of the last days, he said: "It is a great challenge to raise a family in the darkening mists of our moral environment. We emphasize that the greatest work you will do will be within the walls of your home,[11] and that 'no other success can compensate for failure in the home.'[12] *The measure of our success as parents, however, will not rest solely on how our children turn out. That judgment would be just only if we could raise our families in a perfectly moral environment, and that now is not possible.*

"It is not uncommon for responsible parents to lose one of their children, for a time, to influences over which they have no control. They agonize over rebellious sons and daughters. They are puzzled over why they are so helpless when they have tried so hard to do what they should. It is my conviction that those wicked influences one day will be overruled. . . .

"We cannot overemphasize the value of temple marriage, the binding ties of the sealing ordinance, and the standards of worthiness required of them. *When parents keep the covenants they have made at the altar of the temple, their children will be forever bound to them.*"[13]

SOME QUESTIONS AND ANSWERS

This marvelous doctrine can and should provide hope—a measure of peace and rest and assurance—to all who mourn over their wandering sheep. It is a revealed answer to some of the soul's longings for understanding. And yet there are additional questions that beckon for response. Let's consider some of these questions:

1. *Will the power of the covenant coerce straying individuals into obedience?* We all know that even a merciful God will not violate an individual's moral agency, that he will force no man to heaven. Exaltation in the celestial kingdom is reserved for those who chose to go there, not those who were coerced or manipulated into appropriate behavior. We know that the laws of the everlasting covenant cannot violate the principles of justice or the canons of right and wrong. And yet there seems to be, in the sermons and writings of the prophets, the quiet but soul-satisfying message that the alms of the prayers of the righteous do come up into the ears of the Lord of Sabaoth; that righteous parents' loyalty to their covenants will not be overlooked; that no amount of suffering of the faithful in behalf of their posterity will be for naught; and that there is power, remarkable power in the covenant to save those who will be saved. President Joseph Fielding Smith taught: "Those born under the covenant, throughout all eternity, are the children of their parents. *Nothing except the unpardonable sin, or sin unto death, can break this tie. If children do not sin as John says [1 John 5:16–17], 'unto death,' the parents may still feel after them and eventually bring them back to them again.*"[14] As Elder Packer suggested, it may be that the oppressive power of evil in these last days is such that it chokes or restrains the proper exercise of agency. One day that will change.

2. *Isn't the power or spirit of Elijah that which turns our hearts to our deceased loved ones?* The spirit of Elijah does indeed point our minds to those who went before, those who laid the foundation for so much of what we now enjoy. Because Elijah came, we feel prompted and impelled to make available the sweet privileges of the gospel covenant to those who were not so blessed. At the same time, Elijah's power and blessings pertain to the living. President Harold B. Lee explained that Elijah's mission "applies just as much on this side of the veil as it does to the other side of the veil. . . . So, the hearts of you fathers and mothers must be turned to your children right now, if you have the true spirit of Elijah, and not think that it applies merely to those who are beyond the veil."[15]

3. *Isn't is possible that one can stray so far as to forfeit blessings hereafter?* Yes, there are limits, not necessarily to God's mercy but the extent to which mercy can temper justice. In speaking of very serious sins, President Joseph F. Smith explained that a person can and will be forgiven if he repents; "the blood of Christ will make him free, and will wash him clean, though his sins be as scarlet; but all this will not return to him any loss sustained, nor place him on an equal footing with his neighbor who has kept the commandments of the better law. Nor will it

place him in a position where he would have been, had he not committed wrong."[16] President Joseph Fielding Smith declared that "children born under the covenant, who drift away, are still the children of their parents; and the parents have a claim upon them; and *if* the children have not sinned away all their rights, the parents *may* be able to bring them *through repentance,* into the celestial kingdom, but not to receive the exaltation."[17] This is why we teach that prevention is far, far better than redemption. Though we rejoice in the cleansing powers of the blood of our Redeemer, we must, as President Harold B. Lee observed, impress the members of the Church "with the awfulness of sin rather than to content ourselves with merely teaching the way of repentance."[18]

4. *Doesn't the Prophet Joseph Smith's statement regarding the sealing of righteous parents seem to indicate that the parents' calling and election must be made sure?* Reference is in fact made to calling and election in the statement quoted earlier in this chapter. We must, however, keep some things in mind. Latter-day Saints who have received the ordinances of salvation—including the blessings of the temple endowment and eternal marriage—may thus press forward in the work of the Lord and with quiet dignity and patient maturity seek to be worthy of gaining the certain assurance of salvation before the end of their mortal lives. But should we not formally receive the more sure word of prophecy in this life, we have the scriptural promise that faithfully enduring to the end—keeping the covenants and commandments from baptism to the end of our mortal life (see Mosiah 18:8–9)— eventuates in the promise of eternal life, whether that promise be received here or hereafter (see D&C 14:7; 53:7; 2 Nephi 31:20; Mosiah 5:15). "But blessed are they who are faithful and endure, whether in life or in death, for they shall inherit eternal life" (D&C 50:5).

Bruce R. McConkie expressed the following sentiments at the funeral of Elder S. Dilworth Young: *"If we die in the faith, that is the same thing as saying that our calling and election has been made sure and that we will go on to eternal reward hereafter.* As far as faithful members of the Church are concerned, they have charted a course leading to eternal life. This life is the time that is appointed as a probationary estate for men to prepare to meet God, and as far as faithful people are concerned, if they are in the line of their duty, if they are doing what they ought to do, although they may not have been perfect in this sphere, their probation is ended. Now there will be some probation for some other people hereafter. But for the faithful saints of God, now is the time and the day, and their probation is ended with their death."[19]

5. *Don't we believe that if a person rejects the gospel in this life they will reject*

it in the world to come? Isn't it true that if one wanders from the fold here they are not likely to return hereafter? Many years ago while working as a counselor, I encountered a single mother who was struggling to rear three teenagers. We had met for several sessions and she seemed to be making some progress in communicating more love and concern to her children. She came in one afternoon particularly pensive. I sensed that something of substance was weighing on her mind and asked if she wanted to talk about it. She said: "I have a big decision to make." She then reminded me that her husband had been killed in an automobile accident exactly one year ago. "What's the dilemma?" I asked. "I need to decide whether to do his temple work," she responded. "Why is that even a problem for you? Didn't you love him?" "Yes," she said. "I adored him. He was a remarkable human being—a terrific father, a loving husband, a Scouter in the community, a little league baseball coach, an all-around great guy." She paused a moment and then added: "But he was not a member of the Church. He was very supportive of me and the children, was a moral and upright man, and didn't smoke or drink, but he never took the restored gospel very seriously."

I asked again: "Well, what's the problem? Why don't you do his work?" She then told me that one of her institute teachers had discouraged her from doing so. As I recall, his words went something like this: "Look, he didn't accept the gospel here, and so he won't accept it hereafter. To go to the temple in his behalf would be a total waste of time." I was stunned but attempted to hold my composure, especially because the teacher she quoted was well known in the community, and his word was highly regarded. She then asked what I thought. I said: "Oh, I'd probably take a slightly different approach." "What's that?" she asked. "I would go to the temple and see that his work is done for him this afternoon if I could," I said. I explained that we are simply not in a position to judge, to know what's in a person's heart—what they feel, what they believe, what they know. We do not really understand what constitutes a valid opportunity to hear the gospel, when the witness of the Spirit has been felt, or whether the message of the Restoration was even presented in a manner that was intelligible or truly inspirational. As I recall, she saw to it that her husband's temple work was done for him a short time later.

Amulek did teach that the same spirit or disposition we have in this life will be with us in the world to come (see Alma 34:31–35), and the principle is true enough. Continuing in an evil habituated course makes it awfully difficult to change. But is such impossible? We must never deny another person the opportunity to change. People change here. Why can they not change hereafter? President Joseph F. Smith beheld in his vision of the postmortal spirit world how "the chosen messengers went forth to declare the acceptable day of the Lord and proclaim liberty to the captives who were bound, even *unto all who would repent of their sins and receive the gospel.*" Now note this interesting verse: "Thus was the gospel preached to those who had died in their sins, without a knowledge of the truth, or *in transgression, having rejected the prophets*" (D&C 138:31–32; emphasis added). This same principle is echoed in the words of President Wilford Woodruff: "I tell you when the prophets and apostles go to preach to those who are shut up in prison, thousands of them will there embrace the Gospel. *They know more in that world than they do here.*"[20]

So many things can weigh upon the mind and heart of an individual, pressures and challenges and crosses that only God can see and comprehend. Why does a person reject the gospel? Why does a child wander? Can we see the whole picture? Are we in a position to pass appropriate judgment and close the doors to future recovery and reconciliation? I have a conviction that when a person passes through the veil of death all of those impediments and challenges and crosses to bear that were beyond his or her power to control—abuse, neglect, immoral environment, weighty traditions, etc.—will be torn away like a film. Then perhaps they shall, as President Woodruff suggested, see and feel things that they could not see and feel before.

6. *Isn't this risky? Won't these kinds of teachings motivate some young people to neglect their duty and "sow their wild oats?"* I suppose there will always be those who choose to take license in gospel liberty or who show contempt for the saving grace of our Lord by knowingly violating the laws of God. There is always a risk on that end of the spectrum. There is, however, what I perceive to be a greater risk—that well-meaning, hardworking, and diligent mothers and fathers with straying children may draw false conclusions about themselves and maybe even "throw in the towel" in despair. To such persons, the prophetic word concerning the consummate power of the covenant is like manna to the soul, like living water to parched lips. It may also be the case that such doctrine is often more effectively delivered and applied in more intimate settings. Bruce Hafen has written: "I was surprised on one occasion to hear a senior General Authority tell me something in a private conversation that allowed for greater flexibility on a particular issue than I had expected to hear. I told him how valuable I thought it would be if more members of the Church could hear his counsel, because what is said across the desk can so nicely clarify what is said over the pulpit. He replied that private counsel can be adapted to the attitudes and understanding of the person being counseled. If that same counsel were given publicly to an audience that included individuals of

insufficient background or commitment, it might appear to give license to those whose needs require not more flexibility, but less."[21]

7. *Is all of this really fair to those parents who have been successful in rearing their family or to those children who have kept themselves from serious sin?* This may be the most difficult question of all. In this case I think it appropriate to be direct and to the point. Stated bluntly, all of us are guilty of sin. All of us are in need of pardoning mercy. All of us fall short of the divine standard. During a long day of debate with his opponents, Jesus delivered the following parable: "A certain man had two sons; and he came to the first, and said, Son, go work to day in the vineyard. He [the son] answered and said, I will not: but afterward he repented, and went. And he came to the second, and said likewise. And he [the second son] answered and said, I go sir: and went not. Whether of them twain did the will of his father?" (Matthew 21:28–31). One "may wonder why this story does not include a third son who said, 'I will,' and kept his word. Perhaps it is because this story characterizes humanity, and we all fall short (Romans 3:23). Thus Jesus could describe only two kinds of religious people: those who pretend to be obedient but are actually rebels, and those who begin as rebels but repent."[22]

Obviously there are all types and varieties of sin, and some are certainly more serious than others. At the same time, there should be no doubt in any of our hearts that each one of us receives far more of the goodness and grace of heaven than is just. On one occasion I was in conversation with a colleague. We were chatting about life here and the kinds of rewards that can come to us hereafter. I made some offhand and rather flippant comment to this effect: "I just want to get what I deserve." I was startled but instructed by my friend's response: "You had better pray to God that you don't get what you deserve!" Every one of us is and will forevermore be eternal debtors. Indeed, as King Benjamin taught, if we "should serve him who has created you from the beginning, and is preserving you from day to day, by lending you breath, that ye may live and move and do according to your own will, and even supporting you from one moment to another—I say, if ye should serve him with all your whole souls yet ye would be unprofitable servants" (Mosiah 2:21).

Inasmuch as each of us is a recipient of unending and unmerited grace, how can we, in the spirit of Christian charity—or in the attitude of sane discourse—speak of the Lord's pardoning mercy toward wayward children as *unfair?* Of course it's unfair! It's *all* unfair! That a pure and innocent man should suffer and agonize over others' transgressions is not fair. That he who had never taken a backward step should tread the winepress alone, "even the wine-press of the fierceness of the wrath of Almighty God" (D&C 76:107; 88:106) and thereby descend below all things (see D&C 88:6), is nor fair. That the lowly Nazarene should be subjected to the ignominy and unspeakable torture of crucifixion is definitely unfair. But the plan of the Father is not a plan of fairness, at least as we judge fairness from our limited perspective; it is a plan of mercy. The Father and the Son love us in ways that we cannot comprehend. They will do all that is within the bounds of propriety to save as many of the posterity of Adam and Eve as will be saved. President J. Reuben Clark Jr. spoke of the goodness of our God: "I feel that [the Lord] will give that punishment which is the very least that our transgression will justify. . . . I believe that when it comes to making the rewards for our good conduct, he will give the maximum that is possible to give."[23]

CONCLUSION

There is power in righteousness, power that activates God's covenant with his people, power that binds and seals here and hereafter, power that links the children of Abraham, the children of the covenant, together in love and unity. Righteous parents thereby have great positive impact on generations to come. "Ye are the children of the prophets," the risen Lord declared to the Nephites; "and ye are of the house of Israel; and ye are of the covenant which the Father made with your fathers, saying unto Abraham: And in thy seed shall all the kindreds of the earth be blessed. The Father having raised me up unto you first, and *sent me to bless you in turning away every one of you from his iniquities; and this because ye are the children of the covenant*" (3 Nephi 20:25–26; emphasis added).

The pull of the covenant toward righteousness may come from both sides of the veil. The counsel of Elisha the prophet is still timely: "Fear not: for they that be with us are more than they that be with them" (2 Kings 6:16). My friend and colleague Joseph McConkie told me that his grandfather, Oscar McConkie Sr., said to the family just before his death: "I am going to die. When I die, I shall not cease to love you. I shall not cease to pray for you. I shall not cease to labor in your behalf." President Joseph F. Smith, in a general conference address in April 1916 entitled "In the Presence of the Divine," made the following impressive and instructive remarks:

"Sometimes the Lord expands our vision from this point of view and this side of the veil, so that we feel and seem to realize that we can look beyond the thin veil which separates us from that other sphere. If we can see, by the enlightening influence of the Spirit of God and through the words that have been spoken by the holy prophets of God, beyond the veil that separates us from the spirit world, *surely those who have passed beyond, can see more clearly through the veil back here to us than it is possible for us to see to them from our sphere of action. I believe we move and have our being in the presence of heavenly messengers and of heavenly beings. We are not separate from them.* We begin to realize, more and more fully, as we become acquainted with the principles of the gospel, as they have been revealed anew in this dispensation, that *we are closely related to our kindred, to our ancestors, to our friends and associates and co-laborers who have preceded us into the spirit world.* We can not forget them; we do not cease to love them; we always hold them in our hearts, in memory. . . . How much more certain it is and reasonable and consistent to believe that those who have been faithful, who have gone beyond and are still engaged in the work for the salvation of the souls of men, . . . can see us better than we can see them; that *they know us better than we know them.* They have advanced; we are advancing; we are growing as they have grown; we are reaching the goal that they have attained unto; and therefore, I claim that *we live in their presence, they see us, they are solicitous for our welfare, they love us now more than ever.* For now they see the dangers that beset us; they can comprehend, better than ever before, the weaknesses that are liable to mislead us into dark and forbidden paths. *They see the temptations and the evils that beset us in life and the proneness of mortal beings to yield to temptation and to wrong doing; hence their solicitude for us, and their love for us, and their desire for our well being, must be greater than that which we feel for ourselves.*"[24]

"Rewards for obedience to the commandments," Elder Russell M. Nelson explained, "are almost beyond mortal comprehension. Here, children of the covenant become a strain of sin-resistant souls. And hereafter, . . . children of the covenant, and 'each generation [will] be linked to the one which went on before . . . [in] the divine family of God.' Great comfort comes from the knowledge that our loved ones are secured to us through the covenants."[25]

In summary, the Holy One of Israel, who is the Mediator of the Covenant, has extended the promise that when a seal is placed upon a father and mother—a seal that comes through faithfulness to their eternal covenants—their children will be bound to them forever. Even if the children stray for a season, the tentacles of the everlasting covenant will feel after them and they shall, either here or hereafter, return to the fold. We do not fully understand all of the implications of this marvelous promise, but we feel to trust in the ransoming and redeeming power of our Lord who is also our Savior.

"God has fulfilled his promises to us," President Lorenzo Snow explained, "and our prospects are grand and glorious. Yes, in the next life we will have our wives, and our sons and daughters. If we do not get them all at once, we will have them some time, for every knee shall bow and every tongue shall confess that Jesus is the Christ. *You that are mourning about your children straying away will have your sons and your daughters. If you succeed in passing through these trials and afflictions and receive a resurrection, you will, by the power of the Priesthood, work and labor, as the Son of God has, until you get all your sons and daughters in the path of exaltation and glory. This is just as sure as that the sun rose this morning over yonder mountains.* Therefore, mourn not because all your sons and daughters do not follow in the path that you have marked out to them, or give heed to your counsels. *Inasmuch as we succeed in securing eternal glory, and stand as saviors, and as kings and priests to our God, we will save our posterity....* God will have His own way in His own time, and He will accomplish His purposes in the salvation of His sons and daughters.... God bless you, brethren and sisters. *Do not be discouraged* is the word I wish to pass to you; but remember that righteousness and joy in the Holy Ghost is what you and I have the privilege of possessing at all times."[26]

As a personal aside, several years ago my wife and I were struggling with how best to build faith in all of our children and how to entice wandering souls back into Church activity. A caring colleague, sensing the weight of my burdens, happened into my office one day and simply asked this question: "Do you think our Heavenly Parents wander throughout the heavens in morose agony over their straying children?" Startled a bit by the question, I thought for a moment and said: "No, I don't think so. I know they feel pain, but I honestly can't picture them living in eternal misery." Then my friend responded: "Ask yourself why they do not do so and it will make a difference in your life." I didn't get much work done the rest of the day because I spent many hours pondering the question. When I arrived home that evening, I asked Shauna to sit down and reflect on the same question. She answered as I did, and then the two of us set about a prayerful quest for the next several days to understand how it is that our Eternal Father and Mother deal with their pain.

In time it began to dawn on us that the Lord knows the end from the beginning, and that, as Joseph the Prophet declared, all things—past, present, and future—are and were with Him "one eternal now."[27] Perspective. *Perspective.* That was the answer. God deals with pain through and by virtue of his infinite and perfect perspective. He not only knows what we have done and what we are doing, but he also knows what we will do in the future. If in fact, as the prophets have taught, many who are heirs to the blessings of the covenant made with Abraham, Isaac, and Jacob will either in time or eternity be reconciled to and reunited with the covenant family, then all we need to do for the time being is to seek, through fasting and prayer, to gain at least a portion of our God's perspective—his omniloving patience, his long-suffering, his ever-open arms—to gain, in other words, even a glimpse of the big picture as God sees it. Such a perspective will not only serve us well in the midst of our sufferings; it will also empower our souls and fashion us into the image of our Master, who is the personification and embodiment of charity or pure love (see Moroni 7:45–48).

And so, because we are mortal, because we are human, because we cannot see the end from the beginning, when a child wanders we fret and ache and sometimes despair. But there is hope smiling brightly before us, hope that springs forth from the elevated perspective provided by the power of the gospel covenant. President Gordon B. Hinckley, in addressing the Saints in Great Britain, said: "May you be blessed, each of you. May there be love and peace and gladness in your homes. I leave my blessing upon you. May there be food on your table, clothing on your backs, shelter over your heads and a sense of security and *peace and love among your children, precious children every one of them, even those who may have strayed. I hope you don't lose patience with them; I hope you go on praying for them, and I don't hesitate to promise that if you do so, the Lord will touch their hearts and bring them back to you with love and respect and appreciation.*"[28]

"There is never a time," the Prophet Joseph Smith observed, "when the spirit is too old to approach God. *All are within the reach of pardoning mercy, who have not committed the unpardonable sin.*"[29] And so we pray, we fast, we plead, and we implore. And perhaps most important, we love those who wander, and we never, never give up hope. I testify that there is a God in heaven who is our Eternal Father and that he lives in the family unit; that our Heavenly Father knows us one and all by name and knows, perfectly well, of our sorrows and our soul's deepest longings; that Jesus, as the Good Shepherd, will go in search of the lost sheep; that the gospel covenant is as broad and deep and penetrating as eternity; and that there are righteous forces at work that are beyond our capacity to perceive or comprehend. I know, with all my heart, that "the effectual fervent prayer of a righteous man [or woman] availeth much" (James 5:16), and that both in time and in eternity our God shall wipe away all tears (see Isaiah 25:8; Revelation 7:17; 21:4).

We trust in the power of Christ, the Mediator of the covenant, to forgive, to repair, to renew, and to rekindle the gospel light within the hearts of those who stray for a season. And we take comfort in the Master's promise: "Be faithful and diligent in keeping the commandments of God, and I will encircle thee in the arms of my love" (D&C 6:20).

Notes

From an address to Brigham Young University Religious Education faculty, Provo, Utah, 1995.

1. *Teachings of the Prophet Joseph Smith,* 320–21.
2. Ibid., 257.
3. Ibid., 258; emphasis added.
4. Ibid., 320–21; emphasis added.
5. *Words of Joseph Smith,* 240; spelling corrected and emphasis added.
6. Ibid., 241; punctuation corrected and emphasis added.
7. Brigham Young, in *Journal of Discourses,* 11:215; emphasis added.
8. *Words of Joseph Smith,* 241–42; punctuation corrected.
9. *Teachings of the Prophet Joseph Smith,* 149–50.
10. Orson F. Whitney, in Conference Report, April 1929, 110; emphasis added.
11. See Harold B. Lee, in Conference Report, April 1973, 130.
12. See David O. McKay, in Conference Report, April 1935, 116.
13. Boyd K. Packer, in Conference Report, April 1992, 94–95; emphasis added.
14. *Doctrines of Salvation,* 2:90; emphasis added.
15. Harold B. Lee, *Ninth Annual Priesthood Genealogy Seminar–Syllabus 1974, Devotional Addresses 1973* (Provo, Utah: Brigham Young University Press, 1974), 530.
16. *Gospel Doctrine,* 374; see also Spencer W. Kimball, *The Miracle of Forgiveness* (Salt Lake City: Bookcraft, 1969), 310–11.
17. *Doctrines of Salvation,* 2:91; emphasis in original.
18. Harold B. Lee, *Decisions for Successful Living* (Salt Lake City: Deseret Book Co., 1973), 88.
19. Bruce R. McConkie, address given at funeral service for S. Dilworth Young, Salt Lake City, Utah, 13 July 1981, typescript, 5; emphasis added.
20. Wilford Woodruff, as quoted in Boyd K. Packer, *The Holy Temple* (Salt Lake City: Bookcraft, 1980), 206; emphasis added.
21. Bruce C. Hafen, *The Broken Heart* (Salt Lake City: Deseret Book Co., 1989), 4–5.
22. John F. MacArthur, *The Gospel According to Jesus* (Grand Rapids, Mich.: Zondervan, 1988), 167.
23. J. Reuben Clark Jr., "As Ye Sow . . . ," address delivered at Brigham Young University, Provo, Utah, 3 May 1955, 7.
24. Joseph F. Smith, "In the Presence of the Divine," as quoted in *Messages of the First Presidency,* 5:6–7; emphasis added.
25. Russell M. Nelson, "Children of the Covenant," *Ensign,* May 1995, 33–34; citing Joseph Fielding Smith, in Conference Report, October 1950, 13–14.
26. Lorenzo Snow, General Conference address given 6 October 1893, as quoted in *Collected Discourses,* 4 vols., comp. Brian H. Stuy (Sandy, Ut.: BHS Publishing, 1987), 3:364–65; emphasis added.
27. *Teachings of the Prophet Joseph Smith,* 220.
28. Gordon B. Hinckley, fireside address in Crawley, England, as quoted in *Church News,* 2 September 1995, 4; emphasis added.
29. *Teachings of the Prophet Joseph Smith,* 191; emphasis added.

WHAT WE BELIEVE

Sooner or later you and I will be approached by men and women not of our faith, persons either sincerely interested in what we believe or else opposed to much of what we stand for. This is particularly true as the Church grows and as our influence spreads throughout the world. Perhaps it would be worthwhile for us to entertain a few questions about what we believe, questions frequently asked of the Latter-day Saints concerning scripture, God, Christ, and salvation. For example:

1. *How can the Latter-day Saints justify having additional books of scripture and adding to the Christian canon?*

I remember very well sitting in a seminar on biblical studies at an eastern university many years ago. One of the things that stands out in my mind is our discussion of the canon of scripture. For at least two hours the instructor had emphasized that the word *canon*—referring, of course, to the biblical books that are generally included in the Judeo-Christian collection—was the "rule of faith," the standard against which we measure what is acceptable in belief and practice. He also stated that the canon, if the word meant anything at all, was *closed, fixed, set, and established.* He must have stressed those words at least ten times as he wrote them on the blackboard over and over. I noticed in the second session on this topic that the instructor seemed a bit uneasy. I remember thinking that something must be wrong. Without warning, he stopped what he was doing, banged his fist on the table, turned to me, and said, "Mr. Millet, will you please explain to this group the Latter-day Saint concept of canon, given your people's acceptance of the Book of Mormon and other books of scripture beyond the Bible?" I was startled. Stunned.

Certainly surprised. I paused for several seconds, looked up at the blackboard, saw the now very familiar words under the word *canon,* and said somewhat shyly: "Well, I suppose you could say that the Latter-day Saints believe the canon of scripture is *open, flexible,* and *expanding.*" We then had a *really* fascinating discussion!

Joseph Smith loved the Bible. It was through pondering upon certain verses in the epistle of James that he felt directed to call upon God in prayer. Most of his sermons, writings, and letters are laced with quotations or paraphrasing summaries of biblical passages and precepts from both the Old and New Testaments. The Prophet once remarked that one can "see God's handwriting in the sacred volume; and he who reads it oftenest will like it best."[1] From his earliest days, however, he did not believe the Bible was complete or that religious difficulties could necessarily be handled by turning to the Old or New Testaments for help (see Joseph Smith—History 1:12). Nor did he believe in either the inerrancy or the infallibility of the Bible.

"From what we can draw from the Scriptures relative to the teaching of heaven," the Prophet stated, "we are induced to think that much instruction has been given to man since the beginning which we do not possess now. . . . We have what we have, and the Bible contains what it does contain: but to say that God never said anything more to man than is there recorded, would be saying at once that we have at last received a revelation: for it must require one to advance thus far."[2] Occasionally we hear certain Latter-day Saint teachings described as *unbiblical* or of a particular doctrine being *contradictory* to the Bible. Let us be clear on this matter. The Bible is one of the books within our standard works, and thus our doctrines and practices are in harmony with the Bible. There are times, of course, when latter-day revelation provides clarification or enhancement of the intended meaning in the Bible. But addition to the canon is not the same as rejection of the canon. Supplementation is not the same as contradiction. All of the prophets, including the Savior himself, were sent to bring new light and knowledge to the world; in many cases, new scripture came as a result of their ministry. That new scripture did not invalidate what went before, nor did it close the door to subsequent revelation. We feel deep gratitude for the holy scriptures, but we do not worship scripture. Nor do we feel it appropriate to set up stakes and bounds to the works and ways of the Almighty, to tell God, essentially, "Thus far and no more."[3] As the Lord declared through Nephi, "Wherefore, because that ye have a Bible ye need not suppose that it contains all my words; neither need ye suppose that I have not caused more to be written" (2 Nephi 29:10).

In short, we believe God has spoken through modern prophets, restored his everlasting gospel, delivered new truths, and commissioned us to make them known to the world. We feel it would be un-Christian *not* to share what has been communicated to us.

2. What do the Latter-day Saints really believe about God? Is it true that they believe man can become as God?

Joseph Smith's First Vision represents the beginning of the revelation of God to man in this dispensation. We will no doubt spend a lifetime seeking to understand the doctrinal profundity of that theophany. This appearance of the Father and Son in upstate New York had the effect of challenging those creeds of Christendom out of which the doctrine of the Trinity evolved—a doctrine that evolved from efforts to reconcile Christian theology with Greek philosophy.[4] President Gordon B. Hinckley has observed: "To me it is a significant and marvelous thing that in establishing and opening this dispensation our Father did so with a revelation of himself and of his Son Jesus Christ, as if to say to all the world that he was weary of the attempts of men, earnest though these attempts might have been, to define and describe him. . . . The experience of Joseph Smith in a few moments in the grove on a spring day in 1820, brought more light and knowledge and understanding of the personality and reality and substance of God and his Beloved Son than men had arrived at during centuries of speculation."[5] By revelation Joseph Smith came to know that the Father, Son, and Holy Ghost constitute the Godhead. From the beginning the Prophet Joseph taught that the members of the Godhead are one in purpose, one in mind, one in glory, one in attributes and powers, but separate persons.[6]

God is the Father of the spirits of all men and women (see Numbers 16:22; 27:16), the source of light and truth, the embodiment of all godly attributes and gifts, and the supreme power and intelligence over all things. From the book of Moses we learn that among the ancients God the Father was called "Man of Holiness," and thus his Only Begotten Son is the Son of Man of Holiness, or the Son of Man (see Moses 6:57). The title *Man of Holiness* opens us to a deeper understanding of Deity. We believe that God the Father is an exalted man, a corporeal being, a personage of flesh and bones.[7] That God has a physical body is one of the most important of all truths restored in this dispensation; it is inextricably tied to such doctrines as the immortality of the soul, the literal resurrection, eternal marriage, and the continuation of the family unit into eternity. In his corporeal or physical nature, God can be in only one place at a time. His divine nature is such, however, that his glory, his power, his influence—that is, his Holy Spirit—fills the immensity of space and is the means by which he is omnipresent and through which law and light and life are extended to us (see D&C 88:6–13). The Father's physical body does not limit his capacity or detract one whit from his infinite holiness, any more than Christ's resurrected body did so (see Luke 24; John 20–21). Interestingly enough, research by Professor David Paulsen of the BYU Philosophy Department indicates that the idea of God's corporeality was taught in the early Christian church into the fourth and fifth centuries, before being lost to the knowledge of the people.[8]

On the one hand, we worship a divine Being with whom we can identify. That is to say, his infinity does not preclude either his immediacy or his intimacy. "In the day that God created man," the scriptures attest, "in the likeness of God made he him; in the image of his own body, male and female, created he them" (Moses 6:8–9). God is not simply a spirit influence, a force in the universe, or the First Great Cause; when we pray "Our Father which art in heaven" (Matthew 6:9), we mean what we say. We believe God is comprehendable, knowable, approachable, and, like his Beloved Son, touched with the feeling of our infirmities (see Hebrews 4:15).

On the other hand, our God is God. There is no knowledge of which the Father is ignorant and no power he does not possess (see 1 Nephi 7:12; 2 Nephi 9:20; Mosiah 4:9; Alma 26:35; Helaman 9:41; Ether 3:4). Scriptural passages that speak of him being the same yesterday, today, and forever (see, for example, Psalm 102:27; Hebrews 1:12; 13:8; 1 Nephi 10:18–19; 2 Nephi 27:23; Alma 7:20; Mormon 9:8–11, 19; Moroni 8:18; 10:7; D&C 3:2; 20:12, 17; 35:1) clearly have reference to his divine attributes—his love, justice, constancy, and willingness to bless his children. In addition, President Joseph Fielding Smith explained that "from eternity to eternity means from the spirit existence through the probation which we are in, and then back again to the eternal existence which will follow. Surely this is everlasting, for when we receive the resurrection, we will never die. We all existed in the first eternity. I think I can say of myself and others, we are from eternity; and we will be to eternity everlasting, if we receive the exaltation."[9]

We come to the earth to take a physical body, be schooled, and gain experiences in this second estate that we could not have in the first estate, the premortal life. We then strive to keep the commandments and grow in faith and spiritual graces until we are prepared to go where God and Christ are. Eternal life consists of being *with* God; in addition, it entails being *like* God. A study of Christian history reveals that the doctrine of the deification of man was taught at least into the fifth century by such notables as Irenaeus, Clement of Alexandria, Justin Martyr, Athanasius, and Augustine.[10] Because we know that many plain and precious truths were taken from the Bible before it was compiled (see 1 Nephi 13:20–39; preface to D&C 76), we might not agree with some of what was taught about deification by such Christian thinkers, but it is clear that the idea was not foreign to the people of the early church.

For that matter, no less a modern Christian theologian than C. S. Lewis recognized the logical and theological extension of being transformed by Christ. "The Son of God became a man," Lewis pointed out, "to enable men to become sons of God."[11] Further, Lewis has explained: "The command *Be ye perfect* is not idealistic gas. Nor is it a command to do the impossible. He is going to make us into creatures that can obey that command. He said (in the Bible) that we were 'gods' and He is going to make good his words. If we let Him—for we can prevent Him, if we choose—He will make the feeblest and filthiest of us into a god or goddess, dazzling, radiant, immortal creature, pulsating all through with such energy and joy and wisdom and love as we cannot now imagine, a bright stainless mirror which reflects back to God perfectly (though, of course, on a smaller scale) His own boundless power and delight and goodness. The process will be long and in parts very painful; but that is what we are in for. Nothing less. He meant what He said."[12]

All men and women, like Christ, are made in the image and likeness of God (Genesis 1:27; Moses 2:27), and so it is neither robbery nor heresy for the children of God to aspire to be like God (Matthew 5:48; Philippians 2:6); like any parent, our Heavenly Father would want his children to become and be all that he is. Godhood comes through overcoming the world through the Atonement (1 John 5:4–5; Revelation 2:7, 11; D&C 76:51–60), becoming heirs of God and joint-heirs with Christ, who is the natural Heir (Romans 8:17; Galatians 4:7), and thus inheriting *all* things, just as Jesus inherits all things (1 Corinthians 3:21–23; Revelation 21:7; D&C 76:55, 95; 84:38; 88:107). The faithful are received into the "church of the Firstborn" (Hebrews 12:23; D&C 76:54, 67, 94; 93:22), meaning they inherit as though they were the firstborn. In that glorified state we will be conformed to the image of the Lord Jesus (Romans 8:29; 1 Corinthians 15:49; 2 Corinthians 3:18; Philippians 3:21; 1 John 3:2; Alma 5:14), receive his glory, and be one with him and with the Father (John 17:21–23).

Although we know from modern revelation that godhood comes through the receipt of eternal life (see D&C 132:19–20), we do not believe we will ever, worlds without end, unseat or oust God the Eternal Father or his Only Begotten Son, Jesus Christ; those holy beings are and forever will be the Gods we worship. Even though we believe in the ultimate deification of man, I am unaware of any authoritative statement in LDS literature that suggests that we will ever worship any being other than the ones within the Godhead. We believe in "one God" in the sense that we love and serve one Godhead, one divine presidency, each of whom possesses all the attributes of Godhood (see Alma 11:44; D&C 20:28).

In short, God is not of another species, nor is he the great unknowable one; he is indeed our Father in Heaven. He has revealed a plan whereby we might enjoy happiness in this world and dwell with him and be like him in the world to come.

3. *Do the Latter-day Saints believe that salvation comes through their own works rather than by the grace of Christ? Are they "saved" Christians?*

The theological debate over whether we are saved by grace or by works is a fruitless argument that generates more heat than light, much "like asking which blade in a pair of scissors is most necessary."[13] The gospel is in fact a gospel covenant—a two-way promise. The Lord agrees to do for us what we could never do for ourselves, while we promise to do what we *can* do: receive the ordinances of salvation, love and serve one another (see Mosiah 18:8–10), and do all in our power to put off the natural man and deny ourselves of ungodliness (see Mosiah 3:19; Moroni 10:32). We know, without question, that the power to save us, to change us, to renew our souls, is in Christ. True faith, however, always manifests itself in *faithfulness.* Good works evidence our faith, our desire to remain in covenant with Christ, but they are not *sufficient.*[14]

Are we, then, "saved Christians"? Whereas the ultimate blessings of salvation do not come until the next life, there is a sense in which people in this life may enjoy the assurance of salvation and the peace that accompanies that knowledge (see D&C 59:23). True faith in Christ produces hope in Christ—not worldly wishing but expectation, anticipation, assurance. As the Apostle Paul wrote, the Holy Spirit provides the "earnest of our inheritance," the promise or evidence that we are on course, in covenant, and thus in line for full salvation in the world to come (see 2 Corinthians 1:21–22; 5:5; Ephesians 1:13–14). That is, the Spirit of God operating in our lives is like the Lord's "earnest money" on us—his sweet certification that he seriously intends to save us with an everlasting salvation. Thus if we are striving to cultivate the gift of the Holy Ghost, we are living in what might be called a "saved" condition.

One of the most respected Evangelical theologians, John Stott, has written: "Salvation is a big and comprehensive word. It embraces the totality of God's saving work, from beginning to end. In fact, salvation has three tenses, past, present, and future. . . . I have been saved (in the past) from the penalty of sin by a crucified Saviour. I am being saved (in the present) from the power of sin by a living Saviour. And I shall be saved (in the future) from the very presence of sin by a coming Saviour. . . .

"If therefore you were to ask me, 'Are you saved?' there is only one correct biblical answer which I could give you: 'yes and no.' Yes, in the sense that by the sheer grace and mercy of God through the death of Jesus Christ my Saviour he has forgiven my sins, justified me and reconciled me to himself. But no, in the sense that I still have a fallen nature and live in a fallen world and have a corruptible body, and I am longing for my salvation to be brought to its triumphant completion."[15] President David O. McKay taught that "the gospel of Jesus Christ, as revealed to the Prophet Joseph Smith, is in very deed, in every way, the power of God unto salvation. It is salvation *here*—here and now. It gives to every man the perfect life, here and now, as well as hereafter."[16]

In short, salvation is in Christ, and our covenant with Christ, our trust in his power to redeem us, should be demonstrated in how we live. The influence of the Holy Ghost in our lives is a sign to us that we are on course, "in Christ" (2 Corinthians 5:17), and thus in line for salvation.

4. Are the Latter-day Saints Christian? Or do they, as some have suggested, worship a different Jesus?

We believe in Jesus of Nazareth, in the One sent of the Father to bind up the brokenhearted and proclaim liberty to the captives (see Isaiah 61:1; D&C 138:11–18). For us, the Jesus of history is indeed the Christ of faith. He was and is the Only Begotten Son of God in the flesh (see John 3:16; 2 Nephi 25:12; D&C 20:21). While some may exclude us from the category of Christian for this or that doctrinal matter, our behavior must be consistent with our profession; those who claim new life in the Spirit are expected to walk in the Spirit (see Galatians 5:25).

"Are we Christians?" President Gordon B. Hinckley asked. "Of course we are! No one can honestly deny that. We may be somewhat different from the traditional pattern of Christianity. But no one believes more literally in the redemption wrought by the Lord Jesus Christ. No one believes more fundamentally that He was the Son of God, that He died for the sins of mankind, that He rose from the grave, and that He is the living resurrected Son of the living Father.

"All of our doctrine, all of our religious practice stems from that one basic doctrinal position: 'We believe in God, the Eternal Father, and in His Son, Jesus Christ, and in the Holy Ghost.' This is the first article of our faith, and all else flows therefrom."[17]

In the long run, all we can do is live what we preach and bear testimony of what we feel in our hearts and know in our minds. While we do not want to be misunderstood and we certainly would like for others to recognize the centrality of Christ in our lives, we do not require the imprimatur of the religious world to substantiate our claim. We are who we are and we know who we are, and if all the world should think otherwise, so be it. Our primary thrust in the religious world is not to court favor. Our desire to build bridges of understanding does not excuse us from the obligation to maintain our distinctive position in the religious world. Our strength lies in our distinctiveness, for we have something to offer the world, something of great worth. No one wants to be spurned, misunderstood, or misrepresented. But sometimes such is the cost of discipleship (see Matthew 5:10–12).

As to whether we worship a different Jesus, we say again: We accept and endorse the testimony of the New Testament writers: Jesus is the promised Messiah, the resurrection and the life (see John 11:25), literally the Light of the world (see John 8:12). Everything that testifies of his divine birth, his goodness, his transforming power, and his Godhood, we embrace enthusiastically. He has broken the bands of death and lives today. All this we know. But we know much more about the Christ because of what has been made known through latter-day prophets. President Brigham Young thus declared that "we, the Latter-day Saints, take the liberty of believing more than our Christian brethren: we not only believe . . . the Bible, but . . . the whole of the plan of salvation that Jesus has given to us. Do we differ from others who believe in the Lord Jesus Christ? No, only in believing more."[18]

Our conduct and our way of life cannot be separated from our doctrine, for what we believe empowers and directs what we do. A number of years ago an article appeared in *Christianity Today* entitled "Why Your Neighbor Joined the Mormon Church." Five reasons were given:

1. The Latter-day Saints show genuine love and concern by taking care of their people.

2. They strive to build the family unit.

3. They provide for their young people.

4. Theirs is a layman's church.

5. They believe that divine revelation is the basis for their practices.

After a brief discussion of each of the above, the author of the article concluded: "In a day when many are hesitant to claim that God has said anything definitive, the Mormons stand out in contrast, and many people are ready to listen to what the Mormons think the voice of God says. It is tragic that their message is false, but it is nonetheless a lesson to us that people are many times ready to hear a voice of authority."[19] As to the magazine article's claim that our message is false, we must remember that the Savior taught of the importance of judging things—prophets, for example—by their fruits, by the product of their ministry and teachings (see Matthew 7:15–20). He also explained that "every plant, which my heavenly Father hath not planted, shall be rooted up" (Matthew 15:13). Evil trees cannot bring forth good fruit. Works of men eventually come to naught, but that which is of God cannot be overthrown (see Acts 5:38–39; 1 John 3:7).

In short, we proclaim that Jesus of Nazareth is the Christ. We have taken his name upon us, eagerly acknowledge the redeeming power of his blood, and seek to emulate his perfect life.

Let me close by sharing with you three simple suggestions—learned through both sad and sweet experience—on how we might effectively deal with difficult questions posed by those not of our faith. First, *stay in control.* There is nothing more frustrating that knowing the truth, loving the truth, sincerely desiring to share the truth, and yet being unable to communicate our deepest feelings to another who sees things differently. Argument and disputation over sacred things cause us to forfeit the Spirit of God and thus the confirming power of our message (see 3 Nephi 11:28–30). We teach and we testify. Contention is unbecoming of one called to publish peace and thus bless our brothers and sisters. In the words of Elder Marvin J. Ashton, "We have no time for contention. We only have time to be about our Father's business."[20]

Second, *stay in order.* The Savior taught that gospel prerequisites should be observed when teaching sacred things (see Matthew 7:6–7).[21] A person, for example, who knows very little about our doctrine will probably not understand or appreciate our teachings concerning temples, sealing powers, eternal life, or the deification of man. Joseph Smith the Prophet explained that "if we start right, it is easy to go right all the time; but if we start wrong, we may go wrong, and it [will] be a hard matter to get right."[22] It is always wise to lay a proper foundation for what is to be said; the truth can then flow more freely. The Apostle Peter is said to have explained to Clement: "The teaching of all doctrine has a certain order, and there are some things which must be delivered first, others in the second place, and others in the third, and so all in their order; and if these things be delivered in their order, they become plain; but if they be brought forward out of order, they will seem to be spoken against reason."[23]

Third, *stay in context.* As we have already noted, we love the Bible and cherish its messages. But the Bible is not the source of our doctrine or authority, nor is much to be gained through efforts to "prove" the truthfulness of the restored gospel from the Bible. Ours is an independent revelation. We know what we know about the premortal existence, priesthood, celestial marriage, baptism for the dead, the postmortal spirit world, degrees of glory, etc., because of what God has made known through latter-day prophets, not because we are able to identify a few biblical allusions to these matters. Some of our greatest difficulties in handling questions about our faith come when we try to establish specific doctrines of the Restoration from the Bible alone. There is consummate peace and spiritual power to be derived from being loyal to those things the Almighty has communicated to us in our dispensation (see D&C 5:10; 31:3–4; 43:15–16; 49:1–4; 84:54–61). "Our main task," President Ezra Taft Benson explained, "is to declare the gospel and do it effectively. We are not obligated to answer every objection. Every man eventually is backed up to the wall of faith, and there he must make his stand."[24]

I testify to the truthfulness of these remarkable doctrines about which I have written. I know, by the witness of the Holy Ghost to my soul, that God is our Father, Jesus Christ is our Lord and Savior, Joseph Smith was and is a prophet of the living God, and that The Church of Jesus Christ of Latter-day Saints is indeed the kingdom of God on earth. These things I know because I have studied and searched and sought to understand. These things I know because I have read and pondered and prayed and pleaded for light and knowledge. What has come to me is as settling and soothing to my heart as it is stimulating and enlarging to my mind. This work is true, and because it is true it will triumph. The First Presidency of the Church in 1907 declared: "Our motives are not selfish; our purposes not petty and earth-bound; we contemplate the human race, past, present and yet to come, as immortal beings, for whose salvation it is our mission to labor; and to this work, broad as eternity and deep as the love of God, we devote ourselves, now, and forever."[25] I pray that we will come to know what we believe, by study and by faith, and then with boldness but quiet dignity share those saving truths with others.

Notes

From an address delivered at a devotional assembly, Brigham Young University, Provo, Utah, 3 February 1998.

1. *Teachings of the Prophet Joseph Smith,* 56.
2. Ibid., 61; see also Joseph Smith, *The Personal Writings of Joseph Smith,* ed. Dean C. Jessee (Salt Lake City: Deseret Book Co., 1984), 297–301.
3. See *Teachings of the Prophet Joseph Smith,* 320–21.
4. See Adolph Von Harnack, *What Is Christianity?* (New York: Harper, 1957); Edwin Hatch, *The Influence of Greek Ideas on Christianity* (Gloucester, Mass.: Peter Smith, 1970); Henry Chadwick, *The Early Church,* rev. ed. (New York: Penguin Books, 1993), 77, 89–90; Jaroslav Pelikan, *Christianity and Classical Culture* (New Haven: Yale University Press, 1993), 28–29, 74, 84–85, 231–47; Dallin H. Oaks, in Conference Report, April 1995, 112–13.
5. Gordon B. Hinckley, *Teachings of Gordon B. Hinckley* (Salt Lake City: Deseret Book Co., 1997), 236.
6. See *Teachings of the Prophet Joseph Smith,* 370.
7. If the fourteen-year-old Joseph Smith did indeed learn of the Father's corporeality in the First Vision, he did not state it specifically in his various accounts of that vision. The Prophet explained in Ramus,

Illinois, that "the Father has a body of flesh and bones as tangible as man's" (D&C 130:22); that statement was recorded in April 1843. However, the Saints were teaching of God's corporeal nature at least as early as 1836. See Milton V. Backman Jr., "Truman Coe's 1836 Description of Mormonism," *Brigham Young University Studies* 17 (Spring 1977): 347–55; see also *Words of Joseph Smith,* 60, 63–64.

8. See David L. Paulsen, "Early Christian Belief in a Corporeal Deity: Origen and Augustine as Reluctant Witnesses," *Harvard Theological Review* 83, no. 2 (1990): 105–16; "The Doctrine of Divine Embodiment: Restoration, Judeo-Christian, and Philosophical Perspectives," *Brigham Young University Studies* 35, no. 4 (1996): 7–94.

9. *Doctrines of Salvation,* 1:12; see also McConkie, *Promised Messiah,* 166.

10. See Stephen E. Robinson, *Are Mormons Christian?* (Salt Lake City: Bookcraft, 1991), 60–61.

11. C. S. Lewis, *Mere Christianity* (New York: Macmillan, 1952), 154; see also *The Weight of Glory and Other Addresses* (New York: Macmillan, 1980), 18.

12. Lewis, *Mere Christianity,* 174–75.

13. Ibid., 129.

14. See McConkie, *Doctrinal New Testament Commentary,* 2:499–500; Dallin H. Oaks, in Conference Report, October 1988, 78.

15. John Stott, in Timothy Dudley-Smith, ed., *Authentic Christianity* (Downers Grove, Ill.: InterVarsity Press, 1995), 168.

16. David O. McKay, *Gospel Ideals* (Salt Lake City: Improvement Era, 1953), 6; see also Brigham Young, in *Journal of Discourses,* 6:276; 8:124–25.

17. Gordon B. Hinckley, in meeting with Religion Newswriters Association, Albuquerque, New Mexico, 14 September 1997; see *Ensign,* February 1998, 73.

18. Brigham Young, in *Journal of Discourses,* 13:56.

19. *Christianity Today,* 11 October 1974, 11–13.

20. Marvin J. Ashton, in Conference Report, April 1978, 9.

21. See also Boyd K. Packer, *Teach Ye Diligently* (Salt Lake City: Deseret Book Co., 1975), chapter 11; *The Holy Temple* (Salt Lake City: Bookcraft, 1980), chapter 2.

22. *Teachings of the Prophet Joseph Smith,* 343.

23. Peter, as quoted in *Clementine Recognitions* III, 34; as cited in Hugh Nibley, *Since Cumorah,* 2d ed. (Salt Lake City: Deseret Book Co. and FARMS, 1988), 97.

24. Ezra Taft Benson, *A Witness and a Warning* (Salt Lake City: Deseret Book Co., 1988), 5.

25. First Presidency (President Joseph F. Smith, John R. Winder, Anthon H. Lund), in Conference Report, April 1907, appendix, 16; as quoted in Howard W. Hunter, *That We Might Have Joy* (Salt Lake City: Deseret Book Co., 1994), 59.

Chapter 44

THE SECOND COMING OF CHRIST:
QUESTIONS AND ANSWERS

The Doctrine and Covenants is a sacred book of scripture that indeed provides literally thousands of answers—answers to questions that have plagued the religious world for centuries. Mine is a certain witness as to the divine calling of the Prophet Joseph Smith and of the keys of authority that have continued in rightful apostolic succession to our own day. I know, as I know that I live, that The Church of Jesus Christ of Latter-day Saints is, in the language of the revelation, "the only true and living church upon the face of the whole earth" (D&C 1:30). Truly, "the keys of the kingdom of God are committed unto man on the earth, and from thence shall the gospel roll forth unto the ends of the earth, as the stone which is cut out of the mountain without hands shall roll forth, until it has filled the whole earth" (D&C 65:2).

In this chapter I will address the subject of the Second Coming of Jesus Christ. I do so with some fear and trembling, a bit of anxiety that I not be misunderstood, and yet some sense of excitement and anticipation. We are blessed in having modern scripture that provides clarity regarding doctrine; the Doctrine and Covenants is a treasure house of doctrinal understanding, truly a book of answers. Therefore inasmuch as I have supreme confidence in the revelations and in the apostles and prophets who have been charged to interpret those revelations, I proceed. I do so in a rather unusual manner—in a question and answer format. Some of the questions may be answered briefly and quickly, while others require a bit more attention. It would be enjoyable to try to address scores of questions, but given the constraints of time and pages, we will discipline ourselves to consider but a fraction of that number.

1. *What is the Second Coming?* Jesus came to earth as a mortal being in the meridian of time. He taught the gospel, bestowed divine authority, organized the Church, and suffered and died as an infinite atoning sacrifice for the sins of the world. He stated that he would come again, would return, not as the meek and lowly Nazarene, but as the Lord of Sabaoth, the Lord of Hosts, the Lord of Armies. His Second Coming is thus spoken of as his coming "in glory," meaning in his true identity as the God of all creation, the Redeemer and Judge. His Second Coming is described as both *great* and *dreadful*—great for those who have been true and faithful and therefore look forward to his coming and dreadful to those who have done despite to the spirit of grace and who therefore hope against hope that he will never return. The Second Coming in glory is in fact "the end of the world," meaning the end of worldliness, the destruction of the wicked (see Joseph Smith—Matthew 1:4, 31).[1] At this coming the wicked will be destroyed, the righteous quickened and caught up to meet him, and the earth transformed from a fallen telestial orb to a terrestrial, paradisiacal sphere. We will live and move about among new heavens and new earth. The Second Coming will initiate the millennial reign.

2. *Does Christ himself know when he will come?* This question comes up occasionally, perhaps because of what is stated in the Gospel of Mark: "Heaven and earth shall pass away: but my words shall not pass away. But of that day and that hour knoweth no man, no, not the angels which are in heaven, *neither the Son,* but the Father" (Mark 13:31–32; emphasis added). The phrase "neither the Son" is not found in Matthew nor Luke. Christ knows all things; he possesses the fulness of the glory and power of the Father (see D&C 93:16–17). Surely he knows when he will return. If he did not know the exact day or time of his return in glory when the Olivet Prophecy was uttered, then certainly after his resurrection and glorification he came to know. It is worth noting that the Joseph Smith Translation of this verse omits the disputed phrase.

3. *Will all be surprised and caught unaware?* The scriptures speak of the Master returning as "a thief in the night" (1 Thessalonians 5:2; 2 Peter 3:10). It is true that no mortal man has known, does now know, or will yet know the precise day of the Lord's Second Advent. This is true for prophets and apostles as well as the rank and file of society and the Church. The Lord did not reveal to Joseph Smith the precise day and time of his coming (see D&C 130:14–17). Elder M. Russell Ballard, in speaking to students at Brigham Young University, recently observed: "I am called as one of the apostles to be a special witness of Christ in these

exciting, trying times, and I do not know when He is going to come again. As far as I know, none of my brethren in the Council of the Twelve or even in the First Presidency knows. And I would humbly suggest to you, my young brothers and sisters, that if we do not know, then *nobody* knows, no matter how compelling their arguments or how reasonable their calculations. . . . I believe when the Lord says 'no man' knows, it really means that no man knows. You should be extremely wary of anyone who claims to be an exception to divine decree."[2] On the other hand, the Saints are promised that if they are in tune with the Spirit, they can know the time and the season. The Apostle Paul chose the descriptive analogy of a pregnant woman about to deliver. She may not know the exact hour or day when the birth is to take place, but one thing she knows for sure: it will be soon. It *must* be soon! The impressions and feelings and signs within her own body so testify. In that day, surely the Saints of the Most High, the members of the body of Christ, will be pleading for the Lord to deliver the travailing earth, to bring an end to corruption and degradation, to introduce an era of peace and righteousness. And those who give heed to the words of scripture, and especially to the living oracles, will stand as the "children of light, and the children of the day," those who "are not of the night, nor of darkness" (1 Thessalonians 5:2–5). In a modern revelation the Savior declared: "And again, verily I say unto you, the coming of the Lord draweth nigh, and *it overtaketh the world as a thief in the night*—therefore, gird up your loins, that you may be the children of light, and that day shall not overtake you as a thief" (D&C 106:4–5; emphasis added).

To certain brethren who would soon be called to the first Quorum of the Twelve Apostles in this dispensation, the Lord said: "And unto you it shall be given to know the signs of the times, and the signs of the coming of the Son of Man" (D&C 68:11). As we move closer to the end of time, we would do well to live in such a manner that we can discern the signs of the times; we would be wise also to keep our eyes fixed and our ears riveted on those called to direct the destiny of the Church. The Prophet Joseph Smith pointed out that a particular man who claimed prophetic powers "has not seen the sign of the Son of Man as foretold by Jesus. Neither has any man, nor will any man, till after the sun shall have been darkened and the moon bathed in blood. For the Lord hath not shown me any such sign, and as the prophet saith, so it must be: 'Surely the Lord God will do nothing, but he revealeth his secret unto his servants the prophets.'"[3]

4. *Is it true that not everyone will know when the Savior has come?* Once in a while we hear something in the classes of the Church to the effect that not all people will know when the Lord returns. Let us be clear on this matter. There may

be some wisdom in speaking of the Second *Comings* of the Lord Jesus Christ, three of which are preliminary appearances or comings to select groups, and one of which is to the whole world. The Lord will make a preliminary appearance *to his temple in Independence, Jackson County, Missouri.* This seems to be a private appearance to those holding the keys of power in the earthly kingdom. Elder Orson Pratt, in speaking of this appearance, said: "All of them who are pure in heart will behold the face of the Lord and that too before he comes in his glory in the clouds of heaven, for he will suddenly come to his Temple, and he will purify the sons of Moses and of Aaron, until they shall be prepared to offer in that Temple an offering that shall be acceptable in the sight of the Lord. In doing this, he will purify not only the minds of the Priesthood in that Temple, but he will purify their bodies until they shall be quickened, renewed and strengthened, and they will be partially changed, not to immortality, but changed in part that they can be filled with the power of God, and they can stand in the presence of Jesus, and behold his face in the midst of that Temple."[4] Charles W. Penrose observed that the Saints "will come to the Temple prepared for him, and his faithful people will behold his face, hear his voice, and gaze upon his glory. From his own lips they will receive further instructions for the development and beautifying of Zion and for the extension and sure stability of his Kingdom."[5]

The Lord will make an appearance *at Adam-ondi-Ahman,* "the place where Adam shall come to visit his people, or the Ancient of Days shall sit" (D&C 116). For one thing, this grand council will be a large sacrament meeting, a time when the Son of Man will partake of the fruit of the vine once more with his earthly friends. And who will be in attendance? The revelations specify Moroni, Elias, John the Baptist, Elijah, Abraham, Isaac, Jacob, Joseph, Adam, Peter, James, John, "and also," the Savior clarifies, "with all those whom my Father hath given me out of the world" (D&C 27:5–14)—i.e., multitudes of faithful Saints from the beginning of time to the end. This will be a private appearance in the sense that it will be unknown to the world. It will be a leadership meeting, a time of accounting, an accounting for priesthood stewardships. The Prophet Joseph Smith explained that Adam, the Ancient of Days, "will call his children together and hold a council with them to prepare them for the coming of the Son of Man. He (Adam) is the father of the human family, and presides over the spirits of all men, and all that have had the keys must stand before him in this grand council. . . . The Son of Man stands before him, and there is given him [Christ] glory and dominion. Adam delivers up his stewardship to Christ, that which was delivered to him as holding the keys of the universe, but retains his standing as head of the human family."[6]

President Joseph Fielding Smith observed: "This gathering of the children of Adam, where the thousands, and the tens of thousands are assembled in the judgment, will be one of the greatest events this troubled earth has ever seen. At this conference, or council, all who have held keys of dispensations will render a report of their stewardship. . . . We do not know how long a time this will be in session, or how many sessions will be held at this grand council. It is sufficient to know that it is a gathering of the Priesthood of God from the beginning of this earth down to the present, in which reports will be made and all who have been given dispensations (talents) will declare their keys and ministry and make report of their stewardship according to the parable [the Parable of the Talents; see Matthew 25]. Judgment will be rendered unto them for this is a gathering of the righteous. . . . It is not to be the judgment of the wicked. . . . This will precede the great day of destruction of the wicked and will be the preparation for the Millennial Reign."[7] Elder Bruce R. McConkie has likewise written: "Every prophet, apostle, president, bishop, elder, or church officer of whatever degree—all who have held keys shall stand before him who holds all of the keys. They will then be called upon to give an account of their stewardships and to report how and in what manner they have used their priesthood and their keys for the salvation of men within the sphere of their appointments. . . . There will be a great hierarchy of judges in that great day, of whom Adam, under Christ, will be chief of all. Those judges will judge the righteous ones under their jurisdiction, but Christ himself, he alone, will judge the wicked."[8]

The Savior will appear *to the Jews on the Mount of Olives.* It will be at the time of the Battle of Armageddon, at a time when his people will find themselves with their backs against the wall. During this period, two prophets will stand before the wicked in the streets of Jerusalem and call the people to repentance. These men, presumably members of the Council of the Twelve Apostles or the First Presidency—holding the sealing powers—"are to be raised up to the Jewish nation in the last days, at the time of the restoration," will "prophesy to the Jews after they are gathered and have built the city of Jerusalem in the land of their fathers" (D&C 77:15; see also Revelation 11:4–6).[9] They will be put to death by their enemies, their bodies will lie in the streets for three and a half days, and they will then be resurrected before the assembled multitude (see Revelation 11:7–12).

At about this time, the Savior will come to the rescue of his covenant people: "Then shall the Lord go forth, and fight against those nations, as when he fought in the day of battle. And his feet shall stand in that day upon the mount of Olives, which is before Jerusalem on the east, and the mount of Olives shall cleave in the midst thereof toward the east and toward the west, and there shall be a very great valley; and half of the mountain shall remove toward the north, and half of it toward the south" (Zechariah 14:3–4). Then shall come to pass the conversion of a nation in a day, the acceptance of the Redeemer by the Jews. "And then shall the Jews look upon me and say: What are these wounds in thine hands and in thy feet? Then shall they know that I am the Lord; for I will say unto them: These wounds are the wounds with which I was wounded in the house of my friends. I am he who was lifted up. I am Jesus that was crucified. I am the Son of God. And then shall they weep because of their iniquities; then shall they lament because they persecuted their king" (D&C 45:51–53; see also Zechariah 12:10; 13:6).

Finally, and we would assume not far removed in time from his appearance on the Mount of Olives, is Christ's *coming in glory.* He comes in glory. All shall know. "Be not deceived," the Master warned in a modern revelation, "but continue in steadfastness, looking forth for the heavens to be shaken, and the earth to tremble and to reel to and fro as a drunken man, and for the valleys to be exalted, and for the mountains to be made low, and for the rough places to become smooth" (D&C 49:23). "Wherefore, prepare ye for the coming of the Bridegroom; go ye, go ye out to meet him. For behold, he shall stand upon the mount of Olivet, and upon the mighty ocean, even the great deep, and upon the islands of the sea, and upon the land of Zion. And he shall utter his voice out of Zion, and he shall speak from Jerusalem, and *his voice shall be heard among all people;* and it shall be a voice as the voice of many waters, and as the voice of a great thunder, which shall break down the mountains, and the valleys shall not be found" (D&C 133:19–22; emphasis added).

5. *When the Lord comes, who will come with him?* The righteous dead from ages past—those who qualify for the first resurrection, specifically those who died true in the faith since the time the first resurrection was initiated in the meridian of time—will come with the Savior when he returns in glory. The Prophet Joseph corrected a passage in Paul's first epistle to the Thessalonians as follows: "I would not have you to be ignorant, brethren, concerning them which are asleep, that ye sorrow not, even as others which have no hope. For if we believe that Jesus died and rose again, even so them also which sleep in Jesus will God bring with him. For this we say unto you by the word of the Lord, that they who are alive at the coming of the Lord, shall not prevent [precede] them who remain unto the coming of the Lord, who are asleep. For the Lord himself shall descend from heaven with a shout, with the voice of the archangel, and with the trump of God; and the dead in Christ shall rise first; then they who are alive, shall be caught up together into the clouds with

them who remain, to meet the Lord in the air; and so shall we be ever with the Lord" (JST, 1 Thessalonians 4:13–17).

6. *What happens to those living on earth when He comes?* Those who are of at least a terrestrial level of righteousness shall continue to live as mortals after the Lord returns. The Saints shall live to "the age of man"—in the words of Isaiah, the age of one hundred (Isaiah 65:20)—and will then pass through death and be changed instantly from mortality to resurrected immortality. "Yea, and blessed are the dead that die in the Lord, . . . when the Lord shall come, and old things shall pass away, and all things become new, they shall rise from the dead and shall not die after, and shall receive an inheritance before the Lord, in the holy city. And he that liveth when the Lord shall come, and hath kept the faith, blessed is he; nevertheless, it is appointed to him to die at the age of man. Wherefore, children shall grow up until they become old"—that is, no longer shall little ones die before the time of accountability; "old men shall die; but they shall not sleep in the dust, but they shall be changed in the twinkling of an eye" (D&C 63:49–51; see also JST, Isaiah 65:20). President Joseph Fielding Smith pointed out that "the inhabitants of the earth will have a sort of translation. They will be transferred to a condition of the terrestrial order, and so they will have power over disease and they will have power to live until they get a certain age and then they will die."[10]

7. *Is the burning spoken of in scripture literal?* Malachi prophesied that "the day cometh, that shall burn as an oven; and all the proud, yea, and all that do wickedly, shall be stubble: and the day that cometh shall burn them up, saith the Lord of hosts, that it shall leave them neither root nor branch" (Malachi 4:1; compare 2 Nephi 26:4; D&C 133:64). In 1823 Moroni quoted this passage differently to the seventeen-year-old Joseph Smith: "And all the proud, yea, and all that do wickedly shall burn as stubble; for *they that come* shall burn them, saith the Lord of hosts" (Joseph Smith—History 1:37; emphasis added). In the Doctrine and Covenants the Lord of Armies declares: "For the hour is nigh and the day soon at hand when the earth is ripe; and all the proud and they that do wickedly shall be as stubble; and *I will burn them up,* saith the Lord of Hosts, that wickedness shall not be upon the earth" (D&C 29:9; emphasis added), "for after today cometh the burning," a day wherein "all the proud and they that do wickedly shall be as stubble; and *I will burn them up, for I am the Lord of Hosts; and I will not spare any that remain in Babylon*" (D&C 64:24; emphasis added).

The Second Coming of Christ in glory is a day wherein "every corruptible thing, both of man, or of the beasts of the field, or of the fowls of the heavens, or of the fish of the sea, that dwells upon the face of the earth, shall be consumed; and also that of element shall melt with fervent heat; and all things shall become new, that my knowledge and glory may dwell upon all the earth" (D&C 101:24–25; compare 133:41; 2 Peter 3:10). Joseph Fielding Smith wrote: "Somebody said, 'Brother Smith, do you mean to say that it is going to be literal fire?' I said, 'Oh, no, it will not be literal fire any more than it was literal water that covered the earth in the flood.'"[11]

8. *Why will the Savior appear in red apparel?* Red is symbolic of victory—victory over the devil, death, hell, and endless torment. It is the symbol of salvation, of being placed beyond the power of all one's enemies.[12] Christ's red apparel will also symbolize both aspects of his ministry to fallen humanity—his mercy and his justice. Because he has trodden the winepress alone, "even the wine-press of the fierceness of the wrath of Almighty God" (D&C 76:107; 88:106), he has descended below all things and mercifully taken upon him our stains, our blood or our sins (see 2 Nephi 9:44; Jacob 1:19; 2:2; Alma 5:22). In addition, he comes in "dyed garments" as the God of justice, even he who has trampled the wicked beneath his feet. "And the Lord shall be red in his apparel, and his garments like him that treadeth in the wine-vat. And so great shall be the glory of his presence that the sun shall hide his face in shame, and the moon shall withhold its light, and the stars shall be hurled from their places. And his voice shall be heard: I have trodden the wine-press alone, and have brought judgment upon all people; and none were with me; and I have trampled them in my fury, and I did tread upon them in mine anger, and their blood have I sprinkled upon my garments, and stained all my raiment; for this was the day of vengeance which was in my heart" (D&C 133:48–51).

9. *When does the Millennium begin? Why will it begin?* Jesus Christ's Second Coming in glory ushers in the Millennium. The Millennium does not begin when Christ comes to his temple in Missouri, when he appears at Adam-ondi-Ahman, or when he stands on the Mount of Olives in Jerusalem. The Millennium will not come because men and women on earth have become noble and good or because Christian charity has spread across the globe and goodwill is the order of the day. The Millennium will not come because technological advances and medical miracles will have extended human life or because peace treaties among warring nations will have soothed injured feelings and eased political tensions for a time. The Millennium will be brought in by power, by the power of him who is the King of Kings and Lord of Lords. Satan will be bound by power, and the glory of the Millennium will be maintained by the righteousness of those who are permitted to live on earth (see 1 Nephi 22:15, 26).

10. *What are the times of the Gentiles? What is the fulness of the Gentiles?*

How do these relate to the Second Coming? In the meridian of time, by command of the Savior, the gospel of Jesus Christ was delivered first to the Jews and then later to the Gentiles. In our day, the gospel was delivered first to Joseph Smith and the Latter-day Saints, those of us who are "identified with the Gentiles" (D&C 109:60), those who are Israelite by descent (see D&C 52:2; 86:8–10) and Gentile by culture. The gospel is given to us, and we bear the responsibility to take the message of the Restoration to the descendants of Lehi and to the Jews (see 1 Nephi 22:7–11). We therefore live in "the times of the Gentiles." "And when the times of the Gentiles is come in, a light shall break forth among them that sit in darkness, and it shall be the fulness of my gospel" (D&C 45:28). It is a time, in the words of Elder Marion G. Romney, in which "in this last dispensation, the gospel is to be preached primarily to the non-Jewish people of the earth."[13]

In a day yet future, a time when the Gentiles—presumably those outside the Church as well as some from within the fold—sin against the fulness of the gospel and reject its supernal blessings, the Lord will take away these privileges from the Gentile nations and once again make them available primarily to his ancient covenant people (see 3 Nephi 16:10–11). This will be known as the fulfillment or the "fulness of the times of the Gentiles" or simply the "fulness of the Gentiles." Because the people of earth no longer receive the light of gospel fulness and turn their hearts from the Lord because of the precepts of men, "in that generation shall the times of the Gentiles be fulfilled" (D&C 45:29–30). In the purest sense, as we have noted, this will not take place until Jesus sets his foot upon Olivet and the Jews acknowledge their long-awaited Messiah. Thus the fulness of the Gentiles is millennial.[14]

11. *What are we to expect in regard to the return of the ten tribes?* As we all know, there have been numerous legends, traditions, vague reminiscences, and a myriad of Mormon folktales that deal with the location and eventual return of the ten lost tribes, those from the northern part of Israel who were taken captive by the Assyrians in 721 B.C. During my youth in the Church, I was brought up to believe a whole host of things: that the lost tribes were in the center of the earth, on a knob attached to the earth, on another planet, etc. Each of these traditions had its own sources of authority. Since that time, and particularly since I have discovered the Book of Mormon, I have concluded simply that the ten tribes are scattered among the nations, lost as much to their identity as to their whereabouts (see 1 Nephi 22:3–4). Thus it seems to me that the restoration or gathering of the ten tribes consists in scattered Israel—descendants of Jacob from such tribes as Reuben, Gad, Asher, Naphtali, Zebulun, and, of course, Joseph—coming to the knowledge of the

restored gospel, accepting the very points of Christ's gospel (see 1 Nephi 15:14), coming into the true Church and fold of God (see 2 Nephi 9:2), congregating with the faithful, and receiving the ordinances of the house of the Lord.[15] That is to say, the ten tribes will be gathered as all others are gathered—through conversion.

The risen Lord explained to the Nephites that after his Second Coming, once he has begun to dwell on earth with his faithful, "then shall the work of the Father"—the work of the gathering of Israel—"commence at that day, even when this gospel shall be preached among the remnant of this people. Verily I say unto you, *at that day shall the work of the Father commence among all the dispersed of my people, yea, even the tribes which have been lost,* which the Father hath led away out of Jerusalem" (3 Nephi 21:25–26; emphasis added). It will *commence* in the sense that its magnitude will be of such a nature as to cause earlier efforts at gathering to pale into insignificance. The return of the ten tribes is spoken of in modern revelation in majestic symbolism: "And the Lord, even the Savior, shall stand in the midst of his people, and shall reign over all flesh." Further, those who are descendants of the northern tribes shall respond to the gospel message, come under the direction of those prophets or priesthood leaders in their midst, traverse the highway of righteousness (see Isaiah 35:8), and eventually participate in those temple ordinances that make of us kings and queens, priests and priestesses before God; they will "fall down and be crowned with glory, even in Zion, by the hands of the servants of the Lord, even the children of Ephraim," those who are entrusted with the keys of salvation (see D&C 133:26–32).[16] In addition to that portion of the record of the ten tribes in our possession that we know as the Doctrine and Covenants—the record of God's dealings with modern Ephraim—we thrill in the assurance that other sacred volumes chronicling our Redeemer's ministry to the lost tribes shall come forth during the Millennium (see 2 Nephi 29:13).

12. Is it true that every person living on earth must first hear the gospel before the Lord can come? In November 1831 the early elders of the Church were given their authorization to preach the gospel: "Go ye into all the world, preach the gospel to every creature, acting in the authority which I have given you, baptizing in the name of the Father, and of the Son, and of the Holy Ghost" (D&C 68:8). Also: "For, verily, the sound must go forth from this place into all the world, and unto the uttermost parts of the earth—the gospel must be preached unto every creature, with signs following them that believe" (D&C 58:64). It is true that every person must have the opportunity to hear the gospel, either here or hereafter. Eventually "the truth of God will go forth boldly, nobly, independent, till it has penetrated every continent, visited every clime, swept every country, and sounded in every ear, till the purposes of God shall be accomplished, and the great Jehovah shall say the work is done."[17]

Not all, however, will have that privilege as mortals and not all will have that privilege before the Second Coming. Jesus had spoken to the Twelve about the last days as follows: "And again, this gospel of the Kingdom shall be preached in all the world, for a witness unto all nations, and then shall the end come, or the destruction of the wicked" (Joseph Smith—Matthew 1:31). As we have seen, the great day of gathering—the day when millions upon millions will come into the true fold of God—is millennial. But there is more. Elder Bruce R. McConkie explained that before the Lord Jesus can return in glory, two things must take place: "The first . . . is that the restored gospel is to be preached in every nation and among every people and to those speaking every tongue. Now there is one immediate reaction to this: Can't we go on the radio and preach the gospel to . . . the nations of the earth? We certainly can, but that would have very little bearing on the real meaning of the revelation that says we must preach it to every nation, kindred, and people. The reason is the second thing that must occur before the Second Coming: The revelations expressly, specifically, and pointedly say that when the Lord comes the second time to usher in the millennial era, he is going to find, in every nation, kindred, and tongue, and among every people, those who are kings and queens, who will live and reign a thousand years on earth (see Revelation 5:9–10).

"That is a significant statement that puts in perspective the preaching of the gospel to the world. Yes, we can go on the radio; we can proclaim the gospel to all nations by television or other modern invention. And to the extent that we can do it, so be it, it's all to the good. But that's not what is involved. What is involved is that the elders of Israel, holding the priesthood, in person have to trod the soil, eat in the homes of the people, figuratively put their arms around the honest in heart, feed them the gospel, and baptize them and confer the Holy Ghost upon them. Then these people have to progress and advance, and grow in the things of the Spirit, until they can go to the house of the Lord, until they can enter a temple of God and receive the blessings of the priesthood, out of which come the rewards of being kings and priests.

"The way we become kings and priests is through the ordinances of the house of the Lord. It is through celestial marriage; it is through the guarantees of eternal life and eternal increase that are reserved for the Saints in the temples. The promise is that when the Lord comes he is going to find in every nation and kindred, among every people speaking every tongue, those who will, at that hour of his coming, have already become kings and priests. . . . All this is to precede the Second

Coming of the Son of Man."[18] Parenthetically, the revelations declare: "Prepare ye the way of the Lord, and make his paths straight, for the hour of his coming is nigh—when the Lamb shall stand upon Mount Zion, and with him a hundred and forty-four thousand, having his Father's name written on their foreheads" (D&C 133:17–18). This group of 144,000 are high priests after the holy order of God, men who have themselves received the promise of exaltation and godhood and whose mission it is to bring as many as will come into the Church of the Firstborn, into that inner circle of men and women who have passed the tests of mortality and have become the elect of God.[19] I have often thought that the reference to 144,000 high priests called in the last days to bring men and women into the Church of the Firstborn (see D&C 77:11) is a symbolic reference: in that day of division, of unspeakable wickedness and consummate righteousness, temples will dot the earth, be accessible to the Lord's covenant people everywhere, and thus the fulness of those temple blessings will be sealed upon millions of the faithful Saints world-wide by those holding those transcendant powers.

13. *Is the time of Christ's coming fixed, or may it be altered by us?* We hear once in a while the plea for us as Latter-day Saints to repent and improve, that the Lord may come quickly to us. It is true that we are under obligation to be faithful to our covenants, to deny ourselves of every worldly lust and cross ourselves as to the pulls of a decaying society, and to live as becomes Saints. It is true that our labor is to build up the kingdom of God and establish Zion, all in preparation for the Second Coming. The full redemption of Zion is in fact dependent on the urgency with which the Saints of the Most High pursue their sacred duty. Further, our righteous obsession to be a light to a darkened world assures our own readiness to receive the Savior. But the time of his Coming is a constant, not a variable. It may not be postponed because of the Saints' tardiness or sloth, any more than it can be hastened through a burst of goodness. The Father and the Son know when the King of Zion (see Moses 7:53) shall return to earth to assume the scepter and to preside over the kingdom of God. As was the case with his first coming to earth in the meridian of time, so it is in regard to his Second Coming. The Nephite prophets, for example, did not encourage the people to be faithful so that the Lord could come. Rather, they stated forthrightly that in six hundred years he would come (see, for example, 1 Nephi 10:4; 19:8; 2 Nephi 25:19), ready or not! It will be a time. It will be a specific day, a designated hour. That day and that hour are known. The time is set. It is fixed.[20]

14. *The scriptures warn of false Christs and false prophets. How can we know whom to trust? Where do we turn for more insight?* We must keep our eyes fixed on

those charged with the direction of the Church—the prophets, seers, and revelators of our day. What they emphasize in their instruction to us should be what we emphasize. Any who come before the Saints claiming some special insight, gift, training, or commission to elucidate detail concerning the signs of the times, beyond that which the Brethren have set forth, is suspect, is running before his or her file leaders, and his or her teachings are not to be trusted or received. Truly, "it shall not be given to any one to go forth to preach my gospel, or to build up my church, except he be ordained by some one who has authority, and it is known to the church that he has authority and has been regularly ordained by the heads of the church" (D&C 42:11).

With the exception of those few deluded persons who claim to be Jesus, when we speak of false Christs we speak not so much of individuals as of false spirits, false doctrines, false systems of salvation. Latter-day Saints who "stick with the Brethren," who study and teach from the conference reports, the official pronouncements and proclamations, and the monthly First Presidency messages in the *Ensign*—these are they who treasure up the word of the Lord, who will not be deceived or led astray at the last day (Joseph Smith—Matthew 1:37). Elder Boyd K. Packer declared: "There are some among us now who have *not* been regularly ordained by the heads of the Church who tell of impending political and economic chaos, the end of the world. . . . Those deceivers say that the Brethren do not know what is going on in the world or that the Brethren approve of their teaching but do not wish to speak of it over the pulpit. Neither is true. The Brethren, by virtue of traveling constantly everywhere on earth, certainly know what is going on, and by virtue of prophetic insight are able to read the signs of the times."[21]

15. *What are the best sources for understanding the scenes and events incident to the Savior's Coming?* At the October 1972 and April 1973 conferences of the Church, President Harold B. Lee warned the Latter-day Saints about what he called "loose writings" by members of the Church in regard to the signs of the times. "Are you . . . aware of the fact," President Lee inquired, "that we need no such publications to be forewarned, if we were only conversant with what the scriptures have already spoken to us in plainness?" He then provided what he termed "the sure word of prophecy on which [we] should rely for [our] guide instead of these strange sources." He instructed the Saints to read the Joseph Smith Translation of Matthew 24 (which we have in the Pearl of Great Price as Joseph Smith—Matthew), and also sections 38, 45, 101, and 133 of the Doctrine and Covenants.[22] It is of interest to me that President Lee cited primarily the revelations of the Restoration. He did not refer the Church to Isaiah or Ezekiel or Daniel or Revelation. In 1981 President

Marion G. Romney explained: "In each dispensation, . . . the Lord has revealed anew the principles of the gospel. So that while the records of past dispensations, insofar as they are uncorrupted, testify to the truths of the gospel, still each dispensation has had revealed in its day sufficient truth to guide the people of the new dispensation, independent of the records of the past.

"I do not wish to discredit in any manner the records we have of the truths revealed by the Lord in past dispensations. What I now desire is to impress upon our minds that the gospel, as revealed to the Prophet Joseph Smith, is complete and is the word direct from heaven to this dispensation. It alone is sufficient to teach us the principles of eternal life. It is the truth revealed, the commandments given in this dispensation through modern prophets by which we are to be governed."[23]

Even given the divine direction of living oracles and the words of sacred scripture brought forth in this final age, we really cannot plot or calculate the signs of the times or lay out a precise scheme of events. That is, as one apostle pointed out, "It is not possible for us . . . to specify the exact chronology of all the events that shall attend the Second Coming. Nearly all of the prophetic word relative to our Lord's return links various events together without reference to the order of their occurrence. Indeed, the same scriptural language is often used to describe similar events that will take place at different times."[24]

CONCLUSION

We obviously could go on and on. But these feeble efforts at providing answers point us to the glorious reality that modern revelation, especially the Doctrine and Covenants, represents, in the language of Parley P. Pratt, "the dawning of a brighter day."[25] The Doctrine and Covenants is indeed, as President Ezra Taft Benson explained, the "capstone of our religion."[26] It is truly "the foundation of the Church in these last days, and a benefit to the world, showing that the keys of the mysteries of the kingdom of our Savior are again entrusted to man" (preface to D&C 70).

The early elders of the Church were instructed: "Wherefore, be of good cheer, and do not fear, for I the Lord am with you, and will stand by you; and ye shall bear record of me, even Jesus Christ, that I am the Son of the living God, that I was, that I am, and that I am to come" (D&C 68:6). Answer after answer after divine answer concerning such matters as the divine Sonship of Christ, his infinite and eternal atoning sacrifice, the principles of his eternal gospel—these things are made known with great power and persuasion. In addition, the revelations testify:

• that he will come again to reign among the Saints and to come down in judgment upon Idumea, or the world (see D&C 1:36);

• that he will gather his faithful as a mother hen and enable them to partake of the waters of life (see D&C 10:64–66; 29:2; 33:6);

• that Satan and the works of Babylon will be destroyed (see D&C 1:16; 19:3; 35:11; 133:14);

• that this dispensation of the gospel represents his last pruning of the vineyard (see D&C 24:19; 33:2–3; 39:17; 43:28);

• that the elect in the last days will hear his voice; they will not be asleep because they will be purified (see D&C 35:20–21);

• that we will have no laws but his laws when he comes; he will be our ruler (see D&C 38:22; 41:4; 58:22);

• that from the Lord's perspective, according to his reckoning, his coming is nigh (see D&C 63:53); he comes tomorrow (see D&C 64:24); he comes quickly, suddenly (see D&C 33:18; 35:27; 36:8; 39:24; 41:4; 68:35).

My hope is that we will follow the Brethren, search the scriptures, pray mightily for discernment and for awareness and understanding of the signs of the times. That we will be wise, receive the truth, take the Holy Spirit for our guide, and thereby have our lamps filled (see D&C 45:56–57) is my prayer. "Wherefore, be faithful, praying always, having your lamps trimmed and burning, and oil with you, that you may be ready at the coming of the Bridegroom—for behold, verily, verily, I say unto you, that I come quickly" (D&C 33:17–18). In harmony with the soul-cry of John the Revelator, we exclaim: "Even so, come, Lord Jesus" (Revelation 22:20).

Notes

From an address at the Sidney B. Sperry Symposium, Provo, Utah, 19 October 1996.

1. See *Teachings of the Prophet Joseph Smith*, 101.
2. M. Russell Ballard, "When Shall These Things Be?" in *Brigham Young University 1995–96 Speeches* (Provo, Utah: Brigham Young University Publications & Graphics, 1996), 186.
3. Joseph Smith, in *Times and Seasons*, 1 March 1843, 113, as quoted in Kent P. Jackson, comp., *Joseph Smith's Commentary on the Bible* (Salt Lake City: Deseret Book Co., 1994), 109.
4. Orson Pratt, in *Journal of Discourses*, 365–66.
5. Charles W. Penrose, in *Millennial Star*, 21:582–83.
6. *Teachings of the Prophet Joseph Smith*, 157.
7. Joseph Fielding Smith, *The Progress of Man* (Salt Lake City: Deseret Book Co., 1964), 481–82; see also Joseph Fielding Smith, *The Way to Perfection* (Salt Lake City: Deseret Book Co., 1970), 288–91.
8. *Millennial Messiah*, 582, 584.
9. *Doctrinal New Testament Commentary*, 3:509.
10. Joseph Fielding Smith, *The Signs of the Times* (Salt Lake City: Deseret Book Co., 1942), 42.
11. Ibid., 41.

12. See *Teachings of the Prophet Joseph Smith,* 297, 301, 305.

13. Marion G. Romney, in Conference Report, October 1971, 69.

14. See *Millennial Messiah,* 241.

15. See *Teachings of the Prophet Joseph Smith,* 307–308.

16. *Millennial Messiah,* 214–17, 325–26.

17. *History of the Church,* 4:540.

18. Bruce R. McConkie, "To the Koreans, and All the People of Asia," address delivered to returned Korea missionaries, Provo, Utah, 5 March 1971, in Spencer J. Palmer, *The Expanding Church* (Salt Lake City: Deseret Book Co., 1978), 141–42.

19. See D&C 77:11; Orson Pratt, in *Journal of Discourses,* 14:242–43; 16:325; 18:25.

20. See *Millennial Messiah,* 26–27, 405.

21. Boyd K. Packer, in Conference Report, October 1992, 102.

22. Harold B. Lee, in Conference Report, October 1972, 128.

23. Marion G. Romney, "A Glorious Promise," *Ensign,* January 1981, 2.

24. *Millennial Messiah,* 635.

25. *Hymns,* no. 1.

26. Ezra Taft Benson, *A Witness and a Warning* (Salt Lake City: Deseret Book Co., 1988), 30–31.

Scripture Index

OLD TESTAMENT

GENESIS
1:26–28, p. 160
1:27, pp. 482, 548
2:2–3, p. 451
3:7, p. 11
6:9 (JST), p. 236
6:9, p. 523
6:23 (JST), p. 161
12:1–3, p. 80
14 (JST), pp. 122, 123, 131
14:25–36 (JST), p. 34
14:27–32 (JST), p. 32
15:9–12 (JST), p. 148
16:1–2, p. 282
17 (JST), p. 123
17:1–7, p. 80
17:11–12 (JST), pp. 80, 81
18:19, p. 275
21:12, p. 282
25:23, p. 282
25:29–34, p. 283
26:34–35, p. 283
32:24–32, p. 438
50 (JST), pp. 122, 131

EXODUS
3:5, p. 309
14:13, p. 508
16:25–26, p. 451
19:6, p. 36
20:2–6, p. 449
20:7, pp. 445, 447
20:19, pp. 36, 284
33:9–11, p. 59
33:11, p. 430
34 (JST), p. 123
34:1–2 (JST), pp. 37, 284, 454
34:2 (JST), p. 522

LEVITICUS
11:44, pp. 354, 457
17:11, p. 354
19:12, p. 447
19:30, p. 457

NUMBERS
9:15–22, p. 59
11:25, p. 59
12:6–8, p. 430
15:32–36, p. 452

16:22, p. 546
27:16, p. 546

DEUTERONOMY
5:12, 15, p. 451
10 (JST), p. 123
10:1–2 (JST), pp. 37, 284
28:15, 25, 63–64, p. 263
32:7–9, p. 259

2 KINGS
6:16, p. 539

NEHEMIAH
13:15–19, p. 452

JOB
1:1, p. 523

PSALMS
11:2 (JST), p. 323
11:10, p. 492
14:1–3, p. 70
53:1–3, p. 70
102:27, p. 547

PROVERBS
1:7, p. 492

9:10, p. 492

ISAIAH
2:2, p. 240
5:20, p. 348
9:6, p. 309
11:1, p. 61
11:9, p. 271
25:8, pp. 409, 542
27:12, p. 264
29:13–14, p. 27
35:8, pp. 271, 564
43:1–6, p. 264
43:5–6, p. 270
44:1, p. 258
45:4, p. 258
48:22, p. 496
49:6, p. 267
52:1, p. 266
52:2, p. 266
53:2, p. 61
53:6, p. 171
57:19–21, p. 496
61:1, pp. 296, 512, 550
61:1–2, p. 499
65:20 (JST), p. 561
65:20, pp. 271, 561

NEW TESTAMENT

BOOK OF MORMON

DOCTRINE AND COVENANTS

PEARL OF GREAT PRICE

SUBJECT INDEX

Brown, Hugh B.: on Abraham, 219; on eternal families, 292; on the real business of life, 336

Brown, Raymond, on God as spirit, 195

Bruce, F. F.: on papyrus rolls, 5; on canonicity, 6, 131; on Paul, 69–70

Bullock, Thomas, 231

Burgess, James, 35

Bushman, Richard, on Book of Mormon authorship, 109

Butterfly (analogy), 78

Cain, 30–31

Cainan, 160

Calling and election, 57, 201, 202, 203, 219, 273, 376, 535

Calvin, John, 170

Campbell, Alex, 331

Campbell, Alexander, 109

Campbell, Beverly, on men and women, 292

Cannon, George Q.: on faith in the Bible, 13; on Gentiles, 270; on apostates, 364–65

Carter, Stephen L., on secularism, 313

Catholic Church. *See* Roman Catholic Church

Catholic University, 343

Celestial kingdom, 130, 354, 527, 535; vision of the, 127, 245–49, 424

Celestial marriage, 57, 162, 273, 277, 284, 291, 293

Chadwick, Bruce, on personal prayer, 437

Change, through Christ, 75–78

Channing, William Ellery, on Trinitarianism, 115

Charismatic Movement, 312

Charity, 494–95

Children, 248; and the Fall, 175–76; in the resurrection, 250–51; fatherless, 289–90; wayward, 407–9, 413, 532–34, 538–39; covenant of the, 530–43

Christian Fundamentalism, 312

Christianity: true, 328–30; definition of, 338–41; LDS, 341, 550–53; relating to other forms of, 341–46

Christianity Today (magazine), 551

Church Education System, 357, 398

Clark, J. Reuben, Jr.: on the Book of Mormon, 101–2; on a listening ear, 307; on prophets, 418; on punishment and rewards, 539

Claudius, on prayer, 436

Clayton, William, 224, 532

Clement, 552

Codex, 5

Coe, Truman, 226–27

Communication, divine, 382–84

Consecration, 238

Constitution, U.S., 144

Contention, 552

Conversion, 264, 389, 408, 410, 564

Coray, Howard and Martha, 531

Corianton, 110, 172, 366

Cosmic dualism, 88

Council of Trent, 8, 10

Counter Reformation, 8

Covenants: and the Plan of Salvation, 149–50; breaking of, 447–48; comfort in, 495–96; and grace, 499; of the children, 530–43

Coverdale, Myles, 8, 11

Cowdery, Oliver: received priesthood keys, 41, 267; assisted in translating, 121–22; gave heed to false teachings, 417; desired to translate, 418–19; and personal revelation, 421; received witness, 526

Cowley, Matthew, 403

Crime, 315

Criticism, 99–100, 140–41, 364

Crying, 398–99

Cults, polygamy, 291

Cyril of Jerusalem, 7

Damascus, Pope, 10

Danby, Herbert, on dearth of revelation, 65

Davies, W. D., on apostolic witness, 19

Daviess County, Missouri, 165

Dead Sea Scrolls, 401

Death, 539

Death of God Movement, 312, 314

Deseret News, 471

Devil. *See* Satan

Diocletian, edict of, 8

Discernment, 308

Discipleship, 341